W9-CLG-166

COLLECTED WORKS OF ERASMUS

VOLUME 4

THE CORRESPONDENCE OF
ERASMUS

LETTERS 446 TO 593

1516 TO 1517

translated by R.A.B. Mynors and D.F.S. Thomson

annotated by James K. McConica

University of Toronto Press

Toronto and Buffalo

The research costs of the Collected Works of Erasmus
have been underwritten by the Canada Council.

© University of Toronto Press 1977
Toronto and Buffalo
Printed in Canada

Library of Congress Cataloging in Publication Data (Revised)
Erasmus, Desiderius, D. 1536
The correspondence of Erasmus
Vol. 4 annotated by James K. McConica
(Collected works of Erasmus v. 1–   )
Translation of Opus epistolarum Des. Erasmi Roterdami.
Includes bibliographical references.
CONTENTS: [1] Letters 1 to 141, 1484–1500. –
[2] Letters 142 to 297, 1501–1514. –
[3] Letters 298 to 445, 1514–1516. –
[4] Letters 446 to 593, 1516–1517.
1. Erasmus, Desiderius, d. 1536 – Correspondence
I. Title
PA8511.A5E55 1974   199'.492   72–97422
ISBN 0-8020-5366-1

The Collected Works of Erasmus

The aim of the Collected Works of Erasmus
is to make available an accurate, readable English text
of Erasmus' correspondence and his
other principal writings. The edition is planned
and directed by an Editorial Board, an Executive Committee,
and an Advisory Committee.

Contents

Illustrations

Preface

The year that began in August 1515 with the publication of Seneca's *Lucub-rationes* was, famously, the *annus mirabilis* of Erasmus' career. In addition to the Seneca and some other literary works, it saw the momentous publication of the epistles of St Jerome and the first edition of his New Testament, as well as the publication of the *Institutio principis christiani*.[1] In the months following from August 1516 to June 1517, the period covered by the present volume, we are intensely conscious of the impression made by this signal achievement upon Erasmus' contemporaries from letters for the most part full of praise and admiration, although some few show critical reserve. On Erasmus' part, while his scholarly work was not abandoned the pace seems temporarily to have diminished; his attention was drawn rather to the implications for his future of the successes of the recent past.

In CWE 3, we left Erasmus in May 1516 (Ep 445) on the way to the Netherlands to take up his appointment as councillor to Prince Charles. The life and politics of the Netherlands form the background to all that happened in the succeeding year. Prospects of further advancement posed the need for a new dispensation to hold more than one benefice, since as an Augustinian canon Erasmus was technically bound to the obligations of a religious under vows. This was the business that took him to London in August 1516 (Ep 446), a weighty matter that was never far from his mind. By mid-August (Ep 452) he was at Rochester on his way back to the continent, staying with Bishop John Fisher who had enlisted his help in the study of Greek. He left Fisher about 24 August and wrote to Johann Reuchlin from Calais on the 27th (Ep 457). He told Reuchlin of his reception in England with an observation that would serve to describe much of the experience of the year to come: 'The New Testament has made me friends everywhere, although some people protested forcibly, especially at first; but they pro-

* * * * *

1 CWE 3 xi 3n

tested only in my absence, and most of them were the sort who do not read
my work, and would not understand it if they did.'[2]

He named Pieter Gillis of Antwerp as the man to whom Reuchlin
should send his letters, an indication of Erasmus' own uncertainty about
his immediate plans. In theory, as he had told Henry Bullock, he was on his
way to Louvain for the winter, but by the start of October he was having
second thoughts and had settled on Brussels instead.[3] The reason is clear;
he was not certain of his reception by the theologians of Louvain, where
Maarten van Dorp led critical opinion and where Erasmus believed an
examination of his works was threatened.[4] In the end, while negotiating
discreetly with Dorp and his colleagues at Louvain, Erasmus spent the rest
of 1516 and the first half of 1517 in Antwerp, Brussels and Ghent, with the
house of Pieter Gillis as his real base of operations.

There was important business in Brussels, and Erasmus spent the
weeks from early October to the following January there. He was offered a
canonry at Courtrai and also, as it seems, a bishopric, although this latter
scheme fell through.[5] What kept him in Brussels was the prospect of
promotion and the absorbing politics of the Burgundian court where his
patrons, Jean Le Sauvage and Guillaume de Croy were so influential. By 20
January, however, with the loss of his chief companion Tunstall, he abandoned the uncongenial role of the courtier-scholar and wrote to his old
friend Gillis, 'To sit here any longer I simply have no spirits.'[6] He returned
to the happy family setting at Antwerp to complete the work he was
preparing for the Froben press at Basel. While staying with the Gillis family
he dealt also with the flattering if vague proposals that he leave for the court
of Francis I[7] and, in mid-March, received the long-awaited news that Rome
had granted the substance of his petition.[8] He had to return to England to
receive absolution and the dispensation from the hands of Ammonio, his
chief personal agent in the affair, and that ceremony took place on 9 April at
Westminster.[9] The sense of relief and freedom conferred by this papal
favour can be detected at once in the letter Erasmus wrote to Wolsey (Ep 577)
on the eve of his departure from England. He made a perilous crossing on 1

* * * * *

2 Ep 457: 53–7
3 Epp 456: 7, 475: 15
4 Epp 304, 476 introduction, 505: 9–11
5 Ep 475: 2–7
6 Ep 516: 8–9
7 Ep 522 introduction
8 Epp 552, 566
9 Ep 517: 89

May, described in a letter to More in which Erasmus also announced the painting of the remarkable diptych of himself and Pieter Gillis by Quentin Metsys (Ep 584). When this volume ends, the removal of Erasmus to Louvain is still in the future.

While these events were taking place, the scene of his recent success, the upper Rhine, was never far from his mind. Old friends like Willibald Pirckheimer (Ep 555) and Beatus Rhenanus (Ep 460) with other members of the Froben circle wrote to him to keep him informed of their activities and to tell him how much he was missed.[10] Although Erasmus negotiated with Josse Bade in Paris, Martens at Louvain and with the successors to Aldus,[11] it was the Froben press that remained the focus of his scholarly objectives. In addition to revising other earlier works, he continued his translation of Theodore of Gaza, worked at the revision of the *Novum instrumentum*, and prepared the first of his great Paraphrases of the New Testament, that of Romans, which appeared in November 1517.[12] The most momentous humanistic achievement of these months which is also chronicled in these letters was not, however, his own; it was the publication of the *Nusquama* (as it was originally known), the work of his old friend Thomas More, over the production of which as *Utopia* Erasmus maintained, through Pieter Gillis, a benevolent interest (Ep 461). More mysterious was the printing of the celebrated satirical dialogue *Julius exclusus*, constantly disavowed by Erasmus but greeted jubilantly by his friends in Brussels as his own. Wrote Guy Morillon (Ep 532), 'How delightfully and amusingly, and in a word, Erasmically, [Pope Julius] argues with Peter is easier to understand than to explain ....'

Indeed, if Erasmus had been famous before, the meed of tribute now poured in with every courier. Friends prepared the first catalogue of his works (Ep 492); the young Melanchthon, aged nineteen years, sent a Greek poem of praise by way of introduction (Ep 454); Duke George of Saxony would call (Ep 514); the archbishop of Mainz (Ep 578) and the bishop of Bayeux (Ep 489) would give him a permanent home, while the leading humanists at the court of Francis I wrote him of the honour that awaited him in Paris. All proposals were treated with courtesy and reserve; Erasmus' deepest instincts warned him against such entanglements. The letter from Spalatin (Ep 501) which produced the first direct contact with the doctrine of Luther may seem in retrospect a sufficient justification for this caution. For the moment, however, the truest explanation is found in Erasmus' intro-

* * * * *

10 For example, Ludwig Baer on 11 May 1517; Ep 582

11 Epp 472, 546, 588–9

12 Ep 581: 24n; cf Allen III Epp 684: 13, 710 introduction.

duction to his edition of Suetonius, dedicated significantly to Dukes Frederick and George of Saxony (Ep 586). Under the veil of rhetorical courtesy
we find the sharpest condemnation of princely power, a sentiment in
Erasmus that had been nurtured and enhanced by his life among the ruling
families of the Netherlands. On the more positive side of his doctrine we
have in letters to Pieter Gillis (Ep 476) and Wolfgang Capito (Ep 541) two
classical statements of Erasmus' ideals for the men of education and Christian principle upon whom rested his whole programme for the reform of
Christendom. It is symbolically appropriate that this volume should end
with a reaffirmation of these same ideals by his old friend and spiritual
mentor, John Colet in England: 'Nothing can be better, in view of this brief
life of ours, than that we should live a holy and pure life and use our best
endeavours every day to become pure and enlightened and perfected.
These things are promised us by Reuchlin's Pythagorical and Cabalistic
philosophy; but in my opinion we shall achieve them in no way but this, by
the fervent love and imitation of Jesus.'[13]

Like the volume that precedes it, this one reflects an active exchange of
letters. There are one hundred and forty-eight letters over the period from 9
August 1516 to June 1517, an even higher rate of survival than for the
previous period.[14] Again, the survival of much of this correspondence
depends on the preservation of the Deventer Letter-book,[15] the source for
seventy-five of these letters. Most of the others (forty-nine in all) come from
two published collections of the period, the *Epistolae elegantes* and the
Farrago.[16] The remainder come from other letter-collections and from
prefaces to works like the Suetonius. Of the seventy-five letters with manuscript authority in the Deventer Letter-book, seventy-two were published
for the first time in the Leiden *Opera omnia*. Eight letters come from other
manuscript authority and one letter, Epistle 480A, has been redated to 1516
from Allen's assigned date of 1517.[17] To allow the reader to discover the
sequence in which these letters became known the same procedure is
followed that was established in volume 3.[18] The introduction to each letter
cites the first collection in which the letter was printed, along with the
manuscript source, if one exists. Where the introduction to any letter is
silent about both the manuscript source and the collection in which it was

* * * * *

13 Ep 593: 18–23
14 CWE 3 contains 151 letters written over two years; cf CWE 3 xiv.
15 Cf CWE 3 xiv.
16 Cf Ep 546 introduction, CWE 3 Appendix 349–50.
17 Allen III Ep 692
18 Cf CWE 3 xv.

first published, the letter is in the Deventer Letter-book and was first printed by Leclerc in the Leiden *Opera omnia*. If the letter was first published by Allen, the manuscript alone is cited. All the printed letter-collections described in the introductions by short titles are listed in full among the Works Frequently Cited.

The index to this volume, prepared by James Farge CSB, contains references to the persons, places and works mentioned in the volume, following the plan for the correspondence series. When that series of volumes is completed the reader will also be supplied with an index of topics, and of classical and scriptural references. A Biographical Register in preparation under the direction of Peter G. Bietenholz will supplement the biographical information found in the annotation to the letters. The footnotes dealing with technical problems of coinage and moneys–of–account have again been supplied by John H. Munro.

The translation of this volume is the work of R.A.B. Mynors, who has also given invaluable assistance in the task of supplying the text with introductions and annotation. I would also like to acknowledge the assistance of certain other scholars. James D. Tracy kindly allowed me to see, before publication, the manuscript of his book, *The Politics of Erasmus: A Pacifist Intellectual and His Political Milieu*, a study of Erasmus' career in the Netherlands that enlarges greatly our understanding of the connections between his political thought and the complex political developments in the Low Countries during these years. Professor Dr J. IJsewijn of the Katholieke Universiteit Leuven has responded generously to various inquiries about contemporaries of Erasmus in the humanistic circles of the Low Countries. Finally, my colleagues at the Pontifical Institute of Mediaeval Studies, Robert Crooker CSB and Leonard Boyle OP, have given me indispensable assistance in the technical problems of the canon law of Erasmus' dispensations. For the conclusions, which depart from some received interpretations, I take sole responsibility. Other assistance I have acknowledged at the appropriate places in the notes.

The Centre for Reformation and Renaissance Studies at Victoria College, Toronto, and the Thomas Fisher Rare Book Library of the University of Toronto have been valued havens during the three years in which the third and fourth volumes of the CWE were being assembled, and the work could not have been done without them. The editors wish finally to record again their gratitude to the Canada Council, which has made this extensive undertaking possible, and to University of Toronto Press.

Delancey Place   JKM
Philadelphia

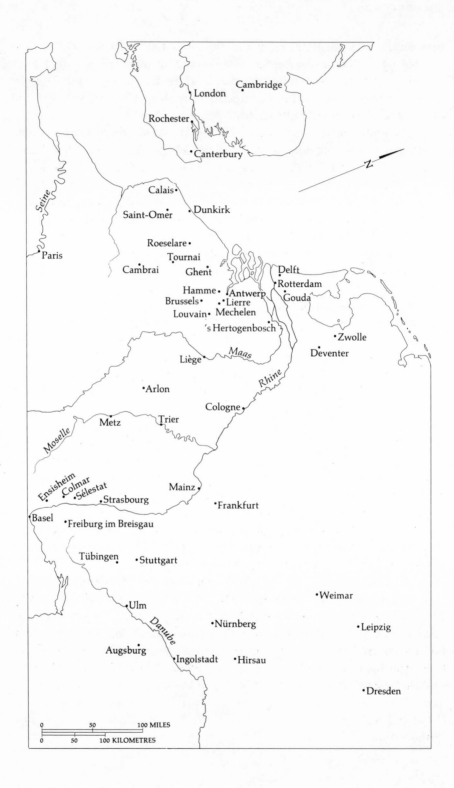

Cambridge

London

Rochester

Canterbury

Calais

Saint-Omer

Dunkirk

Seine

Roeselare

Tournai

Paris

Cambrai

Ghent

Delft

Rotterdam

Hamme

Antwerp

Gouda

Brussels

Lierre

Louvain

Mechelen

's Hertogenbosch

Zwolle

Deventer

Liège

Maas

Arlon

Rhine

Cologne

Metz

Trier

Moselle

Ensisheim

Colmar

Sélestat

Mainz

Strasbourg

Frankfurt

Basel

Freiburg im Breisgau

Tübingen

Stuttgart

Weimar

Ulm

Danube

Nürnberg

Leipzig

Augsburg

Ingolstadt

Hirsau

Dresden

| 0 | 50 | 100 MILES |
| 0 | 50 | 100 KILOMETRES |

THE CORRESPONDENCE OF ERASMUS

LETTERS 446 TO 593

446 / To Leo x   London, 9 August 1516

With this letter we are introduced to one of the leading preoccupations of
Erasmus in these years, the inconvenience caused by his canonical status as a
religious among the Canons Regular of St Augustine, an order which he
joined in 1488 after a year of probation in their house at Steyn. He later claimed
that his original religious profession was not a free act, since it was performed
under various pressures and at too early an age (see eg Ep 447, the *Compendium
vitae* [Appendix] and his letter to Gerard Geldenhouwer of 1524, Allen Ep
1436:19–24). However, the activities of the Canons Regular or Austin Canons,
as they were also known, were in many ways sufficiently flexible and various
to have attracted a man of Erasmus' taste and temperament. Their works
included the service of parishes and convents with teaching in schools and
colleges. Among their incidental responsibilities in England was the mainte-
nance of the shrine at Walsingham, of which Erasmus left such a famous and
critical account in 1526 in his colloquy *Peregrinatio religionis ergo*; cf Ep 262:8n.

Erasmus was ordained priest in the order on 25 April 1492, and the year
following left Steyn to take a post as Latin secretary to Hendrik van Bergen,
bishop of Cambrai (Ep 49 introduction). It was under his patronage that
Erasmus became a student at the University of Paris in 1495 (Ep 43 introduction). During all this time, and through the years immediately following, he
was acting with the permission of the order. In Italy, in 1506, for the first time
he abandoned the religious habit of the Canons, adopting instead the dress of
a secular priest (cf Ep 296 to Servatius Rogerus lines 181–218) which he later
retained in England. In January 1506 he obtained a dispensation from Pope
Julius II (Ep 187A) for tenure of a secular benefice by a religious. Erasmus'
supplication at that time was not in the first place for a dispensation from
defective birth, which in any case had already been granted by his own
superiors (cf Ep 517:11) nor was that the object of the supplication in 1517,
which was rather for habilitation after apostasy and the other technical
charges he had incurred by abandoning his habit, and for a grace to hold more
than one benefice (cf Ep 517 introduction). In both cases, however, the reference to illegitimacy was essential information, because a benefice could not be
granted to an illegitimate without a papal dispensation, and each and every
supplication for a benefice had to mention whether the suppliant was legitimate or not.

Erasmus later invoked the dispensation of Julius II to Servatius Rogerus (Ep
296:196–9) as warrant for his change in dress, which it was not. That this was
an important source of his unease and motive for his seeking a second
dispensation is indicated by the wording of Ep 517:15–20 and by Ep 447:514ff.
Although the dispensation of 1506 does not refer to a change in ecclesiastical

dress, it does indicate approval of the shift implied in Erasmus' abandonment
of his Augustinian habit: a move away from the dependency on his religious
order and in the direction of self-support in the manner customary to secular
priests. Erasmus' lengthy letter to Servatius Rogerus in 1514 (Ep 296) set the
seal on his decision to stay away from Holland and pursue his own career,
rather than 'exchange my studies for drinking parties' (Ep 296:225–6). In the
present letter and in the letter accompanying it to 'Lambertus Grunnius' (Ep
447) Erasmus sets out his case once more. The themes are clear enough and
they are canonically significant as a plea for his cause: his lack of freedom in
entering into the life of a religious under vows for which he was temperamen-
tally and physically unsuited; his reasons for laying aside his religious habit;
and the moral and intellectual dangers that await him if he is forced to
continue to live under his first obligations.

This letter thus resumes the contact of July 1515 (Epp 338–9) when Pope Leo
x had already indicated his willingness to demonstrate his esteem for Erasmus
by some favour. The need to consult with Ammonio about seeking this further
dispensation was perhaps the chief business of Erasmus' visit to England in
August 1516; cf Ep 441 introduction.

The present letter had been composed evidently in draft form in Antwerp
before Erasmus travelled to London; it was in Antwerp that Pieter Meghen
finally brought him the pope's letter of 10 July 1515 (cf Ep 338 introduction).
Erasmus' letter was first published in the *Epistolae aliquot*.

TO LEO X, PONTIFF TRULY SUPREME,
FROM ERASMUS OF ROTTERDAM, GREETING
I thought I should be abundantly fortunate, most holy father, if your
Holiness should have done no more than take in good part the rashness or
the importunity which emboldened me to address a letter of my own accord   5
to the exalted splendour of the papacy and what is grander yet to the
incomparable eminence of a Pope Leo. But this daring, as I see it was, has
been most happily rewarded. My hopes and prayers have been outdone by
your more than fatherly generosity, in despatching of your own free will
two briefs, one of which pays a lavish and impressive tribute to me and my   10
work, while in the other you recommend me carefully and warmly to his
majesty the king. The greatest thing in life is to have earned the approval of
the eternal deity; second to that, at the lowest, I reckon to be approval in the
solemn words of the supreme pontiff – still more the approval of a Leo, of

* * * * *

446:10 two briefs] Epp 338, 339; see introduction.
11–12 his majesty] Henry VIII; cf Ep 339.

one in whom the highest dignity open to mortal men adorns and is in turn   15
adorned by virtues and accomplishments of every kind.

Had your brief reached me in good time (for I was then in Basel), even
the dangers of the journey could not have deterred me from hastening to
pay my duty at your most blessed feet. As it is, I have returned to my own
country and am somewhat restricted by advancing years; still more am I   20
held here by the generosity of princes and tied by what I can only call the
exceptional affection of my native land. For the most illustrious Prince
Charles, the Catholic king, incomparable light and glory of this age of ours,
in whose dominions I was born and of whose father Philip I enjoyed in the
old days not merely the acquaintance but the friendship, invited me most   25
generously in my absence with an annual salary which I neither asked for
nor expected, and on my return, when I was scarcely returned in fact, he
presented me to a rich and honourable benefice. Apart from that, there is
the long-standing favour of the most serene English king, the kindness
shown me by his eminence the cardinal of York, and the old and tried   30
support of the archbishop of Canterbury; and how much these have been
encouraged by the recommendation of your Holiness I have the best of
reasons for knowing. This was all the more welcome to me, and carried the
more weight with them, because it was not won from you by importunity
but freely offered.   35

And so I see clearly the great debt which I owe to your Holiness; and
yet I wish to owe you a debt greater still. In fact it will be a source of
satisfaction to be indebted for all my fortunes and my entire felicity to Leo
and to no one else; and in my view it is no small factor in one's happiness to
enjoy being under an obligation. What I have on my mind will be explained   40
to you by word of mouth by the right reverend father in Christ the bishop of
Worcester, permanent representative of the invincible English king at your
Holiness's court, and in a letter by Andrea Ammonio, your Holiness's
nuncio in England. In this business I make no doubt that I shall experience

* * * * *

24 Philip] Cf Epp 179, 181 introductions.

26 salary] Cf Ep 370:18n.

28 benefice] The prebend of Courtrai; cf Ep 436:6n.

29 king] Henry VIII; cf Ep 272.

30 York] Thomas Wolsey; cf Ep 284.

31 Canterbury] William Warham; cf Ep 188.

36 debt] See Ep 447 introduction.

42 Worcester] Silvestro Gigli, the English agent at Rome: cf Ep 521 introduction.

44 nuncio] Since 1515 as sub-collector of Peter's Pence in England; cf Epp 218 introduction, 517:79 ff.

all the goodness so readily promised me both by that generous nature of 45
yours, in which you approach most nearly to Christ whose vicegerent you
so deservedly are, and by your Holiness's letter; especially since the matter
is of such a kind that it does not concern my own position, in which you
take a generous interest, so much as the good of the world at large, which is
the object of all your watchful care. To obtain this request I might have 50
enlisted, improperly, the support of the greatest princes; but I preferred to
owe this benefit, such as it is, entirely to your kindness and to no one else. I
know of course that it will be too great to be repaid by any service that
mortal man can render, and also that your great position carries with it a
nobility that demands no return of thanks from anyone; but my least duty 55
will be to strive with all my might to prove that you have not bestowed such
outstanding generosity on a man who is wholly unworthy or wanting in
memory or gratitude.

The New Testament published simultaneously in Greek and Latin,
revised by me together with my notes, appeared some time ago under the 60
patronage of your most auspicious name. Whether this work wins universal approval, I do not know; so far at any rate I find it approved by the most
approved and leading theologians, and in particular by that incomparable
prelate, Christopher bishop of Basel, who authorized the publication of the
book. For by this labour of mine the ancient and commonly accepted text is 65
not pulled up by the roots; here and there I correct it where it is corrupt, in
some places I explain its obscurities, and this I do not out of my own fancies
nor, as they say, with unwashed hands, but partly on the evidence of very
ancient copies and partly in accordance with the views of men whose
learning and sanctity alike have been approved by the Church – Jerome, 70
Hilary, Ambrose, Augustine, Chrysostom, Cyril. Meanwhile I am always
ready either modestly to defend my view where I am right, or gladly to
correct it if, being only human, I have made an unwitting mistake.

One volume, while still recent and hot as yet from the press, I sent to

* * * * *

47 letter] Ep 338; see introduction.
49 good of the world] Evidently an allusion to the problem of recruitment to
the monastic life; see Ep 447.
51 princes] The chancery of Prince Charles was, however, busy on his behalf;
cf Epp 475:12, 476:23–4, 519:8. Erasmus' prebend at Courtrai and the prospect
of a bishopric were unquestionably factors in the timing of this appeal; cf Epp
436, 475:5n.
56 with all my might] Literally 'with hands and feet'; *Adagia* I iv 15
61 name] Ep 384
64 Christopher] von Utenheim; cf Ep 305:243n, Allen Ep 598 introduction.
68 unwashed hands] *Adagia* I ix 55

Rome last winter, and suppose that it will have reached your Holiness; and I   75
would now send the other, did I not know that everywhere in the world it is
now familiar. In this I laboured with all the energy that the limits of time
allowed me by the prince and the consideration of my own health permitted; but all the same, I shall never grow weary and never rest until I have so
enriched and polished and perfected the book that it may seem not un-   80
worthy of the Leo who, even apart from his papal dignity, is the greatest of
men. Jerome entire, reborn under favourable auspices as I believe, will see
the light next September, and is most eagerly awaited by the whole learned
world. Henceforward not a page will be issued under Erasmus' name that
will not sing the praises of Leo, a pope as good as he is great. You are far too   85
modest to demand this; it is a tribute to your more than human merits; and
it is for the benefit of the whole world that the example of a pope so
universally admired should be transmitted to posterity. If my natural force
fails me in this task, yet the very greatness of what you have done for me,
the enthusiasm of a heart devoted to you, and above all your transcendent   90
virtues will supply the intellectual force and the eloquence I lack.

My respectful best wishes to your Holiness, and for the revival and
extension of religion and the betterment of the lot of man may Christ the
Almighty preserve you in health and wealth as long as possible.

London, 9 August 1516   95

447 / To Lambertus Grunnius   [London or Rochester?, August 1516]

The following letter was published first in the *Opus epistolarum* by Froben in
1529, a circumstance that assures its authenticity. The facts surrounding its
composition remain conjectural, but the letter is clearly an important if partial
account of Erasmus' early life and religious vocation, connected to his appeal
at this time for dispensation from his early commitments: cf Ep 446:51n.

The name of the addressee is fictitious, alluding to the playful piece, the
'Testament of Grunnius Corocotta the Piglet' mentioned by St Jerome and
cited by Erasmus in his dedication to the *Praise of Folly* (Ep 222:42). He used
the name again to address a group of reforming theologians in the *Epistola
contra Pseudevangelicos*; cf Allen Ep 2440 (5 March 1531).

Erasmus wrote this letter as part of a plan of campaign agreed upon earlier in
London with Ammonio; cf Ep 446 introduction; Ep 451:17. It is conceivable

* * * * *

77 limits of time] Erasmus refers to his appointment as councillor to Prince
Charles; cf Ep 370:18n.
82 Jerome entire] Cf Epp 326, 396.

that it was in intent a memorandum for the instruction and amusement of Silvestro Gigli, bishop of Worcester, who was to put Erasmus' case to the pope by word of mouth; cf Ep 446:41–2. A letter of Erasmus to the pope is referred to in Ep 451:11 and 452:14, and in Ep 453:16 Ammonio calls this letter a 'fiction' (*commentum*). This seems a possible description of this lengthy account of two boys, Florentius and his older brother Antonius, for whom the names of Erasmus and his brother Pieter must be substituted, taking into account the known facts of Erasmus' early life.

In September, Ammonio sent this letter to Rome with Ep 446 and his own covering letter to Leo x, Ep 466; cf Ep 446:43. Some six weeks later Gigli wrote to Ammonio that the matter had been well received, and enclosed a proposed draft for the dispensation; Ep 498:11; 505:5–6. Erasmus made suggestions on this draft and, after it was returned to Rome, the final documents were prepared at the end of January 1517. They reached Erasmus about mid-March (Ep 552). The dispensations are Epp 517 and 518, the former addressed to Ammonio in favour of an unnamed person. Ammonio's subscription to it mentions Erasmus by name, however; cf Ep 517:81. The second letter, to Erasmus himself, contained a general absolution with power to hold ecclesiastical benefices of a specified kind.

Since it is the first of these letters of dispensation (Ep 517), that addressed to Ammonio, that seems to reply most directly to the needs described in the present letter, it is possible that in its original form this letter was written in Ammonio's name; cf also Ep 483:23n. Allen regarded Erasmus as the true author of Grunnius's reply, lines 830–54; an alternative possibility is that it was written by Ammonio soon after the dispatch of his letters as a rhetorical companion to Erasmus' account of himself. Lacking some of the most important original material (none of these documents touches on the question of Erasmus' illegitimacy) which was perhaps conveyed only by word of mouth, we cannot reconstruct the appeal with precision. As we have them, in the form in which they were published by Froben in 1529, the letter and the reply in Grunnius's name are so phrased as to suggest a literary reworking of the whole before it was allowed to reach the public. This impression is heightened by the contrast between this letter, which is vague about the precise favour or favours sought but highly circumstantial in portraying the constraint under which 'Florentius' made his original vows, and the quite specific terms of the dispensations, which allow Erasmus full freedom to pursue the life he had chosen and to support himself appropriately without fear of reproof, yet fall short of the seemingly implicit final petition of this letter – release from his vows as an Austin Canon. For the biographical account known as the *Compendium vitae* which covers much the same ground as this letter, see the Appendix.

ERASMUS OF ROTTERDAM TO LAMBERTUS GRUNNIUS,
A PAPAL SCRIBE

Hitherto, dear Lambertus my most learned friend, I have willingly played
no part in cases of this kind in spite of many appeals, nor have I ever had the
heart to trouble any of my friends; but on this occasion a special obligation   5
has made me desert my principles and has driven me to espouse a cause of
an unfamiliar sort, making trouble for a very old friend like yourself on
behalf of another friend. And so my first request is that you should be
willing to learn the whole story; for I am sure that, if you grant me this, you
will approve the part I have played and will not be unwilling to take a hand   10
yourself, not this time because of our friendship, though I am sure you
would do anything for me, but on the merits of the case. What is at stake is
no goat's wool, as they say, but the welfare of an exceptionally gifted
individual who will perish, buried alive, unless we rescue him. I wish you
knew all that lies behind the story as well as I do; a few words, I am quite   15
sure, would suffice for me to lay the entire case before you. None the less, I
will give such a faithful picture of the whole thing that nothing or at least
extremely little will escape you which you need to know. For the man whose
case I plead has been so well-known to me from boyhood that I am scarcely
better acquainted with myself, and most of what pertains to the case I know   20
not from hearsay but as an eye-witness. And it is such a monstrous story
that I myself can hardly tell it without weeping, and maybe you yourself,
with your kind heart, will find tears in your eyes as you read. But it is the
part of a true Christian, my dear Grunnius, not merely to rejoice with them
that do rejoice but to weep with them that weep.   25
      I am sure that, being the excellent person you are, you will know well
and cordially dislike the impertinence of certain Pharisaical characters who,
as the Gospel records, travel not only over sea and land but through all the
courts of princes, all the houses of the rich, every university, every
drinking-party, that they may inveigle some proselyte into their net; and   30
one can hardly credit the arts with which they lie in wait for the innocence
of young men and maidens. They know the age which supplies an ideal
target for both injury and fraud, so that they can drag them off into a kind of
life from which they may be unable to extricate themselves once they are in
the toils; and no other kind of servitude is so lamentable, for a slave bought   35

* * * * *

447:13 goat's wool] *Adagia* I iii 53; something non-existent, worthless if it did
exist

15 a few words] Literally 'three words'; *Adagia* IV iv 84

25 rejoice *etc*] Rom 12:15

28 Gospel] Matt 23:15

in the open market can at least earn his master's gratitude, and rise from
slave to freedman.

I will not therefore waste your time by telling you what you know well
already, for the whole world is filled with their stratagems on every side.
Was there ever a boy of unusual gifts or honourable birth or ample means   40
whom they did not assail from some ambush, spreading their nets for him
and beguiling him with their tricks, often without the knowledge and
sometimes against the known wishes of his family? Yet though this is more
monstrous than any form of kidnapping, these skilful actors contrive to
label as piety what is really crime. One must flee to Christ, say they, even if   45
it means trampling on one's family, and against the inspiration of the Holy
Spirit parental authority goes for nothing; as if Satan were not to be found
among monks as much as anywhere, or as if all who take the cowl are
inspired by the spirit of Christ, though much the largest crowd is moved by
folly or ignorance or desperation or a desire for idleness and good dinners.   50
That God commanded children to obey their parents is beyond question;
what spirit it is that instigates a man to turn monk is not certain even to the
victim.

You see what a wide field opens before me at this point on a well-worn
theme; but I do not choose to dwell on it, for all men's ears are dulled by the   55
daily complaints of those who have fallen into the snare. Personally, I have
no wish to condemn any man's way of life, nor shall I defend those who,
having begun badly by plunging without a thought into the pit, make a
worse end, escaping not into liberty but into licence to sin. But given the
great variety of bodies and of minds, the same things are not suitable for   60
everybody, nor can anything happen to gifted minds more disastrous than
to be lured by cunning or driven by force into some way of life from which
they cannot extricate themselves. Human felicity consists above all in this,
that a man should devote himself to what he is fitted for by nature. There are
men whom one would compel to adopt celibacy or the monastic life with no   65
more success than one would enter an ass for a race at Olympia or take an ox,
as they say, to the wrestling-school.

Enough by way of introduction. Now listen to the misfortunes of this
excellent young man and to the abominable wickedness of these body-
snatchers. And here let me ask again for your kind attention, for I very   70
greatly desire that what I do should have your approval. One sometimes

* * * * *

36 in the open market] 'off the [stone] counter' on which slaves were exhib-
ited; *Adagia* III i 67

44 kidnapping] *plagium*; cf lines 69–70, 256, 811.

66–7 ox to the wrestling-school] *Adagia* I iv 62

regrets a thing done to satisfy others; what is done from deliberate purpose does not cease to seem right.

There are two brothers, Florentius and Antonius, who is the elder. When quite small, they lost their mother; their father died some time   75 afterwards, leaving a slender estate, but quite sufficient to complete their education, had not the greed of the kinsfolk who attended his deathbed reduced it. Of ready cash there was no trace; but what survived in the way of real property or securities, and so was not equally exposed to the harpies' talons, was roughly sufficient to finish their studies in the liberal arts, had   80 not once again a good part perished through the idleness of their trustees. You know how few those mortals are, who keep a really sharp look-out when in charge of other men's affairs. The trustees had formed the idea of educating them for a monastery, thinking it showed a wonderful sense of duty to provide them with their daily bread. To this the trustees were   85 already inclined, and a certain Warden, a proud man with a great repûtation for piety, had pushed them into it, one of them especially who was the schoolmaster under whom the boys in their earliest years had learnt the rudiments of grammar. This man was commonly regarded as pious and honourable, by which they mean innocent of gaming, wenching, greed,   90 drunkenness and other misdemeanours; but he was a man who lived for himself alone, very mean, in judgment no better than the common herd, and with no respect for education except the confused and scanty sort he had imbibed himself. When Florentius, who was in his fourteenth year, had written him a rather ornate letter, he replied severely that in future, if   95 he sent any letters like that, he must add a commentary; it had always been his own habit, he said, to write plainly and 'punctually' (that was the word he used). He seems to be of the same persuasion as many others I have known, thinking that he sacrificed a victim most pleasing to God if he should have consigned one of his pupils to the monastic life, and is wont to   100 recount with pride how many young men every year he had gained for Francis or Dominic or Benedict or Augustine or Bridget.

And so, when the boys were already ripe for the institutions they call universities – for they were adequate grammarians, and had got by heart a

* * * * *

74 Florentius, Antonius] Presumably Erasmus himself and his brother, Pieter
86 Warden] Or Guardian, the head of a Franciscan house, probably the one at Gouda
87 one of them] Cf Ep 1 introduction.
95 letter] Cf Ep 1 introduction.

great part of the Dialectic of Petrus Hispanus – he nevertheless was afraid   105
that there they might breathe in some spirit from the outer world and refuse
the yoke, and so he arranged for their dispatch to a community of those who
are commonly called the Collationary Brothers, who make their nests in all
parts of the world and earn their living by teaching the young. Their chief
purpose, if they see a boy whose intelligence is better bred and more active   110
than ordinary, as able and gifted boys often are, is to break their spirit and
depress them with corporal punishment, threats and recriminations and
various other devices – taming him, they call it – until they make him fit for
the monastic life. On this ground they are pretty popular with the Dominicans and Franciscans, who say their Orders would soon come to an end if it   115
was not for the young entry bred up by the Brothers, for it is out of their
yards that they pick their recruits. Personally, I believe that even among
them there are some quite worthy people; but suffering as they do from a
lack of the best authors, and living by customs and rites of their own in a
darkness of their own making, so that they have no standard of comparison   120
but themselves – spending moreover a great part of the day in stints of
prayer and various activities – I do not see how they can give the young a
liberal education. Experience shows, at any rate, that no places produce
young men more coarsely educated or more depraved in character.

In such company therefore they wasted two years and more; at least, it   125
was waste for the younger boy, who already knew rather more than his
teachers themselves, at any rate in the subjects they professed to teach him.

* * * * *

105 Petrus Hispanus] Pope John xxi (13 September 1276–20 May 1299) was
born in Lisbon c 1210–15, son to a physician. After education in the Arts
Faculty at Paris (MA c 1240) he migrated to the new University of Siena to teach
medicine. In 1272 he became archbishop of Braga, and was elected pope at the
death of Adrian v. He was killed shortly afterward in the collapse of the ceiling
of the papal palace at Viterbo. He was one of the first western scholars to
comment on Aristotle's *De animalibus* and the *De anima*, and his best-known
works were probably the *Parva logicalia* and the widely circulated *Summulae
logicales*, which was also printed many times in the 15th century. A separate
Dialectica is mentioned by Copinger (2995). He was the author of many other
important philosophical and medical treatises.
108 Collationary Brothers] Or Collationarii. Brethren of the Common Life,
sometimes called by this name owing to their attachment to sermons and
conferences; cf G. Epiney-Burgard *Gerard Grote (1340–1384)* (Wiesbaden 1970)
164 and 39n. They were founded in the 14th century under the leadership of
Geert de Groote (1340–84), canon of Utrecht, to foster a more informed and
devout Christian life and education. See R.R. Post, *The Modern Devotion:
Confrontation with Reformation and Humanism* (Leiden 1968); *Scholen en on-
derwijs in Nederland gedurende de Middeleeuwen* (Utrecht–Antwerp 1954).

One of the teachers was such that Florentius says he never saw such a
monster of ignorance and self-satisfaction. Such men are not seldom put in
charge of boys; for teachers are chosen not by the verdict of educated men   130
but at the will of the General, who as a rule is innocent of humane learning.
The other one, however, who always seemed to take a special delight in
Florentius' gifts, when he understood that the boy's return to his native
place was under discussion, began in private conversations to work on his
boyish mind with a view to his joining their own society, telling him many   135
things about it of the sort that would attract the young. And would that he
had succeeded! – for either a love for the religious life would have retained
him among them willingly, or, had things so turned out, he would have
been allowed to resume his former liberty. For men of this persuasion have
one exceptional advantage, which is a vestige of the early days of religion: 140
they are not bound by indissoluble vows. And if the opinions of truly
religious and spiritual men carried more weight than the judgment of
blockheads, there would in future be no indissoluble vows except the vows
one takes in baptism, especially while mortals continue as prone to evil or
as weak as they are now.   145

So he kept up the pressure with constant exhortations, adding blandishments from time to time and little presents and caresses; and at length
the boy gave him an answer beyond his years – that as yet he knew too little
either of that way of life or of himself, but that as soon as he was grown up
he would consider the question. The man for his part then gave up, for he   150
was neither wholly fool nor knave; but I know members of that society who
have used not only threats and blandishments but terrifying adjurations
and what one could almost call exorcisms and incantations in the endeavour
to browbeat boys not yet turned fourteen, rich and of gentle birth, into
joining their society without the knowledge of their relations. If this is not   155
kidnapping, what is?

So when Antonius and Florentius were back in their native place,
their guardians, who had managed their property, small as it was, with less
than perfect honesty, opened discussions about the monastic life, partly to
secure a more speedy release from their responsibilities and partly because   160
the schoolmaster, who was the only active trustee (for one had been seized
by the plague and died suddenly, without rendering any accounts, and the
third was a businessman who did not take his duties at all seriously)
thought he would make a most acceptable offering to God, as I said before,
if he sacrificed two sheep to Him. Florentius, perceiving that they acted as   165
though their wards had willingly bound themselves to comply, questioned
his brother, who was three years older (he himself having barely passed his
fifteenth year), whether he was really of a mind to be bound willingly in

shackles which later he would not be able to undo. He frankly admitted that
he was moved not by love of the religious life but by fear of his guardians.   170
'You must be quite mad,' said Florentius, 'if out of some absurd misgivings
and fear of men of whom at least you do not have to be afraid that they will
beat you, you throw yourself into a kind of life of which you know nothing,
and from which, once entered, you cannot retreat.' Antonius then began to
argue that their small estate was not only minute in itself but reduced by the   175
negligence of their guardians. 'You have nothing to fear,' said Florentius:
'we will scrape up what is left, and putting all our small capital together we
will set off for the university. We shall not want friends, and many people
who possess absolutely nothing maintain themselves by their own efforts.
In the end, God will be with us if our purpose is honourable.'   180

This reply appealed to Antonius so much that he produced many
grounds for hope which had not occurred to the younger boy. So they
decided between themselves to put off the monastic question to another
time, until having spent as much as three or four years at the university they
would be old enough and have enough experience of life to discern more   185
clearly what best to do. Both held resolutely to this opinion. But the older
was even now tormented by anxiety about the way they should reply to
their guardians, who were busily and seriously pursuing this plan without
having discovered what their wards wanted. So they drew up a form of
words for their reply, which Antonius accepted; only he begged that his   190
younger brother might be the spokesman and answer in the name of them
both, being the more timid speaker, just as he also had less education.
Florentius accepted his proposal, but made his brother promise most
strictly that he would stand fast; 'or else,' he said, 'if I answer and you then
desert me, the entire trouble will fall on my head. Now is the moment to   195
change your mind, if you think you can be driven from your stand either by
soft soap or hard words. For believe me, what is afoot is no laughing
matter.' Antonius swore a solemn oath, and promised he would abide by
what they said.

Some days later, the guardian in question appeared, and after a long   200
preamble about his devotion to his wards and the wonderful zeal and
vigilance he had shown, he proceeded to congratulate them on his having
found a place for both of them among the men who rejoice to be called
canons twice over. At this point the boy Florentius, as they had agreed,

* * * * *

204 canons twice over] The Augustinian (Austin) Canons, or 'Canons Regular' (*canonici regulares*) who lived together according to a rule, and whose
origins went back to the 11th century; cf Ep 446 introduction.

answered for both of them and thanked him for his kindness and care, but   205
said that his brother and he did not think it wise at their age and, besides
that, with so little knowledge of the world, to commit themselves to any rule
of life; they still knew too little of themselves and absolutely nothing of
what they were approaching. (For they had never as yet set foot in a
monastery, nor could they suspect what kind of creature a monk was.) They   210
thought it much better to spend some years in serious studies, and to raise
this business again at a more suitable moment. There would then be a
better chance of success.

The boy's answer, so far beyond his years, deserved a warm welcome
from his guardian, had he been a truly religious man and furnished with   215
the wisdom that comes from the Gospel. In fact, had it so happened that he
found the young men with youthful ardour too ready to accept, it was his
duty to hold them back, and not to trust without question to the enthusiasm
of the moment. But no: he flew into a rage as though he had been punched
in the face, and though normally he seemed a mild man, he was beside   220
himself with anger and scarcely had sufficient self-control not to hit Florentius; but in the most haughty fashion called him a worthless rascal and said
he wanted the 'spirit' (a favourite word with monks, as you know). He
threw up his guardianship, refused to continue as surety to the men among
whom he had bought the boys a livelihood, and assured them that they had   225
nothing left – they could find out for themselves where their next meal was
coming from. With these cruel and violent attacks and many others like
them he belaboured the younger boy and forced him to shed tears (for he
was only a child), but did not force him to let go of the decision arrived at by
the light of reason. 'We accept your resignation as our guardian,' he said,   230
'and acquit you of all responsibility for us.'

On those terms they then parted. The guardian, perceiving that
threats and abuse made no progress, brought in his brother the man of
business, whom I mentioned before, who was a most cheerful and
pleasant-spoken person. They met in an orchard, the boys were invited to   235
sit down, drinks were produced, and after friendly conversation they set
about the business with more care this time, and on quite another tack.
Everything was delightful, there were plenty of tall stories about the wonderful felicity of the religious life, marvellous prospects were spread before
them of great things to come, appeals were added – all you can think of.   240
Beguiled by all this, the elder brother began to weaken, forgetting that he
had more than once sworn to be loyal; the younger maintained his resolve
unshaken. In a word, the traitor betrayed his brother and accepted the
yoke, but covertly laid his hands on such ready money as there was, which
in him was nothing new. And as far as he was concerned, it was a success.   245

Slow-witted he might be, but he was physically strong, had an eye to the main chance and on that was quick and clever, not above stealing money, a sturdy drinker and as a wencher far from idle; in short, so unlike his younger brother that you might think he was a changeling. Nor was he ever anything to his brother but an evil genius. Not long after that, he held the   250
same office among his fellows that Iscariot did among the Apostles. None the less, when he saw his brother piteously caught in the snare, his conscience pricked him and he lamented having undone him by drawing him into the trap. The confession of a true Judas, was it not? And I wish he had followed Judas' example and hanged himself before he did anything so   255
wicked.

Florentius, like most people of a naturally scholarly bent, had no experience of ordinary business and neglected it, and showed surprising innocence (for you can find people whose business sense is full grown before their beards), nor was his intelligence usable except in studies. It   260
was to those that he was entirely devoted and swept away by some natural force; when he was playing with his toys, he was already an academic. He was of delicate physique, though adequate for the activities of the mind; scarcely entered on his sixteenth year; and beyond that, weakened by a quartan fever which lasted already in his boyhood for more than a year,   265
contracted from his mean and illiberal schooling. Which way was he to turn, a boy like that? – On all sides abandoned and betrayed, unschooled in everything, and not exempt from illness? Would you not think enough force had been applied to drive his boyish spirit in any direction one pleased? But he held manfully to the convictions which he had not formed lightly.   270

Meanwhile that stupid guardian, faced with the failure of his undertaking, recruited for the last act of his drama a miscellaneous cast of differing social status and even sex, monks, half-monks, kinsmen male and female, young and old, known and unknown. Among them were some so feather-witted by nature that, except for the respect secured for them by   275
their cloth, they might have appeared in public as itinerant zanies with asses' ears and bells. There were others too who had gone astray, I think, from superstition rather than depravity of will; but what difference does it make to the victim whether it is folly or misplaced zeal that cuts his throat? Think of the battering-rams that thundered there on the poor boy's spirit!   280
One of them painted an idyllic picture of monastic peace, choosing out all its best features (on that principle one could praise a quartan fever) with a generous admixture of falsehood, and concealing the other side of the medal. Another in true tragic vein magnified the perils of this world, as though monks were outside it – their own way of painting themselves in a   285
well-found ship, while all the rest are tossed by the waves and sure to perish

unless the monks offer them a spar or a rope. Another set before his eyes the
terrible torments of hell, as though from monasteries there were no open
road into Tartarus. Another tried to frighten him with fanciful improving
stories, of which they have a large supply. A certain traveller weary with his   290
exertions once took his seat on the back of a dragon thinking it was the
trunk of a fallen tree, and the dragon woke, turned its head back, and
gobbled him up; thus doth the world devour its devotees. A certain man
had once visited a community of monks, but when warmly invited to join
them, he held to his intention and departed; on the way a lion met the poor   295
fellow and tore him limb from limb. There were tales also of miraculous
visions, no less foolish than the old wives' tales of ghosts and goblins. Some
of them wooed him with stories of another kind: of the monk who had some
hours of conversation with Christ every day; of Catherine of Siena, who as a
girl was on such familiar terms with Christ her wedded husband, or rather   300
her lover, that they walked up and down together in her chamber and
sometimes said their hours together. Above all they cried up the monks'
sharing in good works, as though they themselves have a superfluity of
such things, and do not really need the Lord's mercy sometimes worse than
laymen do, or as though there was not in the whole body of Christ a sharing   305
in virtuous acts.

Not to make too long a story of it, every sort of siege-engine was
moved up to attack the mind of this simple-hearted boy, deserted by his
brother's treachery and weakened by ill health, and as much trouble and
pains and vigilance were constantly expended on him as if the capture of   310
some rich city were at stake. Such was the importance they attached, these
ultra-Pharisees, to the taking of one adolescent in order to bury him alive.
Among them were some devoted to the advancement of their own Order, to
which they are so much attached that for the sake of the Order they quarrel
passionately among themselves and virtually disregard their Christian   315
profession. The boy was beyond his years in brains and education and
powers of expression, and they hoped he would somehow prove a valuable
ornament to their society. Such was their famous piety, such their religious
zeal.

I leave much unsaid deliberately, my learned Grunnius, in order not   320
to tire you with the details; and a man of your experience can supply the rest
from what I tell you. Florentius all this time was caught, as the proverb runs,

* * * * *

299 Catherine of Siena] 1347 [1333?] – 1380, daughter of a Sienese dyer and a
Dominican tertiary, she was widely celebrated in her lifetime for extraordinary
sanctity, and known for her visions and mortification. She was canonized in
1461.

between the devil and the deep sea. While he was thus in suspense, looking round to see if any deity might appear, offering some hope of salvation, by pure chance he visited a certain religious house near the city in which he   325
was then living. There he found a certain Cantelius, with whom he had been brought up from infancy. He was some years his senior, had an ingenious mind and an eye permanently to the main chance, but was high-spirited. It was not so much piety as devotion to his dinner and a love of ease that had lured him into the monastery. For he was by nature greedy   330
and extremely idle; his literary education had not made satisfactory progress, but he had a good singing voice and had been musical from an early age. After hunting in Italy in vain for some position, while his parents kept on pointing out their lack of means and their crowd of children, he took sanctuary in the monastic cowl, which has at least this to its credit that it   335
provides a convenient vehicle for the feeding of many creatures who would otherwise starve to death.

At this point Cantelius learnt from their conversation of the great progress that Florentius had made at his books, and thinking at once of his own advantage, he began to exhort him with incredible warmth to come   340
and share his life (he was persuasive by nature), painting a wonderful word-picture of their regular life and building up their blessed peace and liberty and concord – in a word, it was to be fellowship with the angels. Above all he repeated with emphasis what a supply of books there was and how much leisure time for study. He knew the bait with which to catch the   345
young man's mind. In a word, had you heard the man, you would have thought it must be no monastery but a garden of the Muses. Florentius with his frank and friendly nature loved Cantelius with a strong boyish affection, the more so as he had unexpectedly found him again after so long an interval; it is not uncommon at his age to conceive passionate attachments   350
for some of your companions. He had as yet little knowledge of human

* * * * *

323 the devil and the deep sea] Literally perhaps 'between the altar and the knife'; *Adagia* 1 i 15

326 Cantelius] Cornelis of Woerden; cf Ep 296:14n. Erasmus' name plays upon the sense suggested in line 332 ('tantum canendi peritus'), and on the Greek *canthelios*, a pack-ass (and so, a blockhead), with a side-glance at his skill in plain-chant.

350 passionate attachments] There is evidence of this especially in his surviving correspondence with Servatius Rogerus; cf Ep 4 introduction, and R.L. DeMolen 'Erasmus as Adolescent: "Shipwrecked am I, and Lost, 'Mid Waters Chill"' BHR 38 (1976) 7–25.

nature, but judged all others by himself. Cantelius for his part left no stone
unturned, and used every shift to master the boy's mind by his incantations; but he did not succeed.

Florentius came away from that interview only to meet a still heavier   355
attack from the other party; for they had mobilized more powerful siege-
artillery. They impressed upon him the desperate state of his affairs, the
hostility of all his friends, and the starvation (that most tormenting of all
forms of death) which faced him if he did not renounce the world. For that is
how they speak, using 'world' as a term of abuse for those whom Christ   360
redeemed from the world by His blood, and claiming for monks as their
private property what belongs in common to every Christian. After prolonged attacks from them which more distressed than shook him, he returned to Cantelius merely for the pleasure of his company. Cantelius was
now aiming by every means in his power to secure for himself a secret and   365
unpaid tutor; and Florentius had a great gift for friendship, and was easily
persuaded to oblige any casual friend. And so, since there was no end to the
bombardment and no glimmer of hope anywhere, he entered a religious
community, not the one provided by his guardian, but that in which he had
found by chance his old foster-brother. The place was so much decayed, so   370
unhealthy that it was scarcely fit for keeping cattle, let alone for such a
delicate constitution. But at that age he had not learnt to take any account of
diet and climate and physical surroundings. Nor did he go there with the
intention of adopting the religious life, but in order to escape for a time
from those who were bullying him, until time itself should provide some   375
better plan.

Cantelius meanwhile steadily pursued his own advantage, abusing
his companion's simple confidence and readiness to oblige. For Florentius
used secretly to go through a whole comedy of Terence with him sometimes
in a single night, so that within a few months they went right through the   380
principal authors in these furtive and nocturnal sessions, to the great peril
of his delicate health; but that made no difference to Cantelius, who seized
his opportunity, thinking of no one but himself, for self was the only thing
he really loved. Meanwhile, to prevent Florentius from going back on what
he had begun, he was allowed every liberty. The boy greatly enjoyed the   385
pleasant company of his contemporaries. They sang, they played games,
they wrote verses in competition with one another; no one was obliged to
fast, or woken up for the office in the middle of the night; no one rebuked
or chided him, all was friendliness and smiling faces.

* * * * *

352–3 no stone unturned] *Adagia* i iv 30

And so in this thoughtless way several months passed by. But when   390
the appointed day drew near for abandoning secular dress and donning the
habit, Florentius came to himself; he began to sing his old refrain, and
sending for his guardians raised the question of his freedom. Once again
there were cruel threats, and a display of the desperate state of his affairs
unless he continued as he had well begun. Nor was Cantelius backward at   395
this stage in playing his part; it did not suit his book to lose those nightly
lessons which cost nothing. I ask you, was it not mere assault and battery so
to treat a boy by nature simple-hearted, inexperienced and thoughtless? To
cut a long story short, they dressed him in the habit for all his protests,
although they knew that his mind was unchanged. That done, affectionate   400
indulgence was used once more to beguile his boyish mind.

Thus nearly another year passed by in thoughtless levity. But he had
by now almost come to realise that that way of life suited neither his mind
nor his body. For his mind enjoyed nothing except study; and study in that
place was neither respected nor practised. In other ways he was not averse   405
from piety, but he was not much attracted by the chanting and the ceremonies in which almost their whole life consists. Besides which, it is a
common practice to thrust into such communities the wooden-heads and
the half-wits, those who have no tincture of the Muses and love their bellies
rather than their books. Among these people, if a gifted mind appears that   410
is born for the liberal arts, they suppress it to keep it from emerging. And
yet these are the people who insist on despotic rule, and it often happens
that the stupidest man and the most selfish, provided he is of robust
physique, carries the most weight in that society. Now just imagine what
torture it must be for a gifted nature born for the Muses to spend all his life   415
among men like that. Nor is there any hope there of being set free, unless it
falls to one's lot to be made head of a house of nuns; and that is a most
unhappy form of servitude. For besides the continuous responsibility for a
pack of women, one has the relaxing experience of long spells of drinking
every day, not without some peril to one's continence; and it not seldom   420
happens that when their father confessor is stricken in years and useless,
they send him back to his original stable, where he feels all the more
wretched because for some time he has lived to please himself.

Now our young man's constitution was by nature so ill adapted to
fasting that a meal postponed beyond its usual time often endangered his   425
health, though he knew nothing about himself and had no thought for
anything of the kind; he was merely put on his guard by stomach pains and

* * * * *

417 house of nuns] Cf Ep 296:226–30.

a weakness at the heart. This may rouse a sneer from animals of coarser build, which would be wanton even if you fed them on nothing but hay; but experienced physicians are not unaware that this is characteristic of   430
bodies that are rare in texture and have very subtle spirits. In such cases they prescribe food easily digested, taken often and in small quantities, while you may find other men who, once they have filled their stomachs, can last with no trouble longer than vultures. These same constitutions, so the physicians tell us, are most intolerant of cold, wind and mists, and more   435
sensitive to the air around them than to the food inside them. Our young man had another personal difficulty, which dogs him from his childhood to the present day and is incurable. He cannot fall asleep until a late hour, and if his slumber is once broken he takes several hours to get to sleep again. Often he will lament in conversation how he is forbidden to enjoy those   440
golden hours, and has to lose the sweetest part of the day in sleep. Often he has tried to drive out his natural habit by force, but has never succeeded. Further, if he has no supper he spends a sleepless night, and his health suffers for it. For fish he had such loathing as a youth that at the mere smell of it he felt a severe headache and a touch of fever. What could such a mind   445
and such a body do in a monastery, especially in such a situation? He was a fish in a ploughed field or a cow in the sea.

All this was well known to those reverend fathers, and had there been a grain of sincere charity in them, ought they not of their own accord to have come to the boy's rescue in his ignorance or thoughtlessness, and put him   450
right in words like these? 'My son, it is foolish to strive in vain; you do not suit this way of life nor does it suit you. While the question is still open, you must choose some other course. Christ dwells in every place, not here and nowhere else; you can follow religion with success whatever the colour of your garments, if you have the true spirit. We will do what we can to secure   455
your return to freedom with the good will of your guardians and friends. Thus you will not be a burden to us in the future, nor shall we be your undoing.'

Such words would have been worthy of really religious people. But no one gave him a word of advice; instead, they moved up all their engines to   460
prevent the poor tunny from slipping out of their net. One of them said that this was Satan's way: to apply all his arts and all his wiles at such a moment to trip up Christ's new recruit. If he held his own bravely in this conflict, the rest would be easy and even pleasant. The very same thing, he maintained, had happened to him long ago, and now he seemed to live in Paradise.   465
Another tried to fill him with misgivings by displaying the great danger

* * * * *

461 tunny] Cf Ep 451:8; Lucian *Timon* 22.

that St Augustine in a temper would visit some great evil on him in return for
the insult of his abandoning the habit, and of this he recalled several
horrifying examples: one man had contracted an incurable disease, one had
been killed by lightning, one fatally bitten by a viper. He added that the   470
adoption of the habit was a kind of silent vow; this would not be a much
smaller offence in the sight of God, or less disgraceful before men, than if he
had absconded after a full profession. Every possible weapon was brought
to bear on the young man, but none heavier than the fear of disgrace. 'By
now,' they say, 'it is too late to draw back. You have set your hand to the   475
plough, and it is forbidden to look behind you. If you lay aside the habit you
adopted before so many witnesses, you will be a byword for ever more.'
Thereupon they blew up the word 'apostate' to vast and tragic dimensions.
'Where will you go?' say they. 'You will never be able to show your face in
respectable company. Monks will know you have a curse on you; laymen   480
will look askance at you.' Now the young man was girlishly modest by
nature, which made him fear death less than disgrace. On the other side
was the pressure from his guardians and friends, some of whom had
reduced his patrimony by dishonesty. In brief, their importunity was
successful. The young man, with abhorrence in his heart and words of   485
denial on his lips, was compelled to accept the halter, much as captives in
war offer their hands to the victor to be manacled, or men who give way
under prolonged torture do not what they wish but what pleases one
stronger than they.

His mind Florentius might somehow have brought to heel; but no   490
man can remake his body. For the time being the young man did as people
do in prison: he consoled himself with study, so far as the place permitted,
for even that he had to do in secret, while it is allowed to get drunk in
public. So he beguiled the tedium of his captivity by reading, until some
unexpected chance, some god from the machine should show him a hope of   495
salvation. And that came to pass; for he was invited by an important bishop
to join his household, from which after taking orders he proceeded to a
famous university. But for this, that gifted nature would have mouldered

* * * * *

476 plough] Cf Luke 9:62.

495 god from the machine] *Adagia* I i 68

497 after taking orders] The statement that he was ordained after joining the
bishop of Cambrai contradicts the account by Beatus Rhenanus; Allen 156–71
and App V. Erasmus was ordained priest on 25 April 1492 at Utrecht by the
bishop of that see, David of Burgundy, an illegitimate son of Philip the Good.
It is not clear whether he was ordained before or after he first left Steyn to join
the service of the bishop of Cambrai; cf Allen I 588–9 and II 304n.

away among lazy, lascivious men and drinking-parties. Not that he casts
aspersions on his society, but for his nature it was quite unsuitable; it often   500
happens that what is life to one man is death to another. But such is his
modesty and bashfulness that he never speaks of his old community in any
hostile spirit; some people tell more by silence and reluctance than if they
spoke at length. Yet nothing of all this took place without the leave, indeed,
except on the instructions of the bishop who was the ordinary of the place,   505
with the permission of the heads both of the house and of the whole Order,
and with the consent of the whole society. But although his conscience was
clear and he knew that vows taken under compulsion did not bind him, he
made one concession for the time being, partly to his natural modesty,
which was quite excessive and often did him great harm, and partly to the   510
incurable readiness to take offence of ignorant and superstitious people: he
did not change his dress, although often invited to do so by the bishop, his
master.

Somewhat later it so happened that he set out on a long journey to
pursue his studies. There, as the French national custom is, he wore a linen   515
garment over his habit, supposing this by no means unusual in that country. Yet twice this brought him into present peril of his life, because the
surgeons there who tend those sick of the plague wear a white linen scarf
over the left shoulder that hangs down in front and behind, which iden-
tifies them easily so that those who meet or follow them may give them a   520
wide berth. The actual surgeons, if they did not walk by unfrequented
streets, would be attacked with stones by gathering crowds; such is the
horror of death in that country that they are driven to frenzy even by the
smell of incense, because incense is commonly burnt at funerals. On one
occasion when Florentius was visiting a learned friend, he happened to   525
meet two ruffians, or perhaps they were only constables, who with murderous cries drew their swords and would have dispatched him, had not a
married woman who happened to be passing pointed out to them that he
was dressed not as a surgeon but as a cleric. Even so, they went on raging and
did not sheath their swords until by beating on the door (for his destination   530
was hard by) he had secured admission. Another day he was visiting some
fellow-countrymen who were his friends. While he was with them, a great
crowd suddenly came running together from all quarters with stones and
staves, the men madly urging each other on with shouts of 'Kill the dog, kill
the dog!' While this was happening, a priest came up, who merely smiled,   535

* * * * *

517 peril] For an earlier account of this matter to Servatius Rogerus see Ep
296:181 ff.

and said to him, but in a low voice and in Latin 'Donkeys, donkeys!' While
the mob was still seething, a very elegant young man in a scarlet cloak came
out of the house. Florentius took sanctuary with him as if he had been an
altar (for he knew not a word of the language), and expressed his astonishment: what could they mean? 'Of this you may be quite certain' was the   540
reply. 'Unless you take off that linen scarf, one of these days you will be
stoned to death. I give you fair warning. Take it to heart, and look out.' And
so, though he did not take off the linen scarf, he covered it with the edge of
his coat. Great heavens, what a tale of woe, all about something of no
importance at all!   545

This will horrify those blockheads who think the essence of religion
lies in costume; not that I would say it should be lightly disregarded. But the
Carthusians often exchange their habit for a merchant's dress in order to
travel in greater safety to a synod. Canons change or conceal their official
dress either for purposes of study or when they have to make a long   550
journey, on no one's authorization and without attracting any rebuke; for
the linen frock does not carry the same sanctity as the others. For in the old
days canons were not monks, and now they are half and half, monks when
it suits them and when it would make them unpopular, not monks. But it is
an appalling crime for a Dominican or a Franciscan to cast away his reli-   555
gious dress. For the Dominican habit safeguards a rich man's whole house
and brings him prosperity, and when worn for a few years by children in
accordance with their mother's vow it preserves them from sickness and
horrible accidents; while the Franciscan tunic even when put on a corpse
frees the dead man from hell. After all, the supreme pontiff instructs certain 560
monks who had attended some gathering wearing habits of different kinds
that to avoid offence they should all wear the same dress. The papal decretal
threatens dire penalties, not against any who may lay aside the garb of a
religious for honourable reasons, but against those who may do so in order
to secure greater licence to join with laymen in behaving like ordinary   565
people. For linen clothing is not the prerogative of monks, but of bishops
and perhaps in the old days of clerics in general. Nor does Augustine in his
Rule prescribe any form of dress, but instead condemns any particular
attention to it, laying down that clerical costume should not strike the eye,
and that they should aim at pleasing not by their dress but by their way of   570
life; though it is well known that the Rule was written not for men but

* * * * *

559 tunic] For a satirical account of this Franciscan custom see the colloquy
Exequiae seraphicae ASD I-3 686–99.

567 Augustine] Epistle 211.10; CSEL 57:362–4

women; but I am now dealing with those who think it was written for men. In the end, this is the dress worn by the Holy Father when it is his custom to be dressed most like a pope.

Of all this Florentius was well aware; but that he might fulfil all 575
righteousness, he followed the advice of friends, and very easily obtained from the pope permission to use his own discretion in wearing such token of his monastic profession on such part of his body as he might please. Recalled from there to rejoin his patrons, who were neither uneducated nor men of low degree, he adopted the Gallican dress, which apart from a scarf 580
that hangs loose does not differ from the dress of the 'secular' priesthood (such is the ignominious name now given to the duly-appointed ministers of the Church instituted by the Apostles and by Christ). Nor did he do this without taking advice from responsible people. After his appearance in public thus attired, he was told by some very good friends that in that 585
country this costume was quite insupportable, and he must conceal the scarf. He might, you will say, have adopted the costume of the country in all respects; but nothing is more laborious. You need someone to support your flowing train, your left hand has to control a twisting liripipe; for in those parts that is of the first importance – following the example, I suppose, of 590
cardinals. Then the demands of business obliged him to move now and again from one region to another, and change his dress as an octopus changes colour; for the garb that wins respect in one place is thought monstrous in another. Lastly, he was a visitor, and daily in the company of great men, who in matters of dress are difficult to please. So at length his 595
sincerest friends decided that, as his conscience was clear, he must make full use of the papal permission, abandon all his scruples, and resume his freedom, for fear that by so often laying aside and resuming the habit, he might give even greater cause of scandal to malicious tongues.

I will add another point. The kind of life into which he was thrust as a 600
young man gave him so much liberty that it differed little from the unfettered life of a layman; I speak now not of any liberties that he took on his own initiative, but of the liberty allowed him by those in authority. I may point out that in such matters popes are wont to be more ready to grant relaxation than happens when the Seraphic or Carthusian or Brigittine Rule 605

* * * * *

572 women] An error; see Luc Verheijen *La règle de saint Augustin* 2 volumes (Paris 1967) and the review by Edmund Colledge OSA in *Medium Aevum* 39 (1970) 328–32.

575–6 fulfil all righteousness] Matt 3:15

577 permission] See Ep 446 introduction.

605 Seraphic] Franciscan

is breached. Those men do not even accept the pope's authority on such a point, though when he gives them wide-ranging privileges and prerogatives they count his authority sacrosanct and almost set it above Christ Himself.

I will not raise the question here of monastic vows, to which some   610
people attach excessive importance, though this kind of obligation – of slavery, I had almost said – is not found in either New Testament or Old. And then, if the sabbath was instituted for man (Christ is our authority) and not man for the sabbath, much more ought institutions of this kind to give way whenever they interfere with the well-being of a man, and particularly   615
of a man's soul, seeing that Our Lord is speaking of the well-being of the body, for the question at issue was hunger and the healing of a man on the sabbath day. But the men we speak of are the truly Pharisaical characters, those who break God's sabbath to pull out an ox or an ass that has fallen into a pit, and allow a man to perish body and soul to maintain some sabbath of   620
their own.

I will not mention here the great multitude of monasteries in which religious discipline has fallen so low that in comparison with them there is more sobriety and more innocence in a brothel, and all those houses in which, apart from ceremonies and outward show, there is no religious life.   625
This class are almost worse than the other, for lacking the spirit of Christ as they do, it is incredible all the same how they pride themselves on their ceremonies like the Pharisees, locating the whole of religion in externals and for the sake of ceremonial whipping boys to death every day. Though they themselves go through it with marvellous distaste, and would not get   630
through it at all did they not believe that the public would be impressed by the spectacle. And finally, how astonishingly scarce are religious foundations in which life is lived willingly according to the rule of religion, and even in these, if you were to open the Silenus and look inside, if you were to test what you find on the touchstone of genuine piety, it is amazing how   635
little sincerity you would discover! How cunning Satan's arts! How tortuous the heart of man, and how skilful in deceit! And this often imposes even on old men of long experience. And all this they expect to be taken in in a few months by a mere child! And this they call the monastic vocation!

Now let us grant that we can find a religious house in which all is in   640
order: what will happen when the man who has made his profession

* * * * *

613 sabbath] Mark 2:27–8; Matt 12:8, 11–12

634 open the Silenus] *Adagia* III iii 1; the reference here is primarily to the small images or *Sileni*, made so that they could be opened out to display an interior that contradicted the outward appearance.

Matthäus Schiner
A 'Sechser-Groschen' with a portrait of the cardinal;
his motto SOLI·DEO·GLORIA is on the reverse
Münzsammlung des Kantonsarchivs, Sitten

undergoes some bodily change, or when a good head of the house is
succeeded by a numbskull, a drinker, or a bully, or when his fellow-monks
change from good to bad? Let him move, they say, to another house or
another Order. But think with what reluctance they let any of their number   645
go! – While others are much more reluctant to receive him, assuming that
something outrageous must lie beneath the surface if he has left his old
society; and if he gives anyone the slightest cause of offence, he is confronted at once with 'Cannot you go back to your own house?' Besides
which, there is all that intense discussion, which Order is the more severe   650
and which the more relaxed; for everyone wants to make out his own to be
the strictest. So much for that famous facility of changing one's house or
rule of life: the wretched man is at risk once more of falling into yet harsher
servitude. In fact, since most of their recruits are inveigled by fraud, and
then instructed not in the religion of the spirit but in Pharisaism, and forced   655
to obey their fellow-men like slaves, most of them later regret their profession. Fearing therefore that their own orgies may be made public, the
monks retain them by flogging, by laying curses on them, by calling in the
secular arm, by high walls and barriers and imprisonment, and even by
death. Call me a liar if Matthäus, cardinal of Sion, at the dinner-table in the   660
hearing of many people did not mention a place by name, with the persons
and the monastery concerned, where the Dominicans buried a young man
alive, because his father, who was a knight, was demanding with threats
the return of the son whom they had carried off by stealth. And in Poland a
certain nobleman, who in his cups had fallen asleep in a church, saw two   665
Franciscans after the nightly office buried alive. On this point the authority
of the pope carries great weight with them, who as it happens permitted
them to do this without incurring penalties for a breach of their Rule; but
when he frees a man from the tyranny of their precious habit, they tear up
the diploma and put the man who procured it in prison.   670

    And after all this, they boast as founder of their Order of a Benedict or
a Basil, Jerome, Augustine, Dominic, Francis, Bruno. Let them look into
their founders' lives, and see whether they ever laid down or ever did
anything of the kind; and they will find a very different sort of society.
Example, sound teaching, friendly warnings, brotherly correction – these   675

* * * * *

660 cardinal of Sion] Matthäus Schiner of Mühlebach (c 1470–1522) bishop of
Sion in 1499 and cardinal in 1511. He was a noted diplomat who met Erasmus
on several occasions, and suggested his writing the Paraphrase of St Matthew.
The Paraphrases on the Epistles of Sts James and John were dedicated to him.
The horror stories attributed to him here are relayed at greater length in
Erasmus' colloquy *Exequiae seraphicae*.

were the only weapons of government. The man who could not be corrected by methods such as these was cast out of their company, though he might not have left of his own accord; so far were they from retaining a man who wished to leave. I say nothing of all those man-made ordinances, all those different types of dress, all the prayers and the ceremonies, among which 680 the least important of all, costume, has the greatest weight attached to it. Wearing his habit as a religious a man will get drunk every day, he is the slave of his palate and his belly, he goes whoring in secret and openly (not to speak of things far more obscene), he wastes the Church's money in luxurious living, and devotes time to necromancy and other evil arts; and 685 he is a worthy monk and called to be an abbot. The man who for any reason has laid aside his habit they abhor as an 'apostate' – a name which used rightly to be considered execrable, when it stigmatized men who had defected from the religion of Christ to Judaism or paganism. If one were to widen the meaning, everyone who is devoted to the pleasures of the world 690 and its vanities and riches and to the other desires which he renounced at his baptism is an apostate, no better than the other man but more dangerous, inasmuch as large numbers of offenders make the offence seem less heinous. In this way, monks who live an irreligious life (as commonly happens) are doubly apostates, for they have gone back, first on the sacred 695 vow by which they enlisted under Christ, and secondly on the rule of life they have undertaken. These are the men against whom one ought to brandish the accursed title of apostate, were they muffled up in ten cowls.

This being so, my dear Lambertus, what a crime it is by force or guile to get youth and inexperience into the net! If they are openly bad men, as 700 most of them are, this is simply to drag boys down to perdition. If they are neither hot nor cold, how pitiful is the servitude in which they entangle their victims! Suppose, however, that they have an air of virtue to recommend them: such are people's differences in body and in mind, so skilful is pretence, such the inexperience of a mere boy, so indissoluble the noose, as 705 they themselves maintain, that great indeed are the dangers both of mind and body to which they expose the young. The age of puberty, they say, brings with it the power to distinguish good and evil. But puberty does not come at the same age to everyone physically; much less so in mind. Even were there no such differences, it fits a man perhaps for matrimony, but not 710 for monastic vows; some men who have essayed them when something like thirty years old and in other respects fully experienced have retreated before making their profession, saying 'I had not thought it was like that.' In the old days, men were seldom admitted to the priesthood before the age of thirty; are they fit forthwith at puberty for the monastic life? And all the 715

time they impose on inexperience by their misuse of words, speaking of the
world as though they themselves were outside it; of obedience, although
Scripture enjoins obedience to God rather than men; of indissoluble vows,
although they have as yet found no way to distinguish vows soluble and
insoluble, except for Scotus' fancy that a monk's vow is indissoluble be-   720
cause it is taken before God through men; for a vow taken before God alone
is easily relaxed. And yet, seeing that their whole system depends on the
authority of the Roman pontiffs, why do they fart so vigorously in the
pope's face as often as they please? He releases many men from their
monastic obligations, though never without reason; and if he has power to   725
do this, why do they treat his authority on this point as worth nothing? If
they maintain that he has not the power, are they not accusing him of a
serious offence? So as often as it suits them, the pope as the vicar of Christ
can do no wrong; when they think otherwise, he can do nothing.

But I have no mind just now to fight it out against the Orders. Let us   730
grant that different ways of life are suitable, or even necessary, for different
people; let us accept that vows are indissoluble. The more devout and the
more difficult the monastic life, the more cautiously and slowly, and the
later in life, it should be undertaken; early enough if one is not yet forty, in
my opinion. Other vows are not held binding, unless it is established that   735
the man was of sound mind, in full possession of his faculties, and free from
threats and any other form of duress. Are we to call it binding here, when a
boy is driven against his will by flattery and threats, deceit and terror into
the noose? At this point no doubt they will argue that fear is nothing to a
stout heart. They ought rather to ask what are fraud and terror to a guileless   740
inexperienced youth. Besides which, in many of them that lack of guile is
the natural effect of youth and temperament, and it makes no difference if
there is down on their chins. The vow must stand, and stand so firm that for
its sake they must abandon the bride they have never known. Can the law
do nothing?   745

And so, Florentius having been driven into this by so much trickery in
spite of unbroken protest and reluctance, and having done nothing but
wear the habit and kept his conscience always clear, he seems to me bound
by no vow – no more than a man who has sworn a shameful oath to pirates
threatening to kill him. Nor do I doubt that the Holy Father in his goodness   750
will be just as indignant with those slave-dealers as he will be sympathetic
to their victim. The pope, you will say, will have power to give him back his
freedom, so far as any human tribunal can, since his conscience in itself is
clear; even so he cannot restrain men's tongues. And yet, since Christ the
truly supreme pontiff of the Church, and Paul His not unworthy disciple,   755

teach us that we should judge no one, especially in those things that in themselves make a man neither religious nor irreligious, the pope's authority ought to have at least enough weight to turn men's suspicions in a good direction, where to suspect the worst is wicked. But what will become of human affairs, if we are perpetually to give way before the crass opinions and the malignant scurrilities of men like this? When it is human weakness or invincible prejudice, Paul is willing that we should let it be, but only for a season; but to give way before foolish and malignant criticism means to overwhelm the vital force of Christian piety. Christ gave way to Caesar to the extent of paying the tribute-money, and to the Jews in abstaining from forbidden meats. But in healing the sick woman, in giving light to the blind, in restoring the cripple, in plucking the ears of corn, He openly ignored, in fact He deliberately provoked, the protests of the Scribes and Pharisees. And had St Paul not done the same, where would Christianity be now?

But what is their objection – these numbskulls? Did he lay aside his linen dress? How do they know whether he wears it underneath? And if he did lay it aside, how do they know what his reasons were, or by whose authority he did it? If they do not know, why do they pass judgment? And if they know that this was done with the pope's authority, why are they not afraid to reject his jurisdiction, which in other cases they wish to preserve intact? Where do we find in this that marvellous obedience of which we hear so much, while they do not listen to Christ, and rail at the head of the Church and Christ's vicegerent? Where is that simplicity which they advertise with those downcast looks? Where is that spirit that is dead to the world? But let all that go: where is their humanity and the feelings they share with other men? They can be accused themselves of so many crimes not here to be recounted – for they are openly detected in them almost every day – nor will we uncover their unspeakable and secret doings; and yet they never cease to denounce the changing of dress, as though that were an inexpiable offence. What could be more inhuman than to confront someone with his calamity, in which other men's malignity has plunged him? Who is so barbarous as to blame a man for his lameness, when it was a kick from a mule that broke his leg? Who would hold it against a man that he has only

760

765

770

775

780

785

* * * * *

756 judge no one] Cf Matt 7:1–2; Rom 2:1.
762 Paul] Cf Rom 14:1–3.
764 Caesar] Cf Matt 22:15–22; Mark 12:13–17; Luke 20:20–26.
766 sick woman] For these miracles see, for example, Matt 12:1–14, 22, where the evangelist's account comments specifically on Jesus' relationship to the sabbath laws.

one eye, if the other was removed by the enemy in battle? Who would taunt 790
him with epilepsy or leprosy, if he was by nature born like that? Or with
poverty, if he had lost all his belongings in a shipwreck? Real human beings
sympathize with such unfortunates and wish them well and help them if
they can; and the more severe the disability, the stronger their sympathy.
And what greater misfortune could befall a young man of parts than to be 795
pushed into this kind of life? If then it is excessively inhuman to confront a
man with his calamity as though it were a crime, what shall we say of him
who taunts someone for a misfortune which he himself has brought on by
his own wrongdoing? – If, for example, a clumsy surgeon called a man
one-eyed as an insult after his own clumsiness had destroyed the other eye, 800
or if a pirate jeered at a man for being a slave whom he himself had thrown
into slavery. Surely everyone would regard it – and rightly – as outstanding
effrontery to base a charge against another man on a wrong done by oneself.
What else do these men do, who impose on youth and inexperience with
their abominable arts, and then lay their own guilt on others? 805

Do you not perceive here a union of perfect inhumanity with perfect
folly and effrontery combined? The dishonour falls on them, and yet they
want to make someone else feel the shame. For the dishonour is not his who
has fallen into a pit, but theirs who threw him in. He laid aside his habit;
but it was you who forced him to put it on. Whoever thought it wrong for a 810
man taken captive by pirates to make his escape? Not the pirates themselves, I should suppose; and everyone else wishes him joy of it. A man
reckons everyone a pirate who takes away his liberty by force. If you prefer
less prejudiced examples, suppose a shoemaker were angry with a customer for rejecting a pair of shoes that were smart, but a very bad fit; surely 815
he would have the right to reply 'It is yourself you are blaming, for you
made me these shoes. Good-looking I agree they are, but they hurt my feet.'
Nothing prevents an institution from being admirable in itself, and yet for
this or that individual it may be disastrous.

Dear friend, I must conclude. If I have won your approval for my 820
Florentius' case, I beg you urgently to see that this business is put through
as speedily and as much in accordance with my wishes as possible. As for
the expense, you need have no fear; you can take me as surety.

As there seems to be some blank space at the end of this letter, I have
added a few facts which may be needed for drafting the certificate; but I 825
have written them in the cipher which I sent you in my last letter, and even
so you will not find them legible, unless you hold the paper near the fire. I

* * * * *

825 few facts] Presumably concerning his defect of birth, in invisible ink and
written in cipher; the same matters were dealt with explicitly in Ep 517.

shall expect an answer by this courier (for he will stay a fortnight in Rome) or by the next one at any rate. Farewell.

LAMBERTUS GRUNNIUS TO ERASMUS OF ROTTERDAM   830
Never did I take on any business, dearest Erasmus, more readily than what you charged me with, and rarely have I had greater satisfaction from putting through anything, not so much from my friendship with you (greatly as I value that) as from sympathy with Florentius in his misfortunes. I read out your letter from beginning to end in the presence of the   835
pope, several cardinals and other important people. The Holy Father not only seemed to be particularly charmed by the way you write; you would hardly believe how angry he was with those men you rightly call slave-dealers. The more devoted he is to the truly religious life, the more he hates the men you describe, who fill the world with unhappy monks, or bad   840
monks, not without serious loss to the Christian religion. Spontaneous goodness is what Christ likes, he said, not dungeons full of slaves. He gave orders that the licence should be issued immediately, and free of charge; but I gave the clerks and notaries three ducats, so as to get it sooner. You know what a starveling race they are; whether you will or no, you must   845
throw them a few morsels to keep them sweet. The courier by whom you wrote went on from here to Naples, and assured me he would be returning this way; but I do not know what has happened, he has not returned. This present man however presented himself in the nick of time, who is if I mistake not somewhat more reliable than the other, and he will bring you   850
the licence with a copy of it and the papal seal. I have agreed with him for half a ducat, so pray give him no more. Farewell, and give my affectionate greetings to Florentius, whom I now feel I share with you.
      From Rome

                  *   *   *   *   *

844 three ducats] Probably gold ducats of Venice, but possibly ducats of Bologna, Siena, or Hungary; or Florentine florins or Genoese genovinos. Having approximately the same gold content and thus the same value, these coins (and Spanish excelentes and Portuguese cruzados) were then all commonly called 'ducats.' Officially this sum would have been worth 13s 9d sterling = 19s 9d gros Flemish = £6 4s 6d tournois (in France, by royal edict, from 27 November 1516). Cf CWE 1 314, 316, 320, 338; and Ep 463:48n below. Cotton MS Vitellius B iii, f 208v, containing a letter from Gigli to Ammonio of 9 February 1517, sets forth his expenses on Erasmus' behalf. Allen's reading of the manuscript, one of those that suffered in the Cotton fire, was that Gigli had spent 20 ducats (= £4 11s 8d sterling) all told in obtaining the dispensation.

448 / From Johannes Sixtinus to Pieter Gillis   [London] 12 August [1516]

Sixtinus was a native of West Friesland who had graduated from Oxford and
made his career in England; cf Epp 112, 430 introductions. There is no information about the business referred to here.

JOHANNES SIXTINUS TO THE RIGHT LEARNED
PIETER GILLIS
Though I have nothing new to write to you about, having expounded all my
needs pretty fully in a letter sent by Pieter the One-eyed, and then sent you
another recently by a man from Mechelen, by way of increasing my claims   5
to get a letter from you, yet I was unwilling to allow Erasmus, who is so dear
to us both, to return to your part of the world empty-handed. So I make the
same request as in my last: please let me know whether you have been able
to do what I asked you, relying on your well-known kindness, or not so far.
If the business is not done yet, I should like our friend Erasmus to be one of   10
the witnesses. If there is anything here in which my efforts could be of
service to you or your friends, they will always be most readily at your
disposal. Erasmus seems not to think my presence in your parts necessary,
if there is no more on foot than the question about which I wrote to you; so I
have not yet decided whether to come or not. Farewell, and please accept   15
my most cordial greetings.
     12 August

449 / From Henry Bullock   Cambridge, 13 August [1516]

Henry Bullock was the closest of Erasmus' friends in Cambridge; cf Ep 225:5n.
By this date he was lecturing on Divinity as well as Mathematics. The letter
was first published in the *Epistolae aliquot*, October 1516.

TO MASTER ERASMUS, THE SINGULAR ORNAMENT OF
OUR TIMES, FROM HIS FRIEND BULLOCK
Your return to England, most learned of teachers, is exceeding welcome to
all your friends in Cambridge, but above all to me, for I am in many ways
more devoted to you than all the rest. How delighted therefore should I be   5
to see you in Cambridge, so that, if I cannot respond as I would to your

* * * * *
448:4 letter] Sent with Ep 430
4 Pieter the One-eyed] 'Petrus monoculus,' or Pieter Meghen, the scribe and
messenger so frequently referred to in these letters; see Ep 412:47n.

manifold goodness towards me, at least I may show my good will, which is
all I can do; for I long to see you and spend all my time in your company. But
fate prevents me, and fortune that still looks at me somewhat askance;
otherwise, wherever you went, I should resolve to follow you. Here they are   10
keenly studying Greek, and not a little looking forward to your arrival. And
they are great supporters of your edition of the New Testament; what a
book it is! –So elegant, so clear, so delightful and so highly necessary in the
opinion of all men of sound judgment.

But no more of that. There is a young man here whose constant   15
appeals have moved me to recommend him to you, one Edmund Pollard, an
attractive person and a great admirer of yours. He is convinced that his
happiness depends on his being admitted into your household. So if you
would write me word whether you can take him, and mention however
briefly that I recommended him to you (for otherwise he will never believe I   20
have written, I have made so many promises), you will act with your
customary generosity, and I shall be very grateful. Farewell, glory of our
generation.

Cambridge, 13 August

450 / From John Watson   [Cambridge, c 13 August 1516]

Another of Erasmus' friends in Cambridge, John Watson, formerly of Eton
and King's College, was at this time rector of Elsworth, ten miles away; cf
E & C 227, Emden BRUC. The letter was evidently written between the publication of the New Testament and the completion of the edition of Jerome. As
Watson thinks Erasmus is still in England, the date of this reply was fixed
conjecturally by Allen about the time Watson received Erasmus' letter, now
lost. As Erasmus indicates in his answer (Ep 512:30–1) Watson's letter was
delayed in transmission. For Watson see also Ep 275:5n. He died in 1537. The
letter was first printed in the *Epistolae elegantes* 1517.

* * * * *

449:11 studying Greek] Bullock had been a member of Erasmus' small Greek
class at Cambridge; in 1521 he published with John Siberch of Cambridge a
Luciani opuscula (STC 16896), the first English scholar to publish such a translation. The work was the first in England using Greek type. See A. Tilley 'Greek
Studies in England in the Early Sixteenth Century' EHR 53 (1938).

16 Pollard] 'Edmundus Polus arduus,' but no one of this name appears in
surviving college or university records, nor is the name found in Emden.
Allen suggested 'Pollard,' since a Dominus Pollard determined in 1521–2 and
was admitted in 1524–5; see M. Bateson (ed) *Cambridge Grace Book B,
1488–1544* pt 2 (Cambridge 1905) 99, 1220.

TO THE PRINCE OF BIBLICAL SCHOLARS DR ERASMUS
FROM JOHN WATSON

On 11 August I received your letter of 5 June, and believe me, my beloved
teacher, it gave me the greatest joy, for it told me that you were well, and are
in high standing with your prince Charles. You bestowed a rich present on   5
me by sending me a letter, for I do assure you, my feelings for you are such
that I value two or three pages in Erasmus' hand nearly as much as I would
the fattest benefice. You will say with a smile 'How right you are to add that
"nearly"!' I freely confess, I do not entirely despise these external things,
but my love of them is not such as would prefer them to good literature and   10
the friendship of learned men, provided I have enough to live on. Beyond
any doubt I welcomed and valued your letter so highly, that if my prayers
were answered and I were really rich, I would give a gold piece for every
letter.

I wonder daily more and more, my dear Erasmus, to see you grow   15
greater as the years go by, and show yourself daily in a new and grander
guise. You are famous everywhere in Italy, especially among the leading
scholars. It is incredible with what enthusiasm they welcome everywhere
your *Copia* and the *Moria* too as they would the highest wisdom. I have met
many people who seemed to me to regard themselves as better scholars   20
because they know you; and they thought more of me too for the same
reason. Raffaele Regio is still lecturing in Venice on Quintilian, with a
salary and expenses from the city treasury. He is a good scholar and an
adequate lecturer, but falls far short of the other professor there, who
teaches Greek, also on an official salary; I cannot remember his name – he   25
knows you very well and speaks very highly of you indeed. Ambrogio the
physician, whom you mention in your proverb *Dis dia pason*, I had a talk
with almost daily in the druggist's shop at the sign of the Coral, and he

* * * * *

450:3 letter] Lost; Erasmus was at Saint-Omer. Cf Epp 413–17.

5 Charles] Cf Ep 446:77n.

17 Italy] The year before, Watson had travelled to Italy with John Reston and
had visited some of Erasmus' friends in Venice.

22 Regio] c 1440–1520, of Bergamo, who held chairs in rhetoric at Padua and
Venice. In the latter city he edited the letters of Pliny (1490), Ovid's
Metamorphoses (1493) and published notes on Quintilian (1492).

24 other professor] Musurus; cf Epp 512:9 and 223:4n.

26–7 Ambrogio the physician] Ambrogio Leoni of Nola, physician to Aldo
Manuzio in 1507; see Ep 854 introduction.

27 *Dis dia pason*] *Adagia* I ii 63

thought highly of me for your sake; so did Pietro Alcionio, an outstanding stylist in my opinion, and many other people. Aldus' father-in-law, the   30
bookseller at the sign of the Anchor, spoke of you I can't say how often, and
promised you hospitality and every kindness, if it ever suits you to visit
him. Everywhere in all Christendom your fame is spreading; by the
unanimous verdict of all scholars you are voted the best scholar of them all,
and the most learned in both Greek and Latin.   35

In any case, that all should make much of your riches both in universal
learning and in a rare gift of style does not surprise me nearly so much as the
modesty with which you rank yourself below them all, though you are by
general agreement first on every count. It is common for learning of the kind
in which you are so rich to give its owner grand ideas, and not only to make   40
him exceptional but to set a gulf between him and the friendly society
shared by the common run of men. But you are all generosity, you open
yourself to everybody, you are not too proud to be friends with anyone,
provided you can be helpful to everyone. As a result, wherever you may be,
your manner of life is such as to make every part of the Christian world feel 45
that you are present with them, and henceforth your immortal fame and
wonderful works mean that you will live for ever. Your revision of the New
Testament and your notes at the same time have thrown a wonderful flood
of light on Christ, and earned the gratitude of all who are devoted to it. May
God reward you an hundredfold, together with eternal life, for in my   50
judgment you could do nothing more worthy of a Christian teacher. I
happened a few days ago on the *Petty Cato* which you have provided with
brief explanatory notes; you would not believe how much I enjoyed them,
marvelling at so sweet and plentiful a harvest in such a modest field. Do
please add a list of all your writings to one or other of your books. I did not 55
know of this small book, and I fear there may be others too of which I am
unaware. Your Jerome we shall welcome with open arms and every possible
good wish, full of gratitude to the man who has restored him with so much
devotion.

* * * * *

29 Alcionio] Pietro Alcionio (d 1527) of Venice was a pupil of Musurus. He
was reported to have translated Demosthenes, Isocrates and Aristotle, but
only the last is known to have been published (Venice: Bernardinus Vitalis,
April 1521).

30 father-in-law] Andrea Torresani d'Asola; cf Ep 212:6n, 589 introduction.

52 *Petty Cato*] The *Catonis praecepta* or *Disticha Catonis* published in the
Opuscula aliquot of 1514; cf Ep 298 introduction, Epp 435:97n, 480:50.

55 list] Allen conjectures that this request may have prompted Adriaan van
Baerland to compose Ep 492, when he saw this letter during the printing of the
Epistolae elegantes of April 1517 (NK 819).

Peter Falck the Swiss, whom we English called Peter the Great, I like   60
particularly. He took very great pains to look after his fellow pilgrims, and
at the same time was a most agreeable companion. He had in the ship a
monkey with a long tail which was astonishingly clever, gesticulating,
laughing, chattering, jumping about; it was full of tricks that made us die
with laughing every day. Besides that, he is full of interest for novelties and   65
new crafts and inventions: he often wore a pistol attached to his belt, he
made careful notes of the position and names of towns and other places and
marked up his book on the pilgrimage in red ink, and he used to talk to me
of you and boasted that he had once had a letter from you. If you ever write
to him, do please give him my greetings.   70

I congratulate you on your restoration to us, or rather I congratulate us
on getting you back; no one is more delighted. I wish I had a chance of a talk
with you. I believe, if you were to open your heart to me and I to you, you
could not possibly play Thraso, as you often say, nor I Gnatho, if I utter
anything in your praise, for nothing of the sort can happen between true   75
friends, it would more be a crime to hold anything back. I am positively
greedy to see you. If you stay where you are until Michaelmas, I shall visit
you, God willing; or if meantime you think of coming here, which I should
like most of all, no one will welcome your arrival more than I. We shall
pass a really delightful holiday. Whatever I have here that you might find   80
either enjoyable or useful, will be at your service. Farewell.

451 / To Andrea Ammonio   [London, c 14 August 1516]

Letters 451–3 and 455 are closely linked by theme, and the reference to the
New Testament helps to provide a year date, as does the fact that only on this

* * * * *

60 Falck] Peter Falck (c 1468–1519) was the son of Bernard Falck, notary and
secretary of Fribourg in Switzerland. He was a student in Colmar, and in 1492
became a notary like his father. He retained his literary interests and was a
friend of Cardinal Schiner (cf Ep 447:660n). As a result he played an important
part in the diplomatic relations between the Swiss, the papacy and France. In
1515 he travelled on pilgrimage to Jerusalem in the same ship with Watson and
John Reston; cf Allen III xxvi.

64–5 made us die with laughing] Literally, laugh sardonically. A laugh not
'sardonic' in our sense, but convulsive; *Adagia* III v 1

69 letter] Lost

74 Thraso] The proverbial braggart, and Gnatho the lick-spittle; both are
characters in Terence's *Eunuchus*.

77 where you are] At More's house in London

77 Michaelmas] 29 September

visit did Erasmus leave England in August. This letter was left with More in
London (Ep 452:13–4) and like Ep 452, is answered by Ep 453. It was first printed in the *Farrago*.

ERASMUS OF ROTTERDAM TO HIS FRIEND AMMONIO
I hope the hunting in your part of the world has gone as well for you as it has
gone badly for me here. First of all it takes the king out of my reach, and then
it has delayed me several days through the departure of the cardinal.
Besides which, I had made a bid for Urswick's goodwill by sending him a   5
New Testament, and had written to ask for the horse he promised me.
When I went on Monday in hopes of seeing him, he had just dashed off to
the hunting-field, and is not expected back for a week. So that tunny has
thus slipped out of my net. And now on top of that the hunting has
deprived me of you; so what I wanted to say in person I must deal with in   10
writing. Please open the letter to the pope written by my servant; I do not
think it well enough written. If you think it appropriate, have it written out
again more carefully, and add this for the moment to your other kindnesses.
I entrust you with my whole future. I make no bones about asking you, for I
trust you whole-heartedly; I make no magnificent promises, for I would   15
rather thank you in actions, if I can, than words. I at least am full of hope that
our campaign will succeed, not only because it is in the hands of a man very
dear to me, but because that man is Ammonio, who has always been so
successful where Erasmus is concerned. Farewell.
    These two reasons might have kept me in England for a few days: the   20
hope of a horse from Urswick, which beyond doubt he intended to give me,
and the chance of a talk with you, were I not already tired of Britain and
feeling that More's lady somewhat resents me as a guest of rather long
standing. I only hope a favourable oracle may soon return by you. Farewell
again. [1511]   25

* * * * *

451:3 king] Henry VIII
4 cardinal] Wolsey
5 goodwill] Christopher Urswick was a prominent churchman and patron of
humanism; cf Ep 416 introduction.
6 horse] The horse of Ep 416 had died (Ep 452:9).
7 Monday] 11 August in 1516
8 tunny] Cf Ep 447:461n.
11 letter] Cf Ep 447 introduction.
23 More's lady] Cf Epp 236:48n, 232:3n.

452 / To Andrea Ammonio   Rochester, 17 August [1516]

This letter was written while Erasmus was *en route* from London to Dover. He
stopped to visit his patron, John Fisher, at his episcopal see, and was persuaded to stay for a few days to assist the bishop in his study of New
Testament Greek. For other evidence of Fisher's interest in Greek, see Epp
520, 540. This letter was first published in the *Farrago*.

ERASMUS OF ROTTERDAM TO HIS FRIEND
ANDREA AMMONIO
The bishop of Rochester has driven me by his entreaties to stay with him for
ten days, and I have regretted my promise more than ten times over; so that
here too I have felt the truth of the proverb: Promise, and rue it. Meanwhile   5
I am to turn him from a Latin into a Greek – that is the metamorphosis I have
undertaken. I have made a bid for Urswick's goodwill by sending him a
New Testament, in hopes that he would send me in return a new horse; my
old horse, I told him, had died of drink, a common trouble in Flanders. But
he being away in the hunting-field, my hunting proved fruitless. With that   10
in mind I have sent my servant back to your part of the world, and also so
that he might have a word with you; then if you have any fresh ideas, you
can let me know, for I do not leave here before the end of this week. I wrote
to you by way of More before I departed, and left a copy of my letter to Leo,
but not well enough written. In the Muses' name, dear Ammonio, be the   15
good friend to me you always are, and I shall always remember it and be
grateful. Farewell.
      Rochester, 17 August
      Speed, my dear Ammonio, will add very greatly, believe me, to the
value of the kindness you are doing me: the clouds of anxiety in my mind   20
will dissolve the sooner, and if anything does happen to go wrong, I shall be
much safer. Farewell once more.

* * * * *

452:4 ten days] Cf Ep 457:14.
5 proverb] *Adagia* I vi 97
11 servant] John Smith; see Ep 276 introduction and Bierlaire 49–51.
13 end of this week] That is, Sunday 24 August; cf Ep 451:7–8.
13–4 wrote to you] Ep 451
14 Leo] Ep 446

453 / From Andrea Ammonio   Westminster [c 19 August 1516]

This letter plainly answers Ep 452, so the date given at the end is clearly wrong. Ep 455 (23 August) acknowledges receipt of the horse mentioned here. This letter was first published in the *Farrago*.

FROM ANDREA AMMONIO TO ERASMUS OF ROTTERDAM

You seemed to me in such a hurry to cross the Channel that I did not risk asking you to delay even for a couple of days. But risk it I must, evidently, though I know we are not all bishops of Rochester, and that there are very few people as worthy as he is of your society. I have no doubt that your   5
promise will soon be fulfilled without the disasters you speak of. If your hunting went astray, no one will be surprised; you are a man not accustomed to hunt in that sort of chase. In any case, you will say it was a loan at interest. This is surely a new sort of metamorphosis, to turn books into horses; but since I see you need a horse, I will make you a handsome present   10
of a white horse (and you know how much they used to be valued), which has lately arrived from farthest Ireland. Please accept it, such as it is, and rest assured I shall never expect anything in return.

The letter you left with More has reached me safely. I think the first of your two letters to Leo will be enough. On that business of yours, nothing   15
has occurred to me beyond what we agreed on. That fiction of yours I approve without reserve; and about who is to take charge of it, I urge you, as they say, not to lose a wink of sleep; I shall take as much care of it as if my own life were at stake. Only, you must not expect any remarkable speed; the roads are difficult for couriers, and many are frightened by the sons of Mars.   20
In any case, you can be sure I shall not fail to do everything you could expect of your warmest supporter. Farewell, and remember me respectfully to my lord of Rochester.

From Westminster, [25 June, 1513]

454 / From Philippus Melanchthon   Tübingen, 20 August 1516

The author was born Philipp Schwarzerd of Bretten (1497–1560) north of Pforzheim. On his mother's side he was a great-nephew of Reuchlin, who

* * * * *

453:11 used to be valued] See *Adagia* I iv 21.

14 first] Perhaps the first (existing) draft of Ep 446, or Ep 446 understood as the covering letter of Ep 447

16 comment] Probably Ep 447; cf Ep 447 introduction.

18 wink of sleep] Literally 'to sleep on either ear'; *Adagia* I viii 19

Philippus Melanchthon
Replica of a 1529/30 painting by Hans Holbein the Younger
Sir William van Horne Collection, Montreal

fostered his studies and gave him the Greek form of his name. He studied at
Heidelberg and Tübingen (MA 25 January 1514) and in 1518 he became
Professor of Greek at Wittenberg, nothing having come of an earlier proposal
by Erasmus that he should go to Cambridge (Ep 457:61). His later career in the
Lutheran Reformation is famous. At this time he had contributed a preface to
the *Clarorum virorum epistolae ad Ioannem Reuchlin* (Tübingen: Anshelm 1514)
and had taken part in the posthumous edition of Nauclerus' Chronicle (cf Ep
397 introduction). This Greek poem was his first communication with Erasmus and was included by Allen since its signature gives it something of the
character of a letter, and because it was found in the Deventer Letter-book. It
was first printed by Froben with the *Epigrammata* in March 1518.

TO ERASMUS, GREATEST OF MEN, FROM
PHILIPPUS MELANCHTHON   ·

Persuasion once besought almighty Jove
(A clever goddess she, who gets her way):
'Lend me the bowls in which your nectar's mixed;   5
For on Parnassus I would greet my guests,
And serve ambrosia for my loving-cup.'
'Persuasion, dearest child,' with gentle mien
Her sire replied, 'Parnassian guests to me,
As god of hospitality, are dear.   10
Take then a gift, and gladly: take the horn
Of Amalthea, filled with fragrant flowers
By my *Erasmus*, whence the mountain Nymphs
Ambrosian streams, oceans of nectar draw.
Be then this honey-dew the favoured drink   15
Of sweet-voiced Muses and of fairest Loves
And of Desire and of the mistress Graces.
Long may the lilies in Erasmus' horn
Of plenty flower as garlands for the gods.'
Jove's words Persuasion spread among the throng   20
On Mount Parnassus, whose convivial ring
Of deities rejoicing gladly ply
The horn o'erflowing with Erasmus' flowers.
          Tübingen, 20 August 1516

* * * * *

454:12 Amalthea] The she-goat on whose milk the infant Jupiter was fed, one
of whose horns was immortalized by him as the cornucopia or horn of plenty;
Adagia I vi 2

455 / To Andrea Ammonio   Rochester, 22 August [1516]

This letter, replying to Ep 453, was first published in the *Farrago*.

ERASMUS TO HIS FRIEND AMMONIO
My John was clearly in for a good beating, had not More turned up in the
nick of time and rescued him; for the moment he heard I was stuck in
Rochester, he ran down to have another glimpse of his friend Erasmus,
being afraid, one would think, that it may be long before he sees him again.   5
So it was he who recommended my servant to carry off the horse, after you
offered it of your own free will. I perceive that I must be more careful with
you in future; you snatch so eagerly at any chance to make me a present. I
was about to send back your gift even against More's advice, had I not been
afraid that you might suspect I really did not like the horse or did not like   10
being beholden to a man like Ammonio; whereas there is no one I would
rather be beholden to, just as I love no one more sincerely. My life upon it,
dear Ammonio, I set a greater value on your high principles and your true
friendship and am more attached to them than to the whole noisy business
of a position from the pope; nor can I ever think myself denied my due   15
position as long as friends of your calibre are safe and sound. I like the horse
particularly in his spotless white coat; but it is the spotless character of the
giver that recommends him. I would have preferred to make others I could
name stand and deliver – his Eminence of York or Colet or Urswick – but
they have too much sense; though Urswick promises me a splendid horse,   20
and will no doubt be as good as his word, not on the Greek kalends but on
the kalends of October. Farewell, my learned and generous Ammonio. I will
write from Brabant to the Archbishop of York and to Lark.
Rochester, 22 August [1514]

456 / To Henry Bullock   Rochester [22?] August 1516

Since the central portion of this letter closely resembles the *Apologia* prefixed
to the 1516 edition of the *Novum instrumentum*, Allen suggested that that
preface might have been elaborated in the form of the present letter with a

* * * * *

455:2 John] Smith; cf Ep 452:11n. He had accepted the horse Ammonio
offered on Erasmus' behalf but apparently without consultation; cf line 6ff and
Ep 453:10–11.
21 Greek kalends] In Greek, the first of the month is not called by that name,
and so the phrase means 'never'; *Adagia* I v 84.
23 Lark] Cf Ep 283:98n; he was chaplain to the king.

view to publication as a separate defence of the volume. More immediately, the letter answers Ep 449, but line 305 indicates that Erasmus had had another letter from Bullock in which he spoke of preaching. This reply was published by Gillis in the *Epistolae ad Erasmum* the following October. Since Erasmus left London in mid-August and wrote from Calais on 27 August, the date at the end of this letter must be corrected; cf Ep 457 introduction.

ERASMUS OF ROTTERDAM TO THE
DISTINGUISHED THEOLOGIAN HENRY BULLOCK
From your letter it is pretty clear that mine, which I left with Thomas More in London, had not yet reached you. Your long-standing feelings for me, my dear Bullock, I gratefully recognize and welcome. I only wish we might   5
one day return to our old way of life together and those common studies which were so perfectly delightful. I expect to spend the winter in Louvain; you must decide meanwhile what suits you best. That the New Testament as my efforts have restored it should be approved in your part of the world by all the best men, indeed by everyone as you put it of sound judgment, is   10
a great joy to me. Though I have heard from trustworthy witnesses that you have one college steeped in theology whose members are regular Areopagites, and who are said to have provided by solemn resolution that no man bring the said volume by horse, boat, wagon or porter within the curtilage of the said college. I ask you, my learned friend, should one laugh or cry?   15
How their zeal has led them astray! Their prejudice and bad temper hurt no one but themselves: they look askance at what would be very good for them. What kind of men are these, so hard to please that they are provoked by kindness which tames even wild beasts, and so implacable that all that one says in one's defence cannot soften them? In fact, what is much more   20
impudent, they condemn and tear in pieces a book which they have not even read and, in any case, would not understand if they did. They have merely heard over their cups or in little gatherings in the market-place that a new book has come out which tries to peck the crow's eyes out and give all the theologians a taste of their own medicine, and off they go, pursuing   25
with unmixed invective both the author, who has tried with so much nightly toil to be of use to all who wish to learn, and his book, by which they

* * * * *

456:3 left ... More] Cf Ep 452:14.

7 Louvain] Cf Ep 457 introduction.

12–13 Areopagites] Judges of the most grave and revered of the Athenian courts; *Adagia* I ix 41

24 peck the crow's eyes out] *Adagia* I iii 75; Erasmus says in Ep 1479 that he finds the expression puzzling.

might profit. Is that a way for philosophers or theologians to behave? A noisome thing philosophy must be, if it turns out men like that, and a feeble watered-down thing, if it cannot make such men better.   30

Then again, they do not refute and put right what they regard as errors in my work, but merely condemn me for committing them. It is unlawful, they say, to attempt anything of the sort, except on the authority of a General Council. What could be more iniquitous than that? They distort the sacred text every day, consulting no authorities but their own ignorance   35 and rashness; and am I not to be allowed to restore what has been corrupted in accordance with the views of the Fathers, unless the whole of Christendom has been summoned to a Council? You see their policy: the man who removes an error is to be treated worse than he who introduces one, and he who serves the public by his industry worse than he whose lack of   40 thought does it a disservice.

But there is one question I should like them to answer. This same version to which they are so much attached, was it undertaken by a translator authorized by a General Council, or was it published first and approved by the Fathers thereafter? Written first, I imagine, and afterwards   45 approved. But the same thing can happen to this text of mine, not that I desire or demand anything of the kind. Though even that is more than I would concede. It seems to me that it slipped into circulation by being used, and gradually gathered strength as time went by. Otherwise, if it had been approved and handed down by the official decision of a Council, it would   50 have been in general use by everyone. As it is, Ambrose cites one version, Augustine another, Hilary and Jerome others. In fact, there is no general agreement even among copies of our own day.

If, however, they suppose that all is up with Christianity if there is any variation anywhere, we were already exposed to that risk, even if I had kept   55 my eyes shut. 'But this is the text,' they say, 'used by the synods of the Fathers.' Ancient synods or modern? Why should the practice of Councils in antiquity carry less weight than modern practice? – Especially in a subject such as this. Not but what there is a point they ought to prove: that texts cited in the acts of Councils differ from my emended text. What are we   60 to make of the fact that the acts of most Councils were published in Greek? Again, it may well be that texts therein cited in a different form have been altered by someone to agree with our current version, as we find every day in the commentaries of Jerome and Ambrose. About twenty years ago they were printing in Paris service-books and books of hours according to the   65

* * * * *

42–3 same version] The Vulgate bible
63 current version] The Vulgate

use of Trier. The craftsman, who had a mere tincture of letters, found a great many discrepancies and corrected them all against our current version; so he himself confessed to me, thinking he did something admirable.

In fact, I do not find it absurd that something should escape the attention of a General Council, especially in things not necessary to salva- 70 tion. It is sufficient that the actual proceedings of a synod should be exempt from criticism. And after all, why are we in greater distress over a difference of reading in Scripture than over a difference of interpretation? At least the risk in both is equal. Yet we see commentators not merely vary but conflict, constantly. 75

There is another problem, which let them clear up if they can. Do they allow any changes in Holy Writ, or none at all? If they allow any, why not examine in the first place whether it is right or no to make the change? If they do not, what will they make of those passages in which the existence of a corruption is too obvious to be denied or overlooked? Would they rather 80 imitate on this point the mass-priest who refused to change the word *mumpsimus* which he had used for twenty years, when someone told him that *sumpsimus* was what he ought to say? They burst out in horror crying, 'O heavens, o earth! This man is correcting the Gospels!' But with how much more justice one would cry out upon the man who fills them with 85 error, 'Rank sacrilege! This man corrupts the Gospels!' It is not as though I undermine the modern text; I restore the old one to the utmost of my power, but in such a way as not to weaken their new one. Those who do battle for the new one as though for hearth and altar still have what they are so much attached to; they have lost nothing, and have gained something worth 90 having. The text they love they will henceforward read more accurately and understand more correctly.

Suppose I had expounded all the sacred books by way of a paraphrase, and made it possible to keep the sense inviolate and yet to read them without stumbling and understand them more easily? Would they quarrel 95

* * * * *

66 Trier] No such editions appear to survive in R. Proctor *An Index to the Early Printed Books in the British Museum* (London 1960), Polain, or Bohatta's bibliographies of breviaries (1937), missals (1928) or books of hours (1924). Troyes seems more likely.

82 *mumpsimus*] This version of the story precedes that of Richard Pace in his *De fructu qui ex doctrina percipitur* (Basel: Froben 1517), which introduced it to the popular mythology of the English Reformation. See the edition of the *De fructu* by Frank Manley and R.S. Sylvester for the Renaissance Society of America (New York 1967) 65, 103. The reference is to the priest's prayer after the communion, 'Quod ore sumpsimus Domine pura mente capiamus, et de munere temporali fiat nobis remedium sempiternum.'

with me then? Juvencus was actually admired for his courage in putting the
Gospel narrative into verse. Who issues a writ against that excellent divine
Gillis van Delft, who versified almost the whole of Scripture? Every day in
church they sing the Psalms in the ancient version; and yet we possess not
only a revision by St Jerome but his new interpretation made from the   100
Hebrew original. The old version is read in choir, the others in universities
or in private. Neither interferes with the other. In fact, only the other day
Felice da Prato published a new version of the whole Psalter which differs
considerably from all its predecessors. Has anyone ever stirred up trouble
for him? My friend Jacques Lefèvre d'Etaples some time ago did for St Paul   105
what I have done for the whole New Testament. Why should certain people
wait until now to rise in their wrath as though this were something new?
Are they ready to give leave for this to everyone except me? Yet Lefèvre
showed rather more enterprise than I did, for he set his new version
opposite the old, and did so in Paris the queen of all universities, while I set   110
up as no more than a reviser, and either correct or explain a few passages
only. This I say with no desire to make Lefèvre generally unpopular—he is a

* * * * *

96 Juvencus] Caius Vettius Aquilinus Juvencus was a Spanish priest of the
first half of the fourth century who produced a lengthy metrical version of the
four Gospels in order to supply Christian readers with a heroic poem after the
manner of Virgil. It was printed first at Deventer about 1490 (Copinger 3423)
apparently for use in the schools of the Brethren of the Common Life, and was
edited by J. Huemer (CSEL volume 24 1891).

98 Gillis van Delft] A theologian (d 1524) of the University of Paris (BA 1478,
MA 1479) who received his doctorate in theology in 1492, having been rector of
the University from 16 December 1486 to 24 March 1487. He was also dean of
the faculty of theology from 1522 until his death. Among his many writings
were a verse translation of the seven penitential psalms (Paris: Denidel nd),
commentaries on the canonical Epistles (Paris: Bade 28 November 1503) and a
version of the Epistle to the Romans in verse (Paris: Bade 1507). Some letters to
Erasmus encouraging him in his work on the New Testament were still in
existence in 1525 (LB IX 753F) but have since disappeared.

103 Felice da Prato] An Augustinian friar and exegete who was born of Jewish
parents in Prato and died in Rome about 1560. He was educated as a rabbi. In
1515, after conversion to Christianity, he obtained permission from Leo x to
make a new Latin translation of the Bible. Only the Psalter was completed:
Psalterium ex hebraico latine redditum (Venice: Bomberg 1515 Panzer VIII 755).
He also edited a *Biblia rabbinica* in two volumes with a preface to Leo x (Venice
1518, 1521, 1528, 1534; and with many variants, 1525, 1533).

105 Lefèvre d'Etaples] Henri Estienne printed Lefèvre's edition of the Epistles
of St Paul from the Vulgate in December 1512. Beside the Vulgate text there
was printed a paraphrase by Lefèvre called *Intelligentia ex Graeco*, offered
because the Vulgate was not actually the work of Jerome.

distinguished man whose reputation has long outlived any ill will; but I
wish to show how unfair some people are who pick on something which
has long been done by many men without arousing protests, and protest   115
against it when I do it as a sudden innovation. What have students of
Aristotle lost by the appearance of the new edition by Argyropylus,
Leonardo Aretino and Theodore of Gaza? Surely no one wants to suppress
their version or do away with it for fear it may look as though there were
some things which the older generation of specialists in Aristotelian   120
philosophy did not know? Does that reason deter Guillaume Cop from
translating books by Galen and Hippocrates, for fear the world should
perceive that earlier physicians mistranslated many passages?

Someone may say, 'In secular studies this is expedient; but that it
should be done in the Scriptures everywhere and by the first comer is most 125
perilous.' To begin with, I do not make changes all up and down; the mass
of it remains the same, and discussion is confined to a few passages. Nor is
it entirely correct, I think, at least as far as this subject is concerned, to class
me as one of the common herd. I show that in some places slips have been
made by Hilary, by Augustine, by Thomas; and this I do, as is right and   130
proper, with great respect and with no personal attacks, in such a way that,
were they themselves alive today, they would be grateful even to a humble
creature like myself for the way in which I put them right. They were very
great men, but only men after all. Let my opponents show that they were
right, and refute what I say with argument and not abuse; and I shall be   135
much indebted to them. Let those who wish every word that Lyra wrote to
be treated as an oracle defend him in the places where I differ from him. For
to look in Hugo for passages to criticize I regard as a foolish waste of time; I

* * * * *

117 Argyropylus] The Byzantine scholar (1410–90) who taught most impor-
tantly at Florence under the patronage of Cosimo de' Medici from 1456–71.
Later in Rome, he numbered Reuchlin and Poliziano among his pupils. His
surviving lectures are on the various books of Aristotle, and there is conclusive evidence that his real influence was to arouse an enthusiasm for Plato.

118 Aretino] Leonardo Bruni, a native of Arezzo and one of the most brilliant
figures of Florentine humanist culture (1369–1444), he was a prolific translator
from the Greek. See G. Voigt, *Die Wiederbelebung des classischen Altertums*, 3rd
edition (Berlin 1893) vol I, 306–12; Hans Baron, *The Crisis of the Early Italian
Renaissance*, 2 volumes (Princeton 1955) and his *From Petrarch to Leonardo
Bruni* (Chicago 1968).

118 Theodore of Gaza] Cf Ep 233:12n.

121 Cop] Cf Ep 124:18n.

136 Lyra] Cf Ep 372:13n.

138 Hugo] Cf Ep 347:105n.

noted only a few passages that were exceptionally absurd, in order to
encourage caution in those who read such writers with complete confidence   140
and no critical sense.

At any rate, let those who attribute all qualities to authors of that sort
defend their precious darlings, and show that I am all at sea while they hit
the target. But they think it beneath them to descend to these small and
schoolmasterly questions; for so they are wont to refer to those who have   145
had a good literary education, regarding it as a great insult to call a man a
schoolmaster, as though it would be to the credit of a theologian to be
innocent of schooling. Knowledge of grammar by itself is not the making of
a theologian, but much less is he made by ignorance of grammar; at the very
least, skill in this subject is an aid to the understanding of theology and lack 150
of skill is the reverse. Nor can it be denied that Jerome and Ambrose and
Augustine, the principal authorities on whom our theology rests, were all
drawn from the teaching profession. For in those days Aristotle was not yet
accepted as an authority in the theological schools, and the philosophy
current in our universities nowadays was not yet invented. Yet a modest   155
man is glad to be put right by anyone; as Horace puts it,

Though he were blind who shows you where to go,

Yet listen none the less.

Again, even those who reserve this whole matter for authority and not
critical judgment have not much to find fault with in me. Everyone knows   160
that it was provided by this last Lateran Council that a book should be
published after approval by the local bishop or by those to whom he has
delegated his functions. But both the writing and the publication of my
work was done with the cognizance and approval of the bishop of the place,
and no ordinary bishop either, but one who besides his venerable years   165
and his distinguished lineage is remarkable for outstanding sanctity of life
and exceptional learning. And he not merely approved, but offered me
everything one could think of if I had been willing to remain with him, and
on my departure showed me such kindness, such generosity (incomparable
man that he is) that I blush to record it. Even this did not content him; of his 170
own accord he wrote to the archbishop of Canterbury to commend me in
most honourable terms, and to thank him on my behalf. And so my labours

* * * * *

156 Horace] *Epistles* 1.17.3–4
161 Lateran Council] The Fifth Lateran Council (1512–17), which promulgated this ordinance on 4 May 1515
162 bishop] Christoph von Utenheim
171 Canterbury] William Warham; cf Ep 425:32n.

have been approved, if not by a Council, at least in accordance with a
conciliar decision. The authority concerned is such that by himself he ought
to be regarded as the equivalent of many; and his verdict ought to carry   175
even more weight, inasmuch as it was not obtained by humble requests or
services rendered, but was freely offered to a man who almost tried to avoid
it.

    If anyone thinks that one man's authority carries too little weight, the
bishop's opinion has been underwritten by two professors of theology, and   180
those by a long way in the first rank. One is Ludwig Baer, a man by common
consent richly supplied with every form of virtue and knowledge and in the
rough and tumble of philosophy of such experience that at Paris he earned
first place on the list of those qualifying for the doctorate. Such disapproval
did he feel for my work that he offered to share with me all his resources,   185
which are considerable, and of the two prebends which he possesses he
handed one over to me of his own accord. Besides him there is Wolfgang
Faber Capito, whose distinguished knowledge of theology earned him
election to the chapter of Basel, where he holds the office of public preacher.
He is a man who besides the other liberal disciplines has no ordinary   190
proficiency in the three tongues, Greek, Latin and Hebrew, and is of such
integrity, so upright a character that I never saw anything more invulnera-
ble. These are the men on whose verdict the book was published, and their
judgment would inspire complete confidence in the bishop on any subject
however important, if he mistrusted his own opinion.   195

    But it is not as though my work has been condemned by anyone in the
rest of the theological world. Some merely lamented that they had not learnt
Greek in boyhood, and that the book had appeared too late for them to use
it. I could report what was said of my edition by the venerable prior of the
charterhouse at Freiburg, Gregor Reisch, whose opinion carries the weight   200
of an oracle in Germany, or by that eminent divine Jakob Wimpfeling; I
could produce numberless letters from distinguished men, thanking me
because they have risen from the reading of my works, especially what I
have published on the New Testament, both better men and better scholars; were I not afraid that someone might think I showed more vanity in   205

* * * * *

181 Baer] Cf Ep 488 introduction.

184 first place] Cf Ep 413:13–14; Baer is described in the 'Liber receptoris
nationis Almanie' at Paris (Archives de l'Université [Sorbonne] Reg 91, f 29),
against the entry of his inception in 1499 as 'Primus in ordine Theologus anno
1512.'

188 Capito] Cf Ep 459 introduction.

200 Reisch] Cf Ep 308 introduction.

201 Wimpfeling] Cf Epp 224 introduction, 302 introduction.

saying this than regard for the truth. And yet those who have known me well in Germany, and the people in England to whom all my affairs are as familiar as they are to me, are well aware how sparingly I touch on this kind of thing. I am of course reluctant, and for two reasons: one, that I hate nothing so much as boasting, and the other, that I have no wish to cause   210
embarrassment to any of my friends on my account. Not to speak of others, you know, my dear Bullock, what manner of man is that outstanding prelate the bishop of Rochester, chancellor of your university, whether one considers his integrity and true piety or his learning. And are these worthless wretches not ashamed to pursue with their abuse books which so great a   215
man approves and reads?

For that matter, are not these three-halfpenny puppets ashamed to attack as they think fit books which have the approval of the supreme pontiff himself? For unless he approved my work, he could not in any case have said in a letter that he would regard it as a great privilege if I were to   220
offer him the dedication of the whole fruit of my labours. He does more than approve who promises a reward as well. I had set out my plans in a letter to him, enquiring tentatively whether he wished for the dedication. He counterbalanced my single letter at once with two of his own, one a most friendly complimentary scholarly reply to mine, the other a recommendation of me   225
and my learned projects to his serene majesty the English king; with how much emphasis and warmth, you shall judge for yourself, for I enclose a copy of both letters. Both cardinals had replied, Grimani that is, and San Giorgio; but their letters were sent by Andrea Ammonio, who is a particular ornament of your native England, to Richard Pace, the envoy of his king   230
to the Swiss and to Maximilian, for him to hand on to me as I was at that time living in Basel; but up to now they have not yet arrived. Last winter I sent one volume to Leo, to whom it is dedicated, and if it reached him safely, I have no doubt that he will respond to my nights of toil with a handsome reward.   235

What remains then for them to complain of in me? I am not the first to attempt this enterprise, nor did I do so unadvisedly. I have followed the

* * * * *

217 puppets] *Adagia* I viii 10
221 whole fruit] Cf Ep 338:28.
222 letter] Ep 335
224 two] Epp 338, 339
228 both cardinals] Cf Epp 334, 340; Grimani's reply was kept by Ammonio with the other documents from Rome he decided to retain (cf Ep 338 introduction).
233 one volume] Cf Ep 446:74.

decision of the Council. I have won the approval of the best judges at least, if not of everyone. If there were anything irreligious in what I have done, religious men would dislike it; if it were unscholarly, scholars would reject   240 it. But none welcome it more than those who are distinguished by unusual holiness of life and more than ordinary erudition. If my critics are more moved by learning, the most learned men approve it; if by virtue, the most virtuous men approve it; if by authority, bishops approve it and arch-bishops and the supreme pontiff himself. And yet none of these could give   245 me support worth having, if it were known that I had canvassed for the support of any one among them all. Any tributes that have been paid were paid to the facts and not the man.

Many as they are, these considerations do not induce them to wish to unlearn what they have learnt in the wrong way. Are they afraid that if the   250 young are persuaded by them, they themselves will lecture to empty benches? Why do they not rather take into account quite another point? About thirty years ago, nothing was taught in the university at Cambridge except Alexander, what they call the *Parva logicalia*, and the traditional doctrines of Aristotle with Scotistic *questiones*. As time went on the   255 humanities were added; then mathematics; then a new, or at least a new-fangled Aristotle; then the knowledge of Greek; then all those authors whose very names were unknown in the old days even to the brahmins of philosophy Iarcas-like enthroned. And what, pray, was the effect of all this on your university? Why, it flourished to such a tune that it can challenge   260 the first universities of the age, and there are men there compared with whom those earlier scholars are mere shadows of theologians, not the reality. This is not disputed by such of the older men as have an open mind. They rejoice at other people's good fortune, and deplore their own bad luck. Are objectors distressed by the thought that hereafter the writings of   265 evangelists and apostles will be read by more men and read with closer attention? Do they resent that even this space of time should be allotted to the studies to which it would have been proper to devote all their time, and would they prefer to dissipate a lifetime on the puerile niceties of their *questiones*?   270

* * * * *

254 Alexander] Alexandre de Ville-Dieu; cf Ep 31:43n.

254 *Parva logicalia*] More than one medieval textbook of logic bore this title; cf Ep 447:105n.

259 Iarcas-like] Iarcas is the chief Brahman in India, of whom we hear great things in Philostratus' life of Apollonius of Tyana; Jerome refers to him 'seated on his golden throne' in the letter to Paulinus (*Epistulae* 53.1.4).

260 flourished] Cf Ep 457:65–6.

Yet on these grounds at least I do not much regret my nightly vigils. It is common knowledge that before now there have been some theologians so unfamiliar with sacred literature that they never even read the *Sentences* or laid a finger to any part of the subject except their riddling *questiones*. Surely it must be right to recall such people to the genuine sources? For my 275 part, my dear Bullock, I could wish that the labours I have undertaken for the general good, which were by no means inconsiderable, might prove to be of general use. For I look for my whole reward from Christ Himself, if I can only do something to deserve it first; but if it is impossible for me to win general approval, I console myself in the meantime with the fact that almost 280 everywhere I am approved by the men who themselves most enjoy universal approval. And I hope that in future what is now accepted by the best judges may prove to be acceptable to the majority. In other things to be new is the way to be popular, but this work of mine has earned ill will by its novelty. And so I think we shall see the opposite result: they lost their 285 popular appeal as they grew older, and I perhaps shall acquire it. One thing at any rate I foresee: my works, such as they are, will get a fairer hearing from posterity. Not that I can complain even of my contemporaries. They think more highly of me, I will not say than I demand but than I either deserve or can live up to. Diverse and hard to please as are the tastes of 290 mortal men, especially in the domain of literature, it remains true that my writings, which are not irreligious, although inadequate in scholarship compared with the books of others, have not yet been attacked except by a handful of men so captious that they approve nothing not of their own making, so stupid as to be quite insensitive, so idle that they do not even 295 read what they criticize, so ignorant as to be incapable of criticism, so starved of reputation and so greedy for it that they carp at other men's labours in hopes of earning a little glory for themselves. There are even men in this group who condemn and spurn in public what they read with approval at home. It may be a kind of modesty to conceal those who have 300 helped you, but it is the modesty of a man mean and ungrateful. To rend in public the reputation of those whose labours are your standby at home is very far from any form of civilized behaviour; though the man who would serve in Christ's army must swallow this too.

You say you are preaching before public audiences; I think this an 305 excellent plan, and am glad that it goes well, especially since you preach Christ unadulterated, and neither magnify nor advertise the petty clever-

* * * * *

273 *Sentences*] The *Sententiarum libri quatuor* of the 12th century 'Master of the Sentences' Peter Lombard

ness of men. What you write about the boy can be answered very briefly; I
already have more than I need, so far am I from wishing for any further
burdens. Please give my warmest greetings to the friends whom I bear   310
round with me in my heart, Doctor Fawne, the learned John Bryan, that
most cultivated John Vaughan, Humphrey kindest of men, and my old host
Garrett the bookseller; for Watson I hear is away. Farewell, my most learned
Bullock.

    Rochester, in the bishop's lodging, [31] August 1516   315

457 / To Johann Reuchlin   Calais, 27 August [1516]

Erasmus took his leave of John Fisher about 24 August and continued on his
way to the Low Countries. Before leaving England he also wrote a letter to
Sebastiano Giustiniani, Venetian ambassador to England, which was delivered by More but subsequently lost to the record of his correspondence (Ep
461:5). He was now on his way to the house of his old friend, Pieter Gillis, in
Antwerp, and beyond that, to a season at Louvain; cf Ep 456:7. In fact, his
progress to Louvain was very slow, and he spent the rest of 1516 and the first

* * * * *

308 the boy] Cf Ep 449:15–6.

311 Fawne] John Fawne (DD 1510) was a Fellow of Queens' College (1497) who
was vice-president from 1511–13. He was vice-chancellor of the University
from 1512 to 1514, while Erasmus was in Cambridge, and was appointed Lady
Margaret Beaufort preacher on 6 November 1515. He vacated his fellowship in
1514 and held various livings until his death sometime before 1536.

311 Bryan] Cf Ep 262:14. He attended Eton and King's College, Cambridge,
which he entered in August 1510 at the age of 17. In 1513 he became a Fellow of
King's and remained at the College until 1526. He was said to lecture on
Aristotle after the humanist style. Eventually he retired to a living in Essex and
remained a country priest until his death in 1545.

312 Vaughan] Cf Ep 283:142. He was BA in 1500, MA in 1503, and in the year
following he was elected Fellow of Queens' College, where he became in time
bursar and dean (1507–09). He evidently left Cambridge about 1519.

312 Humphrey] Walkden, from the diocese of Lichfield and Coventry, was BA
1504, MA and Fellow of Queens' College 1507, BD 1517, DD 1520. He lectured in
mathematics before 1520 and died about 1525. He owned a Leonicenus *Commentum in Lucanum* (Venice 1475) now in the College Library (Emden).

313 Garrett] Godfrey, born in Limburg, and established in Cambridge by
1503. He died in 1539, and left three presses to his apprentice in his will. He
acted as a messenger for Erasmus, taking his letters to London. See G.J. Gray
The Earlier Cambridge Stationers and Bookbinders (Oxford 1904).

313 Watson] John Watson, formerly a Fellow of King's College, Cambridge; cf
Ep 275:5n.

half of 1517 in Antwerp, Brussels, and Ghent, with the house of Gillis as his
base. It would seem that he actually thought at this point of establishing
himself in the Netherlands, moved no doubt by his old friendships there, by
the proximity of England, by his own origins, and by his recent appointment
to the Council of Prince Charles. For a chronicle of Erasmus' movements in
these years, see M.A. Nauwelaerts 'Erasme à Louvain: éphémérides d'un
séjour de 1517 à 1521' in *Scrinium Erasmianum* ed J. Coppens volume I (Leiden
1969) 3–24.

   This letter, assuring Reuchlin of the good opinion held of him by such
prominent Englishmen as John Colet and the bishop of Rochester–especially
the latter–was printed by Reuchlin in *Illustrium virorum epistolae* ... in May
1519; cf Ep 300 introduction.

ERASMUS TO HIS FRIEND REUCHLIN
No words of mine can possibly express the enthusiasm and the deep respect
felt for you by that great champion of good letters and religion, the bishop
of Rochester, so much so that, though he previously had a very high
opinion of Erasmus, he now comes near to thinking nothing of him in his   5
admiration for Reuchlin – a fact which is so far from consuming me with
envy, that I am simply delighted and do my best, as they say, to spur the
willing horse. He never sends me a letter (and he writes quite often)
without making most honourable mention of you. He had decided to lay
aside his episcopal attire, the linen garment, that is, which they always   10
wear in England, except when they go hunting, and to cross the Channel,
moved by this reason in particular, that he might have the chance of a talk
with you, such is his thirst to learn and his thirst to meet you. And when I
was hastening to take ship, he kept me with him for ten days on the
understanding that we should cross together; only something happened   15
afterwards to make him change his mind. But if he postponed action, his
resolution is unchanged. When I was finally taking my leave, he asked me
anxiously what he could do to give you pleasure. I replied that your position
was not of such a kind as to give you great need of money, but that if he sent
you a ring or something to wear, or some such thing which you could   20
readily accept as a memento of him, it would be most welcome. He replied

* * * * *

457:4 Rochester] John Fisher; cf Ep 432:13.
7–8 spur the willing horse] *Adagia* I ii 46, III viii 32
11 hunting] Cf Ep 451:2–4.
13 to meet you] In the *Spongia* of 1523 (Basel: Froben) Erasmus wrote in
similar fashion of Fisher's great admiration for Reuchlin; LB X 1642C.

that the cost did not trouble him, provided you were pleased. I commended
his attitude; I suspect he will soon come to see you. In the meantime, be
sure to write to me what you would particularly like to be sent; he will spare
no expense. I felt that he had a great desire for those Nile reed-pens, the   25
kind of which you gave me three; and so, if you have any, you could send
him no more acceptable present. Have no hesitation in addressing a letter to
him often, and Colet as well. Both of them have a very high opinion of you;
both are men of the sort who, even if no benefit was to be expected, are
gifted with such eminent virtues and are so well disposed towards you, that   30
a mutual friendship would be right and proper. At the moment both enjoy
very great authority among their fellow-countrymen; Colet is also close to
the king's majesty, and is admitted to the most private converse with him
whenever he pleases.

Leo the supreme pontiff has sent a careful reply to that letter of mine   35
which you have read in print, and no less friendly than it was careful. He
added a second brief, in which of his own accord he recommended me to
the English king in no ordinary terms, and he added specifically that he did
this of his own accord and had never been asked by me or anyone else to do
so. Both cardinals had sent answers; but their letters were despatched into   40
your native Germany to Richard Pace, a distinguished scholar who is now
envoy in Switzerland. Moreover the pope's briefs did not reach me before I
returned to England; had I received them in time, I should perhaps have
dedicated Jerome too to Leo. Scarcely had I returned to Brabant when my
most illustrious Prince Charles gave me a prebend both distinguished and   45
lucrative.

I have revisited England to pay my compliments to my patrons and old
friends; I found them much more affectionate than when I left. The archbishop always treated me with special affection, but now his old interest in
me has so much increased that he might seem to have had very little before.   50
He offered me all he had; I refused money, and when I left he gave me a

* * * * *

25 reed-pens] Cf Ep 194:28.
28 Colet] Cf Ep 106 introduction.
35 letter of mine] Ep 335
37 second brief] Ep 339
40 Both cardinals] Cf Ep 456:228 ff.
45 prebend] That of Courtrai; cf Ep 436:6n.
48–9 archbishop] William Warham, Erasmus' patron of long standing; cf Ep
396.

horse and a most elegant gilt cup and cover, promising that he would
deposit with bankers as much money as I might ask for. The New Testament has made me friends everywhere, although some people protested
forcibly, especially at first; but they protested only in my absence, and most   55
of them were the sort who do not read my work, and would not understand
it if they did.

Write to me often, most learned Reuchlin. Whatever you direct to
Antwerp to the house of Pieter Gillis the town secretary, will certainly be
delivered to me. Farewell, glory of our native Germany.   60

If you send the young man Philippus to the bishop of Rochester with
your letter of recommendation, I assure you, he will be most kindly treated
and advanced to a lucrative position, nor will he ever have the chance of
more leisure for the pursuit of the humanities. Perhaps he is thirsting for
Italy. But in these days England has its own Italy and (unless I am quite   65
wrong) something more distinguished than Italy. Farewell once more.

Calais, 27 August

458 / From Reyner Snoy   Gouda, 1 September [1516?]

Snoy was physician to Adolph of Burgundy, and died in 1537; cf Ep 190: 14n.
He composed a history, *De rebus Batavicis libri xiii*, which was not published
until 1620 at Frankfurt, but Snoy plainly refers to it here. It is not possible
accurately to affix the year date, but Allen assigned the present year on the
grounds that Erasmus was preparing to settle in the Netherlands, and that
Snoy might have taken the occasion to renew their acquaintance.

FROM THE PHYSICIAN REYNER OF GOUDA TO MASTER ERASMUS
Greetings, my dear Erasmus, most learned of men, shall I say, or most
eloquent? You have achieved such a partnership with both Venus and
Minerva, such an alliance between the graces of style and universal knowledge, that all men rightly yield the palm of eloquence to you. I should like to   5
interrupt you for a few moments with this brief letter of mine, knowing that
with your habitual charity you will forgive me. By some curious destiny, I

* * * * *

52 cup] Not clearly identified among his effects; see the discussion by Dr Emil
Major 'Ein Becher aus dem Besitz des Erasmus von Rotterdam' published by
Historisches Museum Basel, 1929.

61 Philippus] Melanchthon, now at Tübingen; cf Ep 454 introduction.

65 England] For this high estimate of learning in England compared with that
in Italy, cf Ep 540:54 ff and 456:260–4.

seem to be the only busybody to attempt a history of Holland in my spare time, and as long as other occupations permitted, I got it all into fifteen books. But, living as I do beneath my own roof-tree, and thus knowing well   10 how slender is my plenishing, alike of words and style, I am conscious of my own lack of skill, and am suppressing it in the belief that it will do my reputation no harm to lay it up for nine years, as Horace recommends. I was inspired to take up this not unlaborious labour by some fragments of my friend Willem Hermans, so torn and fragmentary that they were a riddle for   15 any Oedipus; and on Batavia he had written almost nothing. The first book of my own history gives a clear description of Batavia; the second traces its origins and first inhabitants; the third describes the wars waged by the Batavians against the Romans; the fourth runs from the crossing of the Frisians into England, from whom Willibrord was descended, as far as the   20 Counts; the fifth starts with the Counts.

I am writing to tell you this, most eloquent of men, with no ulterior purpose, and I beg you to take it in good part. Having always been devoted to humane studies, I have loved learning and eloquence from my boyhood with all my heart. I would write more, but my courier's impatience cuts me   25 short. Let me at least beg you for a reply, for I should regard that as a great privilege. Farewell, and my very best wishes.

From Gouda, 1 September

459 / From Wolfgang Capito   [Basel] 2 September 1516

Capito was the name taken by Wolfgang Faber (or Fabri; Köpfli or Köpfel; 1478–1541) of Haguenau near Strasbourg. He studied at Ingolstadt and later at Freiburg (MA 1506, DD 1515) having come probably from a reasonably substantial burgher family. His letter is the first in Erasmus' correspondence to comment on Erasmus' apparently final departure from Basel, and his decision to leave the congenial circle there for an established home in the Netherlands.

* * * * *

458:9 fifteen] *quindecim*; either an error for *quinque*, indicating the number already written, or an indication of the total planned

10 roof-tree] Snoy alludes to Persius 4.52.

13 Horace] *Ars poetica* 388

15 Hermans] Hermans was an intimate friend of Erasmus' youth, who died in 1510. Like Snoy, he was from Gouda. For an account of his unfinished historical work see Allen I page 128.

16 Oedipus] Solved the riddle of the Sphinx.

20 Willibrord] The Northumbrian missionary (658–739) known as the Apostle of Frisia, founder of the see of Utrecht and the monastery of Echternach

In 1512, Capito, who had been ordained priest in 1509, was appointed canon and preacher of the Benedictine foundation at Bruchsal on the Rhine. There he apparently met Conradus Pellicanus and began the study of Hebrew. In 1515 the bishop of Basel, Christoph von Utenheim, appointed him cathedral preacher there. In Basel he also served as professor of Old Testament at the university. In 1517 he was rector, and 1518–19 dean of the Faculty of Theology. Through his knowledge of Hebrew he assisted Erasmus in his work on the New Testament (Ep 456:188), and Erasmus held a high opinion of Capito's grasp of the language (Epp 413:16–17, 541:105–131). In 1516 Capito published an *Institutiuncula* for Hebrew in the Psalter of Pellicanus printed by Froben, and he later (1518) expanded it into a grammar, *Hebraicarum institutionum libri duo*. (Ep 556:26–7n). The lexicon mentioned here (line 184), however, was never completed.

Cardinal Albert offered Capito the position of cathedral preacher at Mainz in 1519, and he left Basel in April 1520. In 1523, increasingly attracted by Luther's views, he removed from Mainz to Strasbourg, where in August 1524 he married. Now publicly committed to the reform, Capito co-operated with Bucer to establish the Reformation in that city. See James M. Kittelson *Wolfgang Capito: From Humanist to Reformer* (Leiden 1975).

WOLFGANG FABER TO ERASMUS OF ROTTERDAM
I am in good health, greatest of men, if you can call it health when one is rather sadly suffering from a desire for one's most desirable Desiderius, without whom no aspirant for a liberal education can find anything enjoyable or gay, especially those who have enjoyed your society beyond all price 5 and your conversation sweet as honey. But what hurts me too most of all is your absence, for while you were here I was prevented by business and poor health from taking full advantage of it. And now that I have recovered my health and see calm water ahead, I have been robbed of my hope of your return by fortune and popularity and the generosity of princes and mag- 10 nates which, lavish as it is, is still hardly adequate to your infinite deserving; and adequate it never will be, unless we suppose that to see our poor Basel robbed of her expectations is an adequate recompense. Yet I still enjoy thus much of my dear Erasmus' favour, that small and speechless as I am, he is yet good enough to write to me, for all that he must be fully occupied in 15 turning away and dismissing those who seek his friendship; for since he cannot give his allegiance to all and sundry, he has chosen one prince, and his native land. Very well, most desirable of men, by all means deprive us of

* * * * *

459:15 to write to me] This is the first surviving letter of their correspondence.

your company, provided it be for your own good and your departure from us
bring you honours and wealth; and we your humble friends, as we sum up   20
our own position, shall not take our misfortune to heart, if outweighed by
your happiness.

Then again, you say in your letter, reasonably enough, that it contributes to the task of establishing true religion and learning that I should long
enjoy good health. For so it is: I am definitely a source of profit to religious   25
studies, I do a real service to the world of letters. And do not think this mere
conceit, for I serve piety and learning equally, and serve them fully, by
summoning the public here to the fullest possible study of Erasmus' works.
I exhort them, I urge them continually to con their Erasmus, to turn his
pages night and day; and with most of those with more than common gifts I   30
secure that Erasmus is the source of all their knowledge, that ocean brimful
of universal learning, that champion of true scholarship. With this Erasmian purpose I shall lecture on St Paul's Epistle to the Romans, beginning
in a few days' time, and I foresee a full and eager audience of volunteers,
attracted merely by the outstanding name of Erasmus. Besides which, in   35
my more elementary class I have arranged that the young boys should be
taught out of Erasmus, that his should be the only name their parents hear
at home, the only one their childish lips praise and extol. And then I seek to
rouse the solemn theologians with a desire to follow your example, openly
telling them that in you the tabernacle of my pilgrimage is pitched, in hopes   40
of developing, in all those in whom resides a love of integrity and learning,
a keen wit like yours, your humanity of spirit, your well-judged sympathy,
your brains, your character, your rule of life. You, I tell them, are the most
perfect, polished product of our age, even of past ages, the universally
accepted model and target of our studies. Not content with this, I pursue the   45
same programme in schools in other places. Is not all this a real service? But
the benefit which is so obvious stems not from a clumsy artisan like myself,
but from a great artist such as you, with a world-wide reputation.

I am delighted to hear that you are at work on a revision of the New
Covenant, and in this I am thinking of the great unskilful public; for they   50
suppose that whatever blemishes you did not remove in your rather hasty
work on the first edition are the result of your critical activity; and if there is

* * * * *

30 night and day] An echo of Horace *Ars poetica* 269

36–7 boys should be taught] With such educational works as the *De copia* (Ep
260), *De ratione studii* (Ep 66), the *Cato* (Ep 298) and the *De constructione* (Ep
341)

49 revision] Cf Ep 417:8.

51–2 hasty work] See Ep 384 introduction.

any conflict between two of your notes, they complain at once that you are
inconsistent and cannot remember what you have written, putting a thing
in one place and then cutting it out in another, staggering along on an   55
unsteady course. The title-page, they say, promises a revision by Erasmus,
based on the Greek and the earliest Latin copies: surely the same man
cannot have written the notes? If the version and the notes are the work of
one man's brain, how could they differ so greatly? These are the sort of
foolish things these home-made critics keep saying. So my advice is – since,   60
incomparably learned as you are, you listen to the humblest counsellors – to
take at least two of your assistants and give them the duty of comparing
most carefully the Greek with the Latin and the notes with the relevant text;
and I should like to see the same done in the Pauline Epistles. For people
often say that your notes on St Paul too are very clearly set out, and they   65
count up in particular the words with which you declare that you have
thrown light on obscurities; but at the same time these words are not in
your translation, although it is no clumsier and no less felicitous than the
version in your notes. But a man of limited intelligence expects them to
agree, especially in a revised edition, and marks down with a touch of spite   70
any disagreements he may have noticed. Pray therefore identify with the
help of your assistants passages which disagree or are clumsily rendered in
the Vulgate version, and bring the whole into agreement with that skilful
pen of yours; make your offspring worthy of its parent and of the pope its
patron, lick it into shape over and over again, experimenting with the   75
language as you so well can. I promise you, nothing will remain that the
demon of fault-finding, Momus himself, could look forward to. As to the
notes, you will give us full measure on St Paul; otherwise the industrious
reader would seek to have the obscurities expounded at greater length
(which you can do as you go along), for he has long grown tired of Lyra and   80
Hugo of Saint Cher and other commentators of that kidney, thanks to you,
having been encouraged by your books to expect more wholesome fare.

* * * * *

77 Momus] The patron of carping criticism; cf Ep 529:90n.

80 Lyra] Cf Ep 166:13n.

81 Hugo of Saint Cher] (c 1200–1263) Theologian and biblical scholar, he held
a doctorate in law and a baccalaureate in theology from the University of Paris
when he entered the Dominican Order in 1225. He played an important part in
the affairs of the Order, and taught theology and sacred scripture at Paris. In
1244 he became the first Dominican cardinal. He is particularly remembered
for his corrected version of the Vulgate, for his Latin concordance of the Bible
(1240) and for his *Postillae*, an exegetical commentary on the whole of Scripture, first printed in the 15th century (Hain 8972–5) and often reprinted up to
the 17th century.

And having foolishly assumed the office of counsellor, I will make
bold to display my folly even more impertinently. I beg you therefore not to
say anything too severe or too openly about the superstition among Chris-   85
tians against certain foods and injunctions to recite some prayer up to a
prescribed number and everything else of the kind, which has been
adopted in credulity or faith from the common usage of our generation.
Thus far you have nobly played the part of Pericles, speaking out in defence
of the truth in a manner that our self-will finds unwelcome, and that with all   90
severity and boldness. To me you seem even now perfectly agreeable, as of
course you are, and indeed mildly disposed even towards those who are
still smarting from wounds inflicted by your eloquent pen; such is your
skill, such the weight of your authority and the more than magisterial
quality of what you write, that not even those who have been attacked and,   95
as they themselves think, hurt by it, know how to protest. But take care:
malevolence will have found an opening, and you may be sure it will cause
you trouble, once it gets an opportunity on any pretext. And so I beg and
pray you, my dear Erasmus, prudent as you are, to man the defences at an
early stage and look to your security; put a bridle of self-restraint, I mean,   100
on your forcible and abundant eloquence, fill us with silent admiration of
the way you restrain yourself. You know, Erasmus, the character and the
sentiments inspired in us by current errors in religious practices and
doctrine. On penance, on the sacraments, on monks with their supersti-
tions and their petty rules, or the widespread misunderstandings regarding   105
the saints, or our feeble attempts to defeat the heretics based on nothing but
forced interpretations of Scripture – on all this, say not a word more, unless
it is hedged about with your wonderful gift of indirect expression. Once
give it an entrance, and the poison of malevolence will force its way into the
heart of things; with its habitual treachery it will spread its policy among   110
the public, and will make out that the bitter passions of a disappointed
mind are true faith and zeal for the right. Then they will denounce the name
of Erasmus, however truly Christian, as a public enemy of Christianity, and
will hold him up to obloquy and condemnation. For it cannot escape you,
best of men, how much those people wish to blacken your fairness of mind,   115
whose murky arts are shown up by your brilliance. And so I would wish to
see your more outspoken remarks on penance modified – say rather, softened by your artistic skill – which I defend all the more zealously, as it is the

* * * * *

89 Pericles] Famous for the 'thunder and lightning' of his oratory

97 will have found] Reading *ceperit* for *coeperit*

117 penance] As on Matt 3:2 (LB VI:17E–F to 18B) where Erasmus places the
emphasis on interior conversion of spirit rather than external works

securest bastion of our position. If however you do not feel free to do away
with what you have said, at least do not add to it. On points of this sort I   120
satisfy many men's doubts on your behalf; I dissipate their more captious
quibbles and infer that your opinion agrees with theirs; by this method I
have extinguished the rising fire of passion in many men. For I earn
confidence with the majority not so much by argument and learning as by
your reputation for a truly religious life, which is my chief asset, as I fight to   125
restore the love of true religion and to defend my Erasmus. I prattle like a
child; but when its parent is listening, what child is ashamed to lisp?

Lastly I must thank you for your kind and friendly letter, with which I
could utterly refute certain obtuse and graceless persons who denied that I
stood well with you. Unless with exceptional kindness you had asked me in   130
that same letter to be your critic, these men (zanies, I should like to call
them) would never understand what in the name of friendship you have
done for a simple man like me; they would maintain that all was done in fear
or poverty. I would rather therefore that they should deny your kindness
towards me than that such idle dogs should see anything sinister or mean in   135
your behaviour. So your letter, much as I appreciate it, shall be seen by no
one, except perhaps Beatus, who is a man of sound judgment and an
honest friend of yours. Suspicious people argue as follows. Because your
New Covenant mentions no theologian by name, nor me either who was in
such continual attendance on you while you were preparing that great   140
work, they suppose that you and I must have fallen out, exactly as though it
would have been typical of you to have loaded the theologians and myself
with eulogies we did not deserve, and as though I had entered that very
busy printing-house in order to get a name for myself and not rather to
enjoy your friendliness, your great qualities, your literary skill. They can by   145
no means be induced to believe that you could have been willing with the
generosity of true genius to say kind things about me which I did not
deserve, and that I refused in fear of being laughed at by those who know
how ignorant I am; that they should think I sought for it rather than allowed
it, I find unwelcome even now.   150

And so I beg and beseech you urgently, dear Erasmus – for you are the
author of such intelligence as I have; to you I rightly owe anything I may

* * * * *

128 letter] Lost

137 Beatus] Rhenanus of Sélestat, Erasmus' close associate at the Froben
press; cf Ep 327 introduction.

139 New Covenant] Erasmus' title for the first edition of his New Testament,
the 'Novum instrumentum'

144 printing-house] The Froben press

become – I beg you to bless your devoted Wolfgang with another letter. I set
you a subject, so that you cannot plead lack of matter as an excuse. We set
out to explain Scripture in its fourfold sense, and not seldom we fall short of   155
all four. Before we have understood the mind of the prophets, we often
misuse their words either to point a moral or to expound the nature of the
Church and other things of the same kind, maintaining that it all flows from
the very heart of Scripture, as though the Holy Spirit had inspired the
prophets with this precise purpose and had never thought of anything else.   160
Then when the truth finds us out or we are proved wrong, we take refuge in
our old stronghold, the variety of senses, not emphasizing the literal, but
the anagogic, tropologic, allegoric meaning; and while we hunt the truth
with nets like this, it gives us the slip. I know the way Scripture works, I
know how it wraps up the nectar of truth in metaphor and allegory, I know   165
it does not shun riddles and indeed invites them from without and collects
them and fills its bosom full of them, as though its purpose were to hide the
truth still deeper. But I think we have to retrace our steps through this
labyrinth with the use of different threads. First by keen judgment, well
equipped with arms provided by the reading of good authors. Next come a   170
richly-endowed familiarity with holy things and skill in handling them,
coupled with a frankness which does not hesitate openly to confess if
anything has eluded its researches. As for moral maxims and the correction
of vice and the arousing of pious motive, nature will pursue all that of her
own accord, of course; but this is not the province of the interpreter, it is the   175
preacher's. Let us therefore pursue one sense only, and that by the best
form of examination we can compass.

But on this point I need your opinion. Please answer, and at one stroke
you will lay me under a double obligation: under your guidance I shall learn
what to treat of in Scripture and how to do it, and at the same time I shall   180
have the means of confuting those who cast doubt on our friendship – by
the evidence of a friendly letter. I am acquiring a certain supply in the way
of Latin, mainly out of your books, and I hope it will be adequate in style
and quantity; for I mean someday to edit a Hebrew lexicon and other trifles
of the kind. My desires are held in check by lack of resources, for I know   185
how little mere industry can achieve in such a sterile soil without real gifts.
If I could use the right word and the stylish word, I should be confident of
doing in the Hebrew field more than even the most learned Jew could easily

* * * * *

155 fourfold sense] An exegetical method chiefly initiated for the Middle
Ages by Gregory the Great (d 604). The senses were the literal, moral, allegori-
cal and anagogic; see de Lubac *Exégèse médiévale* 2 vols (Paris 1959–64).
184 Hebrew lexicon] See introduction.

match. Please do not let my absurd nonsense be tedious and a burden to
you; read it quickly and the tedium will soon be over. Help me to show my   190
friend Rhenanus that I am one of your school.

2 September 1516

Wolfgang Faber, that is, the Smith, is the name I bear commonly, a
barbarous word and most unsuited to my nature, which has nothing of the
craftsman about it. I wish you would make the letters in the name Wolfgang   195
sound a little less harsh, and whatever you call me I shall gladly adopt,
whether Wolfang or something else. Our bishop often speaks of you, and
continually expresses his impatient desire to see his friend Erasmus. You
have left behind you a sort of aura of kindness and courtesy and consummate scholarship, which binds to you magistrates, nobles, prelates and   200
common people. Farewell.

460 / From Beatus Rhenanus   Basel, 3 September 1516

> This letter, also regretting Erasmus' departure from the scholarly circle of the
> Froben press, confirms the impression of Erasmus' intention to establish
> himself in the Netherlands. For Rhenanus see Ep 327 introduction.

BEATUS RHENANUS TO ERASMUS OF ROTTERDAM, GREETING
Sorry as I am that it is not possible for you to move from where you are now,
I am equally glad that the Chancellor of Flanders wishes you well, for the
splendid prebend which he has lately conferred on you is a most convincing
proof of his goodwill. Though, to speak plain, however rich and distin-   5
guished it may be, anyone who accurately reckoned up your virtues and
that depth of learning, greater than has been any man's lot this thousand
years, would find it far less than you deserve. For you deserve the very
highest; just as you are first in the world of learning, so, if you got what you
deserved, you ought to surpass all other men in the dignity of your posi-   10
tion; and that will only happen when the day comes that we hear you have
been made a bishop.

The papal briefs about which you write were delivered here by some
mistake after you had left, but I think Froben sent them to your present
address. Baer is now at Thann, a town not far from here. Christopher   15

* * * * *

197 bishop] See introduction.

460:3 Chancellor] Jean Le Sauvage; the reference is to the prebend of Courtrai:
cf Ep 436.

13 briefs] Cf Ep 338 introduction.

15 Thann] In upper Alsace NW of Mulhouse; for Ludwig Baer see Ep 488
introduction.

bishop of Basel has such a high opinion of you, it passes description. As for myself, since I returned here from home, I have not been lodging with Froben. Thomas Grey has sent me from Paris not so much a letter as a regular book. He made excuses for Faber because he was rather poorly. Give my greetings to that excellent young man John Smith. Farewell.   20

Basel, 3 September 1516

461 / From Thomas More   London, 3 September [1516]

The year-date for this letter, not in the copy in the Deventer Letter-book, is derived from the reference to the *Utopia*. From the frequent references to the work in letters following (Epp 467, 474, 477, 481, 484, 487, 491, 499, 502, 508, 513, 524, 530, 534, 537), it is evident that the first edition, published by Dirk Martens at Louvain, appeared at the end of December 1516. On the historical background see J.H. Hexter 'The Composition of *Utopia*,' Part I of *Utopia*.

MORE TO MASTER ERASMUS, GREETING

I send you my book on Nowhere, and you will find it is nowhere well written; it has a preface addressed to my friend Pieter. Well, you must do what you can for it. I know from experience that you need no urging. I gave your letter to the Venetian ambassador, who seems as though he would   5
have been quite content to accept the New Testament, but Carmeliano

* * * * *

18 Grey] An early associate of Erasmus in Paris; cf Epp 66 introduction, 445.

19 Faber] Lefèvre d'Etaples; cf Ep 445:52n.

20 Smith] An English servant-pupil; cf Ep 276 introduction; F. Bierlaire *La Familia d'Erasme* (Paris 1968) 49–51.

461:2 Nowhere] *Nusquama*, More's first choice of title for the *Utopia*. This indicates that More had finished the work which he had begun in 1514, and that Erasmus was already thoroughly familiar with it; cf J.H. Hexter in *Utopia* xv ff.

3 Pieter] Gillis, Erasmus' close friend of long standing; see Ep 184 introduction, *Utopia* 38–45. More had met him through a letter of introduction written for him and for Tunstall by Erasmus; cf Ep 332:16–19. He was born in Antwerp about 1486 and came of a well-established family; he was now chief secretary to the city. In 1517 he published a study of the sources of the Code of Justinian, the *Summae sive argumenta legum diversorum imperatorum* (Louvain: Martens 1517; NK 15) and with More, he contributed Greek epigrams to the 1518 edition of Erasmus' *Adagia*. See James Hutton *The Greek Anthology in France and in the Latin Writers of the Netherlands to the Year 1800* (Ithaca 1946) 217–8.

5 ambassador] Sebastiano Giustiniani; see Ep 559 introduction.

6 Carmeliano] Pietro Carmeliano from Brescia, whose real family name was 'Fava,' was born in 1451. He was Latin Secretary to Henry VII and (until 1513)

intercepted it. He is entirely devoted to theology, and has performed the task of reading almost all the writers of fashionable disputations, to which he allows so much importance that even Dorp could not allow more. We had a full-dress discussion, each scratching the other's back with formal   10 speeches and long panegyrics. Seriously, however, I like him thoroughly; he seems to me a man of real integrity, very learned, and now most devoted to research in the Scriptures. Lastly, but in my opinion by no means least, he has a high opinion of you.

I have heard nothing yet on business from the archbishop of Canter-   15 bury. Colet had no speech with him about your affair, but he did speak to the archbishop of York, and says he found him so favourable towards you and so eloquent in your praise that he could wish for nothing more, except that some time he should match those splendid words with actions; this I think he will do both soon and generously. That money of yours which you   20 deposited with me my John will give to Gillis at Michaelmas; he will not be coming to Antwerp before then. If later on you publish my epigrams, please consider whether you think it best to suppress those in which I attacked de Brie, for there are some rather bitter things in them; though I might be

* * * * *

to Henry VIII, and an important figure in the introduction of humanism to the English court. He arrived in England at the age of thirty, and little is known of his career up to that time. He worked to secure his position by a series of works dedicated to influential patrons, and may have moved to Oxford in 1483, since he contributed two Latin poems to John Anwykyll's *Compendium totius grammaticae* which was printed there by Theodoric Rood in 1483 (STC 695). Two years later he edited for Rood the *Epistles* of the Pseudo Phalaris; see R. Weiss *Humanism in England during the Fifteenth Century* 2nd edition (Oxford 1957) 170–2. More's is a revealing pen portrait of his personality. In 1485 he returned to London and did editorial work for Caxton. He held several ecclesiastical preferments in addition to his annuity of £40 granted by Henry VIII in 1512, and he died by May 1527.

9 Dorp] Erasmus' critic at Louvain; cf Ep 304 introduction.

21 John] Presumably More's brother, the scribe and secretary (cf Ep 243:2n), since his son by this name was too young for such a task

22 epigrams] Cf Ep 424:90n. They were printed by Froben with the *Utopia* of March 1518; see Ep 550 introduction.

24 de Brie] Cf Ep 212:1n. More refers to epigrams replying to a poem that de Brie, as Secretary to Queen Anne, wrote on the heroism of a French comman-der in the conflict with the English. When More's epigrams were published, de Brie composed a poem, *Antimorus*, precipitating an enduring quarrel with More in which Erasmus tried to play peacemaker; see Rogers Ep 86 and Epp 1093, 1096 below; also M.-M. de la Garanderie 'Un érasmien français: Ger-main de Brie' *Colloquia Erasmiana Turonensia* volume 1 (Paris and Toronto 1972) 359–79.

thought to have been provoked by the abuse he levelled at my country. All   25
the same, as I say, please give them some thought, and in fact all those that
you think might give offence. If besides them any are actually feeble, deal
with them as you may think will be best for me. Quintilian said of Seneca
that he was the sort of man one would wish to use his own brains in writing,
but be guided by someone else's taste; and I am the sort of writer who ought   30
to use not merely someone else's taste but another man's brains. Farewell,
and give my greetings to Dr Tunstall and Master Busleyden.

In haste. London, 3 September

462 / To Wilhelm Nesen   Antwerp, 5 September 1516

This letter was written to accompany the new edition of the *De copia* published by Froben in April 1517. Nesen was a graduate of the University of
Basel and a teacher, and worked as a corrector for the Froben press; cf Epp 260,
329 introductions. Although this letter appeared in the editions of the *De copia*
in March 1519 and February 1521, Froben omitted it in that of May 1526 and
thereafter, since Nesen had died on 6 July 1524, in his thirty-first year. Cf Ep
469 introduction.

ERASMUS OF ROTTERDAM TO HIS FRIEND
WILHELM NESEN OF NASTÄTTEN
Whether it is your critical faculty that prompts you, my excellent Nesen, or
some impulse of affection for me, at least you give me a higher opinion of
my commentaries on abundance of style (which I never thought hitherto as   5
lovable as their compiler's name suggests) by praising them as you do and
getting them by heart and expounding them to your pupils, until they
belong more truly to you by prolonged use than to me as their parent. I have
therefore revised them as you wished, while on shipboard, so that even that
space of time might not be wholly lost to my programme of work. It will be   10
for you to see that they come before the public once again clothed in

* * * * *

28 Quintilian] 10.1.130
32 Tunstall] Cuthbert Tunstall, the English emissary in the Low Countries; cf
Epp 333:19n, 388:114n, 438:13n.
32 Busleyden] Jérôme de Busleyden, provost of Aire and councillor to Prince
Charles; cf Ep 205 introduction.
462:6 name] Erasmus is playing on the associations of his own name and the
Greek *erasmios* (lovable, agreeable) which he uses here.
9 revised] See introduction; the water journey must have been down the
Rhine in May, or perhaps from Calais to Antwerp by barge.

Froben's larger type and as accurate and elegant as may be. Let them at least give pleasure by their appearance if they do not commend themselves to readers by their learning. Farewell, dearest Nesen.

Antwerp, 5 September 1516   15

463 / From Henricus Glareanus   Basel, 5 September 1516

This is a reply to Erasmus' letter written during the summer (Ep 440), in which he invited Glareanus to think of moving his school to the Netherlands. Glareanus was a poet whose talent had attracted Erasmus' admiration; see Ep 440 introduction. This letter was first published in the *Epistolae elegantes* 1517.

TO MASTER ERASMUS FROM GLAREANUS

If you love any man, dearest Erasmus, because he loves you, I certainly ought to be your favourite, for no one (you may safely believe this) is dearer to me than you; and I only wish you could see into my heart as easily as you have so often beheld my outer man. You would see, I promise you, a second   5
Alcibiades, one indeed who far surpasses the first, as far as the true love of men like me surpasses his love for Socrates, or as far as my debt to you exceeds what Alcibiades owed to him. A great thing indeed it was to have learnt morals from Socrates and set one's life in order under his instructions; yet I have had far more from you – besides an infinity of other things,   10
one above all, that you taught me to seek the philosophy of Christ, and not to seek that only but to imitate Him, to worship Him, to love Him. Could anything nobler or more profitable fall to the lot of an ordinary man like me? And so we are not really separated; what you have done for me will not let me forget you. Whatever I do, you are at my side; your image flits before my   15
eyes, ''tis here, 'tis there, continual.' I am never without you, be it bed or board; though you are not here, you rouse me to the pursuit of virtue, you stir up my sloth, you instruct my ignorance; and do you suppose I can fail to love you? How could I? Your absence makes me sad, for which I think no one will reproach me: what greater burden do I bear? I have just said you are   20

* * * * *

12 accurate] For Nesen's earlier responsibility in proofreading Erasmus' edition of Seneca, see Epp 328–30 and, on the shortcomings in this work, Allen Ep 325 introduction.

463:6 Alcibiades] Alluding to the affection he shows for Socrates in Plato's *Symposium*

11 seek ... Christ] *Christum sapere*; this is repeated in Glareanus' poem to Osvaldus Myconius mentioned below at line 73.

16 'tis here] Virgil *Aeneid* 6.122

not absent, but of course you are. Essentially, you are not absent, for you
talk with me every day; and yet you are not here, for I do not see you, nor
enjoy your delightful conversation; and you are also here, for I hear your
words as you speak to me.

I play with words, and foolishly at that, because I love you, and yet   25
with boldness for the same reason; and as I play, tears come into my eyes,
because I love you, my very dear Erasmus. And when I call you very dear,
while other men load you with a thousand other titles, mine is a very special
title, and pays you special honour. What point is there in calling you very
learned, eloquent, erudite, and all the other names thought up not by   30
affection but sometimes by an ignoble desire to please? None of them suits
you better, none describes you so well as the title that comes nearest to
Christ. It was not eloquence or learning on which you taught me to rely, it
was on truly Christian love; and accordingly I owe you a debt of gratitude
the most abundant, undying, superlative and all the other long words our   35
common throng of stylists are so fond of, and which (more to the point) I
pray Christ may repay to you in view of all that you have done for me.

Now I must also answer your letter. When you say that if I were with
you, I could not fail to secure a position, I am truly sorry that I cannot be
with you, but I have good reason for the postponement. My native land is in   40
turmoil. Peace with the king of France is not yet settled, and whether it is
the English or his Imperial Majesty who delays this is uncertain. A mission
from Maximilian has been here and another from England, promising not
money but mountains of gold to keep us from uniting with our French
kinsmen. Some people suspect that the moving force is not instructions   45
from the king in Britain but the cunning of the emperor. At this rate I hope
for peace; and if we do have peace, I expect to find myself in Paris with a
salary of two hundred écus a year. Besides, I have in my house thirty gifted

* * * * *

41 Peace] An alliance between France and the Swiss cantons, signed 29
November 1516 at Fribourg. The alliance was vital to the policy of Francis I
after the election of Prince Charles to succeed Maximilian as Holy Roman
Emperor on 28 June 1519; only Zürich, under the leadership of Zwingli, kept
out of the agreement.

44 mountains of gold] *Adagia* I ix 15: the diplomatic effort to prevent Francis I
from gaining the support of Swiss mercenaries.

47 Paris] Cf Ep 529:112–4.

48 two hundred écus] Probably écus d'or au soleil, whose official value was
raised from 36s 3d tournois apiece to 40s 0d tournois on 27 November 1516.
The salary thus would have been worth £400 0s 0d tournois = £42 10s 0d
sterling = £61 13s 4d gros Flemish. Cf CWE 1 315–16, 321, 336–7; CWE 2 327–40;
Denis Richet, 'Le cours officiel des monnaies étrangères circulant en France au
XVIe siècle,' *Revue historique* 225 (1961) 377–81.

young men, who pay me a hundred and twenty écus a year, though this fee
is not really adequate for the work I put into it. I do beg and beseech you,   50
Erasmus, for you are dear to me as a father, that neither you nor any other
great man who might one day perhaps be my friend will think any the
worse of me for not accepting such a kind invitation. For come Pentecost, if
we are not at peace with the French and if your prince (as I sincerely hope) is
safe and sound, I shall find courage to fly to your side even through the   55
midst of the enemy. Meanwhile, my kinsmen and friends have begged me
not to go away; but I do not commit myself.

The name of Mountjoy cannot fail to be dear to me, until Erasmus
ceases to be so; I have been persuaded to think him an excellent and
exceptional man both by your writings and by a conversation you and I   60
once had together about his merits as a civilized person. Baer was not here
when your letter arrived, and so I have been unable to get any news out of
him. After your departure our logic-choppers so attacked me that they tore
my notices off the church doors and forbade public lectures on Seneca. I
lectured however in spite of them, being afraid of nothing more than that   65
they might induce Baer to share their views; but wishing to steer clear of the
ill-feeling, he had very little to do with the business, though he was
noticeably more kindly towards me as long as you were here.

I would almost not have sent my verses, for they are a youthful effort
and give me no sort of satisfaction as an address to such a great man or, if   70
you reject that as flattery, a great friend. But I hope that you will tear them to
pieces, and but for this hope I should have consigned my nonsense to the
flames. I send some other verses too, a trifle about your departure that I
wrote for Osvaldus, who is a keen follower of yours and my doughty
supporter like great Alcides against the logicians; I have said something   75

* * * * *

49 a hundred and twenty écus a year] A sum worth, as above, £240 os od
tournois = £25 10s od sterling = £37 os od gros Flemish

53 invitation] That Erasmus had apparently extended to come to the Low
Countries, probably on behalf of Mountjoy; cf line 58.

53 Pentecost] 31 May 1517

58 Mountjoy] Erasmus' first English patron, William Blount, Lord Mountjoy,
was praised by Erasmus in the dedication to the *Adagiorum collectanea*; cf Ep
126. In the much enlarged *Adagiorum chiliades*, also addressed to Mountjoy in
1508, this preface was revised; cf Ep 211.

61 Baer] Cf Epp 488 introduction, 460:15.

63 logic-choppers] For background see Ep 328:43n.

65 nothing more] Reading *magis*, not *eos*.

74 Osvaldus] Myconius; cf Ep 861 introduction; the poem follows Ep 440 in
the early editions. Cf Ep 440:15n.

75 Alcides] A name for Hercules.

Bonifacius Amerbach
Portrait by Hans Holbein the Younger, 1519
Öffentliche Kunstsammlung, Basel

about that struggle and also about your most welcome gift of a dial. 'For
Glareanus from Erasmus' has been very prettily engraved on it by the
goldsmith, and it has been kept wrapped all the time in silk. Busche's
poem, which gives me the greatest pleasure, I have copied out as carefully
as I can, considering I had a text that was corrupt; and so I beg you to look   80
through it with your usual care. Your greetings were most warmly received
by Osvaldus, Rhetus and all my pupils, and they have instructed me
unanimously to send you their greetings in return, with every good wish
for your health, prosperity and length of life. You told me to write you a nice
long letter, and I have done so, with more zeal perhaps than success. What   85
else can I do? 'I chatter with the best, speak can I not.' Farewell, dearest
Erasmus, my leading star, my pride and joy.

    From my treadmill in Basel, 5 September 1516

464 / From Bruno Amerbach   Basel, 5 September 1516

This letter from the eldest of the Amerbach sons announces the completion of
the edition of Jerome. In addition to the manuscript version in the Deventer
Letter-book, there is an autograph rough-draft of this letter among the papers
of the Amerbach family in the Öffentliche Bibliothek of the University of
Basel, MS G II 33ª 8; cf AK 563.

Greetings, learned Erasmus. I have made my escape at last from that pitiful
cave of Trophonius, though it has brought me so low that I can scarcely
smooth the wrinkles from my brow. What are you doing now, you ask, now
that you have reclaimed your ancient liberty? After this long exile I have
returned to my studies, and have devoted myself entirely to sound learn-   5
ing; and in particular I pass my days and nights perusing your learned and
eloquent writings, so that to some extent at least I may converse with you,
since
    Clasp hand in hand we may not, nor exchange
    The living voice.   10

    * * * * *

77 engraved] In Greek
78 Busche's poem] Hermann von dem Busche, Glareanus' teacher; cf Epp
440:16n, 830 introduction.
82 Rhetus] Hieronymus Artolf of Chur; cf Ep 440:17n.
86 I chatter] A line from the *Demoi* of the early Attic comic poet Eupolis (frag.
95 Nauck), cited by Aulus Gellius 1.15.12 and by Plutarch, *Alcibiades* 13
464:2 cave of Trophonius] See Ep 439:2n.
9 Clasp hand in hand] Virgil *Aeneid* 1.408–9

William Warham
Portrait drawing by Hans Holbein the Younger, 1527
Windsor Castle; reproduced by gracious permission of
Her Majesty Queen Elizabeth II

For my part, in despair of your ever returning to us, I mean to make for Italy next spring. You will do me a very great service if you will write a letter of recommendation to Bombace and your other friends. I will do my very best to show my gratitude in some other way. You can give a letter to Franz the bookseller at the Frankfurt Easter fair to be delivered to me. 15

I congratulate you warmly on the preferment that has just come your way; God send it may be like a stepping-stone, and we shall soon see you going up higher. Lachner is sending by means of Franz what was missing in the volumes given to the archbishop, and seven works of Jerome in addition; do with them whatever you think best. My brothers Basilius and 20 Bonifacius send their greetings; they are both devoted to you, and each would be content to be your little finger. Our friend Konrad is very sad to think you have so completely forgotten him; you do not even send him a greeting when you write to someone else. Farewell, O Aesculapius of sound learning, and give me your friendship in return for the reverence and 25 respect I feel for you.

Yours sincerely,
Bruno Amerbach
Basel, 5 September 1516

465 / From William Warham to Thomas More   Otford, 16 September [1516]

This letter, number 21 in Rogers, is mentioned in Ep 468:4 as already dispatched.

WILLIAM ARCHBISHOP OF CANTERBURY TO THOMAS MORE, GREETING
Cordial greetings. I have sent Maruffo a letter in which I proposed that he should procure the payment of ten pounds, or twenty if more is needed, to

* * * * *

13 Bombace] Paolo Bombace, the distinguished Bolognese humanist; cf Ep 210 introduction.

16 preferment] The prebend at Courtrai; cf Ep 436.

18 Lachner] Cf Ep 469:11–14.

18 Franz] Cf Ep 258:1n.

19 archbishop] Warham; cf Ep 425:28n.

22 Konrad] Probably Brunner, 'Fonteius'; cf Ep 313:26n.

465:3 Maruffo] Raffaele, a Genoese merchant through whom Erasmus' English annuity was usually paid; cf Ep 387:3n.

4 ten pounds] Probably £10 sterling, which would have been worth, in equivalent silver values, £14 10s 11d gros Flemish or £84 9s 2d tournois. Cf CWE 1 328, 340–4; CWE 2 327–44.

Andr. Ammonius Erasmo.

Vischer, Erasmiana 24.   Allen 466.

Autograph letter, Ammonio to Leo x, September 1516, Epistle 466
Number 1 in a volume labelled *Variorum epistolae ad Erasmum*
Öffentliche Bibliothek, University of Basel

our learned friend Erasmus in Louvain, and promised to repay him as soon   5
as ever I see a letter from Master Erasmus acknowledging receipt. Please
therefore have a word with Maruffo, and find out if he is willing to do this; if
he proves at all difficult, I have given instructions to my servant Henry
Jeskyn, the bearer of this letter, to approach Master Antonio de' Vivaldi and
arrange the affair with him on my behalf.   10

    From my house at Otford, 16 September

466 / From Andrea Ammonio to Leo x   [Westminster][September 1516]

> This is taken from an autograph by the writer, a copy of a letter sent by him to
> the pope shortly after Erasmus' return to the continent, in support of Ep 447; cf
> Ep 478:17–18. It is the first item in a volume entitled *Variorum epistolae ad
> Erasmum*, and on the back of the manuscript Ammonio has written 'Copy of a
> letter to the pope'; it was sent therefore to Erasmus for his own information. It
> is now in the Öffentliche Bibliothek of the University of Basel, Erasmuslade
> D 5, folio 1, number 1.

Most holy Father, etc. It is long since anything arose that seemed to me to
justify the presumption of addressing the throne from which your Holiness
presides over the human race. Now however I feel myself compelled to do
so by a reason which justifies my temerity, and that is that I should
endeavour to add my own recommendation (as I consider all lovers of   5
humane letters ought to do) on behalf of Erasmus, a person already strongly
recommended to your Holiness by his distinction as a man of learning; my
object being that he may be able with a mind more at ease to devote himself
to the republic of letters, and that your immortal Holiness may gain a man of
such quality as your most devoted disciple; not that you could be made   10
greater by any encomium, but because no better offering can be made to
any divinity than the praises of a priest pure in heart and nearest in gifts of
mind to the Deity. In this my confident approach I am filled with hope by
the more than human generosity of your Holiness, accustomed as you are to
lend a ready ear to the petitions even of men of no account, and to encourage   15
learning not only by kind words but by gold and silver. For this last
indulgence, however, Erasmus makes no request, being perfectly content if
he may win your approval, of which (rare as is the boon which he seeks) I
count him worthy, inasmuch as his gifts are likewise rare, and rare benevo-

* * * * *

465:9 de' Vivaldi] A merchant of Genoa resident in London often employed
by officials to provide letters of credit abroad

lence alone can do them justice. The right reverend the lord bishop of   20
Worcester will expound more fully both his petitions and my own at the feet
of your Holiness, etc.

467 / From Thomas More   [London, c 20 September 1516]

> This letter, number 22 in Rogers, is without date in the Deventer Letter-book;
> it is obviously contemporary with Epp 461, 465, and 468. Allen suggested that
> More sent Ep 465 and the remittance as soon as they arrived, about 17
> September, following them shortly afterwards with this letter and, slightly
> later, Ep 468. The present letter accompanied the letter 'to a fellow-
> countryman of mine,' mentioned in Ep 468:8–9.

MORE TO ERASMUS, GREETING

I have received a letter from you written at Calais, from which I gather (and
am glad to hear it) that you had a favourable passage. The provost of Cassel
told me that you had reached Brussels safely before he left home; he is now
here on a diplomatic mission. Maruffo waylaid me recently to complain that   5
by some mistake he had suffered a loss on the payment of your remittance.
Besides which I have sent you another bill of his for twenty pounds of our
money from the archbishop, in the discounting of which I hope you will be
equally fortunate, if you do it promptly before he gives his people instructions to the contrary; for he seems determined to do this. The bearer of this   10
letter will pay Gillis the twenty pounds you left with me, that is, thirty livres
of your money for twenty pounds of ours.

* * * * *

466:21 Worcester] Silvestro Gigli; cf Ep 521 introduction.

467:2 letter] Lost; probably written about the same time as Ep 457

3 provost of Cassel] Joris van Themseke (Georgius of Theimseke); cf Ep
412:58n, LP ii 2303, 2322.

5 Maruffo] On this affair see Epp 387:3n, 388, 412, 424, 465:3n.

7 bill of his for twenty pounds] A bill of exchange for £20 sterling, to be
redeemed or discounted, probably at the Antwerp fair, in livres gros Flemish.
It would have been worth £29 1s 10d gros Flemish (= £168 18s 4d tournois), in
equivalent silver values, but somewhat more in gold values (if specified in
nobles), which had been rising at the Antwerp market since 1512. Cf Ep
463:48n above; CWE 1 336–46; CWE 2 327–44; CWE 3 Ep 424:73–4n; Herman Van
der Wee, *Growth of the Antwerp Market* (1963), II, 133 (table XVI); and Ep
468:3n, 9–10n below.

11 left with me] Cf Epp 461:20–1, 468:12, 481:6–7, 499:7.

11 thirty livres] £30 gros Flemish = £20 12s 6d sterling = £174 3s 10d tournois.
Cf note 7 above.

I spoke with Urswick lately about your horse. He says he will see to it that you get one soon, but that he has not yet found one of the sort he would wish to send you. I sent you some time ago my *Nowhere*, which I long to see 15 published soon, and well furnished too with glowing testimonials, if possible not only from several literary men but also from people well-known for the part they have taken in public affairs – for the benefit especially of one man (you will know whom I mean even if I do not mention his name), who for some reason, which you must guess for yourself, regrets that it should 20 be published before nine years have passed. You will take this in hand as you may consider best for me. Apart from that, I long to know whether you have shown it to Tunstall, or at least, as no doubt you have, described it to him, which I should prefer. For then it will please him twice over: as you recount it, it will appear a much more elegant piece than it did when I wrote 25 it, and you will spare him the labour of reading it for himself.

Farewell.

468 / From Thomas More   London 22 September [1516]

This letter is number 23 in Rogers; on the circumstances see Ep 467 introduction.

THOMAS MORE TO ERASMUS, GREETING

Greetings, dearest Erasmus. My lord of Canterbury has arranged to send you twenty pounds of our money. I have therefore sent you Maruffo's bill and at the same time the archbishop's letter to me, so that you can see how generous he is with his money and how far from stingy I am myself when it 5 comes to paying out other people's. Besides which, you must lose no time in telling his Grace that you have received the money, so that Maruffo may have good cause to demand reimbursement. I have written to a fellow-

* * * * *

13 horse] Cf Ep 451:6.
15 *Nowhere*] *Nusquama*; cf Ep 461:2n.
18–9 one man] Allen suggested that this refers to Colet.
21 nine years have passed] Cf Horace *Ars poetica* 388.
23 Tunstall] Cf Ep 461:32n.
468:2 Canterbury] William Warham; cf Epp 467:7–12, 188 introduction.
3 twenty pounds of our money] £20 sterling. Cf Ep 467:7n, 11n.
7 his Grace] *Episcopus*, i.e. Warham, the archbishop of Canterbury; cf Ep 388:62n.

countryman of mine, who will be collecting some money due to me at your
Fair, asking him to pay Gillis thirty livres gros Flemish, against which he is   10
to acknowledge on your behalf the repayment of the twenty pounds in our
money which you lately left with me.

I sent Latimer your letter, and mine too, about this business of the
bishop of Rochester, but I have as yet heard nothing from him, and nothing
from the bishop either. Colet is very busy with his Greek, in which he has   15
the voluntary help of my friend Clement. I think he will make progress and
achieve his aim by hard work, especially if you encourage him steadily from
Louvain, though perhaps it will be better to leave him to his own momen-
tum. It is his way, as you know, for the sake of the argument to resist those
who try to persuade him, even if their point is one to which he is strongly   20
inclined of his own accord. I have been to see Urswick; he says he has not
forgotten your horse, and will see that you get it soon; and when he does
this, I will see that you know, so that you cannot be taken in by any
substitute.

In haste, from London, the morrow of St Matthew   25

469 / From Wilhelm Nesen   Frankfurt [September 1516]

This letter, as Allen conjectured, was written after Nesen received Ep 462 at
Frankfurt, where he was attending the book-fair with Wolfgang Lachner (line
11n). Nesen did not realize, however, that Erasmus intended to include Ep 462

* * * * *

9–10 at your Fair] one of the four Brabant Fairs: probably the Fair of St Bavon
or 'Bamismarkt,' held at Antwerp from 1 October; or possibly the succeeding
Fair of St Martin or 'Koudmarkt' (Cold Market), held at neighbouring
Bergen-op-Zoom from 11 November.
10 thirty livres gros Flemish] Cf Ep 467:11n.
13 Latimer] William Latimer, a Fellow of All Souls College Oxford, was one of
the most learned humanists in England, from whom Erasmus had sought
advice for his revision of the New Testament: Ep 427. Erasmus evidently
wrote to him after the recent visit to Rochester when he had helped Bishop
John Fisher in the study of Greek; cf Ep 452. It seems from Ep 481: 17–18 that
Erasmus suggested Latimer too might spend some time with Fisher. For
Latimer's comment see Ep 520:12–20.
15 Colet] Cf Ep 471:31–2.
16 Clement] Cf Ep 388:185n.
19 resist] For a like trait of character in Colet see Ep 270:35 ff.
22 horse] For this business see Epp 451:6, 467:13.
25 St Matthew] 21 September

in the new edition of the *De copia* (cf lines 16–18 and Ep 462 introduction). On
returning to Basel, he learned this from Froben and wrote Ep 473, which
repeats some of this letter.

NESEN TO MASTER ERASMUS, GREETING
I am sorry, heartily sorry, that the immortality which you alone would have
been able to bestow has been pre-empted by some distinguished good-
for-nothing; I should have valued it more highly than ten of your golden
rivers, Tagus, Pactolus and what not, and all else that this deceitful world   5
admires. Your *Moria* is not printed yet. Those worthless soldiers who
invaded Lorraine about the time of your departure have prevented Froben
from getting any good paper. But it is now on the anvil, and we shall make
good this negligence by working even harder. There was nothing new at
Frankfurt except a certain Coelius, who has written a universal history in the   10
style of Pliny, if you please. Lachner is sending you as a present seven
complete works of Jerome, and one volume jointly with Franz, out of which
you can make good whatever was lacking in the previous Jerome which you
took away with you, so that you can have eight.

I have not seen the *Copia* yet (for your letter found me at Frankfurt, not   15
Basel), which you say belongs to me. How can it be mine, my dear Erasmus,
when it does not acknowledge me, who am a man of no account in the
literary way, by any letter at the beginning? I will see to it, however, that it
is printed both accurately and as quickly as possible. Lachner urges you
most strongly, if you have put together anything new, or propose to refur-   20

* * * * *

469:2 immortality] Evidently in the dedication of Gaza; cf lines 25–7 below.
5 Tagus, Pactolus] Two of the rivers fabled in Antiquity to run with gold;
Adagia I vi 75.
6 *Moria*] Cf Ep 419:15n.
6 soldiers] Cf Ep 412:5–6.
10 Coelius] Lodovico Ricchieri of Rovigo (d 1525) appointed in 1515 by
Francis I to Chalcondyles' chair at Milan (cf Ep 428:39n). The book mentioned
here is his *Antiquae lectiones* (Venice: Aldus 1516) which led Erasmus to accuse
him of having borrowed extensively from the *Adagia* without acknowledgement.
11 Lachner] He had travelled to the Frankfurt fair together with Nesen; cf Ep
464:18–20.
12 Franz] Birckmann; cf Ep 258:14n.
16 you say] Cf Ep 462:8 and introduction above.
19 Lachner] Cf Ep 473:32–34 where this proposal is repeated in Froben's
name.

Jérôme de Busleyden
Portrait by a Franco-Flemish master, *c* 1480–1500
Wadsworth Atheneum, Hartford, Connecticut
Ella Gallup Sumner and Mary Catlin Sumner Collection

bish anything afresh, to be so good as to let him see it, and he will show his
gratitude somehow or other. Nobody can thank you adequately; for nature
has concentrated all her gifts on you at once, thus proving that she is by no
means barren and worn out, but can still produce a man who is the equal of
them of old time. I am very sorry that the Theodore was dedicated to   25
someone else, some good-for-nothing; I was hoping that it might come
back to us with an inscription to Nesen: how open-minded the man is, I
cannot say, but he is certainly far from ill-disposed. But I hope my friend
Erasmus will do something else to please me.

Farewell, my dear friend, and let the natural goodness of your disposi-   30
tion find a place for me too one day. Forgive my ignorance; I have written
this in the inn at Frankfurt. I will write more fully about everything from
Basel. Everyone here admires you and your great gifts quite particularly.
Give my greetings to my English friend, to whom I would have written had
time not been so short.   35

470 / To Jérôme de Busleyden   Antwerp, 28 September [1516]

Erasmus writes to a man with whom he had been friends since the turn of the
century; cf Epp 157: 67, 205 introduction. Busleyden was the third son of Gilles
de Busleyden, secretary to Philip the Good. His brother François was archbishop of Besançon. Jérôme was now about forty-five years old and an
influential statesman, being an ecclesiastical member of the Great Council of
Mechelen. Like Jean Le Sauvage (Ep 301: 38n) he accompanied Prince Charles
to Spain in 1517 and died there. Erasmus' epitaphs for him are printed in
Reedijk, poems 106–107.

Erasmus' search for patronage in the Low Countries was now nearing a
climax. He had left Basel in May 1516 with the printing of the New Testament
and the edition of St Jerome behind him, to take up the commission which
Jean Le Sauvage, the chancellor of Burgundy, had obtained for him as councillor to Prince Charles (Ep 370: 16–20). He wished to present his treatise on the
education of a prince, written the previous winter, but Froben did not publish
it until late May or early June, after Erasmus left; cf Epp 393 introduction, 407,
419. Erasmus went first to Antwerp to stay with his old friend, Pieter Gillis,
but shortly after his arrival, he paid his respects in Brussels to Le Sauvage,
whom he had first met in Ghent in August 1514 (cf Epp 410 introduction,
301:38, 412: 57–9). After a brief tour in which he visited Mountjoy and the

* * * * *

25 Theodore] of Gaza; cf Epp 428, 575. It was dedicated to Johannes Caesarius.
34 English friend] John Smith; cf Ep 460:20.

abbot of Saint-Omer (Epp 412–17) Erasmus returned to Antwerp. Le Sauvage wrote shortly afterward, on 8 July, summoning him with the news that, if Erasmus was 'determined to remain in these parts and to live a peaceful and pleasant life in honourable leisure' he would cause to be conferred on him 'a prebend or canonry of Courtrai.' There was also the hint of further favour to come (Ep 436: 4–7). By 10 July Erasmus was in Brussels (Ep 438) where he and the chancellor evidently discussed the conversion of the Courtrai living into an annuity, and the prospect of Erasmus receiving appointment as archbishop of Saragossa (Ep 443).

Erasmus then returned to England for a brief visit devoted to removing canonical obstacles to his receiving a major benefice (Epp 446, 447, 451, 452, 453, 455, 466). On the eve of his return he wrote Henry Bullock from Rochester that he expected to spend the winter in Louvain (Ep 456:7). By 27 August he had landed at Calais and his forwarding address was as before, the house of Pieter Gillis, town secretary of Antwerp (Ep 457: 58–60). It was at this stage in his affairs that Le Sauvage summoned him to Brussels once more.

ERASMUS TO HIS FRIEND BUSLEYDEN, GREETING

Actual shortage of funds obliges me to sell my horses. I have emptied all my money-bags buying clothes and arming myself against the approach of winter. I do not fancy riding while naked, and I cannot at the same time both clothe myself and keep horses. I have offers for them, but the onset of 5 winter means that the offers are disappointing. I have no wish to force the animals onto you or to sing their praises; but if you think fit, take over one or both of them, and then fix a price yourself in the light of experience – or even do not fix one. Otherwise I shall turn them loose on the world for as much as I can get, that they may not eat me out of house and home. 10

The chancellor has instructed me to attend in Brussels. What the business is, I do not know. If he sends a second time, I shall take wing; otherwise I shall pack my bags here and move entirely to Brussels in a week's time. This seems to me more and more the best course. I write you a laconic note, because I think I wrote two days ago. Farewell, Busleyden my 15 distinguished friend.

Antwerp, Michaelmas Eve

* * * * *

470:2 horses] Cf Ep 477:31–34.
11 chancellor] Jean Le Sauvage; for his business with Erasmus see Ep 475:2–11.

471 / To Johann Reuchlin   Antwerp, 29 September [1516]

This letter was printed by Reuchlin in the *Illustrium virorum epistolae*, May 1519; cf Ep 457 introduction. It replies to Ep 418.

ERASMUS TO REUCHLIN
After I had got this letter ready against the first offer of a courier, your letter reached me in Antwerp – written in June, and I received it at the end of September. To answer it very briefly, it was my duty, my learned friend Reuchlin, to write and thank you for the manuscript, one of your dearest possessions, which you sent me on loan; but Froben was responsible, who had sent back the volume without letting me know. That my poor stuff should be approved by the vote of a true scholar and a good man like yourself, gives me great joy. Only, when you despise your own work compared with mine, mind that friendship and modesty do not carry you too far. And why do you lament your bad luck? You saw Italy in that blessed age when Agricola flourished and Poliziano and Ermolao and Pico; you are blest with such various and recondite learning; you have been the acquaintance and friend of so many of our greatest men; you are even now so dearly beloved by all our noblest men and our best scholars that, were you their father, you could not be more intimately beloved by all of them. The bishop of Rochester has an almost religious veneration for you. To John Colet your name is sacred. Had not his servant lost your letter, he would keep it, he told me, among his holy relics. I lately visited a very ancient charterhouse near Saint-Omer, a town in Artois. The prior of the house had acquired a remarkable knowledge of Hebrew out of your books without a teacher, and

* * * * *

471:2 courier] A doctor of divinity who is mentioned but not named in RE 231–2.

12 Agricola] Rodolphus Agricola, who had left Italy by the time Reuchlin arrived there; cf Ep 23:58n.

12 Poliziano] Angelo Ambrogini of Montepulciano; cf Ep 61:154n.

12 Ermolao] Barbaro; cf Ep 126:150n.

12 Pico] della Mirandola; cf Ep 126:150n.

17 Rochester] John Fisher; for his admiration of Reuchlin see 432:13–18.

17 Colet] Cf Ep 300:10n.

19 charterhouse] A Carthusian monastery founded at Longuenesse, southwest of Saint-Omer, in 1298. The *Illustrium virorum epistolae* contains a letter from its prior, Jean Quonus, written to Lefèvre d'Etaples in praise of Reuchlin. It is dated 24 July [1514?]; cf RE pp 223 n2; 80 n2.

Johann Reuchlin
Woodcut portrait on p 23 of Part III of Heinrich Pantaleon's
Prosopographiae herorum atque illustrium virorum totius Germaniae (Basel 1566)
Houghton Library, Harvard University

is so devoted to you that he venerates your very name. I happened to have about me a letter from you, and when he saw that it was in your handwriting, he begged and prayed me to leave it with him, putting it to his lips again and again.　25

There are not a few people, my dear Reuchlin, who feel like that about you. That you should feel secure in your own goodness and ignore the malevolence of men, is right. Goodness is her own most plentiful reward. If this generation does not acknowledge you as it should, posterity will do so; in the end Christ will acknowledge you, in whose service you fight your　30
laborious fight. Send Colet a letter, even a short one; old man as he now is, he is learning Greek. The bishop of Rochester also has made good progress. Farewell again, my most learned Reuchlin.

Antwerp, 29 September, from the house of Pieter Gillis, secretary to the Town Council; anything sent to this address will easily be delivered to　35
me.

472 / From Josse Bade　　　　　　　　　　Paris, 29 September 1516

This letter contains several allusions to Ep 434 which had not yet reached Erasmus (cf Ep 477:11). Bade had been a favoured printer of Erasmus prior to 1515, when Erasmus formed his connection with Froben; cf Ep 346 introduction. The *Parabolae* or *Similia* ('Parallels') had first been published by Schürer in December 1514, with his edition of the *De copia*, of which Bade in turn had had the original printing (15 July 1512; cf Epp 260, 311 introduction). Bade complained to Erasmus of the losses he suffered from other printers re-issuing his own publications (cf Epp 263, 346, 434), and Erasmus sent him a revised copy of Schürer's *Parabolae* (not Martens', as suggested by Allen, cf Ep 434:3n) with the suggestion that Bade in turn should reprint that. Bade held strict views on copyright and was reluctant to do so, but nevertheless printed the work in handy form' with a preface of his own, to Pieter Gillis, dated 29 November 1516. Froben followed Bade's text of Erasmus' preface to Gillis (Ep 312) in later editions of the *Parabolae* (February 1518, February 1519, and July 1521) and included a vocabulary by Bade without attribution. In his revised edition of August 1522, Froben acknowledged the authorship of Bade's glossary, perhaps as a consequence of representations by Erasmus, who was by then back in Basel.

* * * * *

31 old man] Colet was about fifty years old; cf Ep 468:15 and, concerning Fisher's studies, Ep 468:13–15.

FROM JOSSE BADE TO ERASMUS, GREETING

Your admirable book, the *Parabolae*, has arrived safely. With your usual
modesty you express the wish that I should do what I can for it; but it is your
book that will do a great deal for my printing-house, except that I have some
misgivings about causing other men to suffer the loss many of them inflict   5
on me. Do you take my point? What I mean is this. Such is your reputation
among your fellow-men, that if you announce a revised edition of any of
your works, even if you have added nothing new, they will think the old
edition worthless; and losses of this kind have been forced on me in respect
of the *Copia*, the *Panegyricus*, the *Moria*, the *Enchiridion* (I had undertaken   10
for 500 copies), and the *Adagia*, of which I had bought 110. It would thus be
greatly to our advantage if you would assign each individual work to a
single printer, and not revise it until he has sold off all the copies; a practice
which you have observed in the *Parabolae* to some extent, if you have given
your previous printer prior warning, and not encouraged Martens to print   15
it. On your own encouragement I sent a fair quantity of your *Panegyricus*
into Germany; but since they had already been printed there, this was owls
to Athens with a vengeance. However, since the *Parabolae* go well with the
Copia, the moment I have a press free, they shall be printed in the same type
and on similar paper.   20
     I have for some time been on the watch for space in the preliminaries
of some rather special book, where I can declare how much I value your
wisdom and your brilliance of style, as the man in the fable did to the
reed-bed; not that this would be doing anything new, or likely to add to
your public reputation, but it would throw a sop to my zealous impatience   25

* * * * *

472:2 *Parabolae*] Cf Ep 434:2n.

10 *Copia*] Cf Epp 434:7, 260 introduction.

10 *Panegyricus*] Cf Ep 179 and the edition by Otto Herding ASD IV-1 1–93.

10 *Moria*] Cf Ep 222.   10 *Enchiridion*] Cf Ep 164.   11 *Adagia*] Cf Ep 211.

15 previous printer] Schürer; cf Ep 311.

15 Martens] Bade had complained about his 1515 edition of the *Parabolae*; cf
Ep 434:3n.

17 already been printed] By Froben, April 1516; cf Ep 179 introduction.

17–8 owls to Athens] In English idiom, 'coals to Newcastle'; cf *Adagia* I ii 11.

24 reed-bed] When the barber of Midas, king of Phrygia, found the king has
asses' ears, he dared not say so and could not keep it to himself, so he uttered
the fact to a hole in the ground. Reeds grew over the place, and as they waved
in the wind, their whispers said 'Midas has asses' ears' (Ovid *Metamorphoses*
11.190).

25 sop] Cf Ep 434:4.

and prevent it from turning to frenzy. I think I mentioned this when I was answering your last letter at some length; and I also entrusted a letter, written with some care, from our friend Budé to the son-in-law of Josse Donaret, the clerk of the Town Council of Ghent, to be delivered to you. Budé is most desirous to know whether it reached you or not. It was written   30 after your arrival in Brabant, about six weeks ago. You will find this servant of mine useful for bringing back an answer.

Farewell, from Paris, Michaelmas Day 1516

473 / From Wilhelm Nesen   [Basel, end September 1516]

For the background to this letter see Ep 469 introduction.

TO MASTER ERASMUS FROM WILHELM NESEN

Although the affairs of mortals are usually such that they cannot at first sight be considered either sweet or sour, to me at least nectar and ambrosia would seem revolting compared with any opportunity of writing to you, and I only wish my ability to do this properly were equal to my desire, and I   5 could open the recesses of my heart with a freedom which is at the moment repressed by my sad lack of skill. You would then see how your friend Nesen, the lowest of the low, would exalt you to a pinnacle of eminence above the greatest. But unfortunately these idle wishes accomplish nothing. That you should have thought of dedicating to me your notes on the   10 ornate style, your *Copia*, fills my heart with a pleasure and secret joy that I can hardly express. It is a wonderful thing, a glory that will make my name immortal, which I think far preferable to the wealth of three hundred Croesuses and Crassuses – not however that anything of the sort is deserved by a simple, humble person like myself, for the last thing my own   15 . qualities have secured for me is an even moderately well-nourished style; but because I am said to have had Erasmus with his more than human gifts as my friend. I will do my very best to see that the *Copia* appears in Froben's type as quickly and as neatly as can be. Your Folly, who is so much wiser than any theologian, is now almost finished. Beatus Rhenanus has held it   20

* * * * *

28 Budé] Ep 435; the figure of six weeks is owed either to a scribal error, Budé's faulty memory, or his ignorance of Erasmus' recent visit in England. The letter did not reach Erasmus until October; cf Ep 434 introduction.
473:11 *Copia*] Cf Ep 462.·
19 neatly as can be] Cf Ep 462:12.
19 Folly] Froben's edition of 1516; cf Epp 328:47n, 419:14n, 469:6.

up for a time half-done with his Latin version of the *Gryllus*, which he hopes
to add to it. Schürer has reprinted your *Enchiridion*.

It is extraordinary (I had almost forgotten this) how like themselves, I
mean how arrogant the theologians are in passing judgment on your Annotations, or rather Illustrations. But by now all the force of this old evil-   25
speaking has evaporated, and the cloud they tried to spread over your fame
has happily blown away. They credit you not only with eloquence, which
they themselves have never achieved, but even with a knowledge of theology, which they pretend to but in reality do not own. Farewell, my life-
giving eloquent Erasmus, and think of me kindly as your protégé. Give my   30
greetings to your English boy.

Froben urges you, if you have anything that you have either revised or
written new, to let him have it; he will repay your kindness with careful
pains and good money.

474 / To Thomas More   Antwerp, 2 October 1516

This letter, which is number 24 in Rogers, was first printed in the *Farrago*. For
the background to Erasmus' financial problems see Epp 467–8.

ERASMUS OF ROTTERDAM TO HIS FRIEND MORE, GREETING
I was already booted and spurred for my journey when two letters arrived
together, but no servant or merchant comes to see me. I showed Maruffo's
bill of exchange to Caspar; it provides for payment in sizeable ducats of full
weight or equivalent value – not valour; you will recognize this time the   5

* * * * *

21 *Gryllus*] Cf Ep 328:48–9n. The translation was not added to the edition of
the *Moriae encomium*.

22 *Enchiridion*] June 1516 edition, a reprint of the second edition of the
Lucubratiunculae supervised by Nikolaus Gerbel of Pforzheim (Strasbourg
1515); cf Ep 445:58n.

24–5 Annotations] To the *Novum instrumentum*; cf Ep 373.

31 English boy] Erasmus' servant-pupil John Smith; cf Ep 469:34.

32 Froben] Cf Ep 469:19n.

474:2 two letters] Epp 467, 468

3 merchant] Cf line 22n.

3 Maruffo] Cf Ep 465:3n.

4 Caspar] According to Allen, possibly the burgomaster of Antwerp; cf Ep
570:3n and CWE 3 350–1. However, this Caspar seems to speak as a banker
rather than an official of the city.

4 ducats] Cf Ep 447:844n.

commercial, not the army word. I asked him what the equivalent was, and he said thirty-seven and a half stuivers. In my view, I said, 'equivalent' can mean only the value fixed publicly by the prince. But, says he, this is our practice. This system of yours is most misleading, I said, for I have no means of guessing your practice from the bill of exchange. And I took my 10 bill back again. Pray tell the man that I have no intention of losing fifteen florins in every sixty nobles. Please ask the archbishop to give the money to you; deposit it yourself with the Easterling Germans; and send me a document against which I can draw it here, unless you know of someone through whom you can send it here more satisfactorily. I have emptied all 15 my money-bags in the process of buying some clothes. Take my word for it, my dear More, I have spent over four hundred florins. The risk now is that in my smart new clothes I shall starve to death. If Tunstall spends the winter here, I shall join him; for he wants that very much. That stupid fool x stirred

* * * * *

6 army word] An echo from Pliny *Historia naturalis* preface 1.

7 stuivers] Silver coins, also known as patards, worth 2d gros Flemish each. By the last Burgundian-Hapsburg monetary ordinance of December 1499, the ducat (and florin) should have been worth 79d gros or 39½ stuivers; or rather, in terms of its gold content relative to that of the St Philip florin, it should have commanded at least that value. The difference evidently represents the charges – about 5 percent – for redeeming the bill of exchange. (On 15 August 1521, an edict of Charles v raised the value of the ducat to 80d gros or 40 stuivers.) Cf CWE 1 327, 331, 337–40.

11–2 fifteen florins … sixty nobles] By florins Erasmus meant either the money-of-account of 40d gros Flemish (livre de quarante gros) or the gold St Philip florin, then worth 50d gros; by noble, he meant either the money-of-account of 6s 8d sterling (half a mark) or the gold 'angel' of the same value, then worth 9s 8d gros Flemish. In any event, Erasmus was exaggerating the potential loss on the exchange: 50s or 62s 6d gros on 580s gros (i.e. 8.6 or 10.8 per cent). Cf CWE 1 312, 318, 320, 325, 327, 336–7; CWE 2 340 (plate).

12 archbishop] William Warham

13 Easterling Germans] Members of the Hanseatic League (in Dutch, *Oosterlingen*); more specifically, merchants from the Baltic German towns.

16 clothes] Cf Ep 470:2–5.

17 four hundred florins] Erasmus probably meant the gold St Philip florins, and thus a sum of over £83 6s 8d gros Flemish = £60 0s 0d sterling = £525 0s 0d tournois (in France, from 27 November 1516). Cf Ep 463:48n above; CWE 1 318, 320, 336–46; CWE 2 327–44.

19 x] Undoubtedly Dorp; this passage and others critical of Dorp were removed from the edition of the *Epistolae ad diversos* printed by Froben in August 1521, doubtless in an effort to preserve the better relations established in 1517; cf Ep 509 introduction.

Christoph von Utenheim
Portrait on glass by an unknown painter, Basel, 1522
Historisches Museum, Basel

up exceptional trouble for me in Louvain, even after we had shaken hands;   20
you shall hear more about this shortly.

While I write this, the Englishmen's host has come to see Pieter Gillis,
offering the price of the books; but of my money not a word. As for Urswick,
mind you keep up the pressure. Jerome will be here in a couple of days,
with a great bundle of letters to me. When I get them, I will inform you,   25
should there be anything that you ought to know. As for your Island, and all
the other things, they shall be taken care of. I write this in the middle of
packing, and expecting to mount my horse any moment. My best wishes,
dearest More, to you and all yours.

Antwerp, 2 October 1516   30

I have arranged for the archbishop, Colet, the bishop of Rochester,
Urswick, and you if you would like one, to be among the first to get copies of
the Jerome. Farewell once more.

Pieter Gillis is devoted to you. You are constantly present with us. He
is delighted with your *Nowhere*, and greets you most warmly, you and all   35
yours.

475 / To Andrea Ammonio   Brussels, 6 October [1516]

This letter announced Erasmus' decision not to go to Louvain after all, but to
remain in Brussels for the winter. It was first printed in the *Farrago*. For the
background see Ep 470 introduction.

ERASMUS OF ROTTERDAM TO ANDREA AMMONIO, GREETING
Are you ready for a laugh? When I got back to Brussels and went to pay my
respects to my Maecenas the chancellor, he turned to the councillors who
were standing with him and said 'Our friend does not yet know what a
great man he is.' Then he said to me 'The prince is trying to make a bishop of   5

* * * * *

22 host] Evidently the keeper of an inn frequented by English visitors to the
book fair, where communications of common concern might be expected. Cf
line 3, Ep 468:7–8.

24 Jerome] Cf Ep 469:12.

26 Island] The *Utopia*; cf 1 35, Ep 461:2n.

475:3 chancellor] Jean Le Sauvage; cf Epp 470 introduction, 301:38n.

5 bishop] Cf Ep 443:19, 460:12. All the evidence suggests that whatever
Erasmus' true attitude, this proposal was taken very seriously by the Council
under Jean Le Sauvage. After this failure the matter of episcopal preferment is
not raised again, perhaps because of Erasmus' candid refusal to give up his
purely literary and scholarly pursuits, which pointed clearly to absentee
tenure: cf Epp 446:51n, 476:27–30, and see the comments of Ammonio, Ep
478:11 ff. and of Mountjoy, Ep 486:11–13.

you, and had already conferred on you a see by no means to be despised (it is in Sicily), but it was then discovered not to be in the list of what they call reserved sees. So he has written to the pope to ask him to let you have it.' When I heard that, I could not suppress a laugh. All the same, it is pleasant to know how the prince feels towards me, or rather the chancellor, who in practice is the prince. I only wish the plot of this comedy may work out all right, for it was at about the same time that I wrote from England and these people wrote from Brabant. I am thirsting to hear how my business progresses.

I mean to spend the winter in Brussels. Anything you send to Tunstall will reach me without delay, for I see him constantly. I have turned somewhat against Louvain. If I were there, I should have to pay my own way and be the humble servant of the university people. The young men would be interrupting me all the time with their chatter: 'Do correct these verses, Just vet this letter for me'; there would be constant demands for different authors; and there is no one there whom it would be any credit or any help for me to know. On top of all this I should have to listen sometimes to the chatter of the theologians, the dreariest sort of men, and among them the egregious x has very nearly got me into trouble; it is a case with him of my having the wolf by the ears, unable either to hold on or let go. Face to face he is all smiles, and uses his teeth behind my back; writes letters full of honey but with more than a little gall mixed in; professes friendship and behaves like an enemy. I have left no stone unturned to cure the defect in that man's nature, for I admire his gifts and appreciate his style, which is elegant by local standards. As I see that this makes no progress, I am resolved to let him alone and leave him to himself until this drunken fit blows over. If only great Jupiter with his famous thunderbolt would plunge this whole race of men into Tartarus: they produce nothing that can make us better men or better scholars, and they are a perfect universal nuisance.

Jerome was on sale in Antwerp even while I was still there. Franz arranges the scenes of this comedy in such a way as to look after his own

* * * * *

8 reserved] For Spanish nomination

12 I wrote] The letters concerning his dispensations; Epp 446, 447 etc.

24 x] Dorp; cf Ep 474:19n.

25 having the wolf by the ears] *Adagia* I v 25

28 left no stone unturned] *Adagia* I iv 30

32–3 plunge ... into Tartarus] So the first edition of 1519; in 1521 this became 'If only great Jupiter would put this whole race of men back on the anvil and remake them.'

35 Franz] Cf Ep 469:12n.

business all the time. He would not even let me see my letters until he had taken care of his own interests – merely said there was a great bundle of letters from Germany for me, among them one from the bishop. You shall have a share of the gossip as soon as I get them. In Antwerp I had what you   40
lately sent to Basel, brought I suppose by Pace; but not a word from Pace himself. Farewell, Ammonio my learned friend.

Brussels, 6 October [1514]

476 / To Pieter Gillis   Brussels, 6 October 1516

This letter was first published in the *Auctarium*.

DESIDERIUS ERASMUS OF ROTTERDAM TO
PIETER GILLIS, GREETING

I have secured a room here, which when the town is so full is extremely difficult, but a very small one; near the Court however and (what com-mends it to me much more) near Tunstall. And so please have my books   5
sent here as soon as you can by either boat or wagon, and at the same time write to me by some other hand to say whom you have entrusted them to and to what address you have told him to take them. Pompilius, I perceive, is up to his tricks; keeping, that is, to his old habits, and so I bear it with more patience. One day perhaps the chance will come to repay him in his   10
own coin.

Do you care to hear something that will make you laugh? What often does not fall to the lot of other men after great and prolonged efforts, has almost come my way while I sleep: his Catholic Majesty has very nearly made me a bishop! Where, you will ask. Not among the farthest Indians,   15
though our friend Barbier gets gold from there, being appointed to rule over

* * * * *

39 bishop] Of Basel, Christoph von Utenheim.

41 Pace] Now at Zürich, he sent these letters which had been by now so long on the way; cf Ep 338 introduction.

476:4 Court] Cf Ep 457 introduction.

8 Pompilius] Allen suggested this name was substituted in printing, possibly for that of Franz Birckmann; cf Ep 475:35–37.

14 Catholic Majesty] Prince Charles as king of Spain. Ferdinand of Aragon had died on 23 January after a reign of forty-one years. He bequeathed Aragon to Charles, and on 14 May Charles was proclaimed king of Castile at Ste-Gudule in Brussels; cf line 22.

16 Barbier] Cf Ep 443; Barbier evidently held ecclesiastical preferment in the Indies; cf Ep 532:31 and Allen Ep 914:6n.

men whom he will never see, but among the Sicilians, who were clever
Greeks once and still are witty and gay. But there was a most fortunate
mistake, which suits me very well; for it was afterwards discovered that the
right of appointing to this honour belonged to the pope. So the king then   20
wrote to the pope to ask him out of respect for himself to let his appointment
stand. This was going forward in Brussels, while I was taking it easy in
Antwerp, amusing myself with reading and writing, and this was why the
chancellor had given orders to send for me; had I had an inkling of this, I
should have taken my time over moving here. When I got here and was   25
congratulated by those who were in the know, and given their best wishes,
I could only laugh. All the same, I thanked them for their kind feelings,
warning them however not to waste vain efforts in future on any business
of this sort, for I was unwilling, I said, to exchange my liberty for any
bishopric however distinguished. There's a daydream for you to laugh at!   30
And yet I am glad to know how such a great prince feels, for he does not as a
rule confer favours except on men whom he knows or at least supposes to
deserve them.

I am most happy, my dearest Pieter, to have relieved you of such a
burden, for I was already developing sympathy for you and your dear wife;   35
and yet, if I was indeed a burden, you cannot say it was my fault. That spirit
of yours with what I can only call excessive affection was never satisfied
with heaping kindnesses on me, and your wife could seldom do enough to
satisfy you, although that is her great object. Now that your Erasmus has
left you, you will have more chance to enjoy her society. How little you and I   40
lose by separation! – and even that much we shall be able to make up by
writing frequently. I hope that your letters will be cheerful and lively; then I
shall know you are in good health, which is nearer my heart than anything.

Good health, believe me, is mainly in your own hands. Most of our
ailments take their rise in the mind, and you will find your work less   45
laborious if you arrange your studies on some rational plan. Your library,
your letters, and all your notes should be arranged in definite places; and do
not be carried away first into one author and then another, but take in hand
one good book at a time and do not abandon it until you have finished it,
making notes as you go along of the things that seem worth remembering.   50
Lay down for yourself some definite course of life, deciding what you wish
to do at what time of day. Do not pile one task on another until the earlier
one is finished; thus you will make the day seem longer, which is now

* * * * *

24 send for me] Ep 436 (8 July 1516)
35 wife] Cornelia Sandria; cf Ep 312:93n.

almost entirely wasted. And since you complain of your memory, I think
you may find it useful to set up a kind of journal for each year (it does not   55
take much trouble), and enter in it briefly day by day anything that happens
which you would not wish to forget. I know some people who have profited
greatly from the time spent on this, among them that distinguished man
François de Busleyden archbishop of Besançon.

But above all I urge you to learn in the conduct of business to follow   60
judgment rather than impulse. If there is anything you do not like, look at
once to see if you can put it right or if the wrong can be made less; and you
will see this more clearly in tranquillity than if you are upset. If anything
can be done, do it; if not, what pray is the use of indignation or laments,
except to make things twice as bad with only yourself to thank? I beg you in   65
the name of our friendship, consider your life and health more important
than anything. If you can maintain your position in life without harming
them, by all means do so; but if not, it is false economy to keep one's
possessions intact and lose one's health and peace of mind. Above all, if you
have too little concern for yourself, mind you do not prove the undoing of   70
someone else as well; for I shall not regard myself as safe and sound unless
you are so too, whom I reckon (as I hope for the love of God) the better part
of me. Do not spend too much time on things of no account. Youth speeds
by, health can break like glass; they must not be squandered. Some things
one ought to look down on, and raise one's spirit to the big things. Seneca   75
and Plato – make them your familiar friends; if you converse with them
often, they will not let your spirit lie down. A truly great spirit should
overlook some wrongs done to it, and to some men's calumnies have
neither ears to hear nor tongue to reply. Make the experiment sometimes:
discover how much more compliance and intelligent courtesy can do than a   80
spirit headstrong and wayward.

As for your excellent father, do all you can to cheer his old age, as I
know you already do, not only because he is your father but as being the
sort of father he is. Keep in close touch with your true friends and dismiss
the pretenders. Give your wife cause to love you, not merely as her bedfel-   85
low, and not merely love you but respect you; give her your confidence, but
share with her only what concerns your family affairs or helps to make life
enjoyable. Maintain your authority over your servants, with this limitation, that the regular running of your household be sweetened none the less
by courtesy and kindness. On your children's education I shall waste no   90

* * * * *

59 Busleyden] Cf Ep 157:67n.
82 father] Nicolas Gillis, the second town treasurer of Antwerp; cf de Vocht
Literae 438.

time in good advice, when your father has set you such a good example.

You see, my dearest Pieter, how wise I am on your behalf, though none too wise on my own; but my foolish remarks are inspired by my affection for you. My very best wishes to you and all yours.

Brussels, 6 October 1516   95

477 / To Pieter Gillis   Brussels, 17 October [1516]

This is the only year in which Erasmus and Tunstall were in Brussels together at this time. It is one of the letters published for the first time by Paul Merula in the *Vita Des. Erasmi Roterodami ex ipsius manu fideliter repraesentata* (Leiden: Basson 1607); cf Allen 146, 575. The letter to which it replies has been lost. In this letter (line 13) it becomes clear that the person whose name had been excised from Epp 474:19 and 475:24 was Erasmus' old critic, Maarten van Dorp; cf Epp 304, 337, 347 and 438.

ERASMUS OF ROTTERDAM TO THE LEARNED MASTER
PIETER GILLIS, HIS INCOMPARABLE FRIEND. IN ANTWERP

Pray hasten to see that Jerome is sent here properly bound for the addition of notes. On the number and arrangement of the volumes consult Pieter; it seems to me adequate to bind them in six. If he gave Franz my letters to the   5
bishop of Basel and to Baer, I have no doubt that they were delivered. I had an idea that I entrusted them to someone else. I am getting the Nowhere ready; mind you send me a preface, but addressed to someone other than me, Busleyden for choice. In everything else I will act as a friend should. Please send here by Franz the *Sententiae Pauli*, so that I can entrust it to   10

* * * * *

477:4 Pieter] Meghen? See Ep 491:4n.

5 Franz] Birckmann; cf Ep 475:35.

6 bishop of Basel] Christoph von Utenheim; cf Ep 305:243n.

6 Baer] Ludwig; answered by Ep 488

7 Nowhere] *Nusquama*, More's first title for the *Utopia*; see Ep 461:2n.

8 preface] Gillis' Preface to Jérôme de Busleyden at the beginning of the first edition of *Utopia* is dated 1 November 1516. On the relationship between the prefatory letters and the work itself, see Peter R. Allen 'Utopia and European Humanism: the Function of the Prefatory Letters and Verses' SR 10 (1963) 91–107.

10 *Sententiae Pauli*] An epitome of the work by that name ascribed to Julius Paulus, the Roman jurist of the early fourth century

Bade, from whom I have now had two letters, and another from Budé, very long but friendly.

Dorp's nonsense you shall hear about shortly. I never saw a man whose friendship was more unfriendly. Tunstall, having read the stuff he addressed to me and his answer to me, abominates the man so much that he 15 can scarcely bear to hear him mentioned. You see how much good he has done! I also answered him in my turn, but assured him that I should waste no time on such rubbish in future. Tunstall has a high opinion of you and admires your gifts more than anyone. Really you are the perfect 'man of good Faith,' if you think that honest dealing should exist not merely, as the 20 old formula has it, between honest men, but with tailors and bargees. You ought to have come to an agreement with the bargeman; as it is, he has named his own figure. And then of the Tournai material I lined my cloak with, only about five ells came back, out of twenty, mind you.

But these are trifles. Our one-eyed Cocles, or Cyclops if he would 25 rather, handed over to me a suit-length of unwashed stuff instead of washed. If you have any reason to want to come over here, you know I shall be delighted to see you. But I should not like you to go out of your way for my sake, if it is not convenient. For I have made up my mind to spend this winter here, and not a moment longer. If you are angry with your servant 30 John, you ought to be angry with me, for it was I delayed him for two days. I have sold one of my two horses, but on such terms that I feel he was thrown away rather than sold; and again the horse I handed over to the abbot of St Bertin's has just as much, I fancy, gone for nothing. Farewell, my incom-

* * * * *

11 two letters] Epp 434, 472

11 Budé] Ep 435

13 nonsense] Erasmus' intimates in England were already aware of the epistolary exchange (Epp 304, 337, 347, and Ep 502:4–9). Such references as this suggest that in 1516 there was another controversy; cf Epp 474:19n, 487:10 f.

21 old formula] Found, for instance, in Cicero *Epistulae ad familiares* 7.12.2

24 about five ells] about 11.5 feet. The Flemish ell = 0.700 metre = 27.56 inches.

25 Cocles] Cf line 4 above.

26 suit-length] Reading *vestimentum*

33 sold] Cf Ep 470:2.

33 horse] Perhaps a horse presented to Abbot Antoon van Bergen (cf Ep 143 introduction) on behalf of Warham, for which service Erasmus himself expected a corresponding gift. Cf Allen Ep 781:33.

parable friend. Give my warmest greetings to your excellent father and your   35
dear wife.

    Brussels, St Luke's Eve

    When you have a suitable man to carry letters, let me use him.

478 / From Andrea Ammonio   Westminster, 20 October [1516]

    This letter, which was first printed in the *Farrago*, replies to Ep 475.

ANDREA AMMONIO TO ERASMUS OF ROTTERDAM, GREETING

I was amused to hear that in your part of the world also you had found a
serious patron, and a patron moreover who, as everyone agrees, can do
what he likes with your prince, a thing of which we cannot but be glad, if
only for your sake. As for the promotion you speak of, though nothing else   5
may come of it for the moment, it is surely a great thing that such prominent
persons should have shown so much good will towards you, and I sincerely
wish you joy, being now filled with a solid expectation that fortune will not
be so unfair to your ability, your learning, and your virtues much longer. If
the Holy Father promotes you like this, I shall think he did it as a tribute   10
more to your merits than to the prince's recommendation. But I am afraid
there will be this against it: he will have no doubt that the prince's favour
towards you will remain constant, and that he will soon have it in his power
to promote you to some other see; and if he does not, I hope the pope
himself will ask him to do so, for I am sure the Holy Father would be very   15
glad to see you exalted, but if possible at someone else's expense rather than
his own. I wrote to him and to my lord of Worcester not long after your
departure.

    You say you mean to spend the winter in Brussels, and I think this is a
good idea, partly to escape the tiresome attentions of the university people   20
in Louvain, and also so that you can often make your self visible in the
bright light of the Court, and thus refresh your friends' memory of you face
to face, and set your sails to catch the breeze of some favouring fortune; you
will be able to be of service both to yourself and to your country, if you can
endure to approach nearer to your patron deity. It will not be a long   25

    * * * * *

478:3 patron] Jean Le Sauvage
17 wrote] Ep 466
17 Worcester] Silvestro Gigli; cf Ep 521 introduction.
25 patron deity] Prince Charles

business, and my view is that you ought to put up with some things and take some time off from your studies, in order to promote the comfort and dignity of the rest of your life. There speaks the practised courtier!

If you let go of your wolf, which in my opinion you can do without any risk, the same fate awaits him as befell Euripides; what he wants is the   30 reputation of having sustained a contest with Erasmus. But be careful to keep your hands off this sore place, for the more you scratch it, the more you will encourage it. Cast this wolf, as they say in Greek, to the crows or to the dogs.

As for your Jerome, I am delighted to hear it has reached you, for this   35 means it will soon be brought over here to us. And so you are not to send me a single page. I am in no hurry, for I have scarcely the leisure to open Cicero a couple of times in a month.

Would you care for some news? The cardinal of Sion (you know, the Swiss cardinal) has arrived here; I have spoken with him, and he strikes me   40 as an able, vigorous, active man, a good speaker, a hard worker and a reasonably good theologian. Your friend More is in excellent shape. Give my cordial greetings to Tunstall; I am delighted that you see so much of him. I should count myself happy, if only I could share in your conversations. Look after yourself, my dear Erasmus.   45

Westminster, 20 October [1514]

479 / From Andrea Ammonio   London, 22 October [1516]

This letter is taken from an autograph manuscript in the Bibliothèque Nationale, Paris: n. acq. lat. 1520, folio 3. Earlier the manuscript seems to have belonged to a volume of documents in Basel dealing with Erasmus' dispensation from Leo x. Like Ep 498, the second in that volume (of which the first is Ep 466), it is endorsed 'Manus Andreae Ammonii' by Erasmus himself. An eighteenth-century copy of it is found in another collection of letters in the Öffentliche Bibliothek, University of Basel, MS G² II 67, folio 82ʳ.

* * * * *

29 wolf] That is, Dorp; cf Ep 475:24n.

30 Euripides] He 'was torn to pieces by the dogs of his patron, Archelaus of Macedonia' (P.S. Allen). The reference here is to Dorp, presumably.

33 say in Greek] Cf Adagia II i 96.

39 Sion] Cf Ep 447:66n; Schiner was in London to secure financial support for the Emperor's policies. See Scarisbrick 63f.

ANDREA AMMONIO TO HIS FRIEND ERASMUS, GREETING

After I had sealed my second letter to you, a courier arrived from Rome with
a letter from the bishop of Worcester, who sends you his greetings and best
wishes, and says that in Rome you have come to life again, for your death
had previously been much lamented. As concerns your business, he writes   5
that the pope read both your letter and mine with pleasure and listened to
our prayers, but that he postponed action until his return. For he was on
vacation more than sixty miles from Rome, but was said to be likely to be
back about 30 October.

The bishop of Worcester expects to get all he asks for, but thinks we   10
shall have to throw a sop of some sort to the datary, to stop him from
barking too much; though just why we should, he does not say. But I have
written to say that he is not to worry about the expense, and that I will
promptly refund here whatever he may have spent over there. So there is no
reason for you to fear any delay; about the end of November or soon after   15
you may expect to have your prayers answered.

London, 22 October

To the most learned and eloquent theologian Master Erasmus of Rotterdam

480 / To Guillaume Budé   Brussels, 28 October 1516

This letter, replying to Ep 435, was first published like that letter in the
Epistolae elegantes 1517. On the correspondence of Erasmus and Budé see Ep
403 introduction.

ERASMUS TO HIS FRIEND BUDÉ, GREETING

I was truly delighted by your last letter, dear Budé, my most learned
friend, for it was not only full of learning, which is normal with you and
so cannot now be any surprise to me, but abounded all through with
such elegance and charm and wit that the gloomiest of men might grow   5

* * * * *

479:2 courier] With letters from Rome dated 27 September, one (from Gigli's
secretary) with news that the pope would stay at Viterbo until the feast of All
Saints; cf LP ii 2394–5.

4 death] For a similar rumour earlier cf Ep 270 introduction.

6 your letter and mine] Epp 446 (and 447), 466

11 datary] Silvio Passerini (d 1529) was apostolic datary, the curial official
through whom Rome since the 14th century had exercised power over individual dioceses. The office had been established within the chancery originally, to administer reserved benefices.

cheerful as he read it. There is a man here called Cuthbert Tunstall, who in
England is Master of the Rolls, and is now his king's representative at the
court of our Prince Charles; besides a knowledge of Latin and Greek second
to none among his countrymen, he has also a seasoned judgment and
exquisite taste and, more than that, unheard-of modesty and, last but not   10
least, a lively manner which is amusing with no loss of serious worth. He
and I share the same table, in which I count myself fortunate, and so we
often relax over one of your letters by way of dessert. For I can hardly
express how much he respects your scholarship, which in any case is
admired by everyone except those who do not understand it. He solemnly   15
swears that of all modern scholars no one writes Greek more expressively or
more elegantly than Budé; yet he does not deny that your Latin is not only
very pure and classical but also rich and eloquent.

Apart from that, I must now reply briefly to your letter, although both
tediously distracted by certain tiresome bits of domestic and Court busi-   20
ness, and in a low state on account of a cold. I must say, this is an agreeable
and friendly thing to do, to ply the whip because my letter was carelessly
written! Pray consider the progress I have made: it is by writing so much
that I have learnt to write badly. How much better you have managed
things, writing carefully and achieving speed as well! Not but what I can   25
deal with this accusation, partly by weakening its force and partly by
turning it against you – what Greek calls ἀντικατηγορεῖν. In the first place,
is it not somewhat inhuman, when a man is busily occupied in the copying
out of great volumes and on top of that sometimes has twenty letters to write
in a single day, to demand that he should take great pains over the penman-   30
ship of his letters as though he had nothing else to do? If I undertook the
labour of copying out my things a second time, the burden would be much
more than I could carry; if I delegated the duty to others, five servants would
hardly be enough. Yet that wife of mine, at whose expense you wax so
merry, barely allows me to keep a single one; such is the hen-pecked life I   35
lead from an imperious mistress rather than a wife. Secondly, how much
you were tormented by my rough notes, as you call them, I do not know.
One thing I do know, that your pure and spotless letter cost me so much
pains that I had to write it out fair with my own fingers to make it legible,
first for myself and then for my scholarly friends; for before I did that, I   40
could hardly read it and no one else could read it at all, not so much because

* * * * *

480:6 Tunstall] On his appointment see Epp 424:89n, 388:114n.
19 your letter] Ep 435 which was not received until now.
34 wife of mine] Poverty; cf Epp 421:140, 435:110.

it was so carelessly written as that you write like no one else. Not but what
you will easily solve this problem if you will take the trouble to write to me
often, for thus I shall grow much more familiar with your handwriting.

When I found you transforming my 'trivialities' into 'certain short 45
pieces,' I recognized at once with a smile Aristophanes' slippery trick of
correcting himself: 'Stole it? No, no! Conveyed it.' On the whole question of
my works, I am delighted to find that you agree with me, so far am I from
protesting; in fact, what you think about my *Copia*, the Lucian dialogues
and the new text of the Petty Cato, I myself believe one should extend to 50
everything else. It is true that the *Adagia* make a biggish book; but the
subject could hardly be more modest. And yet I believe I acquitted myself so
well as to have surpassed all my predecessors, at least those whose compilations are extant. Again, what activity in relation to Scripture could be more
modest than what I have attempted in my New Testament? Fewer nights of 55
toil would have met the case for some far grander undertaking. But suppose
I am born for these humble tasks: what then? I deserve less blame (as I see it)
for attempting tasks of this kind than praise for accepting Horace's advice,
considering 'what can my shoulders carry, and what not,' and refraining
from burdens which I cannot bear. You perhaps should be forgiven if, 60
blinded by immoderate affection for me, you think I can do more than in
fact I can; and I should actually be given credit for measuring myself by my
own foot, keeping my own company, and recognizing 'how scant the gear I
have at home.'

Again, the risk you display before me that by publishing so many 65
minor works I shall get myself a bad name does not move me in the least.
Whatever in the way of notoriety rather than glory has been won for me by
my publications, I would peacefully and willingly dispense with, if I could.
Men's spheres of interest differ and their strength lies in different fields, nor
have all men the same natural bent. For my own part, these superficial 70
subjects are the field in which it suits me to philosophize, and I see in them
less frivolity and somewhat more profit than in those themes which the
professional philosophers find so pre-eminent. Finally, the man whose sole
object is not to advertise himself but to help other people, asks not so much
Is it grand, my chosen field? as Is it useful? I will not shrink from tasks even 75
more despicable than my so much despised Petty Cato, provided I can see

* * * * *

45 'trivialities'] For this theme see Epp 403:135–6; 421:82; 435:74, 93.

46 Aristophanes] *Plutus* 372

58 Horace's advice] *Ars poetica* 39–40

62–3 my own foot] *Adagia* I vi 89

63 keeping my own company] Persius 4.52 (cf Ep 458:10n).

that they help to promote liberal studies. I write these things not for your
Persius or your Laelius but for children and dullards. And remember, my
learned friend Budé, how right Horace is:

Give me three guests, and – O their varying wishes!   80
Three several tastes demand three different dishes.

The *Copia*, which we despise (for on this at least we are of the same
opinion), is much admired by several critics of no common sort, who
maintain that no work of mine was ever so useful or showed greater skill.
Not but what in this respect I do not find your view quite self-consistent.   85
You had attacked me for choosing somewhat humble subjects, and thus
forestalling authors of a lower class; and now you complain that I have not
done justice to the subject of my choice. Yet I think these are two quite
different accusations: 'You have a prosaic mind unaware of its own powers,
and attack subjects unworthy of you' and 'You have chosen a subject such   90
that you cannot do justice to your choice.'

I should not like you to understand from this, my dear Budé, that I am
in any way offended by your letter; only that I love to share a jest or an
argument with a most humorous and also most scholarly friend. The title
seems to you to hold out great hopes; but for the rest, you do not approve   95
my drawing the material from common sources, feeling I suppose that it is
taken from common and widely accessible authors. But if no one else ever
laid down any principles for abundance of style, what would you do then?
Quintilian barely touched on the topic. Trebizond, who pillaged Hermogenes, makes abundant promises on the subject of abundance; but   100
though I pursued his promises until my head spun, I never found anything
on the subject of the slightest importance. In Venice I also ran through
rather than read Hermogenes, nor did I find anything in him that seemed
likely to be of much use. After my work was published I discovered a certain
amount in Rodolphus Agricola, a man who, had the envious Fates allowed   105
him to live longer, would have given Germany someone to match against

* * * * *

78 Persius] Lucilius, the early Roman satirist (cited by Cicero *De oratore*
2.6.25), said he wrote not for scholars like Persius but for ordinary folk like
Laelius. Erasmus has misremembered the exact formula.

79 Horace] *Epistles* 2.2.60–2

99 Trebizond] In his *De rhetoricis praeceptionibus*; cf Ep 36:3n.

103 Hermogenes] This second-century Greek rhetorician was included in
Aldus' *Rhetores graeci*, November 1508.

105 Agricola] His *De inventione dialectica* was published by Martens at Louvain on 12 January 1515; Erasmus' *De copia* had been published by Bade in
Paris on 15 July 1512. See Ep 260 introduction.

the Italians, just as France now has Budé, though no one else. For my own part, I perceived that the addition of examples from the best authors would add greatly to the dignity of the work; but in part I was fearful of making the volumes too big, and in part it would have lost its value for the particular   110
class of reader to whose benefit all my labours were directed. Even now teachers in many places complain that the work is too clever to be understood by readers of moderate attainments.

Again, when you feel for men of moderate abilities whom you would not wish to see deprived of their natural subject, you could use the same   115
argument to discourage me from writing anything at all. Be my chosen subject large, middling or very small, I shall forestall other men of large, middling or small abilities respectively. One thing is common knowledge: 'All men may enter for the prize, who practise the pursuit of poesy.' It is open to anyone even since my *Copia* was published to lay down rules for   120
abundance of style. It is sufficient credit for me to have done so either for the first time or more carefully and accurately than anyone else; which I think you will not deny. But how useless is this plan of which you speak! – to have kept a copy of your letter in draft so that (in your own words) 'I cannot take a too censorious line once a letter has been sealed and sent.' And what good,   125
pray, will this precaution do you, once we have come into open court? You will produce your original hand, I shall counter with the autograph text; you will produce a draft, and I a pure and spotless letter. You cannot deny it; that is how you yourself wish it to appear.

But on those 'trivialities' I have perhaps written too much trivial stuff   130
already. Apart from that, to speak seriously, my excellent Budé, I do recognize up to a point that I have been careless or, I would prefer to say, unsuccessful. All the same, I shall take heart from your letter and perhaps aim at something on a grander scale; and I only hope it may succeed as you are sure it will. Some men make Corinth ..., and we are not all Budés. I am   135
not in that class of people who think nothing right except what they do themselves. I respect your accuracy and diligence, your lofty temper which shows itself equally in your subject-matter and your actual style. My Budé is right to take up these subjects, for he is equal to them; he has the powers needed to unlock the great treasures of rare learning stored up in a common   140
'as.' Such topics suit a man who single-handed fights for the public reputa-

* * * * *

119 'All men] Terence *Phormio* 16–17
126 open court] Terence *Phormio* 282; an account of the collapse of the eloquent young man when brought into court
135 Some men make Corinth] Other men do not; *Adagia* I iv 1

tion of France against the Italians, and can take on Ermolao and Pliny and
their like. In short, that vaulting spirit befits a Frenchman, not a Hollander;
to put it in a nutshell, it suits Budé, not Erasmus.

But in heaven's name, what is this I hear? My wife has been 'pretty   145
much your bedfellow'? How lucky I am not to be jealous! I only wish she
had cleared off somewhere long ago, not to live with you (rather may good
success of every kind take up its lodging with you, in that house which you
have made the home and haunt of the Graces and of every virtue), but with
the Franciscan brethren who have such a passion for her, or anyone else   150
who may love her even more than they do. Though (to be done with fooling)
my modest fortune does not altogether distress me. If it did, I might long
ago have increased my possessions, had I not always been convinced that
money in the hand is better than substantial assets. And that great
Maecenas of mine, the archbishop of Canterbury, supplies me of his own   155
generosity with enough to support my private way of life and a man of my
convictions. Nor do I aim to get something out of his serene Highness my
prince; it merely seemed to me uncivil to refuse entirely to do what little I
can, in the first place for a prince like him and then for my native land which
needed me. What severely plagues me, my dear Budé, is to have Poverty at   160
my side, but not Philology; I have the shadow always with me, not the
substance. How happy should I be if I might have both to share my home!
For that matter, remember that some people may find a lack of consistency
in what you say in your letter – that you have Poverty on your hands, when
at the same time you are building two country-houses fit for Lucullus, as   165
you say yourself.

Furthermore, when you say in your humorous way that there is some
risk of my one day losing my love for the humanities, once I have had the
good fortune to be hung with gold, as far as that goes at any rate I can assure
you there is no need to lose a night's sleep. The times are not such, not such 170
the state of the Court just now, that a good gilding should come the way of
those who seek it as I do, by virtually running away. Up to now, gold has

* * * * *

142 Ermolao] Budé had found Pliny the Elder's *Historia naturalis* a chief source
for his *De asse*, and had made use also of Ermolao Barbaro's important study of
Pliny, the *Castigationes Plinianae*; cf Ep 126:150n, Garanderie 75 n 14.

145 My wife] See 34n above.

155 Canterbury] Warham; cf Epp 188, 255 introductions.

165 Lucullus] The general and statesman of the first century BC, who acquired
great wealth and a rich library in Asia. Plutarch describes his life of luxury. For
Budé's building and comparison see Ep 435:146–9.

170 a night's sleep] Cf Ep 453:18.

been taken off me and I feel a substantial drain, but not the thinnest scrap of gold-leaf has yet appeared. Not but what, though nothing further came to me, I already feel I owe everything either to our excellent Prince Charles or to a man endowed with every virtue in perfection, Jean Le Sauvage, chancellor of Burgundy; who provides our own government with such a pattern as your native France was provided with long ago by that Guy de Rochefort who will be rendered immortal by your praise of him if by nothing else. May your damnable ill-health be damned by Zeus, lord of the thunder (if I may borrow a phrase from Homer), for in my opinion you are worthy to live to the years of Tithonus. But I hope that as the years go by your health will improve, as I know has happened to quite a number of men. As for me, besides the ill-health which is not merely frequent but almost perpetual, I also feel now the assaults of harsh old age, a trouble of nature's own making and therefore incurable.

You are not serious anywhere in your letter, a fact which gave me no little pleasure, for I took it as evidence that my Budé is not only well but cheerful and his own master. Happy man, who can enjoy literature as you do! But nowhere do you seem to me less serious than in the places where you most wish to be thought so. You say you cannot believe that I read your books, unless your name should have come up in conversation and one of my friends had read them aloud to me. Do you suppose me so fastidious that I am reluctant to read anything so scholarly, or so uncivilized, not to say jealous, that I do not enjoy as I should the writings of such a good friend? Let me tell you this: there is not one of your things which is not to be found in my library among my favourite authors. Your Annotations on the Pandects and your *De asse* I regard as oracles, in which I take refuge when confronted with a problem on which the usual authorities are no help. I feel no reluctance and no embarrassment in quoting Budé among classical and time-honoured authorities. Why should we grudge this honour to the living, provided they deserve it? Why not rather pay to learning the same respect which the common people pay to time when, as Horace puts it, they 'look up the date, and merit weigh by age'?

* * * * *

178 Guy de Rochefort] d 1508; secretary of the Parlement of Burgundy under Louis xi and a notable patron of letters, whom Budé honoured in book 4 of the *De asse*. Rochefort was made chancellor of France in 1497 and held the office to his death.

181 Homer] *Iliad* 1.354 *etc*

182 Tithonus] Married the goddess of the dawn and was made immortal; *Adagia* i vi 65

197 Annotations] Cf Ep 403 introduction.

203 Horace] *Epistles* 2.1.48

I have re-read the passages as you told me to, though I had already 205
read them not wholly without attention. For the first of them, humane
studies and those who pursue them owe you no small debt for so manfully
fighting their cause. What you say is perfectly true: no part of the world fails
to produce men of outstanding ability, provided the people are there to
encourage them and bring them on. But those to whom the management of 210
mortal affairs is usually entrusted dislike nothing so much as those studies
without which we are barely human beings. In the second place, I have
often marvelled at your truly French outspokenness, which does not spare
the pope himself. But, for one thing, it is safer and less dangerous to attack
him who is dead; and for another, it is an advantage, at least in one way, 215
that very few appreciate the force of the attack. For though everywhere,
even when deploying all the force of your eloquence, you give the impression of trying to please Apollo rather than Midas, yet on that point you
deliberately put in a touch of Lycophron's obscurity, and made us think of
Loxias or some other riddling oracle. This you do even more in your earlier 220
outburst of indignation, which even I could not understand because, I
suppose, I do not really know the facts, while you suppress the names. Then
again at the end of your work you make a remarkable excursion into
philosophy with your friend Deloynes, whom I have long known from
Colet's account of him, and since then from meeting him first in Orléans 225
and then in Paris. And here too, heavens with what violence and freedom
you rave and thunder against the priests we are blessed with nowadays.

But what a humorous request to make, that I should pass judgment
on your talents, as though I were the man to keep pace with your rare and
almost more than human gifts of mind! In Budé's case a tribunal of most 230
eminent scholars handed down their unanimous judgment long ago. If I
add my signature to their opinion, how much weight can possibly be added
by the vote of one quite ordinary man? If I were to dissent, my conceit
would be insufferable. When I read what you write, my dear Budé, I seem to
see a wealthy householder, not like Lucullus whose house was so full that 235
he forgot what he had and thieves grew rich, as Horace says; but one as
careful as he is rich, who well knows what he has, and by arranging it all in

* * * * *

205 re-read] Cf Ep 435:48 ff.

214 pope] Julius II

218ff Midas] Had asses' ears (cf Ep 472:24n). Lycophron, the late Greek poet,
was rightly famed for his obscurity. Loxias, a name of Apollo, was connected
by the Greeks with *loxos*, crooked (and so, obscure).

224 Deloynes] Cf Ep 494 introduction.

225 Orléans] Epp 130–40

236 Horace] Cf *Epistles* 1.6.45–6.

its proper places has everything at hand like ready cash. You owe this in part to those very careful lists of contents with which you once equipped all your books for this very purpose, partly, and indeed much more, to your memory, which is so fertile and more faithful than any list of contents. So that I perceive you are sometimes almost overwhelmed and weighed down by the wealth of important materials which offer themselves in a dense mass on every side, and you are not allowed to know when to stop. And so it happens maybe that the reader like a squeamish guest sometimes feels the need for rather more control over the material. Besides, you will admit nothing either in matter or expression that you share with ordinary every-day folk and has no distinction, no elegance such as is fetched from the Muses' inmost sanctuary; and so you are never relaxed, never off your guard, but always under pressure and keeping yourself up to the mark. The result must be that no reader can enjoy your work at sight unless he is extremely well-informed and at leisure, and yet is attending all the time; and he has to work almost harder in reading than you did in writing. For long painstaking practice in speaking and writing has bred in you such facility that things flow from your pen without hesitation, which seem to us the polished results of hard work.

I also observe that you take great delight in metaphors and compari-sons, and have a large supply of a most unusual and very telling kind, but that once you have embraced one you can hardly ever be torn away from it; with the result that your whole style seems bespangled with gems rather than picked out with them here and there, and might be thought to part company somewhat with the simplicity of nature. Yet in what is produced by art, men's tastes differ, whereas what comes by nature has some secret power of touching and attracting everyone, and gives much more delight as it makes its quiet way into men's hearts, as though it were akin to them. As for the great love of your own country which you show everywhere, many will give you credit for it, nobody but will readily overlook it; although in my opinion it is more worthy of a philosopher to deal with men and ideas in such a way that we feel this world to be the common homeland of us all, even though I admit France to be the most beautiful region of the Christian world. Besides this, while you often expand into digressions both very scholarly and very entertaining, and spend perhaps rather a long time on them, there is some danger that a reader difficult to please may say to himself: This is all very good and splendid, but (as they used to say What has this to do with Dionysus?) what has it to do with the 'as'? In any case, I

240

245

250

255

260

265

270

275

* * * * *

244 to stop] Literally 'to leave the canvas alone,' as it cannot be improved; *Adagia* I iii 19

275 Dionysus] *Adagia* II iv 57

both perceive, if I mistake not, and approve what you would be at. You had got ready a certain number of passages of the kind, meaning to use them as occasion offered. These you mixed in not unskilfully although the subject might be unsympathetic, that thanks to your skill they might both escape the notice of the profane and be enjoyed by learned and favourable readers; 280 nor would they ever be lost, being intermixed with things the utility of which alone was enough to secure their survival. One problem I have never been able to solve: what was your purpose in publishing a work so distinguished and no doubt sure of immortality without a dedication by name to anyone? For that you had some definite purpose I have no doubt.   285

It has long been clear to me what a fool I am to pass judgment in any form on abilities like yours that are far outside the range of criticism. But what was I to do? Those were my instructions from Budé. I think it less selfish to behave like a fool than to be unwilling to oblige you. I say these things, not because I feel the absence of any intellectual gift in what you 290 write, or am held up by any obstacle. To begin with I should be most uncivilized if I took offence at one or two blemishes in so fair a form; and then I am so fond of my Budé, that even if there were a blemish, I should learn to love it. All the same, I do not think affection for you has blinded me so much that I cannot be sure of having seen one thing clearly: France has 295 produced nothing up to now which can compete with the productions of your intellect; and yet, while leaving them all behind, you daily surpass yourself.

Farewell, and my very best wishes for your house-building. May you achieve all your desires, and one day be able to congratulate me on being all 300 hung with gold, while I salute you as our modern Lucullus.

Brussels, 28 October 1516

480A / From Karel Ofhuys   Paris, 30 October [1516]

This letter, Ep 692 in Allen's edition, has been removed from the year assigned by him – 1517 – to this date, on the presumption that the hand that copied it into the Deventer Letter-book, P.S. Allen's 'Hand A,' was that of Joannes Phrysius, a Frieslander in the service of Erasmus in 1516. He left for England in September 1517, bearing Epp 665–9; cf Allen III Epp 637:13n, 666:7–11, 668:4–7; *Opuscula* 238n; Bierlaire 51–2. The date of the letter cannot be earlier than 1516, since the New Testament had been published, nor later than 1517, the last year for the appearance of Hand A; cf Allen I 604–5.

Allen's reasons for placing the letter in 1517, after the departure of Phrysius for England, are not clear. In his very hesitant account, the only factor that seems to point to that year-date is the calculation of years from the publication of the *Enchiridion* (line 29). Allen himself admitted this was an unreliable

guide. The reference to Erasmus' exchange with van Dorp, on the other hand, points to the earlier date (lines 2–4). Both Ep 304 and Erasmus' reply, Ep 337, were published in the autumn of 1517.

The writer's identity does not unfortunately provide much help. A Karolus Offuys of Brussels is entered in the matriculation register of the University of Louvain on 27 February 1486; cf A. Schillings *Matricule de l'université de Louvain* III (Brussels 1958) 9. The Carthusian Gabriel to whom Ofhuys sends greetings may provide an additional clue. In October 1521 Erasmus wrote some verse for a young Carthusian monk of Scheut, at Anderlecht near Brussels, named Gabriel Ofhuys; cf Allen IV Ep 1239; Reedijk 400. Since Erasmus was in Brussels in the autumn of 1516 this identification would also point to 1516 as the year of composition. Allen also suggested that this was the same Carthusian as the Gabriel to whom Lefèvre d'Etaples dedicated his *Contemplationes Remundi* (Paris: G. Marchant for J. Petit 10 December 1505; cf Allen III 114n) but it should be noted that the recipient of that dedication was a novice at Vauvert, the Paris house of the order at the time; cf Rice Ep 45.

KAREL OFHUYS TO ERASMUS OF ROTTERDAM, GREETING
I have lately read that letter from your friend van Dorp, which, controversial as it was, did not on that account show any less gratitude for your great services; your very full reply I have read carefully, and I agree with it. The New Covenant with your annotations I have long been devoted to, but in   5
such a way that my appetite for reading it grows greater, not less, every day. Besides which there is your very thorough *Institutio principis christiani*, your *Panegyricus* addressed to Prince Philip, your *Moria* so witty and so truly wise (let some worthless dogs bark if they must) – in a word, whatever of yours is to be found for sale in the bookshops here, I am devoted to, more   10
devoted I daresay than anyone. My life upon it if there is any living man, so far as I know, or ever has been one in the past, whose writings could give us

* * * * *

480A:2 van Dorp] The Louvain theologian who had proved himself a telling critic; cf Ep 304 introduction Epp 337, 347, 438.

4 reply] Ep 337

5 New Covenant] The *Novum instrumentum*; the first edition of Erasmus' New Testament; cf Ep 384.

7 *Institutio … christiani*] Cf Ep 393.

8 *Panegyricus*] The *Gratulatorius panegyricus ad Philippum Archiducem Austriae*, published by Dirk Martens in 1504 (NK 837); cf Ep 179, and the edition by Otto Herding ASD IV-1 1–93.

8 *Moria*] *The Praise of Folly*; cf Ep 222.

more vivid pleasure, if we look for a thousand charms of style, or more wholesome instruction if we want sound doctrine.

Some fourteen years ago, if I mistake not, I observed in your *Enchirid-* 15 *ion* how, to make our progress easier, you wanted us to make a close friend of St Paul, to have him always in our pockets ready to 'ply him with nightly or with daily hand,' and ultimately if possible to learn him by heart; and on him – or so you said – you had long been most industriously preparing a commentary. The Lord Jesus knows how I rejoiced at the prospect of a thing 20 so useful, fully believing that no doubt it would soon be published. Weary with waiting, I found it easy to exchange hope for despair. Meanwhile Lefèvre has written the exposition which you criticize in many places, justly but in no unfriendly spirit, so that the author himself does not resent it in the slightest, as I learnt on good authority a few days ago from my 25 friend Bade when we were breakfasting together.

But in reliance on your kindness I must come at length to the object for which I have summoned up the courage in the depths of my ignorance to write you this unpolished letter. You made a promise in your *Enchiridion* and now repeat it in your *Annotations*, I mean your commentary. Dear 30 Erasmus, my most learned friend, if my prayers carry any weight with you, I beg you, and so do many other men, do not delay any longer to share so

* * * * *

15–6 Enchiridion] *Enchiridion militis christiani*; cf Ep 164.

20 commentary] For Erasmus' commentary on the Epistles of St Paul, now lost, see Ep 373 introduction.

23 Lefèvre] Lefèvre d'Etaples, who published an edition of the Pauline Epistles with Estienne at Paris in 1512, a work which Erasmus referred to, with reservations, in his preface 'To the Reader' to Jerome's letters; cf Ep 326:95–111. In Lefèvre's second edition, which appeared (with a colophon date of 1515) late in 1516 or early in 1517, he replied at length to Erasmus' criticisms in the Annotations to the *Novum instrumentum* (1516) while making clear his respect for Erasmus' achievement. He unfortunately allowed himself to describe one of Erasmus' opinions as 'impious,' and the result was Erasmus' *Apologia ad J. Fabrum Stapulensem* published by Martens at Louvain and dated 5 August 1517; see Allen III Ep 597:32n. On the controversy see M.M. Phillips *Erasme et les débuts de la réforme française* (Paris 1934) 23–46; M. Gilmore in *Florilegium historiale* (ed J.G. Rowe and W.H. Stockdale) Toronto 1971, 66; A. Stegmann 'Erasme et la France (1495–1520)' in *Colloquium Erasmianum* (Mons 1968) 285–8.

23 in many places] In the Annotations to the New Testament; see note 30.

30 Annotations] Erasmus' *Annotationes* to his edition of the New Testament, on Romans 1:1 (ed 1516 page 411): 'But I discuss these points more fully in the commentary which I started some time ago on St Paul and with Christ's help shall finish shortly.'

great a blessing with us all. The Christian commonwealth demands it, enthusiasts for the humanities, whose leader you so rightly are in fact and name, demand it with enthusiasm. Farewell, and sometime, when it is 35 convenient, please give my greetings to Gabriel Ofhuys the Carthusian.

Paris, 30 October

Your humble servant Karel Ofhuys, priest

481 / From Thomas More   London, 31 October [1516]

This letter (Rogers Ep 26) answers Ep 474 and was in turn answered by a letter contemporary with Ep 483.

THOMAS MORE TO HIS FRIEND MASTER ERASMUS, GREETING

I am rather late in answering your letter, my dear Erasmus, because I wanted to send you some definite news from Urswick about your horse; but even now I have had no chance to do so, because he had departed for some business of his many miles from town and had not yet returned. When he 5 comes – and I expect him daily – I will get on with it forthwith. The money that you deposited with me has been paid in full to our friend Gillis, I have no doubt; for I have had a letter from my agent written from Antwerp, in which he says that he will pay it over promptly. The letters which you sent for me to read some time ago from Basel I did not dare entrust to this courier, 10 but all the same I will send them shortly, as soon as I have someone whom I can burden with a large bundle. Bedyll has shown me a letter from the bishop of Basel to the archbishop of Canterbury and the archbishop's answer, both in the original hand, and the answer rather too much so, for it is so full of erasures and interlinings as to be perfectly illegible except to the 15 man who wrote it, and I doubt if even he can read it.

Your letter, and mine too, in which we urged Latimer to live for a month or two with the bishop of Rochester, were late in reaching him, because he had already decided to go to Oxford, and he could by no means

* * * * *

481:3 horse] Cf Ep 468:22n.

6 money] Cf Ep 467:11n.

8 agent] Perhaps Birckmann; cf Ep 491:9.

9 letters] Cf Epp 499:28–30, 502:2–4, letters perhaps contemporary with Epp 328 etc.

12 Bedyll] Thomas Bedyll, secretary to Archbishop Warham; cf Epp 387, 426.

17 Your letter, and mine too] Cf Ep 468:13 and note.

be persuaded to put it off for that length of time. You know what immutable   20
laws and ordinances philosophers of this kind lay down for themselves; I
suppose they get satisfaction from this consistency. The bishop is delighted
with your version of the New Testament, though he finds you more
scrupulous than he could wish. He does not like your having kept the word
'sabbath,' and some other things of the kind, which you either did not wish   25
or did not dare to change. But then he does not admit a single word that was
unfamiliar to a Roman's ear. I approved his opinion as far as the history and
ritual of the Jews might permit. But I urged him, and I think he will do it, to
make a note of the individual words which he would wish had been
differently translated, and send it to you with his opinion. I know you will   30
be delighted with this keen interest of his.

   But there are other people, my dearest Erasmus, who have formed a
conspiracy in our midst to read what you write in a very different frame of
mind; and this horrible plan of theirs gives me some concern. Do not
therefore be in a hurry to publish. As for what you have published already,   35
since it is too late for second thoughts, I would urge one thing at least – you
know my devotion and concern for you: I do beg and beseech you to lose no
time in going through and correcting everything, in such a way as to leave
the least possible scope for misrepresentation; for these men are very sharp,
and they have decided to keep a keen look-out for any such opportunity,   40
and seize it greedily and gladly. Who may they be, you ask? I am quite
afraid to name them, for fear your heart sinks in terror before such formidable adversaries; but I will name them, in hopes of making you more
cautious. You know that prince among the Franciscan divines, of whom
you made honourable mention in your edition of Jerome: he has entered   45
into a conspiracy with certain choice spirits of the same Order and the same
kidney to refute your errors in print, if he can find any. And to make this
easier for him and more efficient, they have divided your works among
them, and taken an oath that they will read right through everything with
the greatest care, and not understand anything. There! you see the peril that   50

* * * * *

28 will do it] Cf Ep 520:10–11, 86–91.

44 Franciscan] Henry Standish, a Franciscan friar hostile to new doctrine and
to clerical privilege. He became Warden of Grey Friars, London and in 1505
was made provincial minister. In 1518 he was appointed bishop of St Asaph,
after having acted as the government's spokesman in the Hunne affair in 1515.
In 1527 he was one of Bilney's judges. See Knowles 53–5 and Epp 608, 1126
below. Although an opponent of the royal divorce as one of Catherine of
Aragon's counsellors, he afterward assisted at the coronation of Anne Boleyn.
He died one month after he had formally renounced papal jurisdiction, on 9
July 1535.

hangs over you; and you on the other hand must mobilize all your resources to deal with so great a danger. The fact is, Erasmus, they passed this resolution at some nocturnal session, when they were well lit. Next morning, I understand, when they had slept off their fuddle, forgetting no doubt what they had determined on, and rescinding the resolution which they 55 had after all passed in their cups, they abandoned the attempt and retired again from the study table to the begging-bowl, which they had proved by experience to be far more profitable.

As to the *Epistolae obscurorum virorum*, it would do your heart good to see how much everyone enjoys them, the learned as a joke and the un- 60 learned in all seriousness; these latter, when they see us laughing, suppose we are laughing only at the style, which they do not defend, but consider it is atoned for by the importance of the matter: a flashing blade, they think, lurks in that battered scabbard. I wish the book had been given a different title! – in less than a century scholars dazed with their researches would 65 have failed to detect the long nose of scorn, had it been longer than any rhinoceros's.

I am delighted to hear that Pieter approves of my *Nusquama*; if men such as he like it, I shall begin to like it myself. I should like to know whether Tunstall approves, and Busleyden, and your chancellor; that it 70 should win their approval is more than I dared hope, being men so gifted that they hold high office in their own countries, unless they were to favour it because in such a polity as I have invented men like themselves, so cultivated and so upright, would certainly be at the head, whereas in their own countries, however great they may be (and great men they surely are), 75 they always have to suffer great good-for-nothings as their equals – not to say, superiors – in power and influence. For I do not believe men of their kind are moved by the thought that there they will not have many people under them, many subjects, as kings now call their peoples (something, that is, worse than slaves); for it is so much more honourable to bear rule 80 among free men, and such excellent persons are far from that malignant state of mind which is glad to see others in bad case, provided all is well with themselves. I expect therefore that they will like my book, and very much hope they will. But if the opposite way of thinking is deeply im-

* * * * *

59 *Epistolae ... virorum*] *The Letters of Unfamous Men*; cf Ep 363 introduction.
68 *Nusquama*] 'Nowhere,' the first title for More's *Utopia*; cf Ep 461:2n. 'Pieter' is Pieter Gillis.
70 Tunstall] Cf Ep 499:38–41.
70 Busleyden] Cf Ep 477:8n.
70 chancellor] Cf Ep 475:3n.

planted in them by their own success, your vote will be more than enough   85
for my judgment. We are 'together, you and I, a crowd'; that is my feeling,
and I think I could live happily with you in any wilderness.

Farewell, dearest Erasmus, dear as the apple of my eye.

I have secured a more helpful letter from Maruffo by a direct approach;
this seemed to me both quicker and wiser than to appeal to the bishop again   90
on the subject. Not that he does not give me a kindly hearing on any topic, if
so be it has anything to do with you; but I would rather ask him for more
important things.

From London, in haste before daybreak, All Saints eve

482 / From Simon of Sechsstädtebund   [Brussels? Autumn 1516?]

Little is known of the writer of this letter, who evidently came from Silesia.
The Hexapolis Lusatica (Lausitzer Sechsstädtebund) is a district of six towns
north of Prague and west of Breslau (comprising Kamenz, Bautzen, Löbau,
Görlitz, Lauban and Zittau). If he was seeking employment with his priest
companion, he may be the Simon of Ep 570:2; cf 21n. In a recent dissertation at
Munich, 'Simon Minervius Schaidenreisser, Leben und Schriften' (1962)
12–13, Winfried Zehetmeier has suggested that if Allen's conjecture about the
date and place of this letter are correct, the author was the humanist poet
Simon Schaidenreisser, who was in Brussels in the autumn of 1516.

TO THE MOST LEARNED OF ALL LEARNED MEN,
ERASMUS OF ROTTERDAM,
SIMON OF SECHSSTÄDTEBUND WISHES PERPETUAL FELICITY
I knew already how far you outstrip all the men of our age in ability, in
learning, and in skill in Greek and Latin, but of your kindness I had heard   5
nothing. Now however you have lately given me not merely a glimpse of it
but a vivid picture, by promising me your aid and very present help,
beyond all I could expect as a foreigner and a casual acquaintance, as kindly
and generously as you might to someone who had long enjoyed your
society. I think myself that your more than human mind, which can be   10
nothing else than a fire fallen from heaven, gave you some hidden warning
that this was the Simon who loved you passionately (though as yet he knew
you not by sight but only in your copious productions) and reverenced you

* * * * *

86 'together, you and I] Ovid *Metamorphoses* 1.355
89 Maruffo] Cf Ep 467:5n.
90 bishop] 'Episcopum': Warham, cf Ep 388:66

as his spiritual parent, who for so many years has cherished a constant
desire to see you and to make your acquaintance; and so you thought him a   15
worthy object for the exercise of your generosity. For this I cannot now
adequately express my thanks, but I can swear that I shall be thankful to my
dying day, and shall even seem to some extent to return them, if Cicero is
right when he says that he who feels thankful returns thanks in so far as he
feels them. In any case, since you urged me to open my mind to you, you   20
should know that the theologian with whom I came here is hoping for a
chaplain's post, and if he gets it, I too should wish to spend the winter here,
chiefly with the hope of listening to you and getting to know you better. If
this cannot happen, I am resolved to return with him to my native country,
and none the less to try my fortune on the way. If you will give me letters of   25
introduction to some of your friends, you will put me under a perpetual
debt of gratitude; both this and anything that they may do for me I shall owe
to you. Health and long life to you, leading light of Germany and of the
humanities, and my one refuge in my present afflicted state. The enclosed
poems were put together without Apollo's leave, but take them in good   30
part.

From the convent of the Carmelites

483 / To Andrea Ammonio   Brussels, 9 November 1516

This letter, in which the chief personalities are mentioned in Greek, was first
published in the *Farrago*. It is a reply to Ep 478.

ERASMUS OF ROTTERDAM TO HIS FRIEND ANDREA AMMONIO
A plague on the vacation of our great High Priest, which has delayed my
moment of felicity! Believe me, my dear Ammonio, I have now let go my
sheet-anchor, I have played my last card; and if this does not go as I hope, it
is the end. If it succeeds, I shall owe the whole to your generosity and to the   5

* * * * *

482:18 Cicero] *De officiis* 2.20.69
21 theologian] If the identification of the writer with Schaidenreisser is correct, this may be a young Benedictine by the name of Praus; cf Allen v Ep
1279:10n.
30 poems] The letter is followed by a poem, *Ad Erasmum Roterodamum per-
petuo cognomento polyhistorem*, LB III 1841 D-E.
483:2 High Priest] The pope; cf Ep 479:7–9.
4 sheet-anchor] *Adagia* I i 24
4 last card] *ibid* I iv 32

kindness of the bishop of Worcester; if not, I shall know it is that evil genius
that haunts me, whom I know only too well. I have skilfully recast my
prebend as an annuity. When you advise me to make a nearer approach to
my patron deity, I will do what I can, and more so when the moment comes
that I once hear clearly and wide awake the oracle on which my whole life   10
depends. You know how imperceptive I am, especially in things like this. If
you think there is anything I could do that might please the bishop of
Worcester, please let me know.

Similarly have no misgivings about the money. Even if he of Canterbury were to let me down, there are people here from whom I could get it   15
merely by a nod of the head. There is very great hunting here at present for
everything; but I am at the moment incapable, and this rather distresses
me. Italians, Spaniards, Goths and Danes – I find them all more well-
disposed towards me than my own people, a famishing crowd devoted
entirely to their stomachs. To the chancellor I owe a great debt, and not only   20
I but this whole country. You are right in thinking Tunstall's society a great
blessing to me; I have never yet found anyone more friendly than he is. I
read him that longer letter of yours, and he was greatly delighted by your
talents. I thought him slightly jealous of me, because you wrote him such a
laconic letter; but when I explained how busy you were, he took it very   25
kindly.

The wolf I had already let go of, though only after treating him roughly
in a couple of letters, once I had discovered that kindness on my part only
made him more ferocious. To that libellous Carmelite I never paid any
attention, and yet he too will get, as you put it, the reception from the dogs   30

* * * * *

6 Worcester] Silvestro Gigli; cf Ep 521 introduction.

6 evil genius] Cf Epp 232:1, 281:24.

8 annuity] Cf Ep 436:6n for Erasmus' arrangements.

9 patron deity] Prince Charles; cf Ep 478:25.

14–15 Canterbury] Archbishop William Warham, Erasmus' chief English
patron.

20 chancellor] Jean Le Sauvage; cf Ep 410 introduction.

23 longer letter] Perhaps Ep 466 which is incomplete as we have it, or 447
which may have been in Ammonio's name; see introduction.

27 wolf] van Dorp; cf Ep 480A:2n.

29 Carmelite] Perhaps the 'Carmelita quidam theologus' of Antwerp who
prophesied the coming of the Antichrist as a consequence of the publication of
Erasmus' New Testament; cf Allen III Ep 948:136–44.

30 as you put it] Ep 478:30

that he deserves. The volumes of Jerome are already sold out here; Franz
maintains that he would have made two thousand florins if he had im-
ported a larger supply of copies. What is this I hear? Am I constantly given
out for dead in Rome and coming to life again? No Virbius or Theseus could
do as much. But I shall not feel myself really restored to life until that   35
business of mine is safely concluded. As for you, dear Ammonio, continue
as you have begun, and be my Aesculapius. Farewell.

Brussels, 9 November 1516

484 / From Jérôme de Busleyden   Mechelen, 9 November [1516]

> This clearly accompanied the congratulatory letter contributed by Busleyden
> to the first edition of *Utopia*, addressed to More and dated from Mechelen,
> 1516 (Rogers Ep 27).

JÉRÔME DE BUSLEYDEN TO HIS FRIEND ERASMUS, GREETING
Here at last is the letter that you told me to write, and if I have perhaps done
less well than you expected or than the importance of the subject required,
you have only yourself to thank: it is your own fault for entrusting the task
to such an unpractised writer and one so unsuitable in other ways. I   5
consoled myself with having at least attempted what I could not fully
perform, and even hoped that from this point of view you would not wholly
disapprove of my efforts, but even find them acceptable, the more so since
in making them to please you I have risked my reputation and sacrificed
some self-respect. It is certainly an outstanding and more than obvious   10
proof of my devotion to you, and therefore I trust you will take it in good
part; and much the best way of doing this will be, if you think fit to rub off
the tarnish that lies thick upon it with the keen abrasive of your own
polished style. In the meantime, farewell, and pray commend me to his
excellency the envoy of the English king.   15

In haste, from Mechelen, 9 November

* * * * *

31 Franz] Birckmann; cf Ep 475:35.

32 two thousand florins] Probably the Burgundian-Hapsburg St Philip florins
rather than another gold florin or the money-of-account florin. If so, a sum
worth £416 13s 4d gros Flemish = £300 0s 0d sterling = £2,625 0s 0d tournois.
Cf CWE 1 318, 320, 336–46; CWE 2 327–44; and Ep 463:48n above.

34 dead] Cf Ep 479:4n.

34 Virbius] Hippolytus died, and when restored to life by Aesculapius took
this name; Theseus descended to the lower world and re-appeared.

484:15 envoy] Tunstall; cf Ep 461:32n.

485 / From Alaard of Amsterdam   Louvain, 11 November 1516

The writer was a kinsman of the abbot of Egmond and a scholar who lived at Louvain. He was especially interested in the works of Rodolphus Agricola; cf Ep 433 introduction, Reedijk passim. The letter to which this is the reply has been lost.

ALAARD OF AMSTERDAM TO MASTER ERASMUS

When you set before me Ermolao and Poliziano, those inimitable stylists, as objects of imitation, Erasmus prince of scholars, you give me yet more reason to admire the excellence of your scholarship. First of all, I am reminded that the whole system of our studies rests at the same time on   5
both precept and example, and that in proportion as a man sets before himself as a model a very good author or a very bad one, so he himself turns out either good or bad. My second lesson is that 'Some distance may we go, e'en though no farther.' With you therefore as my leader, 'I must attempt a way to find / Where even I above the ground may rise / And flit victorious   10
o'er the lips of men.' The fact that before now I have sent two or three poor little pieces to the printer causes me great distress. Naturally so, when I reflect that I have invited so many people to witness my own folly by this bid for domestic applause, as Cicero calls it. But what was I to do? I did not wish not to do the best I could, though this in a sense is what I have done; I   15
did not wish to forego the right granted to everyone, or claimed by everyone in the face of opposition, to 'take what risks I would.' After all, everyone in my profession writes something, and 'coins trivial verses at the common mint'; they all wish to put their names forward; and I did not see why I should debar myself, as though I had been born on the fifth of the   20
month, or had started life under some bird of ill omen, from at least trying to 'grate on my scrannel pipe some wretched strains.' 'No blockheads are we'

* * * * *

485:2 Ermolao] Barbaro, the Venetian scholar and diplomatist; cf Ep 126:150n.
2 Poliziano] Angelo Ambrogini, the distinguished humanist of the second half of the fifteenth century; cf Ep 61:154n.
8 'Some distance] Horace *Epistles* 1.1.32
9 'I must attempt] Virgil *Georgics* 3.8–9
14 Cicero] *De oratore* 2.20.86
17 'take what risks] Horace *Ars poetica* 10
18 'coins] Juvenal 7.55
20–1 fifth of the month] A very unlucky day; Virgil *Georgics* 1.277
22 'grate] Virgil *Eclogues* 3.27, joined with *Aeneid* 1.567–8 (Dutchmen taking the place of Carthaginians)

Dutchmen, 'nor so far / From these our coasts does Phoebus drive his team,' so that what is a common gift among other nations must be entirely denied to us. If this is a good thing, I gratefully make use of the common privilege; 25 if it must be counted a fault, I deserve forgiveness all the more, in that I am following a precedent, but not approving of it.

There is a merchant called Pompeius Occo, from Friesland, and he intends to sell all his books to the public without exception. I have just now no access to the catalogue, but I know for certain that in his house more 30 than a thousand books are lying hidden and being gnawed by the worms – really rare books, I mean, and really old ones; and if you can lay hands on any of them, you will not cry out that you have found what children find in beans. The man who keeps Rodolphus Agricola's very rich library so carelessly and in such privacy has barely passed the stage of thumbing his 35 Aesop; he is as rich as a nabob and in his grand way of life a proper Thraso. He lives in Amsterdam, where his house is commonly called the Paradise. I wrote by my courier to ask him to send me a list for your benefit; and as we are old acquaintances, I expect he will do this without delay. Besides which, 'if fate would let me live as I would choose, / and lull my cares to rest at my 40 own choosing,' about the first of January next I shall be moving to take up a chaplaincy in Amsterdam. So if by any chance he does not send it, I shall be able to bring you without fail anything you may want from his library, even if the price is very high. I am very much surprised that, apart from a number of other mistakes in my humble verses, you object in a friendly way to the 45 structure of the line *Vt fles, vt gemis, ut micasque pectus*, seeing that Horace uses a not very dissimilar phrase in *Si tacitus pasci posset* etc.

Our old friend Aurelius Lopsen is in a great state of glee because you

* * * * *

28 Occo] Pompeius (d 1537), a Frisian merchant of Amsterdam, was the nephew of Agricola's physician and friend, and had inherited Agricola's papers from his uncle. For Alaard's interest in Agricola see Ep 433 introduction; Occo willingly placed the papers at his disposal, and generally cultivated the society and favour of men of letters. See P.S. Allen 'The letters of Rudolph Agricola' EHR 21 (1906) 306–8.

33–4 find in beans] *Adagia* II ix 86

34 Agricola] The distinguished Frisian humanist, Rudolf Huusman, 1433–98, who was one of the first to bring humanistic learning to northern Europe; cf L.W. Spitz *The Religious Renaissance of the German Humanists* (Cambridge, Mass 1963) 20–40.

35–6 thumbing his Aesop] *Adagia* II vi 27

36 Thraso] one for display; cf Ep 450:74.

40 'if fate] Virgil *Aeneid* 4.340–1

46 Horace] *Epistles* 1.17.50

48 Lopsen] Cornelis Gerard, who was at the Augustinian convent in the

have abandoned the leopards and given your allegiance to our own lions. But he does not really know the sort of man you are: one who thinks the gods and goddesses of a Court not worth a penny, let alone one who would devote himself to them. Dorp still persists rigidly in his own way of thinking, which you know well; as for the Muses and their followers, 'all's praise and love at home; once out of doors, / 'tis all disparagement and prejudice,' as anyone can see who pays attention and tries to see what is going on. I write this with no desire to pour cold water, but I wish he would remember the story of Dares and Entellus; I should like to see him acknowledge himself beaten, and loudly assail your ears with 'Thou art the greater man; 'tis right for me to obey thee,' O Erasmus. And unless he does this pretty soon, he will deserve to have said of him by way of compliment 'He though defeated has his guerdon due, / Who wins the fame of having fought with you.'

Farewell, dearest Erasmus, and pray be sure of this, that you are dearer to me than any other mortal. Farewell once more.

Louvain, Martinmas 1516

486 / From William Blount, Lord Mountjoy   Tournai, 12 November [1516]

The last letter from Mountjoy to survive up to this date is Ep 215 (27 May 1509). He was Erasmus' first English patron and Lieutenant of Tournai since its capture by the English in 1513.

WILLIAM MOUNTJOY TO HIS ERASMUS, GREETING

Your letter has come, my dear Erasmus, and I am delighted to hear that Jerome is finished. You say the price is high, but I am fully convinced that

* * * * *

district of Lopsen outside the west gate of Leiden, at work on a life of St Jerome; cf Ep 17 introduction; Allen I 92.

49 lions] An allusion to Erasmus' removal from England for the Low Countries, where the lion was featured in the arms of both Holland and Brabant

53–4 'all's praise] Horace *Epistles* 1.19.36

56 pour cold water] *Adagia* I x 51

57 Dares] He was defeated in a boxing-match by the aged Entellus in the fifth book of Virgil's *Aeneid*.

57–8 acknowledge himself beaten] *Adagia* I ix 78

58 assail your ears] An echo of the *Ad Herennium* ascribed to Cicero, 4.52.65

58 'Thou art] Virgil *Eclogues* 5.4 (Erasmus taking the place of Menalcas)

60–1 'He though defeated] Ovid *Metamorphoses* 13.19–20

486:3 Jerome is finished] Cf Ep 477:3–5.

no work by you could be sold for what it is really worth. I have decided therefore in the near future, when I know for certain what it costs, to send 5 for a copy either to Pieter Gillis or to you. So you have moved to Brussels for the winter? This is surely an excellent plan, for you can conveniently transact any business you have with the prince your master, and at the same time enjoy more often the society of my friend Tunstall, who is such an agreeable person and a good scholar. As for your prebend, I hope all is 10 going well, but the bishopric, which is a long way off and supposed to be ill-endowed, I think you are wise to refuse; it will be, as you neatly put it, all kicks and no ha'pence, and more onerous than honorific. I had the *Epistolae* you kindly sent me, and have greatly enjoyed reading them; for I have read a good many, though I have not yet read the whole book right through, and I 15 am very grateful to you for sending me a copy. I told Jean Molinier about Jerome, and he was not sorry to hear the news.

Farewell, and love me as I know you do; and if you have no plans for a visit to Tournai this winter, please be so kind as to visit me at least by letter. Farewell, again, from Tournai, the morrow of Martinmas. 20

Give my greetings to my lord the chancellor.

487 / From Gerard Geldenhouwer Louvain, 12 November 1516

The writer was born at Nijmegen c 1482 and died in 1542. He was the son of the chamberlain to three successive dukes of Gelderland, and his father had asked Herman van Cranevelt, ducal secretary, to have their sons educated together. He therefore began his upbringing with Frans van Cranevelt. He was also educated at Deventer, and in 1501 entered the order of the Crucigeri. For a time he resided at Louvain in the college for students of that order, and he there resumed his connection with Cranevelt. He also came to know many members of the humanist circle, but especially Maarten van Dorp. About 1514 he entered the court of Prince Charles as chaplain, and in 1517 became secretary to Philip of Burgundy, the new bishop of Utrecht.

Geldenhouwer wrote a preface addressed to Maximilian of Burgundy dated 1 August 1514, and another to Philip of Burgundy ('maris praefecto') dated 1

* * * * *

10 prebend] Probably that at Courtrai: Ep 436:5n

11 bishopric] Cf Ep 475:5–6. The only Sicilian bishopric to fall vacant at this time seems to have been Syracuse.

13 *Epistolae*] The *Epistolae aliquot ad Erasmum* (Louvain: Martens October 1516) NK 2939

16 Molinier] Cf Ep 371 inroduction and lines 16–8.

21 chancellor] Jean Le Sauvage

November 1514 for two editions published by Martens of Erasmus' *De con-structione octo partium orationis* (they are NK 4223 and 2889). He assisted in the production of many other of Martens' books, including Erasmus' *Parabolae* (NK 838) and, as we see, More's *Utopia* (NK 1550). See de Vocht *Literae* 609–12.

Geldenhouwer's letter intimates that Erasmus' leading critic at Louvain, Maarten van Dorp, would like to be reconciled with him; cf Epp 304 introduction, 337, 347, 356:8–11, 388:164–171, 474, 475, 485:57–62.

TO MASTER ERASMUS FROM GERARDUS NOVIOMAGUS, GREETING
My friend Martens has undertaken the task of printing the *Utopia* with the greatest pleasure. The plan of the island itself has been drawn out by a capital artist, and Paludanus will show it you; if you would like any alterations, either let me know, or note them on the draft. I will keep the   5
copies of your *Epistolae* most carefully until you get here; if you want them sent to you, they shall be sent without delay. I will take great care to see that *Utopia* makes its public appearance in style, so that readers may get the benefit of it, and not be put off.

Dorp is longing for your visit here, and if you put it off, has decided to   10
come and visit you on his own account. He solemnly swears that he had not shown your letter or his to any mortal man, bar one or two only, and has spread no tales about your work among the theological faculty; he puts the blame on certain people, I do not know on whom. I hope things will reach a stage at which he will take your advice in future; he will never regret it.   15

I am glad you approve of Michael as a theologian; maybe he owes this to Nebrissensis his teacher, for it makes a great difference, by whom one is

* * * * *

487:2 *Utopia*] The *Utopia* was published at Louvain in the autumn of 1516, and Ep 461 indicates that More must have completed the text by early September 1516; cf *Utopia* xv, clxxxiii–v. The woodcut plan of the island referred to here was by Ambrosius Holbein; *ibid* clxxxviii note.

4 Paludanus] Jean Desmarez; cf Ep 180 introduction.

6 *Epistolae*] Cf Ep 486:13n.

12 your letter] Cf Ep 477:13n.

16 Michael] Not identified

17 Nebrissensis] Elio Antonio de Nebrija of Lebrixa in Spain (1444–1522), one of the greatest humanists of his day, studied at Salamanca and Bologna, and held a chair in grammar and rhetoric at the former university. He also served in the household of Diego López de Zúñiga, Erasmus' critic and archbishop of Seville, from about 1486 until Zúñiga's death (1504) when he returned to his teaching. Cardinal Ximénes appointed him to a chair at Alcalá in 1515, when his methods in the interpretation of Scripture, which were close to those of Erasmus, came under attack. His works include an important Latin grammar,

Elio Antonio de Nebrija
Frontispiece to his *Institutiones latinae*, late 15th century;
he is portrayed lecturing in the house of Zúñiga,
his patron, who is seated on the left
Biblioteca Nacional, Madrid, MS Vit. 17–1

taught as a beginner. But I need not tell *you* that. Erasmus, my dear sir, do not take it amiss if I write in this shameless way, and dare to open my mouth in your presence, when you are busy on such very important work. You will 20 forgive my fault, knowing it stems from my affection for you.

Dorp has shown me a book by Pfefferkorn attacking the *Epistolae obscurorum virorum*, in which there lie concealed, according to him, several Bohemian heresies. What shall we come to, if in criticizing trifles of this kind our theological watchdogs do not keep silent but bark so loudly? It 25 would be better to show one's contempt for the thing by ignoring it, than to blow it up ad infinitum by scribbling and wrangling.

So much for the moment, my most learned friend, and I hope you will take it in good part. Best wishes.

Louvain, the morrow of Martinmas 1516   30

488 / From Ludwig Baer   Basel, 12 November 1516

The writer was a native of Basel, born in 1479, who died in 1554. He was educated at the University of Paris (MA 1499) and after taking his Arts degree, proceeded to the DD in 1512 with great distinction. He returned to Basel to teach in the theological faculty of the university of which he was dean in 1514–15; he was rector of the university in 1514 and 1520. He was a convinced opponent of the Reformation, and after its triumph in Basel he withdrew to Freiburg-im-Breisgau (in 1529) where he died. This letter was first published in the *Epistolae elegantes* 1517.

LUDWIG BAER TO THE LODESTAR
OF ALL HUMANE STUDIES, ERASMUS OF ROTTERDAM,
HIS MOST REVERED MASTER AND TEACHER, GREETING
I read your works every day, my dear Erasmus, soul of honour and friend-

* * * * *

a Latin and Spanish lexicon, editions of classical authors, critical notes on Scripture, work as historiographer to Ferdinand and by repute, a share in the Complutensian Polyglot Bible; cf Bataillon 37–47 and P. Lemus y Rubio 'El Maestro Elio Antonio de Lebrixa,' *Revue hispanique* 22 (1910) 459–508, a biographical note, and 29 (1913) 13–120, a bibliographical note.

22 Pfefferkorn] Johannes Pfefferkorn was a Jewish convert of Cologne (d 1524) whose concern to evangelize the Jews after his own conversion (c 1504) took the form of an aggressive campaign against all Jewish learning. In association with the Dominicans of Cologne he set himself in opposition to the policies advocated by Reuchlin. He was caricatured as a main target of the *Epistolae obscurorum virorum* and his defence against that work – *Beschyrmung* – is referred to here.

ship, and always with incredible satisfaction; so I can hardly say how   5
delighted I was by your letter, in which you told me of your prosperous
situation. Friends have all things in common, and so I rejoice on my own
account as I congratulate you, who so well deserve promotion, on the
distinguished and lucrative canonry which the prince has offered you and
on the good success of your affairs. Fortune is wont to play step-mother to   10
all lovers of literature and virtue, but you have not merely despised her, you
have overcome her, and seem to have made her your slave. As for the lunacy
of some of your ill-wishers, who put more work into inventing malicious
criticisms of some part at least of what you write with such polished
scholarship and recondite learning, than they do into a sound understand-   15
ing of it which might do them some good, they are more likely to add to
your success than to impair it. What hope of glory can there be, where there
is no victory? What place can there be for victory, where there is no contest?
And you have no lack, nor ever shall have, of scholarly and distinguished
supporters, although you are your own strongest support, and under God's   20
guidance a glorious victory will always be yours.

Your letter to the bishop of Basel, and the letter from the archbishop of
Canterbury, I took special care to have delivered to his lordship. And the
copies of other letters which you sent me, and which were a most welcome
present, I have shared, as was right and proper, with our common friends.   25
Farewell, and continuing felicity in Christ.

From my home in Basel, 12 November 1516

489 / From Luigi di Canossa   Amboise, 13 November 1516

The Count of Canossa was born at Verona in 1476 and educated at the court of
Urbino, where he was acquainted with Castiglione. He was a papal ambassador for Julius II, and in 1515 became bishop of Tricarico; the following year
he was made bishop of Bayeux. His diplomatic career continued in the service
of France, and from 1523–8 he was French ambassador to Venice; he died in
1532. He met Erasmus in London in 1514 presumably at the house of Ammonio in Westminster, a meeting described in a letter to Ammonio of 1
December 1516 (LP ii 2621; cf 2619). The letter was first published in the
Epistolae elegantes 1517.

TO ERASMUS OF ROTTERDAM FROM LUIGI DI CANOSSA
BISHOP OF BAYEUX, GREETING
My wish, intention and desire has always been, if ever the improvement in

* * * * *

488:9 canonry] Cf Ep 436:6n.
22 letter] Cf Ep 425:35.

my fortunes should make it possible, to devote all my leisure time to
humane studies, and to offer a home to some studious and learned man.   5
And so now I am persuaded that you, Erasmus, are the very man I have in
mind, the one above all others whom I wish to live with me and share my
life, that I might be refreshed by your extraordinary gifts, enjoy your
literary conversation, and feed upon your stores of various knowledge.
Now therefore that by the generosity and favour of his most Christian   10
Majesty (at whose court I serve as envoy of the supreme pontiff) the pope
himself has promoted my unworthy person to the see of Bayeux, I have
decided to inform you at once of this change in my fortunes, and moreover
to issue an invitation which I would urge you to accept, if it is convenient
for you to come and join me, with the prospect of living in my house   15
henceforward. I shall give you, not perhaps entirely the welcome you
deserve, but at least the best reception that my modest resources will
permit, and shall devote myself to giving you satisfaction, as far as I can,
and ensuring that you will never have cause to regret your association with
the bishop of Bayeux. For the time being, until I can provide you with more   20
ample benefices, I offer an honorarium of two hundred ducats annually,
besides the living expenses of yourself and one servant, and also two
horses. Farewell, and let me know your intentions.
     Amboise, 13 November 1516

490 / From Henricus Glareanus   Basel, 13 November [1516]

> The writer, Heinrich Loriti (cf Ep 440 introduction), was indebted to Erasmus
> for support in his career, including a strong recommendation to Urbanus
> Regius for an appointment to the University of Ingolstadt (Ep 394:6). See also
> Ep 463.

TO MASTER ERASMUS FROM GLAREANUS, GREETING
If I am so brief, my dearest Erasmus, you must blame Johann Froben, the
common friend of all devoted to learning. He had told me to write; but said
that in any case the courier would leave in eight days time. And here are
barely eight hours elapsed, and the man is demanding my letter, though I   5
have not yet written a line. I have risen above it, though, thinking it better
to send something, however short, than nothing, and to seize a chance of

          * * * * *

489:21 two hundred ducats] Venetian ducats or similar gold coins, worth
£415 os od tournois = £65 16s 8d gros Flemish = £45 16s 8d sterling. Cf CWE 1
314, 336–46; and Ep 447:844n above.
490:2 Froben] Loriti had become part of the Froben circle when he moved to
Basel in 1514.

writing to you rather than let it go. So make allowances for a young man who is a fool, if you like, but has enough sense to recognize it, and who does not forget that his patron deity is your goddess of Folly.   10

You told me in your last letter to send you the poem that Hermann von dem Busche has written in your honour, and my own poem. I have obeyed with more zeal than discretion, in sending also a piece of lunacy on my part. For I had added a poem addressed to my friend Osvaldus, who is now headmaster of the school in Zürich – without reading it through, I was at the   15 moment so busy. Thus it came about that I failed to detect a disgraceful error in the sixth line from the beginning, for I put *lŏricatus* with the first syllable short, which no educated man can hear without indignation. As a matter of fact, I had written *venenatus* in the margin, but by some mischance I then overlooked it. It is a small mistake, I know; but while an error in something   20 big may be excused, in something small it never is. So it torments me the more that I should make a slip on a point where I deserve to be laughed at rather than forgiven. But you are by nature so kind-hearted and so easily mollified, that you will forgive your humble servant even an error such as this. Only I do beg that the poem itself should be torn up or thrown on the   25 fire or be kept dark as undeserving of the light of day, unless you will put a polish on it; though I wish your polish were employed on something better written.

Of one thing, my dear Erasmus, you may be certain, that I sing your praises everywhere, and never cease to admire what you write; your praise   30 is ever in my mouth; and one thing more than all, that I love you dearly, and for a very good reason, that you, the most Christian of men, have taught me what true Christianity is. Hence my gratitude towards you, which I can feel in my heart, but not express with my pen. I hope for another letter from you at the Frankfurt fair, and I will then send you all my news, which shortness   35 of time does not permit me to think of, let alone to write out. But I am in good health, and so are Rhetus, Osvaldus, Pieter and Valentin, all pupils of mine and most devoted to you, who have told me unanimously to send you their greetings. And so, best wishes for your health too.

Basel, 13 November   40

* * * * *

11 poem] Cf Ep 440:16n.

12 my own poem] Cf Ep 440:16n.

14 poem] *Ad Osualdum Lucernanum Heluitium Elegia Glareani*; Cf Epp 440:15n, 463:74n.

37 Rhetus] Cf Ep 440:17n.

37 Peter and Valentin] Tschudi, brother and cousin respectively of Aegidius Tschudi (cf Allen Ep 618:60) the historian

491 / To Pieter Gillis   Brussels, 18 November [1516]

This letter was first published in the *Farrago*.

ERASMUS TO HIS FRIEND PIETER GILLIS

Great heavens, what fate is bad enough for men who are so slow? If the
Jerome is not bound even now, do all you can to prod those slowcoaches of
yours; and if it is, let me have it as soon as you can. Pieter One-eye is
perhaps laid up, for I hear he was not only robbed but beaten; if so, I am   5
very sorry. I have written to ask Colet to help him. Tunstall is very sorry too.
    I should not like you to be invited here at an inconvenient moment,
but if you have any reason to come, Tunstall will be glad to see you, and you
will bring silver with you and carry off gold. Franz has paid up, he says; but
he denies that he ever pledged his credit for Pieter. I have had a document   10
from Maruffo, in which he has slightly increased the value of the ducats. I
hear Dorp has come to his senses at last. *Utopia* is in the printer's hands.
Best wishes to you and your delightful wife, and be sure to give my
greetings to your excellent parent.
    Brussels, 18 November [1518]   15

492 / Adriaan Cornelissen van Baerland to his brother Cornelis
                              Louvain [c November 1516]

This letter represents one of the first attempts to compose a list of Erasmus'
writings, the kind of catalogue requested by John Watson in August 1516 (cf
Ep 450:54–5). It was evidently done without Erasmus' knowledge, as he told
Watson the following January (Ep 512:31–3). Subsequently, Erasmus had the
list printed in the first edition of the *Epistolae elegantes* (Louvain: Martens,
April 1517) and it was afterward reprinted frequently in the letter-collections.

* * * * *

491:3 Jerome] Cf Ep 477:3.
3 slowcoaches] Literally 'men like Callipides'; *Adagia* I vi 43
4 Pieter One-eye] Petrus Cocles, or Pieter Meghen, the scribe; cf Ep 412:47n.
8 reason to come] Cf Ep 477:27–9.
9 Franz] Cf Ep 481:6–9.
10 document] Cf Epp 481:89, 499:4–6.
11–2 I hear] From Jean Desmarez? cf Ep 496 introduction.
13 wife] Cf Ep 476:35n.
14 parent] His father; cf Ep 476:82n.

The date is derived from the reference (lines 114–5) to the publication of the *Epistolae aliquot ad Erasmum* (NK 2939) of October 1516, and from the fact that it was written in the autumn.

Adriaan of Baerland near Borssele (1486–1538) was a prominent member of the humanist community at Louvain, who at this time supported himself by teaching; among his pupils was Guillaume de Croy, the future archbishop of Toledo (Ep 647 introduction). He inaugurated the lectures in Latin when the Collegium Trilingue of Busleyden was opened, but a year later resigned for the more lucrative practice of private teaching. He was a member of the Faculty of Arts at the University, and on the death of Jean Desmarez he was appointed his successor. He received several ecclesiastical preferments before his death; see de Vocht *Literae*; his brother Cornelis is known only from this letter. He is not to be confused with Adriaan Aelius of Baerland, son of Jacob. See E. Daxhelet *Adrien Barlandus, humaniste belge, 1486–1538* (Louvain 1938).

ADRIAAN VAN BAERLAND TO HIS BROTHER CORNELIS, GREETING
The letter which I had written to that capital scholar Pieter de Schot in Ghent, who taught us both long ago, was forwarded, you say, by the public courier, since you could not take it yourself as I had asked you to do, because my mother was much against it and virtually forbade you to go; she 5
is very fond of you, of course, and did not want you to set out in haste on a journey which is in any case of some length and now made dangerous by the state of navigation. I too am no longer sorry that it turned out like this, for there is scarcely any city in which you could safely have lodged these last four or five months: the plague has been so violent in some places this past 10
summer and this autumn too, and in many has increased so much, and that too in such a secret and insidious way that some people, who thought the whole thing was completely over and safe in shallow water, as they say, fell into danger unbeknownst. You say that you are so much depressed just now that you cannot write to me as fully and carefully as you usually do 15
about the whole state of yourself and our friends. What this means, I do not know, nor what can be the origin of your depression and sadness. You must therefore write me a full account of your troubles as soon as you can, that I may do anything in my power to help you in word or deed.

* * * * *

492:2 Schot] Schoolmaster of Ghent, to whom Adriaan went in 1497 to learn Latin. He later dedicated some translations from Aesop (Antwerp: Martens 1512; NK 26) to Schot.
19 in word or deed] Terence *Heautontimorumenos* 86

You say you wish to know about the works of Erasmus, and I will list   20
them for you in order, though I have not at hand at the moment everything
that great man has written; with which he has so greatly enriched the Latin
tongue that in our own day we need not complain too bitterly of the classical
authors lost in the invasion of Italy by the Goths. First of all then (to turn to
his works) we have the *Enchiridion militis christiani*, a small book of pure   25
gold, and of the greatest use to all those who have determined to abandon
the pleasures of the body, to gird up their loins for the life of virtue and
make their way to Christ, who is the truth and the life. A certain preacher in
Antwerp, a leading man whose name I cannot remember, ascribed to this
book in the old days such an effect on life that he often declared, even in   30
most distinguished company, that every single page gave one material for a
sermon. Then there is his *Panegyricus*, addressed to Prince Philip archduke
of Austria, describing his triumphal expedition to Spain and blessed return
home to his own people. Of this work I think I can truly say what Quintilian
said of Cicero, that it glows with the abundant riches of his immortal   35
genius; he is no cistern collecting rainwater but a live gushing spring. In
this he praises Philip, who is not much more than a beardless youth, and
sets before him a picture of virtue to encourage him to pursue the path of
honour. Then he has also left us a certain number of *Precationes* notable
alike for learning and devotion, addressed to Jesus and His Virgin Mother. I   40
had almost forgotten a second panegyric or, to give it his own title, *Epistola
exhortatoria ad capessendam virtutem* addressed and dedicated to Adolph,
lord of Veere. Attached to the *Enchiridion*, of which I have already spoken, is
an elegant, impressive and beautifully written *Disputatio de tedio, pavore ac
tristitia redemptoris nostri Iesu*.   45

He has also translated numerous dialogues of various kinds by Lucian, in which he seems to me particularly neat and elegant; in fact I think
they deserve to be not only read but learnt by heart by all devotees of
literature, who should have them as companions on every journey. Among

* * * * *

25 *Enchiridion*] Cf Ep 164 introduction.
32 *Panegyricus*] Cf Epp 179, 180 introductions.
34 Quintilian] 10.1.109
39 *Precationes*] Cf Ep 93:113n.
41–2 *Epistola exhortatoria*] Cf Ep 93 introduction.
44 *Disputatio*] Cf Epp 108–11.
46–7 Lucian] Cf Epp 187 introduction, 191–3, 197, 199, 205, 261, 267.

the dialogues is a declamation also by Lucian in Erasmus' version, together   50
with another written in answer to it by Erasmus himself. Those who wish to
write well pore over his compilation *De copia rerum ac verborum commentarii*, which is full of meat. There is also in circulation here a book of *Similia*.
Of Plutarch's works translated by him into Latin I have seen the following:
A short work on the preservation of good health, How a man may distin-   55
guish flatterer from friend, How a man may contrive to profit by his
enemies, On the education of princes, That a philosopher should converse
mainly with princes, Whether Epicurus was right to say that one should live
in obscurity, On the desire of riches. Of the famous poet Euripides he has
produced verse translations of two tragedies, the *Hecuba* and the *Iphigenia*,   60
which show great elegance; one of them was acted and produced in public
here two years ago by several young men of good family, supervised, as you
will remember, by myself.

He has published also a book, *De ratione studii et instituenda pueritia*, in
which he shows the best way to enable children to arrive rapidly at a high   65
standard of instruction. Another work in circulation is *Concio de puero Iesu*,
delivered by a child who exhorts his fellow-children to modesty, forbear-
ance, humility and purity of life. This speech you have no doubt read at
some time, for from your earliest years you have been interested in everything that will help to develop your own character, and have always, and   70
rightly, rejected the bawdy narrative of poets and Apuleius with his most
dangerous anecdotes. Is there, in heaven's name, anything poetry can teach
by such rubbish except to do wrong and to desert the army of virtue to take
sides with vice? He has left also some odes, of the kind written by our
favourites Horace and Prudentius, full of elegance, charm and religious   75
feeling. At the same time he has achieved such heights in prose that one
could justly apply to him what Quintilian said of Plato, that he seemed
equipped not with a mind like mortal men but with some Delphian oracle.

* * * * *

52 *De copia*] Cf Ep 260 introduction.
53 *Similia*] Also known as the *Parabolae*; cf Epp 311, 312 introductions.
54 Plutarch's works] Cf Epp 268, 272, 297.
59 Euripides] Cf Epp 188, 198, 208 introductions.
61 one of them] Perhaps the *Hecuba* is referred to; it was played at the
university in September 1514.
64 *De ratione studii*] Cf Ep 66.
66 *Concio*] Cf Ep 175 introduction.
74 odes] Cf Ep 43:34–5n, Ep 47 introduction.
77 Quintilian] 10.1.81

But to return to his works, he wrote about six years ago, if I remember right, a *Declamatio stultitiae*, by which he earned great and lasting reputa-   80
tion, for the book displayed remarkable learning, great freedom of speech, and more than a little wit and sarcasm. The freedom gave some offence at the outset among those who did not care to have their own foolishness remarked on by Folly; but scholars and all men of good will were highly delighted with an elegant piece that is gay with so much learning and wears   85
its learning so gaily. He has also issued several Chiliads and centuries of proverbs, a work which clearly shows its author's more than human gifts, such is its copious fertility in words and ideas. On publication it gave such almost world-wide satisfaction that within a few years it was reprinted four times by the most distinguished publishers: first in Italy by Aldo Manuzio,   90
a man worthy of immortal memory for his exceptional familiarity with both Latin and Greek; then in Germany, twice by Froben at Basel, and once by Anshelm at Tübingen, both printers of repute. Another neat and concise book is also in circulation *De constructione octo partium orationis*, which most people believe to be his, nor does he absolutely deny this. Then the   95
Disticha moralia, commonly called *Cato*, the *Mimi Publiani*, the *Institutum hominis christiani*. Some *Epigrammata* have also found a public, the author- ship of which he does not deny, but says they were not written for publica- tion.

     Most recently he has broken quite new ground by giving us the first   100
New Testament simultaneously in Greek and Latin, having carefully cor- rected the text in his edition by comparison with the old copies and the early interpreters in both languages, and added annotations, a work which is welcomed with enthusiasm everywhere by all scholars and fair-minded

* * * * *

79 six years] Actually five; cf Ep 222.

80 *Declamatio stultitiae*] *The Praise of Folly*

87 proverbs] Cf Epp 126, 211, 269 introductions.

90 Aldo Manuzio] The edition of 1508; Ep 211

92 Froben] The unauthorized reprint of the first edition of the *Chiliades*, August 1513, and the revised edition of 1515; cf Epp 269, 419 introduction.

93 Anshelm] Cf Ep 397 introduction; his edition of the *Adagia* was dated March 1514.

94 *De constructione*] Ep 341 introduction

96 *Disticha moralia*] These pieces are included in the *Opuscula aliquot* pub- lished by Martens, September 1514; cf Ep 298 introduction.

96 *Mimi Publiani*] The moral maxims of Publilius Syrus

97 *Epigrammata*] The first edition was published with the *Adagiorum collec- tanea* in 1507; cf Ep 126 introduction.

101 New Testament] Cf Epp 373, 384.

men. Next he gave us a new Jerome, so well restored and furnished with   105
summaries and notes that he might seem a different author from the one we
used to read before; for he has further separated out the pieces falsely
ascribed to him and provided his letters with summaries and notes which
are so brief, clear, interesting and elegantly expressed that they give the
greatest satisfaction. As for the valuable notebooks which I have already   110
mentioned on *copia*, 'abundance in both kinds,' I need waste no more
time in telling you to read them, for you gallop unprompted over the Muses'
fields, and need bridle rather than spur. Besides the things I have mentioned, one sees from time to time in the booksellers' shops sundry *Epistolae aliquot Erasmi ad illustres et horum ad illum*. There have been two   115
editions this year of his brief notes on the book commonly called the *Cato*.
This I have expounded to my pupils, hoping by its high moral precepts to
train up their minds in virtue and their tongues in correct Latinity; for to
teach one without the other is to corrupt rather than instruct. He has also
lately revised Seneca, whose text was hitherto in a most parlous state. The   120
first psalm, *Beatus vir*, he has expounded in a most learned commentary. O
how fortunate we are, who have had the good luck in our early years to see,
to con over and to teach works of such perfection!

   This, my dearest brother, is more or less what has come into my
hands; but if you live, you will soon see more. For every day he still writes   125
something fresh, and revises ancient authors whose text is corrupted by the
passage of the centuries or the ignorance and carelessness of scribes; he
truly is a man born for the restoration of humane studies. Mind you always
combine what he writes with your reading of the Ancients; it will be to your
great profit, for thus you will greatly enrich your powers of expression.   130
What you say in your letter, my dear brother, about your not only reading
Justinian's *Institutes* but learning them by heart, gives me great pleasure. I
should not wish you to spend your whole life in the study of the poets,
which the majority of men suppose to lead nowhere. For besides them you
must earn the means of getting a livelihood, and supporting your friends in   135
controversy or litigation. In Cicero, Marcus Cato is highly extolled for
uniting with such consummate eloquence a knowledge of the civil law. He

         * * * * *

105 Jerome] Cf Epp 326, 396.

110 already] line 52

114–5 Epistolae] *Epistolae aliquot illustrium virorum ad Erasmum Roterodamum
et huius ad illos*. Louvain: Martens 1516 (NK 2939)

120 Seneca] Cf Ep 325 introduction.

121 psalm] Cf Ep 327 introduction.

136 Cato] Cicero *De oratore* 1.37.171

also praises Quintus Scaevola as the best orator of all counsel learned in the
law and most learned in the law of all orators. I could recount hundreds of
men to you, had I the time, who have achieved a great reputation in both   140
kinds of study – among the Ancients, I mean, not men of our own time; for
nowadays the most eloquent legal authorities are neglected, and they read
various small-minded glossators, out of whose work everyone constructs
the laws that suit himself, not suiting his behaviour to the laws but the laws
to his behaviour. And so, brother, as you learn the venerable science of the   145
law, mind you follow the more sensible party, that is, the lawyers of our
own day who know how to express themselves. If you do this, you will have
in your maturity the means of helping those in trouble, healing the sick and
raising up the afflicted, as Cicero puts it; and in the old age which I trust you
will reach in due course, you will find your knowledge of the law a source of   150
honour and reputation, as all your friends come to you, seeking your advice
in some concern about their own affairs. For the jurist's house (to finish my
letter with a sentence from Cicero) is the oracle of the whole state.

Farewell, my dear Cornelis, and take in good part this offering of
mine, which I send you as your brother for a token of our relationship.   155
From Louvain

493 / From Guillaume Budé   Paris [26 November 1516]

The date of this letter, which clearly follows Ep 480, has been adjusted from
that in the text (line 570) on the supposition that Budé mistakenly wrote the
present month instead of the month to follow. This allows for the publication
of the *Epistolae aliquot*, which appeared in October 1516, since Budé refers
(lines 47–50) to a printer's error in one of his own letters in that collection.
Although we do not know the exact date in October on which Martens
published the *Epistolae aliquot*, it is unlikely that Budé would have been able
to examine it before the end of October. This letter was first published in the
Epistolae elegantes 1517.

GUILLAUME BUDÉ TO ERASMUS OF ROTTERDAM, GREETING
I re-read your letter from time to time, for its effect upon me has varied.
Sometimes, as I consider how clever you are and the great elegance of what
you write, I think you are making fun of me gracefully; for I am not so
foolishly pleased with myself as not to realize that I am second-rate, though   5

* * * * *

138 Scaevola] Cicero *Brutus* 39.145
148 means of helping] Cicero *De oratore* 1.37.169
152 the jurist's house] *ibid* 1.45.200

you place me among first-class minds. But then again, as I estimate from what you write what a kind heart you have, I accept the letter from you that has reached me lately as not playful but seriously meant. In this to-and-fro of opinion I have decided that it is best to show confidence, foolishly perhaps, in a theologian like yourself, rather than be suspicious and show   10
myself unworthy of you and of friendship itself. And indeed I should run some risk of thinking there was a serious flaw in my character, if I did not believe a friend like you when you write something to me almost on oath. I am therefore determined to believe you, and to trust that you mean what you say. And so I am greatly elated that Cuthbert Tunstall, the English   15
king's envoy, – a man, as you have convinced me, to be specially admired for his unusual and delightful familiarity with Greek and Latin – should of his own accord join you in speaking well of me, especially for my know-ledge of Greek. With the two of you to support me I sometimes do not trust my own judgment, and believe that I too can write letters in Greek, making   20
myself out to be a rival, if you please – I the self-taught, the late learner, who picked up my knowledge where I could find it – of the most famous Grecians of modern times who learnt Greek in childhood. And this I do gladly, I love to do it, when writing to you, for I can trust the good sense of you, the best of men. For I am resolved to open myself wholly to you with   25
complete confidence, in the hope that I who hitherto have had no one but myself to teach me and read with me in either language (a fact I much regret) may now at least at this late hour be improved by your criticism. Indeed, if I find that you ever have time to spare for my interruptions, I shall make you work hard by writing constantly, until you can bear me no longer. What is   30
more, I for my part think it a great thing for us both that a frequent interchange of letters should make our friendship in future famous and a matter of public knowledge.

But pray, my dear sir, if anything gets into circulation through you, see that this does not expose me to criticism. It is only fair that you should   35
protect me against errors such as one expects from a printer, and my own errors too, if need arises; especially if in a letter written in my own hand mistakes have crept in, as they do, and have been overlooked when I read it through. Surely I can demand this of you, to keep my reputation water-tight? – even though I cannot deny the justice of your complaint that letters   40
written in my own hand have given you not a little trouble. When I read that passage in your letter I laughed out loud at the thought that I who write so

* * * * *

493:15 Tunstall] Cf Ep 480:6n.
39–40 watertight] He uses a legal phrase; *Adagia* IV v 37.

badly myself had the nerve to complain of your bad writing, though what is
carelessness in you is in me lack of skill. So if you will bear with me in
future on this point, you are welcome to write how you please; and indeed I   45
on my side am ready to make a compact with you that I shall never again
complain or be complained of in this respect. I have seen one letter of mine
in print among yours in which, though there are many slips, one in
particular annoyed me, where right at the end *quinque* 'five' has been put for
quique meaning 'and when,' to my great detriment: for having been   50
hitherto the father of six sons and one small daughter, I am reduced to five
sons and deprived of a sort of double ration of the *ius trium liberorum*. I shall
therefore bring an action for heavy damages against your printer, unless he
makes good this loss to me forthwith, and I may have to take steps against
you too if I cannot get satisfaction out of him.   55

As for those 'trivialities,' I take it you have quieted down and accepted
my proffered satisfaction. In fact, you yourself read an unhelpful meaning
into it by applying it to, of all things, your notes on the New Covenant, and
again to your *Proverbs*, a book which I am so far from regarding as trivial that I
maintain it to be an important and imposing treasury of words, filled full   60
and decorated and (if you will allow the Homeric adjective) glistering with
good things in both Latin and Greek; though you do seem to me rather
long-winded for a collector of proverbs, if I may have at you in passing,
remembering how you blamed me for not knowing when to take my hand
off the finished picture. How delighted I am that you should say my   65
remarks have somewhat encouraged you to try your hand in future at
subjects which admit of deeper thought! Come on, I will back the success of
this enterprise with all I possess. Is there anything, in heaven's name, in
which you are not likely to succeed, which is within the reach of superlative
gifts brought to a pinnacle of skill and learning? And at this point you start 70
joking, my dear Erasmus! 'I measure myself by my own foot,' you say; 'we
cannot all be Budés.' You really are extraordinary; what a witty and practised ironist you must be! As though anything more uncomfortable could
happen to me than for my foot to be matched against a foot for which
Maximinus' shoe would scarce be big enough. If you and I were measured   75

* * * * *

47 letter] Cf Ep 403:166; the error is corrected in Allen's text (Allen II p 233 line
149) and so does not appear in the translation.

52 *ius trium liberorum*] The privileges of an accelerated political career granted
by Augustus to fathers of three (or more) children

56 'trivialities'] Cf Ep 480:45n.

64–5 take my hand off] See Ep 480:244.

75 Maximinus] A late Roman emperor with enormous feet; *Adagia* I i 21

one against the other, you would necessarily appear three times as large again.

How I admire and venerate your judgment and welcome and respect it, so keen so accurate so swift so ever-ready so consistent! How you surveyed me entire with a single glance and searched me out, leaving no corner unconsidered, unexplored! Certainly this letter of yours has cut short all my hopes of deceiving you in future. With your piercing judgment you have so thoroughly explored all my feelings, like a surgeon with his probe; and, far away as I am, you see into me and through me as though I were under your hand. I have even come to know myself better since you considered me and valued me and sized me up. What a sharp eye you have, and how you hit the target! There is nothing you might not achieve, if you were to aim at more and greater things. If you had read those pieces of mine two or three times and were someone else and not Erasmus, what more could you possibly find to comment on? Yet I am quite certain that you scarcely had time for a cursory glance at the passages I mentioned to you, occupied as your mind was in pressing business. But they say one can tell the lion by his claws; you can tell me and ordinary folk by our fingertips.

At this point I will put a bold face on it, and make the best defence I can before you as my judge, for I can see what it is that you object to, although you conceal this. Your criticisms may be justified and acutely observed, for which I owe you admittedly a great debt of gratitude, since you have done just what I asked of you; but I shall not be deterred, nor give anyone a chance to say that bad as my cause was I could not stand up for myself and win the day, for I am one of those worthy characters who have learnt (I should say, have tried to learn) to make the worse cause appear the better by their presentation of it. But you have made this task hard for me by mixing friend and critic with such cunning and such tact that I could not complain of you even if I wanted to, unless I wished to appear more selfish and sillier than any man who loves to have toadies round him. All the same, I will take up your time somehow, or you may be short of material for an answer to my letter.

You say that things which breathe a native simplicity sink more easily and more agreeably into the minds of men and even encourage the reader to an effort of attention; and that as I have moved a long way from this simplicity, no reader can easily enjoy the perusal of what I write, unless he is both very well-informed and very attentive. This, I think, was the sense

* * * * *

93 the lion by his claws] *Adagia* I ix 34
94 bold face] *Adagia* I viii 47
108 You say] Ep 480:263–5

of what you said, although as I write this your letter is not to hand; it is now
going the round of my friends to be inspected like some picture by Apelles,
for they themselves insisted on seizing it when I showed it them. You add   115
some other remarks to the same effect about my frequent and habitual use
of metaphor; whether you took this to be good or bad, you wished to be
concealed from me, or at least I could not be certain, though I have my
suspicions. Then you add 'What has this to do with it?' I cannot deny this,
and it only remains to try and excuse it somehow, since I have no intention   120
of trying to beg myself off. Though you do not upbraid me with this in a
fault-finding spirit, for you show yourself a critic of exceptional skill, and
things which you might openly have found fault with you put on the credit
side for the moment while you criticize them. The result is that by pointing
out my mistakes within definite limits you seem to exhort rather than   125
discourage me, while none the less making me more careful in future and a
better craftsman, if I can ever learn to listen to my betters.

What then should be at this point my first reply? I know not, unless it
be this: that the manner of writing which would be unacceptable, you say,
to ordinary readers of the book unless they are very well-informed and   130
strictly attentive, was chosen deliberately. I thought it was in my interest at
that date that few should understand me, and that the few should understand in such a way that, if necessary, I could deny in public what each
individual thought I said according to his own interpretation. So I did set
down some things in riddling fashion, which will largely be made clear in   135
the second edition through the mouthpiece of the annotator, so that I may
still be in a position to disown them and remain secure, while at the same
time saying what I want to say for the present; which you understand well
enough, and say I model myself on Loxias in Delphi. You remember that
saying of Solomon's 'It is the glory of God to conceal a matter'? Wise man as 140
he was, he had no wish, when speaking of difficult and secret subjects, to be
understood by the profane or even by men of taste, resembling in that the
other purveyors of oracles. But there are some things, you will say, which it
is desirable that all men should take in, and even in them you do not expose
yourself to be understood by the public, let alone the common herd. Even   145
the subject of my book and the exposition of all that follows from the 'as' and
its subdivisions is beyond the ken of all except men halfway to being
scholars, and even they must read with care and more than once. No one
could find a more intractable subject or set himself a task that demanded

* * * * *

119 you add] Cf Ep 480:275.
139 Loxias] Cf Ep 480:218n.
140 Solomon] Proverbs 25:2

more labour, and carry it through to a conclusion. Nor was it my original   150
intention to try and make it all clear. Hardly any subject has been dealt with
by so many hands to no purpose. You can find no one among scholars of
repute in our own time and earlier who did not take a hand in this, nor
could you find one who did not get it wrong from top to bottom; and yet,
obscure and almost unknown as I am, I think I have mastered this whole   155
subject and made such a success of it, that anyone who tries to refute my
exposition will very soon find himself a self-confident idiot.

On your other points my feeling is this. If I am fond of metaphors and
tropes, I follow the example of the greatest Latin authors, who gave
metaphor first place in the teaching of style and indulged in it extensively in   160
their own writings; and if I am inclined to be high-flown, I do not think I
have done this improperly. Is there any good classical author who did not
try to clothe exalted topics, charged with admiration or passion, in lofty and
splendid language? – unless you think one can be indignant or appeal to the
people without raising one's voice and being audible to everyone who is   165
not stone deaf. As I read your *Sileni* and the *Dulce bellum inexpertis*, which
you have given us as an advance on your polemic against war, I feel that I
have dealt with almost the same subject in a different way. I was indignant
that religion should be mixed up with war, and that that class of men who
are called to be holy should set their hands to the business of making   170
money, when they ought to care for nothing but the way to heaven. I shall
be thought to have taken this topic from you, if anyone reads what we both
write, since I treat the same subject in almost the same fashion. But your
treatment is cautious, conciliatory, simple, popular and well-judged in
every way, as becomes the status of a divine which you have recently   175
adopted; mine is extravagant, unrestrained, enthusiastic, impetuous, de-
clamatory, ornate – I only hope, not vulgar. This, I think, is not unsuitable
for the reason which speaks the language of liberty and prides itself on its
frankness, which you have called truly French. And so I have made liberal
use of tropes and rhythm and all the armoury of speaking for effect, and   180
metaphors too, at any rate when they offered themselves willingly and had

* * * * *

166 *Sileni ... Dulce bellum*] *Adagia* III iii 1, IV i 1

167 polemic] This rhetorical piece is mentioned in the letter to Botzheim of 30
January 1523 as written for Cardinal Riario; cf Allen I 37 lines 7–14; Renaudet
Italie 94. It was never published.

175 status of a divine] Erasmus of course had been a priest since 1492; cf Ep
446 introduction. The reference here is to the prebend of Courtrai; cf Ep
436:6n.

179 you have called] Ep 480:213

not to be fetched. That I went deliberately in search of them or collected
them without restraint or hesitation you will not maintain, for you know
that I do not readily use material and ornament that is traditional and
hackneyed. Nor will you reckon as a tiresome affectation anything that I   185
find in my subject and do not drag in or distort – or else I am much mistaken;
and that this is what I have done is clear from the smooth and steady
movement of my style. You are more tied to principle, your excuse is that
you must do as that Minerva of yours tells you, and you rightly understand
that she is meant to be popular and to please an audience; I should go   190
further and call her senatorial and consular, for such is the welcome that I
see awaiting your work from the public in every walk of life, that I am
already almost jealous of you. But what could I do? The charms of my
subject were too much for me: once I have spread my canvas and been
carried out to sea, I do not think either to shorten sail or maybe to set any 195
limits to my sailing; off I go down the wind, wherever my inspiration
carries me, for rein it in as it warms to its work I cannot; and from time to
time it may be that I am carried off course, if now and again I get over-
excited.

But there is a point that I am willing to leave for you to decide, which   200
now at length seems to come back into my head: that I should keep always
on the same course on which I am once started, with the same breeze
following continually, so that on coming nearer you would feel I was
propelled by sails and not oars as well, nothing, as you know, carrying me
on more steadily than the breeze we call ambition. This is the flattering   205
wind (and it blows smoothly though it may blow strong) on which you
judge I am carried along, with some pitching and tossing maybe, but yet
with following waves that do not incommode me. But you say that few of
my readers can keep up with me as I dash off so far out of their sight. It may
be so; I shall not discuss it with you, for most authors are full of their own   210
ideas. This at least you must let me suppose, that those who once have
caught up will readily devote themselves to the same spirited style of
writing, and perhaps will leave me far behind. You have much more
experience in this race; with your exceptional skill you can manage your
canvas so that you are carried smoothly, evenly, steadily through shallows   215
and deeps, over shoal and reef, and even in mid ocean as you run before the
wind you move with following wave as though it were a river current. This
is a rare endowment, a natural felicity. Nor are you (in passing) left un-
moved by this same breeze of ambition, grand talker that you are; but you
know where you are bound for and how to hoist a modest, more appro-   220
priate spread of sail. So the difference between us is this: you put things
with charm and elegance, in the manner of good conversation, while I

express myself (hold forth, if you like) in rhetorical style, I admit, but in an audible, not a deafening voice. And so, it may be, I am violent and carry my reader away, while you charm him and win him over; I burst in, you worm   225
your way; I sport the full armour of the young and dashing, while you wear a half-suit; your effort is less but well-directed, mine is great but, swing my arms as I may, I do not get the same results as you. In a word, you know better than I what suits the siege, the assault, the defence, you are a laureate of the wrestling-school of philosophy; I have no schooling, and go for my   230
target blinded by enthusiasm.

Even if what you say is true, you cannot, I think, find anything further, anything more serious to bring against me, nor will you say that in this difference of opinion I have 'clad me in shamelessness' rather than valour. It was the same in the great peoples of antiquity: every writer had a   235
character of his own. This has always been nature's way: either we give our faults free rein, or they work to the surface in spite of us. That cautious approach of yours – no emotions, no flashing weapons – suits you well enough; great enterprises, gleaming arms will suit you when you so choose, and you will rise in triumph to the summits; everything in fact will   240
be within your reach, if you make a little effort. I know you as well as you know me. I make more or greater demands upon myself, though I expect nothing that is beyond my powers; you let yourself off too lightly, you are never provoked beyond the bounds of what comes easy, never carried away. No wonder all see with astonishment how you come fresh to new   245
enterprises all the time, as though your spirit never flagged; for you have never made yourself prove how much you can do, you have shown your quality by continuous rather than intensive work, although no one else could do so much. For my part I could not easily be induced to lower my style to the level of ordinary people, writing as I do on dignified subjects of   250
no ordinary kind; it comes easier to model it on those men who have left a great name among posterity. If one day I take up once more the commentary that has lain fallow so long, I will remember that I must use a finer yarn to weave the web which must after all be weighed in the scales of public opinion; in neither style, I think, need I fear that fluency will desert me.   255

* * * * *

234–5 'clad me ... valour.] Homer *Iliad* 1.149,8.262

252 commentary] The *Annotationes in xxiv Pandectarum libros* (Paris: 1508); cf Ep 403 introduction. They formed a commentary to the first twenty-four books of the *Digest* of Justinian (the so-called *Digestum vetus*). Other sections of the Digest were dealt with in the *Annotationes posteriores* of 1526. See D.R. Kelly *Foundations of Modern Historical Scholarship* (New York 1970) 66–76.

253 finer yarn] Horace *Epistles* 2.1.225

But this fluency you seem to find tedious, although in kindness to me you put this as other men's opinion rather than your own. Unless I guess wrong we have the same end in view. I know we both go after reputation of no common ordinary kind, and not by the first route that offers; and you indeed run after it, you never rest. In fact, it is the wish to imitate men of the 260 highest renown for scholarship that makes this battle worth fighting both for us and for all those with a desire for excellence; for all that you, my Socratic enthusiast, began some time ago ingeniously enough to degrade yourself, with a view to playing the part of a theologian or winning approval for your industry from the theologians in your part of the world. You 265 do the same, believe it or not, when in your letter to me you tell me to be content with my own performance.

As for my theoretical argument towards the end of the last book not belonging to my subject, the Roman 'as,' for such seems to be your opinion, why should I enjoy any less licence than you do to combine quite different 270 subjects? Silenus and St Paul (very different characters!), impudent pantomime-artists and solemn heroes, feasts of Bacchus and mysterious Eleusinian rites, – that style of yours joins them together like the best glue: run your nail over the join, and you can neither feel it nor see it. You show us the changing scenery of the world, and have produced new aspects of life 275 that we never suspected before our astonished gaze. What has all this to do with Silenus, or Dionysus himself for that matter? Such is your skill, when you proposed to defend our most sacred altars you had no hesitation in borrowing a starting-point, your actual text as they call it, almost from some bawdy song, and turned it to your advantage with cunning quite excep- 280 tional. Did you find anything like this in my *De asse*? – the purpose of which, I would have you understand, is to open all the sepulchres of antiquity and unlock its secret places, and show that the wealth of the Egyptians and Chaldaeans (as your panegyric puts it), when brought out after all these years into the public view and assessed in money of our own 285 day by me, the only expert money-changer, was much greater than is

* * * * *

269 your opinion] Ep 480:275

271 Silenus and St Paul] A reference to one of the best known of the *Adagia* (III iii 1) in which Erasmus earned much criticism by comparing the Apostles (and St Paul the hermit) with those images of the demigod Silenus which have a ridiculous and despicable exterior, but open to reveal a beautiful image inside. The mention of 'pantomime-artists' is meant to recall the figure of Folly in the *Moriae encomium*.

274 run your nail] *Adagia* I v 91

277 Dionysus] Cf Ep 480:275n.

commonly supposed. To show too that, great as it was, it came to no more than the savings of a charcoal-burner; and that all those who in our day put all their efforts into the pursuit of these gifts of fortune are striving tooth and nail for the donkey's shadow, as the saying goes. And since philosophy   290 can protect its votaries from this mistake, and win true and undying glory for man, I tried to explain what true philosophy is and how the devotees of good literature can aspire to it and achieve it. All this, I think, goes together with my treatise *De asse* and what is there set out, much as light and shade go together in a picture, if only I have been able to achieve a fit and proper   295 balance, as they call it. Was it that I could not express this in spite of all my efforts, or that I could not maintain the efforts with all the power, and indeed all the resources, at my command? You are the man for that, with your practice in flying across the sky, be it darting or gliding, without so much as a wingbeat; while I, in my noviciate as an author, flutter about   300 with much clapping of wings like pigeons at play, as you seem to feel. But one thing I do beg, that you do not count it against me if I have made longish digressions in one or two places, and have inserted like pieces of inlay, in certain places where there were gaps, topics that would not have found such a suitable home in writings specially devoted to them – a fact which   305 you yourself detected with great skill. But I do not wish to conceal from you that my book *De asse* has been published in a second edition much enlarged, in case you have time, I will not say to read it, but to skim it through and read one short page in each quire.

What follows makes me hesitate. 'I observe,' you say, 'that you take   310 great delight in comparisons, and use some which are rare and exceptionally difficult; but when you have once taken one up, there is no tearing you away from it.' Do you wish me to be convinced by these remarks of yours that I have made a very successful use of these figures of speech? For I used to think that a right use of them consisted in not laying aside the metaphor I   315 had adopted until I had finished my sentence and made my meaning clear. Or is it your opinion, as I rather think it is, that I spend more time and trouble on these ornaments than is right and proper, as though I had a mania for figures of speech, and showed complete lack of taste in the way I misuse the decorations of discourse?   320

Related to this fault there is another, that my style is all bejewelled, instead of being picked out with jewels here and there, so that nothing stands out above the rest, although the greatest authorities have held that

* * * * *

290 donkey's shadow] *Adagia* I iii 52
307 second edition] 14 October 1516; cf Ep 435:42n.
310 you say] Ep 480:257–9

writing should be spangled with gems and not set thick with them. My first
answer might be, if I so wished, that I judged these digressions inserted in   325
the book, and the conclusion of the book itself, to be a kind of ornament and
highlight in a treatise dull enough of itself, since without them the exposition of weights and currency and the meticulous investigation of measure-
ment would make very difficult reading. At any rate, it is a pleasure to be
put on my defence before you, my dear Erasmus, as though I had been   330
reported to you as our censor in matters literary, or you yourself in the
exercise of your censorial office had posted my name for having set an
example of fullness of style which is too rich and too brilliant and too
luxuriant, in defiance of the manners and customs of our forefathers, whose
principles are still no doubt accepted as law by scholars of the highest rank.   335
On my side, I am not so far in love with my own or anyone else's faults that,
if the tendency of either my nature or my scholarship had gone that way, I
would not rather be faultless than have to beg pardon and forgiveness for
my faults; but since what I wished most of all has not come my way, I chose
what they call the second best, for such I think it to err on the more liberal   340
side. And who would not rather be called to account for luxury and elegant
extravagance than for a shabby and famished parsimony? I wrote to you
once in jest that I was building country houses to rival Lucullus. You go
further, and compare me with some householder rich as Lucullus, who
knows all the same what he has in store, and has learnt to bring forth each   345
item to be put to its proper use. This I take for no less a tribute than if you
had called me some puritan old Piso in this more licentious age. There is
absolutely nothing here that I could resent: I have found you a critic who is
normally courteous and never hostile, one who never deviates from what is
right and proper and never loses sight of the truth. You could have levied a   350
penalty on me, had you approached what I write in a critical and hostile
spirit, but you allowed friendship to excuse all my shortcomings. Yet I think
no man of good will would have argued that one should not accept and
follow your verdict, had you thought fit to condemn me for a lush and
wanton style. As it is, thanks to your friendly vote, instead of paying the   355
penalty for my bold expressions I shall actually earn credit in the eyes of
those who will read your letter.

So much, as you see, in the way of defending myself; now, I can
converse with you on equal terms. To keep watch over me, and even to find

* * * * *

340 second best] *Adagia* I iv 18
344 Lucullus] Cf Ep 480:165n.
347 puritan old Piso] Calpurnius Piso Frugi, censor at Rome in 125BC; as an
historian he castigated luxury, and his name *frugi* means 'thrifty'.

fault, it is my own regular custom to appoint myself, and to approach my   360
own writings at intervals as though they were by someone else. Even so, I
have never yet regretted giving my nature full rein and following my own
bent; for I write to please myself as well, I am no mere slave of the theatre
and the public, although it is the stalls whose applause I covet, wherein you
sit in the front row. And what you write attracts me more, so clear is it and at   365
the same time so eloquent, while not making things at first glance so
obvious and so subservient to the reader that he is satisfied with a rapid
perusal and hurries on to what follows; although it leaves no sting behind it
for the future but only a pleasant feeling at the time. You for your part are
marvellously clever and successful at retaining your well-known middling   370
level of style, and yet your readers, greedily as they may devour the result,
do not dip into you again maybe for a long time, nor pursue your meaning
by frequent re-reading; as though you were to feel that what can be eaten
without much chewing is easier to digest. I, however, have my eye on
something beyond the pleasure of the moment, I look to the future as well,   375
and reckon that a certain acidity can serve like salt to relieve the sickly effect
of too much abundance. In fact, although I consider myself to owe more to
industry than to natural gifts, I yet feel that nature claims the principal part
in invention, and even when I write as I do now, I check and restrain to no
small degree the force of its free flow. If I begin to use more severe critical   380
standards, who knows but what I may cut out all freedom and abundance of
style? You, I know, succeed in retaining your abundance while setting
limits to exuberance, but then your nature is well balanced and finely
tempered. You remain the servant of your principles, you see clearly what
suits your make-up. And so you never make a longer jump than your   385
training prescribes. But I, lacking as I do your scrupulous eye for the rules,
in my exuberance inevitably overstep the mark. Yet I never expend so much
energy that, in my efforts to overleap the target, I forget that my powers are
limited as I gather force for the jump. This is the error of an ambitious
nature that gives its pen too much play and thrives on activity, not the fault   390
of a mind that is forcing itself to do things beyond its powers; and this I
realize to the full only when the heat of the moment has passed, which
means, long afterwards. Not that you were always immune from this
disorder of the mind, or that I cannot force myself to work in a different
style, if some different purpose should require it, as you will be able to   395
discover from my dialogue with Deloynes at the end of that same book.
Indeed the time will come when, as a result of your advice, or with the

* * * * *

396 Deloynes] See Ep 494 introduction.

maturity that comes with years, I shall take as my models disciplined
authors like you, fine craftsmen of precision in language. As it is, I regard a
welcome for elaboration and complexity of style as a sign of youth, although   400
I draw close to my forty-eighth year, nor could you at least maintain that
this was out of the way and inappropriate to what I have chosen to write. At
least there is no one of the school of Ermolao or Poliziano who would not
aim at this, if you theologians with your solemn faces miscall it verbiage
and fashionable extravagance. Yet they are the men whose wide learning   405
and whose language you normally admire.

　　Again, you find me lacking in restraint in the matter of ornament; so
true is it that you think me wrong not in kind but in degree. True enough: it
is not my habit to bring things in a niggardly fashion out of my copious
store. You too have a store rich above the average; but it is the caution of   410
advancing years that has made you so careful, not nature merely or deliberate choice. You are made more concise every day by your theological
principles, which have I suppose freed you so far from the whip and spur of
ambition that your noble spirit is no longer a slave to glory and reputation,
provided you can contribute to the public good. So at least I have schooled   415
myself to believe, lest I fail to do just as you tell me in every direction. Not
but what in other respects, I think, you have developed not so much a
hatred for Poverty (your wife, as you describe her) as a hopeless passion for
her rival Good Repute (Eucleia call her, not to say Ulysses' nurse Eurycleia);
reasonably enough, since she follows you everywhere like your own   420
shadow. At this point you go on to indulge in quibbling – false modesty,
rather. 'If I undertake great themes,' say you, 'I take them out of the hands of
better men; on moderate themes I forestall no one but men of moderate
talents.' Yes: but suppose there are some tasks which you can achieve and
no one else, and in the meantime, while you devote your efforts to those   425
moderate themes, something happens to you (may the patron deities of
theology avert any such thing!). Who will make good what the world has
lost? Do not you think that in the long run your departed spirit will pay the
penalty for this offence, if you give first call on your great and varied talents

*　*　*　*　*

401 forty-eighth year] Budé was nearing the completion of his forty-ninth
year.
403 Ermolao] Barbaro; cf Ep 485:2n.
403 Poliziano] Cf Ep 471:12n.
418 Poverty] For background see Ep 480:145 ff.
419 Good Repute] For Good Repute Budé uses (as a Latin name) the Greek
word Eucleia; Eurycleia, the name of the nurse in *Odyssey* 19–23, means Wide
Repute.

to subjects not of the first importance and greatest urgency? – which is what   430
the Gospel teaching tells us to do. My own argument is this: it is not for the
first-comer to attack even a modest subject, let alone to aim at what comes
next, which is beyond his reach; and in the same way I think that those who
are better than they are should take up in preference to all else what is in
proportion to their capacity, and the really first-class people should attempt   435
to write on subjects of real importance and distinction. If you are weighed
in the balance with men like that, you might be thought to show a lack of
due order in having set your hand to modest subjects and others of an even
lower class. One might compare the case of a man who, though rich in all
things needful for a life of luxury, yet preferred the casual leavings dropped   440
by the passers-by at some crossroads.

I now come to your point that my building of country-houses in the
style of Lucullus is proof that I have no close acquaintance with your
familiar Poverty. I on the other hand should maintain (and could prove
what I say) that this shows how that runaway character Riches has deserted   445
me (confound him!) and how that Poverty of yours has quickly slipped into
my home in his place (a murrain on her!). What a clever fellow I am! See how
your letter, full as it was of argument, has made me quite a disputant, as I
wrestle with a slippery customer like you who are so difficult to refute. In
my building programme I have unintentionally issued an invitation to   450
Poverty, and when she leaves your house, I fear she will cling to me as her
special victim tighter than any ivy.

My friend Deloynes, who is now in large measure also yours, will
write you, he tells me, a most friendly letter. For it is my custom to show
your letters to him and to several men besides, and to boast of this impor-   455
tant friendship among my other friends. This is my best way of maintaining
my credit and authority among those who think you are our modern Varro,
except that you write much better than he did. At that stage, if I feel some
envy of you, I am obliged none the less to vote for the view held by the
whole body, not going silently into the division lobby but using my voice   460
and all my faculties, so completely have the purity of your style and the
charm of your intelligence persuaded everyone to vote for you. Louis Ruzé,

* * * * *

454 letter] Ep 494

457 Varro] The most learned scholar of Roman antiquity

460 division lobby] A metaphor from the voting in ancient Rome; *Adagia* II vii
12

462 Ruzé] A relation of Budé by marriage and a close personal friend of Budé,
Ruzé died in 1526. He was *seigneur* of Herpinière and Melun. In 1500 he was
municipal counsellor of Paris, in 1511 a member of the Parlement, and later
sub-prefect of the city. He was also a patron of the humanist community at
Paris; cf Allen III Ep 926.

the lieutenant-governor of Paris, immersed though he is in the legal interests dictated by his judicial duties, is yet by nature entirely carried
towards the humanities, in which he qualified long ago as a fluent and   465
elegant composer. He and I are very closely linked in every sort of relationship; Deloynes himself is hardly a more familiar figure to my household and
on my doormat, and it would be hard to say which of them I visit more
frequently. I should count them my Pomponius and my Brutus, if I myself
bore the least resemblance to Cicero; and I should be the sole owner of them   470
both if you, absentee though you are, had not interfered with my possession of my friends, with your insatiable appetite for excellence of every
kind. All the same, as you do not possess them by violence, by clandestine
entry or on sufferance, for you possess them in virtue of offers freely made
by them and open transfer of title, I have no grounds for threatening you   475
with any judge or arbitrator, before whom I can sue you for a decree of
restitution.

Consequently I now propose to form a partnership with you, if you
concur, in all our friends, the more readily as you have already acquired a
title not only to my friends but to myself, so that from now on there is a legal   480
agreement between us for friendship of no ordinary kind expressed in these
words in all good faith; and let us enter into this covenant on the understanding that we shall hold all our possessions in common and shall share
our friends. Although it occurs to me that in this partnership I shall not
contribute my fair and equal share or meet with my deserts, for the persons   485
concerned already have a much greater affection and appetite for your
works than for mine. I perceive therefore that your reputation infringes the
ancient lights not only of myself but, I had almost said, of all our contemporaries; to such a degree are you loved and respected by everyone, that no
one here dares even to voice any criticism, however much he may wish to,   490
nor even to praise you in an uncommittal manner, without being generally
suspected of collusion with the other side.

As for my book, if I did not dedicate it to any individual, I would
rather have you suspect any reason you may choose than explain it to you
myself. Some months ago I met Jacques Lefèvre, while I was on a visit to my   495
country-house, and he then besought me to give you his greetings, and to
put forward his bad health as his reason for not writing to you; he was so
poorly, and still is (he sent one of his friends to see me today) that he cannot

* * * * *

488 ancient lights] As Latin can use *lumina* for reputation or brilliance of style
as well as for the light of the sky, he who casts his rivals' works into the shade
can be compared with the man who obstructs his neighbour's windows,
contrary to the legal rule of 'ancient lights'. The play on words is Ciceronian
(*Brutus* 17.66); cf Ep 494:45n.

495 Lefèvre] For earlier references to his ill-health see Epp 445:33 ff, 460:19.

even write a letter. You know he is not only a good scholar but a very honest
man.   500

At this point, I think, I will bring my letter to a close, although I take
the greatest delight in writing to you and thus beguile the depression
arising from my poor health. But mind you! – in return for this labour I
make it a condition that I receive a letter from you even longer than your
last, and I exercise my right to demand fulfilment. I hope that you will take 505
some holiday from the volumes of Jerome that you have published, and that
during an interval of relaxation we shall have the benefit of your company.
My dear Erasmus, Erasmus mine – Erasmus ours, I ought to say – in the
name of Philosophy the beloved mistress whom we share, in the name of
Zeus god of friendship and of your wonderful reputation which puts in the 510
shade, if I may say so without offence, the fame of our contemporaries and
of my countrymen, in the name of your natural goodness so kindly and
fair-minded and divinely inspired, do not hesitate, do not fail, do not forget
to write and rewrite to me and my friends, and do so often. So may you reap
the return of your many and great exertions. In a word, the more you oblige 515
me in this, the more surely may Poverty, that wife you hate, give you a wide
berth; may she file a bill of divorcement, refuse to cohabit, and never
darken your doors again – always provided she does not migrate to mine.
Mind you are never, never so engrossed that you cannot find the time to
attend to your duty.   520

Farewell then, and my very best wishes, and by all means get yourself
covered with gold, provided you do not get fond of the stuff. As for me, let
God deal with me as He will. Long experience of ill-luck has taught me to
make the best of any kind of fortune; and in any case Philosophy, self-
sufficient and lavish with her gifts, has made me her own by long-   525
continued use and possession. Those who established our legal principles
call a period of ten and twenty years a long term of possession, by which
they laid it down that ownership of property can be acquired by those who
have enjoyed the use of it in good faith. For five-and-twenty years now I
have been in good faith a servant of the humanities, so that though there are 530
many things I lack, I sometimes feel that I am in the position of wanting
nothing – when, that is, my beloved Philosophy has the mastery of my
spirit, having undertaken out of her own resources to provide for me and
those dearest to me. But when three days go by, for any reason, in which I
have not lived with her waking and sleeping, then I do feel how foolish she 535
is (if I dare say so) to lavish her treasures in vain and pride herself on her
generosity to all and sundry. You perhaps, who converse on lofty themes
and have encountered the works of clever men face to face, may have found
a firm anchorage for your hopes in this stormy sea of life. But I, who have

not yet harvested the fruits of philosophy, am so much troubled by affection   540
for the wife who lives with me and for my nearest and dearest. If the time
comes that these purveyors of gold chains begin to claim you as their own
(and God forbid that you should make yourself their slave and chattel of
your own free will!), Philosophy the champion of the rights of men (of
heroes, rather), who has stood by me hitherto in my suit for a declaration   545
that I am a free man, will enter her plea in bar, I do not doubt, against those
who are trying to enslave you, and if they lay claim to you on the ground of
long prescription, she will send these gold-chain merchants packing. But if
you welcome your chains, if you do not refuse to have your free status called
in question, or accept any other affront to what she has taught us, I give   550
notice that you will find me the sternest of your adversaries. So do not say
you were not warned.

The day that I write this, in the afternoon, Josse Bade sent two men of
noble birth round to see me, one of them from Naples, the other a Spaniard;
if I could remember their names, I would put them into this letter. They said   555
they had come to see me out of love of literature, attracted by my reputation,
such as it is. I promised them that I would write to you; for they longed to
see you, as they made quite clear. I had a letter written in draft; this I was
obliged to copy out again on clean paper and, since they said they were
leaving early next morning, I had to work after supper, a thing I never do,   560
being prone to catch cold if any man ever was. If this letter reaches you, let
me know as soon as you can, so that I do not have to lament the loss of my
time, and also my friend Deloynes', who sent me late tonight a letter that
was waiting for a courier. If there are faults in the writing, I see no necessity
to apologize, for I write at night and in a hurry and blinking after my   565
supper. Farewell once more, you and your false modesty, who say you are
no Budé but Erasmus merely, and that it is not everyone's luck (meaning
your own) to make Corinth safely. Farewell yet once again, and never cease
in your setting right of all to do with the humanities and Holy Scripture.

Paris, [27 October]   570
I have a few brief notes on the New Testament, which I was keeping
for insertion in the notes on the Pandects which I one day hope to publish;

* * * * *

553 Bade] The Paris printer; cf Epp 419, 183, 346 introductions.

553 two men] One, probably the so-called Neapolitan, was Mariano Accardo;
cf Ep 544.

563 letter] Ep 494

568 Corinth] See Ep 480:135n.

570 27 October] See introduction.

572 notes on the Pandects] The second edition appeared about 1519.

but after you I shall never open my mouth, for fear of looking a fool if after
Homer I rewrite the *Odyssey*, and in order not, in any case, to advertise my
self-satisfaction. If they can be any use to you, I will make you a present of   575
them, so that they are not wasted.

Let me know your future address.

494 / From François Deloynes   Paris [c 25 November 1516]

The writer (c 1468–1524) had been a close friend of Guillaume Budé since their
youth. They had studied law together at Orléans, where Deloynes subsequently taught. In 1500 he became a member of the Parlement of Paris and
he subsequently resided there. Erasmus apparently met him in the autumn of
1500, and wrote a tribute to him in the *Apologia adversus P. Sutorem* (Froben
1525); cf LB ix 788 B–C. This letter was first published in the *Epistolae elegantes*
1517. It is evidently contemporary with Ep 493, where it is twice mentioned.

FRANÇOIS DELOYNES TO ERASMUS OF ROTTERDAM, GREETING
Perhaps you will wonder, Erasmus most learned of men, what should have
impelled me of all people – endowed as I am with no skill in composition
and united with you by no ties of acquaintance – to take the lead in writing
to you; but your surprise will cease at once, if you have not forgotten a letter   5
you wrote not long ago to that leading light of France, Budé, in which you
say that Colet has mentioned me and that my name is known to you on
other grounds as well. For though I derived great pleasure from your letter,
first because it came from you and then because it was addressed to Budé,
yet, to tell the truth, nothing in it delighted me more than the kind and   10
friendly way in which you came to speak of my humble self. Budé, indeed,
long ago claimed me entirely as his own; but he is no dog in the manger,
and will not refuse to share me, or any other common friend, with you –
such are, I know, his feelings towards you. And again I am bound to love
your friend Colet, distinguished as he is alike for learning and for holiness   15
of life, since it was he who, in your own words, recalled to you the
old-established friendship and familiarity which he and I once enjoyed to
no common degree when we were living and studying at Orléans. Such was
the value which he with his universal generosity set upon our friendship,
and so faithfully did he maintain it, that he speaks of it to you as though it   20
were a thing quite recent, undimmed by any interval of time or space, – so

* * * * *

494:5 letter] Ep 480:224–5
18 Orléans] Colet's stay at Orléans during his study on the continent is known
only from this reference; cf Ep 1211:244 seq., Lupton *Colet* 45.

unlike those who under the charm of new friendships despise or neglect the old.

For who can be so unfeeling or so ungrateful that he does not heartily wish you well as he handles all those outstanding contributions which your 25 gifts and your industry have made to every branch of knowledge? – in which you may be thought to rival Antiquity itself and carry off the prize in front of all the writers of our times, in the opinion of the whole learned world, not mine alone. From darkest depths of ignorance you rescue the noble arts and even sacred studies, and as though they returned from some 30 long exile you restore them to their crown and dignity. Your *Adagiorum chiliades*, your *Moriae encomium*, your *Miles christianus*, your *Novum instrumentum*, and other things of the same kind launched under such happy auspices from your workshop and received with such applause on their arrival here – all these, as far as my leisure permitted, I have read and 35 re-read. I have in my hands the works of Jerome, a formidable task indeed, and too much for the strength of any but our modern Hercules whose name is Erasmus, in which I fancy I see Jerome himself thanks to your care and diligence and unstinting labour returning to the light of day and forestalling in some sort the day of resurrection foretold in Holy Scripture; for now 40 that the corruptions which abounded everywhere have been cleared away, you have dressed him as it were in a new garment of immortality and restored him to his original and native glory. Then there is the help given by your annotations, so learned, so pious, so perfectly made in every way, with which you have so blocked the ancient lights of certain persons with a 45 strong desire to shine, and picked out the crow's eyes, as the saying is, that they are blinded by the splendour of your reputation and humbled by the great force of your eloquence; and so now they are obliged to surrender, to feel pity for the poverty and ignorance of their own generation, and admire the happy state of things today. Yes, you may even see them casting away 50 the coarse (not to say, sesquipedalian) verbiage with which they used to fill their bulging cheeks, and eagerly learning at last to take a just measure of their own abilities.

* * * * *

45 ancient lights] Deloynes uses metaphorically the classical doctrine of 'ancient lights' still familiar in legal circles, which forbade a man to obstruct the access of light from the sky to the windows of his neighbour's house. This is what Erasmus had done – he has put all his neighbours in the shade; cf Ep 493:488n.

46 crow's eyes] See Ep 456:24n.

52 take a just measure] Literally 'measure themselves by their own foot'; Ep 480:62–3

Forward then, dear Erasmus, on your chosen path: cease not to do
yeoman service to literature and theology, to Christian philosophy and the   55
whole polity of the Church. In this you will have the unbroken support of
Budé, and I too, if there is some minute task for me, shall be the devoted
follower of you both, and an energetic, if not eloquent, mouthpiece of your
praise and glory; though I know your achievements are far too great to need
advertisement from anyone, least of all from me. For the rest, I pray to   60
Almighty God that He may continue in you – and I mean both you and Budé
– this spirit of bringing forth new treasures every day, and may grant you
the longest possible period of activity in this life, that as you perform what
you have promised, you may conceive ever greater designs. For what you
have undertaken to produce of your own accord is expected and demanded   65
every day, and there is already some risk that, in Pliny's words, we may
have to serve you with a subpoena. Farewell, and think of me kindly.

When my friend Deloynes was just about to seal up his letter, I
interrupted him, and on his advice now add this greeting to you in my own
hand; which please accept as an old-fashioned token of friendship.   70

Sincerely,

Paris   Nicolas Bérault

495 / From Gerardus Listrius   [Zwolle, end November 1516]

Listrius (Gerard Lyster) was the rector of the school at Zwolle and the author of
an important commentary on the *Praise of Folly*: see J.A. Gavin and T.M.
Walsh 'The *Praise of Folly* in Context: The Commentary of Girardus Listrius'
Renaissance Quarterly 24.2 (Summer 1971) 193–209. He was a native of Rhenen
in the province of Utrecht; born about 1490, he died some time after 1522. He
studied at Deventer and afterward at Louvain and Cologne. On 8 April 1514 he
received his licence and doctorate in medicine at Pavia, and by August 1514
was studying medicine at the University of Basel. During this time he contributed some Greek verses to the title-page of Erasmus' translations from
Plutarch (Ep 272) and he also worked for Froben, correcting the 1515 edition of
the *Adagia* for the press (Ep 269). In 1516 he was appointed rector of the school
at Zwolle, and in 1522 rector of the Latin school at Amersfoort. See also Epp
305:189n, 337:941, 388:183n.

* * * * *

66 Pliny's words] *Epistulae* 5.10.1
72 Bérault] Cf Allen III Ep 925 introduction: Bérault was a native of Orléans
who had moved to Paris about 1512. He was a teacher and the author of many
humanistic editions.

TO ERASMUS FROM GERARDUS LISTRIUS, GREETING

As I read your letter, master Erasmus – for what other name can I use but the
name which is most familiar and most dear to the whole world? – my heart
overflowed with joy: it was so friendly and so like yourself. My life upon it, I
would not exchange it for any gold or jewels. But why does one so tongue-   5
tied open his stammering mouth in the presence of eloquence itself, which
might daunt the utterance even of a regular orator? I know what I will do:
write one word, rustic maybe, but full of the truest feelings to express my
affection for you. Jupiter strike me with his thunderbolt, if there is anything
in the world dearer to me than you are, for whom it would be a pleasure to   10
sacrifice my life, not to mention those external things which are exposed to
the caprice of fortune. Away with all whitewash, all pretence! You know
your friend Listrius to be too sincere to bring himself to any flattery. Indeed
anyone seems to me a brute or a stone who does not admire and venerate a
man as kind, fair-minded, courteous, gifted with all the virtues as yourself.   15
You will say I am talking nonsense. I know there is nothing you more
dislike hearing than the praises you so richly deserve; and so I must refrain,
however reluctantly.

If the theologians are causing trouble, that is no surprise: we know
that dogs will bark. Dorp, to be sure, has caused great surprise here among   20
all the learned besides myself, by his refusal to change his course even after
your divine eloquence and such a friendly approach; these things, if nothing else, will have saved his name from oblivion. Are you sensitive to men's
ingratitude? Master Erasmus, you are too easy-going. If you do not take
care, your modesty will prove the opposite, and your fairness of mind will   25
darken others. With your wisdom and your greatness of heart, you will
easily treat those dogs, those wasps' nests, with the contempt they deserve.

My living conditions here are not particularly attractive, partly because of my unremitting labours hard as iron, partly for my great loss in the
way of reading; for I scarcely have time to glance even sideways at a book.   30
Besides which, I do not see what fortune I am to expect here. Finally, what
little I do get is far from corresponding to their magnificent promises; I can
hardly scrape together two hundred gold pieces a year, and they promised
me four hundred. The only thing that remains, my dear Erasmus, is to
entrust to you my reputation, my fortune and myself, your devoted depen-   35
dant who depends on you alone. You started me on the path of learning,

* * * * *

495:33–4 two hundred gold pieces a year ... four hundred] Probably St Philip
florins, the chief gold coin of the Hapsburg Low Countries, so that 200 florins
= £41 13s 4d gros Flemish = £30 0s 0d sterling = £262 10s 0d tournois. Cf CWE 1
318, 320, 336–46; CWE 2 327–44; and Ep 463:48n above.

you published my name to the world, you were the founder of my fortunes;
would that some day you might finish the work! What could a man like me
have achieved or even attempted without you? Everything I have, such as it
is, I owe to you. For though by your publications and your Herculean   40
labours you have laid all posterity and not merely this present generation
under a debt, I as an individual owe you more than all. Poor creature that I
am, when shall I have the opportunity to show my gratitude in turn?

All scholars and true Christians here are devoted to you, and all the
more zealously do they await your commentaries on the Pauline Epistles.   45
The New Covenant with your explanations is read eagerly here in Greek
even by the aged. Go on your way, master Erasmus, undeterred for a
moment by the shafts of jealousy and rage; though to be sure you have
already reached such a state of virtue that ill will ought long ago to have
given way. You know that to be exposed to calumny, like croaking frogs and   50
barking curs, is a thing you share with Jerome and with Paul and with
Christ Himself. Give your humble dependant what commands you will; I
wish that you could see into my heart. But I begin to talk more nonsense. Let
me have five or six lines in reply!

496 / From Maarten van Dorp   Louvain [end November 1516]

If the opening lines of this letter are read carefully, it does not seem to be a
direct answer to Ep 438, to which at first it seems to refer. Allen suggested that
it replied to another letter written about the same time as Ep 491, in which
(lines 11–12) there is evidence of a spirit of reconciliation; cf Ep 480A introduction.

DORP TO HIS FRIEND ERASMUS, GREETING

What that very kind and also very sincere man Desmarez told you, my dear
and most learned Erasmus, you must please accept as perfect truth. I will
truly maintain the attitude towards you that he said I would; I will keep an
open mind and behave like a true Academic philosopher. Only I do beg you,   5

* * * * *

495:45 commentaries] Erasmus promised these on completing his New Testament; cf Epp 164:41–2, 296:166–8; 334:181.
496:2 Desmarez] Cf Ep 180: introduction; he was from Cassel near Saint-
Omer and had been Erasmus' host at Louvain during the time the *Panegyricus*
was written. He taught in the Faculty of Arts at Louvain and in 1490 became
public orator of the university. He contributed a letter addressed to Pieter
Gillis to the introductory matter of the *Utopia*; see *Utopia* 26–8.

as a man whose fairness of mind we all know, not to think me the immediate cause, if you suffer any criticism or misrepresentation or suspicion
on the part of certain people I could name. When you arrive, we will
consider the wider questions. I shall do my best to show you that I really
have been on your side. In the meanwhile, not a word more. I would only   10
ask you to come to us as soon as you can.

The bearer of this letter of mine is a Bavarian, by name Johannes
Langenfeld, who in my opinion, to judge by what I have learned of him in a
short time, is trustworthy, civilized, frank and learned, and a keen supporter of you and your reputation. He had a great desire to see you and speak   15
with you, and enjoy your society. He begged me for an introduction, being
convinced that a recommendation from me would carry some weight with
you, which no doubt is true. He wants nothing out of you, only to see you
and converse with you and admire you.

Whatever has passed between us, I should like to wipe off the slate,   20
and be friends without reserve. If there is any call for it, in your next edition
you will satisfy all the weaker brethren, if there still are any, who need to be
fed on milk; for like Paul, you must be all things to all men and weak with
the weak. You will find me a Christian and a friend, nor did I ever mean to
be anything else. Best wishes, and be sure to do one thing: have a talk with   25
some of our theologians, and especially with our dean, who is a most
friendly and learned man and has great experience of men and affairs, about
which that excellent scholar, my friend Pierre d'Arras will have more to tell
you. Farewell once more, and let me warmly recommend Langenfeld to you
as an educated and trustworthy person.   30

From Louvain

* * * * *

13 Langenfeld] Known as Longicampianus, Johann Gusebel of Langenfeld in
Bavaria (d 1529) had been educated at various places and was entered in the
matriculation register at Louvain as MA on 16 October 1516. Erasmus urged
him to study with Listrius at Zwolle; cf Epp 500, 504. Eventually he became a
professor of mathematics at Wittenberg; cf Hans Volz 'Johann Gusebel Longicampianus, ein unbekannter Humanist des 16. Jahrhunderts,' E. Geek and
G. Pressler eds Festschrift für Josef Benzing (Wiesbaden 1964) 456–75.
21 next edition] Of the New Testament
23 Paul] 1 Cor 9:22
26 dean] Probably Jan Briaert (d 1520) of Ath in Hainault, a professor of
theology at Louvain; cf de Vocht Literae 62.
28 Pierre d'Arras] Perhaps Pierre Barbier, a graduate of Louvain who was
corrector to Dirk Martens in 1513, and by 1516 was chaplain to Jean Le
Sauvage; cf de Vocht Literae 226–8.

497 / To Jean Desmarez   [Brussels? November 1516?]

This poem is number 104 in Reedijk. The subject of the epitaph was a son of
the count of Chimay who in 1510, while bishop of Cambrai, was created duke
of Cambrai by Maximilian. It must have been written some time between the
death of the bishop of Cambrai (15 August 1516) and the publication of the
Auctarium (August 1518) in which it was first printed.

DESIDERIUS ERASMUS OF ROTTERDAM TO
HIS FRIEND DESMAREZ, GREETING
I send you an epitaph, for I cannot refuse anything to my Desmarez. If you
do not like it (and I do not think you will), remember that it was written by a
theologian – a class of men unpopular, as you know, with the Muses.   5
Farewell.
    1517

EPITAPH IN IAMBIC TRIMETERS FOR JACQUES DE CROY,
DUKE AND BISHOP OF CAMBRAI
    Jacques, the eternal glory of his double race   10
    Of Croy and of Lalaing, now rests within this place.
    A saintly bishop and a famous duke: Cambrai,
    Which was thy greater loss, no man can safely say.
    That day he bade farewell to his mortality,
    When the Maid Mother whom he served rose to the sky.   15

498 / From Andrea Ammonio   Westminster, 4 December [1516]

This letter, a reply to Ep 483, was first published by W. Vischer *Erasmiana*
(Basel 1876) from a manuscript original in the same volume from which Ep 466
comes, Erasmuslade D 5, folios 2–3, number 2, in the Öffentliche Bibliothek of
the University of Basel.

ANDREA AMMONIO TO ERASMUS, GREETING
I write this with some difficulty, being troubled by a touch of the tertian
ague, the result of some digestive upset; while I was trying to cure that by
vomiting and fomentations, it stimulated my bile, which broke out in a
fever, from which I now for the first time seem to feel some relief. I also   5
derived no small benefit from the pleasure of receiving a letter which
arrived recently from Rome about that business of yours. I gathered that

H.H. is wonderfully well-disposed towards you, and I learnt further from
the bishop of Worcester what results it is possible to obtain, or rather, what
has been secured already; which he was reluctant to send, for fear (as is the   10
case) that we might not be satisfied. He also sent me a copy, with the idea
that, if we approve it, we should send it back to him; but if we should like
something different, he urges you to write again to the pope in detail, and
promises that he will follow up your letter with his own representations.
My advice is that you do write such a letter, and another to the bishop of   15
Worcester, to whatever effect you think most appropriate. You will find the
draft I mentioned enclosed with this letter, and in it you will see I have
added some suggestions of my own.

I wanted to consult Sixtinus and asked him to call on me, and he came;
but as it was impossible at that moment to find time to see him, I told him   20
the reason why I had sent for him, and asked him to come another time. He
said he would but he must have been detained, I suppose, by some important business. It occurred to me afterwards that it would be better to leave
the charge of this to you, so that you can discuss your own business
yourself, or entrust it to the judgment of such people as you think best.   25
When, however, you have added or subtracted what seems right, have a
fair copy made of the text that has your final approval, and send it to the
bishop of Worcester in Rome, together with my letter to him, in which I set
down what I think expedient to be done. Mind you do not forget your letter
to the All-highest, and be of a good courage. In a short time you will be a   30
happy man, for your happiness depends on something that is within your
grasp.

To the letter from you which More recently gave me, I have not much
to say in reply, except that the passage about a sort of men born for their
bellies' benefit made me laugh; I am surprised that you were able to silence   35
such a noisy lot, and that they had sufficient self-control to keep quiet. As
for our friend Tunstall, you must not take all the credit; Heaven knows I
have great misgivings in interrupting his very serious business with my
own trifles, so I try my best to take up as few of his busy moments as I can;

* * * * *

498:8 H.H.] His Holiness

9 Worcester] Silvestro Gigli; cf Ep 521 introduction.

11 copy] Evidently a draft for the approval of Erasmus and Ammonio; cf Ep
447 introduction, Ep 505:5.

19 Sixtinus] Cf Epp 430, 448.

34 passage] Cf Ep 483:18 ff.

for myself, I can always find the leisure necessary to intrude with some   40
trivial business one way or another. In any case, now that you have made
me your Aesculapius, have a prize cock ready, which you can sacrifice to me
at short notice. Look after your own health, all the same.

4 December, from Westminster
To the most eloquent and learned Erasmus of Rotterdam DD   45

499 / From Thomas More   [London, c 4 December 1516]

This letter (Rogers Ep 29) was clearly written after More wrote Ep 481 and
before he wrote Ep 502. Allen suggested that it answers a letter contemporary
with Ep 483, which More delivered to Ammonio (Ep 498:33). It may be placed
tentatively therefore with Ep 498, which replies to Ep 483.

MORE TO ERASMUS, GREETING
On the question of your horse, I have seen Urswick. He says he has not yet
found one that he thinks worth sending you, but that, unless he has sent
before then, he will do so without fail next Fair-time. I have lately sent back
to you Maruffo's bill of exchange with a more generous letter, or so he   5
assures me. I could not read it myself, nor could our friend Lily, though he
knows Italian well. The money you left with me has been in the hands of our
friend Gillis for some time now; my agent has returned, and says that he
paid it over.

My friend Palsgrave, whose attachment to you is, as you know, of long   10
standing, is off to Louvain to devote himself to the law, but on the understanding that he means to add to his stock of the humanities in Latin and
Greek, as is his way. He has heard that you will be living there, and in view

* * * * *

42 a prize cock] The sacrifice to the god of healing (cf Ep 483:37); Ammonio
thinks of the last words of Socrates, at the end of Plato's *Phaedo*.

499:2 horse] Cf Ep 481:3n.

5 Maruffo's] Cf Ep 481:89.

6 Lily] Perhaps William Lily, who had studied in Italy; cf Ep 341:18n.

7 money] Cf Ep 467:11n.

10 Palsgrave] John Palsgrave or Palgrave was a graduate of Corpus Christi
College, Cambridge (d 1544) who also studied in Paris. He was tutor in the
royal court to the sister of Henry VIII, the Lady Mary, and in October 1514
accompanied her to France when she married Louis XII. In 1533 he was
collated to St Dunstan in the East by Cranmer, having in the meantime
become tutor to the Duke of Richmond, the king's bastard son. His principal
work was the French grammar, *Lesclarcissement de la langue francoyse* (STC
19166). See McConica 120–1.

of his old acquaintance with you reckons that he can count on you for anything; but all the same (just see how high I am supposed to rank in your 15 favour, a fact in which I exult as much, I swear, as other men pride themselves on the friendship of kings) he has asked me with some urgency to be sure to add my own recommendation to the good will he thinks he already enjoys with you on his own account; he wants to be allowed to enjoy your advice and help in his pursuit of a liberal education. I know, my 20 dear Erasmus, I need waste few words in asking you to assist the studies of a man who is devoted to good literature, full of promise, known to be a hard worker, and his progress hitherto is already familiar to you; one moreover who is both my friend and yours, which means yours twice over; for long ago you took it upon yourself as a sort of regular duty to spend all your time, 25 day and night, in promoting all men's studies. Though, if this can add anything to the heap, I ask you further to give Palsgrave a still more generous share of what you refuse to nobody. I have given him for delivery to you all the letters which were sent to you some time ago by your friends in Basel and have been lying in my hands all this time. This has turned out very 30 conveniently; for no more reliable person could offer himself to carry them, nor could he himself wish for anything more likely to secure him a welcome than a large bundle of letters from very dear and learned friends, awaited for so long and almost despaired of. I have, however, instructed him not to hand them over except against a formal undertaking from you to accept 35 them solely on condition that he is agreeable to you in every respect.

I listen day by day and 'with pricked-up ears I stand,' for news of your Sicilian adventure, which I pray may turn out happily. I had a letter the other day from Tunstall, full of the most friendly feeling; I promise you, his opinion of my republic, so frank and so favourable, cheered me more, 40 dearest Erasmus, than a nugget of pure gold. So you can't think how I now fancy myself; I have grown taller, I hold my head higher, for I have continually before my eyes the perpetual office of prince which my Utopians are planning to confer on me. In fact I see myself already crowned with that distinguished diadem of corn-ears, a splendid sight in my Franciscan robe, 45 bearing that venerable sceptre consisting of a sheaf of corn, and accom-

* * * * *

29 letters] Cf Ep 481:9n.
37 pricked-up ears] Virgil *Aeneid* 2.303
38 adventure] Cf Epp 475:5n, 486:11n.
39 Tunstall] See Rogers Ep 84 for More's reply to this letter.
40 republic] *Utopia*
41 nugget] Literally 'than an Attic talent'
45 diadem of corn-ears] Cf *Utopia* 150–5.

panied by a distinguished company of citizens of Amaurote. Thus equipped, at the head of a long procession, I greet the envoys and the rulers of
other countries, who are greatly to be pitied compared with us, however
much they may foolishly pride themselves on their childish finery and the   50
women's ornaments with which they are bedizened, loaded with chains of
contemptible gold and made to look absurd with purple and gems and other
such airy nothings. Not but what I should be sorry if either you or our friend
Tunstall judged my nature by the analogy of other people's, whose character changes with their fortunes. For my part, although it has pleased heaven   55
to raise my humble self to my present sublime elevation, with which I think
no monarch's place is to be compared, yet you will never find me forgetful of
the old and tried relationship which I enjoyed with you when I was a
private citizen. If you will not find it unbearable to make the brief journey,
and come to visit me in Utopia, I will at once ensure that all mortal men   60
living under my merciful government receive you with the honour due to
those whom they know to be very dear to their own prince.

I hoped to continue this delicious dream a little longer, but alas, dawn
is breaking, and has shattered it and turned me out of my princedom,
recalling me to my treadmill in the market-place. My only consolation is   65
that I see real kingdoms do not last much longer. Farewell, dearest Erasmus.

500 / From Gerardus Listrius   Zwolle [about December 1516]

This letter is dated from the reference to Langenfeld (Longicampianus) in Ep
496:29–30.

GERARDUS LISTRIUS TO MASTER ERASMUS, GREETING
I have done what I could for Langenfeld, whom you recommended to me,
by teaching him Greek; but either because there seemed little to be made
out of it or because it needed so much time, he has turned his attention to
mathematics, which he hopes will be more profitable, and in that subject he   5
seems to me to have made unusual progress. The fathers here, and indeed
everyone of any education, who are very jealous for your good repute, urge
you strongly to write a commentary on the Pauline Epistles, as you have
often promised to do, and when it is written to publish it without delay. My
dear and honoured Erasmus, I speak in all sincerity: you yourself would   10

* * * * *

53 airy nothings] Persius 5.19
500:2 Langenfeld] Cf Ep 496:13n.
9 promised] Cf Ep 495:45n.

hardly believe what a service you would render to the Church, that is, to every thinking Christian, if you would publish those volumes soon. I feel that so many people have been won over and inspired by what you write, and are now devoted to the study of Scripture and the Christian way of life, leaving behind them the husks which the swine did eat, by which I mean   15
the pagan authors. Among these, you have certainly won me for Christ, if Christ by His grace vouchsafes that I should not stray from the path of life which I have set before me. The business of the school distracts me so much that I scarcely have the leisure to open a book now and again at long intervals; but whenever I am able to steal any time from those distractions,   20
it is all spent reading the Gospels and St Paul's Epistles.

I hear from de Keysere that Reuchlin is having his *Ars cabalistica* and *Philosophia Pythagorica* printed by Thomas Anshelm. I have sown the seed of Greek here to such good purpose that the boys can already write exercises in Greek as a matter of course. One thing torments me, that I am not yet in a   25
position to throw out that barbarous logic – the barbarous grammar I sent packing long ago. If a humble friend like myself can be of use to you in any respect, treat me as your devoted servant. You know my feelings. Farewell. From Zwolle.

It is strange, master Erasmus, yet perfectly true: not a night passes   30
without my finding myself in your company. All last night we were to-gether at Basel, if I may even tell you my dreams. So deeply are you implanted in my heart.

501 / From Georgius Spalatinus   Lochau, 11 December 1516

Georg Burkhard of Spalt near Nürnberg (1480–1545) was a graduate of Erfurt and Wittenberg (MA 1502). He made his career as a tutor and secretary in the ducal court of Saxony, where he was instrumental in winning the support of the Elector Frederick for Luther in 1521. His influence at court was also used for the interest of the University of Wittenberg. He translated into German works by Plutarch, Luther, Melanchthon and Erasmus (among them the *Institutio principis christiani*) and wrote a life of Duke Frederick. This letter constitutes Erasmus' real introduction to Luther, appropriately enough over the momentous issue of justification by faith.

* * * * *

15 husks] Luke 15:16

22 de Keysere] Cf Ep 301:39n.

22 *Ars cabalistica*] Published in March 1517 and dedicated to Leo x

23 Thomas Anshelm] The printer, now of Haguenau, associated with Reuchlin; cf Ep 397 introduction.

GEORGIUS SPALATINUS TO ERASMUS, GREETING

While I have long had the most devoted and respectful feelings towards you
as a most learned and distinguished person, on account of your exceptional
scholarship and the many and great services you have rendered to all true
studies and humane learning, I have never heretofore had what I thought a   5
sufficient opportunity to interrupt you, fully occupied as you are with
putting not so much fresh strength as completely new life into the commonwealth of literature, with a letter, for which litter would be a better
name. And so neither our common friend Philipp of Engen nor C. Mutianus
Rufus, my teacher – a learned and honourable man who is not only devoted   10
to you but a former fellow-pupil of yours, if I rightly understood him, in
Deventer school under Alexander Hegius – was able to persuade me to
write to you, though both wrote and urged me to do so in the last few years.
In any case, having lately been urged to pay my respects to you by an
Augustinian priest, as well known for his holiness in life as for his distinc-   15
tion in theology, who is also one of the most sincere upholders of your
reputation, I thought it would be wrong not to seize this opportunity to
write to you, busy though I am, all the more so as I hope for some public
benefit both present and future from the business which has compelled me
to write to you now. So although this Augustinian, who is, I assure you, a   20
man of great intellectual integrity and a most loyal friend, has saddled the
ox (as the saying goes), yet when I remembered the warmth of his kindly
feelings towards me, I thought it better to seem discourteous, if so it turns
out, than not to do a service to a very close friend. If you, with your
exceptional goodness as well as wisdom, understand this letter of mine in   25
the spirit in which it is written, I hope that you will not only add my name
for the future to the standing list of your dependants or supporters, but

* * * * *

501:9 Philipp] Cf Ep 344:52n.

9–10 Mutianus Rufus] Konrad Mut (d 1526) was educated at Deventer and at
the University of Erfurt (MA 1492). From 1495 to 1502 he studied at various
Italian centres, and in 1503 became a canon of Gotha, where he spent the rest
of his life. His correspondence with humanists and reformers is an important
source for the history of the reform movement; see Carl Krause *Der Briefwechsel des Mutianus Rufus* (Cassel 1885), K. Killert *Der Briefwechsel des Conradus Mutianus* (Halle 1890).

12 Hegius] Rector of the school at Deventer; see Ep 23:59n.

15 Augustinian] The text from line 51 to 76 is taken almost word for word from
a letter of Luther to Spalatinus of 19 October 1516; cf *D. Martin Luthers Werke,
Briefwechsel* 1 Band (Weimar 1930) Nr 27 lines 5–16, 25–37.

21–2 saddled the ox] Given a task to the wrong man; *Adagia* II ix 84

moreover will do a service to all devoted students of Holy Scripture and of the pure and unspoilt traditional theology, for all time to come and not merely in this present age – a service all the more effective inasmuch as the   30
subject is of great importance.

After this preamble, as it were, I beseech you in the name of Christ to take my letter in good part, for, as God is my witness, it has no other object except, by introducing me to you, to satisfy the request of a friend, a most religious man, and to enable me to see someday that my acquaintance with   35
a great scholar has been profitable even to posterity. There is no spiteful cunning hidden in my request; no, we are all devoted to you, all of us who have signed on as students of a new and better learning. The output of your gifted mind is held in such high esteem among us that nothing is more eagerly sought for in the fairs or more quickly sold out at the booksellers or   40
more diligently read. My most merciful prince, Duke Frederick of Saxony, Elector of the Holy Roman Empire, who is as eminent for wisdom, religion and learning as he is rich, has in his ducal library every book of yours that I have been able to find, and intends to buy any others that you may hereafter publish anywhere in the world. He has lately seen with admiration the   45
works of St Jerome so well restored in your edition that before you corrected them anyone might have supposed we possessed any author's works rather than Jerome's.

Why do I say this? With this in mind, kindest of men, to make you more ready to be convinced that I write in a friendly spirit. My friend writes   50
to me that in interpreting St Paul you understand justification by works, whether under the Law or of a man's self, as referring to the ceremonial and figurative observances laid down in the Law; and secondly that you would not have the Apostle in his epistle to the Romans to be speaking at all about original sin. He thinks therefore that you should read Augustine in his   55
treatises against the Pelagians, especially the *De spiritu et littera*, also the *De peccatorum meritis et remissione*, the *Contra duas epistolas Pelagianorum* and the *Contra Julianum*, which are nearly all in volume eight, and see how Augustine has added nothing of his own, but follows the sense of Cyprian, Nazianzen, Irenaeus, Hilary, Olympius, Innocent and Ambrose; and then   60
you will not only understand the Apostle correctly but also pay much

* * * * *

51 justification by works] Rom 3.19 ff
58 volume eight] That is, of Amerbach's *editio princeps*; cf Ep 309:9n.
60 Olympius] Known to Luther in the correspondence of Augustine, whose Epp 96 and 97 were addressed to him; CSEL 34:514–20; Pauly-Wissowa Bd 18.1 cols 246–7

greater reverence to St Augustine. My friend, then, simply cannot suppose that justification under the Law or by works refers merely to ceremonies; it consists rather in the keeping of the whole Ten Commandments. If all this could take place outside the Christian faith, even if it resulted in characters 65 like Fabricius and Regulus and the most upright men who ever lived, yet among men it would have no more the true flavour of justification than a service-apple can taste like a fig; his view is that we do not become just by performing just actions, as Aristotle supposed, except in a manner of speaking, but that we become just first and then act justly. For the person 70 must first be changed, and then his works; for Abel was pleasing to God, and afterwards his gifts. Although therefore he both expects and wishes that you should carry world-wide authority, he is afraid that you will encourage people to rush to the defence of the dead, that is, the literal, interpretation, which has filled the work of almost everyone since Augus- 75 tine.

This is the question, most learned of men, which my friend wished to submit to you as a kind of Pythian Apollo through me as intermediary; and I beg you to listen to me, if not for my sake, for that of the whole common-wealth of theology. And so you will give pleasure to us all, and act as a 80 religious man like you should act, if you accept this letter kindly and oblige your honest friend by sending me an answer, however brief, counting this as some return both to my affection for you and to the lively interest and respect that my illustrious prince has for you and Dr Reuchlin and all learned men. For in the list of those who love and respect you I shall never 85 be found among the last. Farewell, most learned of men.

In haste, from Lochau, a castle of Duke Frederick of Saxony, 11 December 1516

It will also give great pleasure to me and all your other supporters in this part of the world, if when you answer you will tell me what you expect 90 to publish after the works of Jerome, and what you have on the stocks now. For you should know that it will give great pleasure to my prince, who is so keen on scholarship and so anxious to learn, if he can take a holiday from

* * * * *

66 Fabricius and Regulus] Fabricius was a Roman leader in the war against Pyrrhus (third century BC); a common type of ancient virtue. Regulus was a Roman general in the first Punic War; his exalted sense of duty is immortalized in Horace *Odes* 3.5.
87 Lochau] A castle of the dukes of Saxony, about 20 kilometres south-east of Wittenberg

graver business and either read something or listen with great satisfaction
to its being read.   95

502 / From Thomas More   London, 15 December [1516]

This letter (Rogers Ep 30) is an important link in the history of the famous
satirical dialogue, *Julius exclusus*, providing evidence of the existence of a
manuscript in Erasmus' hand (line 11). For the text of the dialogue see *Opuscula* 65–124 and Ferguson's editorial introduction on the issue of authorship.
For a general review of the problem and the history of recent scholarship see
J.K. McConica 'Erasmus and the *Julius*: a Humanist Reflects on the Church'
The Pursuit of Holiness in Late Medieval and Renaissance Religion, edited by
Charles Trinkaus with Heiko A. Oberman (Leiden 1974), 444–71. Erasmus
always denied authorship of the *Julius exclusus*, which did not appear in any of
the official lists and collections of his writings. The text of this letter in the
Deventer Letter-book, reproduced here, shows the year date '1517' added in a
later hand; cf Allen I 607.

THOMAS MORE TO MASTER ERASMUS, GREETING
No doubt you have received the letter from me, dearest Erasmus, which
Palsgrave took over to deliver to you, and with it the letters of your friends in
Basel. I am delighted at Dorp's repentance; hard words seem to have
softened him, after kindness had only made him more ferocious. It is a fact   5
that some men are like that by nature: if you yield a little, they grow
insolent, whereas if you treat them with disdain, their spirit is broken and
they trot at your heels. I am woefully anxious, if it could be conveniently
arranged, to read the letters that passed between you in each direction.
    Lupset has given me back some notebooks of yours, which he had had   10

* * * * *

502:2 letter] Ep 499

3 Palsgrave] Cf Ep 499:10n.

4 repentance] Cf Ep 491:11–12, Rogers Ep 15.

9 letters] Cf Ep 477:13n.

10 notebooks] Cf Epp 431:10, 543:39. Erasmus had left compositions dating
back to his first years in Paris (cf Ep 30:16n) with Pace in December 1508; of
these he is known to have recovered only the first book of the *Antibarbari* and
part of the second which was never published. In light of Lupset's involve-
ment with the history of Erasmus' papers, it is relevant to note that in October
1515 he accompanied Pace to Italy, but by June of the next year he had returned
to England. In 1517 he went to Paris to study, and during that time supervised
the printing of the second edition of the *Utopia*.

Letter from Thomas More to Erasmus, Epistle 502
Deventer Letter-book, f 129r-v
Stads– en Athenaeumbibliotheek, Deventer

by him for some time. Among them is the *Julii genius*, and two orations, one on why children's education should start young, and the other a speech of consolation; in your writing, all of them, but first drafts only, and nothing really complete. Aside from these, he swears that none of those things of yours which you want are in his keeping. If you would like these to be sent to you, let me know forthwith.

Linacre will send his Galen-translation to Paris immediately after Christmas to be printed, accompanied by Lupset, who will stand over the printer and correct the proofs. You have no idea how pleased he was with the way you spoke of his books in the letter you wrote me lately; take my word for it, he is all yours, heart and soul. The bishop of Winchester (a man of excellent judgment, as you know), in a large gathering of notables, when some mention of you and your labours came up, declared amid general approval that he found your version of the New Testament as good as ten commentaries: it shed so much light to have the same matter expressed in good Latin without the Greek habits of expression, even if there had been no other faults in the Vulgate that needed to be changed. As for my *Utopia*, your letter gave me hope, on which I batten greedily, and I now expect it daily with the feelings of a mother expecting her son's return from foreign parts. Farewell, dearest Erasmus.

London, 15 December, in haste

I sent your letter on to Latimer, and have no doubt he will do as you wish, and gladly too. My wife bids me send you a thousand greetings, and I

* * * * *

11 orations] The *De pueris instituendis* was written at Rome in 1509 as part of the *De copia* (Ep 260 introduction) and was then developed as the *De pueris statim ac liberaliter instituendis* published by Froben in September 1529; cf ASD 1-2 1–78. The *De morte declamatio*, written at Siena in 1509, was first published by Froben with the *Querela pacis* December 1517. It also appeared in the Froben (first authorized) edition of the *De conscribendis epistolis*, August 1522; cf Allen III Ep 604 introduction.

17 Galen] *De sanitate tuenda* (Paris: G. Le Rouge 1517). A preface by Linacre was addressed to Henry VIII, dated London, 16 June 1517. At one time it was thought Bade would do the printing; cf Ep 534:60–1.

20 letter] Not extant

21 all yours] Cf Ep 388:164n.

21 Winchester] Richard Foxe, founder of Corpus Christi College, Oxford; cf Ep 187 introduction. On the matter of his interest in Erasmus' new Latin version of the New Testament, see CWE 3 page 220.

32 letter] Cf Ep 520:3.

33 wife] Alice, widow of a London mercer, John Middleton; Thomas More took her as his second wife in the autumn of 1511.

am to thank you for your highly polished message, in which you wished her
a long life. She is all the more eager for this, she says, because it means she   35
can plague me all the longer.

503 / From Pierre Vitré   [Paris] 18 December 1516

Vitré was apparently a former pupil of Erasmus, who had been teaching
school in Paris; cf Ep 444.

PIERRE VITRÉ TO MASTER ERASMUS OF ROTTERDAM, GREETING
Cordial greetings, my most devoted teacher. It is a great grief to me that you
should no longer spare me a thought, for in the old days you were the one
person whose support kept me in good health and spirits. I suppose you
sent me here on purpose that I might have to forego the sight of you, which I   5
enjoy so much, and might be forbidden to enjoy the pleasure of your
conversation. Imagine my feelings, when I am greeted everywhere as a
pupil of Erasmus, which I owe to your undying kindness, and yet cannot
display the merest scrap of a letter written to me. You have completely
forgotten me, you are too hard and cruel to a pupil who loves you sadly. As   10
heaven is my witness, while I write, my eyes so fill with tears that I have to
keep my face away from my paper, such is my longing and so madly do I
wish for a letter from you. You will say perhaps that I on my side have not
written to you. But I have, I have, and that often. So I am greatly surprised if
no letter has reached you, or (what I cannot believe) if you have ignored   15
them or treated them as waste paper; though I do know you to be so fully
occupied with important work that you scarcely can find time to scratch
your ear. None the less, you ought to spare a thought sometimes for your
friends, especially for one who has set all his hopes in you alone, and
having enjoyed your help and support and recommendation, looks up to   20
you and reveres you as if you were some deity in human shape.
So please be sure of this, my dearest teacher: if you desert me, it will be
as grievous a blow to me now as it was in the old days greatly to my honour
and profit to be praised by a man like you, no mortal but divine almost, or at
least endowed with divine and immortal wisdom. And so I adjure you in   25
the name of our ancient friendship and of your great gifts, be so good as to

* * * * *

503:5 here] Cf Ep 444 introduction.
8 kindness] Cf Ep 66 introduction.
17–8 to scratch your ear] A phrase in common use, to which in *Adagia* II iii 15
Erasmus produces a parallel from Lucian.

send me at least a message of greeting. This will mean more to me than to be loaded with riches by some generous king. About the work on which I am engaged I will write no more now, for I told you about it in my last letter. I will only say that I am almost worn out by the effort of teaching the young;   30 and when there is any respite, I take refuge with your friend Grey, to have a talk about you since we cannot see you. He is a great friend of mine partly on his own merits but much more because I easily detected that he is a very devoted friend of yours. But time summons me to my regular task, that is, to teach the young. If you love me, dear Erasmus, do not forget your friend   35 Vitré.

From the Collège de Navarre, 18 December 1516

504 / From Gerardus Listrius   Zwolle, 28 December [1516]

This letter apparently accompanied the Greek manuscript of the Gospels which reached Erasmus in January from the prior of St Agnes; cf Ep 515: 5–6. P.S. Allen speculated that the manuscript might have been brought from Rome by Wessel Gansfort, who spent some of his last years at Mount St Agnes; cf Allen III xxvi.

LISTRIUS TO MASTER ERASMUS, GREETING

The moment I had read your letter, dear Master Erasmus, I hastened off to Mount St Agnes in hopes of sending you the Greek Gospels as soon as I could; but, as luck would have it, the prior had lent it to some reverend father near Cleves. I therefore secured a letter from father prior, and dis-   5 patched my servant to the darkest recesses of Cleves. Meanwhile a booksel-ler arrived from your part of the world, who said that there was a wide-spread rumour thereabouts that you had set off for England, and so I wondered whether to send the book or no. But I decided to send it, for most of these rumours have nothing in them. All the same, I fear the book may   10 not be much use to you.

Johannes Langenfeld is toiling away here admirably at both mathema-tics and Greek; but I am overwhelmed by such a mass of work, both for myself and the school, that I have hardly a moment to open a book. It is

* * * * *

31 Grey] See Ep 58 introduction.

504:3 Mount St Agnes] House of Austin canons near Zwolle which was the home of Thomas à Kempis

4 prior] Possibly Gerard of Kloster, a man learned in Greek and Hebrew; cf Allen IV Ep 1116.

12 Langenfeld] Cf Ep 496:13n.

incredible how much reading I lose as a result of this, and the reward is far   15
from adequate to the labour; but I will do as you and the excellent Fathers
tell me to do, and stick to it. For I should like to do as much as even a man
like me can do for the benefit of other men; and since my gifts are too
modest to do this with my pen, I will attempt by teaching and counselling
and a pure and upright life to see if my small powers can serve our German   20
youth. For I have long ago said goodbye, my dear Erasmus, to the world, by
which I mean, to pleasure and ambition.

I have lately been offered by some of my friends a modest canonry at
Utrecht; but as the offer was not entirely innocent of simony, I refused it,
although there was no lack of friends who promised of their own accord to   25
lend me the money. I would rather live Christ's servant in my own proper
poverty, than live the devil's in riches. The prior of St Agnes, your devoted
supporter, is well. He and Father Koechman, with whom I live, who
publicly proclaims your virtues, send their greetings. My own affection for
you needs no testimony in writing, for every man who has been in Zwolle   30
can bear witness to it. Stand your ground, good Master Erasmus, continue
to despise your critics, and give thanks to God, whose will it is that you
should have this in common with Himself, to be ill spoken of by those for
whom you have done most.

Farewell. From Zwolle, 28 December   35

505 / To Andrea Ammonio   [Brussels,] 29 December 1516

This letter seems to reflect Erasmus' expectations of ecclesiastical favours from
the Court in Brussels, and his consequent anxiety to bring the issues before
the Papal Court to a conclusion; cf Epp 470 introduction. It was first published
in the *Farrago*.

ERASMUS TO HIS FRIEND AMMONIO, GREETING
In the name of your own prosperity and my misfortunes (and may heaven
make one permanently your own and the others lighter for me to bear), dear
Ammonio kindest of men, do write and urge the bishop of Worcester to
bring my business to an end, at least in accordance with the draft that was   5
sent here, if he thinks he ought not to trouble Leo further; once that is

* * * * *

28 Koechman] Jan Koechman (fl 1481–1520), sixth rector of the Fraterhaus of
Zwolle in 1491
505:4 Worcester] Silvestro Gigli; cf Ep 521 introduction.
5 draft] Cf the reference in Ep 498:11.

finished, the rest will go all right. Almost all the leading men at this Court are my supporters, and particularly the chancellor and the king himself.

I hear that some theologians, I know not who, are working to secure a public decree delegating the examination of my writings to the university   10
of Louvain and its sister in Cologne. If this comes off, for one thing this will keep them busy for two years, and for another, whoever gives them the task of this examination gives them likewise instructions to learn Greek and Latin, in which they are equally lacking. Though I think this will prove a wind-egg; for all the best people here are on my side, and even among the   15
theologians the leaders wish me well. So-and-so begins to be a laughing-stock; and yet all this time that mischief-maker is getting something out of it in the way of reputation, for before this he was almost unknown in Louvain.

I wrote about my business a few days ago by a courier of Tunstall's.   20
Tunstall has the highest opinion of you and your capacities. They say there is soon to be a meeting of the leading princes at Cambrai, Maximilian, the French king and our Charles; at it there will be a discussion on a permanent peace. I beg you urgently, my dear Andrea, to hasten our business as much as you can. I will see to it that I cannot deservedly be called ungrateful.   25
Farewell.

Morrow of the Holy Innocents, 1516

506 / From Álvar Gómez   [Brussels? end of 1516?]

The writer was Álvar Gómez of Ciudad Real, a Spanish nobleman and poet (1488–1538) who had a long military career and who dedicated a poem, *De militia velleris aurei*, to Prince Charles. It is clear that the work was written in Flanders between the proclamation of Charles as king of Spain and his setting out for the Peninsula in September 1517. A complimentary piece of thirty-seven lines by Erasmus is found in the *De militia* (Toledo 1540); see Reedijk 324 and poem 105. The identification is that of F.K.H. Kossmann in *Het Boek* 26 (1942) 357–64; see also Bataillon 648n. For Erasmus' attitude to the flood of Spanish visitors in the spring of 1517, see Ep 545: 16–19 and Allen III 125 3–4.

* * * * *

8 chancellor] Jean Le Sauvage; cf Ep 410 introduction.
16 So-and-so] Dorp; cf Ep 474:19n. Erasmus' continued expression of dislike for Dorp even after acknowledging his desire for reconciliation (cf Ep 502:4) probably reflects the real cause of his anxiety, the fate of his petition in Rome.
20 I wrote] A reply to Ep 498
22 Cambrai] The conference took place in March 1517.

ÁLVAR THE NOBODY TO ERASMUS OF ROTTERDAM, GREETING

You, Erasmus, are a great scholar, and as such well-known to me; I am a
man by name Álvar whom you do not know. And I am sending you some
verses, which you can use in congratulating our friend Marliano on his
nomination to a bishopric, in which Aesculapius, once regarded by the   5
foolish pagans as the god of medicine, complains that he himself, eminent
physician as he then was, was smitten by a thunderbolt for bringing a man
back from the dead (or so he says); while Luigi Marliano has received a
mitre, and with it, by right of his coronation by the Church, the power of
launching the anathema, that is, of dispatching thunderbolts, even against   10
Aesculapius himself. Farewell, and forgive my irregular and unruly writing, the work of a hand hasty and unskilled, which stumbles after the letters
where it should show them the way.

507 / To Ludwig Baer   Brussels, 1 January 1517

This letter, like that to which it replies (Ep 488) was first printed in the
Epistolae elegantes 1517.

FROM ERASMUS OF ROTTERDAM TO LUDWIG BAER,

FROM THE LOWEST OF THEOLOGIANS TO THEIR CHIEF, GREETING

Whether you are right to congratulate me, my good friend Baer, I do not yet
know; but at least it shows true friendship to dream that a position has
fallen to your friend's lot such as you with your kind heart would wish. But   5
whatever this lot of mine may be, if you knew what I aimed at you would
think it something quite new; if you consider what I deserve you will find it
large; consider the spirit in which I receive it and you will find it is
sufficient; though I have converted the prebend into an annuity, taking a
loss in income rather than lose any of my free time, which means more to me   10
than money. How right am I to be fond of you, kindest of men, who keep up
with me when I am far away with the same warmth with which you always
met me when I was with you. Ill will may very well be earned by men who
make grand claims for themselves or by some rare sort of learning put other
men's reputations in the shade or elbow others out of the way in order to   15
exalt themselves. But what business has ill will with me, who make no

* * * * *

506:4 verses] Printed in LB III^b 1857–8

4 Marliano] See Ep 411:10n. His predecessor in the see died on 18 October
1516. Erasmus was undoubtedly conscious of his influence in the Spanish
court.

507:13 may very well] Reading *mereantur* for *merebantur*

claims and with my modest attainments stand between no man and the
sun, nor do I set myself ahead of any other man or even level with him? I
merely use what little energy I have to aid as best I can the cause of learning.
Some people find me in places too outspoken, too passionate; but only   20
those who do not consider the unworthy treatment meted out to sacred
literature and to the writings of the sainted Fathers. While I was proceeding
with my actual work, the indignation that boiled within me at this monstrous affair was often restrained by reason, but I could not conceal it
everywhere. Even so, I was later made more cautious by some men's   25
astonishing readiness to take offence; for, if it is at all possible, I should
wish to further the advancement of learning in such a way as to irritate
absolutely nobody. If that proves out of reach, my discomfort is somewhat
lessened, first by a good conscience, and then by the approval of those
whom all men most approve. And my hope is that what fair-minded people   30
now accept will one day be accepted by everybody. Far be it from me, at any
rate, ever to accept anything in the way of ignorance or impiety, even in my
own books. Farewell.

　　When you see his lordship the bishop of Basel, play the part of a letter
from me. How well, how well I remember and always shall what I owe to   35
that eminent man.

　　Brussels, 1 January 151[6]

508 / From William Blount, Lord Mountjoy   Tournai, 4 January [1517]

Your letter has come, and with it the book about the island of Utopia which
you sent me; and for both, you may be sure, I am most grateful, since the
letter comes from you, my very dear friend, and the author of the book is a
man I place in the very first rank, both as a scholar and my special friend. I
have not read his work yet, being overwhelmed with business, but I expect   5
to read it soon from end to end, so that though I am not in a position to enjoy
the society of my beloved More, I may at least see his reflection in his
Utopia. Apart from that, I wish very much for news of all your affairs:
whether you are enjoying the society of our friend Tunstall, a man who for
many reasons you must find most agreeable, and whether you have secured   10
possession of the prebend recently conferred on you or some regular allowance from the prince, which would mean profit no less than pleasure. For
though it is far beyond my own capacity to make you rich by any gift such as

*　*　*　*　*

508:1　letter] Not extant

1　book] Possibly sent at this time as a new year's present; cf *Utopia* clxxxiv.

11　prebend] Cf Ep 436:6n.

you deserve, I should not like to seem so ungrateful as not to long for you to
be made happy by others, so that you can at last devote yourself to a life of   15
learned leisure, to the common advantage of all lovers of good literature.
Meanwhile, look after yourself, and remember that if you have any spare
time and are so kind as to visit us, you will give us great pleasure.

As for my return to England, all is still obscure. Please remember me
warmly to his reverence the chancellor. Once more, farewell. From Tournai,   20
4 January

Your sincere friend, W. Mountjoy

509 / From Maarten van Dorp   Louvain [January 1517]

Erasmus visited Louvain briefly in January 1517, probably to establish better
relations with the theologians there, and perhaps at the invitation of Dorp. At
any rate, this invitation from Dorp to Erasmus and Jean Desmarez (Paludanus)
marks a further stage in the reconciliation of the two men; cf Ep 487 introduction. P.S. Allen held that the reference to the purchase of a copy of the Jerome,
which had arrived in the Netherlands in October 1516 (Epp 474, 475), places
the date of the dinner here adumbrated earlier than July, when Erasmus finally
settled at Louvain. A case can be made however for the later date, as was
pointed out by H. De Jongh *Revue d'histoire ecclésiastique* 12 (1911) 115–6.

MAARTEN VAN DORP TO MASTER ERASMUS, GREETING
If I have not yet come to visit you, my dear Erasmus, as I have often wished
to do and as your distinguished merits would make proper, please do not
think me discourteous or neglectful, though I should prefer the latter, but
ascribe it to the business by which I have been hard-pressed for some days.   5
In future, if it will not be a burden on you, I shall be with you often. I am
now writing to ask you to give me the pleasure of your company at dinner
on Sunday, together with Master Desmarez. Athensis will be there, and
several other people who are enthusiastic supporters of yourself and the
scholarship for which you stand. I bought the St Jerome some time ago in   10
quires, for fifteen and a half Rhenish florins, and am reading it with close
attention. Farewell, and count me your friend.

From the College of theologians

* * * * *

19 return] Mountjoy was relieved of his command shortly after this date, and
returned to England 22 January; cf LP ii 2578, 2825.

509:8 Athensis] Jan Briaert of Ath; cf Ep 496:26n. He was probably vice-
chancellor of the University of Louvain at this time.

11 fifteen and a half Rhenish florins] gold florins of the Four Electors (*Renen-*

510 / From Adriaan Cornelissen van Baerland   [Louvain, January 1517]

This letter was evidently written after Ep 492, to which the writer refers (line 6), and before Ep 512 (cf Ep 512 line 33) and thus during Erasmus' visit in January.

FROM ADRIAAN VAN BAERLAND TO MASTER ERASMUS, GREETING
I walked with you yesterday, my most learned Master Erasmus, from your house as far as St Peter's, but after that, when I was hoping for a longer talk with you, you somehow gave me the slip, so I must now commit to paper what I was hoping to discuss with you in person. I have recently composed, 5
by way of practising my pen, two longish letters, one to a brother of mine who is devoted to good literature about your writings, of whose elegance he has always been a passionate admirer like myself; the other to Borssele, my fellow-countryman and a keen supporter of yours, the subject of which is the remarkable kindness I have received from Jérôme de Busleyden. These 10
two letters, I know, are quite unworthy of the attention of a phoenix among scholars like yourself, but I am sending them none the less, to give you at long last an idea of my more than ordinary devotion to you and your incomparable learning. I am no scholar myself, but I love and admire scholars; and among them the first place is yours, and to you I am entirely 15
devoted. It is for you to decide. My letters shall be consigned to the flames if they are no good; if they are any good and are not intolerable, they shall be recalled to the drawer from which I took them to send to you, for print and daylight and the public still frighten them. Farewell, pride of Germany, and let us be friends if I deserve it. 20

* * * * *

sibus), worth £3 14s 11d gros Flemish = £2 12s 11d sterling = £22 17s 3d tournois. The book was thus expensive: the price of 624.3 dozen eggs, or of 401.3 lb of butter, or of 319.2 litres of red Rhine wine in Brabant during 1517. Cf CWE 1 316–17, 336–46; CWE 2 327–44; Ep 463:48n above.

13 College of theologians] This was the Collegium Sancti Spiritus.

510:3 St Peter's] The university church at Louvain; the letter was therefore written during Erasmus' visit in January, since it is prior to Ep 512.

6 brother] Cf Ep 492 introduction.

8 Borssele] Jan Becker van Borssele; cf Ep 291 introduction.

10 Busleyden] The learned ecclesiastical diplomat and patron of scholars; cf Ep 205 introduction.

19 pride of Germany] On this see CWE 3 xii–xiii, Ep 310 etc.

511 / From Augustinus Aggeus   Paris, 10 January [1517?]

The writer was a native of The Hague who had graduated from the University of Paris; cf Ep 291:4n.

TO MASTER ERASMUS FROM AUGUSTINUS AGGEUS
THE PHYSICIAN, GREETING
I have often thought of writing to you, my dear Erasmus, but modesty has restrained me, from fear that with your exquisite taste and almost more than human learning, your ears would be deafened by a letter from me that 5 was uneducated and uncouth to the point of barbarism. So great is the relapse of which I am conscious since I saw you, deprived as I am of your society and of all the advice derived from your wide reading – a relapse in my pursuit of good literature, to which I then made my bow, as it were, from the threshold, under your guidance, and also a loss to my wits, which 10 rust when they are not used. Besides this, when I left you in England and returned with our friend Sixtinus from a kind of exile to my own country and my relatives and friends, I found a state of universal misery and distress, which were whipped up by a party of madmen until they broke out into new storms of war which grew more disastrous day by day. And so 15 the pain of present and the fear of future misfortune (which overwhelmed before my eyes not only friends and relatives but my country and indeed the whole nation) froze the current of my soul 'and the chill blood stood icy round my heart,' so that I had neither opportunity nor will even to think of the Muses and the peaceful pursuit of literature. Those men too who can 20 restore the spirit shipwrecked on such a sea, I mean the philosophers, were not to be had, and this added greatly to my intellectual calamity, for I heard no word of literature or philosophy, but instead only 'Cry havoc!' 'And this was the greatest and most pitiful of my misfortunes. I would write more often to you and at greater length, had not my grief deprived me of all my 25 mental powers, and especially of any fluency in writing.' I borrow Cicero's words, and with good reason, for our plight, I think, is very like; my own affliction seems to me not much lighter than what that wise man thought to

* * * * *

511:10 from the threshold] *Adagia* I ix 91

11 left you] In 1513; cf Epp 273:4, 291:4.

12 Sixtinus] The Frisian scholar and cleric who had made his career in England; cf Ep 430 introduction.

18 chill blood] Virgil *Georgics* 2.484

23 Cry havoc] A reminiscence (in Greek) of Homer *Iliad* 7.279

23–6 'And this was ... in writing'] Cicero *Epistulae ad Atticum* 3.7.3

be the extreme of misfortune. It is you and no one else who can mitigate this
state of affairs, if by the infinitely learned things you write you will comfort   30
your humble friend Augustinus, and tell me where to find the philosophy
with which, as though with oars, I may try to work my ship out of these
breakers, so that I and others with me may not be overwhelmed by this
tempest and sink to the bottom, but may toil at the oar as you advise me,
and work my way into calm water. For though I am for the moment far from   35
the scene of these troubles, while my mission so requires, I am none the less
tormented by the thought of what is happening in my native country to my
own people. I left them at my departure in the greatest misery and distress,
and I suppose with good reason that they can expect nothing but the worst
of fates or have already suffered it, so that I simply cannot say whether it is   40
better to know or not to know what has happened to them.

Farewell, dear Erasmus, and believe me when I say that nothing is
worse for your poor friend than to be deprived of your teaching, your
advice and your companionship, with all that that means of literature and
scholarship and goodness. Farewell once more, and let me have some small   45
supply of these commodities by letter, as I may not have them face to face.
Franz, I think, will faithfully deliver anything. Farewell a third time, for
there is nothing on which I set more store than the welfare of my Erasmus,
the hope, support and glory of good literature.

Paris, 10 January   50

512 / To John Watson   Brussels, 13 January 1517

This letter replies to Ep 450, delayed in its transmission to Erasmus (lines
30–31). It was first printed in the *Epistolae elegantes* 1517.

ERASMUS OF ROTTERDAM TO JOHN WATSON, THE
DISTINGUISHED THEOLOGIAN, GREETING
What is this story, my excellent Watson? Have I shared your wanderings as
far as distant Syria? It is the same with me: I carry all my friends round with
me in my mind, and my dear Watson especially. Wherever I go, I recall our   5
delightful intimacy and those whole nights we spent in agreeable conversation with never a dull moment. It gave me great pleasure too to be reminded
of the old friends in whose society I lived in Venice. The one, by the way,
whose name escaped you was Marcus Musurus. I know the generous

* * * * *

47 Franz] Birckmann; cf Ep 258:14n.

512:4 Syria] Cf Ep 450:60n.

9 Musurus] Cf Ep 223:5n; he was a member of the Aldine academy in Venice.

judgment of your friends: they overwhelm my poor self with their pan-   10
egyrics until some people, heaven help us, even envy me, a thing I had
never thought possible and even now can scarcely believe. That the New
Testament should have your approval, the approval of an honest man and a
good scholar, does not displease me, though I would dare assert no more of
it myself than that I did my level best to use all the little energy I can   15
command in making the philosophy of Christ acceptable to men of open
mind. Your own attitude, my dear John, I heartily approve: that you should
master the labyrinths of Scotism and yet not despise these simpler and more
homespun things, at the same time giving philosophy its due and yet none
the less retaining your free judgment. This sorts well with your character,   20
devout without bigotry, sociable without triviality and strict but not severe. But I must stop, or this will look like no true praise but repaying you in
your own coin. Peter Falck, a man of the highest standing among his own
people, in what he wrote when he returned home had much to say of two
Englishmen, whose names I suppose he had forgotten. Aha, thought I at   25
once, this is my friend Watson; for I had heard of your setting out.

I had already mounted my horse to go to Cambridge when someone
brought the news that the lord bishop of Rochester, chancellor of your
university, would be in London that same day. While waiting for him from
day to day, I wasted some days in London. Nor did your letter reach me for   30
several months. You ask for a list of my writings: unknown to me, that had
been done by Adriaan van Baerland, a man of attractive gifts and an
agreeably free talker, and so I am sending you his letter. Please greet all my
friends by name, although I do not name them as I ask you. Farewell,
sweetest of friends.   35

Brussels, 13 January 1516

513 / From Thomas More   [London,] 13 January [1517]

The references to the contribution of More's friends to the *Utopia* determine
the year-date. The letter is number 33 in Rogers.

MORE TO ERASMUS, GREETING
I suppose that draft from Maruffo must be in the same style as this letter of

* * * * *

23 Falck] Cf Ep 450:60n.

27 Cambridge] No doubt to see Fisher, who had gone for the opening of St
John's College; cf Ep 432:3n.

33 his letter] Ep 492

513:2 Maruffo] The transaction is that referred to in Ep 499:4–6 and in previous letters.

mine, which I shall be surprised if you can read. But you will forgive me, my
dearest Erasmus, for I am under such a constant pressure of business, I have
neither time to write nor energy to think. But if you have received the   5
money from Maruffo, will you write to the archbishop, so that Maruffo can
recover what he has paid. I have written to thank our friend Busleyden. You
must thank Desmarez yourself on my behalf no less warmly than Gillis, for
they wished you to have the credit of what they wrote. You would hardly
believe how devoted to you Linacre is, and what a keen champion of your   10
studies. Why Grocyn was so anxious to meet you, I have not yet been able to
discover, for he has not yet come to London. Farewell, dear Erasmus.

In haste, on St Hilary's Day

514 / From Duke George of Saxony   [Weimar?] [January 1517?]

The bearer of this letter was in the suite of Maximilian in the winter of
1516–17. Maximilian himself was in the Netherlands from 14 January to 1 June
1517, frequently at Antwerp and Brussels during February and March. The
original is an autograph rough-draft in the Dresden State archives, and as
there is no reference to this letter in Erasmus' letter of June (Ep 586) it is
possible that it was never sent, or not delivered. It was published by A.
Horawitz *Erasmiana* (Vienna 1878); the manuscript is Staatsarchiv Dresden,
Loc. 10300, Religions-Zwiespalt mit Dr Martin Luther und andere Sachen,
1521–1545, fol. 180.

Since the report reached me of your eminence over the whole of Germany
and every other nation, and how you are such a brilliant example of
learning and scholarship that you more than any other man might well be
called a light of the world, the desire has grown in me day by day to set eyes
on the great man of whom such things are told, so that my sight might enjoy   5
the feast which has so long regaled my hearing. Hitherto, however, the
opportunity has not been granted me to learn where you were living, and I

* * * * *

6 archbishop] Warham

7 Busleyden] Cf Ep 484; the prefatory material for the *Utopia* contained
Busleyden's letter to More, a letter of Pieter Gillis to Busleyden (Ep 477:8n),
and a letter of Jean Desmarez ('Paludanus') to Gillis. See P.R. Allen '*Utopia* and
European Humanism: the Function of the Prefatory Letters and Verses'
Studies in the Renaissance 10 (1963) 91–107.

10 Linacre] On Erasmus' concern about Linacre's opinion see Ep 388:174–7
and note.

11 Grocyn] One of the first English Greek scholars of note, and an early
acquaintance of Erasmus in England; cf Ep 119:26n.

Duke George of Saxony
Portrait by Lucas Cranach the Elder, after 1537
Bayerische Staatsgemäldesammlungen, Munich

have been unable to visit you. But now, through the honourable Dietrich von Werthern, doctor of laws, my subject and friend, and by way of this unpolished letter and my ill-digested Latin style, I make bold to pay you a 10 visit. He will confirm my sentiments and the strength of my wish to see you; give him your confidence, I beg, and do not send him away empty-handed. Farewell and my best wishes.

515 / From Pieter Gillis   Antwerp, 18 January [1517]

PIETER GILLIS TO MASTER ERASMUS OF ROTTERDAM,
THEOLOGIAN, GREETING

I felt it my duty to write to you, since Nikolaus of Bavaria, who is an expert in astronomy, was leaving for your part of the world. He has with him several astrolabes and spheres to be sold there. He is bringing you a Greek 5 book sent by the prior of St Agnes; I took responsibility for the book, and gave the courier a receipt signed by me. Dirk told me of your warm and friendly reception by the theologians at Louvain, which gave me great pleasure. I hear that my fellow-parent Tunstall has set off. I am sorry for your sake, for I know that he was more congenial to your way of life than 10 most people here. In Paris I got a Suetonius, with Flavius Vopiscus, Spartianus and many others, printed some time ago in Italy; if you would like them to be sent to you, let me know as soon as you can, and I will see they

* * * * *

514:9 von Werthern] Dietrich von Werthern of Schloss Wiehe in Thuringia (1468–1536) was a diplomatist who had been chancellor of the Order of German Knighthood under the younger brother of Duke George, Duke Frederick (d 1510). On Frederick's death he became councillor to Duke George.

515:3 Nikolaus] Kratzer (c 1487–1550) of Munich, who had studied at Cologne and Wittenberg. He is usually thought to have come to England in 1517 or 1518 to join Foxe's foundation of Corpus Christi College, Oxford. However there is no surviving contemporary evidence to connect Kratzer to Foxe's college at that time. What is certain is that in 1519 he entered the royal service as 'deviser of the Kinge's horologes' see Emden BRUO (1974). He also taught in the household of Thomas More; cf Rogers 250 n12.

6 prior] Cf Ep 504:2–3.

7 Dirk] Martens

8 theologians] Cf Ep 509 introduction.

9 fellow-parent] Cf Ep 516:2; Tunstall was godfather to Gillis' newly-born daughter by Cornelia Sandria; cf Ep 312:93n.

9 set off] For Tournai to meet with the Emperor: LP ii 2765–6

11 Suetonius] On these authors see Allen Ep 596 introduction and 48–9n.

Nikolaus Kratzer
Portrait by Hans Holbein the Younger, 1528
Musée du Louvre, Paris

are despatched post-haste. My wife, who is now a mother, and my father
send their best greetings. Farewell, and count me your friend, as I, you well   15
know, am yours.

Antwerp, 18 January

516 / To Pieter Gillis   Brussels, 20 January [1517]

This letter was first published in the *Farrago*.

ERASMUS TO HIS FRIEND PIETER GILLIS, GREETING
I rejoice to hear that you have a daughter, and congratulate you on Tunstall
as a godfather, for he is as good a scholar and as good and kindly a man as
this age can show. Let me see you maintain this principle of alternation in
your family, so that you have an equal number of sons and daughters. My   5
life seems to have come to a halt with the loss of Tunstall, yet I see no refuge.
Mountjoy is too far away. Louvain, although I have made my peace with the
theologians more or less, would give me a grim reception in Lent. To sit
here any longer I simply have no spirits. If without inconvenience to
yourself you could let me have one room which has a privy, maybe I will   10
move over and join you, in order to get ready what I can send to Basel.
Anything you may find you have spent beyond your usual level I wish to be
charged to me; thus I shall not be too much of a burden on you, nor you on
me. Let me know therefore as soon as you can, but do not change anything
in your house until I have had your reply and can reply to you in my turn. Of   15
the money I still hear nothing, and yet it is fairly important for me that it
should not be too long in the banker's hands. My very best wishes to your
delightful wife. The story of my affairs is too long to be entrusted to a letter.
Dining with the chancellor the other day I made a complimentary reference
to you, and he listened rather favourably. Give my greetings to your   20
excellent father, who is now a father twice over. Farewell.

Brussels, St Agnes Eve [1518]

* * * * *

14 wife] Cf n9 above.
14 father] Cf Ep 476:82n.
516:7 Mountjoy] Cf Ep 508:19n.
16 money] Perhaps that mentioned in Ep 513:6

517 / From Leo X to Andrea Ammonio   Rome, 26 January 1517

The background to this letter has been indicated in the introductions to Epp 446 and 447. Unlike the dispensation of Julius II (Ep 187A) and Ep 518 which follows, both of which are entirely in common form, only lines 46–54 and 65–75 of this letter are in common form. The rest is an *ad hoc* papal letter based on the supplication of Ammonio, and it belongs to the special free-style class of letters known as 'Brevia ad principes et alios viros'; see L.E. Boyle OP (to whom I owe this information) *A Survey of the Vatican Archives and of its Medieval Holdings* (Toronto 1972) 65. This class of brief was the preserve of the Domestic Secretary, an office which in the time of Leo X was divided between Pietro Bembo and Jacopo Sadoleto; see line 78.

The letter was a private document meant to be kept by Erasmus and used for his own protection only if the propriety of his clerical status was challenged. Its contents were secret and confidential. With Ep 518, Ep 517 constituted the formal instrument of dispensation sought by Erasmus the previous summer. The pope also sent a private letter to Erasmus accompanying these documents (Ep 519) and Silvestro Gigli five days later sent a personal account of the transactions in Rome undertaken on Erasmus' behalf (Ep 521).

The original of this document is a manuscript in the Öffentliche Bibliothek of the University of Basel, Erasmuslade A.1.4, and it bears subscriptions in the hands of Ammonio and Sixtinus. It was first published by W. Vischer *Erasmiana* (Basel 1876). There is also a copy at Basel in the hand of Ammonio, endorsed by Erasmus 'Commissio.' A duplicate which Erasmus subscribed and left with Ammonio was returned after Ammonio's death by Pietro Ammonio, his cousin, to Erasmus and doubtless destroyed by him.

One of the matters dealt with in the dispensation touches the history of Erasmus' early life and requires some clarification – the matter of his illegitimacy (lines 9–10). There is no doubt that Erasmus was illegitimate, born of a bachelor and a widow, as the matter was stated in the dispensation of Julius II (Ep 187A). The problem had to be dealt with in connection with his supplication as a religious to hold a benefice, or benefices (as in the present instance, cf Ep 446 introduction). There is nothing in these documents, however, to support the view that concern about his legitimacy was the leading or even a prominent motive in his seeking a second dispensation. Those motives, discussed already in connection with Epp 446 and 447, were chiefly the need for habilitation after apostasy and the other penalties imposed by the Augustinian statutes for laying aside his religious habit (lines 15–18), and the need for a new dispensation allowing him to hold more than one benefice. It should be recalled that in addition to his English annuity and the more recent benefits

bestowed in the Netherlands, there was the apparent prospect of a prelacy; cf
Epp 436, 443 and 470 introduction.

In supplicating for the needed dispensation, reference to illegitimacy was
essential information because a benefice could not be granted to an illegitimate without a papal dispensation, although a dispensation to major orders
could be granted by a religious superior (and had been to Erasmus: cf lines
10–14) if no benefice or prelacy was envisaged. Since, strictly speaking, each
and every supplication for a benefice had to mention if the suppliant was
illegitimate, Erasmus also asked that in future, when he supplicated for a
benefice, he would be dispensed from mentioning his status as an illegitimate
and his dispensation from that status with respect first, to major orders;
second, to holding a benefice as a religious (1506); and third, to holding several benefices – the main point of the supplication this time; cf lines 22–26.

As P.S. Allen stated, the present dispensation suggests that he had learned
more of the circumstances of his birth since his original petition to Julius II.
This is scarcely surprising, since he was in his early teens when both parents
died, and after a long absence from the Netherlands he was now back nearer
his own kinship. What had he learned?

Erasmus' own admission in 1524 (see Appendix) that his father eventually
became a priest has led to much speculation about his father's status at the
time of Erasmus' birth. He was described in the dispensation of 4 January 1506
as 'solutus,' ie a bachelor and not a widower. If he had been known to have
been a priest or cleric he would then have been described as such.

In the present dispensation the key phrase is the one here noted (lines
9–10), 'de illicito et, ut timet, incesto damnatoque coitu genitus,' where
(contrary to P.S. Allen) the 'as he fears' is a common euphemism and no
indication of doubt; cf Allen II 434 7n (neither is the new ground a 'contrast'
with that earlier mentioned in Ep 187A, but rather, a more specific allegation).
The phrase indicates simply that there was some relationship of consanguinity or affinity between Erasmus' parents within the prohibited canonical
degrees. The suggestion that this was 'spiritual incest,' indicating that Erasmus' father was in major orders when he was born, is owed, apparently, to J.J.
Mangan, building on a tradition of local gossip; cf Life, Character and Influence
of Desiderius Erasmus of Rotterdam volume 1 (New York 1927) 4–5; cf Allen
147n1. It has often been repeated since but it is based on an incorrect notion of
the canonical background.

The term 'condemned' (damnato) merely distinguishes incest from all other
forms of illicit intercourse, and does not imply sacrilege. The phrase used is
correct for an impediment arising from consanguinity or affinity in a collateral
line. If Erasmus' father had been in sacred orders, he would have been

described as 'de illicito et ... sacrilego coitu'; see F.-X. Wernz and P. Vidal *Ius canonicum* 3rd edition volume v 'Ius matrimoniale' (Rome 1946) Pars Quarta, Caput Praenotiones No 608 (or, page 766 n 4). It must also be pointed out that, even if the phrase did imply 'spiritual incest,' such a relationship could be incurred in a number of ways, including the obligations of godparent to godchild; see G. Oesterle *Dictionnaire du droit canonique* 5 (1953) 1303–4.

It is difficult to believe that in this secret document, intended to serve Erasmus as a final line of defence if his clerical status was questioned, we have anything other than a very exact remedy for the difficulties that troubled him. Otherwise we must suppose that in a matter of the most vital interest to his material welfare, he deliberately deceived the highest authority in the Church in order to obtain a document which, used as intended, would have been useless and even seriously damaging to him if the account of his birth that it contained were contrary to common knowledge as represented in the hearsay tradition later reported at Gouda.

At the very least, it cannot be shown from this document that Erasmus' father was a priest at the time of his birth, and unless firm new evidence can be brought to bear, we are not justified in setting aside for this reason the version of the matter contained in the *Compendium vitae*. There is nothing in the text to suggest that the bond of affinity between Erasmus' parents was particularly close, but it should be remembered that in addition to the many possibilities of relationship offered by extensive families in a small community (from the account in the *Compendium vitae* Erasmus' father was one of ten brothers), by the canon law of the time affinity was established with every act of carnal copulation. Moreover, the statistical chances of incurring a collateral affinity within the forbidden degrees had been greatly enhanced if the mother had a previous marriage.

POPE LEO X

My beloved son, greeting and apostolic benediction. You have lately brought to our attention that there is in your country at the present time an individual distinguished for his learning who in his childhood was made by those who had the charge of him an oblate in a house of Canons Regular, 5
wherein he remained more by reason of menaces and shame and poverty than of his own free will until he made there the profession which canons of that house are accustomed to make. And being thereafter, although he suffers from a disability of birth being the offspring of an unlawful and (as he fears) incestuous and condemned union, advanced in holy orders even 10

* * * * *

517:9–10 unlawful ... union] See introduction.

as far as the priesthood under licence from his superior, upon a summons
from the bishop of Cambrai under licence from the ordinary and from his
superior officers he devoted himself to the study of literature in divers
universities and became a very learned man. Who at length through no
desire of his own but under pressure of events at first concealed and later   15
altogether abandoned the habit which the said canons do customarily wear
and went about for several years and still goes about in the habit of a secular
priest, exposing himself thereby to apostasy and all the other sentences
censures and ecclesiastical penalties imposed by the regular statutes of his
order upon those guilty of such conduct; and now wishes for the peace of   20
his soul and the avoidance of greater scandal to continue in the said secular
habit and that he may be absolved from apostasy and other sentences
censures and penalties and rendered capable of holding any benefices
whatsoever, and that it be permitted him in any request for letters apostolic
to make no mention of his disability of birth and of any dispensation of this   25
kind. And you have caused the request to be submitted to us, that of our
apostolic charity we should agree to confer upon yourself licence and
authority to give him absolution and dispensation in respect of the matters
aforesaid and to grant him an indult to this effect.

    We therefore being moved by the man's other virtues of which we   30
have heard and by his prayers in this regard authorize you, if the said canon
(whose name and surname with his qualities and disabilities in this regard
we take as already known) should humbly so request, to absolve him by our
authority on this occasion at the least from the apostasy and the sentences
censures and penalties aforesaid in the form commonly used by the   35
Church, enjoining salutary penance upon him in proportion to his guilt and
such other penalties as may properly be enjoined according to law, and to
give him dispensation as follows. In the first place, in respect of the
aforesaid irregularity if he has contracted any such after the imposition of
sentences censures and penalties by celebrating masses and other divine   40
offices (provided it be not in contempt of the authority of the Keys) or in
other ways intruding upon them. Secondly, that he may have permission to
reside for the term of his life outside the houses of his aforesaid order in any
convenient place of good repute living reputably in other respects, to wear a
symbol only of his former habit as a regular canon beneath the reputable   45
garb of a secular priest, and to accept and retain freely and lawfully any
benefices whatsoever of whatever kind whether secular or regular of any

* * * * *

11 summons] Cf Ep 447:496.
15 pressure of events] Cf Ep 296:214.
41 Keys] The symbolic expression of the authority of the see of St Peter

Letter of Dispensation for Erasmus dated 26 January 1517,
sent by Leo x to Ammonio, with autograph subscriptions by
Ammonio and Sixtinus, Epistle 517

At one time in the possession of Erasmus; now MS Erasmuslade A.1.4
in the Öffentliche Bibliothek, University of Basel

... pueritie per eos, qui eius curam habebant, oblatus fuit Monasterio Canonicoz regulariu, in quo potius minis, pudore & egestate, qz sponte

... um pateretur & illicito, & ut timet, incesto damnatoqz coitu genitus, ad omnes et sacros et pbratus ordines promotus de licentia sui superi=

studio operam dedit, & in virum doctissimum euasit: ac tandem non affectate, sed per occasionem coactus habitu peridcos Canonicos ge=

apositorian & alias sententias, censuras & poenas ecclesiasticas in Italia presumentes & ex institutis dicti ordinis regularibus latas incurrendo,

...ententiis censuris & poenis absolui, & ad bñficia quecunqz obtinenda habilitari, sibiqz indulgeri, ut in quibusuis impetrationibus litez apticaz

...abssoluendi, ac cum eo super premissis dispensandi, et illi indultu hmoi concedendi licentiam & facultatem concedere de benignitate aptica

... Canonicus cuius nomen & cognomen ac qualitates & defectus hmoi pns expressis habemus, id humilr petierit, eum ab apostasia ac

...ipsi pro modo culpe poenitentiis salutaribus, & aliis, que fuerint de iure iniungenda; secunqz super irregularitate predca, si quam sen

...tis immiscendo, contraxit: qzq extra Monasteria dicti ordinis in locis ad hoc conuenientibus & honestis, & alis honeste uiuendo quoad

... deferre: ac quecunqz, & qualiacunqz bñficia ecclesiastica, secularia & quorumuis ordinu regularia, et si secularia Canonicatus & prebendaz

...dignitas eclesiis, uel eaz perpetue vicarie, Regularia uero Prioratus & prepositura prepositatus dignitates, et conuentuales curatos et electiue

...pere & retinere, libere & licite ualeat, dispensare, abolereqz omnem inhabilitatis & infamie maculam siue notam per eum premissoz

...ca Sede uel eius legatis seu alis quomodolibet impetrandis uel sibi concedendis de defectu & dispensatione predcis, et si alis

...sit Canonicus regularis nullam decetero mentionem facere teneatur, litteresqz ipse propterea subreptitie uel inualide nullatenus

...e libere & licite ualeas, aucte aptica licentiam & facultatem concedimus. Non obstantibus bo: me: Otthonis & Otthoboni in

...tibus, necnon statutis & eclesiaz, ac Monasterioz & ordinu predcoz, uiramento confirmatione aptica uel quauis firmitate alia

...ce & expressis habentes, illis alis in suo robore permansuris, hac uice dumtaxat specialr & expresse derogamus, ac defectu

...xxvi Januarii. M.D.xvii. Pontis mi Anno quarto

...H. & Erasmu Roterodamu humilr a nobis petite a sma excommnicationis, ceterisqz censuris eclesiastis

...ri & alignot annos mordens absoluimus & forma ecetis consueta inc nõ inc eodem senuin familiari, et phatorum

...e re fide per me proprria manu scripsi in Domo pñs meç in stello S. Stephani ppe westmñ Dni

...dibs inseruiens, ut maiore fide faceret, et sua manu sbscriberet.

...positz absolutioni ac dispensationi in oibz et pz onē dum sit ut pfertur pp pfatum diium Collectore ptino die et

...diem Ideo luc inē subscripsi meua gpa in fidem et testimoniu pmissoz rogatus et   Ja. Sadoletus

order, provided they be conferred upon him lawfully in other respects or he be elected presented or otherwise promoted and instituted thereto, even if the secular be canonries and prebends dignities rectories administrations or offices, including those with a cure of souls and elective office in cathedrals and metropolitan or collegiate churches or perpetual vicarages thereof, the regular to include the office of prior or provost and conventual dignities including those with a cure of souls and elective, all spot or stain of incapacity and infamy acquired by him for the causes aforementioned being done away. Thirdly, that henceforward in any application to be made by him or on his behalf to the apostolic see or its legates or in any other way for any letter concerning any grant or judicial decision or in the granting of the same he be not obliged in future to make any mention of the said disability and dispensation, even if on any other occasion he should for any reason have been refused any dispensation in this regard by reason of his concealment, nor of the fact that he is a canon regular, and that the letters themselves should by no means be deemed for this cause to be spurious or invalid, but in all and every respect should have the same validity as if he had been born in lawful wedlock. All this notwithstanding the constitutions of the late Otto and Ottoboni legates of the apostolic see in the realm of England and other constitutions provincial and synodical and ordinances apostolic, together with the statutes of churches monasteries and orders aforesaid deriving their force from oath apostolic confirmation or any other authority and any privileges and indults apostolic which may have been granted to them: from all of which, holding the tenor of them all to be for the present purpose sufficiently well known, without prejudice to their continuing validity in all other respects, we do on this occasion and on this occasion only specifically and expressly make exception, as also to the disability aforesaid and all other considerations to the contrary whatsoever.

Given at Rome at St Peter's under the ring of the Fisherman on the twenty-sixth day of January in the year 1517, being the fourth year of our Pontificate. Ja. Sadoletus

* * * * *

66 Otto and Ottoboni] This reiterates the provisions in Julius II's dispensation of January 1506; cf Ep 187A: 32–4. It allows Erasmus specifically to hold a living in England; cf Ep 255. Otto, cardinal deacon of St Nicola, was papal legate of Gregory IX in England; his legatine council of 1237 and that of the later legate Ottobuono Fieschi (who was later Pope Adrian V) in 1268, issued the most important legislation of its kind in medieval England.

78 Sadoletus] Jacopo Sadoleto (1477–1547) was a distinguished humanist, exegete and ecclesiastical reformer who became bishop of Carpentras (1527) and a cardinal (1536); see R.M. Douglas *Jacopo Sadoleto 1477–1547 Humanist and Reformer* (Cambridge Mass 1959).

I therefore, Andrea Ammonio, collector in the realm of England of our most holy Father Pope Leo the Tenth aforesaid, etc. hereby absolve our humble 80 petitioner Dr Erasmus Rotterdam in the form commonly used by the Church from the sentence of excommunication and all the other ecclesiastical censures by him incurred through his abandonment of the habit proper to his monastic profession, going about for some years in the habit of a secular at grave risk of apostasy, and give him dispensation by apostolic 85 authority in each and every respect in accordance with the power and authority granted to us and hereinbefore written. In testimony whereof I have written this with my own hand in my prebendal lodging in the chapel of St Stephen's at Westminster on the ninth day of April in the year 1517. I have also requested Dr Johannes Sixtinus, doctor of canon and civil law, 90 who was concerned in all the business aforesaid, to add weight to this testimony by appending his signature.

And I, Johannes Sixtinus, doctor of canon and civil law, having been present at the aforesaid absolution and dispensation in each and every respect while they were performed by the aforesaid master collector in the 95 year day and place above-written, and having seen and heard them so performed, have therefore as required and requested subscribed this with my own hand in witness and testimony of the preceding.

To our beloved son Andrea Ammonio, our notary and collector

518 / From Leo x   Rome, 26 January 1517

Like that of Ep 517, the original of this letter was in Erasmus' possession; it is now in the Öffentliche Bibliothek, University of Basel, Erasmuslade A 5, and was first published by W. Vischer *Erasmiana* (Basel 1876).

POPE LEO X

My beloved son, greeting and apostolic benediction. The integrity of your life and character and other estimable evidence of your uprightness and virtue, in respect of which you have been recommended to us by credible witnesses, incline us to visit you with special grace and favour. Hence it is 5 that we, wishing to show you gracious favour, on whose behalf as of a man acceptable in his sight we have received a humble petition from our most beloved son in Christ Henry viii illustrious king of England, and absolving

* * * * *

90 Sixtinus] See introduction and Ep 112 introduction.
518:8 Henry viii] What intervention the king supplied is unknown; cf Ep 519:7. Allen suggested that it might have been a statement about the customs of English canons in the matter of dress; cf Ep 296:205–18.

you by the terms of this letter and declaring you absolved for the future from
each and every the ecclesiastical sentences censures and penalties of ex-   10
communication suspension and interdict and any other which may have
been imposed upon you by the law or by man for any occasion or cause (if
you are held bound in any way by any such) as far as is necessary for the
effectiveness of these presents and no farther, do now in virtue of our
apostolic authority by the tenor of these presents and as a gift of special   15
grace give you dispensation as follows: to accept and if they be incompatible to hold simultaneously for the term of your natural life all ecclesiastical
benefices whatsoever and whatsoever be their number and quality with or
without cure of souls even if they be two parish churches or perpetual
vicarages thereof chantries free chapels hospitals or annual duties normally   20
assigned to secular clerks by way of perpetual ecclesiastical benefice, together with any dignities rectories administrations or offices in cathedral
(including metropolitan) or collegiate churches, even be they chief and
principal dignities, including those with a cure of souls and elective office,
provided they be conferred upon you lawfully in other respects or you be   25
elected presented or otherwise appointed to them and instituted thereto:
and simultaneously or successively whether simply or by way of exchange
to resign these as often as you wish and in place of that one or those
resigned to receive in like manner and retain together freely and lawfully for
the term of your natural life one or more other ecclesiastical benefices   30
whatsoever and whatsoever be their number and quality, be it or they
similar or dissimilar, up to the total value of one thousand gold ducats,
provided always that among the incompatible benefices there be not more
than two parish churches or perpetual vicarages thereof: notwithstanding
the constitutions and ordinances general and special of any General Coun-   35
cil or any other such of apostolic authority and those of Otto and Ottoboni of
blessed memory formerly legates of the apostolic see in the realm of England and any others promulgated in councils provincial and synodical,
together with the statutes and customs of churches in which the incompatible benefices aforesaid may be situate, whether they be ratified by oath by   40
apostolic confirmation or by endorsement of any other kind, and all other

* * * * *

32 one thousand gold ducats] Venetian ducats or similar gold coins, worth
£229 3s 4d sterling = £329 3s 4d gros Flemish = £2,075 0s 0d tournois. Cf CWE 1
314, 338–9; and Ep 447:844n above. A letter from Gigli to Ammonio dated 9
February 1517 (LP ii 2895) speaks of sending 'another brief which dispenses
him to have a thousand ducats.'

things contrary to the contents hereof: provided always that the incompatible benefices aforesaid be not thereby defrauded of their due service and that the care of souls therein (should any such be incumbent upon them) be by no means neglected.   45

Given at Rome at St Peter's under the ring of the Fisherman on the twenty-sixth day of January in the year 1517, being the fourth year of our pontificate.

Ja. Sadoletus

To our beloved son Erasmus son of Roger, of Rotterdam, clerk of the   50
diocese of Utrecht

519 / From Leo x   Rome, 26 January 1517

This personal letter from the pope accompanied the dispensations granted by Epp 517 and 518. It was published the same year in the *Epistolae elegantes* 1517.

LEO, SUPREME PONTIFF, TO HIS BELOVED SON
ERASMUS OF ROTTERDAM

My beloved son, greeting and Apostolic benediction. The uprightness of your life and character, your exceptional learning, and the outstanding merit of your virtues, which are not only strongly corroborated by the wide   5
renown of your published works but also commended to us by the opinion of the most learned men, and not least by letters from the king of England and from his Catholic Majesty, make us wish to encourage you with some singular and special favour. We have therefore gladly acceded to your request, and furthermore will display our concern for you more fully, when   10
you give us the opportunity or chance brings it within our reach. For we judge it right that your sacred industry, which toils unceasingly for the common good, should be urged on by suitable rewards to yet greater undertakings.

Given at Rome on the twenty-sixth of January 1516/7, in the fourth   15
year of our pontificate.

* * * * *

50 Roger] The only authority for this information. In the *Compendium vitae* (see appendix) Erasmus calls his father 'Gerardus,' and Allen suggested that his full name was Rogerius Gerardus; cf Allen I Appendix 1 577–8.
519:8 Catholic Majesty] Cf Epp 475:5n, 476:20.

520 / From William Latimer   Oxford, 30 January [1517]

This is a reply to a letter written by Erasmus on receipt of Ep 481 from More; cf Ep 502:29. A copy is included in the Deventer Letter-book, but it was first published in the *Farrago*. For Latimer see Ep 468:10n.

WILLIAM LATIMER TO THE RIGHT EMINENT
MASTER ERASMUS, GREETING

I have received your letter, dear Erasmus most learned of men, dated 21 November, in which you thank me warmly for having promised my assistance (or so you say) in the correction of your New Testament, although, so far as I know, I never did anything of the kind. Not that I would not gladly have done so, had I supposed it would be useful to you; but after all the learning and all the diligence which (as I understand from the preface) you had lavished on the work, I saw that I could make no changes except for the worse and add nothing that would not be superfluous. In any case, it was my friend More, I have no doubt, misled you, in order to put you under some obligation to me, however mistaken. For he spoke to me seriously on this same subject when I was last with him in London, and also about the bishop of Rochester, about whom you too had written to me some months before. As it happened, however, I read that letter for the first time on the day I met More, so he took the opportunity to discuss both topics with me in some detail. I said no obstinately on both: I knew I could do nothing to help the bishop in such a short space of time (for he asked me to give him a month), and on the other point I could see clearly that my labour would be superfluous. Whereupon he left me to decide as I would about the bishop; but as for you, he began to urge me more and more to help you if I possibly could, and give you any assistance in my power in the revision of this New Testament of yours. I owed this, he maintained, to your exceptional generosity or to our familiar friendship, to the affectionate kindness you have always shown me, and to the common interest of all those, he said, who would profit by your labours; and he produced many other reasons which I confess to be true and weighty, though for me at least they would be quite unnecessary, if I thought I could do any good.

For of good will, dear Erasmus, there is in me no lack, nor ever will be, either to advance your reputation if opportunity should offer, or to assist you if I can help in any way. But having been for eight or nine years so

* * * * *

520:8 preface] Ep 373
14 bishop of Rochester] John Fisher
14 had written] Cf Ep 468:13n and lines 40f below.

immersed in other pursuits that all this time I have read hardly a page of
Greek or Latin, as this letter will demonstrate clearly enough even if I do not
mention it, what should I, or indeed what could I, promise, in answer to a
request from More or a demand from you? – I who am greatly ashamed (for   35
one must, I think, speak the truth) even to address a man like yourself who
write so well, to put it no higher. Unless I had understood from your letter
that you were expecting something from me greater than it was right for me
to promise or possible for me to perform, I should not even have written you
this letter. And the reason why I have so far sent no answer to your other   40
letter is, that I felt myself such a stranger from this whole field in which I
might have helped. Formerly, this would not have escaped the suspicion of
negligence and ingratitude; but now, when I make a clean breast of it, I
deserve to be forgiven. And besides this interruption in my studies, which
I believe to be the greatest of all enemies to scholarship, there is another   45
obstacle in the way of my doing what you ask, which is perhaps even more
serious. It is this: that almost all those who have left any written comment
on the Scriptures have used words and forms quite different from those of
the classical Greeks, and are so far from the language of the Ancients, on
which I once spent much time, that there is little enough in them that I can   50
understand and nothing I dare guarantee; for neither the forms of speech,
on which alone the sense sometimes depends, nor the peculiar meaning of
the words are sufficiently familiar.

Though even if they were extremely familiar to me and nothing had
been lost through the interruption of my studies which I spoke of, what   55
after all have you left for me or for anyone else to do? To your consummate
learning and eloquence, in which by common consent you are supreme,
you have added enough industry and diligence to satisfy not only the keen
and careful reader but the most meticulous and pedantic critic. I do not
mention the various editions of this New Testament current in antiquity, of   60
which some traces yet remain in the Fathers; I say nothing of the various
and sometimes contradictory readings in the text, on which it is difficult to
form a judgment because of the authority and exceptional learning of the
men by whom they are transmitted to us; I pass over the commentaries of

* * * * *

32 other pursuits] Latimer's interests in these years must be conjectured. His
fellowship at All Souls College Oxford was vacated by 1497. In 1513 he was
incorporated MA at Oxford, having returned from Ferrara with that degree,
and he was appointed tutor to Reginald Pole. In 1516–17 he was renting rooms
at Canterbury College. P.S. Allen suggested that the 'other pursuits' had to do
with music, following a comment about Latimer's interests in Richard Pace's
De fructu; see the edition by Frank Manley and Richard S. Sylvester (New
York 1967) pages 47 and 155 (note). See also Ep 207:25n, Emden BRUO II.

some modern scholars besides; all these things I do not doubt that you have 65
inspected and examined and weighed in the balance. Who, in short, could
wish for greater industry than you display in your revision of the New
Testament? – above all in adducing, correcting and explaining the most
approved authors; and in those few words how much toil there lies and how
much care and what a deal of anxious thought! I say nothing of all those 70
famous names – Origen, Chrysostom, Cyril, Jerome, Ambrose, Hilary –
whom few divines of our generation read, and none can understand. And
then to return to the Greek original (which means to abandon the runlets,
and go back to the fountain-head), and where necessary, even to the
Hebrew; whether you do this single-handed or, as you put it, with your 75
faithful Theseus! And not content with all this, you add the genuine and
uncorrupted testimony of the most ancient manuscripts, without which it
may be that in other authors you have toiled in vain. But in all this I know
not which to admire more, your diligence in the pursuit or your lucky skill
in finding; such is the scarcity of the books you want, the Greek especially, 80
in this world of ours.

And so, after your exceptional and meticulous diligence, such as no
one else, I think, could have contributed to so great a task, there is no reason
why you ought to expect anything from me, especially in view of my great
ignorance of the language and the degree to which I have forgotten almost 85
all humane letters. Nevertheless, I shall read this work of yours with minute
attention; but I shall read it not for your benefit but for my own, in hopes of
learning from it. Not but what it will also be a great pleasure to read
anything of yours, my dear Erasmus, and if I chance upon something I do
not like – which I foresee will certainly be very little, and more likely 90
nothing – I shall not hesitate to write and tell you; which, if I remember
right, I also promised our friend More that I would do, so do not think you
ought to upbraid him seriously for not doing as he said.

You often write to me about the bishop of Rochester, showing a
special degree of affection and good will towards him; and at the same time 95
you show a remarkable desire to promote the study of Greek, in trying so
hard to make it familiar to such a leading bishop who excels in learning of
every kind; under his patronage it will be not merely safe from ill-natured
persons and detractors, but welcome and popular in almost the whole of
England. Who would dare attack it, if the bishop were on its side? or who 100
would not be willing to welcome it if he knew it had the blessing of so
eminent a prelate? On this point, I observe that both you and our friend
More expect some help from me, thinking that I can perhaps be of some

* * * * *

75 as you put it] Epp 334:135, 335:288

assistance in this enterprise, and even that I have a duty to help from love
for my native country. On this I hope, in the first place, and indeed I beg,   105
my dear Erasmus, that you will not think me so disobliging and so churlish
or so far removed from all decent feeling, as to be unwilling at the request of
two very dear friends to undertake to work through one book with him or
endure one month's work; for I know that I owe you both far more than
many months could repay. Secondly, do not think me fool enough not to   110
wish to do a service to a man of his great position, and earn with so little
effort the good will of a bishop who is not only distinguished for learning
and saintliness of life but very influential and well thought-of – the more so
as he is, as you say in your letter, and it is the common report, which I
readily believe, a man very appreciative of such things. Nor, thirdly, am I so   115
careless that I could willingly miss a golden opportunity, when in helping
one man I can promote the cause of humane studies and bring great
distinction to my country, actually with very little effort.

But there is another point, my dear Erasmus, which holds me back,
and discourages me from complying with your complimentary proposal: I   120
know that in so short a space of time I am sure to disappoint both you and
the bishop. Greek is a complex and many-sided business, as you know, and
more than a little involved; and though it is toilsome rather than difficult,
yet it needs time, at least until it can be got by heart. Do not think I judge
other people's mental powers by my own slow pace. I am sure, and have   125
been told so by many people, that the bishop is unusually able and capable
of greater undertakings than that you now propose. You write of his
willingness, and how greatly he longs to learn Greek, and from this I see
clearly that he will also work very hard; and all this shows me that I can hope
for as much progress as anyone could hope for from a man of considerable   130
powers, great industry and an incredible desire to learn. But how great that
progress can be in so short a space of time, I find it hard to say. You seem to
hope for much; and I too think it will be much in relation to the time
available, but small in absolute terms. I remember how Grocyn, a man (as
you know) of very wide learning, with great and well-exercised powers of   135
mind, devoted continuous labour to this same language for two years on
end, even after he had learnt the rudiments, and that under outstanding
teachers, Demetrius Chalcondyles and Angelo Poliziano; how Linacre too,
a man of great quickness of mind, spent the same number of years or even

* * * * *

134 Grocyn] Cf Ep 513:11n.
138 Chalcondyles] Cf Ep 428:39n.
138 Linacre] The distinguished English humanist and medical scholar; cf Ep
119:27n.

more under the same masters. Of myself I say nothing; after six or seven 140
years I confess without shame that there is much I do not know. Tunstall
and Pace I do not count, for they were held back longer perhaps than their
intelligence required by the ignorance or idleness of their teacher. As for
More, you know yourself how quick he is, what a forceful mind he has, and
with what energy he addresses himself to anything once he has started; in a 145
word, how much he resembles you. I do not want to broach that topic, for it
is unnecessary to mention you and your brilliant mind, and might run close
to flattering you. But neither of you, I think, will say that he ran through
these difficulties so fast that after a month or two he could go where he
would without a guide; the more so as one meets so many meanders and 150
side-turnings everywhere that they might lead even an expert astray. So, if
you want the bishop to make progress and arrive at some results in the
language, make him send to Italy for someone well versed in all this, who is
also willing to stay with him long enough for him to feel himself strong and
secure, so that he can not only creep along but raise himself and stand up 155
and even go forward. In this way, it seems to me, you will do more for his
future skill in the language than if, while he is lisping still and can barely
utter childish cries, you abandon him like a baby in its cradle. Farewell.

Here's a great long letter for you, my dear Erasmus, to make up with
too much verbiage for my silence this long time past. But you have only 160
yourself to thank: you have written to me on this topic so often, that I had to
send you a lengthy reply. Farewell once more.

Oxford, 30 January

521 / From Silvestro Gigli   Rome, 31 January 1517

For the setting of this letter see Ep 517 introduction. Gigli (1463–1521) who
came from Lucca, succeeded his uncle Giovanni Gigli as bishop of Worcester
and papal collector in England in 1498; he was resident in England from
1505–12. He then returned to Italy as the representative of Henry VIII at the
Lateran Council (LP i 1083) and later acted as English agent at the court of
Rome. It seems from Ep 552:4–5 that this letter was edited at line 11ff before its
publication in the *Epistolae elegantes* 1517.

* * * * *

142 Pace] The royal secretary and diplomatist; cf Ep 211:53n.
153 Italy] Compare this with the opinion of Erasmus expressed in Epp
457:64–65, 540:54ff.

SILVESTRO, BISHOP OF WORCESTER AND PERMANENT ENVOY OF
HIS BRITANNIC MAJESTY TO THE HOLY FATHER,
TO ERASMUS OF ROTTERDAM, GREETING

Such is my respect for you, and such the fraternal feelings I must hold
towards you, that it was a great pleasure to have been given the opportunity   5
to be of service to you, for I have always admired exceedingly your exceptional learning and outstanding virtues, and could desire nothing more
than to be able to express my very warm disposition in your favour. Being
given the opportunity, therefore, I hastened to open your business, and
had a long and interested discussion with the Holy Father on that subject.   10
He gladly granted your request forthwith, partly from his natural kindness
of heart and partly because of the singular and special good will he feels
towards you in particular for your exceptional gifts. But, as you know,
business of this sort needs many hands to put it through. Besides which,
one or two people were not wanting, who tried to hold the matter up; but   15
thanks to the continuing favour of his Holiness we brought the whole thing
to the conclusion we were hoping for. It was no failure of effort on my part
that prevented a more speedy outcome; but a touch of ill-health and the
troubles in the Duchy of Urbino caused his Holiness no small inconvenience, and were the reason why it took longer to complete than I wished. For   20
the rest, I am eternally grateful for the very good opinion which you have
formed of me, as I learn from your most kind and welcome letter, though I
ascribe this to your kindness and not to my own deserts. Such as I am,
however, pray believe that I am entirely devoted to you. And if in any
respect you think that I may be able to be of service to you or your friends,   25
you can rely on me, as you would on your own brother. Farewell, and pray
count me your friend.

     Rome, 31 January 1516   Silvestro II, bishop of Worcester

522 / From Guillaume Budé   Paris, 5 February [1517]

This is the first of a group of letters (Epp 522, 523, 529, 531, 533–5, 537) all of
which were printed in the *Epistolae elegantes* 1517 and all of them having to do
with the Collège royal, the foundation that was to develop into the Collège de
France. This letter crossed Ep 531, and Budé had as yet had no reply to Ep 493
except the brief note mentioned in line 2 below. Because of the special
circumstances he describes, he at once wrote this letter, an attempt to interest

* * * * *

521:19 Urbino] In pursuit of family and papal power, Leo x had expelled
Francesco della Rovere from Urbino and on 18 August 1516 invested Lorenzo
de' Medici as duke in his place.

Erasmus in the service of Francis I. On the foundation of the Collège see Abel
Lefranc *Histoire du Collège de France depuis les origines jusqu'à la fin du premier
Empire* (Paris 1893) and 'La fondation et les commencements du collège de
France' *Le Collège de France (1530–1930) livre jubilaire* (Paris 1932) 25–58; cf
McNeil 46–8, and A. Stegmann 'Erasme et la France (1495–1520)' in *Colloquium
Erasmianum*, Actes du Colloque International réuni à Mons du 26 au 29 octobre
1967 (Mons 1968) 283–5, 296; M.-M. de la Garanderie 'Les relations d'Erasme
avec Paris ...' in *Scrinium Erasmianum* I (Leiden 1969) 44–9.

GUILLAUME BUDÉ TO ERASMUS OF ROTTERDAM, GREETING
As I write this I am full of anticipation, as a result of your brief note which
read as though you expected shortly to find time to write a really long letter.
At the same time I long to know the reason why Tunstall the Englishman,
his king's envoy in your part of the world, an excellent scholar so they tell   5
me, is proposing of his own accord to write to me, which means to make me
an offer of friendship, though I am quite unknown to him and to almost all
learned men except those who know me by sight. In the meanwhile, as (if I
rightly understand it) my turn to write has not yet come, I was quite content
to forego writing, as far as you are concerned, being a very dilatory corres-   10
pondent even in my mother tongue, and a great one for doing nothing and
putting off, even if, when I do write a letter, I do not really know when to
stop, as you have already discovered. And an opportunity of the kind has
suddenly presented itself, which I must seize on with a will.

Yesterday to amuse myself (a thing I rarely do) I had decided to spend   15
some hours in the afternoon going round the bookshops. In the shop of that
well-known bookseller Jean Petit I found one Guillaume Petit, who is, I
think, a kinsman of his, an especially important man and an excellent
theologian, an honour to his brethren, whom they call the Dominicans or
Friars Preacher, who is now the king's confessor, an office for which I have   20
coined the phrase pillow-chaplain. He is the only preacher to whom the
Court and the royal household are willing to listen on the great festivals,
and it was the same in King Louis' time – a man exactly formed by nature for

* * * * *

522:6 proposing ... to write] Ep 571

17 Jean Petit] A celebrated bookseller and publisher; cf Ep 263:15n, Ph.
Renouard *Répertoire des imprimeurs parisiens* (Paris 1965) 339–41.

17 Guillaume Petit] He was born at Montivilliers and died in 1536; in 1502 he
became a doctor of theology at Paris, having been a member of the Dominican
Order from about 1480. In 1509 he was appointed confessor to Louis XII, an
appointment continued by Francis I. He was active among the Paris printers
and humanists in promoting publication of important theological works,
including patristic editions; in 1528 he was made bishop of Senlis. See Quétif
II 100–102, Renaudet *Préréforme* passim.

pulpit oratory. He is not only very friendly with me and likes my friends,
but I respect him particularly for this reason, that he has great experience in   25
the acquisition and hunting down of scarce books; I nearly said, in skim-
ming the cream off libraries, except that it is hard to say whether he shows
more acquisitive spirit in getting his hands on every book or generosity in
sharing them and lending them to his friends. In short, he offers many
reasons, many traits of character to make me love him; yet I could dislike   30
him (I will be quite frank) for one thing alone. I have no other reason to fall
out with him, except that he is too much attached to one Erasmus, a
foreigner, whom I am now beginning to look askance at for the excessive
reputation with which he floods not only Germany (I will say nothing here
of other countries) but even my native France; with the result that he puts   35
into the shade what little reputation we had, and compels us to be obscure
and to seem so. Not that Budé can sue him for ancient lights with any
plausibility, having gained so much extra illumination from his published
works.

To return to my subject, Guillaume Petit spoke with me to this effect.   40
The day before yesterday, I think it was, he assured me that the topic of
learned men was raised in the presence of the king. Thereupon there was
much talk of Erasmus and others, of Budé perhaps; and the king, inspired, I
hope, by the goddess Minerva, observed that he had it in mind to attract
picked men to his kingdom with generous offers, and to set up in France   45
what I may call a nursery-bed of scholars. When Petit heard this (he had
long been on the look-out for an opportunity, for he is a supporter of all
learned men but in particular admires your learning and your industry and
sings their praises), he gave it as his opinion that Erasmus should be sent
for before anyone else, and that Budé would be an excellent go-between,   50
being a very close friend of Erasmus through their common devotion to
Latin and Greek and for other reasons. In the end, he said, the king with an
outburst of enthusiasm was brought to the point of saying (for there were
other people present who are friendly to the humanities and to you) that he
wished an offer to be made to you by me on his behalf: if you could be   55
induced to leave your present abode and devote yourself to learning here as
you have been accustomed to do where you are now, he himself would
undertake to confer on you a benefice worth a thousand francs and more.

In this you will understand that my own credit is engaged only to the

* * * * *

58 a thousand francs] Guillaume Budé was probably using the term *francicos*
as the popular synonym for the French livre tournois. The gold franc à cheval
was last struck in November 1423; but some gold francs were evidently still
circulating in early sixteenth-century France. Cf CWE 1 318, 336–44; Epp
463:48n above and 575:52–3n below.

extent that I play the part of an intermediary and not a principal, and pass 60
on in good faith what I have learnt from him. I have not, as the saying goes,
personally inspected the property, and this initiative by the prince had
nothing in it for me; nor will it have, I am sure, for I feel my whole way of
thinking is so different, and indeed averse, from that of the Court and all
proceedings of this kind, and the spirit which heaven (if I rightly under- 65
stand it) has conferred upon me is one that can neither give satisfaction in a
Court nor receive it. And yet I must do violence to this spirit of mine and
indeed to my whole nature, if I plan to increase my stature with the
trappings of the goddess Fortune; though many people wish this might
happen to me and think that it ought to. I do not agree with them, for I know 70
myself better and more fully than they do and at close quarters. Your
situation is quite different: no one will expect anything from you except
what you can provide easily and with a light heart. If it were possible for our
monarchs to fill the records of their largesse and their generosity with the
names of laymen as freely as they can with religious and spiritual names, I 75
too, married man though I am, might think it worth while to invest a little
hope in waiting for windfalls. As it is, the style of the life I have embarked
on, and my centres of interest, are such that neither in Court matters nor in
public affairs either is there anything for me, be it seedtime or harvest. As a
result, many men who do not understand my point of view suppose, and 80
often say, that I am pursuing interests likely to lead to fine words rather than
a fine income; all the same, I promise myself an abundant harvest there-
from, which will be the stay of my old age and even contribute something in
the way of livelihood or reputation to my grandchildren and their descen-
dants. But I place above all else what will supply food for the mind and will 85
also contribute to the achievement of eternal life and the highest good.

At this point you will perhaps ask what advice I have for you. What
could it be but to accept this offer forthwith and whole-heartedly? First,
because I should like to think you so disposed, for my sake if nothing else;
secondly because, if you accept, you will do as much for your honour and 90
reputation as for your worldly prospects. Just think, in heaven's name,
what a distinction! How it will redound to the high standing and prosperity
of scholars as a whole, if learning like yours recommends you to the greatest
and most illustrious of monarchs and he seeks you out and summons you to
a land afar off! The monarch in question is not merely French, which is 95
already a great thing in itself; he is Francis, a name introduced by him for
the first time into our royal house and, we may fairly conjecture, full of

* * * * *

61–2 I have not ... property] A legal formula; cf Cicero *De oratore* 1.58.250.
79 seedtime or harvest] *Adagia* I vi 82

promise of great things. True, he knows nothing of literature, a normal quality of our kings, by a tradition which I myself do not much approve; but he has a natural sense of style, is clever, seemly, of gentle and easy access   100 and freely approachable, generously endowed by nature with rare gifts of body and mind, and an enthusiastic admirer of such ancient princes as have ever won fame by great heart or high exploits. Besides which, he has the wherewithal to be generous, if any king ever had, having recently on the first of January entered into a rich and most ample inheritance free from   105 indebtedness and all impediments; nor is anyone more freely and openly generous than he. As far as one can make out, he desires to be the founder of a famous institution, in order that in future the liberal arts may actually seem to have some profit in them, as has not been normal hitherto; and this is the best possible way of shedding lustre on the memory of his reign.   110

But what makes me undertake that all will go well for you is the fact that Petit who is, as I say, the king's pillow-chaplain, will be regarded, I believe, by the whole tribe of learned men, and truly good men as well, as a sort of agent for the public, making an offer on behalf of us all, and an assiduous remembrancer, so to say, who will not allow our prince to forget   115 his splendid proposal – one who is also particularly well-disposed towards you personally and what you write. Then there is the bishop of Paris, Etienne Poncher, a man of great learning and of settled and saintly character if ever a bishop was, of exceptional ability and powers of work, who in the conduct of diplomatic missions everywhere on both sides of the Alps has   120 risen through every level of seniority and gained experience in all the offices of state; one who inspires and encourages literary men, and for this and other reasons is well known and highly thought of in Italy, and with whom I am proud to claim kinship. This man is reported to be at the moment on an

* * * * *

104–106 having recently ... all impediments] The inheritance of Francis I from Louise of Savoy (d September 1531). The passage was inserted in *Epistolae latinae et graecae* which is dated February 1531 (Renouard *Imprimeurs* 650). To take issue with P.S. Allen's suggestion that Budé (who was in a position to be well-informed about events at court) referred to a false and preliminary rumour of her death, it may be pointed out that in France, Easter did not give place to 1 January as the beginning of the year until 1564. If so, the edition of Budé's letters by Josse Bade appeared in February 1532 and 'the first of January' in the letter could have been added to the proofs. Mme de la Garanderie in her recent edition of the correspondence (p 99n) favours the view, rejected by Allen, that the allusion is made to the death of Louis XII in 1515.

118 Etienne Poncher] Cf Ep 529 introduction.

124 kinship] Reading *cognationem*; Budé's grandmother was a Poncher (Allen II 573n).

assignment in Brussels, where he is awaiting the emperor in order to give   125
an account of his mission; and I expect he will already have invited you to
come and see him, if you have been in Brussels, such are his feelings
towards you, as I learnt from him when he passed through here rapidly on
the way to perform his task. He is, as I learn from his brother's son, who is
said to be a favourite, a keen reader of your books, in what time he can take   130
from the pressure of essential business. The nephew saw your edition of the
New Testament the other day, open, in his private chamber. For he too is
against those defenders and champions of so-called tradition (which is
really deep-dyed and hopeless ignorance) who, like 'reeking old Saturn
with his rheumy eyne,' as the saying goes, stand out against you and Truth,   135
that returning exile, and he is always ready to use his great authority in
defence of you and the truth.

Nor need you suspect that the king's proposal is a matter of impulse
rather than settled judgment and policy; for this same bishop told me, when
we were talking about you and about authors of the first rank, that the king   140
is now much concerned to promote literature of a higher and more polished
kind and that his Majesty had spoken with him about securing scholars of
eminence. I told him that you could be invited to France with a distinguished offer, and promised that I would take care of this, if things should
have turned out that way, and would be successful; I said you had studied   145
for a long time in Paris, and knew France as well as the land of your own
childhood. In my opinion he will give you the greatest support. And
furthermore, he himself enjoys very great influence with the prince, for he
has been admitted to the prince's most intimate council together with the
few whom the Ancients called 'apolecti,' men on the short list. You will   150
make up your mind about this, and then please write either to me or to

* * * * *

125 assignment] To secure the adhesion of Emperor Maximilian to the treaty
signed by Prince Charles and Francis I at Noyon, 13 August 1516. The emperor
agreed on 14 February and these negotiations culminated in the Treaty of
Cambrai, 11 March 1517.
126–7 to come and see him] Erasmus had met him by the time he next wrote to
Budé: cf Epp 531:618ff; 569:44ff.
129 son] François Poncher (d 1532) a canon of Paris who became bishop in
1519. In 1511 Girolamo Aleandro dedicated an edition of Sallust (Paris: J. Bade)
to him. In 1526 he was charged with simony and treason and he died in prison.
130 favourite] Literally 'does not take his eye off him'; *Adagia* v ii 50
135 saying] *Adagia* II i 75
150 'apolecti'] Cf Livy 35.34.2 and 36.28.8 where this is the reading of some
early editions (Allen). The true reading is *apocletas*.

someone else, if you think anyone is more your friend than I am, in order that, if you accept this offer, that is, if you think it worth accepting, the prince may bind himself by a new and more concrete proposal, by the agency in particular of the man at whose prompting I write this letter. For I 155
myself particularly wish this business to go through without your being misled in the least at any point.

I believe Guillaume Cop, the king's physician, a good scholar in both Latin and Greek and your friend and well-wisher, intends to write to you on this subject, and maybe others on instructions from the prince, or even his 160
Majesty in person. It is remarkable how devoted the tribe of Guillaumes is to you and to the humanities, for now you have three of the name all pursuing your interests in this same affair. But Etienne Poncher (and Etienne means 'the victor's crown'), if as I hope he has spoken with you, offers a most favourable omen for a complete and happy outcome of the 165
whole enterprise. However that may be, if you were to write a letter of thanks to the king himself, you would give him pleasure and do yourself credit. 'O joy, o rapture unconfined,' as it says in the comedy. 'How can Earth deep enough her gaping mouth' open to swallow up those prating crows, whose eyes you pick out every day? These mendacious characters, I 170
mean, who are set in opposition to you and begrudge you the reputation and the universal applause that you enjoy. Yet I myself, if the truth be told, am sometimes inclined to envy you, kind and considerate towards me though you always are, and to have some second thoughts about the excessive praise I was in such a hurry to lavish on you when we were 175
discussing those men who have reached the summit of humane learning. Is it surprising that I should take all this applause somewhat amiss, when you are so much more famous than I am? and that too when my own country-men are the judges in this contest. What a hapless foolish fellow I am! I the devoted patriot (a thing for which you are inclined to criticize me), always 180
impetuously ready to support my fellow Frenchmen, am not given my deserts even by the verdict of my own people. But, my dear friend, you

* * * * *

155 man] Cf lines 17ff.

159 intends to write] Ep 523

160–1 his Majesty] Francis' letter of invitation did not come for six years; cf Ep 1375 (7 July 1523).

168 comedy] Aristophanes *Peace* 291

168–9 'How can Earth] Virgil *Aeneid* 4.24

170 crows ... pick] Cf Ep 456:24n.

180 to criticize] Cf Ep 480:265–271.

must not be envious of me in return, for there is nothing in my situation to deserve it: I am, I maintain, not a success, and many of my friends (with whom I think you agree) believe that I am not treated as I deserve. And yet will you, for pity's sake, be cursing your own Poverty? Do not let her come anywhere near me! 185

Enough of this nonsense. When writing to you I cannot refrain from provoking you with a pleasantry or two, being a man made up of quips and cranks yourself – off with you, hell for leather, as the saying goes. Every good wish, my dearest friend, and may success and happiness ever attend on all your efforts. 190

Paris, 5 February

523 / From Guillaume Cop   Paris, 6 February [1517]

Cop, the distinguished physician and old friend of Erasmus (cf Epp 124:18n 305:208n), writes to Erasmus to second the offer conveyed by Budé; cf Ep 522 introduction. This letter was first published in the *Epistolae elegantes* 1517.

GUILLAUME COP TO HIS TEACHER ERASMUS OF ROTTERDAM,
GREETING

If after so much encouragement from you I have never answered your letters, please understand there was no other reason except my crass and barbarous ignorance, which was ashamed to prattle in your learned ear, as you might easily understand without a word from me. But at this moment I am obliged to break silence by his Majesty, and you shall hear briefly what it is all about. Guillaume Petit, a doctor of divinity who is the king's confessor and very zealous for your reputation, and François de Rochefort, the king's tutor in childhood and now an abbot, who often praises you to the skies among the nobles here, both went to the king when he was attending Mass, and persuaded him with many arguments to invite you to France. When he understood the extent of your consummate learning, the king at once instructed me to write to you and sound your feelings on the subject, whether you would be willing to live in France, and what conditions would retain you here. His most Christian Majesty promises that, if you decide to come and live among us, he will give you such generous 5

10

15

* * * * *

190 off with you] literally 'Let the horseman scour the plain', do what you are so good at; *Adagia* I viii 82
523:9 de Rochefort] François du Moulin de Rochefort (d 1526) was almoner to the king of France and abbot of St-Maximin at Micy-sur-Loire.

treatment that you will never repent of your decision. And so please let me
have an answer. I have not yet been able to see your Aphorisms.

Farewell, from Paris, 6 February   20

524 / From Antonius Clava   Ghent, 6 February [1517]

Antonius Clava of Ghent was a member of the Council of Flanders; cf Epp
175:13n, 301:39n. His anticipation of More's *Utopia* provides the chief clue to
the year-date of this letter, which was first published in the *Epistolae elegantes*
1517.

ANTONIUS CLAVA TO HIS FRIEND ERASMUS, GREETING
If I have written nothing to you so far, most learned Erasmus, the tragic
death of my sister, who died a little before I had your letter, and this intense
cold are responsible; I am in any case a very bad correspondent, and they
have made me so lazy and stuffy and full of yawns that you would think, as   5
the saying goes, that I lived on a diet of venison. But how are you? And are
you right to complain of my long silence? You never sent any previous letter
to your poor friend Clava, nor even a message of greeting, so far as I know;
yet I am such an admirer of your virtues and your learning, that I hardly
dare interrupt you when you are so busy on holy things and on your fruitful 10
researches, in which I know you are so profitably immersed to the great
advantage of humane studies. You ask about Robert de Keysere, and I can
tell you what he is doing. He is now making a very vigorous attack on
Roman law, as it is something he must maintain with constant energy and
resolution. You will agree that this is a great programme, and worthy of a   15
man of his imperial name. He has also written, as he told me some time ago,
to our common friend Erasmus, and would like an answer very much
indeed.

I am looking forward eagerly to Thomas More's merry book on the
new island of Utopia, which I expect hourly, for I instructed a bookseller   20
with whom I am very friendly to send it me as soon as ever he could. You say
you are still at seedtime and do not know what you will reap. Be of good

* * * * *

19 Aphorisms] The *Institutio principis christiani*, in its heading described as
'aphorismis digesta'; cf Erasmus' own account, Ep 393:69.
524:2 written nothing] In answer to the letter mentioned in Ep 525:4
5–6 as the saying goes] *Adagia* II vi 61
16 imperial name] Cf Ep 525:4–5.
16 written] Cf Ep 525:2–3.

cheer: you have a chancellor who is most humane, and a king who not only
likes learned and upright men but is also most generous. With these to rely
on, why do you think one must despair? If you do not get what you deserve   25
for all the divine and sacred seed you sow continually, I do not doubt that,
whether you will or no, you will reap a heavy and copious harvest of the
worldly and fleshly (to use the Apostle's word) and human sort. For the rest,
de Keysere greets you warmly, and your humble friend Clava recommends
himself to your protection; and we beg and pray that you will commend us   30
to our common master, the king's most excellent chancellor. Farewell, most
learned Erasmus.

Ghent, 6 February

525 / From Robert de Keysere   Ghent, [c 6 February 1517]

Robert de Keysere, formerly a schoolmaster at Ghent, was a printer who had
published the first edition of Erasmus' *Concio de puero Jesu*; cf Epp 301:39n, 175
introduction.

ROBERT DE KEYSERE TO MASTER ERASMUS OF ROTTERDAM, GREETING
Greetings, sweetest Erasmus. I should be glad to know whether my worthless productions have reached you. You rouse my feelings when you say in
your letter to Clava 'He ought to be doing something worthy of a name like
that.' What you are alluding to, I do not know. When Clava writes back that   5
I am vigorously attacking the law of the Caesars, that is no more surprising
than that everyone in Ghent at the moment is frozen stiff. I was never more
ashamed of my distinguished name and my glorious house than I am today,
since for three years now I have been unable to find anyone to share it with
me. One of my friends was removed by the common lot of all men, as they   10
call it; the other is now so much pierced and overwhelmed by the cold, that I
am entirely confined to my old empty 'Lynx,' with nothing to console me

* * * * *

23 chancellor] Jean Le Sauvage
23 king] Charles
28 Apostle's word] 1 Cor 9:11
525:3 productions] Cf Ep 530:14–15.
4 letter] That which is answered by Ep 524
7 frozen stiff] Cf Ep 524:3–4.
10 common lot] Reading *communis*
12 'Lynx'] A 13th-century house to the north of St Michael's church

but my own penury, like a snail in its shell. You add some irony to the
situation, by not recommending us to my friend the chancellor, or you will   15
not be able to, given the opportunity. I shall revive, however, when you get
a letter from Caesar; at the moment this is only Robert writing. Farewell, O
champion of the humanities.

From Ghent, at the sign of the Lynx

526 / From Pieter Gillis   [Antwerp, early February 1517]

PIETER GILLIS TO HIS FRIEND ERASMUS, GREETING
I am very sorry to hear that illness keeps you where you are. How could I not
be sorry, when the better half of my soul is sick? I hear that Tunstall has
returned from Tournai. My neighbour, who brings you this letter, wants a
recommendation to you, in hopes that you will recommend him as warmly   5
as you can to Tunstall, with whom you have so much influence. Your
company, dear Erasmus, will be a very great pleasure. I am sorry you dislike
your native land; but we will speak of this when we meet. Elias and men of
his kidney will never take me in again. Once bitten, twice shy. There are
some Prognostics on sale here under Ortwin's name; I never saw anything   10
more ridiculous, if you compare them with the forecasts of the physicians
here. The object of this nonsense I do not know; I send you a copy to amuse
you, in case you can take any pleasure in this kind of nonsense. My wife and
my parent send their greeting. Farewell.

* * * * *

526:2 illness] Cf 528:10–11, 530:7, 531:659–60.

4 returned] He reached Brussels on 27 January; LP ii 2847.

8 Elias] A person otherwise unknown

10 Prognostics] *Gemma prenosticationum* supposedly of Ortwinus Gratius (c
1480–1542) was a lampoon against a favourite target of the *Epistolae
obscurorum virorum*, an associate of Pfefferkorn; cf Ep 487:22n. Gratius was the
translator of Pfefferkorn's works into Latin and hence the butt of ridicule, but
his scholarly editions of classical authors show his serious interest in
humanism. His *Fasciculus rerum expetendarum seu fugiendarum* of 1535, re-
printing various works on the need for Church reform, was put on the Index in
1564: cf Jedin vol 1287n. See Dietrich Reichling *Ortwin Gratius, Sein Leben und
Werke: Eine Ehrenrettung* (Heiligenstadt 1884). A recent study that illuminates
the early career of Gratius is Charles G. Nauert Jr 'Peter of Ravenna and the
"Obscure Men" of Cologne' in *Renaissance Studies in Honor of Hans Baron*, eds
A. Molho and J.A. Tedeschi (Florence 1971) 609–40.

527 / From Willibald Pirckheimer   [Nürnberg, February 1517?]

It is quite possible that this letter should be dated 1516, in which case it would
be the letter to which Pirckheimer refers in Ep 409:1–3. This was the view of
Reich and Nichols, and is the place assigned to it in LB. P.S. Allen thought it
might equally refer to the imminent resignation of Richard Croke on the eve of
his return to Cambridge: see Allen II 453. Since neither argument is conclusive
the letter has been left where Allen put it. Apparently Pirckheimer copied out
the extract from Emser's letter and added his own note to Erasmus.

HIERONYMUS EMSER TO WILLIBALD, GREETING
If you ever write to Erasmus of Rotterdam, recommend me to him, though
he does not know me, and tell him at the same time that if he has any wish to
see the university at Leipzig and what the people are like in Meissen, I will
arrange with our illustrious prince that this is made possible for him by an   5
adequate salary every year or a proper sum for the expenses of his journey;
and let me know what he thinks of this.

WILLIBALD TO ERASMUS, GREETING
Hieronymus Emser, a licentiate in law, a good scholar and one of your keen
supporters, councillor of Prince George, Duke of Saxony, has written this to   10
me among other things. I wish you had a desire to see Saxony, so that you
might travel by way of Nürnberg, and then we could have a talk.

528 / To Thomas Grey and Pierre Vitré   Brussels, 13 February 1517

This letter, replying to Epp 444 and 503, was first published in the *Epistolae
elegantes* 1517.

ERASMUS OF ROTTERDAM TO HIS FRIENDS THOMAS GREY AND
PIERRE VITRÉ, GREETING
Your letters reached me on the same day, full of complaints at my failure to
answer. Besides these most recent letters of protest, or rather of rebuke, I
have had at least two from you, one from each, that is, which I have not yet   5
answered; but, if I remember rightly, I did send you greetings in a letter to
Bade. Nor is my affection for you any the less if I seldom write; so distracted

* * * * *

527:1 Emser] Cf Ep 553 introduction.
528:3 letters] Perhaps Ep 503 and another from Grey which is lost
5 two] Epp 444, 445

am I, partly by the disturbance of life at Court, partly by the unkindness of fortune, and to some extent also by my studies, that I am not really my own master. As I write this I am very poorly, not with the phlegm but more probably the plague, from which very many people are now suffering.

You lament, my dear Vitré, that I sent you where you are now in order to deprive you of my company; but you know yourself that it was the ill will of certain people that drove you from Calais, a result I always expected. And I only wish that you now enjoyed the sort of position I always wished you might have. All the same, it is something to live in one's own country, especially a country like yours, and you will make your lot more tolerable if you are willing to be what in fact you are. If there is anything in which you may need my help, try the experiment whether I am the same Erasmus I have always been. Letter-writing is a duty, but I could not possibly answer everyone, even if I did nothing else.

Your warmth of feeling, my dear Grey, and your affectionate heart are more welcome to me than I can say. I am sincerely delighted to hear that your son shows such promise. You say you are devoting yourself particularly to religion, to something, in fact, which will bring you happiness in life and a still happier deathbed; and this is wise of you, in your own interest you cannot do better. Though you for one will survive in your children, in whom you are a father twice over; for not satisfied with launching them into the world, you ensure that they are reborn in Christ. My best wishes to you both. Equally dear as you are both to me and to one another, it seemed right to join the two of you likewise in one letter.

Brussels, 13 February 1516

529 / To Etienne Poncher   Antwerp, 14 February 1517

The recipient, bishop of Paris from 1503–19, came from a wealthy family which had connections with that of Guillaume Budé. He rose through several government posts, was chancellor of the University of Paris (1501) and of the Duchy of Milan (1503) and ambassador to Italy (1511). In 1519 he was transferred to the archiepiscopal see of Sens. See Renaudet *Préréforme*. Erasmus has left Brussels as he had planned to do; cf Ep 516. This letter was first published in the *Epistolae elegantes* 1517.

* * * * *

10 very poorly] Cf Ep 526:2n.
16 one's own country] Cf Ep 444:19.
18 willing to be] Martial 10.47.12

Antwerp
A view of the harbour, *c* 1518–1540, by an anonymous master
National Scheepvaartmuseum, Antwerp

TO THE RIGHT REVEREND FATHER IN GOD ETIENNE PONCHER,
BISHOP OF PARIS, ENVOY OF HIS MOST CHRISTIAN MAJESTY
TO THE CATHOLIC KING

Respectful greetings, right reverend father and excellency. That France is
far the most flourishing realm in the Christian world is common know-   5
ledge; but in this respect it seems to me exceptionally fortunate, in that it
has a prince who is most Christian in fact as well as title and is richly
endowed with all the gifts that truly beseem a king; who is moreover in the
prime of life, so that there is good hope that your native Gaul and we, her
neighbours and friends, shall enjoy this felicity for many years, indeed for   10
ever. A nature upright and vigorous, a mind worthy not merely of a king
but of such a king as he: spirited and ambitious, yet fully sympathetic with
the humanities in their widest sense, and then again upright and
straightforward but yet watchful and wise in the highest degree; for in the
recent conflict with the Swiss he showed clearly enough that, though fully   15
prepared and ready to make war if he cannot secure peace, he yet greatly
prefers peace to war. He counts it far more important to make his realm rich,
glorious and splendid with excellent laws, exalted standards of morality
and every honourable form of culture than to extend the boundaries of his
dominions. He understands of course that these alone are the true orna-   20
ments of a kingdom, these are its real wealth and the true glory that the
passage of the centuries can never dim.

And so he is not satisfied to have strengthened his kingdom with
proper defences, unless at the same time he sees it enriched and distinguished with men whose scholarship and integrity are alike outstanding,   25
judging that this above all others is the way to be a great and prosperous
king, if his subjects are not as numerous but as good as they can be. Many of
these he has with him already – among the first the incomparable Guillaume Cop, champion and leader in the field of medicine, who is claimed in
rivalry by both France and Germany. Then there is Guillaume Budé, most   30
certainly the glory of France, who long ago by universal consent of the
learned world snatched from the grasp of the Italians the victory in both the
ancient tongues, surpassing all others in his mastery of Latin no less than in
Greek he surpasses himself. None the less, he looks elsewhere: every day he
invites some foreign scholar with tempting offers, recalling in this point as   35
in others the long-forgotten example of the most famous monarchs of
antiquity. If among such people he does not hesitate to think of me as well, I
am conscious on my side of the debt I owe to his intentions, and wish I were

* * * * *

529:15 conflict with the Swiss] Cf Ep 360:5–6; the negotiations after Marig-
nano were finally concluded on 29 November 1516 (Ep 463:41n).

capable of justifying the judgment of so illustrious a prince. The generous
opinion of certain persons lays on me a burden of reputation which I could   40
not accept without gross egoism, nor live up to without being a quite
different man from the self I know. In other ways, I have always loved your
land of France, and it is specially dear to me because I spent there some
delightful years with freedom to study the best authors. But now my age
counsels me not to change my country, so that even had I not chosen this as   45
my home, I should still be obliged to settle wherever old age might have
chanced to overtake me. Besides which, I am bound by the generosity of our
excellent Prince Charles and his zeal for the promotion of humane studies,
which agrees so closely with the policy of your king that he seems engaged
in competition with him for the honour of so doing. Consequently, I can   50
send no definite answer on this point for the moment, except my sincere
recognition of your excellent king's goodness towards me and my
gratitude, which is no less than if I were already enjoying his generous
offer, with the assurance that I shall not fail in future to comply with the
wishes of so great a prince, who invites me with such uncalled-for generos-   55
ity, provided I can do so honestly and in good faith. If this opportunity is
denied me, I shall not feel I owe any less to France; and you in turn will not
take it amiss, if I do not perform what is outside my reach. My feeble body I
cannot put at all men's service, my mind and its fruits I can.

Apart from that, when I see his Majesty and you, right reverend   60
Father, devoting so much effort to the adornment of your land of France
with really good and cultivated men, the name of Henricus Glareanus
comes appropriately to mind. I came to know him long ago when I saw
much of him in Basel, and in my opinion he is as much the man you want as
anyone could be. Here is a brief but most reliable account of him. By birth a   65
Swiss (for that country too begins to add distinguished learning to its
renown in arms), in the prime of life, being not yet past thirty, of robust
health, and a very hard worker, he has spent some years already in teaching
the liberal arts first in Cologne and then in Basel, and not without great
success. He is a doctor of what they call the Seven Arts, and not (like the   70
majority of men of that rank) in name alone. In sophistic philosophy he was
an expert, but having seen the error of his ways is now an enemy and a

* * * * *

46 old age] He was still under fifty.

62 Glareanus] Heinrich Loriti; cf Ep 440 introduction.

70 Seven Arts] Traditionally, the disciplines preparatory to the study of
philosophy: grammar, rhetoric and logic (the *trivium*), arithmetic, geometry,
music and astronomy (the *quadrivium*).

71 sophistic philosophy] Cf 328:43n.

renegade. Theology he has not merely paid his respects to from the threshold, but at one time had advanced into the inner shrine; taking a dislike, however, partly to the frigid quibbling which now secures almost 75 all the applause in the schools, and partly to the infinite disputes and differences between theologians, he retreated, deciding to draw Christ from the fountain-head and not from their standing pools. For this purpose he set about acquiring Greek with enthusiasm. He is a poet of considerable charm, and in this field was once crowned with the laurel while still very 80 young at Cologne by Emperor Maximilian. In prose his performance shows no lack of talent or of learning, though sometimes one might wish he had more experience and practice. He has a great knowledge of history, and in music, geography and all the other subjects that are commonly called mathematical he is most experienced, for this is the field in which he is a 85 specialist.

Then again, he has such a high standard of character and conduct, a rare gift in men of this sort, that not only in thought but even in talk he abhors all trace of anything improper, while he is passionately devoted to true personal religion. Momus himself would have no fault to find in him, 90 except for the way he lets himself go against those prickly sophisters, if we are to call this a fault and not good judgment on his part; for you know how proud and conceited such men are, except for those who have combined a more liberal education with the study of philosophy. Against them Glareanus does battle with no less spirit than Hercules at grips with his 95 monsters and, rant as they may, he has the lungs and voice to match them, and above all the invincible spirit of a true Hercules. For this reason there is not much love lost between him and the theologians, not the scholarly sort, with whom he gets on very well, but those one could name who beyond the mumbo-jumbo of some pointless *questiones* have learnt nothing. He finds 100 them all the easier to rout and cut to pieces because he was once familiar with their strongholds himself. Though like other things this fire and fury, this divine frenzy if you like, becomes daily more temperate with age. Apart from that, he is as far as could be from all self-conceit and pomposity, having very easy ways, adaptable to any sort of society. Bid him sing, and 105 he will sing without hesitation; if you would rather he read, he will read. If

* * * * *

73–4 from the threshold] Cf Ep 511:10n.
80–81 very young] Aged 24 years
90 Momus] Patron deity of quibbling criticism: *Adagia* I v 74

you feel like levity, he can be a very merry fellow; but should you wish to be serious, he will at once become quite different. And yet, adaptable as he is, he is incapable of flattery.

If you wish to know how he stands in the world, he is quite uncommit- 110 ted: not given to excesses, no admirer of money, not hampered by a wife nor bound by any vows save those of baptism. He wrote to me lately that he would have an annual salary in France from the royal exchequer as soon as peace should be made between you and the Swiss; and I am delighted to hear that this has now happened. If he has taken this up, I beg your 115 Lordship to be so good as to make his acquaintance, and see whether I have painted a misleading picture; if he has not arrived, you should take steps to have him sent for, and that on honourable terms. I know what his gifts are worth; but he is a most modest man, and will be content, I believe, with a hundred écus à la couronne, which, believe me, will be well spent. I know 120 the value of Horace's advice, that we should consider more than once whom we commend to whom; but in this man I have no fear 'lest others' errors make me blush for shame.' Normally it is those whose introductions are accepted who say thank you; but I expect to be thanked myself, once you know my friend Glareanus as well as I do. In this matter if you wish me to do 125 anything, give me my orders. For if invited in a letter from me, he will come all the more readily and rapidly (not to rate my influence too highly), especially if I give him the picture of you that I have given you of him. But mind you, he should not be summoned in a letter that is empty-handed; journey-money should be added as a kind of earnest of the rest that is 130 promised him.

You see how frankly I write to you, as though I had forgotten your high position. So spoilt have I been by your kindness, which has taught me this lack of shame; you must either forgive it entirely, or take a great part of the blame at least upon yourself.   135

Farewell, from Antwerp, 14 February 1516

Erasmus of Rotterdam

* * * * *

112 lately] Ep 463:47–8

119–20 a hundred écus à la couronne] gold French coins (*coronatis*), then worth £29 11s 8d gros Flemish = £20 16s 8d sterling = £195 0s 0d tournois. On 27 November 1516 a royal edict raised the value of the écu à la couronne from 35s 0d tournois to 39s 0d tournois. Cf CWE 1 315, 336–37; CWE 2 340 (plate), 327–44; and Ep 363:48n above.

121 Horace's advice] *Epistles* 1.18.76–7 .

530 / To Antonius Clava   Antwerp [c 14 February 1517]

This letter was first published in the *Epistolae elegantes* 1517. It replies to Ep 524.

ERASMUS OF ROTTERDAM TO ANTONIUS CLAVA, MEMBER OF THE COUNCIL, GREETING

I would offer you consolation, my distinguished friend, on your sister's death, were I not convinced that the sorrow of it, which in other men is softened and removed by mere passage of time, has in you been comforted 5 long ago by your unwavering philosophy. As for me, I have been so much distracted on all sides by illness, by the effort of research on more fronts than one, and by frequent changes of abode, that I have been almost beside myself. Yet through it all I have never forgotten my friend Clava, the most sympathetic patron of men of letters because of course he is so well-read 10 himself. I have actually written to you once or twice.

That our friend Robert should have several strings to his bow is good; my view is that after trying everything he will find the right solution eventually. He sent me not so much a letter as, in his own words, a tragedy, an Iliad of misfortunes; but his humour made a very good story of it. But it is 15 not yet clear to me which of them did me the greater disservice, the man who attacked me so severely as an enemy or he who overpraised me in public as a friend, and thereby misrepresented me and made me unpopular; for nothing sharpens the tooth of envy among one's fellow-men more than excessive praise. We find that intolerable in great men, men whose 20 quality should be beyond the reach of ill will, and so it is less surprising if they cannot tolerate the praises of a man like me who scarcely rises into mediocrity. Or rather, if that parson let fly at me like that, I owe this to the man who sang my praises. 'Goodwill untimely differs not from hate.' What was the point of dragging you into such nonsense when you were busy on 25 better things? It was a waste of time to write and describe to me the ravings of one party or the other among themselves. The poets tell us that Jupiter himself cannot please everyone, rain or shine. I for my part have done what I could, and shall do more in the future, to give all men satisfaction; until that time I console myself partly with a good conscience, partly with the 30 knowledge that all the best judges at least do not disapprove of me, and

* * * * *

530:12 Robert] de Keysere; cf Epp 524, 525.
15 Iliad] *Adagia* I iii 26
24 'Goodwill untimely] A Greek line often in Erasmus' mind; *Adagia* I vii 69
27 the poets] Theognis 25–6; *Adagia* II vii 55

maybe I shall win general approval as soon as envy falls silent after my death.

When you have read More's *Utopia*, you will feel you have been suddenly transported into another world; everything there is so different. 35 About the harvest I am to reap I am not much concerned, provided my expenses do not exceed my income. I have enough to satisfy my present frame of mind and my retired life, and my days on earth will soon have shot their bolt. Moreover you will find that I even enjoy casting off the burden of reputation, and virtually accepting Epicurus' rule, to live unseen. By the 40 way, I am now expecting a letter from you half in Greek, now you are already in your third year as a Grecian. Give my warmest greetings to de Keysere. The chancellor is your sincere well-wisher.

Farewell. From Antwerp

531 / To Guillaume Budé   Antwerp, 15 February 1517

> This letter, a reply to Ep 493, was first published in the *Epistolae elegantes* 1517. The fair copy sent to Budé was copied out by Erasmus' host in Antwerp, Pieter Gillis; cf Ep 534: 66–8.

ERASMUS OF ROTTERDAM TO HIS FRIEND GUILLAUME BUDÉ,
GREETING

Really, my most learned Budé, what princely generosity! You have repaid my ill-educated letter with one of such exquisite learning, giving me like Glaucus in Homer more than gold for what was hardly bronze, and have 5 rewarded my mediocre performance with something so flowery and so long, it was not a letter, it was a volume, or rather a thesaurus, in itself. In the name of all the Muses, how much learning there is in it, and of no ordinary kind! What classic eloquence, not at all of our own age! Could anything be more elegant, more charming? How truly like yourself you are, 10 how eminently you put the true Budé on paper! I would support this opinion of mine with the votes of many other readers; but there are so few in this part of the world who can follow your bilingual letters – they would not understand them very well, if I mistake not, if you wrote in one language. Cuthbert Tunstall at any rate, whose judgment as an individual I 15 find worth as much as constant sounding of other opinions, was so ravished, so enchanted, so inspired by your letter, that he simply devoured it – read it is not the word – and re-read it three or four times, nor could it be

* * * * *

531:5 Glaucus] Gave Diomede gold armour in exchange for a suit of bronze; *Adagia* I ii 1.

extracted from him anyhow except by threats. Indeed, had he not suddenly been called away from Prince Charles to Emperor Maximilian and soon   20 overwhelmed with great tides of business, he was already squaring up to write to you. For he did not think it proper to start a friendship with a man eminent in so much besides literature and of such recondite all-round scholarship by sending an unpolished letter; while I made much of your friendly disposition and urged him to write for the moment whatever might   25 come into his head. But he is a better scholar than I am and so has a clearer idea of your gifts, and therefore his respect and veneration for you is a more solemn thing than mine.

As for my own judgment, how others value it I know not. You at any rate cannot reject it altogether, for you asked for it yourself; it was you   30 dressed me in the lion's skin and made me play Aristarchus to what you write. I for my part do not enter my name on the list of learned critics; but I should like to be numbered among your friends, below the rest as far as you like in every other respect, but in devotion to you I undertake to yield to no man. Yet I am not, I think, such a stranger to the Muses of good literature   35 that I do not have some idea of your most rare and almost more than human intelligence, for what is exceptionally prominent and brilliant can usually be detected even by men of defective vision. Nor on the other hand am I so much dazzled by devotion to you that affection blindfolds me and I cannot see clearly, as often happens when judgment takes its cue from affection.   40 Conversely, when affection is prompted by judgment, so far is love from being blind that nothing has keener sight, and it then ensues that the greater our affection, the keener our vision and the more reliable our judgment.

Some time ago I thought I detected that you were challenging the   45 Italians in this field, and a noble contest it is, but exceptionally difficult; to be quite frank, I almost despaired of your success. But now I perceive you are so successful that I think in these days there is no one among the Italians so self-centred and self-confident that he would risk a challenge to Budé, and compete with him in a field he has made his own. I speak with no party   50 spirit, and mean no offence to Italy, for I am her keen supporter and rate her very highly. Who would be ready nowadays to descend into this arena, when we see those heroic and by common consent quite inimitable figures

* * * * *

20 called away] Cf Epp 515:9, 526:3–4.
22 write to you] Cf Ep 571.
31 lion's skin] *Adagia* I iii 66
31 Aristarchus] The prince of ancient critics; *Adagia* I iii 10, I v 57, I ix 41

Ermolao Barbaro and Angelo Poliziano far surpassed by you equally in the
mastery and free use of both ancient tongues? Happy indeed is France, and   55
what airs she would give herself if she knew her own resources! But such is
human nature: as Horace says, when excellence is with us, we resent it, or at
least pay no attention; but 'reft from our sight, we seek her jealously.'

    If it should come about that my present feelings should be shared by
France as a whole, Budé's famous figure would be set up in solid gold in all   60
our greater churches; though in fact those statues will have a longer life
which are set up in his honour in the hearts of all learned men, and will
stand for ever. Some men will find flattery in my words and others arrogance, I know full well; but only those who have never got to know your
exquisite works or at least do not reach their level. Anyone who has done   65
both will exempt me forthwith from either criticism.

    After this you say in jest (for what else can it be?) that I wish to obstruct
your ancient lights – your high lights, rather. I will tell you briefly, dear
Budé, just what I think. If there has hitherto been any drag on your
reputation, nothing can be blamed for this except the fact that up to now   70
very few mortals can keep pace with your new and recondite erudition;
when that moment comes, my life upon it, the lustre of your name will
promptly dazzle us all, and you will put into the shade the fame of everyone
everywhere who has any reputation now. All the same, we shall have no
right of action against you, if I may for the moment include myself among   75
men of some reputation, which truly makes me a minnow among the
Tritons. For in your business world, the men who build higher than is right
secure an advantage for themselves by inflicting harm on their neighbours
and profit themselves out of other men's loss. In this field the opposite is
true: he who interferes with another's monopoly of the light does him a   80
service, not an injury, and the man whose own light is obstructed enjoys
no less light as a result – perhaps indeed rather more – but what brilliance
he has of his own is now less outstanding. There is therefore no question
here of an action for damages, no more than the lesser stars could complain
when they fade and are put out at the sudden rising of the sun. And yet one   85
may find people who in their selfishness have got it so wrong, that they

* * * * *

54 Barbaro, Poliziano] Cf Ep 493:403.

57 Horace] *Odes* 3.24.31–2

67–8 obstruct ... lights] Erasmus again uses the analogy between blocking a
neighbour's 'ancient lights' and obscuring his reputation or criticizing his
brilliance of style; cf Ep 493:488n.

76–7 minnow among the Tritons] Literally 'blue pimpernel in the salad,' a
Greek proverb of someone overplaced; *Adagia* I vii 21

think other men's gain is a loss to themselves. For my part, ill-fated as I am in other respects, I think myself not wholly unfortunate in this, that my friends' success gives me even more pleasure than my own, and I am not incensed when my enemies have a reputation provided they do some   90 service to the cause of good letters. And I wish we might see even now the success which I believe awaits the humanities in the near future, so that a man like myself, who am credited by some people with a modicum of learning and reasonable powers of expression, may come to seem an ignoramus and quite speechless and tongue-tied.   95

And now to answer bit by bit several sections of your letter: if it should ever befall me to be tried on a capital charge, I could ask for no better counsel than my friend Budé: you show such cunning in defending yourself as you do, not satisfied with refuting all my arguments, unless you had turned all my weapons clean against me, and converted me in a moment from judge   100 into defendant. Your whole defence is based on the idea that I must either let you go scot-free or condemn myself inevitably in any sentence which I may pass on you. Observe the power of your own enviable eloquence: you put the judge in jeopardy while the accused remains secure, and make him think himself lucky if only he is allowed to let the accused go free without   105 running any risk himself. At this point, when you match me in a contest against yourself, I at once think, my dear Budé, of that Greek proverb about the ant and the camel, or any pair more ill-matched than they. Tell me, what resemblance or relationship of any kind is there between us, except perhaps this spirit that is not averse from the humanities? Make light of your success   110 as far as you can, self-taught as you may be and a late beginner: in one point at least I go one better than you – I have never been taught anything, and am quite uneducated. Nor do I believe that you set up this comparison on purpose, because you thought these humble resources of mine were comparable in any way with your own riches, but to make your own brilliance   115 more striking by setting me alongside it, on the same plan, I suppose, as painters are said to follow in using shadow in their work to emphasize what they wish to stand out, and as some ingenious ladies to impress the beholder with their beauty (which is excellent in its own right) take care to bring plain serving-women with them. Poliziano, I think, did much the   120 same when he wove other men's letters to him in with his own, which was almost without precedent. There are men in that book whose self-conceit he could not have shown up so clearly in any other way, and others again who

* * * * *

108 the ant and the camel] Typical of great inequalities; *Adagia* I v 47
111 self-taught] Cf Ep 493:21.

write very well when left to themselves, but when compared with him
strike one as inarticulate.   125

In saying this I do not suggest that you are not brilliant enough in your
own right, and need me like a patch of shadow to set you off; this is a device
intended, I believe, to correct the errors of certain people, and at the same
time to lighten for me the load of a reputation I do not deserve. For there are
people who think much too highly of me, some of whom you yourself have   130
given away, Deloynes I mean and Ruzé, who regard me, you say, as the
Varro of our age, except that I can write better than he could; for it would not
be proper to suggest that you put that in out of your own head as though
with a little flattery you could make them more acceptable. There are some,
on the other hand, who denude me of everything; to one party there is   135
nothing I do not know, and to to the others I know absolutely nothing. Nor
is it yet clear to me which do me the greater disservice, the spendthrifts
whose generosity loads me with exaggerated tributes which I could not
possibly accept unless I were singularly conceited or completely shameless,
or those whose jealousy strips me so bare that there is absolutely nothing   140
left. On the one hand, I have not the effrontery to demand a place in the
world of letters like that taken by Achilles or Diomede on the field of battle;
but on the other, I am not so ignorant of my own capacity as to put Thersites
above me. And yet it troubles me not a little that I can neither be indignant
with those whose affection and high opinion of me blinds their judgment,   145
unless I would rather incur the stigma of gross discourtesy, nor prove those
others wrong, whom in some ways I am more disposed to favour because
they seem more to bear out my own opinion. This, to be sure, is one reason
why I love you too, my dear Budé, that you disagree with those who admire
me excessively; for so I understand your meaning when you say you are   150
somewhat jealous of me in this respect. I would rather have your jealousy,
which means your critical opinion, than the enthusiastic support of other
men, which makes me truly unpopular, though I deserve every man's pity
and no man's jealousy. If I think well of myself, it is with this limitation:
what Socrates said of himself with false modesty, I think I can very nearly   155
assert with truth and sincerity of myself: the one thing I know is that I know
nothing. Maybe I shall not convince other people, but you at least will I

* * * * *

131 Deloynes ... and Ruzé] Cf Epp 493:462ff, 494 introduction.

143 Thersites] An ugly, ignoble and contentious character in the second book
of the *Iliad*; *Adagia* IV iii 80

150 your meaning] Ep 493:458-9

155 Socrates] Plato *Apology* 21D

157 you at least] Reading *certe*

hope believe me in this, my dear Budé, if you believe me at all: I never brought anything to such a degree of finish that I was really satisfied with it. To this someone might instantly retort: Why then overwhelm us with this 160 flood of books, if you think none of your work is any good? To begin with, I cannot sleep – an excuse already used by Horace. And then, if I summon up my courage to write something, it is other men's amazing impudence that drives me to it who, though they cannot write and have read nothing, have the effrontery to teach what they do not know. You get the urge to write 165 from Pliny and Ermolao and Poliziano; in me the passion is aroused by Passavanti and Hugo and their like, the compilers of summaries; for though more than tongue-tied compared with your great scholars, in this unmusical company even a lark like me dares to give tongue.

But to return to my subject: although I see it must do great damage to 170 my reputation, yet I rejoice meanwhile to be in some fashion matched against my Budé, especially when you do this yourself with such learning, in heaven's name, and such eloquence and so divinely that nowhere do you show more clearly how far I am beneath you as when you put me on the same level as yourself or even (the Muses help us!) higher. And yet all the 175 time, as I say, I preen myself on gaining for the future at least this much, that, though I retire defeated, yet it will be told how I was matched against Budé, the champion of scholars, like some Thersites against Achilles. What matter the outcome? – I was matched, all the same. There are some men whom it is a discredit to have beaten; others whom it is creditable enough 180 to have been beaten by, and this degree of glory is sufficient for my way of thinking. Why should I not confess my ambition to you, the dearest of my friends? – since you, as you say in your letter, have opened your whole self in good faith to me. You say that I have not so much developed a hatred for my wife Poverty as a passion for her rival Good Repute; which you would 185 certainly not have written, I am quite sure, if you had a fuller and more intimate knowledge of me. As a young man I was not untouched by the

* * * * *

162 Horace] *Satires* 2.1.7

167 Passavanti] Jacopo (d 1357), a Dominican friar of Florence who wrote *Lo Specchio di vera penitenza* which was first printed at Florence 12 March 1496; cf Quétif I 645^b–6^a, II 821^a.

167 Hugo] Cf Ep 347:105n.

167 summaries] Cf Ep 575:34–5.

169 even a lark] The Greeks thought the crested lark a poor songster, and a lark singing in unmusical company is the equivalent of our 'the one-eyed man is king in the country of the blind'; *Adagia* II ii 92.

185 rival] Cf Ep 493:419.

wish to be famous, and that not seriously, to be sure; and now there is
nothing I would rather do than lay aside the reputation, such as it is, which
is the only reward my labours earn for me, and even that is corrupted and   190
soured by no small share of ill will, so that there is not a little more bitter
aloes than honey in it – either lay it aside, if that were possible, or shed it in
the place where those stags of yours shed their antlers; I swear by
Philosophy, the beloved mistress whom we share, if you do not trust me
except on oath. On this point, then, though I entirely differ from you, yet I   195
could not deny that my mind is assailed by a great feeling of satisfaction
when things written by people like you either speak well of me or at least do
not reject me; for the acquaintance and affection of such people is, I believe,
an important part of one's felicity. And your style, taken by itself, I like and
respect so much that even a rebuke couched in such language is a pleasure,   200
even a wound dealt by a weapon of such distinction. For it does not escape
my notice on how many points you attack me in your letter while defending
yourself, and how you and your pleasantries give me a good shake-up and
make fun of me. But you are welcome to do this often, provided you do it in
the same elegant fashion – though your style now is most friendly too; such   205
is the affection I feel for your gifts. Nor shall I have any misgivings in future
about provoking your criticism in one way or another. Now that I have
started, I am resolved to make a clean breast of everything. I was well aware,
dear friend, how easily appeased you are by nature; and yet I had my
doubts whether I might give offence by my bold criticism of what you   210
write, just as though I were some Areopagite, a regular Aristarchus, instead
of Erasmus, that three-ha'penny character. But now that my temerity has
turned out so well, I shall have no hesitation in future in inventing accusations, provided that my shameless behaviour is allowed to extract letters
such as these from my dear Budé.   215

As it is, your counter-attack having turned me from judge or pros-
ecutor into defendant, I shall clearly not attempt to counter such a massed
and well-drilled phalanx of arguments in the open field and in a pitched
battle, which even Xerxes could hardly do; but at least I shall turn skir-
misher and try to raid several divisions of your army and harrass it,   220
assailing it now on one side and now on the other and pulling out the mare's
tail gradually hair by hair. On one at a time I shall perhaps make some
impression, though I cannot prove a match for all at once. First of all, take

*****

191–2 more bitter aloes than honey] *Adagia* I viii 66
211 Areopagite] A solemn judge; cf Ep 456:12–13n.
211 Aristarchus] A severe critic; cf 31n above.
221–2 mare's tail] *Adagia* I viii 95

my introduction, in which you say that I indulge in quibbling, or rather in
false modesty. Your evasive action is neat enough, provided I let you get   225
away scot-free with something which you take for granted exactly as
though it were common ground between us – that there is something useful
I can do which no one else can. And yet this is precisely the point that I
consistently and explicitly deny over and over again, for it cannot stand up
against even moderate arguments. 'Suppose there are some tasks,' you say,   230
'which you can achieve and no one else.' Suppose the heavens fall. Besides
which, before you match my modest style with your splendid eloquence,
you should perhaps have explained more precisely where you suppose that
grandeur you speak of to be situated. If you mean in the nature of the
subject-matter, I have as yet undertaken nothing sufficiently exalted to   235
demand anything in the tragic vein. Nor is your 'as' an exalted subject in
itself, except in so far as it is a difficult one; it is your treatment that exalts it.
Otherwise, I think the best is always greatest. But if you suppose grandeur
of style to lie in the actual forms of expression, my own conviction is this: I
think that style of writing most exalted which is most effective in recom-   240
mending its chosen subject; for on this point I differ somewhat from
Quintilian, who held that nothing should be called eloquence which lacks
the power to compel admiration. For since much of the art lies in concealing
art, because any suggestion of artifice makes the speaker less credible, I do
not see how a style can be effective which parades itself and shows off.   245
Clothes can be at the same time both splendid and, in spite of that,
convenient; eloquence cannot be suitable at the same time both for moving
the hearers and displaying the speaker's skill. The best shot is not the man
with a bejewelled quiver and the grandest possible bow, but he who hits
the target most infallibly. Your great philosopher is not the one with the   250
finest grasp of Stoic or Peripatetic doctrines, but he who exemplifies the
principles of philosophy in his life and character, which is philosophy's
true aim. In the same way, the task of the consummate orator is fulfilled by
the man who has carried conviction. If this were not so, would not one look
foolish who set out to recall the multitude from the fever of war to a great   255
desire for peace, and by an elaborate rhetorical speech persuaded them only
that he was a very clever and well-read man? That was not the point at issue.
The theatre too does not seek to arouse admiration by any and every means.
The player is damned who seeks to catch the eye of his audience with some

* * * * *

225 false modesty] Cf Ep 493:421.
231 Suppose the heavens fall] *Adagia* i v 64
242 Quintilian] 8.3.6

rich alien setting when he should have invited its applause by the acting   260
and the play. Personally, if our object is grandeur of style, I think that
splendour of language has very little to contribute, nor is much to be gained
from rhetorical devices unless they are grounded in the subject-matter, not
the words. It makes no little difference whether it is the play or the splendid
setting that you admire. Professors of rhetoric, at any rate, themselves agree   265
that the natural style of speaking wins the highest praise. Yet nothing could
be less remarkable; for who would remark the art of what he supposes to be
a natural product? And they differ by absolutely the whole gamut, the thing
they put first and the thing you seem to accept; not to mention meanwhile
that it is very foolish to admire what you do not understand. It follows that   270
clarity should be the chief aim of everyone who wishes his style to be
admired.

You yourself know already that all this passion for polishing one's
style was scarcely accepted in the old days by men of sound judgment, and
professors of rhetoric who are most eloquent in other respects have   275
difficulty in convincing us that the art of oratory serves any useful purpose
or is worthy of a man of high character. I think it all the more unfair of you to
demand a power of expression actually proper to the stage from a Christian
theologian, while Cicero expects a gentile philosopher to have none at all,
content if he makes himself understood. But your aforesaid teachers of   280
rhetoric who, as is fair enough, are all for the importance of the subject they
profess, do not, even so, approve the exquisite elaboration of style that you
have in mind, except in one department only, panegyric. Nothing, I suppose, could be further from this than a style wholly employed in teaching,
and what is more, not in teaching any subject you may choose (for the   285
causes of thunderbolts or earthquakes might furnish forth a splendid
paragraph), but things intrinsically small and ordinary, and moreover so
difficult and involved that, no matter how distinct and lucid and simple and
appropriate your exposition may be, even an attentive reader will scarcely
grasp them. If ever there are occasions when the difficulty of the subject   290
seems to demand a very easy style, this at least was one of them, in order to
spare the reader the twofold discomfort first of subject-matter and then of
exposition; while, since everything is mutually interdependent and so the
reader must press on impatiently to the conclusion, this did not seem the
moment to delay his progress by putting rough places and muddy bottoms   295
in his way. Besides which, if that style is most generally acceptable which
keeps closest to the matter in hand, can it be appropriate, I ask you, to

* * * * *

268 the whole gamut] *Adagia* I ii 63

appeal to the people (your own phrase) on such a barren topic? For it does not immediately follow that what is most difficult is also at the same time most exalted; on the contrary, we usually find that the most difficult things 300 are those which are most minute. This class of subjects, all the same, has its virtues; but in my opinion they include brilliance and grandeur least of all.

I now appeal, dear Budé, to your own intelligence. Would you tolerate Euclid holding forth on geometrical figures with all the display of rhetoric you recommend? But you were not unaware of all this, I fancy, when you 305 had some piece of work finished at all points and wished to submit a specimen of your gifts to the plaudits of the learned at any rate; and it was your cunning plan to interlard your *De asse* with digressions, like grass-plots in a sea of brambles, to give the reader wearied by the thorny subject somewhere to rest and breathe again. You threaten to accuse me of having 310 done the same in the *Chiliades*, unless I cease to accuse you, for you say that in my *Sileni*, forgetting what I have set out to do, I make the world my stage; in the *Dulce bellum inexpertis* I make war on those warlike characters of yours; in the *Scarabaeus* I am full of merry tricks; in the proverb *Spartam nactus exorna* and many others I harangue the reader. How gladly, if I could, 315 I would admit to the same defect as you, provided only that it had brought me the same success! Though, if I wished to quibble, I could reply that your case is not entirely similar to mine. Your *De asse* all holds together like a chain, so that there is not the same scope for longer digressions. The system of my *Chiliades* is such that, whenever you have finished an adage, you can 320 imagine that you have come to the end of the volume. And many topics come one's way which almost invite one to deliver an harangue. Tell me, by all the Muses: when, after starting from the subdivisions of the 'as' in purely instructive style, you come on near the end of the work to settle down to that long conversation with your friend Deloynes about the condi- 325 tions and the manners of modern life, are you not afraid that some critical croaker might throw that question of Horace in your teeth?

An amphora it was when it began;
As the wheel spins, why does a jug result?

Pliny also ranges widely in his history of the world, on a theme immensely 330 wide, it is true, but more briefly than either of us, and less often than I do.

* * * * *

298 your own phrase] Ep 493:164–5

310 threaten to accuse] Cf Ep 493:265ff.

312–15 *Sileni ... Spartam nactus exorna*] *Adagia* III iii 1. IV i 1, III vii 1, II v 1

327 Horace] *Ars poetica* 21–2

330 Pliny] The Elder; his *Naturalis historia* in thirty-seven books was dedicated to the future emperor Titus. It embraced a wide diversity of subjects.

So does Seneca in his enquiry into natural causes, but somewhat in-
frequently. You can see how much more sparingly I have allowed myself
this liberty on the New Testament, although there too the subject is not of
such close texture as yours of the 'as'. I hear that some people take the same   335
view of your annotations on the Pandects which, though they brought you
a great reputation, would have earned, they think, a somewhat higher one,
had you cut out the good things from your very well-stocked larder which
you pile on our plates rather than set before us, like some over-lavish
Lucullus rather than an industrious chief butler, and had contributed to the   340
common stock those things in particular which properly pertained to your
chosen subject; to give an example, if, when expounding the nature of
vindicta, you had not promptly heaped up together what is to be found
anywhere in any kind of author about *vindicare, vindicta* and *vindiciae*, but
only what properly belonged to the elucidation of that passage. As it is, no   345
one feels that erudition is lacking; but at the same time, the greedy reader or
the busy one or those who are merely difficult to please object that this is a
great big book, and yet only a few passages out of so many are fully treated.
Not but what the things you bring in by force are learned enough to leave
the reader who has leisure and an open mind with no regrets for the extra   350
work you have given him.

    But I now return to the question of style. I know, well do I know, dear
Budé my most learned friend, that with your natural fluency you can
succeed in any style if you do but wish to; you yourself suggest this, and it
means that a man like you, since you can do whatever you wish, should   355
wish only for the best. Personally, I have never accepted the stumbling
tongue-tied fashion of some men we know, who wish us to recognize as an
important factor in scholarship an inability to express oneself or (what in
my view is more pitiful) a foul style full of monstrosities. Language above
all is the mirror of the mind, and the mind should be without spot; if then   360
we hold it a fault in a man if his clothes are filthy, I think it more incumbent
on a good man to develop a pure clean style, and to this end I have always
striven since my boyhood, so far as the land of my birth, my generation, my
position in life, and above all as far as my scanty natural gifts permitted.
And yet, though I saw that an artificial style wins such solemn approval   365
from established men, I always aimed at pure and not elaborate language,
and a solid masculine style, rather than something brilliant or theatrical,

* * * * *

332 Seneca] The *Naturales quaestiones* in seven books
336 annotations] Cf Ep 493:252n.
340 Lucullus] Cf Ep 493:344n.

one designed to convey the subject-matter before displaying the writer's
gifts. Such was my aim; whether I achieved it, I know not. It may be that,
while in pursuit of this ideal, I have fallen, as so often happens, into another   370
fault that stands close to my target, a thin ordinary obvious style, a mere
taste of which will more than satisfy the reader, like that tree of whose fruit
they say no man eats more than once; for there is nothing there that any man
of more than average taste would wish to meet a second time, nor does it
leave any sting behind to be effective later, but merely sounds smooth for   375
the moment. Such, roughly, are the colours in which you paint me, my dear
Budé, and for all I know you may be absolutely right. I attach more weight to
your judgment taken by itself than to that of a crowd of other men. But,
while I have no desire for an elaborate style, I should like, if I could, to
achieve one that was pure, appropriate, easy and clear; though when I say   380
easy, I do not mean lacking in sinews and barbed points when the subject
calls for them. If I fail to achieve this, the fault lies with my endowments, not
with my determination. All the same, just see how unfairly I am treated
meanwhile, when they find fault with me on both counts. People like you,
the class of true scholars, criticize me as lacking in energy, as spineless, as   385
like a sluggish stream; by my own colleagues here I am blamed, and blamed
every day, for driving the common reader right away by too much elaborate
ornament in the shape of rhetorical figures and rare words; and notes are
called for to explain my notes. What was I to do? I moderate my style in such
a way as to oblige neither party entirely and yet make some concession to   390
both. Besides which, a man has, I think, achieved something worth having
who persuades his reader to devour his whole book eagerly and hurry on to
the end without slackening speed. I suspect too that it is safer to help one's
reader on his way with an easy style than to frighten him away with a
difficult one, and a more tolerable fate never to be read a second time than   395
not to be read at all. Not but what those whose easy style wins them readers
do also secure a second reading. After all, whose style moves more easily
than Cicero's, and who has more enthusiastic readers?

The qualities you ascribe to my patroness Minerva are your own
affair; I know from experience how ungenerous she is. What you say about   400
my position as a theologian and about the rules which bind me more than
they do you, and compel me to be more cautious, has this much truth in it,
that I am allowed less licence to go wrong than you, since forgiveness is less
easy to come by, but I am not obliged to write worse. As far as concerns the

* * * * *

376 you paint me] Cf Ep 493:365–9.
400 What you say] Ep 493:412ff.

liberty I allow myself, I am never gross or subversive (two faults which a   405
man of principle must strictly avoid), but in many places I do write with
great freedom, and sometimes suffer for it: such are the troubles stirred up
for me by these cursed vain talkers into whose company I pray that you, my
excellent Budé, may never fall; for no living creature by land or sea is more
abominable. Again, if you think that old age makes me more restrained, I   410
raise no objection; nor is it so surprising if there happens to me what
happened, as we can see, to Isocrates and Lysimachus and Cicero himself. I
only wish it might happen to me as it did to them, that advancing years
should make me not only write more equably but (in spite of that) write
better! Not but what, if you choose to reckon up our ages, there is not much   415
difference, unless either you or I have done the sum wrong; for I am in my
fifty-first year and you, according to your letter, are not far from your
forty-eighth. And so, though I have aged much more than you, I am not that
much older. But I will own up to you in private what does make my style
somewhat worse than it was. You know how writing is made more vigor-   420
ous by reading, just as manuring restores fertility to a field, and fields are
allowed to rest every other year that they may not grow unproductive from
continuous cropping. I, on the other hand, for several years now have been
continuously tilling this field of mine, which in itself is grudging and of no
great fertility, until it is nearly worn out, giving it no rest in the way of   425
holidays, no manure in the way of reading, to help it out. For the desultory
reading which got together my *Chiliades* and the notes on the New Testament and the Jerome is so far from restoring the vigour of the mind that you
would be hard put to it to find anything else so bad for one's memory or
mental alertness. And then that kind of subject in itself does not admit any   430
splendour of language. You are lucky, my dear Budé: you have been
allowed to choose a subject which provides you with a proper field or
theatre, in which to give the world a sample of your rare learning and
literary skill. I happened upon these topics of mine, though there was no
kind of writing whatever for which I was less fitted by nature; and yet, once   435
I had done so, I had to serve my term with the play and scenery as they were.
I undertook several subjects on the entreaty of friends, so that I have

* * * * *

409–10 more abominable] An echo of Aristophanes *Plutus* 443

410 if you think] Ep 493:410–12

410 old age] For Erasmus' age see Garanderie 113n. For that of Budé cf Ep
493:410n. This passage (lines 416–18) suggests the year 1466 as his birthdate,
but it is only one of several inconsistent estimates.

437 entreaty of friends] As with the *De conscribendis epistolis* commissioned
by Robert Fisher and Mountjoy; cf Epp 71, 117.

scarcely had the good fortune hitherto of being active in my own field and
following my natural bent, if I have such a thing; not to complain, at the
same time, that these studies bring no credit, especially in my own country,   440
and also that men's critical standards are false. Who is there now whose
approval you would value? Whose plaudits would you seek as you give
your steeds free rein?

Again, not wishing to be rebuked for inability to take your hand from
the canvas without defending yourself, you accuse me in passing of being   445
too much inclined to proverbs. It is not quite clear to me whether you are
criticizing me for an immoderate use of adages or an unduly painstaking
and pedantic collecting of them. I do remember, and freely admit, that there
was a time when I used to make a special point of bringing them in as
though they were my peculiar property; but later I realized this, and began   450
to use them more sparingly. Further, I was encouraged to collect them by
two men especially. One was Robert Gaguin, who long ago (concealing
what he thought himself under the mask of other men's opinions) reported
that critics blamed me because that first collection of mine was so meagre,
and I had included only a few items out of so wide a field; the other Polidoro   455
Virgilio, a good scholar and now a good friend of mine, who spread it
abroad that I was following in his footsteps, and imitating another man's
work rather than creating my own, though I had published my book, such
as it was, several years before I knew the name of Polidoro. In the end,
when I got access to Polidoro's book, the printer's imprint was enough to   460
show that I preceded him by several months, while he published his work

* * * * *

438 my own field] *Adagia* III vi 62

444–5 hand from the canvas] *Adagia* I iii 19

445 you accuse me] Ep 493:63

452 Gaguin] Gaguin (1433–1501) was a leading figure among the Paris
humanists when Erasmus first made his appearance there; cf Ep 43 introduction.

454 first collection] The *Adagiorum collectanea*, a work of 152 pages, published
in 1500; cf Epp 126, 211 introductions.

456 Virgilio] c 1470–1555, born in Urbino and educated at Padua, he passed
into the service of Pope Alexander VI and, through the patronage of Adriano
Castelli, collector of Peter's Pence, to England as deputy-collector in 1502.

461 preceded him] Erasmus is wrong, no doubt through ignorance of the first
edition of Virgilio's *Proverbiorum libellus*, published by Christoforo de' Pensi,
Venice 1498 (Hain 16009). The second edition from the same publisher was
dated 6 November 1500; cf Ep 126:112–13n, and D. Hay *Polydore Vergil*
(Oxford 1952).

in Italy and I mine in Paris. And yet a certain Lucas of Poland, a theologian
in Louvain – a man who had I suppose no reason to attack the humanities
except that he himself had pursued them for many years without success
and clearly without the blessing of the Muses – used obstinately to assert   465
that I was using other men's discoveries to advertise myself. While trying
with excess of zeal to escape these criticisms, I fell, it is clear, into another
trap close by, and began to be extravagant instead of meagre. Though my
purpose was not to sweep up everything so indiscriminately – carte
blanche, as the phrase goes – that I could not bring myself to reject much   470
which was to be found in the Greek collections, for I had my suspicions that
some of it had been picked up from the dregs of the public in our own day,
and some had been invented with more zeal than discretion.

Then again, to my argument that it makes no sense for a man to have
Poverty living with him and yet to be laying foundations on the Lucullan   475
scale, your reply takes the form of suggesting that this by itself shows that
Riches has left your house and gone off heaven knows where (confound
him!) and Poverty moved in to take his place. Fair enough, provided you do
not reckon estates and country houses among your assets, though this was
the principal source whence rich men got the name *locupletes*.   480

This is quibbling, best of men, and not argument; but I took a fancy to
it, partly because you asked for it, or because it is a pleasure to rattle on on
any subject to a friend like you, or because I thought it would reduce the
value of your triumph even more if I let you win by default. In any case,
there is nothing of yours that I do not quite specially both approve and   485
admire; and while I have always done so, now that I see you at daily closer
range and with deeper insight, I love and respect you all the more. It is not
only that you are a most finished scholar, endowed with more than human
gifts and judgment to match, as is shown by your books, filled as they are

* * * * *

462 Lucas] Lucas Walters (d 1515), apparently from Konitz, near Danzig, a
Scotist theologian who taught at Louvain from 1499, taking his doctorate in
1512. He was one of the correctors of Lefèvre d'Etaples' edition of Johannes de
Sacrobosco's *Sphera* (Paris: [Johann Higman for] Wolfgang Hopyl 12 February
1495); cf Rice Ep 8 and p 28. His associations suggest that he might have
known of the original edition referred to in note 461. See H. de Vocht *Jérôme de
Busleyden* (Turnhout 1950) 460n.

469–70 carte blanche] *Adagia* I v 88

471 Greek collections] The collectors of proverbs (Zenobius, Diogenianus,
Suidas) who were one of the principal sources of the *Adagiorum chiliades*; but
in particular the near-contemporary Apostolius, whom Erasmus accuses more
than once of collecting colloquial material of his own day.

476 your reply] Ep 493:417–8

484 by default] *Adagia* I v 80

with a wonderful store of universal learning; it is the man of integrity and   490
principle displayed by your passionate attacks on the corruption of the age.
If there are any faults, on top of that, in form or fulness of expression – and I
do not think there are; but if there are any, they are in the first place
honourable faults, as you quite rightly say yourself, and then they are
employed so felicitously that I would much rather, to be sure, have your   495
mistakes than other men's successes. Among so many kinds of authors I find
none less tolerable than those Ciceronian apes, a class to which I find
Pontano comes very close – for those who copy Apuleius and their peep-
show miracles are scorned even by children. But you show such marvellous
judgment in being highly-finished and elaborate without sacrificing clarity   500
and ease, eloquent and copious without losing sight of your theme, brilliant and wide-ranging with no loss of energy and force, rich in image and
ornament in such a way that it is always the scholarship and not the flowers
of speech that men admire. Only Budé can do this. But just as it is not for a
man of my modest attainments to envy your happy state which none of us   505
can copy, so you must think the best of us and not despise writers of my
stamp and class, especially as you admit that each man's style and manner
of proceeding have always been as much his own property as his face and
voice. You have preferred to be understood by scholars, at any rate; I, if I
can, by the great majority. Your intention is to win your point; mine either   510
to instruct or to persuade – though these objects you achieve as well, with
much besides. Your enlarged edition of the *De asse* I had given instructions
for the purchase of, some time ago, and now at long last, as I write this, I
have extracted it from the grasp of the men who bind books. And so your
industry levies a double charge on us; and I hope you will frequently do so.   515
The two editions I shall read from cover to cover, but with the help of
someone to read with me, to discover more precisely what you have
thought fit to change or add. The reading will make me, if not really
accurate, at least a little less inaccurate. Your annotator I recognized at once
by his style; he is very like the author himself, and I can say for myself 'For   520
thief to thief is known and wolf to wolf.'

   For the very scholarly and very complimentary letter that Deloynes has

* * * * *

494 say yourself] Ep 493:336ff
498 Pontano] The Neapolitan humanist; cf Ep 337:355n.
512 *De asse*] The edition published by Bade, 14 October 1516
520 thief to thief] *Adagia* II iii 63; Erasmus seems to wish to attribute the
   marginal notes to Budé himself, despite acknowledgement in the new edition
   of Josse Bade's authorship; cf Garanderie 84n.
522 letter] Ep 494

written me I am grateful to you too, for I guess that you encouraged him to write. Otherwise how could a man of such importance, distracted with important business, take it into his head to write? Here truly, if anywhere, is the life of the gods! How else can one describe the daily converse and amusing company of such friends as this in a most delightful garden of the Muses? The stories, the conversation and the flights of fancy that you must enjoy, with wit and humour such as Cicero used to exchange with his dear Brutus and Pomponius! For I have no hesitation in setting Deloynes and Ruzé above even Brutus and Pomponius, if you are ready to be equated with Cicero, whom at least in this age of ours you so recall. Here we have nothing of the sort, and somehow the humanities still have a somewhat cool reception. The reason is, I think, that Maecenas and his like are out of fashion, and it is the enemies of good letters who hold sway. One man of great distinction, one might say, Jean Le Sauvage the chancellor of Burgundy, is devoted to the interests not only of his country but of liberal studies too; but we are in great part deprived of him by the public business of the realm. You know that no blessing can be fully enjoyed without someone to share it. Had Tunstall not happened to be here, I should have had no one with whom I could have tasted the full sweetness of your delightful letter. Now I most willingly accept the offer you make to me, that henceforth we should fully share the property in all our friends in common. What richer source of profit could be offered me? At least as far as I am concerned, I will make it my business to see that anyone who has any affection for Erasmus shall also think most kindly of Budé. I have made bold to write to Deloynes, either because he himself writes to me so affectionately in the first place or because you urge me to it so much that I should be ashamed not to comply. Otherwise, to tell the truth, you could not have found a surer way to deter me from writing than to start off with a letter like that. If I had as much care for my reputation as you suppose, I assure you that neither Philosophy that mistress whom I share with you, nor Jupiter the patron god of friendship, nor thought for my own name which you make out to be so distinguished, nor that fertile genius which you ascribe to me in more than human measure would have made me so forget my proper modesty as to reply to such polished letters. As it is, being the most devoted possible supporter of your reputation and myself already having almost my fill of fame, I write you this all the more readily because I foresee that everyone in future will admire your eloquence with increased enthusiasm

525

530

535

540

545

550

555

* * * * *

547 Deloynes] Ep 535

when they observe that Erasmus, whom up to now they thought was   560
eloquent, was simply tongue-tied when you spoke.

All that passage about my gilding and my voluntary servitude made
me laugh. Either you are astonishingly ignorant of my nature or you are
very cunningly pretending to be so. Hitherto it has been seedtime for me
here, and what manner of harvest I shall reap I know not. Even now I live on   565
my own juice like a snail, or rather feed myself by gnawing my own arms,
squid-fashion, except that I have been promised a salary from the prince's
exchequer, and have now been given one prebend, which I have myself
converted into an annual payment. A great deal happens here; but O! the
great crowd of vultures! and I am made to be anything sooner than a   570
vulture. If anything could have turned my mind away from literary studies,
either this unsteady health of mine would have done so long ago, or the
great malevolence of this ignorant body of vain babblers whose wickedness
has nearly had me pelted with stones.

Those same men who had visited you where you are now came to call   575
on me in Brussels; and the sight of them gave me pleasure up to a point
because what they said refreshed my memory of you, and in part distressed
me because they brought no letter from you, though they gave me hopes of
a letter. One of them is Mariano, a Sicilian with much of his countrymen's
traditional charm, a good scholar and an open-hearted man, clearly born for   580
friendship, and his society gave me no little pleasure.

As for the mistakes in the printing of your letters, you are right to
protest. The same thing had also roused my ire; but we only have one
printer here, and the sort of printer we deserve. In any case, the publication
of the letters was in the charge of Pieter Gillis, the secretary of the Antwerp   585
city council, a scholar and a civilized being who is devoted to your reputation, and I did not really know about it, though I had my suspicions and
acquiesced in it rather than wished for it, because I wanted all scholars at

* * * * *

562 that passage] Ep 493:521–2

566 my own juice] *Adagia* II viii 80

567 squid-fashion] During its winter sleep the squid gnaws its tentacles, a
habit well-known to Greek poets; eg Hesiod *Works and Days* 524 etc.

567–69 salary ... payment] Reference to Erasmus' appointment as councillor
to Prince Charles (cf Ep 370) and to his annuity from the living at Courtrai (cf
Ep 436).

575 same men] Cf Ep 493:553n.

579 Mariano] Accardo; cf Ep 544.

582 mistakes ... letters] Cf Ep 493:35–9.

584 sort of printer] Martens; cf Ep 263:10n.

the least to read your letters – if for no other reason, in hopes that the sight of
you so far surpassing us might rouse people in my country from their sloth,   590
and that the brilliance of someone as wide awake as you might disrupt their
heavy slumbers. Yes, you were deprived of your legal rights as a father of
three and robbed of one of your six children: you have a right of action
against me, because it was my mistake. But this loss shall very soon be
repaired; I undertake to see to it, and that forthwith.   595

    If you are willing to pass on to me your notes on the New Testament,
have you thought how much this precedent will embarrass the men who go
out of their way to claim other people's work as their own, or keep exclusively to themselves whatever they may possess in the literary way? You
really are the most open-hearted of friends and the most utterly immune   600
from the infection of jealousy! It is a true word that authors love their works
as they would love their own children. But you do not hesitate to defraud
your son in order to enrich me, and while most men fight for reputation as
they would for their lives, you are content to transfer your own reputation
to a friend. Who would not love, who would not be devoted to such a man?   605
But do not do this, my dear Budé. It is not in my nature to set myself off with
other men's valuable property, although in Hebrew I have submitted to a
certain amount of assistance; but on a small scale and with no attempt at
concealment. At the same time I should be doing a grave disservice to all
who wish to learn if I took for myself topics which I know will be more   610
profitably treated by you. Finally, when you have published them yourself,
they will be mine no less than yours, and I shall be free to use them, coupled
with the name of my friend Budé; wherein I am not so much honest as
thoughtful of my own reputation. All I really had in mind was that you
should have a taste of my work, and warn me if you thought anything   615
lacking or did not like anything, that I might be able to get it right in the next
edition which I am preparing.

    I do not yet know whether I ought to thank you on another count, that
that paragon of all the virtues the bishop of Paris, who is now your king's

* * * * *

592 legal rights] Cf Ep 493:47n, 52n.

596 notes] Cf Ep 493:571.

607 in Hebrew] Erasmus had received help with Hebrew both in the edition
of Jerome and in that of the New Testament, from the Amerbachs and from
Oecolampadius; cf Epp 324:28n and 34n, 373:81n.

616–7 next edition] This appeared in February 1519; it was announced almost
immediately after publication of the *Novum instrumentum*; cf Epp 417 (to
William Latimer, June 1516), 421:76–7 (to Guillaume Budé, June 1516).

619 bishop of Paris] Etienne Poncher; cf Epp 522:118–130, 529 introduction.

envoy to ours, credits me with some standing in the humanities. Thank you   620
I would, to be sure, had you not overdone it, so that I have more reason to
complain of you, for having led such a great man into serious error; and had
you not laid on my insufficiency, which ought to be well known to you, a
burden of expectation which I cannot bear. But whatever this is, whether
kind or officious – whether, that is, you have done me a service or made a   625
mistake – you share the whole thing with Lefèvre and Cop, or so I thought I
understood from what the bishop said. At least it was an exceptional
pleasure to make the acquaintance of such a religious, scholarly and
civilized person; and I can hardly express how much I am indebted to him,
for he not only spoke highly of me and granted me the privilege of his   630
conversation and even of sharing his table (in the poets, as you know, those
whom the gods are so kind as to invite to dinner become gods themselves),
but also invited me in the name of his most Christian Majesty to come and
share your beloved France if my prince would give me leave.

Your news of Jacques Lefèvre's ill-health, and how long-continued   635
and almost unbroken it has been, was very painful hearing; for he is a man
of such saintly character, so civilized and so scholarly, and has done so
much for learning and all who wish to learn, that he deserves never to grow
old or die. I was however encouraged by the bishop, who told me he is now
a little stronger.   640

You had demanded, my dear Budé, a letter longer even than yours.
Well, good luck to you, here is one as huge as it is ill-written. In quantity I
can easily match you; in quality how can I? Pray consider whether it be
expedient for the future to challenge your Erasmus to write at length. To
make you even more fearful of this for the future, I will add a finale. There 645
are some Italians here who object to the epigram on the title-page of your *De
asse*, where you add that it is easier to make fun of such things than to make
them, like the people who with a touch of arrogance criticized Venus'
sandal when they could find nothing to complain of in herself. I said I
thought it a waste of time to trump up some charge on a thing that the   650
printer might perhaps have added out of his own head. Let them rather
attack, I said, the work itself, and if they could find one stone in it they could
pull out, no doubt the whole structure would come tumbling down. You see

* * * * *

626 Cop] Cf Ep 522:159–62.

635 ill-health] Cf Ep 493:495n.

648–9 Venus' sandal] Momus, the god of carping criticism, could find no fault
with Venus, until he determined that her shoe squeaked as she walked
(*Adagia* I v 74).

651 printer] Josse Bade; cf Ep 346 introduction.

what confidence is bred in me by your high standards; I am not afraid to encourage the first comer to attack you, knowing you can only gain in 655 reputation. I hope the same thing will not happen to me.

I had already sent you a short letter as a sort of forerunner of this; and though this is rather late in following, you would agree it had come promptly if you knew how many days I have been suffering from the rheum, an almost universal plague, from which after a month I am hardly 660 recovered. On top of that was frequent moving back and forth. Farewell, scholar and friend beyond compare.

Antwerp, 15 February 1516

532 / From Guy Morillon   Brussels, 18 February [1517]

The writer, who died in 1548, came from a Burgundian family and first appears in Paris, where in 1507 and 1508 he undertook several editions of the classics for his pupils. By June 1515 Morillon was living in Brussels. He entered the service of Le Sauvage and like his colleague, Pierre Barbier (cf Ep 443 introduction), he accompanied the chancellor to Spain in 1517. Cf de Vocht CTL 3 44–50.

GUY MORILLON TO HIS FRIEND MASTER ERASMUS, GREETING
Our theological friend had to depart suddenly, and could not answer your letter, so he laid on me the duty of sending a reply; in fact, he told me to act as dean of Utopia while he is away. He also entrusted me with the staff of a theological Mercury, with the idea that I should possess the power to open 5 and shut the gates of promotion; it is just my bad luck that I am the one who is always left outside. You see, dear master, what a very great man he must be, if his absence and nothing else can make me so important. Wherever I go, everybody greets me kindly, addresses me with respect, invites me to dinner, asks me endlessly what has happened in this or that piece of 10 business. Bundles of letters make their way to me from all directions. In short, your friend Guy has become a man of business, in other words a theologian, except that in the meantime there is a strange silence on the subject of ducats. Perhaps they do not suppose the deputy of Utopia has any interest in such things. In that case the duties entrusted to me are more 15 onerous than honorific. I can hardly persuade myself that our theologian in

* * * * *

657 short letter] Cf Ep 522:2.
660 rheum] Cf Ep 526:2.
532:2 theological friend] Pierre Barbier; see introduction, Ep 565.

Guillaume de Croy
Portrait by an unknown artist; date unknown
Institut Royal du Patrimoine Artistique, Brussels
Copyright: ACL

person would long be able to endure such an uproar of business, unless his
exhaustion were refreshed from time to time by the goddess queen of earth
and heaven whom they call Money. For by the kind favour of this deity he
wrote to you recently in letters of gold, so do not think I am making it all up.   20
I wish you would teach me by what sacred rites or magic arts I could make
her my parent instead of my stepmother; for my master's theological principles do not seem very successful.

But to be a little more serious: I treated you to a little banter, in order to
answer to the name of 'crony' with which you were so good as to honour me   25
in your letter. How I have enjoyed the *Julius*! I paid it the tribute of a
continuous chuckle; how delightfully and amusingly, and in a word, Erasmically, he argues with Peter is easier to understand than to explain. The
chancellor thinks the world of it. He hurried off this morning at six o'clock
to Cambrai with my lord of Chièvres and that well-known theologian from   30
the Indies; they expect to return in a few days time, unless there is some real
agreement between the monarchs, which we foresee will not go beyond
looking at one another and exchanging a few words. Otherwise they will
wait at Cambrai for his Majesty the emperor and our king. I will give the

* * * * *

26 *Julius*] The satire *Julius exclusus*; cf Ep 502 introduction.

30 Cambrai] Cf LP ii 2940, 2943.

30 Chièvres] Guillaume de Croy, lord of Chièvres (1458–1521), was the leading member of a powerful family which had opposed the centralizing policies
of Charles the Rash (1433–77), the last of the Valois dukes of Burgundy, and
now supported the Hapsburg policy in return for a share in government.
Guillaume de Croy became the leader of a 'national' party in the imperial
council, along with Le Sauvage, Busleyden and others; cf Epp 301:38n,
332:3–4n. The persistent refusal of the Estates General to vote funds for a war
against Guelders (see Ep 549:29n) had forced Margaret of Austria to appoint
Chièvres first chamberlain and thus Prince Charles' official guardian until the
household ordinance of 1513 (Ep 332:3–4n). In the reorganization of government following the emancipation of Charles from his minority, Chièvres was
reappointed first chamberlain while his collaborator, Jean Le Sauvage, became chancellor of Burgundy. Chièvres resisted renewal of the alliance with
England against France once the Anglo-Burgundian commercial negotiations
were completed in January 1516, and negotiated the Treaty of Noyon with
France, by which Charles was to marry Francis I's infant daughter Louise.
This left Charles and his government in the Netherlands free to take up the
claim to the kingdoms of Aragon and Castile left to Charles with the death of
Ferdinand of Aragon, February 1516.

31 Indies] Another reference to Barbier; cf Ep 476:16n.

34 king] Charles; cf Ep 332:3–4n.

works of Jerome today to your host Maarten, as instructed by our theolo-   35
gian, so that they may reach you with the rest of the baggage. I hope your
very kind host where you are now, Pieter Gillis, and his wife and the rest of
the family are all in the best of health, and Joannes especially. My betrothed
hopes you are well. Farewell, dear master.

    Brussels, 18 February   40

533 / To Francis I   Antwerp, 21 February 1517

> This eulogy of the king as a guardian of international peace and patron of
> letters was perhaps prompted by Budé's report (Ep 522:40ff), to which Eras-
> mus alludes (lines 31–2), that the king wished to attract him to Paris. It may be
> observed that it also conformed to the policy of Guillaume de Croy, lord of
> Chièvres (Ep 532:30n), and of his associate Jean Le Sauvage, who together
> dominated the policies of the court. European peace was, of course, an
> obsessive concern of Erasmus. The letter was included in the *Epistolae ele-*
> *gantes* 1517.

TO FRANCIS, MOST CHRISTIAN KING OF FRANCE,
FROM ERASMUS OF ROTTERDAM, WITH HUMBLE DUTY
Many as are the princes famed for piety and warlike prowess who have
been bred in this glorious realm of France, by common consent the most
prosperous of all realms, it has been left for you, Francis, of kings alike best   5
and greatest, to deserve in full measure, as it seems to me, that splendid title
of Most Christian King, which is the peculiar property of the French kings.
Christ Himself, king of kings and lord of lords, desired that His followers
should be recognized by no distinguishing mark except the mutual harmony between them; and you, once you had shown by a war against the   10
Swiss that you lacked neither spirit nor resources for a war, chose none the
less to devote all your energies to quelling the tumults of war in perpetuity,
that the leading princes of Christendom might henceforward be united in
perpetual peace among themselves. In your wisdom you cannot fail to see

* * * * *

35 Maarten Davidts (d 1535) a canon of the collegiate church at Brussels with
whom Erasmus stayed in 1516; see Pl. Lefèvre 'Martin Davidts, un ami
d'Erasme à Bruxelles (d 1535)' *Ephemerides theologicae Lovanienses* 42 (1966)
628–36.
38 Joannes] Joannes Phrysius; he entered the service of Erasmus in Antwerp
about September 1516; cf F. Bierlaire *La Familia d'Erasme* (Paris 1968) 51–2.
38 betrothed] He married Elizabeth de Mil about June 1517; cf Ep 587.
533:11 Swiss] Cf Ep 529:15n.

that from the discord between kings one with another the decay and   15
destruction of all that is good descends once and for all upon the life of men
together with a flood-tide of all that is evil, while if their hearts and their
resources are once united in sincere peace and amity, we shall see the return
of a sort of golden age, in which there will be a simultaneous flowering of
religion, good laws and liberal arts in every form, which always are the   20
companions and the nurselings of peace. With that right royal mind of
yours you understand and perceive clearly enough that your way to felicity
and greatness as a prince lies not in the multitude of your subjects but in
their virtue and prosperity. And to promote this result your Majesty with
unsleeping vigilance, rich though your kingdom is in men who excel in   25
virtue and knowledge of every kind, is yet always ready to invite others
from every quarter with the most generous rewards, in order to render a
kingdom already richly furnished with such ornaments richer still; for you
well know that distinction in such things adds a truer and livelier lustre to
your realm than wealth or trophies, pyramids or other masses of masonry   30
however grand. As furthermore your Majesty is good enough to include my
name among their number with an invitation that does me the greatest
honour, I see clearly how great a debt I owe to that spirit of yours which is as
generous as it is lofty. I only wish I had the vigorous intellect and the
copious learning that in part at least might answer the expectations of so   35
great a prince, and gifts of eloquence sufficient one day to immortalize your
heroic virtues and your shining glories in panegyrics not unworthy of
them, above all else the restoration of peace, this divine blessing which the
Christian world owes principally to your efforts. And I beseech Almighty
God that, it having pleased Him to awake these noble ambitions within   40
your heart, He may prosper them and bring the same to good effect. True
indeed are the words of that great peace-loving king: the hearts of kings are
in the hand of the Lord, and He turneth them whithersoever He will. For
who can doubt that the mind which is in you was inspired by Him? And so
there is good hope that He who begins to bestow this new felicity upon the   45
Christian world, and bestows it through you above all, will vouchsafe by
your devotion and your perseverance to make this blessing our own for
evermore. May He long preserve and bless your Majesty, illustrious king,
in health and wealth of every kind, for the benefit of your dominions and
indeed of the whole world; to whom I profess my entire devotion.   50
    Antwerp, 21 February 1516

        * * * * *

    42 great ... king] Prov 21:1

534 / To Guillaume Budé   Antwerp, 21 February 1517

This letter, which replies to Ep 522 and was written the same day as Ep 533, indicates Erasmus' concern about the reported interest shown by Francis I in attracting him to Paris. His guarded response reflects clearly the immediate negotiations with Jean Le Sauvage for a position in the Netherlands. This letter too was published in the *Epistolae elegantes* 1517.

ERASMUS OF ROTTERDAM TO HIS FRIEND BUDÉ, GREETING
Scarcely had I at last got free from that very prolix letter, which you will find dreary reading if I may judge by the tedium I suffered in the writing of it – scarcely had I sealed it when your second letter reached me, in which you indicate his most Christian Majesty's intentions towards me. To this I must   5
send you a laconic reply, partly not to be the death of both of us equally with this tedious flow of words, and partly because at the same moment I have to write to many other people. The king's intentions are truly worthy of a prince, and of such a prince as he, and I am bound to admire and welcome them. The exalted opinion which he has of me I owe principally to you and   10
my other friends, who depict me not as I am but as you wish me to appear. In doing this you run, of course, no small risk, not only at my expense but also at your own. Not but what the same subject had already been opened with me in detail on the king's behalf by his distinguished representative the bishop of Paris, a man of whom you give an accurate and vivid picture   15
in your letter. It would take too long to set down in a letter, like a man asking counsel's opinion, the arguments that dispose me to accept and those which dissuade me. Your own opinion I can see quite clearly, and I think it even more likely to be well-advised as it came from a man who is not only very wise but very fond of me; for if there is any place for the Greek proverb   20
which says that the gifts of an enemy are no gifts at all, I think it applies in the giving of advice. In any case, I am deeply obliged to all of you, and above all to your most generous and excellent king; but for the moment I can give no definite answer, until I have taken advice from the chancellor of Burgundy, who is now absent on a journey to Cambrai. In the meantime,   25
while I think the question over carefully in my own mind and ask the views

* * * * *

534:2 letter] Ep 531
15 bishop of Paris] Etienne Poncher; cf Ep 529 introduction.
20 proverb] *Adagia* I iii 35
25 Cambrai] Cf Ep 532:30n.

of my friends, he will I hope have time to return; and as soon as I know what he thinks, I will give you my opinion without reserve. All I will say for the moment is this, that I have always been fond of France for many reasons, but now it has no greater claim on my affection than its possession of Budé, 30 and you cannot alienate me from it or make me what you call a foreigner, for if we are to believe the geographers, Holland too belongs to Gaul.

You put me in mind just now of something at which I have often wondered – the great support I owe to the tribe of Williams, whether this is due to some kind of fate or merely accident. Long ago when I was barely ten 35 years old I had a favourite playmate called Willem. At fifteen I had a friend of my own age whom I loved more dearly than myself. He was followed by Willem Hermans, a good scholar whose hymns I think you have seen; after him, William Mountjoy, my continuing and most faithful Maecenas; then William Latimer, in mastery of Latin and Greek not inferior to Linacre and a 40 true theologian, by which I mean integrity as well as learning, and specially devoted to me. Then there is William Grocyn, whose epistle prefixed to the *Sphere* of Proculus you possess. And think how many Williams are out-weighed by that supreme William, the archbishop of Canterbury! And again Guillaume Cop: I love everything about him so whole-heartedly that 45 the mere mention of his name refreshes me. Of you, I will speak in your presence with reserve. But I am even richer than I had supposed. I was not aware that that distinguished theologian of whom everyone speaks, Guil-laume Petit – a misnomer: in his outstanding merits he is great, not small – is so much my friend. But wait! I have not yet listed all my Williams, for in 50 Basel there is Wilhelm Nesen, a passionate lover of the best literature and so devoted to me that I could with perfect justice call him my Pylades; he would have no hesitation in facing any mortal danger for his friend Erasmus.

* * * * *

32 Holland] Cf Ep 321:16n.

38 Hermans] Cf Ep 33 introduction; for his *Silva odarum* see Ep 49 introduc-tion.

39 Mountjoy] Cf Ep 79 introduction.

40 Latimer] Cf Ep 207:25n.

42 Grocyn] Cf Ep 118:26n.

43 *Sphere*] Linacre's translation of Proclus' *De sphaera* published in *Astronomi veteres* by Aldus, October 1499

44 Canterbury] William Warham; cf Ep 188 introduction.

45 Cop] Cf Ep 523 introduction.

49 Petit] Cf Ep 522:17n.

51 Nesen] Cf Ep 329 introduction.

From your ambassador I learnt that Paolo Emilio is at last publishing   55
his history of France; for it cannot fail to be a work of the highest finish,
being the result of more than twenty years' labour by a man as learned as he
is industrious. As for Thomas More's *Utopia*, if you have not yet had a
chance to see it, mind you buy a copy and do not grudge the leisure to read
it, for you will not regret the trouble taken. I hear that Thomas Linacre's   60
works will shortly appear from Bade's press, and the news greatly delights
me. Nothing from that man can, I think, fail to be masterly in every way. In
heaven's name, what an age will soon be upon us! How I wish I might be
young again!

Pieter Gillis my host, as a devotee and a great expert in the humanities   65
and a leading admirer of yours, tells me to give you his best wishes. He had
copied out that very long letter with his own hand, though very busy with
other things, since I had no time to write it fair, and I had sent one of my
servants to Louvain while the other was having trouble with his eyes.
Farewell.   70

Antwerp, 21 February 1516

Cuthbert Tunstall has been torn away from me by Emperor Maximilian; now that he has been attached to the emperor as envoy, and a successor
appointed to be with our Prince Charles, he has ceased to live any longer in
the one place. It is a kind of life that I should not altogether dislike, provided   75
my library could accompany me wherever I went. If he comes here I will
speak to him, and otherwise I will write to him in his absence about his
sending you a letter. Farewell once more.

* * * * *

55 ambassador] Poncher; cf line 15.

55 Emilio] Cf Ep 136:2n.

61 works] His translation of Galen's *De sanitate tuenda*; cf Ep 502:17n. It was
actually printed, not by Bade, but by Guillaume Le Rouge.

67 long letter] Ep 531

69 servants] One of them was Joannes Phrysius; cf Ep 532:38n.

73 successor] This was William Knight (1476–1547), a lawyer and distinguished royal servant. He was a scholar of Winchester and fellow of New
College, Oxford, where he took his DCL by 1507. He had studied law also at
Ferrara in 1501. By March 1513 he was chaplain to the king and he then
embarked on an active diplomatic career. In February 1514 he was ambassador
to Margaret of Savoy in the Low Countries and in 1515 he was authorized to
treat with Charles about renewal of the 1506 treaty; cf Emden BRUO II 1063–4.
Among his many ecclesiastical promotions, in 1517 he was made canon of St
Paul's London, and in 1541 he was appointed bishop of Bath and Wells.

78 letter] Ep 571

535 / To François Deloynes   Antwerp, 21 February 1517

This letter replies to Ep 494, and is referred to in Erasmus' letter to Budé of 15 February (Ep 531:547). It would seem therefore that the final paragraph and date were added later. It was published in the *Epistolae elegantes* 1517.

ERASMUS OF ROTTERDAM TO HIS FRIEND MASTER
FRANÇOIS DELOYNES, GREETING
I perceive, Deloynes my most distinguished friend, how great and complex is the debt I owe to Guillaume Budé, the glory and incomparable ornament not only, as you so rightly say, of your native France but of this whole age of   5
ours; for not content with giving me his support which carries so much weight with scholars everywhere, and distinguishing me by a series of most exquisite letters, he makes me rich and happy with the gift of so many friends. And in heaven's name, what friends! Should I not be right in thinking that a great addition had been made to my worldly wealth, when   10
Guillaume Petit, François Deloynes, Louis Ruzé are added to the number of my friends and can be counted in the inventory of my possessions? For when I name those three names, ye gods, the outstanding gifts and rare accomplishments I sum up in those few words! Nor is the profit which I owe him limited to them, but he has made a formal agreement with me that,   15
whatever friends we may possess anywhere in the world, shall by the principle of Pythagoras be held in common by us both. His credit is of course as high as anyone's; but even so I have an agreement to this effect in writing in his own hand, should he wish to go back on it. I will endure anything rather than allow myself to be done out of this valuable property,   20
now that I have once taken over possession.
     To the distinguished tribute paid me in your letter I have nothing to reply, except that you are wrong about me, though I know the error is most kindly meant. And then I gather that you not only read all my books but examine them too with a critical eye. Should I call myself happy to be   25
thought worthy of such an honour by men of the highest learning and authority, or unhappy to have fallen, being the man I am (for I am not ignorant of myself), into the hands of such keen-eyed critics? Whenever I think of this, just imagine my feelings of shame! I feel like exclaiming, 'This

* * * * *

535:11 Guillaume Petit] Cf Ep 522:17n.
11 Ruzé] Cf Ep 493:462n.
17 principle of Pythagoras] Friends have all things in common; *Adagia* I i 1.
18 agreement] Ep 493:478ff

was not written for readers like Deloynes, the Laelius and Persius of our time   30
and more; this was meant for raw recruits in the army of learning, or at best
for certain thick-headed and ungifted theologians, who in old days had to
take refuge fruitlessly in purveyors of the *Catholicon* or the *Mammotrectus* as
though they were the true tripod of Apollo. It was their Cimmerian darkness on which I aspired to shed a little light. Why must you grandees, you   35
leading nobles and patricians force your way into a dinner cooked for the
common herd? It was not to please your palate that I dished up these greens.
I see all too well how much more care I must take in future over my work, if I
ever publish anything again.'

A few months ago when I was in Colet's company I spoke of you, and   40
he knew the name Deloynes at once and seemed much pleased to be
reminded of an old acquaintance. It was charming of Nicolas Bérault to
recall in his postscript the old custom of giving tokens of friendship. I well
remember, when long ago I was in Orléans and about to set out for Italy,
how I enjoyed his hospitality and was entertained by him for several days   45
in the most generous and friendly fashion. Even now I fancy I can hear that
clear and rapid articulation, the charming cadences of that musical voice,
and the classical purity of that ready flow of words. I see that friendly face,
beaming with courtesy, without a trace of self-importance; his charming
sympathetic ways, so easy and so unlikely ever to get on one's nerves. What   50
is more, he offered me a silk shirt as a kind of leaving present when I was
about to depart, and I had great difficulty in persuading him to let me refuse
it. So it is a pleasure to acknowledge his token; his greeting I gladly accept,
and send him mine in return with interest.

If you object that this letter is none too long, read the one I have sent to   55
Budé and you will have no more complaints; for since the rule that friends
have all things in common is now in force, anything I send him in the way of
a letter you must take as written to you too. Farewell, O learned counsel
without peer, and be sure to greet Ruzé on my behalf.

Antwerp, 21 February 1516   60

* * * * *

30 Laelius and Persius] Cf Ep 480:78.
33 *Catholicon ... Mammotrectus*] Cf Epp 26:100n, 337:330n.
42 Bérault] Cf Ep 494:72n.
44 long ago] Cf Ep 194 introduction.
55 the one] Ep 531

536 / To Maarten van Dorp   Antwerp, 21 February [1517]

Erasmus writes to his critic at Louvain; cf Ep 304 introduction, and Epp 337,
347, 438, 496 and 509. This letter was first published in the *Farrago*.

ERASMUS TO HIS FRIEND DORP, GREETING
In other departments of learning, I agree that what you say is true: the man
who disagrees does one no harm, in fact he often does good. In this field, he
who disagrees does so not in order to make himself out the better scholar
but to prove his adversary no Christian. Even if this is not his purpose, yet   5
at the time in the eyes of the ignorant public he puts his opponent in the
wrong, and gives a handle to that perverse class of men who batten or push
themselves forward upon the misfortunes of others. Not that I have ever
had many suspicions of your own attitude, but perhaps I was better acquainted with human nature, and considered the circumstances of the case   10
in more depth than you. If any men are tormented by the fact that we agree,
let us do our best, my dear Dorp, to cause them more and more distress;
those who take pleasure in the misfortunes of others do not deserve to have
anything go right for them. Gossip you need not fear; no man in the world is
less moved by such things than I am. Those who are well disposed to their   15
Erasmus will easily grow fond of Dorp too, if they feel that you and I are
sincerely friends. Yesterday I had two letters from More. Within a couple of
days a man will set off to take my reply, in which I will add what you wish;
in fact I had already said something about our reconciliation before I had
any instructions from you. I have an invitation to France in letters from   20
many people, with magnificent promises, and that too on the king's
behalf; but I am not prepared to take the stage afresh. My mind demands a
peaceful retreat; my time of life, or rather my health, insists on my taking
things quietly. Pieter Gillis was delighted to have your greetings, and sends
his affectionately in reply. If you have anything for England, let me have it   25
as soon as possible, and I will see that it goes. Of Athensis I hear nothing but
good, and cannot hear too much; give him my warmest respects. Farewell.
    Antwerp, 21 February

* * * * *

536:3 does good] Cf Erasmus' earlier remarks to Desmarez, Ep 180:16–19.
18 my reply] The letter mentioned in Epp 543:2, 545:2, 7–8
19 had ... said] Ep 502:4
21–2 king's behalf] Cf Epp 522, 533.
26 Athensis] Jan Briaert; cf Ep 509:8n.

674

91

Erasmus Gulielmo Copo suo S. D.

O felicem Galliam tali principe, O te fortunatum, istiusmodi patrono. O me beatum tanti monarchae favore. Ceterum ad tuas litteras quas regis tui iussu scripseras ad me, nondum licet recti quippiam respondere. Sed brevi statuam, ac renuntiabo Lutetiam huius honoris usura fruar, quod laudatissimo hominum genere, laudatissimo regi placuerim: pro cuius vita...

Bene vale.
Antverpiae ... Cal. Mart. An. M.D.17.

Audio iam et gaudeo, Thomae Linacri lucubrationes ... di Lutetiae. Utopiam Mori, si nondum legisti, fac requiras, si quando voles ridere, imo si fontes ipsos ... ... Rursum vale

Lettre d'Erasme
célèbre humaniste hollandais
(1467-1536)

Autograph letter, Erasmus to Guillaume Cop;
Antwerp, 24 February 1517, Epistle 537

Bibliothèque Municipale, Nantes, MS 674 f 91

537 / To Guillaume Cop   Antwerp, 24 February 1517

This is the last of the letters printed in the *Epistolae elegantes* 1517 and referring to the foundation of the Collège royal; cf Ep 522 introduction. It replies to Cop's invitation in Ep 523. The autograph original is in the Bibliothèque Municipale, Nantes, MS 674 f 91.

ERASMUS TO HIS FRIEND GUILLAUME COP, GREETING

Happy indeed is France in such a prince! Fortunate are you in a patron of such quality, and blest am I in the favour of so great a monarch! That being said, as regards the letter which you wrote me on your king's instructions, I cannot yet send a definite reply, but I will shortly make up my mind and   5
report to you. Till then I shall enjoy a kind of interest on this distinguished offer from the feeling that men of the highest reputation have secured me the favour of the most highly reputed of kings, for whose generosity towards me I owe a debt I shall neither conceal nor forget for ever. I have thanked his Majesty in a letter as best I could; Budé told me to. But you will   10
do it more skilfully by word of mouth, and please thank not only the king but that distinguished theologian Guillaume Petit and the reverend father François de Rochefort, who have been led astray by affection into so kindly misleading the king on my behalf. When you express the wish to see my aphorisms, you must not suppose them of the same class as those of your   15
great Hippocrates; this is something quite different. But if you ask for a small book by Erasmus on the education of a Christian prince, you will find it more quickly under that title. Farewell.

    Antwerp, 24 February 1516

    I hear, and am of course delighted, that Thomas Linacre's works are   20
printing in Paris. As for More's *Utopia*, if you have not yet read it, be sure to ask for it when you want to be amused, or more truly, if you wish to see the very wellsprings of all troubles in the commonwealth. Farewell once more.

* * * * *

537:10 letter] Ep 533
12 Guillaume Petit] Cf Ep 535:11n.
13 de Rochefort] Cf Ep 523:9n.
15–6 your ... Hippocrates] Cf Ep 124:18n.
20 Linacre's works] Cf Epp 502:17n, 534:61n.

538 / To Luigi di Canossa   Antwerp, 24 February 1517

On the recipient of this letter see Ep 489 introduction. It was first published in
the *Epistolae elegantes* 1517.

TO THE RIGHT REVEREND LUIGI DI CANOSSA,
LORD BISHOP OF BAYEUX,
FROM ERASMUS OF ROTTERDAM, GREETING

I congratulate you on your promotion, as a man whose deserts have secured
him this high position from the favour of Leo, a pontiff truly supreme, and I   5
highly approve your generous attitude towards humane studies. Next to
that, I must thank you warmly for your high opinion of me or, to speak more
truly, for the friendly errors which you entertain about me; and I consider
myself as much indebted to your kindness as if your offer – a most generous
offer, clearly more than I deserve – had been already accepted. Only, in the   10
absence of the chancellor of Burgundy, whose doing it was that I was
originally invited to join the household of the Catholic King Charles, I am
unable to return a definite answer for the moment. But I will do so shortly.
Meanwhile pray continue your kind feelings towards Erasmus, who is
yours wherever he may be. Best wishes to your Lordship, to whom I profess   15
myself entirely devoted.
            Antwerp, 24 February 1516

539 / To Andrea Ammonio   Antwerp, 24 February 1517

This letter was first published in the *Farrago*.

ERASMUS TO HIS FRIEND ANDREA AMMONIO, GREETING

You would hardly credit, dear Ammonio, how close I have come to a
blazing outburst of hostility from the theologians here. In Louvain they
were creeping up on me with their knives drawn, in a conspiracy (what is
more) led by Athensis, who was all the more dangerous because he was an   5

* * * * *

538:11 absence] Cf Ep 532:29ff.
11 whose doing it was] Cf Epp 370:18n, 460:3; for the chancellor, Jean Le
Sauvage, see Ep 410 introduction.
539:4 with their knives drawn] Literally 'in the spirit of gladiators'; *Adagia* I iii
76
5 Athensis] Jan Briaert of Ath; cf Epp 509:8n, 337:393.

enemy disguised as a friend. They were also trying hard to work on the
prince, so as to have his authority as well as the pope's on their side. But in
the end I went to Louvain myself and blew all the clouds away, ending up
on most friendly terms with the theologians both great and small. Their
machinations at Court were kept in check partly by the good will of the   10
nobility, who have a particular dislike of all divines, and partly by the help
of the learned, among whom the bishop of Chieti was conspicuous.

I have been expecting the message of salvation for a long time now. If
it fails me, your Erasmus is lost like the beans at the end of the row, and
nothing remains except for you to write his epitaph. Personally I would   15
rather have gone to Rome twice than be tormented by this long dreary wait.
I do not say this to lessen the value of what you have done. I know this delay
is not what you wanted. It is my own destiny. I entrusted Jerome to the
booksellers so that I could send him bound; they put me off with words, as
is their custom. If you have not yet bought it, I will send one; besides   20
which, any money you demand will be forthcoming. All the same, I shall
never cease to feel that I owe this kindness entirely to you. Only make haste
to give me security before Easter, and prove yourself a true Aesculapius.
Should anything transpire to give me cause for despair, it will be part of
your kindness to relieve me of my empty hopes as soon as possible; though   25
what I know of you forbids me to despair. In France they offer me mountains of gold; but my hands are tied. If you have anything that can restore
me to life, send it by More, unless you have a more likely envoy. Farewell.

Antwerp, 24 February 1516

* * * * *

8 went ... myself] Cf Ep 509.

12 bishop of Chieti] Gianpietro Carafa; cf Ep 287:9n. He was a founder of the
Theatines.

13 message of salvation] The letters from Leo x, Epp 517–9; cf Ep 447 introduction.

14 your Erasmus] Written in Greek, 'Εράσμιος, meaning lovable; cf Ep
462:6n.

14 like the beans at the end of the row] Which get trodden on; *Adagia* IV iv 72

19 put me off] *Adagia* I v 49

21 money] For the dispensation; cf Epp 479:10–1, 447:844n.

23 Easter] 12 April 1517

23 Aesculapius] Cf Ep 483:34n.

26 France] Cf Epp 522 and following.

28 by More] Cf Ep 498:33.

540 / To William Latimer   Antwerp [February 1517]

This letter was first published in the *Epistolae ad diversos*.

ERASMUS OF ROTTERDAM TO WILLIAM LATIMER, A THEOLOGIAN
IN WHOM THERE IS NO GUILE, GREETING
What a pleasure it was, learned friend Latimer, to recognize in your letter to
me your charming fairness of mind and more than maidenly modesty,
combined with Christian wisdom! You mention no man except to speak   5
well of him, and show such wisdom in the way you do so. And then, far as
you are from parsimony and meanness in praising other people, how little
you claim for yourself! Apart from that, when it comes to finding excuses
not to do something for me, I wish you did not write so well. I thought I had
collected solid arguments in plenty to persuade you to help me with the   10
revision of my New Testament, and in the second place to devote at least a
month's work to that incomparable bishop who wishes to add Greek as a
sort of coping-stone to his pyramid of learning; for in both you were likely
to assist the common cause of the humanities. In reply, you press me with
such serried ranks of argument that it was at once clear to me how tongue-   15
tied and barren I am compared to you. All the same, my excellent Latimer,
you are welcome to carry off the prize for eloquence on this topic, if only in
your turn you will give me leave to carry off the service I demand; and I shall
appreciate it all the more if it is clearly not wrung from you by argument but
given me of your own free will out of pure kindness of heart.   20

And as far as I am concerned, you do at last almost promise something,
and I accept what you undertake, though I fear that your contribution will
not be much more help to me than Rhesus and his men were to the Trojans
long ago, for Froben's printing-house has long been clamouring for the
copy. But as concerns the bishop of Rochester, I differ from you even more.   25
You think it better simply not to attempt the business, unless having started
you can finish it. You recommend that some distinguished expert in Greek
should be sent for from Italy, who will not let the bishop go until he is far
advanced and fully-fledged in this field of study. But that, my dear Latimer,

* * * * *

540:3 your letter] Ep 520
12 bishop] John Fisher; cf Ep 520:94.
18 service] That is, assistance in revision of the *Novum instrumentum*; cf Ep
520:4ff.
23 Rhesus] Arrived at Troy too late to help the Trojans; *Iliad* 10.435ff

is easier said than done; I was in favour of doing, as it says in the comedy,   30
'the best we can.' Italy is a long way away and has rather fewer distinguished scholars now than it had when you were there; and there is some
risk that we may send for a man of distinction and be given some
jackanapes. You know the Italians, and the immense rate at which they
expect to be hired if they are to emigrate to the barbarians, even those of   35
moderate ability; not to mention for the moment that those who do reach us
who are well equipped in the humanities do not always bring with them a
character to match. And you know the bishop's high standards. The result
is, that while we are discovering who is the best man to send for, and there
are consultations between the two sides about fixing his salary, and prep-   40
arations are made for his journey, a good deal of time is wasted.

I know it has been wisely and truly said that before starting one should
take counsel, but counsel once taken, one should waste no time in doing
what has been decided on. But I see many men take counsel and nothing
else, so that it is already too late to carry out the decisions they have   45
eventually come to, like men who spend so long wondering whether they
wish to get married and then whom they wish to choose out of so many, that
time flitting stealthily away leaves them too old to marry before they can
make any definite choice. Nor am I willing to suspect you of any touch of the
prejudice of some ordinary people, who admire nothing unless it has been   50
fetched from afar. Anyone is an Italian to me, who is a genuine scholar,
even if he was born in Ireland. Anyone is a Greek who has worked hard and
successfully at Greek literature, though he may not wear a beard. For my
part, I support the reputation of Italy for this reason if no other, that I have
had a better reception there than in my own country. But to say honestly   55
what I think, if I could get Linacre or Tunstall as a teacher, to say nothing of
you, I should not feel the need for Italy. And so I urge you to consider, first
whether it is not rather unwise to seek abroad for what you have at home,
and then whether to despise some modest thing which you badly need,
merely because you have no chance of the very best, or reject anything in   60
the way of capital unless someone guarantees a very profitable investment
for it. Grocyn himself whose example you cite, did he not start by learning

* * * * *

30 in the comedy] Menander *Sententiae* 273
31 Italy] Cf Ep 520:153n.
42 truly said] *Adagia* II iii 70
56 Linacre] Cf Ep 520:138n.
56 Tunstall] Cf Ep 480:6n.

the elements of Greek in England? Afterwards he set off for Italy and was taught by the best people; but all the time he profited by what he had learnt earlier from such teachers as he had. With men of outstanding ability, even 65 to have shown them the way is often a very great step forward.

On one point I agree with you: it is highly desirable that even the first rudiments should be learnt from a master of the art, if only this is possible. If that cannot be, it is better to make a start somehow than to remain entirely ignorant, especially in this field. It is a fairly troublesome business to learn 70 to recognize the shapes of the letters at sight, to pronounce readily, to decline and to conjugate. Do you think a man has achieved nothing who has digested all this tedious stuff? In fact, when I ask you for a month's work, I hope secretly for three months, although I have not the face to demand it. If I am unlucky in that, I am full of hope that someone will turn up meanwhile 75 who can build on the foundations you have laid. Should that hope entirely deceive me, yet such is his powerful intelligence and such his passionate desire to learn that I am confident he will by his own resources gain at any rate a working knowledge. And maybe he is content with that, for the only reason why he wishes to learn Greek is to be able to spend his time with 80 more profit and more sure judgment on the Scriptures. And then, suppose none of this comes his way, what shall we have lost? The bishop's studies may gain very little by it; yet it will be no small encouragement to the ambitions of the young, if they see such an eminent man taking up Greek. Besides which, it makes a difference in every subject if you start early, and 85 in this case the bishop's age makes me feel very strongly that the business should not be put off.

I will draw to a close; but there is one warning I must utter. Do not allow your excessive diffidence, and a degree of modesty that is almost immodest, to distract you to some extent from advancing the cause of 90 scholarship. Some people, like me, attempt more than they should; but it is not yet clear to me who make the greater mistake, those who attempt nothing for fear of doing something wrong, or those who from an ill-judged passion to do good sometimes fall down. The one party teaches many excellent lessons, though everything may not go as they would wish; and then 95 by their keenness they rouse and put an edge on the zeal of other people. The others, by reserving what they have for their own benefit, deserve more blame, to my thinking, than notorious misers who are watchdogs rather

* * * * *

63 in England] At Oxford, not from Cornelius Vitellius, as stated by P.S. Allen, but perhaps from John Serbopoulos or Emmanuel of Constantinople; cf R. Weiss *Humanism in England During the Fifteenth Century* 2nd edition (Oxford; Blackwell 1957) 147–8, 173–4.

than owners of their money. For the money they accumulate, if it does
nothing else, at least passes at their death to different people who can use it;   100
from the deathbed of the others nothing passes to an heir, unless they have
put down their ideas in writing. This, my dear William, is what I fear may
happen to our friend Grocyn, and I should be sorry if the same fate befell
you too. Farewell, best and most learned of men, and do not be slow to do as
you have promised.   105

Antwerp, 151[8]

541 / To Wolfgang Capito   Antwerp, 26 February 1517

For the recipient of this letter see Ep 459 introduction. It was first printed in the
Epistolae elegantes 1517. The sentiments expressed here form a classic statement of the aspirations and programme of humanistic reform.

TO THE DISTINGUISHED THEOLOGIAN
WOLFGANG FABER CAPITO OF HAGUENAU,
A TRUE EXPERT IN THE THREE TONGUES,
FROM ERASMUS OF ROTTERDAM, GREETING

I am not overmuch in love with life, my learned friend Wolfgang, perhaps   5
because I have lived nearly long enough to suit myself, being now in my
fifty-first year; perhaps because I see nothing in this life so splendid or so
delightful as to arouse much desire in a man sincerely persuaded by the
Christian faith that those who have pursued godliness with all their might
in this world have a much happier life than this waiting for them in the   10
next. At this moment, none the less, I should almost be willing to grow
young again for a space, for this sole reason that I perceive we may shortly
behold the rise of a new kind of golden age. So great is the heaven-sent
change we see in the minds of princes, who bend all their powers to the
pursuit of peace and concord under the leadership above all of Leo, pontiff   15
supreme in more than name, and Francis king of France, most Christian
monarch as much in his distinguished record as in his solemn title. Francis
has the spirit and the resources needed for waging war to an extent unsurpassed by any other prince; but he considers in a responsible way the
immense damage done to the strength and the resources of Christians by   20
these disagreements and conflicts among princes, and on the other hand
the strength and the encouragement they offer to the enemies of our religion. He remembers, what is an even greater scourge, how every vestige of

* * * * *

541:7 fifty-first year] Cf Ep 531:410n.

Maximilian's *Triumphwagen*
Albrecht Dürer, 1518
Graphische Sammlung Albertina, Vienna

true religion, of just laws, of civilized behaviour, of high moral standards
and of liberal arts among the incessant clash of arms is either killed outright   25
by a licentious soldiery, or at best is brought to the lowest ebb; while in
their place a whole host of evils and calamities sweeps all at once like a flood
over the lives of mortal men. And so there is nothing he will not do, nothing
he will not tolerate from others in his zeal to abolish war and cement a
lasting peace, submitting voluntarily to men to whom he could not have   30
been expected to submit, had he preferred to think of his own exalted
position and not of the common good of the world at large. This is not the
only field in which he shows a truly exalted and right kingly spirit.

And so, now that I see the greatest princes of the world, Francis king of
France, his Catholic Majesty King Charles, Henry king of England, Em-   35
peror Maximilian, tearing out by the roots the nurseries of war and binding
peace in chains, I hope, of solid adamant, I feel the summons to a sure and
certain hope that besides high moral standards and Christian piety, the
reformed and genuine study of literature and the liberal disciplines may be
partly reborn and partly find new lustre; the more so, since this object is   40
now pursued with equal enthusiasm in different regions of the world, in
Rome by Pope Leo, in Spain by the Cardinal of Toledo, in England by King
Henry, eighth of that name who is something of a scholar himself, in our
country by King Charles a divinely gifted young man, in France by King
Francis who seems as if born for this very purpose and even offers the most   45
generous rewards to attract and woo men of distinguished integrity and
learning from every quarter, in Germany by many other eminent princes
and bishops and especially by Emperor Maximilian who in his old age,
wearied by so many wars, has decided to relax in the arts of peace, which
will prove both more appropriate to his time of life and more beneficial to   50
the Christian world. So it is to their piety that we owe the spectacle of the
best minds everywhere rising as though at a signal given and shaking off
their sloth, as they set themselves in concert to restore the humanities. How
else can one describe the way in which so many good scholars are attacking
this splendid programme, dividing the task among themselves in different   55
ways, not with zeal merely but with considerable success, so that we have

* * * * *

42 Toledo] The great Cardinal Ximénes (1436–1517), confessor and councillor
of Isabella of Castile, who was the architect of religious reform in Spain. He
was made archbishop of Toledo in 1495, and cardinal in 1507. His most
notable achievement was the foundation of the University of Alcalá and the
promotion there of the scholarly work that produced the polyglot bible known
as the Complutensian Polyglot; cf Ep 384 introduction (p 220). After the death
of Ferdinand in January 1516 he became regent of Castile and Aragon.

the almost certain hope of seeing every subject come forth into the light of day reformed and purified? To begin with, that elegant literature which has so long been reduced almost to extinction, has now for some time been studied and absorbed by Scots and Danes and Irishmen. As for medicine, 60 what champions it can number! In Rome Niccolò Leoniceno, in Venice Ambrogio Leoni of Nola, in France Guillaume Cop and Jean Du Ruel, and in England Thomas Linacre. Civil law is being restored in Paris by Guillaume Budé and in Germany by Udalricus Zasius; mathematics in Basel by Henricus Glareanus. 65

Of course the science of theology was rather more of a business, because this has hitherto been taught as a rule by obstinate opponents of the humanities, and those who defend their own ignorance the more successfully as doing so under the cloak of piety, so that the ignorant public is convinced by them that religion is in danger if anyone sets out to attack 70 their barbarous style. For humble and uneducated folk are their favourite audience for appeals to the public and calls to start throwing stones, if they foresee a risk of its appearing that there is something which they do not know. Here too I am confident of success, as soon as knowledge of the three tongues proceeds to secure public recognition in the universities, as it has 75 already begun to do. For even in this faculty, those with most learning and least prejudice are some of them helpful, and some approve it in principle; and in this business, an active part has been played by Jacques Lefèvre d'Etaples, besides other people, by a man whom you remind me of not only in your name but in many of your gifts. As for me, I have been allotted, as 80 was to be expected, a very humble part in this enterprise, and whether I have contributed anything, I do not know. At any rate I have roused the passions of those who do not wish the world to change its ways, as though my efforts too, such as they are, had brought some influence to bear.

* * * * *

61 Leoniceno] Niccolò, of Vincenza (d 1524); he taught medicine at Ferrara, where Erasmus met him in 1509; cf Ep 216A:21n.

62 Leoni] (d c 1526) taught medicine at Padua and subsequently at Naples. After 1507 he was in Venice as physician to Aldus' household; cf Ep 854.

62 Cop] Cf Ep 523 introduction.

62 Du Ruel] Physician to Francis 1 and translator of Dioscorides; cf Ep 346:13n.

64 Zasius] Cf Ep 303 introduction.

65 Glareanus] Cf Ep 440 introduction.

75 universities] With trilingual foundations, notably at Alcalá and Louvain

76 this faculty] That is, of theologians

78–9 Lefèvre d'Etaples] Cf Ep 315 introduction.

80 your name] Capito's name too was Faber; cf Ep 459 introduction.

Though I at least did not undertake this from a firm belief that I was capable 85
of anything distinguished in the way of teaching – I enjoyed paving the way
for others who had greater projects in hand, so that, with fewer boulders
and bogs to impede them, they might find it easier to introduce their
splendid lofty programme. And yet this industry of mine, such as it is, is
not unacceptable to scholarly fair-minded critics, and no dogs bark at me 90
except a few blockheads who are rejected even by uneducated people who
have a little common-sense. The other day a man here before an audience of
ordinary folk, in a sermon in fact, lamented in a voice breaking with
emotion that sacred literature was finished, and with it the theologians who
had hitherto carried the Christian faith on their shoulders, now that men 95
had appeared who corrected the holy Gospels and even the Lord's Prayer
itself, exactly as though I find fault with Matthew or Luke, and not with
those whose ignorance or carelessness has corrupted what those writers set
down correctly. In England two or three people loudly complain that it is
monstrous if a great man like Jerome has to take lessons from me, as though 100
I altered what was written by Jerome and did not rather restore what he
wrote. And yet they think themselves great theologians, the men who make
this nonsensical chatter, which would be rejected with scorn by a fuller of
even moderate sense.

But now that I have handed over this sphere of activity, much more 105
accessible than it used to be and not a little less exposed now to unpopularity, gird up your loins, my excellent Faber, and seize the torch which I pass
on to you! I have done what I could, ill-starred as I am; you, I think, possess
in an eminent degree what we see is needed for this splendid task. Young in
years, still vigorous and fresh; physically energetic and able to face hard 110
work; equipped with a fertile mind, keen judgment, no ordinary skill in the
three tongues, and sufficient gifts of style to adorn your subject and not
merely to convey it; a lofty spirit with no greater ambition than to do some
service to the whole race of mortals; a situation not perhaps highly lucrative, but adequate at least and even honourable – you have a position of 115
authority, won mainly by your own merits, as holder of the office of
preacher under our distinguished bishop Christoph of Basel in his celebrated cathedral church, and above all a character so upright, a reputation

* * * * *

92 a man] The same mentioned in Allen III Ep 948:104; cf also Ep 483:29.
99 In England] For example, Henry Standish; cf Ep 481:44n.
107 torch] *Adagia* I ii 38
117 preacher] He was appointed cathedral preacher in 1515; cf Ep 459 introduction.

so spotless, that the most shameless purveyor of scandal would hesitate
before speaking ill of Faber. Aulus Gellius tells us how long ago a good and   120
acceptable proposal was rendered futile by the bad character of its pro-
poser; and in the same way the fruits of study are quite rightly made more
attractive by the reputation of the man who recommends it. It will also tell
in your favour that, apart from that more recondite learning of your own
you also enjoy an unsurpassed familiarity and mastery in the subjects   125
popular in our universities, the only subjects all other men approve; so that
they cannot suggest (as they love to do) that you turned aside into this
different field of study after failing to make a success of the traditional
course. He makes the most effective champion against error who is most
familiar with it; no one cures a disease better than the man who has most   130
experience of it.

   Not that I would wish to see the kind of theology which today is
established in our universities abolished; I want it to be enriched and made
more accurate by the incorporation of ancient and genuine texts. For there
need be no weakening in the authority of Scripture or of theologians, if   135
some things are read in future in more accurate form which used hitherto to
be corrupt, or some things better understood on which the majority of
teachers hitherto were deluded; in fact they will carry all the more weight in
proportion as they have a more genuine understanding of sacred literature.
The shock of the first encounter, which Terence calls the sharpest, I have   140
supported myself; though this ordeal, like others, you were best able to
withstand, equipped like some Geryon with the three tongues or rather,
armed with three swords and triple shield. Besides which I foresee that men
will not be wanting to play the part of Theseus once you are engaged upon
this task. And then you have such a steadfast spirit that it will be easy for   145
you to despise the unpopularity that commonly arises from outstanding
merit, just as light must cast shadows, and such charm of manner that you
can be on good terms with the most difficult of men. In a word, all seems to
me to promise the greatest success. There is still one misgiving in my mind:
that under cover of the reborn literature of antiquity paganism may try to   150

* * * * *

120 Aulus Gellius] 18.3
140 Terence] *Phormio* 346
142 Geryon] A mythical Spanish king with three bodies
144 Theseus] Had a reputation for assisting other heroes in their exploits
149–70 There is still ... laborious toil] Erasmus evidently feared that, just as
excessive enthusiasm for pagan learning might lead to a revival of pagan
culture (with Italy, perhaps, in mind) so the new vogue for Hebrew studies,
once its fruits escaped the close circle of biblical scholarship, might lead to a

rear its ugly head, for we know that even among Christians some scarcely
acknowledge Christ in more than name, and under the surface are rank
heathens; or that the rebirth of Hebrew studies may give Judaism its cue to
plan a revival, the most pernicious plague and bitterest enemy that one can
find to the teaching of Christ. For such is the nature of human affairs: never   155
was good so successful that something in the way of evil did not try to creep
in under cover of it. I could wish that those frigid sophistries could either be
quite cut out or at least were not the theologians' only concern, and that
Christ pure and simple might be planted deep into the minds of men; and
this I think could best be brought about if, aided by the support of the three   160
tongues, we drew our philosophy from the true sources. But I pray that in
avoiding one evil we fall not into another that may be worse. There have
lately been published several pamphlets which breathe the unadulterated
air of Jewry. I watch our great hero Paul toiling to defend Christ against

* * * * *

revival of the abuse he most disliked, religious legalism. 'Judaism' to Erasmus
was a spiritual phenomenon rather than a social or 'racial' issue, a problem
within Christendom: the habitual tendency to substitute legalism and the
satisfactions of formal devotional observances for a personal and faithful
following of Christ. His attitude derives from a deep Paulinism rather than
any notable interest in or concern about the Jewish community or its worship. Characteristically patristic in outlook, Erasmus seems to have held that
Judaism, displaced in the providential plan by the New Covenant of Christianity, was no longer important as a living faith. The attitude expressed here
finds an early parallel, for example, in the letter of St Ignatius of Antioch to the
Magnesians (x.3): 'It is monstrous to talk of Jesus Christ and to practise
Judaism. For Christianity did not base its faith on Judaism, but Judaism on
Christianity, and every tongue believing in God was brought together in it'
(translation of Kirsopp Lake *The Apostolic Fathers* 1 Loeb Classical Library
[New York 1912] 207; cf F.X. Funk *Die Echtheit der Ignatianischen Briefe*
[Tübingen 1883] 169–70).
   This passage might also be compared to Erasmus' comments on the many
passages in the Epistles of St Paul where there is a sharp contrast between
Christian liberty and the adherence to old rituals of the Judaizing party among
the early Christians. Among other such texts, Erasmus' Paraphrase on
Romans 4:17 states: 'The Jews think that they are alive and that they amount to
something. They detest the Gentiles as if dead and worthy of nothing good.
But the summons of God accomplishes more for the Gentiles than their own
ancestry accomplishes for the Jews' (LB VII 790F). Again, the Paraphrase on
John 1:5 runs as follows, 'But against this living and eternal light they [the
shades of this world] are powerless. The Jews, the philosophers, the rulers and
all those who have devoted themselves to things that perish have striven to
confound it, but it conquers ...' (LB VII 501A).
157 sophistries] Scholastic refinements derived from the use of Aristotelian
(and thus pagan) logic in theology.

Judaism, and I feel that some men I could name are slipping back into it   165
secretly. Then I hear of people who have other schemes afoot which can add
nothing to our knowledge of Christ but merely throw dust in men's eyes.
This makes me wish all the more to see you take up this task, for your
genuine devotion will have no aim in view, as I well know, save Christ
Himself, the sole object of all your laborious toil.   170

Give my particular greetings to our reverend father Christoph
bishop of Basel, and give my best wishes to all my other friends especially to
Ludwig Baer, Henricus Glareanus, Beatus Rhenanus, the Amerbach
brothers, Wilhelm Nesen, to those learned lawyers Dr Lukas and Dr
Gerard, to the bishop's official and to all the others whose most delightful   175
society I so much enjoyed when I was with you.

Farewell. From Antwerp, 26 February 1516

542 / To Henricus Afinius   Antwerp [February] 1517

Afinius (Hendrik van den Eynde) of Lier, 17 kilometres from Antwerp, was
chief physician of that city. This is a complimentary epistle introducing three
Questions – on medicine, astronomy and metaphysics – publicly disputed by
Afinius at Louvain on 19 December 1516. They were printed in Antwerp by W.
Vorsterman, 4 April 1517 (NK 42). There is a close similarity to Ep 541. Pieter
Gillis too contributed complimentary verses introducing the volume, and
Franciscus Colibrantius, secretary of Antwerp, added a letter of eulogy.

Afinius had studied both Arts and Medicine at Louvain, where he enrolled
in the Faculty of Arts on 31 August 1499 (see A. Schillings *Matricule de
l'université de Louvain* III [Brussels 1958] 191, 324). In the autumn of 1517 he
presented Erasmus with silver cups, and the next year Erasmus dedicated to
him his *Encomium medicinae* (Basel: Froben 1518). This text was republished in
the *Epistolae ad diversos*.

* * * * *

173 Baer] See Ep 488 introduction.
173 Rhenanus] Cf Ep 327 introduction.
173–4 Amerbach brothers] Bruno and Bonifacius; cf Epp 331, 408 introductions.
174 Nesen] Cf Ep 329 introduction.
174 Dr Lukas] Klett; cf Ep 316 introduction.
174–5 Dr Gerard] De Lupabus, dean of the Faculty of Law at Basel in 1508 and
1513
175 bishop's official] Johann Heigerlin, known as Johannes Fabri; cf Ep 386
introduction.

ERASMUS OF ROTTERDAM TO THE DISTINGUISHED PHYSICIAN
HENRICUS AFINIUS OF LIER, GREETING

Happy indeed is this age of ours, dearest Henricus, in which the enlightened study of literature blossoms so wonderfully everywhere. This we
owe principally to the generosity and goodness of princes, who have begun 5
to concern themselves with the rewards and honours due to outstanding
minds, especially since, as though some divine power had altered their
intents, they have begun to concentrate all their policy on anchoring peace
in the world with everlasting chains. In winter all is withered and laid low,
and the north wind is king with his cruel snow and ice and hail; but when 10
the sun returns, bringing the charms of spring, all revives and is green
again, and men's energies are roused from their former sloth to the age-long
task of cultivation, one ploughing, another pruning his vines, one grafting
and another manuring. So it is with humane studies, which in wartime are
neglected and virtually dead, but put forth new shoots under the favour and 15
liberality of princes. For now Pope Leo, pontiff supreme on many counts
but on this count especially, issues to all Christians a public call to mutual
harmony; now Francis king of France, most Christian monarch not in title
only, devotes all his strength to the same end, zealously advancing the
excellent policy of that best of shepherds, while his Catholic Majesty King 20
Charles and Emperor Maximilian are devoted to the cause; and so all the
liberal disciplines can breathe again, for they have always been the nurs-
lings of peace, as flowers are of the breezes of spring. Now gifted minds
bestir themselves to take up interrupted tasks. One gives theology its life
again, another physic; one restores to the light of day the authors who were 25
like to perish from neglect, another clears up those beset with errors; each
man has his task. In a word, while all is activity everywhere, as though men
were trying to mend what had been torn apart by war, there shines forth all
that wisdom which your master Galen defines as 'a knowledge of the affairs
of gods and men alike,' complaining that it was despised and neglected in 30
his time, as it has been in ours.

For the rest, if you have lately begun to add to your earlier studies in
astronomy and medicine the study of Greek, which can contribute so much
to every branch of learning but particularly medicine, I have the highest
praise for your judgment and enterprise, and I congratulate you on your 35
good fortune in starting this in good time while still in the prime of life. The

* * * * *

542:21 Maximilian] Cf Ep 532:34; Maximilian had agreed to take part in the
conference at Cambrai in December 1516; cf LP 2667.

29 Galen] This has not been identified.

same objective has been attacked by the leading physicians of our time, Guillaume Cop, Ambrogio Leoni of Nola, Niccolò Leoniceno at a more advanced age, yet not without success; for Thomas Linacre and Du Ruel were fortunate enough to learn their Greek earlier. Marcus Musurus of   40
course is Greek by birth as well, and in scholarship Greek through and through. In no art is a mistake more perilous than in medicine. No wonder if the most intelligent of our physicians are adding Greek to their other fields of study; and soon, I believe, it will be thought impudent to call oneself a physician without it. It is at least far from negligible to be able to   45
listen to the founder of the art, Hippocrates, and next to him Galen, Paulus Aegineta, Dioscorides speaking in their own language. But as it is uncivil to deprive a man of his vote without due notice and to throw off the bridge, as it were, everyone who has not had the luck to learn Greek, so it is reasonable that such men should gladly put up with a warning from me. Farewell.   50
Antwerp, 1517

543 / To Thomas More   Antwerp, 1 March 1517

This letter (Rogers number 35) first appeared in the *Farrago*.

ERASMUS OF ROTTERDAM TO HIS FRIEND THOMAS MORE, GREETING
I sent you recently a bundle of letters with a copy of the *Utopia* by the hand of a man who said he was a particular friend of yours, and would have given him more to carry but I did not like to. Having now secured another courier,

* * * * *

38 Leoni] Cf Ep 541:62n.
38 Leoniceno] Cf Ep 541:61n.
39 Linacre] Cf Ep 520:138n.
39 Du Ruel] Cf Ep 541:62n.
40 Musurus] Cf Ep 224:5n.
47 Aegineta] Paul of Aegina (c 625–c 690) was an Alexandrian physician and surgeon, whose *Epitomae medicae libri septem* was the last medical encyclopaedia of the ancient Greek world.
47 Dioscorides] Pedanius Dioscorides (c AD 40–c 90) was a Greek physician. His *De materia medica* was for centuries the leading pharmacological text.
48 throw off the bridge] *Adagia* I v 37
543:2 recently] Probably about 13 February; cf Ep 558:2.
2 *Utopia*] Probably a copy for More's use in revising the text for the new edition forthcoming; cf Ep 550 introduction.
3 a man] Cf Ep 545:2.
4 another courier] Cf line 28n and Ep 545:3.

I send all the Reuchlin pieces in one volume, which please pass on to the   5
bishop of Rochester on the understanding that he reads them and sends them
back as soon as he can, for some of them are not to be found anywhere. For
your part you should read the *Propositiones* of a true theologian, the Depths
of Wisdom and the Articles edited by Arnold of Tongeren. I enclose a letter
to Marliano, having heard that he suspects the first book of the *Utopia* of   10
coming from me, and I should not like that to get about for nothing is more
baseless. That dialogue of Julius and Peter, I understand, is already in the
hands of the chancellor, and delights him hugely. I expect the *Moria* daily.
Send your revised *Utopia* here as soon as you can, and I will send a copy for
the printer either to Basel or, if you prefer, to Paris. If Ammonio has   15
anything, please have it sent to me as soon as you can, for the prince is
preparing to depart, and where I shall go or when I am uncertain. A vast

* * * * *

5 Reuchlin pieces] Evidently a collection of some of the fugitive pieces printed
on Reuchlin's behalf

6 Rochester] John Fisher, who had long interested himself in Reuchlin's
difficulties; cf Epp 300:8–9, 324.

8 *Propositiones*] *Articuli sive propositiones de Iudaico favore nimis suspecte ex
libello theutonico domini Ioannis Reuchlin ... (cui Speculi ocularis titulus inscriptus
est) extracte, cum annotationibus ... Arnoldi de Tungeri.* Cologne: Quentel 28
August 1512

9 Arnold of Tongeren] Arnoldus Luydius (d 1540) studied at Cologne (MA
1489) where he became a professor of theology and in 1521 was rector. An
esteemed theologian with a command of Hebrew and, for that reason, appointed a judge in the Reuchlin controversy, he attracted the enmity and
criticism of the humanist's opponents.

10 Marliano] Cf Ep 411:10n.

12 dialogue] The *Julius exclusus*; cf Ep 502 introduction.

12 I understand] Cf Ep 532:29.

13 chancellor] Jean Le Sauvage

13 *Moria*] Perhaps Froben's undated edition; cf Ep 419:14n.

14 *Utopia*] Cf line 2.

15–6 has anything] That is, from Rome, concerning Erasmus' case; cf Ep 447
introduction, and the opening of Ep 505 to Ammonio.

16 prince] Charles

17–8 vast sum] In 1515 the Estates of Brabant had granted the prince an annual
subsidy of 150,000 gulden = £25,000 gros Flemish = £17,187 10s 0d sterling =
£145,161 tournois. Cf CWE 1 323, 340, 347; and Ep 474:11n above. The Estates
granted an additional sum the next year to help pay for Prince Charles' journey
to Spain. Then on 23 February 1517 the Estates were asked to renew the annual
subsidy for three more years.

sum of money is being demanded from the people and, what is more, immediately. The request has been accepted by the nobility and the prelates, the only people, that is, who will pay nothing. The cities are consider- 20
ing the question now. The emperor, who is normally unarmed, is now here with a body of troops splendidly equipped, and the country round is full of bands of soldiery, though where they come from and in whose name is uncertain. I pity this country gnawed by so many vultures! How happy it would be, if only the cities would agree among themselves! 25

Let me know whether my lord of Canterbury and Colet still have the same feelings towards me, and the bishop of Rochester too, about whom I wrote to you lately. The father of the man who brings this letter asked me to an excellent dinner; he is well-to-do and respected, and spoke at length about all you had done for him. Please help me with your advice. I shall 30
soon arrange for the printing of another volume of letters to bring them before a larger public. I enclose Budé's latest. May Maruffo get what he deserves with that bill of his! – for I can make nothing of those sauls of yours anywhere, unless I set off for Bruges. Farewell, my sweetest More.

* * * * *

20 cities] At the time of writing, the four chief cities of Brabant – Antwerp, Louvain, Brussels and s'Hertogenbosch – were deliberating on their response to the request mentioned in note 15. On 27 March, with the Estates convened again, they acceded to the request.

26 Colet] Cf Ep 468:15n.

28 The father] Johann Crull, a commercial agent, and a citizen of Antwerp; cf LP ii 2190.

31 another volume of letters] The collection *Epistolae elegantes* (1517) published by Martens at Louvain (NK 819). It had a preface by Pieter Gillis addressed to Antonius Clava of Ghent, and dated 5 March 1517, from Antwerp. It contained four letters from the *Epistolae ad Erasmum* of 1516 (NK 2939) and thirty-one new letters written by or to Erasmus during his recent stay in the Low Countries; cf CWE 3 348–9. Although Gillis' preface (CWE 3 351–2) claimed that the publication would not please Erasmus, this passage makes it clear that Erasmus was at least partly responsible for it. When Ep 543 was published in the *Epistolae ad diversos* (1521) this passage was suppressed; cf also Ep 546, for evidence of Erasmus' complicity.

32 Budé's latest] Ep 522

32 Maruffo] Cf Ep 465:3n.

33 sauls] Allen suggests that Erasmus' term *Saulos* meant 'possibly the English double sovereign' [sic: the sovereign or double ryal]; but neither the NED nor Schrötter's *Wörterbuch der Münzkunde* (1930) offers any support for that theory – nor indeed do they offer any clue as to Erasmus' meaning. Perhaps Erasmus was making a pun on 'sols' – shillings. Cf CWE 1 329–30; Epp 467–8, 474 above.

Antwerp, 1 March   35
Franz is with you at the moment. If the archbishop's Jerome is not yet
complete, he is the man to ask, for he is under obligation to complete it.
Send me back the originals of the letters which I now send you, and the
things you had back from Lupset; but mind it is by safe hand. Best wishes
again to you and yours.   40
  1516

544 / From Mariano Accardo   Brussels, 1 March 1517

Mariano Accardo (d 1521) of Noto was possibly one of the two men of noble
birth mentioned by Budé as sent by Josse Bade and desirous of meeting
Erasmus (Ep 493:553). His call on Erasmus in Brussels in February 1517 is
described in Ep 531:579–81. He had been in the service of his fellow-citizen
Rinaldo Montuoro, bishop of Cefalù in Sicily, and on the bishop's death (in
October 1511) he returned to Sicily and entered the service of the viceroy Ugo
de Moncada, whom he accompanied to the court of Brussels in 1517.

FROM MARIANO ACCARDO THE SICILIAN TO
ERASMUS OF ROTTERDAM, GREETING
While you were here, maybe I did not come to see you very often, but it was
easy for me to enjoy your delightful society, and so, when you were not at
hand, I bore it with equanimity. But since your departure I am consumed   5
with such a longing to see you that I suffer torments of impatience for not
being permitted to do what I could do at will during your stay. Nor is that
all. I much regret that while you were here I often missed an opportunity to
hang greedily upon your lips, when there was so much to learn and to
enjoy. What an idle creature I was, unworthy of the friendship of so great a 10
man! Who can forgive me for preferring a lot of rubbish to all the treasures
of antiquity? But it is useless to blame me for my irreparable loss, when I
have no chance whatever of making good the irrevocable waste of time, for
which I am alone responsible. It is better to come and see you, instead of
envying the good people of Antwerp and especially Pieter Gillis, such a   15
well-bred man and such a good scholar and, to put it in a word, one who
fully deserves your friendship and your good opinion. I wish I could

* * * * *

36 Franz] Birckmann, the Cologne bookseller and agent in Antwerp; cf Ep
258:14n.
36 archbishop's Jerome] Warham had originally received four of the nine
volumes; cf Ep 413:34–5.
39 Lupset] The writings referred to in Ep 502; cf Ep 502 introduction and 10n.

discover, by way of a letter from you, whether you mean to visit us in the
near future. If only you would say 'Patience! for soon I shall be at your side!'
If on the other hand you mean to leave us for some time in the dark, I shall   20
hurry to visit you, that the light of your countenance may banish the
darkness by which I am blinded. Till then farewell, honour and glory of our
times, together with your *fidus Achates*, to whom I send special greetings.

Brussels, 1 March 1517

545 / To Thomas More   Antwerp, 8 March 1517

This letter, number 36 in Rogers, was first published in the *Farrago*.

ERASMUS OF ROTTERDAM TO HIS FRIEND THOMAS MORE, GREETING
I have sent two bundles of letters, one by a merchant I know and the other
by a son of Johann Crull, whom you had helped. To this man I entrusted a
volume in which were the pieces by Reuchlin which the bishop of Rochester passionately wanted; by the former I sent Reuchlin's book, translated at   5
my own expense. Send a *Utopia* at the first opportunity. There is a councillor in Antwerp so much struck with it that he knows it by heart. Dorp's
letter to which you replied was copied by your people in such a way that the
Sibyl herself could not read it; I wish you would send it me less badly
written. Please write fully at the first opportunity about everything; for here   10
a great revolution seems to be in prospect, unless I am quite wrong. Best
wishes to you and all yours.

The bearer of this is an excellent young man, to whom Sixtinus has
promised something or other. In reliance on this he is making for England,
not knowing that a simple promise gives rise to no legal claim; but all the   15
same encourage Sixtinus to do more for him. If Vives has been with you

* * * * *

544:23 *Achates*] Pieter Gillis, Erasmus' old friend and host in Antwerp; cf Ep
516:9–11.

545:2 the other] Ep 543: cf Ep 543:4, 28n.

4 pieces by Reuchlin] Cf Ep 543:5–7.

5 book] Probably the *Augenspiegel*; cf Ep 300:3n. It was written originally in
German.

7–8 Dorp's letter] Ep 347; More's reply to it is Rogers 15.

16 Sixtinus] Cf Ep 430 introduction.

16 Vives] This is the first mention in the correspondence of the great Spanish
humanist Juan Luis Vives. De Vocht argued (*Literae* xlix 7n) that More's letter
to Erasmus of 26 May 1520 (Allen IV 1106), expressing surprise at the excellence
of Vives' *Declamationes syllanae* (Antwerp: Hillen van Hoochstraten April 1520

often, you will easily guess what I have suffered in Brussels, where I have
had to cope every day with so many Spaniards come to pay their respects, as
well as Italians and Germans. Farewell once more.

Antwerp, 8 March 1517   20

546 / From Rutgerus Rescius   Louvain, 8 March [1517]

The writer was a corrector for the press of Martens, whose printing of the
Epistolae elegantes, which appeared in April 1517, is at issue here; see CWE 3
Appendix, Ep 543:26n. Rescius (Rutger Ressen), who died in 1545, was born
in Maaseik in Limburg, on the river Meuse. He was a pupil of Girolamo
Aleandro at Paris (BA 1513–14) and afterward studied law at Louvain, supporting himself there by working for Martens and by teaching. In September 1518
he was appointed to the new chair in Greek at Busleyden's college; see Gerlo
5150; de Vocht CTL I 277–9 and *passim*, 2 *passim*.

TO MASTER ERASMUS OF ROTTERDAM FROM RUTGERUS RESCIUS,
GREETING
In your letter to Wolfgang Faber, O universally learned Erasmus, there is a
passage not far from the end, of which we can make absolutely nothing. It
begins: 'Tum audio nonnullos alia quaedam moliri, quae ad Christi cog-   5
nitionem nihil adferant, sed *funcios* tantum offendant oculis hominum.' I
showed it to Desmarez and Nijmegen, and they were stumped by it, just as I

* * * * *

NK 4062) and professing not to know Vives at all, makes it certain that this
reference cannot be to Vives, but rather to 'Pollio,' the name substituted in the
text printed in *Epistolae ad diversos* (Froben 1521). This supposes a needless
contradiction between More's account and Erasmus' phrase here, and seems
too abrupt a dismissal of the text in the *Farrago* (Froben October 1519) where
the identification is strengthened by the addition in the margin, 'Lud. Vives.'
    It seems altogether likely that Erasmus, having come to admire Vives (cf Ep
1107), decided in 1521 to tone down what had been published in October 1519,
and substituted the name 'Pollio,' possibly referring to Catullus 12.6. Here,
the Pollio who was afterwards famous from Virgil's fourth eclogue, is introduced as 'a young man filled with charm and wit'; both More and Erasmus
seem to have been impressed with the combination in Vives of intelligence
and wide learning with what they regarded as youth. For Vives' connections
with the English humanists, see McConica *passim*.
546:3 Faber] Capito; Ep 541:166–7
7 Desmarez] Cf Ep 180 introduction.
7 Nijmegen] Gerard Geldenhouwer, born at Nijmegen and known as
Noviomagus
7 stumped by it] *Adagia* I iv 99

had been; but they thought we should make no rash changes, and advised
me to show you the passage before printing it. Dorp conjectured that we
ought to read 'fumos tantum offendunt.' Dirk has therefore left this part of   10
the letter to be printed later, and sends you the actual copy, begging you to
let him know what you want done about the reading in this place as soon as
possible. He would also be glad, if there is anything that could conveniently
be added to the preface of the letters, if it might be sent him. He kept for it a
whole page blank on both sides, while it will hardly fill half of it. Farewell,   15
my walking encyclopaedia.

Louvain, 8 March

547./ From Riccardo Bartolini   Antwerp [March 1517]

These lines were written to solicit an interview with Erasmus. It seems that
after this was arranged, Bartolini was unable to keep the appointment and
wrote Ep 548 to apologize, sending with the letter Ursinus' *Genethliacon* (Ep
548:5n).

Riccardo Bartolini (d 1529) was a native of Perugia, where he taught at the
university and held a canonry. He served on embassies to Florence and Rome,
and by 1515 had become chaplain and secretary to the powerful Cardinal
Matthäus Lang, bishop of Gurk (cf Ep 549:52–3n). With Lang he travelled in
1515 from Augsburg to Vienna for the meeting of Maximilian with the two
Jagiello kings of Poland and Bohemia-Hungary to draw up agreements on the
Hapsburg succession. This journey was described in an early work, the
Odeporicon (Vienna: Vietor 13 September 1515). He also wrote court poetry,
including an epic – *Ad divum Maximilianum Caesarem Augustum de bello Norico
Austriados libri duodecim* – on the war of succession between Bavaria and the
Palatinate in 1504–05. In 1517 he was crowned poet laureate personally by the
emperor in Antwerp. In 1519, having been offered the chair in rhetoric there,
he returned to Perugia to resume his teaching career.

TO ERASMUS, KINSMAN OF THE MUSES,
FROM RICCARDO BARTOLINI

Erasmus, if you've time to spare,
Give me I beg, dear sir, a share.
I will a leading Grecian bring,   5
Learned, well-born and quite the thing.
* * * * *

9 Dorp] Maarten van Dorp, Erasmus' old critic at Louvain; cf Ep 304 introduction.

10 Dirk] Martens

15 whole page] Folio a^2; see CWE 3 349.

No frowning now in that stern face!
Put off hard work a little space.
'Tis no whole day for which he pleads;
A third, a fifth is all he needs.   10
Say yes! – and choose the time to suit you;
He asks leave only to salute you.
So well he loves your master-mind,
He's sure he will a Plato find,
A saintly Socrates in you   15
And sacred Phocis' prophet too.
Don't think he means to give offence
Or treat you with malice prepense.
Sure, 'tis your learning charms his heart,
In which you bear the leading part,   20
Beat all the world of scholars down,
And win yourself a heavenly crown.
In you has generous Nature sited
(With unremitting toil united)
What others scarce by drudging gain.   25
Thrice, sevenfold blest may you remain!

Lines written at Antwerp extempore, therewith to request an interview.
Farewell.

548 / From Riccardo Bartolini   [Antwerp, c 10 March 1517]

See the introduction to Ep 547; this letter was first published in the *Epistolae
elegantes* 1517.

RICCARDO BARTOLINI TO ERASMUS OF ROTTERDAM, GREETING
I would have come to you, dearest Erasmus, had I not been prevented by a
courier who announced that he was off next day. I should be sorry, however, to deprive you of your proper tributes, so I am sending you a number
of well-turned lines in celebration of your birthday. The author is Gaspar   5

* * * * *

548:5 well-turned lines] A *Genethliacon Erasmi* composed about February
1517 by Gaspar Ursinus Velius (Kaspar Bernhard 1493–1539) of Schweidnitz;
cf Allen III Ep 851:1, Reedijk 399–400. It was printed in the *Epistolae elegantes*
1517 (NK 819) and in subsequent editions, and also by Ursinus in his *Poemata*
(Basel: Froben March 1522). It seems from his text that Velius thought Erasmus
had just reached his fiftieth birthday.

Velius, a young man of no small skill in Latin and Greek, a member of my
master's household and very devoted to you at a distance. He wrote to ask
me to underline anything that I thought not very successful. I read the
whole thing rapidly; but when I read them with more attention a second
time, I marked a few things right at the very beginning; not that I thought   10
they needed the rod from me, but so that he might have the benefit of your
opinion, if anything in the correction of his work needed redoing. I have
not been able to complete my task; the burden now falls on you, since the
lines are written to celebrate your birthday, of ensuring that they are as
faultless as possible before they see the light. Of his gifts I can say this, that I   15
have found no one in Germany like him. Farewell, and let Paulus and
myself have a letter from you sometime.

    Riccardo Bartolini

549 / To Riccardo Bartolini   Antwerp, 10 March 1517

Erasmus' prompt reply to Bartolini's letter was first published in the *Epistolae
elegantes* 1517.

ERASMUS OF ROTTERDAM TO RICCARDO BARTOLINI,
LEADING SCHOLAR IN BOTH GREEK AND LATIN, GREETING
I was remarkably taken, my learned friend Bartolini, with Gaspar Velius'
hendecasyllables. Everything runs with such classical ease that one can
easily detect a vein of talent which is not merely elegant but fertile and full   5
of promise. However, I must be sparing in my praise of a man who has so
heaped praises on myself. How I wish he had devoted this labour to
some more rewarding subject! Happy indeed would Germany be, if she

* * * * *

6 Velius] Velius (see note 5) was born about 1493 and died on 5 March 1539.
He matriculated at Cracow in 1505 and at Leipzig in 1508, but evidently took
no degrees. Like Bartolini (Ep 547 introduction) he entered the service of
Matthäus Lang, bishop of Gurk, and he accompanied him to Italy where he
studied Greek under Scipione Fortiguerra (Carteromachus) at Bologna. In the
same year, 1512, he went on to Rome. In 1515 he was at Vienna with Bartolini;
he matriculated at the university there, and he remained in Vienna for a year,
not accompanying Bartolini to the Netherlands.
16 Paulus] Paulus Ricius, who died after 1541, was a Jewish convert whom
Erasmus had met at Pavia, and who had published various works drawing on
Hebrew literature in support of Christianity. Now settled at Augsburg, he
was working at a Latin translation of the Talmud at the request of Emperor
Maximilian, to whom, in 1516, he was appointed court physician.
549:4 hendecasyllables] Cf Ep 548:4–7.

could at long last be quit of war. And there is some hope that our princes in
their wisdom will soon bring this about, although among the common herd   10
there are still people who try to kindle a war against the French. A godless
idea indeed! Is the Christian world to be leagued together against the most
spotless and most flourishing part of Christendom? France alone remains
not infected with heretics, with Bohemian schismatics, with Jews, with
half-Jewish marraños, and untouched by the contagion of Turkish   15
neighbours, as are some other countries which everyone can recognize for
himself without naming any names. Nowhere else is there a more impressive council, a university with a higher reputation or higher standards;
nowhere is there greater respect for the law, or a like spirit of unity in the
whole kingdom. Who more deserve to rule than those who best know how   20
to? And at the same time what a disastrous policy for us is this of working
towards a war! We are at all points such close neighbours to the French that
we ourselves are almost Gauls as they are, and it would from the start be
civil war if we fought Gaul against Gaul. Besides which, what can be better
policy than to share mutual good will with your nearest neighbour, and so   25
powerful a neighbour too? And those men are so much blinded by their
hatred of the French that they promise themselves a certain and rapid
victory, forgetting how many years we have struggled unsuccessfully in
Gelderland; for in Friesland the outcome is still uncertain. But suppose we
were indeed victorious, what could better answer the wishes of the Turks   30
and any who hate the name of Christ even more than they do, than for the
fairest and strongest portion of the Christian world to be laid waste with fire
and sword, and the flower of our religion to be shamefully trodden under
foot? Almighty God forbid that their lunacy should be supported by fortune's favour or the policy of princes. But this is outside my province.   35
    As for the publication of the poem, how can I favour the idea when,
scholarly as it is, it says so much about me that is false? The only result
would be to make the writer famous and myself absurd. I should be happy
to promote his reputation, if I could lose my sense of shame. Your departure

* * * * *

15 half-Jewish marraños] These were the Spanish Jews, *conversos*, forcibly
baptized after the edict of 1492 but who continued Jewish worship.
22 close neighbours] Cf Ep 534:32.
29 Gelderland] Burgundian sovereignty was not achieved in Gelderland and
Friesland until 1523; cf Ep 584:40–41. The Duchy of Guelders, a French dependency, bordered on its western frontier with north Brabant and south Holland. The counts of Holland had also long sought to assert their claim to
overlordship of Frisia, and Chièvres relied on an accommodating policy with
France to help remedy the situation without the expense of war.

Johann Huttich
Model for a medal by Friedrich Hagenauer, 1532
Staatliche Museen, Berlin

I will endure as best I may, if you are soon restored to us, for I should like to   40
see more of you and to get to know Velius besides. Furthermore, I was so
much attracted by Paulus Ricius in our recent conversation, that I have
a kind of great thirst for more frequent and intimate talk with him. Besides his knowledge of Hebrew, what a lot of philosophy he knows and
theology too! And such an upright character, a great desire to learn, an open   45
readiness to teach, a modest manner in debate. Personally, I liked him long
ago at first sight in Pavia, when he was teaching philosophy there; and now
that I see him at closer quarters, I like him still more. At last I find in him an
Israelite indeed, and he answers truly to his given name, for all his pleasure
and his toil, his leisure and his business hours alike are spent upon the   50
Scriptures. He has a mind that deserves honoured leisure in the highest
degree. To that most learned Maecenas of all men of learning, the cardinal of
Gurk, pray give my humble duty. Farewell.

Antwerp, 10 March 1516

550 / To Johann Huttich(?)   Antwerp [March?] 1517

This is the preface to the *Convivium*, Erasmus' translation of Lucian's Banquet,
added to Froben's edition (December 1517) of the translations made by More
and Erasmus from the dialogues of Lucian. The first work in the volume is the
Querela pacis, followed by the *Declamatio de morte*, and it was intended to
include, besides the Lucian, More's *Utopia* and the epigrams by the two
friends. But Froben concluded the volume with More's *Lucubrationes* and
published the *Utopia* and *Epigrammata* in a separate volume the following
March; see the account by C.R. Thompson in *The Complete Works of St Thomas
More* 3 (New Haven 1974) lix–lxiii.

The date of the preface is conjectural. It may be fitted into this period (cf Epp
543:2n; 551:12–13) or after Erasmus' return from England when he was as-
sembling the volume for Froben (Epp 584:18–20; 597). The recipient of the
dedication, called Joannes Eutychius, was apparently the resident of Mainz (cf
Allen Ep 614:8n) mentioned in Allen Ep 614:8. Allen tentatively identified him
with Johann Huttich (c 1488–1544) of Mainz, author of *Collectanea an-
tiquitatum in urbe atque agro Moguntino repertarum* (Mainz: Schöffer March
1520) in the preface of which he speaks familiarly of Erasmus.

* * * * *

42 Ricius] Cf Ep 548:16n.

49 Israelite] John 1:47

52–3 cardinal of Gurk] Matthäus Lang; cf Epp 547 introduction, 548:6n. Lang
(1468–1540) was the son of a burgher of Augsburg, and had risen to become
chief councillor of Emperor Maximilian.

ERASMUS OF ROTTERDAM TO HIS FRIEND JOHANN HUTTICH,
GREETING

This dialogue of Lucian, Huttich my learned friend, is a most skilful performance, in that the drawing of so many and such different characters is so
wonderfully lifelike; but even so I have met people who thought it ought to   5
be suppressed, because it tears to pieces philosophers of every kind with
such freedom and in such a spirit of carnival. I on the other hand think it
more proper to be indignant with the standards of our own day, in which
we see the schools of philosophers and theologians squabbling between
themselves even more like children, and waging no less internecine war; in   10
fact those who profess religion fight as bloody battles among themselves as
ever Lucian reported from that banquet, whether it were truth or fiction.
This small work, which lacked a master when I chanced upon it and yet
seemed to me to need a patron, I have dedicated to my friend Huttich. May
you enjoy the good fortune which your name seems to promise; and so   15
farewell.

       Antwerp, 1517

551 / To Andrea Ammonio   Antwerp, 11 March 1517

    We do not have the letter to which this letter replies; it was first printed in the
    Farrago.

ERASMUS TO HIS FRIEND AMMONIO, GREETING

Whether you are right to rebuke me is not yet clear, but at least your
consolation is both affectionate and stylish. Otherwise I might be reduced
to reiterating the familiar 'In my place, you would sing a different tune.'
Indeed, if blindness towards Erasmus took the same form in everyone as it   5
does in you, I should be much less ineffective. Your warmth of feeling, your
sense of duty towards me I might almost say, I am, heaven be my witness,
quite ashamed to thank you for. Your goodness feels too great for conven-
tional expressions of gratitude, and to repay it is beyond me. I will try, all
the same, if only life be granted me. About Sixtinus you feel what I have   10

     * * * * *

    550:7 in such a spirit of carnival] *Adagia* I vii 73

    15 which your name seems to promise] The recipient's name is Latinized as
    Eutychius, which is close to the Greek *eutyches*, fortunate.

    551:2 rebuke me] Erasmus was uneasy about the outcome of his appeal to
    Rome; cf Epp 505:2ff, 539:13ff. It should be realized that he had not yet
    received Epp 518, 519 and 521; cf Ep 552.

    4 'In my place] Terence *Andria* 310

    10 Sixtinus] Sixtinus was a witness to the dispensation; cf Ep 517:93–8.

always felt. So the hope that you offer me shall be my support till further
notice. I am entirely immersed in composition, for I am getting ready some
things to send to Basel. The king of France invites me to his country with the
promise of a thousand florins yearly; I have sent a letter in reply designed to
give no definite answer. The theologians are now actually trying to get me   15
to move to Louvain, and one offers me a hundred florins of his own money.
More is the man; you will get the whole story better from him. Farewell,
dear Ammonio, and continue your efforts to rescue your thrice-wretched
Erasmus. Antwerp, 11 March

    I am a little impatient with the business that prevents your whole   20
mind from being given to the Muses, as it should be. I observe that More
too, who used to be impregnable, is swept like you into stormy water.
Personally, I am what I always was, and have 'sold all my goods to buy my
Phrygian cap.' Farewell once more. 1516

552 / To Andrea Ammonio   Antwerp, 15 March [1517]

> Erasmus refers to the receipt of Epp 518, 519 and 521. This letter was printed in
> the *Farrago* but omitted in all subsequent editions.

ERASMUS TO HIS FRIEND AMMONIO, GREETING
I have had a letter written in the pope's name, and another from the bishop
of Worcester, which is most friendly but has a certain smell of coin about it –

    * * * * *

12–3 some things] Cf Ep 550 introduction.

14 letter in reply] Ep 533

14 a thousand florins] Erasmus is evidently using his monetary terms (*mille
florenos*) loosely, because in Ep 522:58 Guillaume Budé had stated that the
benefice offered by the king of France was worth 'a thousand francs [probably
livres tournois] and more.' A sum of 1000 florins or ducats would have been
worth £2,075 tournois; a sum of 1000 St Philip florins, £1,312 10s 0d tournois
(or £150 sterling). Cf also CWE 1 336–46; and Epp 447:844n, 463:48n above.

16 a hundred florins] In view of Erasmus' previous use of the term florins, no
value can be safely attached to this amount. But since he is speaking of
Louvain, perhaps this time he did mean the St Philip florins of the Hapsburg
Low Countries (which were worth £20 16s 8d gros Flemish = £15 0s 0d sterling
= £131 5s 0d tournois).

24 Phrygian cap'] The sign of a freed slave; Erasmus has in mind Martial
2.68.4.

552:2 a letter] Epp 518, 519

2 another] Ep 521

he makes so much of what has been granted and complains that the datary
is so hard-hearted. He encloses a copy of a brief addressed to you, but   5
corrected apparently in accordance with my changes. But he added that I
must go and see you. If this is necessary, let me know as soon as you can,
though I really hate that Channel crossing. Never mind, I will face it, I will
be a second Theseus who, according to Virgil 'so oft by that sad road goes
and returns,' and do what I have to do in person. If it is not necessary, tell   10
me what you would like me to do and how much is to be paid; but find out
from Sixtinus whether the brief is in order, for he already knows about
Erasmus' misfortunes. When I discover, dear Ammonio, kindest of all the
mortals I have ever met, how I can possibly repay, or rather, show myself
conscious of the spirit you have shown towards me, if I do not drop   15
everything else and do all I can, you will be welcome to enter the name of
Erasmus among the most ungrateful men alive. Farewell.

Antwerp, 15 March

553 / From Hieronymus Emser   Dresden, 15 March 1517

Emser (1478–1527) of Weidenstetten near Ulm, studied Arts at Tübingen and
later at Basel, where he took his MA in 1499. For a few months in 1500 he was
tutor to Bruno and Basilius Amerbach, and he later assisted Johann Prüs of
Strasbourg in editing the works of Pico della Mirandola (15 March 1504). The
next year he entered the service of Duke George of Saxony and received
various ecclesiastical promotions. His good reputation among the humanists
is indicated by Willibald Pirckheimer's account of his qualities in Ep 527;
Pirckheimer dedicated to him a translation of Lucian's *Rhetor* (Haguenau:
Anshelm January 1520). Emser later became a prominent defender of Catholic
orthodoxy against Luther.

* * * * *

4 makes so much] Cf Ep 521:11ff.
4 datary] Cf Ep 479:11n.
5 copy of a brief] Ep 517
6 corrected] Gigli had sent a suggested draft of the dispensation for Erasmus'
inspection; cf Epp 498:11 and 505:5–6.
9 Virgil] *Aeneid* 6.122; Theseus is mentioned in that line, but these words are
used of Pollux, who took turn about with his twin Castor to spend time in
Hades.
12 brief] Ep 518
13 misfortunes] Perhaps a reference to the circumstances of his birth; cf Ep
517:9–10n. The phrase was written in Greek.

HIERONYMUS EMSER TO MASTER ERASMUS

Greetings, Erasmus, chosen vessel, and next after Paul as teacher of the
Gentiles! Your publications, for all that I read them with sore and bleary
eyes, I revere like something straight from heaven. Each of them breathes
your unique brand of learning, to which your 'Christian Knight' adds   5
Christian piety complete. Two years ago, when it was hard to find in these
parts, I gave it to a publisher to be reprinted, and prefixed an epigram, a
rude thing, of my own:

> Learning with piety our sires did wed;
> We keep the letter, but the spirit's fled.   10
> Not the good life, but knowledge is the cry;
> In vain he's wise, who's wise he knows not why.
> How well Erasmus treads the ancient ways! –
> Tunes lyre and voice alike to sacred lays;
> His silver tongue adorns with golden heart;   15
> Spoils the Egyptians, and gives God His part.
> Sell all thou hast and buy him, as you're bid:
> Pearls of great price within this field are hid.

May the God of heaven and earth, who has filled you with the spirit of
wisdom and understanding that you might open your mouth in the midst   20
of the congregation, preserve you for the resurrection of ancient Christianity and the ruin of your detractors, who like wolves and wild asses in
sheeps' clothing assault Christ's fold.

Apart from that, master Richard Croke, an Englishman who has been
sowing the seeds of Greek here for two years to the general satisfaction and   25
has an excellent reputation personally, and who is now on his way back to
England and promised to take this letter to you, will tell you by word of
mouth of a proposal that you should come here, which has long been greatly
desired by our illustrious prince and the entire nobility. On this subject I
beg you urgently to write to me at Leipzig and let me know your mind, and   30
how much money would secure a favourable answer; and when I know

* * * * *

553:2 chosen vessel] Acts 9:15

5 *Christian Knight*] The *Enchiridion militis christiani*; cf Ep 164 introduction.

7 to be reprinted] The edition of V. Schumann, Leipzig 27 August 1515. It has
a preface by Emser and the epigram quoted here on the title-page.

18 Pearls of great price] Matt 13:46

24 Croke] Croke had been at Leipzig for two years, and now left for Cambridge; cf Ep 415:13n.

28 you should come here] Cf Ep 527.

that, I will leave no stone unturned, until we can welcome you here in the north with the honour you deserve. Farewell, and let me have an answer.

From Dresden by Meissen, 15 March 1517

554 / From Hieronymus Dungersheim   Leipzig, 18 March 1517

The writer of this letter was a theologian at Leipzig who became rector of the university in the summer of 1510. He came from Ochsenfurt on the river Main, born 22 April 1465, and studied both Arts and Theology at Leipzig, then continued his theological training at Cologne and Siena (DD August 1504). He published various works dealing with traditional theological questions, and 1518–19 engaged in controversy with Luther. He died at Leipzig in March 1540.

HIERONYMUS DUNGERSHEIM TO ERASMUS OF ROTTERDAM, GREETING

Pray do not take it amiss, dear sir – for I have great respect for you – if I, who am perhaps a stranger to you, presume to interrupt you with a letter; it is the desire to know the truth that prompts me. As I read your edition of the New 5 Testament and the notes, I came upon the place where it says 'Who, being in the form of God, thought it not robbery to be equal with God, but made Himself of no reputation' and so on, in the second chapter of Philippians, where you repeat your same version in the notes and suggest that the clause 'thought it not robbery to be equal with God' should be understood of 10 Christ, inasmuch as He is man. For you say 'He speaks of Christ as being man, nor is the clause otiose in the Greek, for he is explaining why he said 'robbery,' no doubt meaning this same thing, 'to be equal with God.' He did not lay claim to equality with God, but demeaned Himself.' So you say at that point. On the other hand, our forefathers, who were not ignorant of 15 Greek – among them Fathers of the Church and famous scholars, Jerome, Ambrose, Hilary, Augustine, Leo and others – assert that in this phrase the Apostle is speaking of the divinity of Christ, and speaking with an authority of which they make the greatest use against the Arians, who, as you know, denied the equality of Christ with the Father in accordance with a 20 nature divine as well as human, and laid down the blasphemous principle that there were degrees within the divine nature. But these holy men and many others take the Apostle to mean that Christ did not think it robbery to be equal with God according to the form of His deity, in which He is the

* * * * *

32 leave no stone unturned] *Adagia* I iv 30

same with God the Father according to the essence of His deity, and equal to   25
Him according to the distinction of persons, since there cannot be but one
form of the deity, which is God Himself or the essence of deity. And in this
they uttered Catholic doctrine beyond a doubt.

I say this, not because I have failed to notice that you forewarned the
reader that in certain passages you have for good reason deserted the   30
accepted text and the doctors who followed it; but since this passage which I
have just referred to seems to me to contain a very important principle of the
Faith, so much so that many authors, and especially Augustine in the
seventh chapter of book one of his *De trinitate*, seem to regard it as 'a kind of
touchstone for use everywhere in Scripture in settling the question in what   35
respect our Lord is less than the Father, and in what respect equal' and what
follows; for Augustine himself suggests that the Apostle at this point clearly
approved this distinction. Jerome too, in the edition which he published
with notes, and which is in circulation in print in a revision by yourself,
puts down this text of the Apostle in the wording used by the Church, and   40
says in his commentary: 'Many understand this passage to mean that Christ
humbled Himself according to His divinity, that is, according to the form,
according to which He did not lay claim to equal equality with God, which
He possessed by nature. And He humbled Himself, not emptying Himself
of the substance but declining the honour, by taking upon Himself the form   45
of a servant, that is, the nature of man.' So too Hilary who, as Jerome says
against Rufinus, translated Origen's Homilies on Job etc., and made extensive use of the Greek homilies in his own works in Latin. In his book against
Emperor Constantius, who was an Arian heretic, he writes among other
things: 'So you forbid things to be said that are not in Scripture; and yet you   50
yourself use words not in Scripture, and what is in Scripture you do not
repeat. You wish it to be predicated of the Son that He resembles the Father,
in order not to listen to the Apostle when he says 'Who being in the form of
God, thought it not robbery to be equal with God, but emptied Himself,
taking upon Himself the form of a servant.' Christ does not seize what was   55
already His, to be in the form of God. It is not 'equality with God' to be in
the form of God, unless you say that it means equality with man to be in the
form of a slave. But if Christ in the form of a servant is man, what else is He
in the form of God except God? So you wish the resemblance to be predi-

* * * * *

554:39 by yourself] In the edition of 1516, vol ix fol 179^v
554:48–9 book against Emperor Constantius] *Contra Constantium Impera-*
torem, against the Emperor Constantius ii, about 360 AD; PL 10
53 Apostle] Phil 2:6–7

cated of Him, to avoid including in your beliefs 'And let every tongue   60
confess that Jesus is Lord in the glory of God the Father. How deceitful is
your pious hope,' and the rest of the passage. Do you think that Constantius, who was a Greek and very well-disposed towards the Arians, and had
Arians too to assess the weight of what was written against him, – do you
think he could have concealed this, unless this sense, which is derived by   65
the saints from our passage in the Apostle, were definitely contained in the
Greek? Even if the sense were altered, simple-minded people might be able
to suspect it from the rest of the passage, the saintly Doctors notwithstanding. For brevity's sake I omit others – Ambrose (who translated most of it
from the Greek) in his letter to Bishop Sabinus, Pope Leo (who also knew   70
Greek) writing to a Greek emperor, Pope Gregory on Job, Rufinus (whose
great skill in Greek is well-known) in his exposition of the Creed. All these
and many others make use of this text and cite it for the same sense, as if that
sense followed from it like what I have already quoted. Most important of
all, who can doubt that the Church of Rome has followed this interpretation   75
from the most ancient times, seeing that many of the saints who follow it
lived over a thousand years ago? Nor is it certain that the native Greeks who
in our own time have become members also of the Latin church, among
them Cardinal Bessarion, a very great scholar in both languages, have
declared that this passage, which is read in the liturgy, needs emendation.   80
Valla too in his notes made no alteration with respect to that passage, except
that he thought *sentiat unusquisque* a better reading than the plural *sentite
singuli*, and that he said most Greek codices read *considerate*, σκοπεῖτε. And

* * * * *

60 'And let every tongue] Phil 2:11

69–70 Ambrose ... letter] Cf Ep XLVI, PL 16 1194–9.

70 Pope Leo] Ep 165 Ad Leonem Augustum c vii; PL 54 1165C–67A

71 Pope Gregory] *Expositio in librum B. Job* II c 23; PL 75:576

71 Rufinus] *Liber de fide* PL 21 1146 C

73 as if] Reading *ceu* for *seu*

79 Bessarion] 1403–1472; Bessarion, a humanist and theologian, was born in
Trebizond and educated in Constantinople. He was made archbishop of
Nicaea by the Emperor John VIII Palaeologus, whom he accompanied to Italy
to negotiate a common front in the face of the Turkish threat from Asia Minor.
A champion of union between the Greek and Latin churches, he remained in
Italy and was made a cardinal by Pope Eugenius IV in 1439. He was one of the
leading sponsors of Greek scholarship, especially of the Platonic tradition.

81 Valla] His notes were edited by Erasmus and published by Bade, 13 April
1505; cf Epp 182,3.

what Lefèvre d'Etaples has does not, I think, go against the opinion of the
saints as I have given it.   85

There seems also to be some reason behind this; for otherwise, it is
clear, the Arians, who undermine the divinity of the Saviour, would have
no small excuse for their mistake. For if (as the saints understand the
evangelist St John to hold in his fifth chapter) the Son is equal to the Father,
yet is not equal to Him according to His assumed nature (which nobody will   90
deny), He will be equal to Him in respect of His divinity. And so, if what
the Apostle says about equality is not to be understood of the divine nature,
as you propose, why did he himself put forward this about it quite un-
necessarily? Why did the saints who knew Greek do so, using the words of
the Apostle in the wrong sense, and that too in matters of faith and against 95
the Arians, who perversely denied the equality of which we speak? Or, if
the Apostle meant that it was not in respect of the form of His divinity that
Christ thought Himself equal with God, that He might not commit a
robbery, it follows that He is not identical in substance with God the Father;
which is the rankest Arianism. For the Arians, most of whom were Greeks,   100
felt the force of the Scriptures and were unable to deny that Christ is God,
and they also confessed that He is like unto the Father. But they talked
nonsense about a God who is less than the Father, presumably in respect of
His having some sort of share in the Godhead, and like Him in respect of
imitation, far above everyone else and yet not consubstantial. If therefore   105
Christ is said to have been unwilling to think Himself equal to the Father, in
order not to commit robbery, since this, as has been said, is obviously true
of His human nature (and it is something that ought not to happen), it must
be understood of the divine nature; which is, as I said, Arianism. It seems
therefore that we must follow the saints and understand this of the divine   110
nature, that being in the form of God He did not commit robbery, thinking
Himself in respect of it to be equal with the Father. Finally, if He thought it
robbery that He should be equal with God, He will appear Himself to have
detracted from His own divinity, for in truth He is equal with God. For
Christ is one; and once that has been made clear, it is perfectly correct to say   115
'This man is equal with God' – equal of course in respect of His divine
nature; for that 'this' stands for the underlying basis of the divinity, that is,
of the Word. Therefore even when it is not to the point, there is a sharing of

* * * * *

84 Lefèvre] In his commentaries on the Pauline epistles published in Paris,
December 1512, by Estienne; cf Ep 304:100n.

89 St John] 5:18ff

93 about it] Reading *praemisit* for Allen's *promisit*

117 for that 'this'] Reading *quoniam illud* for Allen's *quamlibet*

specific properties. Either then He did not think it robbery that He should
be equal with God in respect of His divine nature, which is the Apostle's   120
meaning as it has been understood by the saints; or, if He did not think that
He was equal with God, then He thought it was robbery, detracting from
Himself as I have already said; and even to contemplate this is impious.
Therefore what the Apostle says about Christ not thinking it to be robbery,
must not be understood of His human nature.   125

But I should wish these to be regarded as hasty thoughts, jotted down
as they came into my head, O friend very dear to me in the Lord. I beg you
therefore to think kindly of them, long-winded though they are, for I have
had no time to think and set them out with more method. I have not yet
made such progress in Greek with that generous and scholarly man Richard   130
Croke, my revered master, as to be able to sit in judgment between one
interpretation and another. In writing this I have preferred, as was right
and proper, to follow the authority of the saints. The same man has promised to take this letter to you and to bring back your reply, which please do
not grudge me. Farewell.   135

From Leipzig, 18 March, the year of Christ made man 1518

555 / From Willibald Pirckheimer   Nürnberg, 20 March 1517

As with Ep 385 (cf introduction) there is a copy of this letter in the Deventer
Letter-book as well as a manuscript among the Pirckheimer papers: Stadtbib-
liothek Nürnberg, Nürnberg STB PP No. 329. The letter should be considered
with Epp 527 and 553.

WILLIBALD PIRCKHEIMER TO ERASMUS, GREETING
Although I have no reason, dear Erasmus, most learned of men, to send you
a letter, all the same, for fear that our friendship in its early stages should
falter, I wanted to write you these few lines, that you might understand how
very far I am from forgetting you. I hear you have finished a new book, and   5
will soon be setting off for Basel to hand it over to the printers. I asked you
some time ago to come and see us too, if you conveniently could. Let me
repeat this invitation, and urge you again, if you can spare even a little time,
to visit your friends – you have made a great number by your writings and
all your other merits – and give them the chance to see you face to face. I am   10
quite sure you will not regret it, for besides the pleasure you will give to all

* * * * *

124–5 Therefore ... nature] The Latin of this sentence is untranslatable, and
presumably corrupt.
131 Croke] Cf Ep 553:24n.

your friends, you will see many other things that will interest you, and
especially such a city-state as, if I may say so, you have never yet seen in
Germany. In fact, although this country in years gone by had been infested
with robbers as a result of frequent wars, all is now peace, and things are so   15
safe that you need have no fear for your own security. Let us therefore have
the answer to our prayers; nothing can happen that could give us greater
pleasure. Farewell, my excellent Erasmus; may you live long and happy, as
much for the benefit of all the friends of learning as for your own. Let me
know sometime what you have in hand. Farewell once more.   20
    Nürnberg, 20 March 1517

556 / From Beatus Rhenanus   Basel, 22 March 1517

Beatus Rhenanus was Erasmus' associate and collaborator at Basel; cf Ep 327
introduction.

BEATUS RHENANUS TO ERASMUS OF ROTTERDAM, GREETING
Your honours and your prosperity give me infinitely more joy than any
pleasure I could get from successes of my own. Everyone must be pleased to
see such a complete scholar praised, glorified and honoured, the highest by
the highest, the most eloquent of authors by the most powerful of princes.   5
Everyone who reaches us from your part of the world tells us how high you
stand in the regard of King Charles, how all those councillors in their gold
chains respect you, how the rest of the throng of courtiers look up to you,
how you enjoy the special regard of everyone who has any love of virtue or
store of learning. And so I hope we shall soon see that you, who hitherto   10
have promoted the study of sound learning so successfully with all that
tireless labour and midnight oil, will shortly be able to enhance its status by
your authority. For if Charles wishes to honour literature, is there any way
in which he could give a clearer proof of his good will than by promoting
you to some illustrious dignity? There is in you such learning, such elo-   15
quence, such wisdom as all of us can admire who run this race in any part of
the world, and no one has yet equalled or perhaps ever will. In this way
Pope Leo lately made Marcus Musurus an archbishop, a most generous
prince honouring a most learned man. Again, Christoph bishop of Basel
does not cease to think very highly of your work and to speak of it with great   20

    * * * * *

556:18 Musurus] The Greek scholar and member of the Aldine Academy. He
was promoted to the see of Monembasia on 13 June 1516; cf Epp 223:5n, 574.
556:19 Christoph] von Utenheim, a good friend of the humanist community;
cf Ep 305:243n.

respect. All studious men admire you and look up to you. The Muse herself, as they say, now lives again; everyone is learning Greek; Rudolf von Hallwyl, a man of noble spirit and lineage and custos of the cathedral here, grows young again as he learns the rudiments of Greek, being already, I think, past five and fifty.   25

Our friend Volaganius intends to publish three books of the Elements of Hebrew next month. Froben has printed this winter at his press the *Lectiones antiquae* of a certain Coelius in sixteen books; but if there is any learning in them, we must thank the authors from whom he took it, for he himself shows bad judgment, and as for the writing, it is neither adult nor   30 entirely sound. One can see this from his childish prefaces, for that is all I have sampled so far. You have seen the man in Padua; for he taught there a long time as a private tutor, but in those days had no reputation. Really, when compared with this man, you and Rodolphus Agricola are more than Cicero or Lysias or Demosthenes. Compared with anybody, for that matter.   35 Hutten has written to me lately from Bologna. May you ever enjoy good health and unbroken good fortune, my teacher and second father. Give my greetings to that excellent young man, John Smith. Commend me to Master Dorp and to Gillis the secretary of Antwerp. I have sent you a poem by Philippus Melanchthon; that's a very learned all-round young man.   40 Farewell, most eloquent of men, and keep a warm corner for your Beatus.

Basel, 22 March 1517

* * * * *

22 Rudolf] Johann Rudolf von Hallwyl, Aargau (c 1462–1527) was provost of the cathedral and also of St Ursicin's at Basel. He died a canon of Basel, where the cathedral contains a monument to him. His scholarly industry was praised by Capito: cf Ep 561:63–7.

26 Volaganius] Capito was searching for an elegant version of his name, Wolfgang; cf Ep 459:195–7. This may have been intended as a suggestion.

26–7 Elements of Hebrew] Two books of his *Hebraicae institutiones* were published by Froben in January 1518.

28 Coelius] Cf Ep 469:10n.

34 Agricola] The great Frisian humanist of the previous century; cf Ep 23:58n.

36 Hutten] This letter is lost. Hutten was in Italy from the autumn of 1515 to the summer of 1517, and in Rome until the summer of 1516, when he went to Bologna. Cf Ep 365 introduction.

38 John Smith] One of Erasmus' servant-pupils; cf Ep 276 introduction.

39 poem] Ep 454

557 / From Bruno Amerbach   [Basel, c 22 March 1517]

On the friendship and earlier association of Erasmus with Bruno Amerbach
see Ep 331 introduction. The writer's rough draft (AK 580) is in the Öffentliche
Bibliothek of the University of Basel, MS G II 33ª 9.

If I assail you again, most learned Erasmus, with an illiterate letter, the
reason is partly that I may not seem negligent in keeping our friendship in
repair, and partly in hopes of extracting a letter from you if I keep it up. For I
set so high a value on your letters, that I would not exchange them for all the
wealth of Croesus, and those you have sent me I keep more secretly than   5
gold itself. So I think myself in this one thing quite rich enough, if I can fill a
cabinet with your elegant and learned letters. There is a friar here of the sort
they call Franciscans, who is preparing to attack your Testament on some
points of Hebrew. The donkey puts his head through the window.
     I thought you ought to be warned of this. For Beatus and Fabricius,   10
who are great men in the learned way, do not think it worth while to warn
you about such small things.

558 / From William Warham   Canterbury, 24 March [1517]

The last previous letter known to have come from Warham is Ep 425; see also
Ep 465 to Thomas More. He had been archbishop of Canterbury since 1503 and
had long been one of Erasmus' most steadfast patrons. From him Erasmus had
the living of Aldington in 1512; cf Ep 188 introduction.

WILLIAM ARCHBISHOP OF CANTERBURY TO ERASMUS, GREETING
Most learned Erasmus, I have received your esteemed letter of 13 February,
in which you explain what expectations smile upon you from all sides; and
the news made me wish that I could congratulate you fully and unreser-
vedly on your good fortune, the promises having all come true. For there is   5
no one whom I would sooner wish to see well treated. If those expectations
look for certain as though they would succeed, I would not dissuade you
from embracing fortune's favours and making the most of them; in this

* * * * *

557:9 The donkey ... window] A Greek proverb of uncertain meaning, which
can be used of those who bring frivolous accusations; *Adagia* I iii 64.
10 Fabricius] Capito again; cf Ep 556:26n.
558:2 letter] This was probably one of those sent in the packet to More; cf Ep
543:2.

field, whatever happens, you will always find me the same that I promised I
would be when you were over here, a friend unshakeable in the face of time   10
and circumstance. I would gladly invite you to return soon to England, that
in this my retreat from public business I might enjoy your delightful
society. But I am unwilling to interrupt such expectations, and to be the
occasion of your losing some piece of good fortune which at the moment
may lie in good measure within your reach. But if, after the prince has left,   15
you cast your eyes this way, I will make it my business to provide a retreat
convenient for your studies.

About your annuity there is no need for anxiety. I sent instructions to
Maruffo within the last ten days to arrange for the money to be sent you,
and he undertook the task of transmitting it free of interest and commission   20
in the manner and form agreed between yourself and him. If there is
anything else I can do to oblige you, you will have only yourself to blame, if
you do not ask me without hesitation.

Farewell, from Canterbury, 24 March

559 / From Sebastiano Giustiniani   [London, March 1517?]

In his letter to Thomas More from Antwerp, written at the end of May (Ep 584:
49–53), Erasmus reported that he had lost this letter and asked More to let him
have it back, supposing presumably that he had left it in More's house. He
may also have left a transcript of Ep 574 which was probably communicated to
him on dispatch, although Erasmus might only have heard of it and not yet
seen it, if it was not sent until 22 April and Erasmus landed in France on 1 May
(Ep 584:2). More sent the letter (or perhaps a copy from Giustiniani's draft)
along with Epp 574, 590–2 and perhaps 593 in a bundle with Ep 601 (16 July
1517).

Giustiniani evidently wrote this letter some time after Erasmus left London
in mid-August 1516, judging from the tone of his opening lines. He still
believed that Erasmus had dedicated the edition of Jerome to Leo x (lines
28–9) as he announced in Epp 334–5, but this does not assist in a more precise
dating of the letter since Ep 396 was at the end of volume 1 of the Jerome and
Giustiniani might well have failed to understand that it was the preface to the
whole edition. Erasmus was still not expected back in England (by Warham:

* * * * *

15 prince] Charles
19 Maruffo] Cf Ep 387:3n. The dispute about payment of the annuity, due
each year at the feast of the Annunciation, 25 March, had been going on for a
year; the record begins with Ep 388 from Thomas More, February 1516.

Ep 558) as late as the last week in March, so that the present dating of the letter
marks the latest likely time of composition.

There are two copies of this letter in the Deventer Letter-book made by
different scribes; the same is true of Epp 574 and 601. There are no differences
of any substance between them, and this circumstance seems to suggest that
the duplication was a mistake in Erasmus' personal secretariat. Hand B was
evidently inexperienced, and Ep 574 is the earliest letter in this hand (Allen I
605).

Sebastiano Giustiniani (1460–1543) was a member of a distinguished Venetian family, and the resident ambassador in England for Venice from January
1515 to October 1519. Erasmus had sent him a copy of the *Novum instrumentum*; cf Ep 461.

SEBASTIANO GIUSTINIANI, KNIGHT, VENETIAN AMBASSADOR,
TO ERASMUS OF ROTTERDAM, GREETING

When you departed, my dear Erasmus, I supposed that you would not be
long absent; and if your absence were prolonged, I hoped that at least you
would make good my loss by writing to me. But I now see that there is no   5
remedy for my regrets, though nothing causes me more pain and grief than
longing for you: you are not able to cheer me by your conversation, not
being present, and you are not willing, being absent, to do so by correspondence. If you cannot be with us here, if it is not possible for you to
comfort me face to face, I have been ready to blame the state of your affairs,   10
which perhaps do not permit your return. But that you should be unwilling
to relieve my unhappiness at least by writing, I cannot help being indignant
with you; for no period of life should be free from the call of duty, and I
cannot think you have so much business that it can turn your mind away
from me and from our common friendship, which I shall always maintain   15
enduring and entire, unless you give it up or fall away. Deprive us, Erasmus, if you will, of the charms of your society, which I was hoping to enjoy
for a long time; deprive us of your letters and of the delightful products of
your genius; you cannot delete and blot out from my mind the record of
your name and the pleasant memory of our friendship, which I shall   20
preserve as long as I live. On this at least, if you allow it no other sustenance,
my mind shall feed. And I thought it well to do what parents sometimes do,
when bereaved of beloved children: having lost their society, they recall
how they behaved and repeat what they said, and they have pictures of
them drawn, so that the memory of what they were and the contemplation   25
of their likeness may be some sort of compensation for their loss. And so I
take refuge in your wonderful book of *Adagia* (since I cannot listen to you), I

read and re-read some of your letters to Pope Leo, to whom you dedicated
Jerome (as you rightly say) reborn, to several cardinals, and lastly to your
benefactor the archbishop of Canterbury; whom you have so carefully   30
painted and so cunningly modelled, that the greatness of his reputation is
to be measured by what your strong and skilful portraiture has secured for
him. How fortunate for you both! that he should have you to praise him,
and that you should have been ready to win praise yourself by praising
him, securing your own immortality while you devote yourself to his   35
immortal fame.

It is indeed surprising, the quality and quantity of what is wrought in
your workshop. You take your patron, the archbishop of Canterbury, a man
subject to the same fate as other men, and content to remain within the
boundaries of Britain, and set him up like some deity to be adored; you   40
make him immortal, and spread his name through the whole world. He
does indeed deserve to be chosen by you with good reason as a subject for
your anvil, your skill and industry, and I think he has the treatment he
deserves, when he has such a Phidias or Apelles or Pyrgoteles to make his
statue and paint him and cast him in bronze. Though he may shine by his   45
own light, none can deny that he shines more brightly thanks to you and
your glorious art. I myself have always valued him, and still do so, as much
as I thought he deserved; and that means very high indeed. But now that
you have drawn his image in your writings, you have impressed it on my
heart to an extraordinary degree; not as a likeness engraved on copper or cut   50
in marble, in which our approval is all for the artist's skilful touch, for this
sculpturing of yours displays the excellence of the artist and his sitter, and
inspires feelings towards both of you in us as we admire it, so that I now
love and reverence him, whom I seem scarcely to have loved before. And
you I admire so much that I can hardly think you mortal. Nor have I any   55
reason to regret my judgment in thinking such men worthy of respect. One
of you is looked up to and admired by the whole world for his great virtues
and his admirable learning and wisdom, as you have extolled them; the
other, by his knowledge of all the liberal arts, the integrity of his character

* * * * *

559:28 letters] Epp 333–5
28–9 dedicated Jerome] An error, doubtless derived from Ep 334:161–4
29 as you rightly say] Ep 335:343ff
30 Canterbury] Probably Ep 396; cf introduction.
44 Phidias *etc*] Phidias was the greatest sculptor of antiquity; Apelles the
painter and Pyrgoteles the sculptor were the only artists allowed by Alexander
the Great to represent him.
53–4 I now love ... before] The text of this sentence is uncertain.

and his incomparable literary skill, is quite without peer and must be   60
regarded as one of the new wonders of our age.

But to return to my starting point, I feed on these crumbs of yours,
since you deprive me of the daily pleasures of your table; I shall drink plain
water, unless you allow me a taste of the good Falernian which you keep to
yourself. When you do so, this will make up for the loss of your society,   65
which I miss so much, and I shall drink draughts of it sufficient to indem-
nify me for what my thirst costs me now. In the meantime, I shall read from
end to end and preserve with affectionate zeal such portions of the rich
stores of your library as you were willing to deposit with me, for fear that
over and above the loss of yourself I may incur another misfortune, that I am   70
left with nothing from your pen that I can read. I do not expect you to come
yourself, unless you have to come for some personal or business reason; I
ask for nothing that belongs to you, for I need nothing; it is a letter that I
demand, from which I may gather the charms of your conversation, as
though I were plucking sweet flowers from some delightful meadow to   75
weave into chaplets to adorn a scholar's brow, and therewith may feed my
mind and relieve my regrets. Perhaps you suppose that such things can be
no benefit to my present distemper, having been endowed by nature with
no power to cure sickness, since they do not possess those prime qualities
whence medicines derive their force; and you may think that I ask for a   80
medicine that can do no good. This would not be unreasonable, my dear
Erasmus, if you supposed me a victim of the headache or stomach-ache, or
oppressed by shortness of breath or tormented by internal pains or suffering from a looseness which must be checked. It is not troubles of this kind
that torment me: my sickness is of the spirit, a kind of severe pain caused by   85
your absence gives me no rest, which will cease, I do not doubt, as soon as I
cease to love you. But how can I cease to love you as long as I live, unless
there ceases to be anything in you that I can love? If I must do without you,
who can offer a rich objective for my affection, I must needs be in pain. But I
am in pain, not because I love something I must do without, but because I   90
must do without something I love. You, however, will be without fail my
Aesculapius. You will skilfully cure my sickness, if you supply me with
what I love; but you will never remove the cause of my pain, save by the
application of what I love; for my pain will leave me, if love restores you to
me.   95

Enough of this elegant foolery; but what I have said under this foolish
mask you must please take seriously. I want nothing more from you than a

* * * * *

67 my thirst] Reading *sitis* for *sit*
76 scholar's brow] Horace *Odes* 1.1.29

letter, or any other of the usual products of your workshop, which I often call Latin at its best. There is no need for you to deprive me of the privilege of your letters, from which I can learn how you find yourself in mind and body, and how fortune has been treating you. I simply cannot fail to regret the state of things, in which you are not being treated as I feel you deserve: light is not divided from darkness, the poet's laurel is enslaved to gold, and he who burns the midnight oil must labour by day as well. If I were my own master, dear Erasmus, and if a breeze of fortune blew which would distend and fill my sails, I would so alter things that you would not call his grace of Canterbury your patron, but would yourself be called patron by others. Farewell.

560 / From Petrus Mosellanus   Leipzig, 24 March [1517]

This letter was carried by Croke along with Epp 553 and 554, to seek Erasmus' acquaintance for its writer. Petrus Mosellanus was the name used by Peter Schade (c 1493–1524), who came from Bruttig on the Moselle, about forty-five kilometres above Coblenz. He came from peasant stock and obtained his early education with difficulty. In 1512 he matriculated at Cologne and was a pupil of Johannes Caesarius (cf Ep 374 introduction) and Hermann von dem Busche. He had settled at Leipzig in April 1515, and when Croke returned to England, succeeded him as lecturer in Greek at the university.

PETRUS MOSELLANUS TO MASTER ERASMUS, GREETING

Such is my natural modesty, Erasmus most eminent of scholars, that, unimportant as I am, I have never yet dared to write to you and men like you without very good cause; but there are many reasons why I should break my own rule at this moment and boldly interrupt you with an illiterate letter. First, I was encouraged by your well-known kindness, which is said to surpass even your exhaustive learning. And then the willing horse was spurred on by Richard Croke, a young Englishman distinguished alike for his lineage and his knowledge of Greek and Latin in Germany as well as in his native Britain; for as we talked about books, your name often came up, and each time he did not fail to urge me and encourage me to make myself known to you. You would not be displeased, he said, nor should I regret it, because you were kindness itself, nor could anyone even among ordinary men be more approachable. My friend Croke added that he knew Erasmus well enough to ensure a warmer welcome for a letter from me, if for no other

* * * * *

560:7 willing horse] Adagia I ii 47
8 Croke] Cf Ep 227:31n.

reason, because he would be the bearer, for at that moment he was about to leave for home. Stimulated by this encouragement, I snatched up my pen, scribbled these few lines, and entrusted them to Croke for delivery.

If I did wrong, it is your friend Croke you must pardon for my error; he was the moving spirit, the coryphaeus as the Greeks call it, who made me so   20
bold. You must also make some allowance for the warmth of my feelings towards you, which you can gauge from this, that in the course of seeking your acquaintance I have been ready to wear the mask of effrontery. Lastly, if that is not enough, I will appeal to Theophrastus, who will put a more respectable interpretation on the impertinence, if you will have it so, with   25
which I pursue your friendship; for your Plutarch quotes him as saying that friends should have nothing in common more than their friends. I have so many friends in common with you, and those of no ordinary kind, that one could make a list of them: Reuchlin the alpha and first of scholars, Willibald Pirckheimer who stands high among the learned, Philippus Melanchthon a   30
young man whom you too must reckon most promising. If you admit all of these, pray suffer the name of Mosellanus too, of whom they already approve, at least to be entered on the list of those who cordially admire your works and long to be friends with their author. Farewell, great glory of our times.   35

From Leipzig, where I give public lectures in Greek and Latin to the best of my power, 24 March

561 / From Wolfgang Capito   [Basel] 24 March 1517

This letter is contemporary with Ep 556, as the citations from the *Hebraicae institutiones* indicate; cf Ep 556:26–7n.

WOLFGANG FABER TO MASTER ERASMUS, GREETING
A second passage in your notes, which I myself thought not wholly safe from criticism, has meanwhile been picked out by an obscure but impertinent individual, who in several places reflects on your modesty and your

* * * * *

26 Plutarch] *Moralia* 490E, citing Theophrastus fragment 75
29 Reuchlin] The distinguished Hebraist; cf Epp 300, 457 introductions.
30 Pirckheimer] Cf Ep 318 introduction.
30 Melanchthon] Cf Ep 454 introduction.
561:3–4 obscure ... individual] Mentioned by Bruno Amerbach; cf Ep 557:7–9.

incomparable gifts, and much more offensively on Oecolampadius, who   5
helped you, as you confess in another place, in distinguishing the mean-
ings of the Hebrew. 'Erasmus' he says 'set many men to rights on points of
Greek, and needs setting right himself in Hebrew,' with other insolent
smears of the same kind, with which the silly fellow, as though to curry
favour with me, attacked you in a long-winded letter to me that was quite   10
without decent feeling. The passage is in the first chapter of Matthew,
where you seem to correct St Jerome, I mean, on the word הָרָה (page 237);
'הָרָה' you say, 'is rendered by St Jerome "will conceive," although as the
Hebrew points – two camez – indicate, it is present tense. It would be past, if
there were one camez.'   15

Roused partly by the impertinence of such a man, and in part more or
less by accident, I am preparing an introduction to Hebrew in three books.
In the first book, chapter 14, where I state various principles relative to the
pointing, I have used this passage from the prophet as an example; it is in
my second canon. I will remind you in passing of this peculiarity of the   20
sacred language. In my first canon, I wrote as follows: 'The perfect preterite
usually has a kametz under the first syllable and a patha under the second, as
in שָׁמַר, and they retain the same points in all the persons of both singular
and plural.' And further on I have laid down canon two, which is more to
the point, precisely for verbs ending in he and aleph, as follows: 'No verb in   25
the preterite whose last syllable ends in aleph or he allows a patha under the
letter immediately preceding – in the final syllable, that is – but exceptionally admits, and indeed always requires, a kametz, as in הָרָה, "has conceived." For so it reads in the seventh chapter of Isaiah; and it is worth
while to enquire more closely into a sentence from so great a prophet. For St   30
Jerome, following the Septuagint, rendered הָרָה "shall conceive," with a
verb in the future, following a very common tradition among the Jews of
which they cite an example from the לוחות grammar, as they themselves call
it. In accordance, they say, with the nature and tense of the first verb, all
verbs of whatever tense that follow in the same period, which they call פָּסוּק,   35
should be explained. Thus in this passage of the prophet it runs
לָכֵן יִתֵּן אֲדֹנָי הוּא לָכֶם אוֹת הִנֵּה הָעַלְמָה הָרָה וְיֹלֶדֶת בֵּן וְקָרָאתָ שְׁמוֹ עִמָּנוּ אֵל: and here
the first verb, יִתֵּן, that is, "will give," is future; therefore הָרָה, "has

* * * * *

5 Oecolampadius] Johann Hussgen (1482–1531); for his work on the Novum
instrumentum see CWE 3 passim. Cf Ep 563 introduction.
5–6 who helped you] Cf Ep 324:31n.
30–1 St Jerome] In the 1516 edition, volume v folio 15
36 prophet] Isaiah 7:14

conceived," which is past tense, and again יוֹלֵדֶת, "brings forth," which is
present, are even now explained as futures by a number of good scholars,' 40
to whom this principle of interpretation seems acceptable. I myself rule it
out on arguments of some weight, as being beneath the dignity of sacred
language, and immediately add a defence of what you have put against the
malice of inferior people. The better sort you yourself vanquished long ago,
and I am quite capable of providing these donkeys with the thistles they 45
prefer. Being ignorant myself, I can do battle with the ignorant, so that the
lid will fit the pot all right. I will add my actual words: 'It must already be
clear to you that a man is not talking, as they say, through a brick wall, who
has rendered every word of this prophecy according to its natural sense,
contrary to the mode of interpretation current among the Jews, who main- 50
tain that the verbs of the whole sentence should follow the natural sense of
the first verb.' And later on I adduce you as agreeing with my own opinion,
in the words 'Nor does my friend Erasmus, a most gifted critic, seem to
attach much importance to this formula of interpretation, which twists the
later verbs all through the period to suit the first verb.' 55

Admirably learned as you are, you must take my self-confidence in
good part – my obstinacy, if you like to call it so – in venturing to interrupt
your studies with all this empty chatter. Forgive the inexperience of a
humble friend, who wastes your time on trifles, because the delightful
courtesy with which you temper your awe-inspiring intelligence has en- 60
couraged me to this audacity. In any case, your works with their infinite
learning and sincere piety are still winning you new friends, even in your
absence. Here in Basel Johann Rudolf von Hallwyl, that canon whom you
thought by no means in favour of humane learning, is a complete Erasmian.
Though in his fifties, he devotes himself to commentaries, and this winter 65
has picked up a sound knowledge of the rudiments of Greek, so that he may
be fit to read the New Covenant. In a word, he talks of Erasmus everywhere

* * * * *

40 good scholars] Matthaeus Adrianus, the Hebraist (fl 1501–21), and the
Carthusian Gregor Reisch (Ep 308 introduction) are cited in support of this
view in the *Hebraicae institutiones* folio 1². For Adrianus see de Vocht CTL
241–56.

45 donkeys] *Adagia* I x 71

47 actual words] *Hebraicae institutiones* folio 1²

48 brick wall] *Adagia* III iv 54

52 later on] *Hebraicae institutiones* folio 1² verso

63 Rudolf] Cf Ep 556:22n. In the *Hebraicae institutiones* folio A³ Capito praises
him for devotion to *'vetustior theologia.'*

and dreams of him; besides which he has a great-nephew, a boy of great promise, and he has given orders for him to be nurtured on the sweet fruits of Erasmian scholarship, for which purpose he is busy trying to collect all   70 the books you have edited. He is a great admirer of the *Moria*, and more devoted than anyone to your book on the prince.

I tell you this to show you how to infer from one example what a high value is set on you by all the others, and the veneration they all rightly feel for the perfect image of virtue and scholarship which you have carved upon   75 the great pyramid of your works and entrusted to the judgment of the world. I will write sometime more carefully, when I have more spare time. Farewell, this Tuesday after the fourth Sunday in Lent 1517.

Froben is in a hurry to be off.

562 / From Johann Reuchlin   [Tübingen?] 27 March 1517

This letter is a reply to Ep 457.

JOHANN REUCHLIN TO ERASMUS OF ROTTERDAM, GREETING
That letter which you wrote me on the spur of the moment on 27 August all among those robbers on the beach at Calais is more than I could answer adequately even if I had all the Muses at my elbow, such is your native force and fluency. I am slightly ashamed to write you anything of my own, and   5 am not easily induced to write often, unless you swear by all the gods to take my incompetence in good part. I do not wish to be reminded of the warning in the old story: If you had kept your mouth shut, you would still have passed for a philosopher. Do not have any doubts about me on that score, dear Erasmus, my best hope. In front of everyone else I am fairly confident,   10 of which there is visible evidence at the moment, for I am sending you this book, *De arte cabalistica*, which I dedicate to Leo x. If you think it worth

* * * * *

68 great-nephew] Hartmann von Hallwyl; the *Hebraicae institutiones* are dedicated to him, as was Oecolampadius' *Graecae literaturae dragmata* (Basel:
Cratander and Cruftanus September 1518). The preface states that Hartmann
had used this Greek grammar so much that others were asking for it, and
shows that he was reading Basil, Chrysostom, Origen and Gregory with
Capito. He matriculated at Leipzig in the summer of 1521, and later became
bishop of Basel.
72 book on the prince] *Institutio principis christiani*
79 to be off] To the Frankfurt book fair; cf Ep 326A:16n.
562:2 letter] Ep 457
562:6 by all the gods] Literally 'by a marble Jupiter'; *Adagia* II vi 33
12 *De arte cabalistica*] Cf Ep 500:22n.

reading, you will find it needs the polish that only you can give it; but, though I cannot write, I could not refrain from doing as others do, and offering to the great patron of the humanities, to whom all the authors of our 15 day dedicate their productions whatever their merit, even these barbarous products of a man from Swabia.

You speak of that sainted bishop and champion of liberal studies the bishop of Rochester, and I should like you to know that I regard him, not only with deep respect, as I am bound to do, but also no less with affection. 20 But such a warm recommendation frightens me, and I do beg you not to let him grow too fond of me. You know well enough that distance lends enchantment. If he sees me one day close to, and takes a dislike to me, as does happen sometimes, the devil will be in it. I told Thomas Anshelm to send a copy of my *Cabalistica* for each of you from the March fair in your part 25 of the world, together with this letter from me. When the books reach you, keep one copy for yourself in memory of me, and send the other carefully to my lord of Rochester, so that he may know that I have by no means forgotten your encouraging words about him.

I am travelling away from home, and weary from my journey, so I can 30 write no more just now. Once I get home, I will pick up the threads, if God permit, whom I pray to take good care of you. My very best wishes to you, and please share my prayers for your welfare with his lordship of Rochester.
27 March 1517

563 / From Johannes Oecolampadius   Weinsberg, 27 March 1517

This letter, which was first printed in *Farrago*, is also in the Deventer Letter-book. For Oecolampadius see Epp 224:30n, 354:6n. Ep 605 is the reply.

TO ERASMUS FROM OECOLAMPADIUS, GREETING
Where in the world, my source of glory and delight, am I to look for you? To what ill-defined messenger shall I entrust my all too definite longing for

* * * * *

19 Rochester] For an earlier account of Fisher's interest in Reuchlin see Ep 324:5–25.
24 Anshelm] The printer at Tübingen, Reuchlin's friend and publisher; cf Epp 300, 397 introductions.
25 the March fair] The Easter Fair or 'Paesschenmarkt,' one of the four Brabant Fairs, held at Bergen-op-Zoom from mid-March until the beginning of May. Cf Ep 468:9–10n above.
30 travelling] Geiger in RE 237 suggests that Reuchlin was perhaps visiting Anshelm at Tübingen.
563:2 glory and delight] Horace *Odes* 1.1.2

Johannes Oecolampadius
Portrait by Hans Asper, undated
Oeffentliche Kunstsammlung, Basel

you, that he may pass it on to the Desiderius I so much desire? There are no
signs of any courier; and what purpose could a courier serve with such a   5
rustic letter, too inelegant to make its bow before the elegant Erasmus? I
could, it is true, keep my scribbling close within the narrow walls of my
hermit's cave; but love is too active, he will not stay at home, he abhors
silence, his passion and anxieties all go for naught unless they are known to
the object of his affections. Where in the world then am I to look for you?   10
How well off I was in Basel, what pleasures I then had within my reach, I
understand now I am far away, and like the Phrygians see sense too late. But
it is foolish to put Destiny to rights. You will be close enough, if I can be sure
you know that in spirit we can never be parted. In other ways your heroic
virtue is fixed and lives before the eyes of my heart (you must excuse the   15
Hebrew idiom), your affection is alive before me and your virtues bright,
the charm of your conversation still delights my ears, they are still assailed
by your copious proverbs and resound with the praises of those great men,
statesman More and saintly Colet. Your aphorisms ring in my head, and
one especially, one golden word that cannot be too highly valued, that we   20
should seek nothing in the Scriptures saving only Christ. These things are
so vividly present with me now, that I seem still to hang upon your lips, and
you are as much with me as I am myself.

Sometimes I forget my own humble state, carried away by my admiration for you, when I put to my lips that small, but sacred and very dear   25
pledge of our friendship, the beginning of the Gospel according to St John,
and with that in my hands, the most sacred oath a Christian can take, I
devote myself to the name of Erasmus. I should have given it to my mother,
did I not value you so much. I had hung it on my crucifix, before which I tell
my beads, that I might commend you and your fortunes to Him (for so you   30
asked, and so charity requires), and that your memory might not be parted
from me even in my sacred moments. Rashly, however, I showed my
treasure to my friends, boasting that it came from my dear friend, and so
some harpy has removed it, which is no small grief to me but there is small
risk that I shall forget you. I had thoughts of adding the letter you wrote me,   35
from Speyer I think, were I not afraid of thieves; so I read it in secret, and
put it to my lips from time to time.

* * * * *

12 Phrygians] *Adagia* i i 28

24–5 admiration] Oecolampadius' admiration for Erasmus is evident also in
his *De risu Paschali* (Basel: Froben 1518) where (page 15) Erasmus is praised as
the most learned and elegant of all mortals.

36 Speyer] Presumably when Erasmus left Basel for the Netherlands in the
spring of 1516 (Ep 410); Oecolampadius had only arrived in Basel in the
previous autumn (Ep 358:7).

What need of this? How could I ever forget that special document and tribute to our friendship, in which you call me your Theseus? For though unequal to such an onerous, not to say honourable, task, I have not forgot-   40
ten the promise I made when we parted, that I would do my best to make what you said about me prove true. I try indeed, maybe without much success. Much is denied me by the barrenness of my wits, and much by my doubtful health. And yet my health has many advantages, for it detains me at home in fetters of gold. I am comparing Jerome's versions with the   45
Hebrew originals, which are almost never out of my hands. I have with me a young man called Johann Brenz, who is as industrious as he is enthusiastic in studies of all kinds, and is your great admirer. He and I are preparing an index to the genuine works of St Jerome. I am also trying my hand at a tragedy, *The Nemesis of Theophilus*, but it goes rather slowly; I have not yet   50
seen the end of the second act, though there are nearly 1500 lines. I have taken on too great a task for my modest gifts, and what the end will be, I doubt. And so it would have been better not to mention it, for fear it may end in the waste-paper basket; but I thought of my promise, and had to report it. For I will try, God willing, to prove that your praise of me was not   55
ill-advised. I have had several letters from Philippus Melanchthon. He always speaks of you, always with admiration; always asks to be commended to you. He richly deserves your affection; he will make a second Erasmus, in eloquence, in ability, in learning, and in manner of life. If any German can, he will make a new Erasmus. I do not doubt that Beatus has   60

* * * * *

39 Theseus] Cf Ep 373:75–6.

47 Brenz] Brenz (1499–1570), born in Swabia at Weil der Stadt, west of Stuttgart, was at this time a student with Oecolampadius at the University of Heidelberg. In 1518 he was teaching Greek there to Bucer (BRE 79). He later became a disciple of Luther and a leading architect of the evangelical church polity.

49 index] This was printed by Froben in May 1520.

50 *Nemesis of Theophilus*] While this play does not seem to survive, the prologue of the *Nemesis Theophili*, addressed to Pirckheimer, is printed by Johann Heumann von Teutschbrunn *Documenta literaria* (Altdorf 1758) 319–21.

54 waste-paper basket] Literally 'lest it fall upon the sponge.' Ajax took his own life by falling upon his sword; the Emperor Augustus wrote a tragedy about Ajax, and when he abandoned it (and, as it were, wiped the slate clean), he said that his Ajax had fallen upon his sponge; Suetonius *Divus Augustus* 85.2.

56 several letters] Not in Bretschneider's edition

60 Beatus] Cf Ep 556:39–40.

spoken to you on his behalf, and better than I can. Remember that in this letter I write not as a stylist but as a friend quite free from guile, and imagine, dear Erasmus, that I am always present with you. Farewell, most excellent Erasmus, crown of my head, as they say in Hebrew.

From my native retreat in Weinsberg, 27 March 1517   65

564 / From Mariano Accardo   Brussels, 1 April 1517

For an account of Accardo see Ep 544 introduction.

MARIANO ACCARDO TO HIS FRIEND ERASMUS, GREETING
Being very conscious of the weakness of my feeble powers, most excellent sir, I have often lamented the mortality of my name. I saw that not merely must my reputation after my death be submerged in the waters of Lethe, but that even during my life my name was wrapped in darkness and blotted   5
out in complete obscurity. But you, the very child of fame, take steps to comfort my legitimate regrets, by giving me the gift of immortality, however much undeserved and in despite of fate, in two letters from you. For if your writings, which know not death, make mention of me, who can doubt that my name will be immortal? But mind you, I am more ambitious, to be   10
quite frank, than either I could express or you believe. There is nothing I want more than that the men of our generation should not be aware of your inborn habits of being much influenced by friendship and going too far in the praises of your friends. You will easily impose on posterity: they will know your judgment in literary matters to be in every way impeccable, and   15
will suppose that when you praise your friends you are equally free from deceit. Drawn onward by this hope, I have thrown to the winds the diffidence inspired by your most exquisite letter. For I cannot deny that those who know us both, when they read it and see me dressed in these peacock's feathers, will detect the jackdaw; posterity however will declare I   20
must have been a peacock, and will count me fortunate to have been praised by so great a man (of which my ghost will be very proud). And so, having been made immortal by your kindness, I offer you undying thanks for having rescued me from the indignity of oblivion, and for the honourable mention you made of me in a letter to Budé I shall most willingly repay you   25
when I can. For the moment I am overwhelmed with business, and the

* * * * *

564:8 two letters] Lost
20 peacock's feathers] Phaedrus 1.3 (cf *Adagia* III 6 91).
25 letter to Budé] Ep 531:579–81, published just at this time

affairs of Sicily are keeping me so fully occupied that I scarcely have time to
breathe. When I can extricate myself, I shall come and see you, hoping to
make a third in the friendship of Erasmus and Pieter Gillis, which is the
most desirable and precious thing that could happen to me. Meanwhile   30
please send me a letter, and as long a one as possible. The longer your letters
are, the more I enjoy them, and they possess the special quality that one
never has too much of them but they make the load of business at once seem
lighter. Farewell, chief ornament of both Greek and Latin, and love me, as I
know you do. Please give my best wishes to Pieter Gillis.   35

From Brussels, in haste, 1 April 1517

565 / From Pierre Barbier   Brussels, 3 April 1517

Barbier was secretary to Jean Le Sauvage; cf Ep 443 introduction.

PIERRE BARBIER TO MASTER ERASMUS
Greetings, most learned Master Erasmus. I had two letters from you some
days ago, to which my reply is perhaps a little more belated than you may
think reasonable. The cause of this, you may be sure, is the difficulty of
approaching my master, and also my absence from here for several days. It   5
was of course a delight to both Guy and myself to have you here for a time,
but it is far more delightful to know that, though unfortunately you cannot
be here, you are now better, and have accomplished so much in the way of
writing in so few days. For though we so much enjoyed seeing you every
day and sharing a joke with you and often hanging on your learned lips, yet   10
all that was confined to us alone; but the voyage on which you are now
engaged with favouring winds can be unwelcome to no one and will be
most profitable to us all. Besides which, we would far rather you were well
although not here, than have you here and have you ill. I have spoken with
my right honourable master about sending you new money in time for   15
Easter, as a fresh start. He urged in reply that you ought to be willing to

* * * * *

565:5 master] Jean Le Sauvage, chancellor of Burgundy; cf Ep 410 introduction.
6 Guy] Morillon, also in the service of Jean Le Sauvage; cf Ep 532 introduction.
8 better] Cf Ep 526:2.
8–9 so much ... writing] Is this an ironic reference to Erasmus' epistolary
campaign, making widely known the invitations that had come to him from
France? Cf Epp 529, 531, 533, 534, 536, 537, 551.
15 new money] To start the new Christian year; the reference is to Erasmus'
salary as councillor cf Ep 370:18n.
16 Easter] 12 April

accept patiently a postponement until Pentecost; for it is not the custom, he says, to pay stipends except at the end of the year. But when that time comes, you will meet with no refusal that might stop your receiving the fixed stipend for a year and a half.   20

For Jerome's works I will promptly send the money if you have sent them off, although I may not have had them yet. If you send your *Moria* with the Jerome, I will remit the money at the same time as the rest. Guy himself sends you cordial greetings, and so does my brother. Please convey my compliments to Master Pieter Gillis, your delightful host, whose agree-   25
able company has given you new life. And so farewell for the present, dear Erasmus, my most learned master.

Brussels, 3 April 1516

566 / To Leo x   Brussels [c 4 April] 1517

This letter replies to Epp 518 and 519 which reached Erasmus between 11 and 15 March (Ep 552). As Erasmus had feared, he had to return to England to receive from the hands of Ammonio the absolution and dispensation granted by the pope. He left Antwerp about 1 April (Ep 572:16–7, 17n) and this letter must have been written shortly afterward. The formal ceremony with Ammonio took place at Westminster on 9 April, as Ammonio himself testified (Ep 517:79–80).

If Erasmus had reached Brussels by 3 April, Pierre Barbier did not know of it (cf Ep 565), so the conjectural date of composition selected is 4 April. This letter and Ep 567 must have been written hastily while Erasmus was on his way to England. Conceivably, business with the chancellor (cf Ep 565) might have dictated this plan of travel, but it was the ordinary route from Antwerp to the Channel ports for London. This letter and Ep 567 were both published in the month of April in Louvain, among the *Epistolae elegantes*. It follows that Erasmus must have taken special pains to see that the text of these important letters were sent at once to Dirk Martens, and Ep 546 shows how closely they worked together on the construction of the volume. It is likely that he sent with them copies of Epp 519 and 521, kept with him until answers were written, since they occupy the page before Ep 566 in the *Epistolae elegantes*. If Martens had no earlier reason to expect these additions he may have received them with mixed feelings, since on 8 March his people had written (Ep 546) asking for more material for the preface to fill an unforeseen gap, as though they thought they had most or all of the copy for the volume.

* * * * *

17 Pentecost] 31 May
24 brother] Probably Nicolas Barbier; cf Allen III Ep 613.
25 host] Since early February; cf Epp 529, 544:23n.

TO LEO, PONTIFF TRULY SUPREME, FROM ERASMUS OF ROTTERDAM,
GREETING

It is always the same, most blessed Father: your incredible goodness and
mercy surpasses not only what I deserve but what I desire. The limited and
partial request which was all that I had the courage to make has been   5
answered by your generosity lavishly and in full. Nor did you wish to
conceal from me the names of those to whom I owe this benefaction, though
I myself desired to owe it entirely to your Holiness and no one else. I knew
that his Catholic Majesty had written to recommend me to you, but in
another case; and yet that too was done not only in my absence but without   10
my knowledge. To the king of England I was indebted on many other
grounds, but of his suffrage here I was hitherto entirely unaware. Only too
well do I understand, most holy Father, how heavy and how complex is the
burden on my shoulders. First of all, I must strive with might and main to
profit from the privilege you have generously conferred upon me in a   15
manner worthy of both giver and recipient. And then I must try at least in
part to justify the recommendation of these great princes, since you have
been willing to give them a share in the credit of your benefaction. Last of
all, I must try to find – I will not say some service I can render, for who can
render a service to Christ or to the pope, who stands nearest to Him? – but at 20
least some evidence of a grateful heart, that may correspond to the greatness
of the benefit I have received: This, I perceive, will for a start be hard
enough; but then to correspond to the eminence of a Leo, who is in all
respects so great that he surpasses other Roman pontiffs as far as the dignity
of a Roman pontiff surpasses all other men – this will be harder still.   25
Whether I can achieve this, I do not know; but at least I shall try, in such a
way as to show all men that only strength is lacking, if life be granted me.
And I shall have nothing more to live for, if I live long enough to enshrine
for posterity the more than human virtues of our good and great Pope Leo.
He attacks an arduous task with less risk of failure who attacks it with a will 30
and knows how heavy his new burden is. If my own proper forces fail me, I
shall ask scholars for their help and support, for nowhere is there one who
does not confess how much he owes to your religious fervour, that champion of the public peace which has always been the nurse of honourable
studies. In the meantime I can enjoy the sense of my own personal good-   35
fortune, in having won the approval not merely of a supreme pontiff, but of
a Leo, whose gifts give him supremacy over them all; and no less the

* * * * *

566:9 Catholic Majesty] Charles as king of Castile; cf Ep 413:44n.
9–10 in another case] That of the Sicilian bishopric; cf Ep 475:8.

good-fortune of this age of ours, which has good hopes of becoming an age of gold, if such a thing there ever were. For in this age, under your most auspicious leadership and through your saintly wisdom, I foresee that three 40 of its greatest blessings will be restored to the human race: that true Christian piety which in so many ways is now decayed, the study of the humanities in part neglected hitherto and in part corrupted, and that public and perpetual harmony of the Christian world which is the fountain and the parent of religion and learning. These will be the undying trophies of Leo 45 the Tenth; these will be enshrined for ever in the works of the learned and will shed eternal lustre on your pontificate and your family. I pray Almighty God that He may preserve this mind in you unchanged, and may vouchsafe you a long sojourn in our midst, that all things may be settled to your heart's content before you, our Leo, make your long-deferred return to heaven.   50

Brussels, 1516

567 / To Silvestro Gigli   Brussels [c 4 April] 1517

This letter replies to Ep 521; for the circumstances of its composition and publication see Ep 566 introduction.

TO THE RIGHT REVEREND FATHER IN CHRIST SILVESTRO,
BISHOP OF WORCESTER, ENVOY OF
HIS BRITANNIC MAJESTY TO THE SUPREME PONTIFF,
FROM ERASMUS, GREETING
You have doubled the value of what you have done for me, my lord bishop, 5
by adding to the great service which you have rendered to my undeserving person a letter full of friendly feeling. I have heard much, and from many sources, of your singular good will towards men of learning; but I now find that all reports fell short of the reality, for you seem to me designed by nature for the express purpose of earning universal gratitude. What would 10
you not be ready to do for others, if you do so much for a man called Erasmus whom you scarcely know by sight? And so it no longer surprises me that you should have found equal favour and equal good will long ago from that most intelligent of kings, Henry seventh of that name, and now from the eighth Henry, a son so like his father, nor that Pope Leo regards 15
you with singular affection. You and he have so much in common. In both of you, virtue has been tested by extremes of fortune and emerged the brighter for it; you both have the same passion for doing good to all men in

* * * * *

50 long-deferred return] An echo of Horace's words to Augustus (*Odes* 1.2.45)

Henry VII
Portrait by Michel Sittow, 1505
National Portrait Gallery, London

private and in public; both have the same wonderful mildness and generosity of temper. The pope I have thanked by letter as best I could, but it will be 20
better done by you, that he may learn how grateful I am from the man whose doing it was that I am so much beholden to him. I know you will be ready to add this small appendix to your acts of kindness towards me, which are so great already. My respectful good wishes to your Lordship, to whom I profess myself entirely devoted. 25

Brussels, 1516

568 / From Guillaume Budé   Paris, 5 April [1517]

This letter replies to two letters from Erasmus which do not survive; they were evidently written after the dispatch of Ep 534.

BUDÉ TO ERASMUS, GREETING

I have had two short letters from you, one, which was half in Greek, without day or year, the other written on the feast of the Annunciation. I have already answered the first one, saying that I was not at that time in a position to answer it, since as yet I had heard nothing definite; to the second 5
I have hardly anything to reply, from the day when I first showed your letter to the king up till now. For the Court has been out of town, and the king himself has spent most of his time on the move, or rather, galloping round the places where the stags shed their horns, and I could not stay in the country all that time; until I again fell in with the man who was to introduce 10
me, and met the king on his way to church. As it happened, his confessor, Guillaume Petit, was there, and he thought I should speak to his Majesty there and then; which I did not think a good idea, because I wanted to get away from the flies. The king was then in the district of Saint-Maur, where I have a country-house which is not yet finished; and when he knew who I 15
was, he said 'Where is that letter from Erasmus I told you to translate?' So I produced it, and he said he would read it, and went on to Mass.

On his way back, I met him again contrary to my intentions, in the company of Guillaume Petit and the man who introduced me, who is also a friend of mine and a great supporter of yours, and one who looked forward 20

* * * * *

568:7 king] Francis I
10 man] François du Moulin de Rochefort; cf Ep 523:9n.
12 Petit] Cf Ep 522:17n.
14 flies] Cf Plautus *Poenulus* 691 (Allen), but the sense is not clear.
14 Saint-Maur] Visited by Francis I from 6–19 April
15 country-house] Cf Ep 435:146n.

to seeing your works, as those of a future member of the king's court; for so I allowed him and one or two other people to delude themselves, one of whom is the man who taught the king his rudiments when he was a child (he is my guide in these things, and the man who first introduced me to the king). So the king then said 'What are Erasmus' intentions? It is by no means clear from the letter he wrote me.' 'Indeed,' said I, 'from your Majesty's letter it is far from clear.' 'Did he write anything more definite to you?' I gave the best answer I could, and what I thought most conducive to the plan you and I are hatching in secret; when the other person present, the king's tutor in his boyhood, broke in with 'Sire, if your Majesty has a design to invite Erasmus to come and live in your kingdom, this man,' pointing to me, 'will bring it off if anybody can; for the two of them are very close and dear friends.' I had boasted in the course of conversation that I could arrange this in my position as an old friend, if I knew that the king's intentions were honourable and adequate; for this was my plan, formed since I got your letter written in Greek, but no one else knew of it, because I did not want to betray your feelings and the state of affairs where you are now. That was what you asked me to do. So when he said that, the king turned to me and said 'What about it?' 'Sire,' I replied, 'if you instruct me to treat with Erasmus as a plenipotentiary and write to him once and for all, I think I can promise that he will put himself in my hands and not reject my advice.' 'That,' he said, 'is what I want you to do,' and went straight off to dinner with no more for me to go on than that. At this I was somewhat cast down, and said to the men who had introduced me that, unless Erasmus were given some more reliable security, I would never mention the subject to him; for I saw no prospects here firm enough to justify a man in forfeiting his bail.

Yesterday I went to see the bishop of Paris on your behalf; but after waiting more than three hours I had some difficulty in finding a free moment amidst serious and difficult business. I told him the whole baffling story, and also showed him your letters. It would take too long to tell the whole thing; what matters is that he has an exceptionally high regard for you, supports your interests without any concealment, and mentions you in every other sentence at the dinner-table. When the conversation turns on questions of this sort, he says he will try his luck, and let me know. In brief,

* * * * *

26 letter] Ep 533

30 tutor] See note 10; M.-M. de la Garanderie *Christianisme et lettres profanes (1515–1535)* (Paris 1976) II 35.

46–7 forfeiting his bail] *Adagia* I viii 18

48 bishop of Paris] Etienne Poncher; cf Ep 529 introduction.

I would say the state of affairs here is such that one must not hope too much, but I think the question is still undecided, and therefore it is right to hope.

I leave tomorrow, or even today, and thought it well to send this interim report, so that meanwhile you can explore things in your part of the world and take advice about conditions here. This much I cannot refrain   60 from adding. In the name of our old friendship I assure you, it sometimes occurs to me to abandon all the subjects to which in the old days I devoted too much effort, and valued them above everything, which on top of my state of health have tied me down with this accursed poverty. If you think fit, you had better write to the bishop of Paris. Someday, maybe, I shall   65 advise you to write to the king again, if I see that the affair has not been simply forgotten. I do not expect to return before the 22nd, or even the 24th, of April.

Your old pupil, Germain de Brie, archdeacon of Albi, is a great supporter of yours; he is now chaplain to the queen. I had great difficulty in   70 getting back from him the letter you wrote me. He is a good scholar in both Greek and Latin, and I should love him dearly, if he did not love you so much more than me. Farewell.

Paris, Palm Sunday

569 / From Germain de Brie   Paris, 6 April 1517

The writer was a French humanist and priest with educational background in the law. He was born in Auxerre about 1490 and died in 1538. He and Erasmus had met in 1508 in Venice; cf Ep 212: 2n, Rogers 212. After de Brie's return to France he had become secretary to the queen, Anne of Brittany, and since 1514 he had been a canon of Auxerre. This letter, first published in the *Farrago*, opens a correspondence which lasted until Erasmus' death. It is part of the production associated with Ep 522 and the effort to interest Erasmus in coming to France; it was probably sent to Erasmus with Ep 568. De Brie was about to become involved in a literary quarrel with Thomas More; cf Ep 461: 23–4; Allen Ep 620 (the reply to this letter, which did not reach de Brie); L.B. Bradner and C.A. Lynch eds and trans *The Latin Epigrams of Thomas More* (Chicago 1953) xxix–xxxi. The author's repeated allusions to the *Adagia* recall the fact that Erasmus placed three of de Brie's poems, two of them in Greek, at the head of the *Adagiorum chiliades*. See M.-M. de la Garanderie 'Un érasmien français: Germain de Brie' *Colloquia Erasmiana Turonensia* (Paris; Toronto and Buffalo 1972) vol 1 359–79.

* * * * *

69 de Brie] Cf Ep 212:2n; Ep 569 introduction.

GERMAIN DE BRIE TO ERASMUS OF ROTTERDAM

Etienne Poncher, bishop of Paris, has very lately returned to us from your parts, having successfully completed his mission to the emperor. This bishop of ours enjoys the admiration and respect and even reverence of this country to a degree which it is very hard to describe. And rightly too, for it 5 is beyond question that the bishop of Paris alone surpasses and leaves far behind all the other bishops of France, be it said without offence, as a man of honour and courtesy and wisdom, in the simplicity, moderation and uprightness of his manner of life, in the versatility, openness and high quality of his mind, and in his incomparable knowledge of civil and canon 10 law, of theology and philosophy and almost all the learned disciplines. It is not without reason that he has always hitherto stood first in the list of those whose wisdom, prudence and sound judgment govern the great fabric of this kingdom. Three successive kings of France, one after another, have already entrusted him with great authority in all that came before them, like 15 some wise Nestor chosen to guide their counsels, and they have always held him in great esteem and honour; so often have they proved and tested our bishop's loyalty, and observed and experienced his prudence and his ready foresight in business of every kind. Besides all this, in all the great affairs of the state – a stormy sea, one might more truly say, in which he is 20 continually not only fully engaged but almost overwhelmed – he alone of all our bench of bishops not merely respects aspirants to sound learning or summons them to him, but spurs them on with rewards and earns their gratitude by his generosity, attracts them by his courtesy and wins them over by his kindness, fosters them with his authority and shields them with 25 his prestige, enhancing their status by his own reflected glory. And all this he does with one end in view, that in every respect he may play the part in our society of a benefactor without parallel towards all those in whom he finds the combination of scholarship and high character. Happy indeed, and far the most fortunate of countries, will France be, if she can find ten 30 further patrons of literature to match the one she has already, men whose generous support can at long last rekindle the humane studies and the liberal arts, quenched by the meanness and hostility of our modern princes, and bring them forth, as the saying goes, out of the shadows into the light of day.   35

* * * * *

569:3 mission] In March 1517, Francis I had met Emperor Maximilian with Margaret of Austria and Charles, to arrange for imperial accession to the Treaty of Noyon; this is known as the Treaty of Cambrai; cf Ep 532:30n.
34 saying] *Adagia* I ii 82

But you must not wonder, Erasmus most learned of men, why I have embarked on this panegyric of the bishop for your benefit; for, if he has ever done anything for any man of letters, I do assure you that most recently he has shown abounding and open-handed generosity towards you above all. For this I too am more beholden to him on your account than ever I was before, believing as I do that whatever distinction and honour and advantage is ever bestowed on you, is bestowed no less on the nine Muses, whose most distinguished servant and incomparable high-priest you are. Let me explain then, Erasmus, what sort of debt you owe the bishop of Paris and how exceptional it is. When he first returned to us from the mission of which I spoke, it was his special and favourite occupation to speak of you, my friend, more than of anyone else, to extol your learning and your brilliant style alike in Greek and Latin, both publicly and in private, loud and clear, and sing your praises in full-throated strains, as the saying goes. He had previously read a great many of your books, but, so he says, had never met you personally. It is surprising how delighted and triumphant and in a way content he is, now that he has met the great man face to face on his own ground, and enjoyed your society and conversation as much as he wished, which he says was very often. There is no praise he does not bestow on you, no compliment he does not pay you. I have a fancy to add here what he says about you; but pray let it be clear that in this flattery finds no place at all.

'Erasmus' great reputation had preceded him, but I found him greater still; for why should I not use the same language of Erasmus that Pliny, we find, once used of his admired Iseus? What truly Attic grace, what eloquence worthy of Nestor, what rare learning of another age than ours! Never did the world on our side of the Alps produce anything more richly gifted with every literary endowment than Erasmus, if I may say so without offence. This age of ours has had two great leaders in the humanities, Ermolao Barbaro and Angelo Poliziano – such fertility of invention was theirs, such keenness of judgment, such eloquence, such familiarity with the languages and with the whole range of knowledge. These men found Latin after long years of squalour crumbling under the rust of barbarism, and tried to restore it to its pristine brilliance; nor was their attempt unsuccessful, for Latin owes as great a debt to them as to the most effective

* * * * *

39 open-handed] Literally 'using both hands'; *Adagia* I ix 16
49 full-throated strains] *Adagia* I v 96
59 Pliny] *Epistulae* 2.3.1
61 Nestor] *Adagia* I ii 56
65 Barbaro, Poliziano] Cf Epp 126:150n, 129:154n.

of their predecessors. And so they have won for themselves immortal glory and renown, and the memory of Ermolao and Poliziano will remain for ever enshrined in the hearts of all educated men, immune from extinction by time, chance or fate. In my time I too have seen in Italy with my own eyes several famous men of high literary reputation, in whom was learning of no   75 common kind and keen judgment and rare eloquence; but this I must say, with no desire to offend and asking pardon of the Italians, whose staunch supporter I was long ago and whom I always respect greatly in the field of learning: Erasmus it is alone who wins the palm against all men on both sides of the Alps, Erasmus alone eclipses every other light by the splendour   80 of his learning and his style, and pecks out the crow's eyes, as the saying has it.

'Even now I seem to see Erasmus himself speaking; in heaven's name, how apt and to the point, how scholarly it all is, so elegant, so exquisitely turned, and yet so clear and so precise! He has the greatest fluency, abun-   85 dance and resource; his language is pure and lucid, unforced and melodi-ous; his expression appropriate, sinewy, well thought-out and forcible; his reflections unfamiliar and far from obvious. Words never fail him; and such words! such choice, such workmanship, such perfect Latin, and all this in such plentiful supply! Never was there so rich a store of eloquence; his   90 familiar conversation, however much unprepared, gives evidence of wide reading and great erudition; his incredible memory can supply him with recondite things to say with not so much as a syllable at fault – in a word, you would think some Attic Muse herself was speaking, and no mortal man. How he makes rhetoric do his bidding, how precise his knowledge of   95 the art! Fully at home as he is in all its principles, he can take all its figures of speech and various styles of composition, and bend them back and forth like wax just as happens to suit him. One would swear it was Demosthenes, or a greater than Demosthenes if such were possible. Then he has a special intimacy with all the poets, both Greek and Latin, and writes verse in both   100 languages of which no one would be ashamed; as he plies his skilful pen, Apollo smiles approval and all the Muses vie with one another to inspire him; for in this field I think he challenges the ancients themselves.'

'Again, that Erasmus has no ordinary knowledge of theology is proved by his very numerous writings on the subject, and I too, who have   105

* * * * *

81–2 saying has it] Cf Ep 456:24n.
95 how precise his knowledge] *Adagia* I v 91

tried a fall with him in that field, can be a well-informed and truly Attic witness. For Erasmus has not, as some perhaps suppose, merely set his lips to the cup of theology, but has made his way into the sanctuary, into its inmost heart. Philosophy too, the queen of the arts, he has not merely greeted in passing and, so to say, from the threshold: he knows all its 110 mysteries and professional secrets, all the discoveries bequeathed to us by the genius of Plato, the intellect of Aristotle, or any other masters of philosophy. And in this great and many-sided equipment in all humane subjects, who can be found who dares to challenge Erasmus and enter the arena against him? – unless it were perhaps some weakling Thersites, 115 presuming to take on an Achilles or a Diomede and destined very soon to throw away his spear in disgrace and quit the arena, covered entirely in confusion. I gave the man himself an invitation from the king, and on a king's generous terms, to come and live with us in France, adding some separate promises of my own; and he would have come without reluctance, 120 except that he has already bound himself to his own sovereign, his Catholic Majesty, and his good fortune – his merit, rather – has secured him several supporters who have the prince's ear, men of great distinction and leaders of the Court, thanks to whose favour and countenance he hopes at no distant date to gather the harvest of his researches and the fruit of all his 125 toil.'

Such are the tributes, and more like them, which the bishop of Paris does not cease to pay you openly, to your great credit. I know of course that you deserve every word of them and that he has simply painted you in your true colours; yet, for my part, I think you owe his lordship more than 130 ordinary gratitude, and that on two accounts. For one thing, though under no obligation from any other cause, he has been so free and generous in offering you his assistance, and so frank in making his feelings towards you widely known of his own free will. And then again (and this you should value highly), it has been your good fortune to deserve the esteem of a man 135 who is himself highly esteemed and a model of excellence of every kind; for

* * * * *

106–7 truly Attic witness] *Adagia* I viii 25
107 set his lips] *Adagia* I ix 92
110 from the threshold] *Adagia* I ix 91; cf Ep 511:10n.
114–5 enter the arena] *Adagia* I ix 83
118 invitation] Ep 529 is Erasmus' reply to this invitation, conveyed in Brussels or Antwerp.
130 true colours] *Adagia* I iv 6

no praise so truly deserves the name as that uttered by a man who is praised himself. In any case, my dear Erasmus, two reasons in particular have made me testify at this moment to his praise of you. One is, that I can be above all others a fair-minded and trusty witness with access to Jove's records, as the saying goes, since I have more than once been present when the bishop of Paris himself was speaking on this subject, for I am often in his company; he welcomes not men of letters only but lovers of literature as well, among whose number (may it please the Muses) I too claim a modest place. The other, that I thought it very important for you to know who it is to whom you are most indebted and who has a special lien on you, so that you can either express your thanks for the services he has done you or even, given the opportunity, one day return them. For I well knew, and had in fact discerned long before, that you are by no means of an ungrateful disposition. Add to this a thing which I too suspected, that you would find evidence from me on this point less dubious than anyone else's, and so you would decide (as is in fact true) that in view of my long-standing loyalty to you and our mutual friendship I have told you the whole story frankly and openly, adding no fancy colours but simply as one who, as they say, 'takes figs for figs and calls a spade a spade.'

For I am not the man, believe me, to wish to impose on you in any way, or to attempt to butter you up with false praise and soften you into a state of self-admiration. I have always regarded you as very far removed, unless I am wrong, from any such condition; you have always valued your endowments at the price of your real talents and your proper merit, needing no support other than yourself, unless perhaps, if you will allow me at this point to borrow a thought from Homer, 'changed art thou, friend, from what thou wast before,' and since the last time I saw you something has happened to your character and the modesty and, to speak frankly, the simplicity that were natural to you. For you let me take the further liberty of plucking you by the ear from time to time, and reminding you briefly of the old days, when we were companions and friends in Venice. I, under my

* * * * *

141 saying] *Adagia* I viii 24

146 special lien] *Adagia* I vii 51

154 as they say] *Adagia* II iii 5

160–1 needing no support] The phrase is from Cicero *Epistulae ad familiares* 5.13.1.

162 Homer] *Odyssey* 16.181

166 by the ear] To the ancients the ear was the seat of memory; *Adagia* I vii 40.

167 Venice] De Brie was a servant-pupil there of Johannes Lascaris; cf Epp 269:55n, 461:24n.

beloved Johannes Lascaris (I call him mine, as my teacher and almost my
second father), was beginning to work on Greek, though still little more
than a beginner in Latin; while you were living with Aldo Manuzio and   170
producing before a delighted audience of gods and men those famous,
faultless monuments of your learning, which even in those days was
unique in both Greek and Latin. Prominent among them are your four
chiliads of proverbs, a work considered not by me alone but by the learned
world to be bedecked with such erudition in both languages, adorned by   175
such various reading, and seasoned with such charm and eloquence, that to
a competent and unbiased critic it would suffice by itself to make perfectly
clear how far Erasmus outstrips all other entrants in the literary race, as far
as the trumpet drowns the flute or the chatter of crickets overbears the
buzzing of bees. I can only say that anyone who does not admire it has   180
either not read any of it, or if he has read it, his eyesight in these matters is at
fault. For, to mention this merely in passing, what could show more
scholarship, more eloquence, more abundance and elegance of style or
purer latinity than all those digressions of yours? – in which you present us
with Erasmus in his true colours, a second Quintilian using all his powers. 185
  This was followed by the *Moriae encomium*, the *Miles christianus*, the
Testament in both languages, the *Christiani principis institutio*, the works of
Jerome restored and set in order, and much else of the same kind. In the
name of all the Muses, what a welcome these earned from all lovers of
humane letters in these parts, what an enthusiastic and affectionate recep-   190
tion! What can we suppose to be the result of all this, except the clearest
indication of the fertile genius, the keen critical sense, the exquisite taste,
the more than human memory, the unfailing eloquence, the learning in
both Greek and Latin, the practised and powerful pen, the universal knowledge which endow and glorify the name of Erasmus? In heaven's name,   195
who can any longer deny that in Erasmus' breast and bosom there wells up
an unfailing fount of undying eloquence that spreads far and wide? – from
which so many different brimming rivulets flow in abundance to irrigate
the green fields of scholarship. Who can deny that, while in many other
men one finds eminent gifts and qualities of eloquence, some here some   200
there, in Erasmus alone one finds them all, a great pile, an ant-heap, an
ocean of all the virtues.

* * * * *

174 chiliads of proverbs] The *Adagiorum chiliades* of 1508; cf Ep 211 introduction.
187 both languages] The *Novum instrumentum*, with Erasmus' edition of the
Greek text and his new Latin translation
201 great pile *etc*] *Adagia* I iii 31, 32, 29

As for me, my most learned friend, I understand well enough that what you write is intelligible only to keen-sighted readers, and that such a delicate repast fit for a king (to speak truly, such food for the gods) is not   205
meant for an appetite like mine. And yet (blessed heavens) how could I keep my hands off such a feast, hungry and thirsty as I am? I read most diligently and peruse with passion all your works; though I have read each one now ten times over, I never grow tired, and fresh admiration overcomes me every time. The oftener I look into them, the more closely and carefully I   210
read them, the more pleasure and sympathy and delight they rouse within me. Immortal gods, how should they not delight me? Look at my friend Deloynes, a man with whom I am on intimate terms and whom I see almost every day, such an old and kind friend is he, and Ruzé too, who shows me exceptional good will, both men of high standing and patrician rank, and   215
well thought-of in literary circles: they find your books not merely sympathetic and delightful, they are so overcome and ravished by them that Erasmus is their one favourite author and they think him worth all the other moderns put together. How can I regret it if I take such eminent men as my models and follow their well-marked footsteps? – to say nothing for the   220
moment of that distinguished figure Guillaume Budé, the outstanding ornament of my native France and her unparalleled glory in the field of letters. With his frank and open character, he treats the three of us as his close friends, and we revere him as our teacher – if I may say so, our Apollo; nor does he ever cease to recommend to us your scholarship, your mul-   225
tifarious breadth of reading, the force and abundance of your style. He expresses a high opinion of all your writings and casts his vote for them, as the saying goes, with enthusiasm. For our part, in this respect as in others, we follow Budé as our critic of keenest scent, our true touchstone of Heraclea; such is our reverence for him or his authority.   230

And so, my most distinguished friend, suspecting as I do that to a man as busy as you are, and accustomed to devote what little leisure you may get to reading the most elegant authors, I have written already at such length as can only sicken and disgust you, I will bring my letter to a close. Let me first, however, make one thing clear: long as I have been deprived of your   235
society, and great as is the distance that separates us, in spite of this I have your memory always with me as something sacred in my mind and heart,

* * * * *

213 Deloynes] Cf Ep 494 introduction.
214 Ruzé] Cf Ep 493:462n.
227 vote] *Adagia* i v 53
229 keenest scent] *Adagia* ii viii 59
230 Heraclea] *Adagia* i v 87

and my affection and respect for you are just the same as if I had enjoyed your company face to face every day down to the present. I am not the man to forget or neglect my friends when we are far apart; never was there a time   240 when I did not hate that maxim 'Friends dwelling far away are no true friends.' Yet my great desire, the thing I long for more than I can say, is that our king's intentions towards you, which are surely by no means to be despised, and his promises, which will not I think be found wanting, may be able, if anything can, to tempt you to come and live with us in France;   245 and this for many reasons, but especially that you may have the most perfect opportunity to put to the test my loyalty and affection for you and (may I add?) my readiness to share at any rate everything which Fortune has conferred on my modest and undeserving self.

Farewell. Do not forget my affection for you, and give me yours in   250 return.

Paris, 6 April 1516

570 / From Johannes Ammonius   Edingen, 6 April 1517

The writer of this letter was identified by Allen (IV xxvi) with Johannes van der Maude or van den Sande, also known as De Arena. His Greek ánd Latin names were literal translations of Sande: Dutch *zand* meaning arena. He was a brother of Levinus Ammonius, author of Ep 1463. Both brothers were Carthusian monks. Johannes was professed at Herne, a small village north of Edingen or Enghien, on 11 November 1500, in the convent Domus Capellae, and died 27 October 1543. See J. De Grauwe *Prosopographia Cartusiana Belgica* (Ghent 1976), nrs 1357, 2023.

JOHANNES HARENACEUS TO ERASMUS OF ROTTERDAM, GREETING
A priest called Simon, of the family of that excellent man and sound lawyer Caspar van Halmale sheriff of Antwerp, was staying with me for a night during Lent. In the morning I asked him for news of Erasmus, for my first question is usually about some learned man or other; and he replied that   5 Erasmus was very well, and was living in Antwerp with Pieter Gillis, a man of very good judgment and chief secretary of the city. 'I often have a friendly

* * * * *

241 maxim] *Adagia* II iii 85
570:3 Halmale] A prominent townsman who held the offices of sheriff and burgomaster several times. About 1514 he was sent to Bremen to allay tension between the Hansa and the city of Antwerp. He died in 1530. Pieter Gillis' preface to the *Epistolae ad Erasmum* (October 1516) is dedicated to Halmale. Cf also Ep 474:4n.

Cuthbert Tunstall
Portrait by an unknown artist; date unknown
Collection of J.R. Chichester-Constable, Burton Constable Hall, Yorkshire

talk with him,' he added, 'sometimes in my house, sometimes in his lodging, and even sometimes elsewhere.' 'Please,' I said, 'when you have the chance, give him my greetings, and in these words, if you see fit: "A   10 certain Carthusian of Domus Capellae sends you his greetings, Erasmus, because he has warm feelings towards you, and urges you, if you are ever travelling in that neighbourhood, to be so good as to put up at Domus Capellae and visit the brethren who think so highly of you."'

Such was the greeting I sent, most learned Erasmus, and if it seems   15 unduly forward, I beg you of your kindness to put the blame on my enthusiasm. If it were not for that, I ought not to trouble you, for I know of the distinguished works you have in hand. Until then, I shall think highly of you and speak well of you, and hope and pray that all good things may be yours, as I have done hitherto, thus playing the part of a true friend.   20 Farewell, dear glory of our generation, and think warmly of me if you can, as I do of you.

From the house of Capella diuae Mariae near Edingen, 6 April 1517

571 / From Cuthbert Tunstall to Guillaume Budé   [Antwerp, April 1517]

This is a letter written at the insistence of Erasmus; cf Ep 572:2–5. Along with its reply (Ep 583), it was included by Erasmus when he published his own correspondence in the *Auctarium*. It had already been written when Ep 572 was sent, but it was probably not dated very early in April since it did not reach Budé until 6 May (cf Ep 583:53).

Erasmus was eager to promote an intimacy between Tunstall and Budé, as he had already done successfully between Thomas More, Tunstall and Pieter Gillis; cf Ep 332. Tunstall (see Ep 207:25n) was a valued diplomat in the royal service at this point in his career, and had belonged to the English mission sent in May 1515 to negotiate a new commercial treaty with the Burgundian Netherlands; cf Epp 332, *Utopia* xxixff. When those negotiations were finished in January 1516, Tunstall was sent back to Brussels to seek a renewal of the alliance against France (cf Ep 388:114n). On 13 August 1516 the Treaty of Noyon was signed between representatives of Charles and Francis I, but the English mission remained and in November 1516 a new pact was drawn up between England, Prince Charles and the Emperor; this was ratified by Maximilian the following May; cf Charles Sturge *Cuthbert Tunstall* (London 1938) 46.

Tunstall and Erasmus met on 3 June 1516 in Brussels (Ep 412), and the following October Erasmus wrote enthusiastically to Budé about the charm and learning of his new friend (Ep 480:6–18). Tunstall was particularly interested in the subject of ancient coinage about which Budé was such a distinguished authority; cf Epp 403 introduction, 584:20–22.

CUTHBERT TUNSTALL TO GUILLAUME BUDÉ, GREETING

I had intended, learned sir, to write to you at leisure of my own accord, and now I have been driven to do so, at an exceptionally busy moment, by a series of letters from Erasmus, who has promised you, he says, that I shall write soon. So, in order to release my friend from his promise, I am obliged 5
to do forthwith what I had in any case decided to do in due course. For in a letter to you he cites me as an authoritative witness to your skill in Latin and Greek, and you take his word for it and do not despise me as a critic, as though you accepted me as a member of some panel of competent judges; and at this point I thought modesty demanded imperatively that I should 10
withdraw at the earliest moment from the arena in which two heavyweights of our generation in the literary way were competing in an interchange of most friendly letters, each passing scholarly criticisms on the other – not for me to play the literary critic with Erasmus or deliver an opinion on Budé when he comes up for audit. Each of you is an ornament to his native 15
country and enjoys a world-wide reputation; each carries such authority among the learned that any opinion on a literary topic expressed by either of you receives such universal support, that it seems to take rank as a decision binding on all future cases. I might well therefore seem as mad as any Orestes if I, who have no skill in either tongue, set myself up as judge 20
between men whose knowledge of both is beyond all cavil. But my state resembles that of those who look with enthusiasm at great pictures, though they themselves cannot paint and have never learnt to draw an outline or lay on the different colours or make the right allowances for light and shade in producing the effect they seek. If such men, when confronted with pieces 25
distinguished by some kind of beauty which attract all beholders, are the only people who do not praise them, they may give the impression that they are envious. And I, if I do not burst out in praise of things that I read with admiration, unskilled in words as I am, shall hardly escape the suspicion that I am jealous. Very well then, if I must mingle my own opinion of you, 30
for what it is worth, among those of more important critics, I think that you two have done more towards the revival of that antique eloquence that has been out of fashion for many centuries, more towards the revival of humane

* * * * *

571:4 letters] Cf Ep 572:2–3.
4 promised you] Ep 531:15ff
7 letter to you] Ep 480:15ff
8 not despise me] Ep 493:15ff
11 heavyweights] Literally 'Milos.' Milo of Crotona was the proverbial strong man of antiquity.
20 Orestes] The proverbial raving madman of antiquity

studies than – if I may say so without offence – all your Perottis and
Lorenzos, yes, and men like Ermolao and Poliziano and all the others who   35
were in the field before you. They amused their leisure moments by concen-
trating on such points as took each man's fancy, and collected interesting
observations which hold the reader by the mere charm of variety, like
people in some pleasant meadow gathering only the choicest flowers. But
you two with your Herculean and unwearying efforts have valiantly at-   40
tacked and routed hordes of barbarians more numerous than Xerxes' army,
and have already won almost complete victory, one of you in our churches
over those who profaned all that was holy, the other in our lawcourts over
those who were the ruin of all judicial process. They wrote to beguile a
reader's leisure, you to attract the serious student. Their work contributes   45
to the elegance of life, but life can be lived without it; you give us things
without which the life of man does not deserve the name. They laboured
with success to keep us on the right path even in comedy, light verse and
history; it was your common aim to expel error from the whole of human
life. Their productions were such as will be read by few, and men of leisure   50
at that; yours, such as any man however full of business will wish to have at
hand. You two have certainly equalled and perhaps surpassed their splendid record in the restoration of ancient texts, and your triumphs were
beyond the reach of men who lost hope when they saw the formidable
greatness of the task.   55

    And indeed, though one may read what they have written with the
greatest attention, how little is the progress we have made towards rich and
accurate powers of expression! How long do we allow barbarism to hold
sway in lawcourt and in church, where so much of our time is spent? Yet, on
the other side of the account, if eloquence is once restored to church and   60
courts, what place will ignorance still find to hide its barbarous head? A
smattering of Scripture is the common property of every Christian who can
read and write; and those who carry the study of the Scriptures further,
think themselves sufficiently instructed if in the end they acquire something of their style. In the lawcourts, the style of eloquence used in every   65
country in the administration of justice dictates to a great extent the language of ordinary people; for all are driven by necessity to learn the style
without which they cannot conveniently defend their rights, and all would

* * * * *

34 Perottis] Niccolò Perotti of Sassoferrato (1430–80), a student of Guarino
and Vittorino da Feltre. Cf Ep 117:49n.

35 Lorenzos] Lorenzo Valla (1406–57) the great philological critic; cf Ep
20:100n.

35 Ermolao, Poliziano] Cf Ep 569:65n.

give the impression of being able to speak like the leaders in the courts. It is
hopeless therefore to devote one's efforts to the restoration of Latin, and all   70
one's attempts will prove in vain, unless one can first reintroduce a purer
style into the church and the law.

      And so, when the two of you entered on the true path to glory, you saw
that these were the places that must be cleaned up first. And if you have
achieved immortal fame, it is because you could not be deterred from a   75
purpose so valuable by the immensity of the task, the difficulty of making
headway nor despair at ever finishing – no, not by the ranks of barbarism
massed before their camp and ready to fight as it were for hearth and altar,
not by the great number of augurs (shall I call them?) trying to scare you
with the name of religion, nor by the emblems of the civil power. Erasmus,   80
working through authors of every kind, has collected the proverbs of
antiquity, which gave the impression that there were almost as many
riddles as there were adages and plunged the reader in darkness; and these
he has expounded for those who wish to learn like a modern Oedipus of
amazing energy. At the same time he has published many other remarkable   85
works, some with quite modest titles, which not only are of the greatest
assistance to those who aim at higher things but have formed a kind of
practice-ground, rendering the author himself equal to the task which he
has made peculiarly his own, the exposition of the Scriptures. You for your
part have shown no less energy in exploring all the classics, and having   90
acquired equal fluency in both languages by making many versions from
Greek into Latin, you made it your business to emend the Pandects, an
enormous work with as many mistakes in it as its laws have clauses and a far
larger number of errors by its commentators; and in revealing the errors of
Accursius and reinstating the original meaning you expended far more   95
labour than Hercules himself when he cleared the dung from the Augean
stables. In your exposition of the 'as' and its parts, you have given us back
the ancient weights and measures like a reforming magistrate, a work of
more than Herculean effort in which you have far surpassed what your
contemporaries could have expected. Who would ever have thought that a   100
subject in which all hope was abandoned, dead and buried, plunged in the
deep oblivion of so many centuries and quite given up by so many scholars
for lost, would one day return into the light? Who could have attempted
such a thing without criticism of his rashness, or promised such a result
without our laughing at him? Would anyone have borne with your attack   105
on the problem, unless you had produced the result before announcing that

* * * * *

95 Accursius] Francesco Accorso (1182–1260), author of the *Glossa ordinaria*; cf
Ep 134:30–1n.

you were going to try? In the rest of your commentaries you leave others far behind, in this one you unquestionably surpass yourself.

But what is this I see in the letter from you to Erasmus which he gave me to read? Do you not say that you are entirely self-taught, and came by 110 your present wealth of knowledge without instruction from any teacher? – a fact which, did not your transparent character rule out any suspicion of falsehood, would be hardly credible. For my part, I was overcome with admiration of you, as I reflected that the effort you have expended in reading through so many authors, which was barely credible already, had 115 been greater than seems within one man's compass; for self-taught as you are, you leave so far behind you men taught by the most scholarly masters, even men of unflagging industry. But then, when I think of all the difficulties you have surmounted, I feel that it was some divine providence that made you do without teachers. How much of our diligence goes for naught 120 as we sit under them, while we listen with careless and inattentive minds to them while they hold forth! – believing everything they say although, for fear of our supposing there is anything they do not know, they often for effect teach falsehood as though it were truth and things doubtful as though they were certain. Hence it is that the errors implanted in our minds while 125 they were still young grow up with us, and once they have struck deep root you will try in vain to pull them up; so ashamed are we, as Horace says, when we are old 'to own that what we learnt as beardless boys is good for nothing.' But you were anxious to learn, and your lack of teachers obliged you to have an eye for details, to accept nothing as certain that you had not 130 ascertained, and never to trust your own judgment rashly; to pause at things which others skate over without a thought, and not proceed until you had examined them and weighed them up and inspected them closely and compared them with like things elsewhere. And many were the disadvantages it held for you, you say? Just think of the incredible advantages it 135 was to mean for other people! It has taken a long time to digest that labour, as you have contrived to do; but the glory you have won from it is immortal, and such glory is not to be had save by great exertions. Posterity will be in your debt for a new atmosphere in the courts, the restoration of the 'as' it will owe to you. Like a new Servius Sulpicius dawning among us, 140 you are healing the breach between civil law and eloquence, which have for many centuries been separated.

* * * * *

109 letter] Ep 493:21ff
127 Horace] *Epistles* 2.1.84–5
140 Servius Sulpicius] One of the great Roman jurists, consul in 51BC

The news you added at the end of your letter, that you are preparing new notes on the Pandects, filled me with incredible joy. I was wondering why, when you have been carried out to sea by such a favourable breeze, you should have cast anchor when the course of your important labours is but half done; and wishing as I did to introduce myself among your friends, I had decided to take as my subject for addressing you the need to finish what you had begun. That my subject should have been forestalled is a great pleasure to me. If you resume the voyage of your own accord, you will pass more easily through the stormy sea of difficulties and reach the haven where you would be. Besides which, Minerva usually adds grace more readily to a subject of her own choosing. How great the pleasure I take in your commentaries you can gauge from this. In my young days, after a brief taste of the humanities I was reduced on the advice of my friends to the study of civil law, as being more likely to increase my worldly goods. My teachers were the leading men of the time in Italy, regarded by all as Scaevola and Papinian come to life; and from time to time I used to take them up when I saw them dragging some wretched law by the scruff of the neck into their own way of thinking, which would have meant something quite different if their brutal methods had allowed it – and all the time they would boast that they had unearthed (for pity's sake!) the law's true meaning, when it would have been nearer the truth to say they had completely buried it. This monstrous treatment roused me, and I put them right in their delusion, now and again about the true reading, which would occur to me in the course of my considering the corrupt passage, and sometimes about the true meaning. Whenever I did so, they thought me as arrogant as I thought them ridiculous; for to them it was an unpardonable crime for anyone to impugn the sacrosanct authority of Accursius, by whose lightest word they had sworn. And so, as I lamented the sad state of the times as it then was, I prayed that we might live to see some champion of the truth enter the lists, to bring back the daylight and drive out this darkness from the civil law. And this at last has come to pass by the goodness of Almighty God, who has sent us a Budé, I had almost said, down from heaven. For who is it who bundles out of the courts the barbarians who sully the purity of the civil law with their sordid 'interpretation' and often give us some

145

150

155

160

165

170

175

* * * * *

143 at the end] Ep 493:571ff

158 Scaevola] Quintus Mucius Scaevola, consul 117BC, one of the most famous of the Roman jurists

158 Papinian] The most famous name in the history of Roman jurisprudence (put to death AD 212); cf 180n.

159–60 scruff of the neck] *Adagia* IV ix 50

absurd enigma in place of the law? Budé, of course. Who 'cuts the law's knots, makes riddling statutes plain?' Who starts classical eloquence on a new career in the courts? Budé. Who is it who welcomes Scaevola, Papi- nian, Ulpian, Paulus and the other great authorities in the civil law, who 180 have so long languished in captivity among the barbarians, and as they return home from bondage to their native land introduces them once more into the courts? Surely his name is Budé.

Forward then, learned sir, with all success, as you have begun, and win this glory, which others have left untouched, entirely for your rightful 185 own. Your learning will ensure that nothing is left unexplored, your gener- ous mind will share all its discoveries with those who wish to learn. As for your letter to Erasmus, I admired it so much that I never saw anything of yours more elegant, more brilliant, or with more display of scholarship in every line; for Greek and Latin compete in it on such equal terms, that it 190 would be hard to say whether the writer's mother tongue were Greek or Latin. On one point all will agree, that it is the work of a great scholar, whom one would hardly think a man of our own day. Farewell.

572 / From Cuthbert Tunstall   Antwerp, 22 April [1517]

Tunstall (cf Ep 571 introduction) was apparently enjoying a respite from his tour of duty accompanying Emperor Maximilian through the Netherlands; cf Ep 584.

CUTHBERT TUNSTALL TO ERASMUS OF ROTTERDAM, GREETING
I have had two letters from you, my dear Erasmus, in both of which you urge me to write to Budé; which I did some time ago in the middle of a great press of business, partly to make the acquaintance of a good scholar, and partly to release you from your promise. Only, you perhaps promised that I 5 would pay in gold, and I had some difficulty in finding ready cash in copper. He must make the best of it; that was the only coin I had in my money-box that I could produce. So I foresee that your credit with Budé will suffer a serious blow, by my having so greatly deceived the expectation

* * * * *

177–8 'cuts the law's knots] Juvenal 8.50
180 Ulpian] A famous Roman jurist, pupil of Papinian, murdered in AD 228
180 Paulus] Julius Paulus, contemporary of Papinian, a voluminous writer on the civil law
572:2 two letters] Lost
3 I did] Ep 571

aroused by your letter. Did not Thales the Milesian declare that one must   10
avoid making promises on behalf of other people? Be warned by this risk,
and do not put yourself forward as a guarantor when you need not. Learn,
after all this time, to make less extravagant claims for your friends. In your
second letter you ask what I advise about your going to France, where new
prospects, you say, are opening before you; and I deliberately postponed   15
my answer in hopes of telling you what I think face to face. But you had left
here the day before I arrived. I have been here already for three weeks on
account of the Easter festival, though otherwise expecting to change my
abode at any moment, for I now play in a touring company, not the fixed
affair I was used to in Brussels. So you will forgive me for not having   20
warned you of my arrival, for I myself had no idea when it would be until
the day I received orders to come here. The moment I dismounted from my
horse, I gave one of my servants the task of seeking you all through the
town, and not returning till he had found you. He brought from our friend
Gillis the sad news that you had left the day before, but you were expected   25
to return shortly. Six days later I heard from some English merchants that
you had crossed to England, and had been seen by them at Dover when you
had just landed from the ship. So my hope of meeting you soon is ended,
and I must tell you in absence what I had meant to say by word of mouth.

For my part, dear Erasmus, I want to see your affairs prosper no less   30
than my own, and if a position offers itself that is good enough for you, I
should think you ought not to despise it. But in heaven's name what solid
hope can there be for you in France, when those of their own people who are
devoted to humane letters can scarcely find patrons? – a thing which Budé
himself, the glory of his native land, laments to some tune in his writings.   35
In that country knighthood is held in high honour; and it is a rule among the
French in the present state of society (if one can believe what one hears) that
a knight must be uneducated, or must conceal his education, for fear that

* * * * *

10 Thales] *Adagia* i vi 97

17 I arrived] Tunstall's travels included these stops: 12 March, Brussels; 22
Lierre; 24–25 Brussels; 27 Mechelen; 29–30 Lierre (LP ii). On 1 April (LP ii 3101)
Tunstall and his companion were summoned by the emperor to Antwerp, and
presumably arrived within twenty-four hours. Erasmus' departure may thus
be dated 31 March or 1 April.

17 three weeks] Tunstall left Antwerp for Brussels on 28 April (LP ii 3180,
3210). Easter fell on 12 April in 1517.

19 touring company] Cf Ep 584:43.

25 Gillis] Erasmus' host; cf Ep 565:25n.

26 Six days later] Letters from Greenwich, England, dated 3 April, reached
Tunstall on the 8th; LP ii 3126.

one dedicated to knightly pursuits should be thought more ready with the
tongue than with the sword. As for their theology, you know already what   40
value they set on learning in that Sorbonian bog. But your friend, you say,
was told to write to you by the king. Yes; but has he any more influence
with the king of France than a certain person, whose name I cannot recol-
lect, with your own king? – you know what I refer to. From your letter I
could not see clearly enough on what basis this expectation rests. I have a   45
suspicion that your friends in France, who long to see you, in order to make
their invitations more attractive have magnified the king's instructions in
their letters, and made an elephant out of a gnat. And there is another thing
occurs to me. I have often heard you say that the French climate, mild as it
is, disagrees with you and is bad for your health; and will you at your age   50
trust yourself to a place which you found barely tolerable in the flower of
your youth? I think it a better plan to spend the rest of your days in comfort
either in your native country or in some other which you have learnt by
familiarity to like as much, rather than to risk your health by going into
foreign parts in pursuit of new expectations. A man such as you, my friend,   55
can never lack for friends or money.

Such is my opinion, which I would have expressed more fully in
conversation. But as I am at the moment rather fully occupied, I thought
even a Laconic letter would be better than to say nothing and seem to
neglect a friend who had asked my advice.   60

Farewell. Antwerp, 22 April

573 / From Cornelis Batt   Groningen, 22 April 1517

Cornelis was the son of Jacob Batt (or Badt), secretary of the town of Bergen-
op-Zoom; cf Ep 35 introduction. The probable reply to this letter – and
perhaps to a second from Batt at a later date – is Ep 839, dated 29 April and,
from internal evidence, of the year 1518. It is conceivable that this letter may
have been delayed in transmission to Erasmus, or that he put off replying until
he was about to leave the Netherlands for Basel.

* * * * *

41 Sorbonian bog] Cf Ep 403:15.
41 friend] Tunstall was thinking of Guillaume Petit (cf Ep 522:17n, 44–52) or
Budé (cf Ep 568:38–42).
43 certain person] Possibly referring to the influence of Le Sauvage with
Charles
45 rests] Reading *innitatur* for Allen's *invitatur*
48 elephant out of a gnat] *Adagia* III i 27
52 youth] Cf Epp 124:6–12, 146:18–20.

TO MASTER ERASMUS OF ROTTERDAM HIS PATRON
FROM CORNELIS BATT, GREETING

You know, most honoured Master Erasmus, the many problems that beset
me, and you have done all you can to help me by recommending me in
writing to distinguished men and by advice and assistance, not, I fear, for   5
any merit of my own but from an affectionate recollection of my father Jacob
Batt, who while he lived was not least among your friends. If therefore, as
an excuse for expressing my gratitude, I send you an account of my present
circumstances, I am confident that you will take it in good part and will not
abandon a man whom you once took under your protection. In the first   10
place, then, I delivered the letters you gave me in London in accordance
with the addresses on them, except one to Johann Reuchlin, which I forwarded by Franz the bookseller. Your friend Jan van Borssele showed me
kindness as a result of your recommendation. The Lord of Veere did not
give me a penny, but I have not lost hope of something generous from him.   15
And so at the same time, having nothing to hope for in Veere, I set out for
Groningen in Friesland, at the suggestion of a certain Jan Brecht, headmaster of the school at Antwerp and one of my supporters, who gave me letters
of introduction to some citizens of Groningen; and this was a better plan
and more successful than my former trip to England, for I was appointed   20
second master in the school there, and can easily provide myself with both
food and clothes. For I live with a leading burgher, who provides me with
board and lodging in return for the private tuition of his sons. I also receive
payment from the youth of Groningen for teaching the seventh form, most
of which goes on clothes; which leaves me little hope of saving much.   25

* * * * *

573:11 London] If this letter was written in 1517 (see introduction) this visit (cf
lines 20, 53) may be dated in May 1514, when Erasmus was probably in
London with letters to answer from Reuchlin and Jan Becker van Borssele (cf
Epp 290, 291). He evidently gave Batt letters of introduction to Adolph of
Burgundy (Ep 93 introduction) and Jan Becker (cf Ep 320:30n), and his reply to
Reuchlin (cf Ep 300:39n).
13 Franz] Birckmann; cf Ep 258:14n.
13 van Borssele] Cf 11n.
14 Veere] Adolph of Burgundy, heer van Veere; cf Ep 301:42n.
17 Brecht] Johannes Custos (de Coster) of Brecht, north-east of Antwerp (d
1526). In 1496 he was first in promotions in the Faculty of Arts at Louvain. He
was master earlier of the Latin school at Groningen. Pieter Gillis dedicated an
edition of the *Epistolae* of Poliziano (Antwerp: Martens 4 May 1510; NK 1745) to
Brecht, who was himself the author of a well-known Latin syntax.
24 seventh form] The highest was probably the first form, as at Deventer.

Besides which, I do not seek for great preferment, unless perhaps it were a chaplaincy without cure of souls; and this is my third year spent in Friesland in these conditions. That is why, best of patrons, I wanted very much to ask you, if you were able easily and without any loss on your side to get me any preferment where you are – for you know my capacity, and what I am suited for – do not hesitate to write to me. For if you think it a good plan, I will return to your part of the world, the more readily as I have heard that you mean to stay in Brabant, my native country, and at the same time because I am uncertain about war here. If, however, you advise me to stay here, please do not fail to write a line in answer to your humble friend Batt, for a letter from you will be more welcome to me than many gold pieces; for by this I shall count myself happy, and think you have paid the debt of friendship to my father. And your letter, if you do write, can be deposited with Franz, the bookseller in Antwerp; for I have made arrangements that Paul the bookseller, who handed this letter to Franz, will collect from him your letter to me and bring it here.

It only remains to express my gratitude for all your kindness; for repay you at present I cannot, which grieves me much. What can I do? If I promised that I would trumpet forth your praises, you have a most unworthy herald, and you are world-famous already. But I will do as a grateful man should, and never cease to acknowledge the kindness you have shown me, for you were so fond of my father Jacob Batt while he was alive, that since his death you have generously transferred all your kindness to me as his son, not for any merits of mine but for the love of God and pity for man's estate and also in memory of the mutual affection that was between you – so generously that you never did more for him than you have for me. My friends in Louvain can bear witness to the gold pieces you so generously gave me. Then, when in some fit of madness I came to England, you did not spurn me; in fact you sent me home with plenty of journey-money and many testimonials. But I say nothing of this, because I know you dislike to have your generous actions listed, and are content to enjoy the feeling that you have done a kind deed. And so in return for all these kindnesses I shall never forget, as long as these eyes remain open, to pray to Almighty God, unworthy sinner though I am, that all may go well with you, that you may enjoy length of days to do good to more and more men, and may overcome all your ill-wishers. Farewell, from Groningen 22 April 1517.

Ever your devoted follower

* * * * *

34 war] Cf Ep 584:40n.

Quare referta cùm malis sint omnia,
Vitam vt citò obeas leuissimis, pete
Quo tunc beatus, hic quod haud vales, agas,
Ito, & precare mutuum Demetrio.

Marcus Musurus.

MARCVS Musurus genere Cretensis, exactæ diligentiæ grammaticus, & raræ felicitatis poeta, in gymnasio Patauino aliquan diu Græcos authores interpretatus, secunda perspicacis ingenij fama ad integram doctrinæ maturitatem peruenit: sed sæua con iuratione externarum gentium afflictis bello Venetis inde exturbatus, ita tranquillum otium quæsiuit, vt Græco carmine diui Platonis laudes elegantissimè decantaret. Extat id poema, & in limine operum Platonis legitur, commendatione publica cum antiquis elegantia comparan.

Marcus Musurus
Portrait engraving by Tobias Stimmer from p 57 of Paolo Giovio's
Elogia virorum literis illustrium (Basel 1577)
Rijksmuseum, Amsterdam

574 / Niccolò Sagundino to Marcus Musurus   London, 22 April 1517

This appreciation of the learning and reputation of both Erasmus and Thomas
More was written by a Venetian ecclesiastic in the embassy of Sebastiano
Giustiniani to England 1515–19; cf Ep 559 introduction. Sagundino, who died
in 1533, was one of the secretaries to the Signoria by December 1511. For
Musurus, the celebrated Greek scholar from Crete, see Ep 223: 5n: he was in
Venice from 1509–16, after 1512 as professor of Greek. During this time he
completed his edition of Plato, published by Aldus in September 1513, making available for the first time in print the Greek text of the *Dialogues*. He also
completed the *editio princeps* of Alexander of Aphrodisias' *Commentaries on
the Topics of Aristotle* (Aldus, February 1514). In 1516 he was summoned by
Leo x to participate in a newly-formed papal Greek institute at Rome, and he
apparently left Venice to take up that post in the latter part of 1516; cf D.J.
Geanakoplos *Greek Scholars in Venice* (Cambridge, Massachusetts 1962) chapter 5 and 158:n156. There are two copies of this letter, as of Ep 559, in the
Deventer Letter-book.

TO THE RIGHT REVEREND FATHER IN CHRIST MARCUS MUSURUS,
WORTHY ARCHBISHOP OF MONEMVASIA
FROM NICCOLÒ SAGUNDINO, GREETING
I was filled with longing for a letter from you, most learned of prelates, and
my devotion to you and the respect and reverence I always feel for you,   5
coupled with your kindly feelings and exceptional generosity towards me,
gave me confidence that you would reply to the letter I sent you, I think, on
10 August last. Pray do not think that anything could have befallen me at
this time more delightful or welcome or honourable than such a blessed
letter. But amid my regrets at this frustration of my hopes and my silent   10
meditation over many possibilities, suddenly I learn from a letter from my
friends in Venice that you have lately received from our most holy father
Pope Leo a most honourable summons to leave Venice and come to Rome,
where you have, they tell me, been appointed under most favourable
auspices and consecrated archbishop of Monemvasia. This news, as was   15
right and proper, gave me the greatest delight, not so much from the
knowledge of your new and exalted situation (of which you have long been
adjudged most worthy, incomparably endowed as you are with charm of
character, rare learning and eloquence, wisdom, prudence and integrity) as
because I see in it a great encouragement to all devotees of great literature.   20

* * * * *

574:15 Monemvasia] Cf Ep 556:18n.

574 NICCOLÒ SAGUNDINO TO MARCUS MUSURUS 1517338

When they see you raised to such an eminence, and enjoying in the pope's counsels the influence which you deserve, they will know without doubt that the Muses, who have been in our day cast down from their lofty eminence and pitifully confounded, will be raised up and re-established in their ancient supremacy and peace. This fills me with hope: I believe that when the world of scholars sees that some honour and reward have come the way of humane studies, and that men can be found to play the part of Maecenas here and there, many will arise to play the part of Maro. So I rejoice on my own account, and truly and sincerely wish you joy; I hope that the dignity that has been happily conferred on you will so prosper, that it may prove a step towards the highest honours, coupled with great distinction for your name and outstanding glory for the humanities, together with continuing happiness for your friends and dependants, in whose number I include myself.

But I would have you know, kindest of prelates, that though nothing can happen to me more delightful than to hear news of your welfare, than that you should reap a rich and richly-deserved harvest from your strenuous husbandry and after being so severely tossed by wind and wave should reach a haven of peace and tranquillity, none the less I must inevitably be tormented by thoughts of the young men in Venice who burn with the love of humane letters. Daily you used to nourish them with copious feasts of nectar; they hung upon your lips and venerated you as a second Demosthenes or Cicero; and now they are bereft and deprived of you, a great and good man and a shining light of our generation. Yet you have left in Venice a very prosperous and fertile field, in which some young plants of great promise were growing under the tendance of your most skilful hands, who should one day be of great use, profit and glory to the famous Venetian republic and to yourself; and now, deprived of such a husbandman and destitute, they may well be obliged to fear icy planets, excessive heats, and rainstorms suddenly descending from on high. Woe is me too, for I shall be bereft of my great solace and robbed of the light without which I must needs grope blindly and leave the path. But yet I have a far from negligible hope, which somewhat consoles and cheers me – that with the help of heaven I may see you in Rome and talk with you face to face, enjoying your most valuable companionship and following you in admiration as a neophyte might his deity. For I have long harboured a resolution to go to Rome; and now the pleasure of seeing and admiring you pricks me and burns in my veins. But enough of this.

* * * * *

28 part of Maro] An echo of Martial 8.55.5

As for me, I still tread British soil, and shall do so until the decree of
our illustrious senate grants me the longed-for leave to return home. But my   60
mind, I assure you, is on fire to return; for I cannot endure to be deprived for
so long of the sight of my dear ones and the delightful face of my beloved
country. In the meantime, however, I shall do all I can to see that no day
slips by without some offering to the Muses. For I often meet Erasmus, who
has been sent for, I suppose, by this truly god-like monarch, filled at all   65
points with every kind of virtue, and has recently arrived. I am confident
that he will have no mean success with the king; for you know yourself,
most learned bishop, how well he deserves all the good fortune that can
befall a human being. You know his most exact and most elegant learning in
both Latin and Greek. You are aware also of the world-wide respect and   70
admiration he inspires. I thought he ought to know of your happy promotion to an archbishopric; and being the most humane person that he is, he
was at once delighted, and greatly pleased at your success. For Thomas
More, one of the leading citizens of London, was present at the time, a real
pattern of nobility of character and much devoted to you by name; he is   75
well-known, and I do not doubt you will have heard of him. You could not
find or even imagine, I assure you, a more agreeable, charming and amusing man; his wonderful elegance as a writer, his noble periods, his choice of
words and well-rounded sentences are universally admired, but not more
so than his keen mind and his polished Latin, set off by fairness, humour,   80
wit and courtesy. For I am entirely devoted to this man, my dear archbishop, I am his vassal and his slave for life, and I often relax in his
delightful company as one might lodge in some beautiful place. Such is his
kindness that he gave me a most friendly and affectionate reception; so that
I never see him without his sending me away better informed and more   85
attached to him than ever. And this learned man congratulates you most
warmly on the dignity you have so happily attained.

It only remains for me to beg and beseech you as warmly as I can to let
me have the favour of one of your heavenly letters; and if I get this from you,
I shall count myself the happiest of men. Farewell and best wishes, O   90
leading light of learned men; bear with the nonsense of your Niccolò as you
read it, and keep me always in your mind.

London, 22 April 1517

* * * * *

64 Erasmus] On the topic of possible preferment in England see Epp 517:66n,
577. The real purpose of Erasmus' visit, to receive absolution from Ammonio
(cf Ep 552), was of course unknown to Sagundino.

575 / From Beatus Rhenanus   Basel, 24 April 1517

For earlier letters from Rhenanus see Epp 460, 556.

BEATUS RHENANUS TO ERASMUS OF ROTTERDAM, GREETING
Bruno brought me your letter on Good Friday. There is no reason to be sorry
that the first book of your Theodore has been published here. The book had
been brought here by some printer from Louvain with the intention of
selling it, and unless Froben had acquired it himself by giving the man a   5
copy of the New Covenant, it would very likely have been printed by
someone else, for many people were after it. Send along any more Theodore
you may have that has been translated, and it shall be printed immediately.
Nesen has explained Lachner's intentions in a letter he wrote you from
Frankfurt. Whatever you send them, new compositions, revisions, transla-   10
tions, your own or other people's, they will gladly accept and will show
themselves truly grateful. There was very nearly war between Froben and
me, while I was trying to get your *Bellum* printed by itself. Froben appeared
at my house quite out of breath, begging and beseeching me to let him have
some little thing of yours to print, that he might not be obliged to take a   15
holiday after your *De copia* while Lachner is on his way back from
Frankfurt. This is his regular practice – never to come and ask for copy until
he already has no work left to keep his men busy. I produced your *Sileni*,
which he accepted. Next morning I went down to the works. Goodness me,
what uncalled-for complaints I found waiting for me, about himself and   20

* * * * *

575:2 Bruno] Amerbach; cf Ep 331 introduction.

2 Good Friday] 10 April 1517

3 Theodore] Erasmus' translation of the first book of the Greek grammar of
Theodore of Gaza, published initially by Martens in July 1516, NK 3051.
Froben brought out a new edition of the book in November 1516 and reprinted
it in 1518; cf Ep 428 introduction.

6 New Covenant] The *Novum instrumentum*, the first edition of Erasmus' New
Testament

7 any more Theodore] Erasmus translated the second book in the summer of
1517.

9 Nesen ... intentions] Cf Ep 469 introduction, line 19ff.

13 *Bellum*] This lengthy Adage *Dulce bellum inexpertis* (*Adagia* IV i 1) was
printed by Froben in April, following shortly on the publication of the *Sileni*
(*Adagia* III iii 1). The *Scarabaeus* (*Adagia* III vi 1) was printed in May, annotated
by Beatus Rhenanus, as was the *Sileni*.

16 *De copia*] The new edition published by Froben in April 1517; cf Ep 462
introduction.

me! Did I think he was a publisher of the class who print ballads in the vernacular? He had no interest in small stuff like this, and it was pretty unfriendly of me to provide him with a few pages and not great tomes. Froben made me more than a little heated with all this fuss; but since your interests, or rather, the interests of educated people were at stake, I kept a   25
tight hold on myself, and by prayers, threats and blandishments at length secured that the *Bellum* and *Scarabaeus* should be printed at the same time. They are afraid that this publication may harm your *Proverbs*.

It is impossible to say what a passion they have for really huge tomes. So they were easily induced to print Coelius. Coelius' work, which had not   30
yet been seen here, was recommended by Johannes Oecolampadius. When it arrived, I advised them to reproduce it in a small number of copies. They preferred their own opinion and that of their other advisers. What they liked about Coelius was that it was a compilation. Lachner thinks of nothing but summary compilations – Gabriels, Spieras, Brulifers. This summer he   35
wants the house of Froben to produce the *Compilatio solennis* ('Solemn' is in the title) of some Spaniard named Álvar, a papal penitentiary, on the power of the pope and cardinals; what will come of this I do not know.

* * * * *

30 Coelius] Cf Ep 469:10n.

35 compilations] Cf Ep 531:167.

35 Gabriels] Gabriel Biel (c 1420–1495) of Speyer, a professor of theology at Tübingen from 1484 and in his last years a member of the Brethren of the Common Life, was one of the most important theologians of his day. The work referred to here is no doubt his *Collectorium* of Ockham's commentaries on the Sentences of Peter Lombard. This was first published at Tübingen (Hain-Copinger 3187) and later in Basel by J. Wolff (1508–1512). See the edition by W. Werbeck and Udo Hofman, Tübingen 1973.

35 Spieras] Ambrogio Spiera (d 1477?) of Treviso, a Servite, wrote a *Quad-ragesimale de floribus sapientiae*, first published at Venice in 1476, then by Wolff at Basel in 1510, 1515.

35 Brulifers] Etienne Pillet Brulifer (died c 1497) was a Franciscan and doctor of theology of the University of Paris. His voluminous commentaries on the Sentences were printed by Wolff at Basel in 1501 and 1507, and published also at Venice (1501, 1504) and Paris (1521, 1570).

37 Álvar] Álvar Pelayo (Alvarus Pelagius) (d 1349) was a Spanish Franciscan and theologian who became penitentiary to Pope John XXII from 1330–40. He wrote a *Compilatio solennis de planctu ecclesiae* on the state of the church and the power of the popes and cardinals. It was published at Reutlingen in 1473, Ulm in 1474, Nürnberg in 1489, Lyon in 1517 and Venice in 1560. Froben abandoned his plans to print the work (cf Ep 581:8–9), no doubt because of the immense size of the *Compilatio*.

Chrysostom too is to be published, but in that small type in which they
printed Jerome's commentaries. What a sorry spectacle! Fortune plays her   40
tricks here, just as she does in the rest of human affairs. Impostors, men of
straw and drones have their books printed most successfully, while the
books of scholars are completely neglected. As though it were not enough
that in their position in life scholars should be nearly always inferior and
the others everywhere in great prosperity: even after death they must feel   45
her tyranny in their literary remains.

Your books on *Copia* have been printed, quite neatly. I did something
for them in my afternoon walks, on which I sometimes drop into the Froben
press. He has a reader not without some knowledge, who even allows
himself to be put right, and if there is anything he does not understand,   50
tries to learn without hesitation from Faber or Bruno or me. Glareanus will
be off to France before the first of June; he is to have a hundred and fifty
francs a year. There has happened to him what you always said would
happen: he has become completely humane, kindly and mild, and more so
every day. He has not been ashamed meanwhile to ask me often, if he came   55
across something in history or grammar that he did not know; and the other
day when he was attacked by Wimpfeling, he thought nothing of it in a
noble and really Christian spirit. Our friend Fabritius Capito's *In linguam
Hebraicam institutiones* will be published very shortly. If you wish anything
of yours or your Lucian translations to be published here, write to the firm 60

* * * * *

39 Chrysostom] Cf Ep 581:6. This was the second attempt to publish a collected edition of the works of Chrysostom, earlier undertaken by Wolff and
Lachner (Basel 4 December 1504). Froben's edition was more complete and
appeared in five folio volumes, July–October 1517.

49 reader] This was Wolfgang Angst of Kaysersberg; cf Ep 363 introduction.

51 Faber] Capito; cf Ep 459 introduction.

51 Bruno] Amerbach

51 Glareanus] Cf Ep 529:62ff.

52–3 a hundred and fifty francs a year] Beatus Rhenanus was probably using
the term *francos* as the popular synonym for the French livre tournois (as in
much previous correspondence). If so, a sum of £150 tournois would have
been worth, in equivalent silver values, £25 16s 8d gros Flemish or £17 15s 2d
sterling. Cf CWE 1 318, 336–44; Ep 146:9n; and Ep 522:58n above.

57 Wimpfeling] Cf Ep 224 introduction; nothing else is known of this matter.

58 *In linguam*] Cf Ep 556:26–7n.

60 Lucian] Cf Ep 550 introduction.

and say you would like it. Baer is at Thann. Give my greetings to your
friends. Farewell, beloved as a father and honoured teacher.

Basel, 24 April 1517

I hope John Smith is well.

576 / From John Watson   Peterhouse, Cambridge [April 1517]

This letter was evidently written by Watson from his old college during
Erasmus' visit to England in 1517, probably shortly before Henry Bullock
wrote Ep 579. For Watson see Ep 450 introduction.

JOHN WATSON TO MASTER ERASMUS, GREETING

How generous and friendly of you, kindest of teachers, to find time to write
something to a person like myself, who can make no return for all you have
done for me either by some service that might give you pleasure or by some
gift that might square the account; all I can do is to vie with you in spirit and   5
good wishes. I am most grateful to you for not criticizing my letter for fear
you deter me from writing, and actually praising it to encourage me, though
you administer a few buffets to keep me from getting above myself. For
when you call me a Scotist, if I judge rightly, you suggest in a roundabout
way that I am a Dunce and have been wasting my time. I frankly confess, I   10
am not as much of a Scotist as I could wish, though I have decided not to be
more of a Scotist than I am at the moment; for I have formed a solemn
resolution to devote the rest of my life exclusively to biblical and sacred
studies. But to give you, as a friendly and fatherly observer, a true idea of
my humble self, I am neither Thomist nor Scotist, nor first one and then the   15
other, but quite simply a nobody, a blockhead. I only wish I could prove
myself truly and sincerely a Christian.

I am very glad to hear of your good fortune, and shall rejoice still more
when the hope deferred which now depresses you has been turned into
reality. I shall pray constantly that this may happen, and specially that some   20
good fortune worthy of you may come your way here, so that you may be an

* * * * *

61 Baer] Cf Ep 488 introduction.

64 Smith] The English servant-pupil; cf Ep 276 introduction.

576:9 Scotist] Cf Ep 512:18.

18 good fortune] Perhaps Watson refers to the proposal for a bishopric, news
conveyed to Ammonio in October 1516; cf Ep 475.

19 hope deferred] Proverbs 13:12

ornament to this kingdom and a great strength to your friends, of whom you have many here. I have been given a living within seven miles of Cambridge. It has a pretty parsonage, and makes a reasonable contribution to my living expenses, being worth twenty of our pounds on top of all the   25 annual dues; but in this first year that now is, something like a half share will go on repairs to the house. If this can contribute at all to your pleasure or profit, it shall be yours, you and I will share it; and the same for anything else I possess. I wish you would come and visit us here, as soon as ever your business permits. If I were not tied up with so much business myself, I   30 would fly at once to your side to enjoy your company. Farewell, kindest of benefactors.

From Peterhouse in Cambridge
Bullock I hear is sick, but I do not know what is wrong with him.

577 / To Thomas Wolsey   London [c 28 April 1517]

This letter, written on the eve of Erasmus' setting sail from England, must be ascribed to 1517, the only year in which his patron, Lord Mountjoy, was in London at the time of Erasmus' departure. Erasmus made a short stay at Rochester with John Fisher, encouraging him further in his study of Greek (cf Epp 520, 540, 592) and reached Calais on 1 May (Ep 584). Erasmus' confident tone in dealing with the powerful Wolsey over some proposal to provide for him in England (cf Ep 574:64–5) shows his new self-confidence after the favours shown him in the Netherlands and the successful outcome of his request for a dispensation from Rome.

TO THE MOST REVEREND CARDINAL OF YORK
FROM ERASMUS OF ROTTERDAM
Most reverend Father, with sincere greetings. Though I was previously not unaware of your Eminence's kindly feelings towards me, I learnt of them more fully today in a conversation with the right honourable Lord   5 Mountjoy. I should have offered my thanks to your Grace in person, but the wind that is now blowing and the books which I have abandoned for so long have for some time been demanding my return, and I knew that while your Eminence is storm-tossed on such a sea of business you are fully occupied. The remainder of this business can be dealt with by correspon-   10

* * * * *

23 living] The rectory of Elsworth to which Watson was inducted 30 November 1516.
25 twenty of our pounds] £20 sterling = £29 1s 10d gros Flemish = £168 18s 4d tournois, in equivalent silver values. Cf CWE 1 340–6; CWE 2 327–44.
34 Bullock] Cf Ep 579.

dence. When you have decided how much you think sufficient for my
leisure, it will be my business to secure my release from my prince on terms
appropriate to departure from an excellent master who has treated me well.
In any case, whatever be the outcome, I shall always be grateful for the
king's indulgence and the very great good will shown me by your Emi-   15
nence; and I pray that you may both be long preserved in health and wealth
by the Almighty.

London, [1515]

578 / From Heinrich Stromer   Frankfurt, 30 April 1517

Heinrich Stromer (1428–1542) of Auerbach studied at Leipzig where he eventually became professor of pathology (1516). Among other works he edited
Lefèvre d'Etaples' introduction to Aristotle's De anima (Leipzig: Thanner 30
March 1506). By August 1516 he had become physician to Albert of Branden-
burg, archbishop of Mainz. Through all his later career he remained a close
friend of Erasmus and was in Basel at the time of Erasmus' death, perhaps as a
personal physician.

HEINRICH STROMER, PHYSICIAN, TO MASTER ERASMUS, GREETING
Most learned and eloquent Erasmus, the bearer of this letter, Richard
Croke, an active supporter of your reputation, has encouraged me to bom-
bard your exquisite ear with this nonsense of mine. I wrote to your honour
before the first of January to say that the most reverend the archbishop of   5
Mainz, my very kindly master, greatly desires to know you and to have you
with him, and there was much else which the sudden departure of my
messenger prevents me from repeating. May I beg you to reply to my earlier
letter; you will give great pleasure to my master, and no less to myself. The
other things that I ought to write about you will learn from the croakings of   10
Croke. Farewell, O luminary of the whole world.

Frankfurt, on the last day of April. Croke will not let me write any-
more.

579 / From Henry Bullock   Cambridge, 1 May [1517]

The writer, who had studied Greek under Erasmus at Cambridge (cf Ep 449
introduction), seems tacitly to acknowledge Ep 456; in any event the letter
must have been written in 1517, the only year after the publication of the New
Testament in which Erasmus revisited England.

* * * * *

578:3 Croke] Cf Ep 227:31n; he carried this letter with Epp 553, 554.

TO THE RIGHT LEARNED AND ELOQUENT MASTER ERASMUS
FROM HENRY BULLOCK, GREETING

Recently, on the occasion of a sermon at what they commonly call the Friars
Preacher, Bryan and I – he is on many counts my dearest friend in the world
after yourself – were talking together as our habit is, and among other   5
things he told me that you had safely returned to England; and heartily
glad, in the name of all the Muses, I was to hear it. I would have written you
a letter for him to take, had he not left me at such short notice. As it is, I am
compelled to borrow the pen of a stranger, for I am suffering from some
severe complaint which, in company with other misfortunes, has pitilessly   10
brought me so low, that I despaired of life, and for some days the doctor
thought me more likely to survive than I did. But now, thank heaven, I am a
little better. The severity of my disease was considerably increased by the
extraordinary ingratitude of the age we live in, which so much grudges
scholars – yourself especially – what they deserve. How I wish greater   15
resources could find their way to those who would have the knowledge and
the will to use them! As it is, those who have the power, did they not lack
the will, are so astonishingly mean, that you might as well expect the
magnet to let fall the iron as them to let go of one trumpery coin, unless one
were to put both energy and impudence into one's begging or were as great   20
a toady as any Gnatho in the play and a worse liar than the Cretans. Such
faults as these are so abhorrent to my spirit, that I would rather bravely go
hungry than use disgraceful wicked arts and even sacrifice my freedom, in
hopes to get some wretched sum that would scarcely meet my needs.

I have been lecturing for some months on St Matthew's gospel, in   25
which I have had more help from your very elegant brief notes than from the
lengthy commentaries of several other men, and specially on the most
knotty points. By some chance I have acquired a very ancient copy, which
in almost every place where you say that the older Latin codices read
so-and-so, agrees; and I have demonstrated this to my audience. In my   30
daily Masses, while I had my health, as was right for a pupil bound to you

* * * * *

579:3–4 Friars Preacher] That is, the Dominican priory, on the site of which
Emmanuel College now stands.

4 Bryan] John Bryan was a London boy who had gone to Eton and thence to
King's College Cambridge, where he commenced BA in 1515 and, in 1513,
became a Fellow. He was said to lecture in the university in the new style, on
the text of Aristotle rather than the scholastic commentators. See E&C 218, Ep
262:14.

10 severe complaint] Cf Epp 576:34, 580:24–6.

21 Gnatho] The toady in Terence's *Eunuchus*

26 brief notes] That is, his annotations

by so much kindness, I have remembered not you alone, but all those who
were long ago, as I know well, your supporters, or still are. I pray Almighty
God may keep you long in health and wealth, O pattern of all learned men.

Cambridge, 1 May   35
Your friend Henry Bullock

580 / From Henry Bullock   Cambridge, 4 May [1517]

This letter was evidently written shortly after Ep 579, answering a letter from
Erasmus in which he apologized for including Ep 449 in the *Epistolae aliquot* of
October, 1516.

BULLOCK TO ERASMUS, GREETING
No more of this, I beg; I never heard anything more ridiculous. Heaven save
me from the disgrace of not wishing a letter of mine to be printed, though
not very good Latin nor written with such care as I could wish; which you
answered with a very long and friendly one, as elegant, so everyone agrees,   5
as it was searching. So far was I, to tell the truth, from resenting it, my most
learned master, that I would gladly have given a great part of what little I
possess to purchase anything of the sort; and this I would have proved in
action, had my opportunities been equal to my wishes. No, much more was
I surprised by your generosity, to which history offers no parallel, and your   10
singular modesty, in that you were not too proud to share your reputation
and your immortality with a nonentity like myself, and were willing to
lighten my darkness with your own brilliance. For when I consider that
feeble shadow of scholarship, to achieve which I nearly lost the sight of one
eye from those tiny Greek letters and did lose my health, I seem compared   15
with you to be a tiny brook to your great ocean. No, this is all a figment,
invented by some jealous person who cannot bear to see so much honour
come my way. Some people really enjoy telling lies, though they get nothing out of it; others are roused to spread scandal by jealousy. I know you are
too sensible to believe one party, and too soundly based to be shaken by the   20
other. No man shall ever take you from my heart, such as it is. There is
nothing I more pray for daily than the chance of showing what my feelings
are towards you.

My sickness gets better slowly, and the distemper which pounced
upon me so swiftly and without a moment's thought is now in the throes of   25
deciding whether it is yet ready to leave me in peace. Farewell, O rarest
glory of the Muses.

Cambridge, 4 May
Bullock, your devoted pupil

581 / From Beatus Rhenanus   Basel, 10 May 1517

This letter resumes the account of affairs in Basel begun with Ep 575.

BEATUS RHENANUS TO ERASMUS OF ROTTERDAM, GREETING
When I heard that Johann Weiler, a citizen of Basel who was born in
England, though his father was German, was setting off for Antwerp, I
could not let him go without a letter from me to you. For I can now say rather
more clearly what I wrote somewhat obscurely to you in my last letter. The   5
Chrysostom is now printing, in the small type on two presses. Besides
which the *De homine* of Galeotto of Narni is being printed, on two presses
also. The *Solennis compilatio* of Álvar seems, as far as I can make out, to
have come to a bad end. We are daily expecting a great parcel of work from
you; and as soon as it arrives, everything else shall be put on one side, and   10
the house of Froben will print nothing that is not Erasmus. They are
surprised that you have not yet sent anything, but think that the carrier
must be on his way. I have told Baer to write. Our friend Capito is now
rector of this university; he too is going to write to you. We were all sorry to
hear that for the third time some people who are up to no good had made   15
free with your name in the rubbish they write – I mean the new series of
Epistolae obscurorum virorum. If it gives them any pleasure to behave in this
lunatic way, they might leave other men's names out of it.
      I think you must some time ago have received the *Copia* printed here,
with a letter from me from Cologne. Lachner tells me to send you his   20

* * * * *

581:2 Weiler] He is mentioned in BRE 124–5 as lending money to Beatus
Rhenanus in 1519; cf also BRE 143.

7 Galeotto] Galeotto Marzio (1427–c 97) of Narni in Umbria was a pupil of
Guarino at Ferrara 1447–50. After teaching for some years at Padua and
Bologna he sought ecclesiastical promotion at the court of Matthias Corvinus,
king of Hungary, in the years from 1465 to 1473. The *De homine* was written at
the beginning of that period. On returning to Italy he was imprisoned by the
Venetian inquisition for heresy in his treatise *De vulgo incognitis*. He was
released on the intervention of Lorenzo de' Medici and Corvinus in 1478. He
later returned to Hungary and travelled eventually to the court of Charles VIII.

  8 Álvar] Cf Ep 575:37n.

13 Baer] Cf Ep 575:61.

13 Capito] He was elected rector 1 May 1517 for the next half-year.

16 new series] The second part appeared early in 1517 according to Böcking
(P.S. Allen); cf Ep 481:59n.

20 letter] Ep 575

20 Lachner] Cf Ep 469:11n.

regards. He promises to show his gratitude for all the work you have done. About the revision of St Augustine's works you shall have some news in September; for he will discuss this question at Frankfurt with Koberger from Nürnberg. Your paraphrase on the apostolic Epistles is eagerly awaited; besides which the work on letter-writing and the *Antibarbari* and   25
the *Copia* revised and enlarged are badly wanted by all who wish to learn. The Englishman called Thomas Grey wrote to me the other day for advice, whether he should take refuge here if war breaks out between France and Britain. I shall send him my opinion by Glareanus, who is now in his home country taking the waters, so as to be fit when he sets out for France later   30
this month. After that he will go and see you, wherever you are, in Antwerp or Brussels or Bruges. I am enclosing a copy of a letter to Johann Froben from Francesco Giulio Calvo, a bookseller in Pavia. Farewell and best wishes, my beloved master and honoured teacher. Greetings to John Smith, our English friend.   35

From Basel, 10th May 1517

* * * * *

22 St Augustine's works] Apparently a proposal to revise Amerbach's edition of 1506, but nothing came of it at this time. A complete edition of Augustine revised by Erasmus was published by Froben in 1528–9 in ten volumes.

23 Koberger] This is Johann, first cousin to the notable Nürnberg printer Anton Koberger (c 1471–1513). After Anton's death, Johann carried on the firm on behalf of Anton's sons; Benzing 330.

24 paraphrase] The first of these, on Romans, was written at Antwerp probably in May and June 1517, and printed by Martens at Louvain in October and November 1517 (NK 846). Froben brought out his first edition of the work, a reprint of Marten's *editio princeps*, in January 1518, and a new edition in November 1518; cf Allen III Ep 710 introduction.

25 letter-writing] The *De conscribendis epistolis*; cf Ep 71 introduction.

25 *Antibarbari*] Cf Ep 30:17n.

27 Grey] Cf Ep 58 introduction.

29 Glareanus] Cf Ep 440 introduction.

33 Calvo] Francesco Giulio Calvo (d 1545) from Pavia was well-known among humanist writers. About 1518 he changed his name from Giulio to Minutio (BRE 168 in a letter re-dated by P.S. Allen to c August 1518). He later settled in Rome as a printer. The original of the letter to Froben mentioned here is in the Öffentliche Bibliothek of the University of Basel, MS G II 33, 24; cf AK II Appendix pages 525–7. Calvo announced his intention to establish himself as a printer at Genoa, and proposed that he and Froben exchange their publications.

34 Smith] Cf Ep 575:60–64.

582 / From Ludwig Baer   Basel, 11 May 1517

This is the letter referred to by Beatus Rhenanus (Ep 581:13), replying to a
letter of Erasmus which does not survive; for Baer see Ep 488 introduction.

LUDWIG BAER TO MASTER ERASMUS, GREETING
Your letter of 13 March, my dear Erasmus, which was full of charm and
clearly showed your affection for me, gave me more pleasure than I can say,
and you could hardly believe what an impatient desire it aroused in me to
see you; for while you were here, though you are our most perfect scholar in   5
the humanities and my own teacher, I am ashamed to say that I saw less of
you than I should have, and now that you are no longer here, I miss you
from the bottom of my heart. But, for all my bad management, I derive
much consolation (giving true friendship its proper weight) from your
success, and all the invitations and generous promises you receive from the   10
king of France, from numerous bishops, from the cardinal of Toledo, from
English and other leading men. Still, I wish you could give up all that,
provided you could do it without loss, and come back to us in Basel! Where
though it is true that no fortune adequate to what you deserve now presents
itself, yet you will, as you know, have a position that takes account of your   15
high standing, in a healthy and beautiful place – a position honourable and
secure, free from anxieties and interruptions and truly happy, such as the
Muses most wish for. Your host Johann Froben, a man of the highest
integrity, longs to see you so much, that he has often said to me he would
give you a hundred gold pieces a year for the rest of his life, if you would   20
come back here and live with him. As far as I am concerned, I offer and
present all my own fortune, such as it is, and myself to use as your own.
Others too will greet you with much kindness and generosity, so that I trust
you will lack nothing here that you could need for your literary work and for
the happiness of both the inner and the outer man. Do therefore let me   25
know sometime, with your usual kindness, whether any hope remains of
your return to us, and if I can do anything to oblige your lordship, let me
know, and it is as good as done.
    As far as concerns the state of Upper Germany, a serious conflict seems

* * * * *

582:11 Toledo] Francisco Ximénes de Cisneros; cf Ep 541:42n. It is clear that he
had invited Erasmus to Spain; cf Allen III Epp 597:48, 628:53, Bataillon 82–8.
20 a hundred gold pieces] Indeterminate gold coins (*centum aureos*), but
possibly Rhenish florins of the Four Electors. If so, a sum then worth £147 10s
od tournois = £24 3s 4d gros Flemish = £17 1s 8d sterling. Cf CWE 1 317,
336–46; Ep 509:11n above.

to be arising between a certain Franz von Sickingen and the cities of the   30
empire, unless the emperor can intervene and quell it. Apart from that,
there is a great and serious scarcity here of wine, wheat and almost every
article of human food, and far worse appears to hang over us, to repress the
wickedness of men, with many another plague sent from heaven, unless
Almighty God turns a pitying eye upon us, whose mercies are over all His   35
works. Our friend Glareanus and many other young men from Switzerland
will soon be setting out for the University of Paris, to be maintained there
by grants from the king. The right reverend the bishop of Basel was cheered
by your greetings and by your letter to me, and has told me to send you his
most cordial greetings in return. If anything else happens that you should   40
be told of, I will let you know. Meanwhile, since I cannot see you face to
face, I shall steadily read those wonderful learned works of yours and
contemplate your finished scholarship and your inmost mind. Best wishes
for your continued prosperity, greatest of men.

    From my home in Basel, 11 May 1517   45

583 / From Guillaume Budé to Cuthbert Tunstall   Paris, 19 May [1517]

> On the background to this letter, and for the circumstances of its publication,
> see Ep 571 introduction.

GUILLAUME BUDÉ TO CUTHBERT TUNSTALL, GREETING
At one stroke, most learned Master Cuthbert, you have released Erasmus,
your friend and mine, from his promise, and so much attached me to you
that I could not be more closely and definitely bound to you by the ties of
any relationship in law or kindred. In no way could you be added to my list   5
of friends with better prospects or with greater honour than by giving me a
sample of your gifts and of your learning in a letter so authoritative, so
pithy, so full of good will and a kind of elegant humane sincerity, which you
wrote, I know, under great pressure of your own affairs, or rather of your
prince's. As for your prince, I reckon that one day he will owe his greatest   10

    * * * * *

30 Sickingen] Franz von Sickingen of Schloss Landstuhl (1481–1523) was a
free knight of the empire who acquired much wealth from marauding cam-
paigns against various rulers and Rhenish cities. On 25 March 1517 he had
plundered a train of merchants from South Germany near Mainz and subsequently attacked Landau. He was later retained by Maximilian.
35 mercies] Psalms 144 (145):9
38 bishop of Basel] Christoph von Utenheim; cf Allen III Ep 598 introduction.
583:10 prince's] Henry VIII

renown to this cause in particular, that he has shown such skill in choosing
for the conduct of missions on his behalf men of outstanding scholarship
and wisdom; and if he has in his realm at this moment two or three like
yourself, he must also be supremely fortunate. For myself, as I read over
your letter from time to time, I feel how much I owe to the friendship of   15
Erasmus, with whom I lately agreed that we would share our friends, as
either of us should acquire them; it was, I think, in the letter which you say
gave you so much pleasure. How can I fail to think that I have secured a
generous increase in my resources and a stout bulwark against misfortune?
Is there any agreement, any contract, any trading venture that could make   20
my situation easier and better equipped or my domestic circumstances
more prosperous (and my plan is to raise the house of Budé not by pompous
foundation-works but by solid achievements of intelligence and industry)
than this association with Erasmus and this sharing of our friends that we
have agreed upon? – for it is on their favourable judgment that I hope   25
posterity will accept the design of what I build. In fact I would not hesitate,
if it were lawful, to swear by Jupiter Philius, guardian and interpreter of the
law of friendship: so highly do I value this agreement that, if the offer were
now made to me, in modest circumstances as I am, I would refuse a rich
estate, if it meant repudiating the pact with Erasmus which has already   30
brought me so much profit. I am prepared for Erasmus to expect me to be
grateful to him for himself and his friendship in perpetuity, for no reason
except that it has given me you, at least if he does so without underrating
me, for never will anyone establish a greater claim upon my gratitude,
'were his gifts countless as the grains of sand.' Yet even so my score against 35
Erasmus is not unlevel, whether you judge the value of friendship by things
that actually happen or by openness and honesty of heart; for I have
contributed all my friends to the common stock, outstanding men in other
ways, and in friendship especially reliable, though not all have yet declared
themselves to him, any more than his friends have declared themselves to   40
me. For that is how I hope to see the business go on either side: that as soon
as possible, or given a suitable opportunity, either on their own initiative
or in answer to a summons they will give in their names to the pool.
Further, I should not like you to think that the part of my fortune which I so
loyally contribute to the common stock is worth little, or of little value to me; 45
please remember that a great part of my worldly possessions consists in my
friends, unless these friendly words and faces are a great imposture. I only

* * * * *

16 lately agreed] Cf Ep 493:478ff.
35 'were his gifts] *Adagia* i vii 87

wish that of men like you 'ten such had I to counsel and befriend me.' Certainly I have invested more effort (which I regard as my substitute for great resources) in the acquisition of friends than in buying land.   50

That letter of yours, so pleasant and agreeable, full of honey, sweet as sugar yet not without a pinch of salt and seasoned with a surprising acidity in its opinions, reached me on the sixth of May, when I had returned to town not many days before and was at the moment not in the best of health, which made me somewhat depressed, and slack and dispirited when it   55 came to starting work. At first I devoured your letter at speed and almost in one breath; then I read it over and over again and savoured it afresh, and was gradually (no, rapidly) so much renewed and cheered by it that to my own surprise I found all my depression and sloth cleared away and all my energy restored. One thing made me slightly ashamed, that I could not   60 recognize in myself the outstanding gifts and accomplishments with which you credit me. But this too was a keen incentive to revive my zeal for hard work and arouse the concentration which, to speak frankly, has always been encouraged by the ambition to distinguish myself. And the sparks of this ambition are, I perceive, engendered by nature in minds that were far   65 from ignoble and mercenary, to judge by those authors whose writings now form the canon of literature and give their grandeur to our liberal studies. Not but what I have always held that any man of high character should enter on this pursuit of glory with one limitation: men who strive for intellectual distinction ought always to take more account of posterity, and of a reputa-   70 tion that will last for many centuries, than either of the judgment of their own age and their contemporaries, which tends for the most part to be neither disinterested nor fair, or of immediate rewards. You remember the line (and what a stimulus it is!): 'Thus will men speak; my name shall never die.' Whereas I think that that short-term reward is exactly as if I were to   75 covenant at a one-year, two-year, three-year or four-year term, as the draftsmen in our civil law express it, or slightly longer, as a satisfactory return for so much labour endured for so many years – a return which cannot be paid in full except by payments in perpetuity; or, to speak more appropriately, if I covenanted for certain annual payments of a negligible   80 amount in all future years to be made to me in advancing years and cease on death. And though I always hope that the day of death has not yet arrived (an error among mortals that dies hard), yet I know that from the start of my life it has been getting nearer. And so, although I would rather have this

* * * * *

48 'ten such] Homer *Iliad* 2.372
74 'Thus will men speak] Homer *Iliad* 7.91

reward in the way of reputation promised for some future date rather than   85
paid now, yet all the same the fact is that I rejoice to see some breath of fame
rounding my sails as I go along, and that if I can catch even a light breeze in
the way of some slight reputation, I feel my labours lightened in the
struggle.

Not that I should like you to think, or any other scholar and   90
philosopher for that matter, that I judge this intensive industry to have no
other object than to commend one's name and reputation to posterity,
which is a chancy business to be sure, and not worth a thought if one were
to rate the affairs of mortals at their true and proper value and not weigh
them in the misleading scales of popular opinion. Philosophy has its own   95
scale of values, unknown to the market-place and the lawcourt, because it
sets a price equivalent to the minimum upon transitory objects which are
bound to perish with the lapse of time, and a price equivalent to the
maximum upon those that are eternal (not to go beyond the language of the
legal draftsmen). From time to time Philology, my second wife, assures me   100
that the benefits of this kind of valuation will at length inure to me as part of
her dowry; whom I love not as other men do in this country of ours but – so
my friends and kindred tell me with some irritation – with an absorbing
passion. Ever since I brought her into my house, or so they say, I have never
been thought to devote proper attention to my own prospects or my health.   105
Let this, rightly or wrongly, be held against me as the father of six sons and
one small daughter, by men who consider that they have proved their own
worth if they know how to run a banking business and build up a patrimony on the most ample scale. Never mind: not my wife's embraces and
the endearments of my children, not the persistent demands of my financial   110
affairs, no threat or ultimatum from physicians, not sickness with all its
tedium and its torment has ever been able to persuade me or compel me to
refrain from consorting with my Egeria day and night, at home or abroad,
in city or country. Even at that moment twelve years ago when I married a
wife, the mother of my children, against the expectation of almost all   115
devoted husbands I never wrote her a bill of divorcement. This was my
chosen course of action: to have a lawful wife to bear me children, and by

* * * * *

113 Egeria] A Roman fountain-goddess, whose grove was visited for inspiration (according to the legend) by King Numa. Used as a courtesy title for
female companions where the relationship is entirely or principally intellectual, and the woman perhaps of higher standing than the man.

114 twelve years ago] This passage offers the only evidence for the date of
Budé's marriage. His wife, who was fifteen years old at the time, was Roberte
Le Lieur.

Philology to procreate books to win me an eternal name, if my modest gifts should prove equal to my industry, and to be immortal offspring. As it is, I have produced rather more children than I have books, indulging the body 120 perhaps more than the mind. Hereafter I hope, as my body grows weaker, my mind will become keener and more active day by day. It is impossible for the two of them to be equally productive both at once, but as one's bodily powers begin to reach their retiring age, the powers of the mind will be mobilized for full activity. But as my studies have proceeded (I might 125 fairly say, progressed) along their course, I have often been restrained, and almost forced to retreat, by ill-health, which has caused me so much trouble that more than once I have felt the urge to break off the course of life upon which I was set, and the temptation to abandon myself in a fit of the sulks to sloth and illness henceforward. Under the burden of such prolonged and 130 tedious ill-health who would not submit either to the dogmas of the physicians or to the prayers of his wife or to the warnings of his friends, as though he had given up literature for lost? At least, had not philosophy been in my horoscope, I should long ago have shown the door to my beloved Philology and confronted her, to use the traditional formula, with a dissolution of 135 conjugal rights.

So I did not forget, when I uttered those earlier words, that the study of literature rightly and duly conducted is, we must hope, a source of that well-tempered life of which one hears so much in lectures on philosophy, especially for a man who is initiated into orthodox philosophy and cleaves 140 with locked grip, as they say, to its principles, or, if I am to speak strictly according to the book, a source of the image and phantasm of that well-tempered life, since its true and complete self is not, I think, to be had in this life of ours – by which I mean that perfect peace of mind which cannot be said to be complete in all its parts until the passions have been disciplined 145 and tamed by the force of reason and all the senses have been drilled into obedience to a mind at peace with itself. We have it on the authority of St Paul, the master-builder of true religion and piety, that we are threatened by a pitiless enemy who is also the perpetual prince of darkness, whose guile advised and instigated that primal disobedience; against whom he 150 tells us to be constantly on the watch, and never relax at any time and close our eyes, for he is the sort of enemy who may lose a battle now and then but is never defeated in the war. There he stands, poised to make the most of every opportunity and from time to time stirring up great and unexpected disorder in our affections; and it is impossible that any man should feel 155

* * * * *

147–8 St Paul] Cf Eph 6:10–18.

confident of being protected right-and-tight against his attacks, as though
he had secreted himself safely within the ramparts of philosophy and in the
very citadel of the well-tempered mind, while there are no defences which
our enemy cannot penetrate. Have we not a notable example in that same St
Paul, whom even the privilege of grace beyond the normal did not exempt   160
from service in this war?

But I fear that I have slipped unknowing into the fault of being tedious
and foolish, when in a letter which should be brief I take a fancy as I go
along to play the philosopher, although a mere beginner in philosophy.
And so I return to your letter, in which it seems to me very humorous that   165
you appear to pit Erasmus against Budé, like one Milo against another in
some kind of ring under Pallas' aegis, where Mercury is the promoter and
judge and referee and you are a spectator, ready, what is more, to applaud
either side and doubtfully prepared to favour both. In that part of your letter
you naturally earned my gratitude, and yet there is very little danger that   170
you will have offended Erasmus. Erasmus is so fair-minded that he will
have no complaints even if I am put equal with him, for he would not
complain if you put me first, now he has settled into that spirit of Socratic
irony and, like a comic actor, taken the natural smile from his face – I am
afraid to suggest that he is brazening it out, for he would maintain that by   175
calling me in one word quite uneducated he has put out of court all the
descriptions I would apply to myself such as 'a late learner' and 'self-taught'
and even 'badly taught.' As for me, did I not prefer to believe that in your
judgment of me you are both of you wrong and simply do not know what
you are talking about, however sharp your eyesight in criticizing other   180
people, I should protest that you are a pretty pair of humourists and in
league against me. What? Should I dare to try a fall with that redoubtable
Milo, unless I were quite sure he meant to spare me many tight holds and
not use all his thews against me, and in general to moderate that invincible
strength of his to something which an average man like me can manage?   185
'Weaker am I, and would be that much stronger' to have my prayers fully
answered. I should think myself extremely well done by and be quite
satisfied if I could play second fiddle to him, a kind of sub-Milo or Milonias-

* * * * *

156 right-and-tight] A Roman legal phrase, used of premises in good repair;
Adagia IV v 37
159–60 St Paul] 2 Cor 12:1–10
166 Milo] See Ep 571:11n.
175 brazening it out] *Adagia* I viii 47
186 'Weaker am I] Homer *Iliad* 16.722

ter. Tell me, how on earth can any athlete not make a perfect fool of himself
and deserve the jeers of the crowd who, though he may perhaps not be   190
wholly lacking in muscle, yet has never learnt the skills of the wrestling-
school, which offers such prizes to cunning and hard work, under the
masters of the art? Though when I assert this of myself, you seem to think
this is all of a piece with my character, rather than something like the truth.
One thing I would gladly try to get out of you, that if you can ever put your   195
public duties behind you and find a little leisure for light relief, you who
now have time only to watch our contest for your own amusement should
descend from your pedestal or your flight of steps into the arena, and give
us a taste of your mettle. For I consider that you ought not to be solely a
spectator, you should actually be one of what they used to call seeded   200
players, who sat there not merely to see the fun but as reinforcements and
reserves, not to let the winner be too confident of victory from the start, and
to give the vanquished the consolation of seeing someone tackle the victor.

　　　And, as I read your letter, I no longer take Erasmus' word for it, great
authority as he is, when he expresses the highest opinion of you; I believe   205
my own eyes. I am not influenced in my own judgment by gratitude for
your friendly feelings, as anyone might suspect that Erasmus was when he
wrote to me about you. You seem to me to understand all the arts of this
style of wrestling so well, that I must needs suppose that you learnt them
from a master whom you can be proud of, and would make a much better   210
and more adequate match for that Milo of ours, always assuming that any of
us can keep up with him. For Erasmus seems to me no longer an ordinary
Milo, but some famous all-rounder with a universal reputation, a man who
has travelled all the world over, leaving evidence of his great gifts
everywhere, and has won nearly all the classic races; who has competed in   215
both fields, sacred and profane, and in every sector of the great cycle of
knowledge to which they give the name encyclopaedic, and has proved
himself everywhere. To say nothing of his *Panegyricus* and his *Miles chris-*
tianus and the whole roll-call of his many famous works and his *Moriae*
encomium, which is favourite reading with everyone keen on these things,   220
when I look at that Iliad, so to call it, of elegance in Greek and Latin that he
calls his *Proverbs*, I seem to see Minerva's own arsenal of language. Or again,
it is Mercury's own standing salt-cellar – Mercury the god of eloquence – a
masterpiece of craftsmanship in which even so the material vies with the
making, from which those who would be eloquent or amusing can help   225

* * * * *

200–01 seeded players] *ephedros*
218–19 *Miles christianus*] The *Enchiridion*
222 *Proverbs*] The *Adagia*

themselves to purest Attic salt when they need to make an effect. At one time, it is all the delights, all the allurements of plausibility, Persuasion's very marrow; sometimes it is like the display of notable furnishings in unlimited choice, brought from afar out of historic and expertly chosen stores (and never were things brought forth in such close-packed profu-   230
sion), exposed to view in the spacious establishment of some rich merchant, eloquently catalogued and arranged to make them look their best. In that volume, and in some other books of his, you can find all the apparatus on which those two elegant ladies, Poesy and Eloquence, rely for their exquisite complexions and their jewels, all the cosmetics and the finery   235
deployed by their handmaid whose name is Charm to give them their finishing touches, those ornaments which the master-craftsmen in language – the quaint artificers of words, as they are called – used in old days to improve the market for their writings.

> There Love and Longing lie, there Dalliance lurks,   240
> That steals men's senses, be they ne'er so wise.

Again, when I read what he has published on the New Covenant, the instrument of true religion and piety, and what he has done for St Jerome's works (on whose interpretations almost alone rests our understanding of the divine law), with his immense labours of elucidation and explanation,   245
of setting in order and renewing and virtually resurrecting, then I feel how fortunate is this age of ours, and our successors, to have that sacred body of doctrine, the source of our rule of living and of dying, rightly and duly ordered and indeed restored to us. At the same time I rejoice to see those men put in their places who have that old-fashioned smell, the patrons and   250
defenders of inarticulate senility, of learning clownish and tongue-tied, who are at the same time obstinate critics of a civilized style; who think nothing sacred unless its language is unshaven and unwashed; who believe that Philosophy herself, who discovered and enriched all the liberal arts, the champion and interpreter of all that is serious and honourable, is   255
debarred from using all polish and elegance of language and expression by the decrees of some orthodox council, got together from the elder statesmen of what they call the major countries. As though, if it ever became the practice to put Philosophy on the stage in some theatrical impersonations (as happens in this country as part of the licence traditionally allowed to   260

* * * * *

238 quaint artificers of words] The word (*logodaidalos*) comes from Plato *Phaedrus* 266E.
240 There *etc*] Homer *Iliad* 14.216–7, of Venus' girdle
250 old-fashioned smell] A Greek phrase, from Aristophanes *Clouds* 398

students at the Feast of the Kings, which they call the Epiphany), the producer ought not to dress her as a tragic or historical character, but bring her on as a comic buffoon in a booth at the fair.

So it is a pleasure as I read his work to observe how those home-made Stoics who used to display a barbarous and clamorous flow of words before   265
an admiring public are now sent packing with all their quillets out of the ranks of the learned, and indeed thrown off the bridge on which stand all supporters of good literature, so that those who once were supposed to hold the citadel of philosophy and to have the right to be heard first on all academic questions, are now declared by common report to be blind as old   270
Saturn with his bleary eyne, as the proverb has it – as least among all those who aspire to be thought in any sense cultivated men. Is there any man so much hated by the Graces from his cradle that he is not now disgusted with that crass and darkling form of science, ever since even the Scriptures have been purged of it by Erasmus' efforts and have recovered their original   275
clarity and brilliance? Though that other object is far more important which he achieved at the same time, that the sacred truth itself should emerge from those Cimmerian shades, even if theology has not yet entirely sloughed off the filth of academic sophistry, to shine once more. If this ever happens, it will be due to the moves first made in our own time. At least we have   280
already made this much progress, that some of them seem to be putting off that scornful conceit of theirs and silently admitting they were wrong, and some, whose age and manner of life leave it open to them, seem to be regretting their lot, and now accept and welcome humane studies and give them their support. That I have attempted to do the same in the literature of   285
civil law, and with the same success, will be found credible by posterity, I hope, when they read the tribute paid me in your letter, if it ever sees the light.

As for me, while I write these lines, I am moved to smile at the vanity and folly of men who habitually value the worth of everyone they meet by   290
the way he looks or walks. On this point I will borrow the language and opinion of a man in authority whom I could name, an experienced judge of men, who not long ago saw a good deal of Erasmus. 'Who is there,' he used to say, 'who has ever thought of forming an estimate of Erasmus from his general appearance and bearing, and all the chance physical effects to   295
which men are subject, and has no suspicion that this is the famous

* * * * *

267 thrown off the bridge] A Roman phrase of uncertain origin; *Adagia* I v 37
270–1 old Saturn] Cf Ep 522:136n.

292 man in authority] Perhaps Etienne Poncher; cf Epp 522:119ff, 531:619ff
and 569:36ff.

Erasmus, who would think that a man who behaves just like other men is a Mercury in speech, a Genius in intelligence, Venus and the Graces in the charm of his style, carrying the goddess of wisdom herself in his head as Jupiter once carried Pallas?' And in spite of this Erasmus dares to speak of   300
me as no longer an equal but even (Christ and the truth forgive me!) as a greater man than himself, as though I were ignorant both of myself and him – a man who has either discovered or introduced the admirable principle (of which he has left an example to posterity), that no man can rightly call himself a theologian and proceed to lecture on the Scriptures and expound   305
them in public, before he is sure that he has duly washed his hands in every fountain of the Muses. I only wish I were as near to being his equal in merit as I am in age, as I see from the place in his letter where he jests about old age and senility – unless it is proper to believe what he says about the soil of his intellect being worn out by continuous cropping. That passage, like many   310
other things in his letter, was admirable enough, but I could not agree with it; it was clear to me that his intellect itself is so fertile and the riches and scope of his learning are so great, that the field can bear a continuous harvest of all that is good, and has no need to be periodically enriched by the study of this or that subject as by a kind of irrigation continually   315
renewed. For the nature of an exceptional and gifted mind, if I mistake not, resembles a highly fertile soil: its power of annual bearing produces a crop that is not lush, but shows no sign of falling off.

Like that is the highly-gifted nature from which, as from some flourishing and extensive estate of inexhaustible fertility, Erasmus has now   320
for many years gathered a rich harvest of that solid and well-defined reputation which will endure down the centuries. Not but what in writing to him I always take the line of spurring on his restless spirit, and declaring that all that diligence and industry does not satisfy me, unless he under-takes greater enterprises every day, such as suit his eminent gifts and such   325
as no spirit however exalted could ever regret. Hence that difference of opinion between us, in which I say that I simply will not accept as major works a large output of small or middling pieces, judged by the standard of Erasmus' own capacity, even if they are properly finished approved and of good merchantable quality, to use the traditional formula; for I maintain   330
that a man with such a lofty swift-winged capacious versatile mind, polished on every workbench of the Muses, ought now to undertake enter-prises of the grandest scale. From this same cause arises that skirmishing between us in letters which you, I observe, contemplate with amusement,

* * * * *

311 his letter] Ep 531:410ff
322 down the centuries] Silvius Italicus 12.312

but which of late seemed likely to break out into open conflict at any   335
moment, as appears from the immense letter in which he routed all my
forces of argument at the first impact. I had indeed determined to get
together what remained of my army, to make good my losses and try my
luck once again. But I was discouraged from doing so by my friends, who
saw that in the end I should be unequal to the contest, if after an interval of   340
rest he should have warmed to his work again, for they recalled Homer's
words 'Let two fight side by side: 'tis better so' in this kind of struggle. And
then I did not think he made sufficient allowance for my ignorance or my
countrified roughness, being himself a master of all the arts of wit and
polish. For though I seem to myself in everything I write to him to be quite   345
straightforward, yet I know not how, either in taking advantage sometimes
of the rights of friendship or in some other way, I fall unwittingly into some
extravagant remarks, at which he takes offence as though they were cunning criticisms of him or double-edged expressions; or at least he pretends
to take offence. This is an instance of what I said above: I am like one of   350
those athletes they called unschooled, who do not know what is at the same
time both seemly and effective for the purpose in hand. The result is that,
while I enjoy scribbling to exercise my spleen, he seems to allow more scope
either to resentment or to some ill-timed suspicion, whether I sometimes
take it into my head to suspect this quite wrongly or whether he, as a   355
veteran competitor and in this department clearly an old hand dealing with
one who is still a tiro like myself, thinks this is the way to correct and cure
my somewhat impetuous attacks – and this I would much prefer to suppose.
If our mutual suspicions in this matter should prove misdirected, you as an
expert not only in civil law but in friendship would, I like to think, arbitrate   360
between us, or liquidate our dispute and make it up. I at least should be
very happy to have you do this, nor do I think you would favour him more
than me, even if he is an old friend of yours and, as he tells me, almost a
boon-companion – which he rightly thinks a feather in his cap. But do not,
good scholar that you are, do not I beg you think what I have said about   365
suspecting him to have taken offence is seriously meant, for nothing is
further from my thoughts. But I should be glad if you could persuade
Erasmus that some such suspicion is the reason why I do not reply to the
voluminous letter in which he routed and put to flight all my brilliant
inventions, to which I had devoted a good deal of trouble. I would rather   370
have him suppose that I conceded victory to him and gave way before his

* * * * *

336 immense letter] Ep 531
341–2 Homer's words] *Iliad* 10.224–5
350 said above] Cf lines 191–2.

authority while my forces were still intact, than that I threw in the sponge
at the moment when I could sustain his attacks no longer. I wrote to him
some time ago and shall, I hope, write again; but I shall choose some other
topic which I find easier to manage and, if the opportunity presents itself, I   375
will catch him on the hop. At least I shall not commit the mistake of
attacking him seriously unless he is off his guard and weary; though when I
lately said that I hoped to wipe out my earlier defeat, a man not without
experience pulled me up, being jealous for my reputation, with these words
of warning: 'What man art thou that dar'st to cross him thus?' And when I   380
gave him a rather bold reply out of the comedy: 'Nothing today, but shall be
great tomorrow,' he replied: 'Hapless the sires whose sons shall challenge
him.'

For I am really and truly grateful for the confidence you show in me as a
straightforward person, when you believe the fact which I had lamented in   385
passing when writing to Erasmus – that I had no teacher, no one to read
with me but myself; did I not suspect from time to time that you find that
easy to believe, basing your judgment on the style of what I write; in which
I have a haunting fear that you may perhaps have found something ill-
disciplined in the structure, some touch of roughness in the form, seeing   390
that it has never felt what they call the file and spokeshave of the critic's
bench nor the correction of a teacher. But then again you seem to me not to
feel this at all, for you even tell me to be proud and pleased on this score, and
to thank providence precisely for this absence of teachers as a very great
blessing. What cheerful advice, so encouraging, so artful! – to turn my   395
shortcomings into advantages, and show me that what I used to think
highly discreditable, or at least a thing that must be hidden if concealment
had been possible, is useful and honourable and something to be proud of!

But stay a little, for I have taken it into my head to give you the whole
story, a rather long-winded narrative, now that I have found in you some-   400
one to console me with such kindness and such skill. I had said I was
self-taught and a late learner, and not only had had no teacher but had come
to the humanities very late in life. I can now say in more detail that I learnt
my elementary letters and made my first steps in grammar, as the way then

* * * * *

372 threw up the sponge] *Adagia* I ix 78
380 'What man art thou] Homer *Iliad* 21.150
381 out of the comedy] Aristophanes *Knights* 158
382 'Hapless the sires] *Iliad* 21.151
386 no teacher] Cf Ep 493:26–7.
402 self-taught] Cf Ep 493:21.

was (and life was much simpler then), in this city from an elementary-   405
school master of the ordinary kind, and when I had scarcely begun to
stammer Latin, I turned over as the custom is (plunged in would be more
accurate) to the study of law, with a saving of time which in any case cost me
dear. After wasting three years on that subject, I returned home and bade
farewell to book-learning, devoting myself to the pursuits of uneducated   410
youth, or at least of youth that has done with education and has now
secured its freedom, until after some years under the paternal roof I set
myself to study privately, far from all the assemblies of university students
in this city, inspired only by the example of my father, who spoke highly of
learning – for such was his nature – and was a great buyer of books. There I   415
began, as often happens, with all the worst authors, and in my unwisdom
greedily drank the glossators to the dregs; but at length I perceived my
mistake, turned over to books of a better sort, and gradually threw off the
dregs with which my inside was awash – though the old 'Come tell me,
Muses' had taken deep hold of me.   420

But lo and behold, another handicap! When I had once said farewell to
the devotees of hawking and hunting, six and twenty years ago, and had
begun to devote myself with some success to books, as I said, and not to
instructors, I immediately secured the help of a certain Greek (or rather, he
secured mine, for I brought him a substantial income), who knew Greek up   425
to the point where the classical and vernacular tongues part company, or a
little beyond it. The torments I endured at this man's hands by his teaching
me things I soon had to unlearn (but he did know how to read very well, and
had an excellent accent) I could not easily recount on three sheets of paper;
while all the time I, who had heard that he was the only Greek in France,   430
supposed he must for that reason be a very good Greek scholar, and he, as
he showed me Homer and ran off various celebrated authors, 'telling the
tale of every man by name,' could see that I was madly enthusiastic. On top
of which I made the mistake of thinking that what was mere ignorance in
him was deliberate mystification, intended to retain me all the longer as his   435
paymaster and virtually his bondservant in my eagerness. At length the
state of literature in this country grew brighter in a few years by contact

* * * * *

406 master] There is little more information on the early education of Budé;
see Ep 493 introduction.

419–20 'Come tell me, Muses] Homer *Iliad* 2.484

424 a certain Greek] Georgius Hermonymus of Sparta; cf McNeil 9–10. He
was a papal diplomat who had settled in Paris to make a living teaching Greek;
cf Ep 149:77n.

432–3 'telling the tale] Homer *Iliad* 22.415

with Italy, and a supply of books in both Greek and Latin gradually came in; and I struggled to recoup the losses of those early years spent in ignorance. I spared no outlay in the purchase of expensive books and no labour in getting them by heart, and every day I forced myself to do fully the work of a day and a half, abandoning all holidays. Thus I reached the point first of all of setting myself to unlearn what I had been taught wrong – and even that first stage in learning the language gave me much trouble, for I had learnt nothing except the rudiments, and even there I had learnt the wrong things in the wrong way; then of listening no further to my Greek teacher expounding a text, even though he used to come to me to try and sell me books which I wanted to buy or write books for a price he had named outright. What do you make of this, my ingenious friend? Can you once more maintain that what I reckon as handicaps were really blessings in disguise, or will prove so?

And then there is the ill-health which is not so much acquired, in my view, as congenital and inborn: how much trouble do you suppose that has caused me? For it has always followed me more closely than my own shadow, wherever I went or whatever I set myself to do. Indeed it has been the more tiresome for this reason: ill-health is responsible for the bad reputation which literary studies have enjoyed for more than fifteen years now among both my physicians and all my acquaintance whether friends or strangers, as crazy and disastrous; even more so the study of Greek as a dreadful frenzy that must be exorcized, even though of late it has begun to seem respectable and desirable. Not however that I would wish you on that account to strike me off the list of first-line troops, as one whose training is home-made and academic; for even so I feel myself capable of being enrolled among the younger men, having begun to take my place among those on duty neither prematurely nor without success, as I willingly believe on the authority of yourself and Erasmus and of other men as well. In the meantime I have twice visited Rome and the famous cities of Italy, where I did not so much sit at the feet of their learned men as see them through the lattice (and no great number of them), and paid my respects to their professors of the humanities as it were from the threshold, so far, that is, as

440

445

450

455

460

465

470

* * * * *

448 write books] Oxford Bodleian Land. graec. 7 is a copy of the collection of Greek proverbs ascribed to Diogenianus, written by Georgius Hermonymus and bearing Budé's coat of arms.

452 ill-health] On Budé's puzzling and disabling ailments see McNeil 7; L.-F. Flutre 'L'étrange maladie de Guillaume Budé' *Aesculape* ns 28.1 (1938) 3–6.

467 visited Rome] Budé visited Venice in 1501, and in 1505 he was a member of a French embassy to Julius II; cf McNeil 13–14.

468–9 through the lattice] *Adagia* III i 49

470 from the threshold] Cf Ep 511:10.

was possible for a man ranging rapidly through Italy with no official facilities. At home too I have sometimes enjoyed the society of scholars, among whom I attached myself especially to Johannes Lascaris, a Greek by nation and an excellent scholar in both tongues, who has now been ap-pointed by the pope head of the Greek school in the city. He was eager to do   475
all he could for me, but was not able to give me much help. Though he spent most of his time in the king's entourage sundered from this city by many miles, and I was constantly in the city and rarely with the king, he gladly did the one thing he could, like the courteous man he was, now and then reading some text with me when we were together – a piece of good fortune   480
that did not come my way a score of times – and in his absence trusting me with shelves full of books and leaving them with me. My apprenticeship, at least, I served without a teacher.

So there, kind friend, is the course of my studies, which made an easy start under an indulgent father, who let me have what I wanted – how   485
fortunate this was, I do not know. I lost my father fifteen years ago, and suffered many handicaps, for I found fortune unkind in many ways; but all the same I strove with oar and sail to complete the voyage I had undertaken. Only one thing, like 'the little fish that men call remora,' held me back most mischievously, the ill-health of which I spoke. Nothing did so much to   490
narrow and bring down the eager spirit with which I devoted myself to these studies, as the continual thought of death that hourly hung over me, as I remembered how often my breathing was interrupted and began again. My father was well off, and left me heir, not to the whole of his estate, for the eldest of my brothers had taken half by right of primogeniture; from my   495
mother's estate I inherited the same proportion four years later. This more or less was the basis on which rested the course of life I had embarked on, together with additions of one sort or another; but all the time with the

* * * * *

473 Lascaris] He was brought from Italy by Charles VIII; Budé would have had contact with him before his return there in 1500. They met again in Rome in 1505; cf 467n and McNeil 10–11, Ep 269:55n.

485 father] Jean Budé, who died 28 February 1502, was descended from a line of court officials dating back to the late 14th century. Guillaume was the fourth son among eighteen children.

488 with oar and sail] Every means in my power; Adagia I iv 18

489 remora] A small fish which, it was thought, could attach itself to the keel of a big ship, and bring it to a halt even under full sail; see Apophthegmata 603A.

495 eldest of my brothers] Dreux (1455–1528) succeeded his father as trésorier des chartes and audiencier de la chancellerie; cf McNeil 3–4.

496 mother's estate] That of Catherine Le Picart, who died 2 August 1516. Her mother was a Poncher.

limitation that I owed nothing to the generosity of kings or of fortune. And in the course of my studies I lost much of my patrimony by neglect of the proper economy of a good citizen, although I did escape shipwreck.

What follows in your letter gave pleasure not to me so much as to some of my friends, who hope that providence will grant you many blessings in return for it. You urge me not to grow weary in the exposition of passages in the law and in correcting errors of long standing, and you congratulate me as though you thought that the justification for my laborious efforts had been to undermine the authority of men who, as scholars now agree, were greater experts in Accursius than in civil and Roman law. And yet, while I have never seen any cause to regret those labours, for many reasons but particularly because the benefit of them was commonly said to be widespread and available to the majority of people interested, yet I find it somehow distasteful to revive an activity which I gave up long ago and have now virtually abandoned, and which, as I remember, made a stormy start in its early stages. In that, I recognize of course my own responsibility and ask pardon for it, if it is not too late; for I was not strong enough to control the enthusiasms of those early days and refrain from pleading the cause of jurisprudence as though my audience were a council of experts in antiquity, coupled with hard words for the men who were not afraid to diminish and encroach upon the majesty of the civil law. It is true that I saw a few people bringing this accusation against them; but I knew that as yet no one had arisen to challenge them by due process of law, and go on to pursue them on indictment with a detailed examination of their offences before an attentive jury and judges retiring to consider their verdict. I took the initiative in speaking against them with more readiness and more energy than I could produce now for re-opening the case. Should anyone else arise to claim the right to succeed me, I have researches of another sort already started, which have turned my mental energies away from the study of the law in a quite different direction; and I prefer to write on subjects which are not circumscribed by such narrow boundaries. The mind cannot move freely and exercise itself, when it has put on flesh and is in high fettle from wide and prolonged reading, like a horse feeling his oats, unless it has a spacious subject like free and open fields in which to gallop. I know that this is sometimes the fault of an undisciplined mind that allows itself imprudent liberties; but if I took it into my head to control my impetuous pen and make it observe some standard of moderation and discipline, not only should I deprive it of all its energy and perhaps make it feeble and listless, but I should also run counter to my genius and my patron Minerva – a fact I mean to make the most of in the case in which I long ago took Erasmus to court.

* * * * *

508 Accursius] Francesco Accorso; cf Ep 571:95n.

But I cannot spare myself this labour and follow my own inclination, which would decline the task, because of the demands of my creditors (so to call them) – for they serve a writ on me from time to time in respect of my rash promise – and because of the keen students of the law themselves, who to my great surprise and embarrassment have made peace with me of their own accord and have readily abandoned their action for damages against me. And this, though they themselves thought my offence was heinous and even a form of sacrilege, since I had attacked the majesty of their special deities. This was no tribute to my popularity or influence, but rather to the truth, which even they are gradually beginning to accept. At the same time, you advise and encourage me to do so, and of this certain men of good judgment are aware, who admire your letter as though it were some remarkable object from foreign parts. And so I suppose I can hardly avoid returning for some few months to that treadmill, and making some perfunctory additions to the first edition of my annotations, unless I happen to discover that someone else has forestalled me, as I have long hoped would happen.

I know that I have exceeded the limits of a letter, for 'from head to foot I have the story told' of my early life, as Aristophanes puts it. But you have said that you enjoy my letters, and I find pleasure in conversing with you. You did me the honour of taking the initiative, and have thus put me on my mettle; and it was proper for me to add something by way of a bonus, as the more generous debtors do; nor could I possibly have repaid at the same length what I owe for such an elegant and friendly letter. Lastly, it is a condition of this letter that I get a second letter from you, and many more, when leisure permits, if they are to be of the same fabric as your first one. I propose to dedicate my casket of special sanctity for letters (I hope) from you and Erasmus, and I shall treasure them as a kind of symbol of a friendship with two great men, formed by friendly exchange of letters and maintained by acts of mutual and honourable courtesy. And these letters I shall leave, I hope, as legacies of special value to the dearest of my children.

Farewell, from Paris, 19 May

This letter, I know, will be a trouble to you, being so foully ill-written. But I think I deserve to be forgiven for this fault by you, since Erasmus, that great man, has seen fit to forgive me. For as you seem to be as kind and charitable as he is, I cannot think that you would endure to seem less ready to forgive. Farewell once more, O pillar of your country, and give my greetings to our common friend who has just returned from England.

* * * * *

549 to do so] That is, continue his legal scholarship; cf line 506–7.

557 Aristophanes] *Plutus* 649–50

576 common friend] Erasmus; see Ep 584 for his return to the continent.

584 / To Thomas More   [Antwerp, 30 May] 1517

This letter (Rogers Ep 38) describes Erasmus' crossing from England, and can be dated even more precisely by the reference (line 27) to the departure from Antwerp of Matthäus Schiner, Cardinal bishop of Sion; cf Ep 478:39n. The painting of the diptych by Quentin Metsys, reproduced on pages 370–1, is also announced. The letter was first published in the *Farrago*.

ERASMUS OF ROTTERDAM TO HIS FRIEND MORE, GREETING
On the first of May, with the wind increasing and by now actually against us, in the middle of the night I was roughly put ashore from a ship's boat not without peril under some cliffs on the French coast not far from Boulogne. The wind soon became very rough, and for the rest of our journey was made 5 worse by our being so near the coast. It has caused many deaths in these parts from inflammation of the throat and lungs, and still does.

Pieter Gillis and I are being painted on the same panel, which we shall soon send you as a present. But it so happened, very inconveniently, that on my return I found Pieter seriously ill, even dangerously, from some 10 sickness I know not what, from which even now he has not properly recovered. I myself was in capital health; but somehow the physician took it into his head to tell me to take some pills to purge my bile, and the advice he foolishly gave me I was fool enough to take. My portrait has already started; but after taking the medicine, when I went back to the painter, he said it 15 was not the same face, and so the painting was put off for several days, until I look more cheerful.

Your *Epigrammata* and *Utopia* I have sent to Basel by my own servant, whom I had maintained here for several months for that purpose, together

* * * * *

584:8 panel] The portrait of Erasmus reproduced in this volume is that known as the Barberini portrait; that of Gillis is from a private collection in England. The portrait of Gillis shows him holding a letter with the handwriting of More carefully reproduced, and has been held to be the original. The Barberini portrait of Erasmus has been presumed also to be the original, although this has recently been questioned; see M.M. Phillips 'The Mystery of the Metsys Portrait' *Erasmus in English* 7 (1975) 18–21; see also A. Gerlo *Erasme et ses portraitistes* 2nd edition (Nieuwkoop 1969) 9–17, and G. Marlier *Erasme et la peinture flamande de son temps* (Damme 1954) 90. Erasmus is represented commencing his Paraphrase on the Epistle to the Romans, which was done in Antwerp at this time. The finished versions were sent to More in September; see Allen III Ep 654.

14 My portrait] Cf Ep 591:16–22 for Giustiniani's reaction.

18 *Epigrammata*] Published by Froben with the *Utopia* in March 1518; cf Ep 550 introduction.

with some things of my own. Tunstall is in splendid health, in fact posi-   20
tively triumphant: he has acquired while here such a quantity of ancient
coins. He has read through my *Copia*, and highly approves of it. My
panegyric in praise of Philip fills him with admiration. He has worked
through the whole of Budé's *De asse*, and has written to him, but he has not
yet answered.   25

The cardinal of Gurk left here several days ago, the emperor, I am told,
being not very pleased with him. His eminence of Sion left yesterday. I
dined with him that day, and had a long discussion with him about the
New Testament, and then about the war. He lets fly in public against the
French, and frankly, as becomes a Swiss. He said that the Germans are   30
aiming at the subjection of all kings to the emperor. The emperor goes to
Mainz, for there they say there is to be a meeting of the ruling princes of
Germany. Our Charles is holding a council in Ghent, which the emperor
did not attend. They say he departs without being really satisfied even now.
Goodness me, was there ever a man displayed bad temper more success-   35
fully than he? Peace was in train even with the people of Gelderland, and on
terms moreover which were most favourable to the emperor; but he
stopped it for fear we might have no war anywhere. Philip bishop of
Utrecht has entered his cathedral city under the happiest auspices and with
splendid pageantry. The duke of Gelderland is said to have got together   40
eight thousand men for an attack on Friesland.

Tunstall is thankful to have at last finished with his part in that
travelling show. If he returns to you, there is no point in my writing this;

* * * * *

23 panegyric] Cf Ep 179 introduction.

24 *De asse*] On Budé's work see Ep 403 introduction.

24 has written] Ep 571

26 Gurk] Matthäus Lang; cf Ep 549:52–3; LP ii 3200, 3208, 3295.

27 Sion] Matthäus Schiner; cf Ep 447:660n; LP ii 3269, 3301, 3303. On the
dinner meeting see also Allen III Ep 948:94–103.

33 Ghent] The court arrived there between 17–25 May; cf LP ii 3251, 3283.

38 Philip] Of Burgundy, an illegitimate son of Philip the Good. Erasmus
dedicated the *Querela pacis* to him. The entry referred to here was on 19 May
1517, shortly after the former soldier was named to the see; cf Ep 603 introduction.

40 duke of Gelderland] Charles d'Egmont, hertog van Gelderland (d 1538) was
an ally of France against Hapsburg interests in the Netherlands. On his
resumption of arms in violation of an unexpired truce, see LP ii 3283, 3300.

43 travelling show] His tour of duty following Emperor Maximilian through
the Netherlands; cf Ep 572:17n, 19. His mission was ended when the emperor
left for Germany; cf Ep 585:4n, LP ii 3300.

Erasmus
Portrait by Quentin Metsys, 1517, known as the Barberini portrait
Galleria Nazionale d'Arte Antica, Rome

Pieter Gillis
Portrait by Quentin Metsys, 1517
Private collection, England

but if he stays over here, I am resolved wherever he may be to pass the time
in his company. Otherwise my plan was to spend the summer in Louvain,   45
which even the theologians are urging on me. Only x still raises some
objection or other, with an eye to his reputation, for fear he may be thought
inconsistent. Mind you do not do me out of that letter from you which you
showed me when it was half finished. If the letter from Giustiniani the
Venetian ambassador is in your possession (for I have lost it), please let me   50
have it back; if not, ask that very civil man Master Niccolò, his secretary, to
send another copy to me here together with his own letter of congratulation
to Marcus Musurus. I will write at greater length within the month, when I
send the picture. No news yet of the horse, though now is the time it would
have been useful. Best wishes to you and your delightful wife and your dear   55
children. Pieter Gillis and his beloved Cornelia send their warmest greetings to you and your wife.

    1517

585 / From Antonius Clava   Ghent, 4 June [1517]

For Clava see Ep 524 introduction.

ANTONIUS CLAVA TO MASTER ERASMUS, GREETING
I am well, most learned Erasmus, and rejoice to hear that you can say the
same. Our friend de Keysere departed eleven days ago to join the Kaiser,
taking with him the emperor's son Leopold. We are looking forward to his
return, and hope that he will be with us again shortly. Master Pierre Barbier   5
is looking after your interests most faithfully and is extremely anxious to see
your situation more distinguished and more dignified. My lord the chancellor, distracted as he is by a mass of daily business both difficult and diverse,
listens with great interest whenever your name comes up, as it does fairly
often, and regards you with favour out of the ordinary. He is fully inclined,   10

    * * * * *

46 x] Maarten van Dorp; cf Ep 474:19n.

48 letter] Ep 559

51–3 Niccolò ... Musurus] Ep 574

56 Cornelia] Sandria

585:3 de Keysere] The printer; cf Ep 525 introduction.

4 Leopold] Of Austria, illegitimate son (c 1504–1557) of Emperor Maximilian;
he accompanied his father as far as Maastricht. De Keysere presented the
emperor with his *De nuptiis Leopoldi*.

5 Barbier] Cf Ep 443 introduction; he was evidently with the chancellor in
attendance on the court; cf Ep 584:33n.

so far as I can guess, to do something for you, when some opportunity or
lucky chance smiles on the idea. I wish your friend Clava possessed resources to match his good will towards you and his affection and respect
and keenness for your promotion.

The letters you mentioned I have not seen anywhere, and I long to see   15
them and read them through. You will discover from Barbier's letter the
steps that we thought would be to your advantage. So I hope to see you here
soon, and at the same time beg you not to stay with anyone but me. You will
find a cheerful host, very attentive to your needs. Till then, farewell, and
give my warmest greetings to my dear friend Pieter Gillis, your delightful   20
host.

From Ghent, 4 June

586 / To Dukes Frederick and George of Saxony   Antwerp, 5 June 1517

This is the preface to Suetonius, edited by Erasmus with the *Historiae Augustae scriptores*, printed by Froben in June 1518 and by his successors in July
1533. The earliest source for the text is a manuscript in the Öffentliche Bibliothek, University of Basel, Erasmuslade c 6. This is written in Hand D of the
Deventer Letter-book (Allen I 605) and revised by Erasmus with amplifica-
tions of the text.

Frederick the Wise (1463–1525), Elector of Saxony, was the patron of Luther;
his cousin Duke George (1471–1539), however, enforced the Edict of Worms
(1521) and remained a loyal Catholic and supporter of the Hapsburg dynasty.
See also Ep 588:61n.

TO THE MOST ILLUSTRIOUS DUKES OF SAXONY,
FREDERICK ELECTOR OF THE HOLY ROMAN EMPIRE, ETC, AND
GEORGE HIS COUSIN, FROM ERASMUS OF ROTTERDAM, GREETING
Men who are placed by Fortune's suffrage at the helm of world affairs
cannot be expected, O paragons of honour, Duke Frederick and Duke
George, to possess a meticulous and accurate knowledge of academic sub-   5
jects; for we often see that one who has grown old in them actually loses
touch with the common feelings of mankind, so far they are from fitting
men to hold the reins of government. And yet I differ emphatically from

* * * * *

15 letters] Probably the *Epistolae elegantes*, which bore a dedicatory letter from
Pieter Gillis to Clava.

17 see you here] As councillor to Charles; cf Ep 370:18n.

20 Gillis] Erasmus had clearly returned once more to his customary host in
Antwerp.

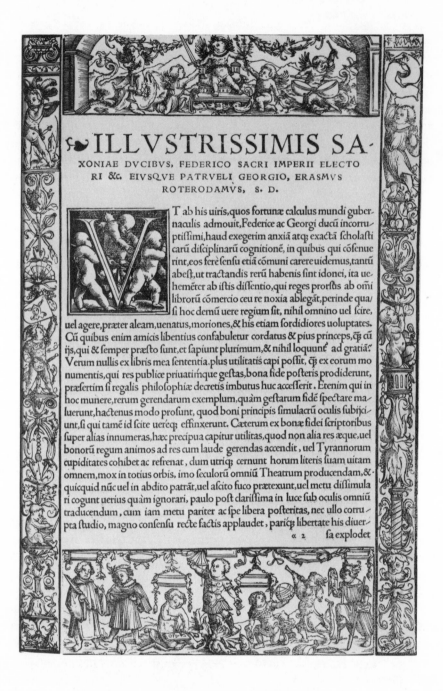

✢ILLVSTRISSIMIS SA-
XONIAE DVCIBVS, FEDERICO SACRI IMPERII ELECTO
RI &c. EIVSQVE PATRVELI GEORGIO, ERASMVS
ROTERODAMVS, S. D.

T ab his uiris,quos fortunæ calculus mundi guber-
naculis admouit,Frederice ac Georgi ducũ incorru-
ptiſſimi,haud exegerim anxiã atqʒ exactã ſcholaſti
carũ diſciplinarũ cognitionẽ, in quibus qui cõſenue
rint,eos ferè ſenſu etiã cõmuni carere uidemus,tantũ
abeſt,ut tractandis rerũ habenis ſint idonei, ita ue-
hemẽter ab iſtis diſſentio,qui reges prorſũs ab omͥ
librorũ cõmercio ceu re noxia ablegãt,perinde qua-
ſi hoc demũ uere regium ſit, nihil omnino uel ſcire,
uel agere,præter aleam,uenatus,moriones,& his etiam ſordidiores uoluptates.
Cũ quibus enim amicis libentius confabuletur cordatus & pius princeps,cɜ̃ cũ
ijs,qui & ſemper præſto ſunt,et ſapiunt plurimum,& nihil loquunt̄ ad gratiã?
Verum nullis ex libris mea ſententia.plus utilitatis capi poſſit, cɜ̃ ex eorum mo
numentis,qui res publicæ priuatimʠque geſtas,bona fide poſteris prodiderunt,
præſertim ſi regalis philoſophiæ decretis imbutus huc acceſſerit. Etenim qui in
hoc munere,rerum gerendarum exemplum,quàm geſtarum fidẽ ſpectare ma-
luerunt,hactenus modo proſunt, quod boni principis ſimulacrũ oculis ſubijci-
unt,ſi qui tamẽ id ſcite uerèqʒ effinxerunt. Cæterum ex bonæ fidei ſcriptoribus
ſuper alias innumeras,hæc precipua capitur utilitas,quod non alia res æque,uel
bonorũ regum animos ad res cum laude gerendas accendit, uel Tyrannorum
cupiditates cohibet ac refrenat, dum utriʠ cernunt horum literis ſuam uitam
omnem,mox in totius orbis, imo ſeculorũ omniũ Theatrum producendam,&
quicquid nũc uel in abdito patrãt,uel aſcito fuco prætexunt,uel metu diſſimula
ri cogunt uerius quàm ignorari, paulo poſt clariſſima in luce ſub oculis omniũ
traducendum, cum iam metu pariter ac ſpe libera poſteritas, nec ullo corru-
pta ſtudio, magno conſenſu recte factis applaudet, pariʠ libertate his diuer-

α 2   ſa explodet

Historiae Augustae scriptores, preface, with decoration by
Ambrosius Holbein (Basel: Froben 1518)

those who would shelter monarchs entirely from any contact with books as   10
from some noxious thing, as though it were the hallmark of a king to know
nothing and play a part in nothing except games of hazard, hunting,
buffoonery and pleasures more sordid even than these. What better friends
could an intelligent and pious prince choose to converse with than those
who are always at hand, always full of wisdom, and never speak merely to   15
give pleasure? But no books in my opinion have more to offer than the
works of those who have transmitted to posterity a true account of events
public and private, especially if a man before he comes to them is steeped in
the true principles of kingship. For those who in performing this task have
chosen as their theme an example of what ought to happen rather than a   20
faithful account of what did happen, among whom is Herodotus, are of use
to this extent and no more, that they set before us the image of a good
prince, provided it is skilfully and truly displayed. But faithful historians,
besides their value in other ways, can render this service in particular:
nothing is more effective in inspiring a good king to actions that will bring   25
him praise, or in curbing and limiting the appetite of tyrants; for both see
that the historians will soon put their whole lives upon the stage before an
audience of all the world and indeed of all future generations. Whatever
they do now in secret or cover up with some fictitious pretext or force men
through fear to pretend ignorance of it though they cannot help but know,   30
must, they are well aware, be soon displayed in broad daylight for all men
to see, when posterity, freed now from hope and fear alike, and warped by
no prejudice, will praise with one voice what has been well done and with
no less liberty of judgment will condemn and execrate what has not. I
cannot believe that any tyrant (for I will not use the word prince) has so   35
entirely put off the common feelings of humanity that he would find life
enjoyable, if he knew that his name would be as hateful to posterity in every
age and country as we find the names of Nero, Caligula, Heliogabalus,
Commodus, Domitian and Julian, the very mention of whom, as though
they were monsters rather than princes, now rouses loathing horror and   40
disgust. Vitellius while still alive paid the proper penalty for his mis-
government of the Empire, and Nero would have done the same, had he not
been appalled by the horrible nature of the punishment and chosen to be
his own executioner. And would that their example might still take effect
today, should there (which God forbid!) arise anyone like them. As it is,   45
nothing is so immune from punishment as an offence for which no
punishment however grave would be adequate – the guilt of a ruler who has
misused his power.

    Now as regards the other qualities of an historian, the value each of us
would attach to other writers is a matter of individual judgment. One point   50

is, I think, agreed among all educated readers: that for truth of narrative the
first place must be assigned to Suetonius who, as has been wittily said,
wrote the lives of the emperors with the same freedom with which they
lived them. Suetonius was almost equalled in this good quality by Aelius
Spartianus, Julius Capitolinus, Aelius Lampridius, Vulcatius Gallicanus,   55
Trebellius Pollio, Flavius Vopiscus, though in power of expression and
polish of language they are much his inferiors. And so they deserved – or so
it seemed to me – that their writings should be most dutifully preserved by
those who wish to learn; for it is to their sense of duty that we owe the
accurate knowledge of those great events which survives to our own day.   60
Suetonius for his part was preserved already by some kindly god from
widespread corruption, and now by the efforts of scholars and my own
efforts is available, if I mistake not, pure and intact. In this task I was aided
by a very old copy from the library of a monastery at Tournai, in the country
of the ancient Nervii, known as St Martin's, access to which I owe to the   65
right honourable William Mountjoy, then his king's viceroy in that city. In
the other historians I had no such assistance, and did the only thing I could,
which was to present them at least with many fewer mistakes than before.
All of them I have decided to submit to the public under the recommendation of your famous names, being moved to this bold course either by the   70
support you have given me or by my natural devotion to good literature, in
order that men distinguished by lineage and wealth may learn more and
more to ponder them, and to use them as a mirror for the amendment of
their own lives and behaviour. In the first place, when we see how a change
of constitution in the Roman world cost so much human life, this will   75
discourage a religious prince at any rate from hasty innovations. And then
it repays the trouble to watch how human affairs sway up and down as
though in some great Euripus with its tidal ebb and flow, unless this surge
is restrained and disciplined by the solid wisdom and inflexible virtue of
princes.   80

Another thing moves one to astonishment, that in all those princes
scarcely can a few be found who are tolerable and very few who are

* * * * *

586:54–6 Aelius … Vopiscus] The six authors of the *Historiae Augustae*, lives
of later Roman emperors (AD 117–284), of small historical value, and included
with Erasmus' edition of Suetonius, in Froben's publication of June 1518

64 old copy] The Tournai manuscript, according to M. Ihm's edition of Suetonius (Leipzig 1927 p vi), has not been identified.

66 Mountjoy] Erasmus' early English patron; cf Ep 301 introduction.

78 Euripus] The strait between the island of Euboea and the Greek mainland;
Adagia I ix 62

virtuous; most are not simply vicious, but mere monsters, mere plagues of
the human race, and many of them mad. Never had any age beheld such a
calamity, enslaved as the whole world was to a single raging beast, and   85
singing between its groans with Carion the slave in Aristophanes ''Tis
hard, 'tis hard ...' And yet monsters of this kind, blackened with parricide,
sacrilege, incest, in a word with infamy of every kind, were presented with
temples altars and divine honours by their fawning subjects, who paid to
worldly success, or rather, to wickedness the tribute normally reserved for   90
outstanding merit. After this, who will work his way to an immortal name
by virtuous deeds, if heaven is opened to men who were not worthy to set
foot on the earth? If Domitian and Commodus, criminals both, usurped the
title of god even in their lifetimes, clearly this was not effrontery so much as
some unquestionable frenzy. Another point: the reason why it came about   95
that good princes were so hard to find is not yet clear to me. Could it be that
great position of itself brings many things with it which can corrupt a
nature well born and virtuously brought up? A man will believe this more
easily if he considers that Nero in his youth won universal praise, and that
the most pestilent man whom the world has yet seen gave hopes to start   100
with that he would prove an excellent prince; and again that, long after him,
Geta's brother Bassianus was an excellent and virtuous man as long as he
was a private citizen, but a wicked emperor. Could it be that, like ships so
big and bulky that they will not steer, the task of ruling the whole world is
too big to be encompassed by one man's mind; for we know that it is very   105
difficult to govern well a single household? And so even a man who
sincerely wishes to do right is sometimes forced to say, in Virgil's words,

> The driver's team now carry him away,
> Nor will his chariot the reins obey.

It was because he understood this, I imagine, that Octavius Augustus, who   110
was an educated and clear-sighted man and (something you will seldom
find in those early emperors) of uninterrupted sanity, thought more than
once of laying down the load of empire, and would have done so, had he
found anyone upon whose shoulders the burden could have settled without
disaster to the commonwealth. This was why later emperors, unequal to the   115
stormy seas of business, sought to divide the burden of the empire between
several men; or perhaps this is more properly to be ascribed to causes many
of which, but not all, are listed by Flavius Vopiscus in his life of Aurelian.
Even so, in such a throng of wicked princes, you may find policies worthy of

* * * * *

86 Aristophanes] *Plutus* 1
107 Virgil's words] *Georgics* 1.514

a high-principled ruler, you may hear the language of a model prince, and   120
discover patterns in which you can find no fault. Among pagans you may
find some who in the spirit of a Christian ruled for the common weal, not for
themselves; who sought no other recompense for the heavy burdens of
government than the gratitude of their fellow-men; who set the public good
above their affection for their children and even above the security of   125
themselves and their families. Happy indeed should we be, if every Christian prince showed with regard to his own domains the spirit which
Octavius, once established, or the two Tituses or Trajan or the two An-
toninuses or Aurelius Alexander showed towards the whole world!
Another thing is surprising too, that men could be found bold enough to   130
address to an emperor a book about his predecessors which displayed not
merely freedom of speech but actual contempt. Today there are rulers who
insist that we should write about the most depraved of monarchs with deep
respect, their object being to prevent a precedent for freedom of speech
from recoiling on themselves. But it is much more to the point to watch in   135
these examples how the name of emperor, which the world once held sacred
and august – and even now it moves the emotions of many men as something solemn and venerable, though scarcely anything remains except the
shadow of a mighty name – crept into the world from a disgraceful origin,
from criminal activity in Julius first, more criminal after him in Octavius,   140
Lepidus and Antonius. Truly there is no limit to Fortune's caprice in human
affairs! The authority which the common consent of mankind was later to
place on a level with the gods was founded and consecrated by impiety,
murder, parricide, incest and tyranny. These were the prospering omens
under which the majesty reverenced by the kings of the whole world first   145
took its rise. It was born in crime; its growth was almost more criminal. An
army of barbarians, itself a sink of iniquity, often chose a master for the
world not by their votes but by raging insurrection, and as a rule there was
no right of succession other than the murder of a predecessor. These were
the conditions in which an emperor's reign in the old days began; and even   150
so it had all the time to be purchased at such a price as the troops' insatiable
greed might fix. Nor did it suffice to vent their fury on a single head.
Children, kindred, friends – the merciless slaughter extended to them all
and often, with vengeance swinging as it often does from one side to the
other, uncounted leading men and women were piteously murdered by   155
their bestial cruelty. Often the contest between several claimants was the
cause of universal chaos, and so at every new succession to the empire the
whole world was shaken to its foundations. Supreme power was in the

* * * * *

139 shadow of a mighty name] Lucan 1.135

hands, not of the senate or people of Rome, but of a mercenary and criminal
soldiery. An emperor ruled on such conditions only, and only for so long a   160
time, as had won the approval of those monsters, who could endure no
emperor good or bad for very long. One was too stingy, another too
extravagant to please them; a third had more education than they liked; this
one was too much ruled by his mother, that one too strict a disciplinarian;
one unwarlike, one too fond of fighting, one too much disposed to listen to   165
the senate; one was handicapped by a name, another by kindred unpopular
with the rank and file. The lightest cause, no matter what, sufficed to serve
them as a death-warrant for the ruler of the world.

Finally, granted that there might be no reason for it, it was profitable
for them to change the emperor from time to time. Their insatiable hunger   170
for money used to incite them to a change of régime. The man they had by
now sucked dry was slaughtered as of no further use, and another was sent
for, to be stripped of everything and then slaughtered in his turn. And thus
it happened that for some men their tenure of the empire lasted only a few
months, for some only a very few days; so that, as I read, I often wonder   175
how there was anyone at that time willing to take his turn of empire, when
they might have learnt from so many examples the conditions on which the
empire must be held. And it was this sort of office, marketed like this or,
more truly, let on a short lease, to which they gave the name of empire. Sad
and pitiful indeed was then the state of things! Gone was the authority of   180
the senate, gone the laws, gone the liberty of the Roman people. An
emperor thus created ruled a world enslaved, and was himself the slave of
creatures such as no honest men would be willing to have among the slaves
in his household. The emperor was feared by the senate, and lived himself
in terror of that criminal military mob; the emperor laid down the law to   185
kings, and accepted laws dictated to him in his turn by an army of mercenaries. The supreme power in the world depended on a few armed and
desperate men. A glorious monarchy indeed, such as all men might covet!
And yet there was a strange kind of compact between the emperor and the
soldiers who were his masters, for we read sometimes of their submitting to   190
be decimated by a man whose throat they would soon be cutting when it
suited them, as though they had agreed to be master and slave by turns.

My object in saying this is not to suggest that the power of the Caesars

* * * * *

193 My object] This whole paragraph, down to line 233 'from seeming right,'
appears in the Froben Suetonius of June 1518; in the Basel manuscript, which
has autograph corrections, there are only a couple of sentences: 'This being so
– and it cannot be denied – one must consider whether we should desire such
an empire, if it had lapsed long since and we could restore it to our liking. If no
man in his senses could wish anything of the kind, how much less could he
wish ...'

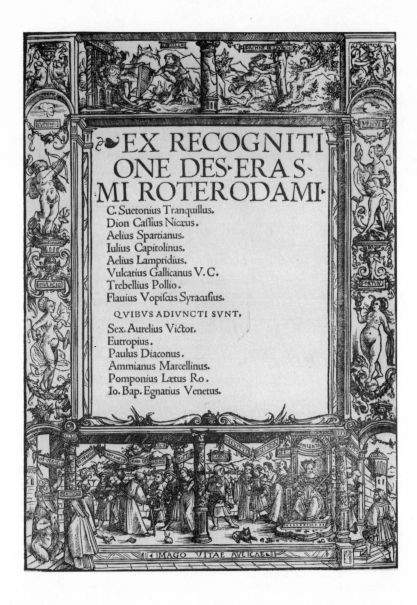

Historiae Augustae scriptores, title page, with decoration by
Ambrosius Holbein (Basel: Froben 1518)

lacked legal foundation, for authority born in force and the right of con-
quest, and even in crime, if it gradually wins the consent of the multitude   195
and strikes root, can become lawful. Otherwise, if one were to trace the rise
of governments from their earliest beginnings, one would find few of
legitimate birth. There is point in Octavius' remark about Cato: 'The man
who allows no change in the present shape of the commonwealth seems to
me a good man and a good citizen.' He admitted obliquely that Julius had   200
wrongfully seized sole power; yet none the less a constitution which had
been remade and was now established ought not to be altered once again. It
is generally agreed that no dominion has spread more widely or lasted
longer than the Roman empire, though the imperial power lay at first in
senate and people, and supremacy was concentrated in an individual not   205
suddenly but by slow degrees. Yet neither the senate nor any of the emperors held sway over the whole world. Apart from the fact that there were
some whole regions that never recognised the Roman rule, not the least part
of the world was then unknown. To speak of the antipodes was thought
prodigious folly, and the earth was thought to float upon the ocean as a ball   210
would float on water, with only some hill projecting; indeed, unknown
countries are discovered in our own day, the boundaries of which no one
has yet been able to trace fully, though they are known to be of enormous
extent. But the majesty of the Roman empire gradually faded in the brilliant
light of the Gospel, as the moon fades before the brightness of the sun.   215
Finally it was swept away by the flood of the barbarian invasions, and after
many centuries restored by the Roman pontiffs more in name than in
reality. For what else could they do? At least it was right to transfer the right
of election from a military mob to certain specific princes, who could be
relied upon to give the world, with a full and proper sense of responsibility   220
and no interference from hopes of reward, the prince whom they knew
most likely to be a blessing to mankind. For if the laws threaten such dire
penalties on those who elect an abbot or a bishop for a corrupt consideration, be it money or anything else, how high should be the standard of
integrity among those whose votes will choose a prince with such wide   225
jurisdiction! Otherwise, it would be far better to take a prince by right of
birth than owe him to a corrupt election. And so, as it is the part of a good
citizen not to wish to change the present shape of the commonwealth, so it
is the part of a good prince to govern his dominions by the laws which he
has inherited.   230
    Whether that ancient empire should be restored as it was once, is an
open question. For my part, I do not think any intelligent man would desire

* * * * *

198 Octavius' remark] Macrobius 2.4.18

this, even if wishes could put it back; so far is it from seeming right to defend and revive an institution which for many centuries now has been largely outdated and non-existent, at the price of a great upheaval in human 235 affairs and very great loss of Christian lives. Remember, even among pagans, the spirit of a man like Otho who, rather than buy the empire at the cost of so many other men's lives, preferred to take his own, and showed in this if nothing else that he deserved to be emperor, if Fortune smiled on merit. Is it not enough for every region to have its own master, unless the 240 individual regions have yet another over them, and the people's slavery is redoubled if the supreme power should fall into the hands of a wicked prince? I say this with no wish to deny that monarchy is the best form of commonwealth, provided the monarch follows the example of the eternal Deity and surpasses everyone else in goodness and wisdom as far as he 245 does in power; but partly because, men's natures being what they are, I doubt whether we could be so fortunate, and partly because, even if we were fortunate enough to get such a prince, I do not think the mind of one mortal man capable of such extensive rule. Suppose it were, when will a prince living far away, let us say in Constantinople, learn what is happen- 250 ing among the Ethiopians or on the Ganges? And if he discovers, when will he send help? For a man who limits a great emperor's part to the exaction of revenue is anything rather than a true emperor. The world will not greatly feel the absence of such a monarch, if Christian princes are united in concord among themselves. The true and only monarch of the world is 255 Christ; and if our princes would agree together to obey His commands, we should truly have one prince, and everything would flourish under Him. If, however, human appetites are to be the mainspring, we shall be carried to and fro and tossed in the eternal flux of things. And yet we can secure a great part of this felicity for ourselves, if we all agree to work together for what is 260 essentially the best. And I for my part think no commonwealth will be happy, until princes who have had an honourable and Christian education take up with the reins of kingship a spirit worthy of a king, measure all their policies against the public good, avoid like the plague every form of tyran- ny, and strive each for himself to hand on the kingdom that has fallen to his 265 lot not larger but better to his successor; all endeavouring with one accord not to win wars but to see that wars do not happen; not to equip themselves with armed forces, but to contrive that they should need none. Let them study to achieve greatness by the arts of peace, which are based on wisdom and on the powers of the mind. For my part, if change were possible 270 without public upheaval, I would judge it to be of great importance for the peace of the Christian world that limits should be laid down for every jurisdiction by specific treaties in accordance with the public good, and that

these once determined should be neither contracted nor expanded on any
pleas of relationship or previous agreement, the system of ancient rights   275
and claims being completely done away with, which every ruler commonly
uses as a pretext to suit the circumstances, when he is ready to go to war.
Should anyone perchance protest that princes are being deprived of some
right which belongs to them, I would ask him to consider whether he thinks
it fair that for the sake of such rights, whether authentic perhaps or in-   280
vented, the Christian world should be a scene of endless conflict of
weapons impious and murderous, so many harmless persons should be
ruined or done to death, so many innocent women should be brought to
misery and dishonour – in a word, that the whole tragic series of evils which
every war brings in its train should be let loose on human life. For these are   285
the sources from which almost all the wars which I have seen in my lifetime
unquestionably took their rise. But it is not merely unnecessary, it might
even be thought impertinent to write this to you two, who are princes
above all as wise as you are eminent, and moreover (a very rare thing in
your station in life) eminently equipped with the resources to be found in   290
books. For your distinguished gifts, Frederick, are so outstanding that it is
no wonder if their fame has reached even my humble level. And you,
illustrious George, who are in every way so like your famous cousin – in
effect a brother – I came to know on a closer view when you were governing
our neighbour, Friesland. And so I bid your Highnesses farewell, examples   295
of true felicity, illustrious in your lineage but far more so in your gifts of
mind. Christ the Almighty keep that same mind in you, and keep you safe
for the benefit of Christendom; and may He vouchsafe us many princes like
you.

     Antwerp, 5 June 1517

587 / From Guy Morillon   Ghent, 5 June [1517]

    For Morillon see Ep 532 introduction.

GUY MORILLON TO MASTER ERASMUS, GREETING
Paris has won his Helen! I have married a wife, dear master, and would now
try to describe her to you, did I not hope that you would soon be coming
here, and so I shall show her to you. The expression on the chancellor's face

    * * * * *

295 Friesland] Erasmus' friends must have given him an account of George's
vigorous government of Friesland, which he resigned, after a decade, in May
1515.

as he read your letter and his feelings towards you, you will learn from our 5
theologian's letter. All your well-wishers are unanimous that you ought to
come here forthwith, before the chancellor himself sets out on his journey to
Spain. Please, dear master, allow yourself in this matter to be guided by
your friends. All else that may be to your advantage you will better hear face
to face. My wife calls me incessantly to come to bed. Farewell, my master. 10
From Ghent, the 5th June.

Tell Pieter Gillis, your most kindly host, that my wife and I drink to
him with no heeltaps.

588 / From Giambattista Egnazio   Venice, 21 June 1517

The Venetian scholar Egnazio, originally Giambattista Cipelli (c 1473–1553)
took the humanist name of Baptista Egnatius; he made the acquaintance of
Erasmus when the latter was working at the printing house of Aldus; cf Ep
269:56n.

BAPTISTA EGNATIUS TO HIS FRIEND ERASMUS, GREETING
Ulrich von Hutten, a much gifted man, so far as I could guess from one
meeting with him, both in character and learning – one would know him for
a disciple of Erasmus – brought me greetings from you. I welcomed him
warmly in the first place for your sake, as was reasonable, but soon his 5
quality and his charm made him no less welcome on his own account, than
from your recommendation. He told me a budget of news, with the warmest references to his affection for you; among other things, that you had
been summoned to act as tutor to his royal highness Prince Charles on the
most flattering terms. The joy that this news gave me I can hardly express. 10
For I thought to myself not, as most people do, what great promotion and
wealth you might gain from the post, for these you, with your great heart
and high standards, have always despised; but that under your rule and
guidance the most distinguished prince on earth might easily receive such
education and training as would make him worthy of the succession to 15
those great dominions and to the empire; and then he will turn all the might
and all the policy of that rich monarchy away from what are now worse than
civil wars into a righteous campaign against a pagan foe, and will love and
cherish good letters and all who practise them. For I have no doubt that your
king is so much gifted by nature, that with only very little effort on your part 20

* * * * *

587:5–6 our theologian's] Evidently Pierre Barbier; cf Ep 585:5, 16.
588:2 von Hutten] See Ep 365 introduction.
10 terms] Cf Ep 370:18n; the appointment was to the prince's council.

he will not be slow to produce the most prolific results; while you, I know, are endowed with such wisdom and experience of affairs that you will have followed not so much your own private advantage as the public weal. Do all you can therefore, dearest Erasmus, with the extensive authority which you have already so deservedly acquired and remembering the great expecta-   25
tions which you have aroused everywhere, to make the prince worthy of you as his tutor, of the name of Christian, and of his great forebears, so that his grandfather Maximilian might fairly have the same reason to rejoice that is reported of Philip king of Macedon: 'he would,' he might say, 'be profoundly grateful to the gods not so much for the birth of the royal child as   30
that Charles was born in your lifetime.'

   But more of this on another occasion. I must now come to the letter you sent me some time ago. You have heard, you say, that I have become Aldus' successor as literary adviser to the business, and am so much better than he that, good though he was, there is no comparison between us. For my part,   35
my dear Erasmus, I do not welcome praise which is combined with asper-
sions on someone else's reputation, nor would I ever think so well of myself as to suppose myself equal to Aldus, let alone superior. To say nothing of the rest, who is Aldus' equal for hard work and endurance and late night sessions? Who has his enthusiasm in the cause of good literature? I excuse   40
you, I say no more; I know your affection for me and your great natural kindness, far more than I deserve. But I would not take on that task, even temporarily. I have set my hand to a few things only, more in hopes of arousing you and others like you than because I felt capable of it myself. And in any case, we have to deal with a head of the firm who, to put it   45
mildly, thinks of private rather than public benefit, and whose wealth and position I should find easier to praise than his generosity and sense of obligation towards men of learning. But if only I had here, not Homer's 'counsellors ten,' but two or three like yourself, and if there were any prospect of the rewards rightfully due to so much toil and effort, I would not   50
hesitate to promise that very soon the business could pick up so much, it would be so right-and-tight that you would have no reservations to make

* * * * *

29 reported] By Aulus Gellius 9.3.6, in the original Greek, which Egnazio quotes
32 letter] This letter does not survive, but it was presumably written before Erasmus' journey to England in April.
45 head of the firm] Presumably Andrea Torresani; cf Ep 589 introduction.
48 Homer's] *Iliad* 2.372
52 right-and-tight] Cf Ep 583:156n.

except timber and minerals. But at the moment the thing is run with such avarice and such jealousy that I cannot protect my rights even by the traditional five-foot limitation.   55

You speak of sending to us some of the things you have written; it will be a very great pleasure to see them, and we shall take care that they are printed very accurately. Nothing will give me greater joy than to work hard for the honour and glory of my beloved Erasmus. Asola and his family are very keen on this; they and the boys send you most cordial greetings.   60 Meanwhile please read as carefully as you can my Caesars and the other things, which Ulrich will be bringing to you, and do not hesitate either to make plenty of corrections or to tell me frankly what you think of them. Farewell.

Venice, 21 June 1517   65

589 / From Andrea Torresani   [Venice, c 21 June 1517]

Andrea Torresani of Asola in Lombardy (1451–1529), known as Andreas Asulanus, was the father-in-law and partner of Aldus; cf Ep 212:6n. He was slightly younger than Aldus, who married his daughter Maria in 1499.

ANDREAS ASULANUS TO ERASMUS, GREETING
I was remarkably pleased with your letter to Egnazio, because I learnt from it that you are in good health and think kindly of me. It gave me great pleasure that you should approve our publication of Lucian's dialogues in your translation, which is as accurate as it is elegant, and of the *Moria*, that   5 invention of yours which is such a worthy specimen of your high principles and your wit; I hear it wins high praise from our most distinguished and prominent politicians. The invention of it all is so brilliant, the working out

* * * * *

53 timber and minerals] *ruta caesa*, another formula from Roman law; *Adagia* IV iv 38
59 Asola] Andrea Torresani; cf Ep 589 introduction.
60 boys] Aldus' sons
61 Caesars] The *Historiae Augustae scriptores* printed by the Aldine firm with a colophon dated July 1516; cf A.A. Renouard *Annales* 76 number 4. In the Froben printing (Ep 586 introduction) the preface to the reader, dated 23 June 1518 and perhaps written by Erasmus, explains that Egnazio's *Caesares*, which he received through Frankfurt, was useful, but that the volume was already far advanced before it reached him.
589:4 Lucian's dialogues] In May 1516; see Renouard *Annales* 76 number 2.
5 *Moria*] In August 1515; see Renouard *Annales* 73 number 7.

so successful, and the execution so finished, that there is nothing to touch
it. For my part, dearest Erasmus, how can I fail to have the warmest feelings   10
for a man with such gifts as yours? I hope you are convinced that there is
nothing I wish for more than to be able to contribute something to your
reputation, whether in deed or word. It cannot have escaped you that I have
always thought it the proudest moment of my life, in the days when we had
the support of several books from you, to do the best I could for all you great   15
men. At the present time this is my dearest ambition. Hence it is that I have
decided to write to you with a proposal which I hope will not be unwelcome, for it can do you nothing but credit. You know, I think – in fact I am
sure you know, and must have heard from many people by letter and in
conversation – that Marcus Musurus has been appointed to the pope's new   20
college; and also that this place is very short of people who have had any
experience in that class of composition. Now I hear from everyone capable
of forming any judgment of a man's abilities, that no one could fill this post
or perform its duties better than you. All sound judges agree that this
honourable position should be awarded to you. I am therefore writing to try   25
to discover what your opinion may be. If you agree, I mean about your
being engaged as Orator in either Greek or Latin, I will propose it to the
Three Hundred (they are the council responsible for business of this kind).
Above all else I beg you to do me the kindness to send me back word how
you feel about this, especially as there is nothing I would not do for your   30
sake that might conduce to exalting your position in the world. What you
write about your *Proverbs* is welcome news; also about your other works
which are brought to such a high degree of finish. This too is most highly
welcome; for, as Erasmus says in his *Proverbs*, Africa always offers something new. Send them to us as soon as you have someone to whom you can   35
safely entrust them. I will take care to see them published in such a style as
will make it clear I have been as much concerned for the reputation of my
press as for the glory of Erasmus, whose distinction never fades. Farewell,
dear Erasmus. All I can do is at your disposal. Farewell.

I had already finished my letter when I remembered something I   40
wanted to tell you; hence this postscript. You know (for you were here just

* * * * *

14 in the days] Cf Ep 211 introduction.

20 Musurus] Cf Ep 574 introduction.

20 pope's] Reading *pontificium* for Allen's *pontificum*; cf Ep 574 introduction.

32 *Proverbs*] It seems that Erasmus may have proposed a new edition of the
Adagia to be printed by Torresani. However, the next edition was printed by
Froben in November 1517. The Aldine edition of September 1520 (Renouard
Annales 89 number 2) was a reprint of this Froben edition.

then) how much time Aldus, my dearest and most delightful son-in-law, spent on correcting Terence. What a wonderfully gifted man! I cannot mention him without singing his praises first. And so kind! His name, my dear Erasmus, always brings tears to my eyes. And then the Plautus, how   45 much effort he expended on that, in which you gave him a great deal of help, for he used you to stick together, as it were, the lines of that Latin Siren. These two I should like to publish for the benefit of all persons interested. Please allow me therefore to take advantage of your kindness in this matter. I beg you by the splendour of the Latin name, of which you   50 have always been such a keen supporter: send me anything you may have in the way of an ancient manuscript, which we can use as a sort of bear-leader for the manuscript we have here, or anything else you may have that could help to put a polish on our work. I want to do all I can to finish it in a careful and stylish manner, which will increase our standing in the eyes of   55 all the best judges. Farewell.

My sons send you their very best wishes, and I have passed on your greetings to them. Aldus' sons, Manuzio the eldest and Antonio and Paolo, send you their respects.

* * * * *

43 Terence] The first Aldine Terence is dated November 1517 (Renouard *Annales* 80 number 5). Francesco Torresani, Andrea's son, states in his preface that Aldus had promised an edition.

45 Plautus] Francesco Torresani's preface to the first Aldine edition of Plautus, July 1522 (Renouard *Annales* 94 number 2) states that a text prepared jointly by Aldus and Erasmus was the base of this edition.

47–8 Latin Siren] This is the title applied to P. Valerius Cato, the grammarian, as a master of poetry, in a couplet preserved in Suetonius *De grammaticis et rhetoribus* 11. It conveys a note of irresistible charm, not, to a modern reader, the first quality of Plautus' admirable comedies. They required 'sticking together,' because medieval ignorance of metre had left the text in rags.

58 Manuzio] Manuzio de' Manuzii, the eldest son, became a priest and lived on his family patrimony at Asola. He died in 1568; cf Renouard *Annales* 391.

58 Antonio] The second son who became a bookseller in Bologna. He died in 1558 or 1559; cf Renouard *Annales* 392.

58 Paolo] The third son, born in 1512, who died in 1574. He took over management of the Aldine press in 1533 and became one of the most famous printers of his time. He was also renowned as a scholar, especially for his work on Cicero. In 1561 he removed the family press to Rome at the request of Pope Pius IV, to undertake the printing of texts of the Church Fathers, and to become the unofficial printer of the Roman counter-reform. See Renouard *Annales* 425–60.

590 / From Niccolò Sagundino   London, 22 June 1517

This letter was written by the Venetian diplomat (cf Ep 574 introduction) after the receipt of Ep 584 in London. It was forwarded by More in July (Ep 601) together with Epp 591, 592 and (probably) 593.

TO THAT SINGULAR ORNAMENT OF THE REPUBLIC OF LETTERS
ERASMUS OF ROTTERDAM, FROM NICCOLÒ SAGUNDINO, GREETING
A raw recruit like myself who tries at this stage to address such a prince of scholars may well be deterred by shyness almost beyond the limits of courtesy, by the knowledge of my own attainments (which are non- 5
existent), or by your own lofty genius and the great splendour of your reputation; for who is there so deeply versed in eloquence and gifted with so keen and powerful a mind, that he can write to you without a tremor? And yet, my dear Erasmus, all these feelings are overcome by your excep- tional goodness and unlimited good will, which have inspired in me such 10
confidence that without a touch of embarrassment I send you this poor letter, which might otherwise be taken for effrontery. How so, you will ask? Yesterday I was in company with a capital scholar and most civilized man, in every way without peer, to wit Thomas More, and he read me your most elegant letter; after which he handed it to me and I re-read it on the spot two 15
or three times with unspeakable delight. To say nothing else, why in God's name should you ask me to send you that letter of mine, which I wrote to Marcus Musurus to congratulate him? Why, as heaven's my witness, I think it hardly deserves a single perusal by a man of ordinary attainments, much less to be sent to Erasmus, who is in my opinion far the most learned man 20
who ever was, is or ever will be, to be re-read by him. Still, I would rather do as you ask and send you something which I know to be quite unworthy of your attention, than refuse to oblige you and withhold it as I ought. You will therefore find two copies attached to this letter, one of that really most admirable letter written by his excellency my master, which you say you 25
have lost, the other of my own worthless effort.

Besides which, I wish you to understand, dearest Erasmus, that if you could look into the very centre of my inmost and most secret heart, you would infallibly see your own name written there, and never will it fade

* * * * *

590:12 letter] Ep 584
15 letter] Ep 574
24 really] Reading *vere* for Allen's *verae*; his master was Giustiniani; cf Ep 591.
25 admirable letter] Ep 559

until that heart itself ceases to beat – that name which deserves the highest   30
possible renown, and has made its rapid and triumphant progress from
Ocean to the far land of Egypt by its own unaided merits; yet wherever I
may be and in whatever company, I shall never until I die have enough of
exalting it and magnifying it as it deserves with all the tributes in my
power. And if by any chance I have to enter the lists against some carping   35
Zoilus, I will play my part manfully with words, aye and with fisticuffs and
cudgels too, should need arise. In return for which, dear Erasmus, I ask for
no reward except your affection, the honour of being sometimes recalled to
memory when I am absent from you, and permission to count myself
among your friends. Besides which, I would ask you, and indeed adjure   40
you, to answer this foolish letter of mine, did I not recognize that I am
unworthy to receive one of your heavenly letters. For my own part, I live my
usual life here and devote myself whole-heartedly to literature, for wanting
that this life would certainly be impossible. Apart from that, most learned
of men, I can hardly say what nectar sweet as honey I sip from your most   45
delightful *Chiliades*, rich source of nectar as they are, what lovely flowers of
every kind I gather thence like a honey-bee, carrying them off to my hive
and building them into the fabric of what I write. To their perusal I have
devoted two hours a day. In heaven's name, my dear Erasmus, what
splendid things you write! what fertility of genius they display, what   50
brilliance of language and what honeyed fluency of style, what force, what
charm, what inexhaustible delight! Blessings attend upon you, for you are
unique! You, you alone seem to me wise, and no one else; no one but you
deserves the title of the Muses' favourite child.

But what purpose do I serve in praising you, who am tongue-tied   55
myself? for your outstanding virtues and your distinguished intellectual
gifts could not be fitly praised and glorified by anyone, unless at least he
possessed your eloquence and unexampled sense of style. It is my misfortune that I cannot enjoy your society and the incomparable pleasures of
your conversation. Happy indeed should I be and fortunate beyond mea-   60
sure, dear Erasmus, if over some years I could win my way into intimacy
with you, and live with you, and offer you my most loyal service. But since
the duties of my post do not permit, I shall read and re-read, I shall embrace
and hold fast that golden work, your really more than human *Adagia*,
whereby you have not only equalled but far out-distanced the classic   65
monuments of antiquity, and such other ripe fruit of your studies as is to be
found over here. With these honey-sweet delicacies I shall gorge myself,

* * * * *

36 Zoilus] The bitterest of ancient critics, often wrong; *Adagia* II v 8

and assuage my longing in the best way that may be open to me: day and
night I shall ponder in my mind and foster in my heart the sweet memory of
your name, with the result that, though not in actuality, at least in recollec-   70
tion Erasmus will be always with me.

Farewell, true light and glory of our world. May happiness be yours,
and prove a blessing to your friends and to posterity. To you sincerely and
permanently I offer devote and dedicate myself. You will do me a further
kindness if in your own words, and with the greatest respect, you will   75
convey my humble and unfailing duty to my lord the bishop of Chieti, who
so richly deserves the panegyrics with which you laud him to the skies.
Dearest of men, once more farewell.

London, 22 June 1517

591 / From Sebastiano Giustiniani   London, 29 June 1517

> Like Ep 590, this was written after the receipt of Ep 584 in London and was sent
> by More with Ep 590 and a copy of the rough draft of Ep 559; cf Ep 559
> introduction.

SEBASTIANO GIUSTINIANI, KNIGHT, AMBASSADOR OF VENICE,
TO ERASMUS OF ROTTERDAM, GREETING

From your letter to my friend More, dear Erasmus, I learn that my letter has
gone astray and that you are very anxious for a copy of it. I am sorry about
this, but it pleases me to this extent, that you should openly express the   5
wish to have in your possession a token of my affection and definite
trustworthy evidence of my feelings. So I send you a copy of the letter you
have lost, and am adding this to play the part of a messenger and assure you
that I am well; also that I pray you may enjoy good health of a kind you will
never get from those pills of yours which that fool of a doctor gave you to   10
take. In future, my dear Erasmus, pray do not entrust your health so
imprudently to a penniless pill-monger, for not the whole of France nor
Germany could make up for the loss of you. I know that, though cast up like
a shipwrecked sailor on a rocky shore, you none the less by prayer and

* * * * *

76 bishop of Chieti] Carafa; cf Epp 287:9n, 539:12n, 591:79ff.

77 panegyrics] Cf Ep 335:261–79. Printed in the *Damiani elegeia* in August
1515.

591:3 letter] Ep 584, which supplies some of the topics treated here

3 my letter] Ep 559

12 pill-monger] The Latin has a play on words: 'more mendicant than
medico.'

fasting survived the perils of the storm, and have your picture of the wreck   15
already painted and ready to be fixed in the temple – but that it looks most
unlike you. Nor is there any reason to ascribe the badness of the likeness to
the pills which purged you more violently than they should have, and
reduced you to a shadow of your former self: it was the caution of the
painter, reproducing a man who supposed that votive pictures of this kind   20
have some force in the avoidance of shipwreck, and not Erasmus, who on
such a question could not, the painter thought, share the popular delusion.
He did well: it was to protect your reputation that he depicted someone else
instead of you. Mind you keep clear of shipwreck in future, for there's no
help in a picture; beware of Aeolus when he is angry, and Neptune in a   25
tantrum, even though you may have some Juno at your side to pacify and
soften the violence of both (if we may believe the fables of antiquity about
the gods); for do not suppose yourself safe under the protection of your dear
Pallas – Neptune hates her. Give the physicians a wide berth; they treat a
man and his horse, and don't know the difference. Fees and not physic is   30
what interests them. Sometimes they give you garlic when it should be
aloes. You would have done better to stick to pullets instead of pills. Away
with the painter who usually puts a cypress instead of a man; no one will
ever have told the likes of him to take the cloth off his picture or drive away
the flies so that the birds may have a proper chance to test his grapes. It is   35
surprising that you should have been mixed up with all this; more so, to be
sure, that you should have got free.

Thus far, dear Erasmus, I have taken the liberty of being humorous
once again, not in your own charming way, for your humour is seasoned
with more salt than there is in all Ibiza. I continue my daily reading of your   40

* * * * *

15 picture] A reference to the widespread ancient practice of commemorating
an escape (especially from shipwreck) by setting up a votive picture in a
temple

19 shadow] Cf Erasmus' account of his purgation on the eve of the portrait
sitting; Ep 584:12–4.

26 Juno at your side] Reading *praesentem* ... *Junonem* with the Deventer
manuscript for Allen's *parentem* ... *furorem*; the allusion is to Virgil *Aeneid*
1.34–156.

31 garlic] That is, substituting a cheap for a costly ingredient.

33 cypress] Horace *Ars poetica* 19–21

34–5 cloth ... grapes] Pliny *Historia naturalis* 35.65–6; the rivalry of Zeuxis and
Parrhasius produced a painted curtain that deceived one artist, and painted
grapes which the birds tried to eat.

40 more salt ... Ibiza] Salt has for centuries been the main export of this
Balearic Island.

Adagia with the greatest pleasure, and chuckling as I find myself throwing
over all the things that used to satisfy me. And though the adages you have
got together from Greek and Latin sources are quite delightful and a great
help to both learning and liveliness, so that one's style is better nourished
and more readable, yet what you add to your adages is far better still. The   45
scholarship, the variety, the force, the abundance of the language, the
delightful gaiety which beguiles the reader with its wit and humour and
refreshes his weariness – all this is quite extraordinary. They are all comparable with the great works of antiquity, but some especially – the *Bellum
dulce inexpertis*, the *Aut regem aut stultum nasci oportet*, the *Speude bradeôs*   50
and more besides – not only compete (I would think) with the ancients but
leave them far behind, notwithstanding even the venerable authority of
those classical writers; for if your work were compared with theirs with the
authors' names suppressed, at no point would a fair-minded reader not
prefer your modern inspiration to their ancient majesty. As a rule I am   55
reluctant to read modern authors, and I sometimes tell my son and secretary
that, as there are so many classics on whom I can and should model myself,
there is no need to go looking for other footsteps for me to follow. But when I
look into what you write, all the things that other people admire because
they are protected by the prestige of antiquity seem to me now, I confess, to   60
be somehow worn out and negligible. There have also come into my hands
several of your letters, the most scholarly and elegant things, even when
compared with Cicero's letters to Atticus, that I have ever read or heard of.
    Why do I waste time in holding a candle to the sun, a silly and indeed
idiotic thing to do, when nothing is forged in your workshop that is not   65
inspired? Plainly, you have given so much new brilliance to the Latin
language, that I think you have done more to make it new and splendid than
it has done to make you famous. For myself, as I read your works, my eyes
are dazzled and I see visions, my mind is stupefied with admiration, so that
I am all fired with an incredible enthusiasm for you. Nor must you think   70
that I write of you thus from a desire to please, like some Gnatho out of
Terence who does not so much make a fool of his Thraso as send him
headlong; this office I resign to others who are poles apart from me in
character and in the theory and practice of living. I am no Gnatho, nor are
you a Thraso; Giustiniani I, who know not how to deceive, and you   75
Erasmus, kindly enough, but not deceived by my affection nor misled in

* * * * *

62 letters] Perhaps the *Epistolae elegantes*
64 holding a candle] *Adagia* II v 7
71 Gnatho] Cf Ep 450:74n.
72 Thraso] The boastful soldier in Terence's *Eunuchus*

your judgment. But those others take in hand the life of the great men whom they flatter and turn its gold to common brass instead of adding to its lustre.

Enough of this. I should be most grateful, if you happen to meet the bishop of Chieti, a man whose scholarship matches his integrity, if you 80 would give him my greetings. Perhaps he may return your attentions; he does not listen to me, for I am waiting for an answer to several letters, as though he set no value on my affection and admiration for him, which in such a kindly nature seems hardly possible. But what the reason can be for this long, not to say obstinate, silence, is far from clear; when he was the 85 nuncio here, I do not think I gave offence in any way. I am, as you know, of an inoffensive disposition. I desire rather to bind other people to me by acts of kindness than to render myself unpleasant to them. It may be that he has to consider his public position. I too am and have been for a long time the representative of my republic, but I never thought that a reason for abrogat- 90 ing the laws of friendship. I am afraid that like a hedgehog he wishes to cover up the mild and friendly side of his nature with sharp projecting spines which are safe from attack; for he conceals his open and charming character, wearing the severe frown and beetling eyebrow of the magis- trate. If by any chance he thinks I treated him with insufficient courtesy, 95 and did not show him the respect I should have shown him while he was here, then I complain that I am being badly treated: I did nothing to offend him, unless it was inadvertently, which I do not suspect. But if he has taken offence at anything I have done, he ought to have told me, and not broken off our friendship, as it says in the adage about not breaking bread; I do not 100 think, all the same, that he would make these excuses, if there were abso- lutely no underlying causes for complaint. But why this field, which others find so smiling and so fertile, should for me be so full of weeds, cannot fail to be a source of wonder to me and no less of regret. If I better understood the nature of the ground, I on my side would till it more industriously to win a 105 better harvest; for the harvest of friendship is mutual agreement, equal response of feeling, and a common readiness to do things for one another. The field is tilled by exchange of letters, by freedom of conversation (given the opportunity), by the giving and receiving of counsel and by common

* * * * *

78 turn ... to brass] Reading *obaerant* with the manuscript; this is surely what Giustiniani intended, although *obaeratus* in classical Latin means 'heavily in debt.'

80 bishop of Chieti] Cf Ep 590:76n.

100 not breaking bread] A maxim of Pythagoras, thus explained in *Adagia* I i 2

studies; finally, by continual rivalry, but without jealousy, in the pursuit of   110
excellence. For the nature of the soil dictates the cultivations. In acquiring
friends one should show discrimination; once one has discriminated, one
should keep them; the friendship, if it continues, should be nourished,
encouraged and cultivated; if it weakens, it ought not to be unravelled or
cut short, but patched, restored, re-knit and supported. Such has been the   115
opinion of wise men.

I myself cannot fail to regret my loss of the society of such a man; in
that small compass are all the qualities that pave the way to virtue – and
virtue speeds our journey towards felicity. In him are a most charming
character, singular integrity, an air of authority matched with a proper   120
courtesy and a humorous cheerfulness matched with authority, precise and
varied learning: nothing is lacking – philosophy, law civil and canon, a
knowledge of Greek and Latin worthy of a native speaker, theology the end
and goal of all kinds of knowledge. All that he ever does is gauged with the
square of reason and made straight against the plumb-line. Every moment   125
and attitude is graceful and becoming, modest and well-bred; his voice in
conversation always musical. Besides, he is not like that image cast from the
golden vessel kept by Amasis for base purposes: his home is elegant, all full
of coats-of-arms and hung with distinguished portraits of his family; no
one need be surprised if I am unwilling to let friendship with such a man   130
languish and die through neglect or interruption. He was the man whom I
had chosen as my pattern, whom I would strive to imitate; he spurred me on
to the pursuit of excellence. I am therefore resolved to take particular pains
to repair the loss of such a friend and restore him to his setting like a
dislocated limb. If he allows this to happen, my plan will prove a great   135
success; if he does not agree to return my affection, he will at least provide
an opportunity to be quit of him, a knife with which to amputate the limb
that I despair of, not without pain but without fault on my side. Thus I shall
at the same time mourn my loss and be indignant with him for spurning my
friendship. You know, dear Erasmus, my feelings towards him, which I   140
have expounded at excessive length; pray do your best to make them clear
to him, vivid and prominent. In the meanwhile maintain your affection for
me, and be sure that it is returned. Farewell, great bulwark of the republic of
letters, my distinction and the half of my soul.

London, 29 June 1517   145

* * * * *

128 Amasis] A king of Egypt in Herodotus 2.172

John Fisher
Portrait drawing by Hans Holbein the Younger, *c* 1528
Windsor Castle; reproduced by gracious permission of
Her Majesty Queen Elizabeth II

592 / From John Fisher   Rochester [c June 1517]

For Fisher see Ep 229 introduction. This letter seems to respond to the first
news of Erasmus' journey back to the Low Countries, news contained probably in a letter written at the same time as Ep 584. More's reply to that is Ep 601
(16 July 1517), accompanied by the letters from the Venetians (Epp 559, 574)
requested in Ep 584, and P.S. Allen surmised that the present letter was that
referred to by More at the end of Ep 601; Allen Ep 601:59n. It may therefore, be
dated in June or July. The reply is Ep 653.

JOHN, BISHOP OF ROCHESTER TO MASTER ERASMUS, GREETING
I was very sorry to hear of the perils of your crossing, and am correspond-
ingly glad that you had escaped safe and sound. There was a certain justice
in your being punished for the great haste in which you left me, when you
might have stayed here in peace, safe from any tossing on the deep.   5
    The book on the Cabala which you say Reuchlin is giving me has not
arrived yet. Your friend More has sent me his letter, but is still keeping the
book, as is his way; this is just what he did long ago with the *Speculum
oculare*. I am deeply obliged to you, my dear Erasmus, for many other
kindnesses, but especially because you make such efforts to have Reuchlin   10
bear me so carefully in mind. He is a man whose acquaintance I heartily
welcome; and for the time being, until I have read the book and can write to
him, please tell him I am as grateful to him as I believe to be possible.
    The New Testament, as translated by you for the common benefit of us
all, can offend no one of any sense; for you have not only shed light on   15
countless places in it by your scholarship: you have appended an absolutely
fresh commentary to the whole work, so that it can now be read and enjoyed
by anybody with much more pleasure and satisfaction than before. I rather
think, though, that the printer nodded from time to time, for when I was
exercising myself in reading St Paul as you recommend, I often found that   20
he had left out Greek words and sometimes whole sentences. I owe you
another thing too, my dear Erasmus, that up to a point I can make conjectures in places where the Greek and the Latin do not entirely correspond. I

* * * * *

592:6 Cabala] Printed by Thomas Anshelm at Haguenau, March 1517, it
represented an esoteric method of interpreting the Old Testament, believed to
reveal hidden doctrines to its initiates.

6 giving me] Cf Ep 562:24ff.

7–8 keeping the book] It would seem from Ep 593:6–7 that the culprit was
Colet.

8–9 *Speculum oculare*] The Latin version of Reuchlin's *Augenspiegel*; cf Ep 290
introduction.

wish I had been able to have you for a few months as my tutor. Farewell and
best wishes, from Rochester.   25
    John Roffen
    your grateful pupil

593 / From John Colet   London [c June 1517]

> This letter was written at the same time as those preceding; for Erasmus'
> earlier relations with Colet see especially Epp 106 and 260.

JOHN COLET TO MASTER ERASMUS, GREETING

I am mildly annoyed with you, Erasmus, for sending your greetings in
letters addressed to others and not to me. I have complete confidence in our
friendship, but this greeting at a distance and in other people's letters
makes other people suppose that your affection for me has diminished. I am 5
a little annoyed also on another point, that you sent Reuchlin's *De arte
caballistica* to the bishop of Rochester and not to me, not that I was against
your sending it to him, but I should have liked to have had one book from
you myself at the same time. My friendship with you is such a source of
pleasure to me, that I am sorry when I see you thinking less of me than of 10
other people. That particular book reached me first, and I had run through it
before it was given to the bishop. I dare express no opinion on it. I
recognize my own ignorance, and how blind I am in such a recondite
subject and in the work of such a great scholar. Not but what, as I read, some
things struck me as more remarkable in language than in content. For, as he 15
shows, there is something mysterious in Hebrew words, the way they are
both written and put together.

    My dear Erasmus, of books and knowledge there is no end. Nothing
can be better, in view of this brief life of ours, than that we should live a holy
and pure life and use our best endeavours every day to become pure and 20
enlightened and perfected. These things are promised us by Reuchlin's
Pythagorical and Cabalistic philosophy; but in my opinion we shall
achieve them in no way but this, by the fervent love and imitation of Jesus.
Let us therefore leave all these complications behind us, and take the short
road to the truth. I mean to do this as far as in me lies.   25
    Farewell, from London.

* * * * *

593:7 not to me] Cf Ep 592:6–9.

COMPENDIUM VITAE
ERASMI ROTERODAMI

This document was published by P.S. Allen in the first volume of the *Erasmi epistolae*, pages 46–52, along with other material of a biographical nature; it belongs with Ep 1437 to Conradus Goclenius, dated 2 April 1524. Because of the close relation between this text and that of Ep 447, which it largely overlaps, it appears as an Appendix to this volume as well.

The *Compendium vitae* was first published by Paul Merula at the University of Leiden from a manuscript he thought to be an autograph: *Vita Des. Erasmi Roterodami ex ipsius manu fideliter repraesentata* (Leiden: Basson 1607). Merula's manuscript was still in existence in 1649 but has since disappeared. Another manuscript exists in the Oesterreichische Nationalbibliothek, Vienna, MS Lat. 9058. For Allen's account of the history and authenticity of the document see the introduction to the *Compendium vitae Erasmi* I 46 and Appendix I of that first volume, 575–8.[1]

The editors accept the view that the *Compendium vitae* was composed by Erasmus for his friend and confidant Conradus Goclenius when Erasmus' health had been failing for some time, for the use of his biographers after his death; cf Allen IV Ep 1437:121n. There is no question that there are difficulties about the authorship, and we may hope that there will be fresh light on the subject from the manuscript edition announced by L.M. Tocci.[2] The style of the document is the most conspicuous problem, and suggests that the author was jotting down notes on a subject that was to be written up by others. The jerky sentences and loose structure are quite unfamiliar from Erasmus' letters, but there is no comparable document to set beside this one, and they need cast no doubt on its authenticity, for the criticisms of its Latinity recorded by Allen (I 575) are nugatory; additional examples are adduced by Crahay; see note 1.

Both the *Compendium* and the letter in which it was embedded have a brief heading in Greek which ties them closely together, and this seems unlikely to be the work of anyone but Erasmus himself. In addition, the views I expressed on the dispensation from Leo x in the introductions to Epp 446, 447, and 517 argue for the substantial accuracy of this biographical account on the issue of Erasmus' paternity. The problem of the omission of Erasmus' older brother Pieter is considered in place. There is no doubt that the *Compendium vitae* is highly tendentious as an account of Erasmus' early life, but it cannot be dismissed as a pastiche without any independent authority.

JKM

* * * * *

1 The assertion of Dr J.B. Kan of Rotterdam that the present work was a forgery by its editor Merula is discussed by P.S. Allen in these notes. Since Kan's death, the most important discussion questioning the authenticity of the *Compendium vitae* is that by Roland Crahay 'Recherches sur le compen-

dium vitae attribué à Erasme' *Humanisme et Renaissance* 6 (1939) 7–19, 135–53. Crahay's objections are accepted by R.R. Post 'Quelques précisions sur l'année de la naissance d'Erasme (1469) et sur son éducation' BHR 26 (1964) 489–509. Post, however, admits that the account in the *Compendium vitae*, 'authentique ou non, ... est basé sur l'idée qu'Erasme naquit en 1469' (page 502) and thus that it supports the main contention of his article. Crahay's objection that the *Compendium vitae* contains no account of the difficulties experienced by Erasmus at the time of writing is answered by James D. Tracy 'Bemerkungen zur Jugend des Erasmus' *Basler Zeitschrift für Geschichte und Altertumskunde* 72 (1972) 222. I find, moreover, that Crahay's view that the document was composed after Erasmus' death at 'une époque plus tardive' is too imprecise as it stands to be convincing. Margaret Mann Phillips, accepting Crahay's view, has printed a posthumous life of Erasmus (not however by an anonymous hand) composed from published sources, in BHR 34 (1972) 229–37; whether the *Compendium vitae* can be explained adequately as such a pastiche may perhaps be questioned. Dr Cornelis Reedijk indicates his acceptance of the authenticity of the *Compendium vitae* in 'Erasmus' Final Modesty' *Actes du congrès Erasme* (Amsterdam 1971) 174. The most serious problem posed by the contents of the *Compendium vitae* remains that of the suppression of Pieter Gerard's identity in the events of Erasmus' early years, discussed below 88n.

A more recent analysis deserving attention is that by Robert Stupperich, 'Zur Biographie des Erasmus von Rotterdam. Zwei Untersuchungen' in *Archiv für Reformationsgeschichte* 65 (1974), where the relevant section is that on 'Erasmus und das Corpus iuris canonici' pages 19–29. Criticizing the account of Erasmus' early vocation in the *Compendium vitae*, he cites legislation of Gregory IX with the contention that an illegitimate could only make his way to the priesthood through joining a religious order (page 22). The canon in question (x.1.17,1) although in the Decretals of Gregory IX, is actually a canon of the Council of Poitiers in 1087, the purpose of which was to end the custom whereby sons, illegitimate or not, could succeed fathers in benefices. The canon is not specifically directed against illegitimacy as such. In fact, canonists commonly held that any bishop could dispense a simple illegitimate for ordination to major orders, and although a papal dispensation usually was necessary for sons of priests, it was also held that in cases of need or usefulness (or for any other just cause) a bishop could dispense with these too for major orders: see Hostiensis (d 1271) *Summa aurea* (Lyon 1542) folios 371–38r, especially 37va, which opinion became commonly accepted. It is not possible thus to argue that Erasmus entered the Augustinian Canons only because religious profession offered him the only access to the priesthood.

Finally, Stupperich's contention that, by his dispensation, 'Papst Leo x. sprach ihn am 26. Januar vom Mönchtum frei' (page 29) cannot be accepted in the literal sense that is apparently intended. As is indicated in the introduction to Ep 447, Leo x's brief to Ammonio did not dispense Erasmus from his vows. It gave Ammonio the right to absolve Erasmus from his various irregularities; it gave Erasmus the right to live outside the monasteries of his order for the rest of his life, to wear the dress of a secular priest, to be promoted to any benefice open to secular priests, and, when applying in future for any such benefice, the right not to specify his illegitimacy and his dispensation

Natus est in uigilia Simonis et Judę, suxputat annos
circiter quinquaginta septem. Mater dicta est Margareta
filia medici cuiúsdam Petri, ea erat è Septimontio uī,
go Zeuenberghen. fratres illius dúos uidit Dordraci penè
Nonagenarios. Pater dictus est Gerardus, is clam habuit
rem cúm dicta Margareta spe coniúgij, et sunt qui
dicant intercessisse uerba. Eam rem indignè tulerúnt
et parentes Gerardi et fratres. Pater erat Elias
mater Catharina uterqz peruenit ad extremam senec,
tutem. Catharina xenè usqz ad nonagesimúm quíntúm
annúm. fratres erant decem, nulla soror, ex eodem
patre et matre omnes coniúgati. Gerardus erat natú
minimus úno excepto, uisum est omnibus, ut ex tanto
múmero únús Deo consecraretúr. Mosti affectus senúm
et fratres nolebant minúi rem. sed esse apúd quem cō,
uiuarentúr. Gerardus uidens sese de his ^{modis} omnib. excludi
à matrimonio magno consensu omnium, fecit quod solent
desperati clam aufúgit et ex itinere misit parentrb.
et fratrb. epistolam cúm manú manúm complexa
addito elogio Valete núnqz uos uidebo. Jnterim tamē
relicta est sperata coniúnx grauida, puer alitús
apúd auiam, Gerardus romam se contúlit, illic scri,
bendo (nam tunc nondúm erat ars typographorúm)
rem affatim parauit. Erat autem manú feliciss,
ma et uixit iúueniciter mox applicúit animúm ad
         ho

Compendium vitae, opening page
Oesterreichische Nationalbibliothek, Vienna, MS Lat. 9058

from it (as he was in law bound to do) and the right not to specify the fact that he *is* a canon regular ('et quod sit canonicus regularis' Allen Ep 517:55; CWE 4 Ep 517:62).

2 The following information was provided in a personal communication: Luigi Michelini Tocci *L'apparato autografo di Erasmo per l'edizione 1528 degli 'Adagia' e un nuovo manoscritto del 'Compendium vitae'* Rome, Edizioni di Storia e Letteratura 1977.

A BRIEF ACCOUNT OF THE LIFE OF ERASMUS OF ROTTERDAM,
MENTIONED BY HIMSELF IN THE PRECEDING LETTER
The life to be kept secret

Born in Rotterdam on the eve of SS Simon and Jude. Reckons he is about 57 years of age. His mother's name was Margaret, her father a physician named Pieter. She was from Septimontium, commonly known as Zeven- bergen, and he saw two of her brothers at Dordrecht who were nearly ninety years old. His father's name was Gerard. He lay with Margaret secretly, in the expectation of marrying her. Some say they were already betrothed. This was received with indignation by Gerard's parents and his brothers. Gerard's father was called Elias and his mother Catharine; both lived to a very great age, Catharine till she was nearly ninety-five. There were ten brothers, but no sister, born of the same parents, all of them married. Gerard was the youngest but one. All agreed that out of so large a family one should be consecrated to God. You know how old men feel. And his brothers wished to have no reduction in their own patrimony, but someone with whom they could always be sure of a dinner. Gerard, finding himself entirely debarred by general consent from matrimony, did what men in despair often do: he ran away, and on his journey sent a letter to his parents and brothers, with two clasped hands on it, and the legend 'Farewell, I shall never see you more.'

Meanwhile the woman he had hoped to marry was left expecting a child.

* * * * *

3 The life ... secret] In Greek

4 eve] Evidently during the night of 27–8 October; he celebrated his birthday on 28 October.

4–5 about 57 years of age] On the much-discussed issue of Erasmus' year of birth see R.R. Post 'Quelques précisions ...' and Epp 531:410, 548:5n.

7 Dordrecht] Perhaps in 1498; cf Ep 76:19.

9 in the expectation] *spe conjugii*; the theory that Erasmus' father was already a priest cannot be reconciled with this statement. If, however, there was an obstacle of affinity, that obstacle might have been removed by dispensation, a procedure that would have required, in all probability, the co-operation locally of both families. Cf Epp 446, 447 and 517 introductions.

The boy was brought up by his grandmother. Gerard made his way to Rome. There he earned enough to live on as a copyist, for the art of printing as yet did not exist. He wrote a very expert hand. And he lived as young 25 men will. Later he turned his mind to honourable studies. Of Greek and Latin he had a good knowledge. In the law too he was more than commonly proficient. Rome in those days was wonderfully blest with learned men. He heard Guarino lecture. All the classical authors he had copied with his own hand. His parents, when they learned he was in Rome, wrote to him that 30 the girl he hoped to marry was now dead. Supposing this to be true, in his grief he became a priest, and devoted his whole mind to religion. On returning home, he discovered this was a fraud. But she was never afterwards willing to marry, nor did he ever touch her.

For the boy he arranged to provide a liberal education, and when he 35 was scarcely more than four years old he sent him to an elementary school. In his early years the child made very little progress in those tedious rudiments, for which he had no natural gift. In his ninth year he sent him to Deventer; his mother went with him as guardian and guide of his tender years. The school there was at that time in a state of barbarism (a standard 40 text was the *Pater meus*; they were forced to learn the paradigms, the textbooks being Eberhard and John of Garland), except that Alexander

* * * * *

29 Guarino] Guarino de' Guarini of Verona (Ep 23:78n) had a younger brother teaching at Ferrara.

31 girl] *puella*; cf *vidua* in Ep 187A.

36 elementary school] A school attached to St John's Church at Gouda; cf Ep 1 introduction; Post 'Quelques précisions ...' 495–6.

38 rudiments] These studies 'in litteris inamoenis' were apparently in the Dutch vernacular; classical studies at Louvain were 'literae amoeniores.'

38 ninth year] Allen, accepting 1466 as Erasmus' birth-date, placed this arrival in 1475; Post, arguing for 1469 as the year of birth, dates the beginning of the Deventer schooling in 1478; 'Quelques précisions ...' 497–8, 506.

39 Deventer] According to Beatus Rhenanus, Erasmus was a chorister in the chapter school at Utrecht between his schooling at Gouda and his arrival at Deventer. He would have been there at the same time as the famous organist and composer Jacob Obrecht; cf Allen 156 and note; Post 'Quelques précisions ...' 496.

41 *Pater meus*] As interpreted by F.M. Nichols, this obscure reference to a school text refers to a concord set for declension in Latin grammar (Allen).

42 Eberhard] Eberhard of Béthune, a twelfth-century grammarian, author of *Graecismus*, a Latin grammar in verse; cf Ep 26:100n.

42 John of Garland] (c 1180–1 1258) An Englishman who taught in Paris and whose *Dictionnarius*, *Compendium grammaticae*, and *Accentuarium* became standard works in the Middle Ages.

Hegius and Synthen had begun to introduce something of a higher standard as literature. At length his playmates, of whom the older ones were in Synthen's class, gave him his first taste of better teaching, and later he sometimes heard Hegius, but only on high days when he lectured to the whole school. Here he reached the third form; then the plague, which was raging there, carried off his mother, leaving her son now in his thirteenth year. As the plague grew daily more and more severe, the whole house in which he lived was deserted, and he returned to his native place. Gerard when he heard the sad news fell ill, and shortly afterwards died. Both were not much over forty. He set up three guardians, whom he thought most reliable. Of these the chief was Pieter Winckel, at that time master of the school at Gouda. He left a moderate estate, had his guardians managed it in good faith. And so the boy was removed to 'sHertogenbosch, being now old enough for the university. But they were afraid of a university, for they had already decided to bring up the boy for the life of a religious.

45

50

55

* * * * *

43 Hegius] Alexander, rector of the school at Deventer from 1483–98; cf Ep 23:59n. Erasmus could not have known him there for long; cf Post 'Quelques précisions ...' 498.

43 Synthen] Johannes, born in Delden in the east Netherlands (d 1498). He wrote a commentary on the *Doctrinale* of Alexander de Villa Dei which was published at Deventer in 1488 and again in 1500 (NK 2276), 1501 (NK 70) and 1503 (NK 2278). I am indebted to E.J.M. van Eijl for pointing this out. From the account here it would seem likely that he taught only in the first and second forms, given over to philosophy. Boys in the third form would be considered ready for university; cf Post 'Quelques precisions ...' 501–2; J.D. Tracy 'Bemerkungen ...' 227–8.

48 mother] There was a severe epidemic of plague at Deventer in 1483. From this point to 'canonical habit' (line 112) the text is adapted from Ep 447, a few passages being almost word for word. There are some additions, however.

54 guardians] Cf Ep 1 introduction. The chief was Pieter Winckel, master of the school at Gouda. The first surviving letter in Erasmus' correspondence was written to Winckel evidently in the summer of 1484, shortly after the death of Roger Gerard, the boys' father.

55 's Hertogenbosch] Also known as Bois-le-Duc. In reference to speculation about the possibly profound influence of the Brethren of the Common Life on Erasmus, it may be noted that this is the only period when he is known to have lived in one of their hospices, for perhaps two full years. The boarders would have taken most of their classes at the municipal school of St John; Erasmus was quite likely by this time too advanced in his Latin studies to do so, a circumstance that would certainly have added to his boredom and resentment. See R.R. Post 'Studien over de Broeders van het Gemene leven' *Nederlandsche Historiebladen* 2 (1939) 150–1, and Edmund Colledge OSA 'Erasmus, the Brethren of the Common Life and the Devotio moderna' *Erasmus in English* 7 (1975) 2–4.

There he spent, or rather, wasted about three years in a house of the
Brothers, as they call them, in which Rombold was then teaching. This sort
of men now spreads widely through the world, though it is disastrous for   60
gifted minds and a mere nursery of monks. Rombold, who was much struck
by the boy's gifts, began to work on him to join his flock. The boy pleaded
the ignorance of his youth. At this point there was an outbreak of plague;
and after suffering for a long time from a quartan fever, he returned to his
guardians, having by now also acquired some fluency of style derived from   65
a few good authors. One of the guardians had succumbed to the plague; the
other two, who had not managed his affairs very skilfully, began to treat
with him about the monastic life. The poor youth, who was weak from the
fever which had held him for more than a year, felt no dislike of religion,
but he did dislike a monastery. They therefore allowed him a day to think it   70
over. All this time the guardian put up people to tempt and threaten him and
bring pressure to bear on his innocent mind; and in the meanwhile he had
found a place in a monastery of regular canons, as they are commonly
called, in a house near Delft, called Sion, which is the chief house of that
chapter. When the day arrived on which he had to answer, the youth   75
answered sensibly, that he did not yet know what the world was, or what a
monastery was, or what he was himself; and so it seemed, he said, a better
plan that he should still spend some years attending lectures, until he might
know his own mind better. When he saw the young man persist in this,
Pieter suddenly lost his temper. 'I see,' he said; 'I have wasted my labour in   80
securing you a place like that with so much entreaty. You are a worthless
fellow, and have a spirit of perversity in you. I resign my office as your
guardian. You can fend for yourself.' The youth replied that he accepted his
resignation, being now of an age when guardians were no longer necessary. When the man saw that threats got him nowhere, he suborned his   85
brother, who was also one of the trustees, and a man of business. He set to
work with blandishments, and was supported on every hand by those who
had put him up to it. The boy had a companion, who betrayed his friend,

* * * * *

59 Rombold] This individual is otherwise unknown.

75 chapter] The congregation of which Sion was the head included the priory
of Steyn (line 91). When Erasmus entered the house at Steyn his older brother
(by three years) Pieter, whose existence is not acknowledged in the *Compendium vitae*, was already a monk at Sion. Cf Ep 3 (to Pieter Gerard) introduction
and the note to line 88 below.

80 Pieter] Winckel; cf 54n above.

88 a companion] The only guarded reference in the *Compendium vitae* to his
older brother Pieter; cf 15n. The author's reticence about the existence of his

and the fever still lay hard on him; but even so, a monastery had no appeal, until by some chance he visited a house of the same Order at Emmaus, or 90 Steyn, near Gouda. There he found one Cornelis, who had been a friend of his and shared a room with him at Deventer. This man had not yet taken orders; he had visited Italy, but had returned without learning much. With an eye to his own advantage he began to draw a most eloquent picture of a very saintly way of life, with plenty of books, leisure, tranquillity, and a 95 society like that of angels, everything you can think of. The young man was drawn to his old companion by fond memories of boyhood; he was lured on by some people and driven forward by others; the fever lay heavy on him. So he chose this place, being disgusted with the other, and of the moment all was made pleasant for him, until he should take the habit. Meanwhile, 100 young as he was, he realized how far the place was from true religion; and yet he inspired the whole community to study harder. Though he made preparations to leave before his profession, he was restrained partly by natural shyness, partly by threats and partly by necessity.

He made his profession. At length he had an opportunity of becoming 105 known to Hendrik van Bergen, the bishop of Cambrai. The bishop was hoping for a cardinal's hat, and would have had one, had he not been short

* * * * *

brother is regarded by some as a serious objection to accepting the authenticity of the *Compendium vitae*; see for example Crahay 'Recherches' 137–8. Allen suggests reasons for supposing that Erasmus himself would have wished to suppress his brother's part in his early story; cf Allen I 577. I would add that even if Pieter were still alive there is no evident reason why Erasmus should have wished his brother's name to appear in this account, where it could only have brought embarrassment, even if Erasmus' attitude to their early choice of vocation had been by this time more sympathetic. It should be noticed also that since Pieter was a professed religious (75n), their common defect of birth would have involved him in the same canonical difficulties faced by Erasmus if Pieter had been promoted to any prelacy like that of abbot. In appraising the tone of this account it must be remembered (as with Ep 447) that his purpose was less to give a full and impartial history of his early years than to justify Erasmus' dispensation with the argument that his decision to take vows was neither free nor informed.

91 Steyn] The priory had been founded in 1419 and was situated within a mile of Gouda in the parish of Haastrecht. It was dedicated to St Gregory, but from its nearness to Gouda it was known as Emmaus. In 1549 the monastery burned to the ground and the site was acquired by the town council of Gouda; it is now occupied by a farmhouse; cf Allen I 583.

91 Cornelis] Possibly Cornelis Gerard who was ordained to a different house in the same congregation but who seems to have moved about; cf Allen I 92.

103 profession] In 1488

106 Hendrik van Bergen] See Ep 446 introduction.

of ready money. For the purpose of this journey he needed a good Latin scholar. So our man was sent for by him, with authorization from the bishop of Utrecht, which was sufficient by itself, but he also secured the 110 approval of the prior and of the general of the Order. He joined the bishop's household but none the less still wore his canonical habit. When the bishop had lost his hope of a hat, and perceived that the young man's devotion to them all left something to be desired, he arranged that he should go to Paris to study. He was promised an annual subvention, but nothing was ever 115 sent. Great men are like that. There in the Collège de Montaigu, as a result of rotten eggs and infected lodgings, he contracted an illness, a morbid influence on a constitution until then quite free from taint. So he returned to the bishop. His reception was complimentary. He recovered his health at Bergen. He revisited Holland with the intention of remaining with his own 120 people. But on their unsought encouragement he went back to Paris. There with no patron to support him it was a question of survival rather than study; and as the plague was continuous there for many years, he was obliged to return every year to his native country. Theology repelled him, for he felt himself not disposed to undermine all its foundations with the 125 prospect of being branded as a heretic. At length, when the plague continued for a whole year, he was compelled to move to Louvain. He had previously visited England to oblige Mountjoy, who was at that time his pupil and later his Maecenas, though more of a friend than a benefactor. In those days he won the good opinion of all men of standing in England, 130 particularly because, although robbed on the coast at Dover, he not only sought no revenge but published a short work not long after in praise of the king of England and the whole country. At length he was invited with generous offers to return from France to England, and it was at that time that

* * * * *

110 bishop of Utrecht] David of Burgundy, illegitimate son of Duke Philip the Good (d 1467), bishop first of Thérouanne, then of Utrecht

116 Collège de Montaigu] Cf Ep 43 introduction.

119 the bishop] Cf Ep 76 written from the bishop's library in Brussels in the summer of 1498.

127 Louvain] Cf Ep 95:51.

128 Mountjoy] Cf Ep 79 introduction.

131 robbed] Cf Ep 119.

132 short work] The poem 'Prosopopoeia Britanniae,' written in the autumn of 1499 shortly after Erasmus' visit to the royal children at Eltham palace; cf Ep 104, Reedijk 248–53.

he secured the friendship of the archbishop of Canterbury. When the offers 135
did not materialize, he set off for Italy, which he had always had a great
desire to visit. He spent a little more than a year in Bologna, his life being
already at its turning-point, for he was now about forty. Thence he moved
to Venice, and published his *Adagia*; from there to Padua, where he spent
the winter; thereafter to Rome, where a substantial and favourable reputa- 140
tion had preceded him. Raffaele the cardinal of San Giorgio had a special
feeling for him. Nor would he have failed to secure a lucrative position, had
he not been summoned back to England on the death of Henry vii and
accession of Henry viii by letters from friends, full of generous promises. In
England he had decided to spend the rest of his life; but as these promises 145
were no more kept now than before, he retreated to Brabant, having been
invited to the court of the present Emperor Charles, whose councillor he
became through the efforts of the lord chancellor, Jean Le Sauvage. The rest
you know.

The principles behind his change of costume he has explained in the 150
first of the pamphlets in which he answered the attacks of Lee. His personal
appearance you will describe yourself. His health was always delicate, and
thus he was often attacked by fevers, especially in Lent on account of the
eating of fish, the mere smell of which used to upset him. His character was
straightforward, and his dislike of falsehood such that even as a child he 155
hated other boys who told lies, and in old age even the sight of such people
affected him physically. Among his friends he spoke freely – too freely
sometimes, and though often deceived he never learned not to trust them.
Having a touch of pedantry, he never wrote anything with which he was
satisfied; he even disliked his own appearance, and his friends' entreaties 160
barely prevailed on him to let himself be painted. For high office and for
wealth he had a permanent contempt, and thought nothing more precious
than leisure and liberty. A charitable judge of other mens' learning, he
would have been a supreme encourager of gifted minds had his resources
run to it. In promoting the study of the humanities no one did more, and 165
great was the unpopularity he had to suffer in return for this from barba-

* * * * *

135 Canterbury] William Warham; cf Ep 188 introduction.

137 Bologna] Cf Ep 200 introduction.

150 change of costume] See Ep 446 headnote; the reply to Lee was the *Apologia
... nihil habens neque nasi neque dentis ... qua respondit ... duabus invectivis ... Lei*
(Antwerp: M. Hillen 1520 NK 782).

156 hated other boys] This phrase is taken almost word for word from the
Spongia adversus aspergines Hutteni (Basel: Froben 1523; LB x 1663F–1664A).

rians and monks. Until his fiftieth year he had attacked no man, nor did any
man attack him in print. This was his intention: to keep his pen absolutely
innocent of what might wound. Lefèvre was the first to attack him; for
Dorp's efforts were suppressed. In reply he was always courteous. The sad   170
business of Luther had brought him a burden of intolerable ill will; he was
torn in pieces by both sides, while aiming zealously at what was best for
both.

* * * * *

167–9 Until ... might wound] Allen describes this passage as 'plainly a reminiscence'; cf Allen I 52.

169 Lefèvre] In the second edition of his commentary on the epistles of St Paul
(Paris: Regnault 1517) Jacques Lefèvre d'Etaples had replied to some criticisms
made by Erasmus in the *Novum instrumentum* concerning Lefèvre's views on
Hebrews chapter 2. In his reply Lefèvre accused Erasmus of holding an
'impious' opinion; Erasmus' indignant rejoinder, the *Apologia ad Jac. Fabrum
Stapulensem*, was published at Louvain by Martens in August 1517 (NK 777); cf
Allen III Ep 597:32n.

TABLE OF CORRESPONDENTS

WORKS FREQUENTLY CITED

SHORT TITLE FORMS

INDEX

TABLE OF CORRESPONDENTS

WORKS FREQUENTLY CITED

This list provides bibliographical information for works referred to in short title form in the headnotes and footnotes to Epp 446–593. For Erasmus' writings see the short title list, pages 419–22. Editions of his letters are included in the list below.

AK	Alfred Hartmann ed *Die Amerbachkorrespondenz* (Basel 1942–)
Allen	P.S. Allen, H.M. Allen, and H.W. Garrod eds *Opus epistolarum Des. Erasmi Roterodami* (Oxford 1906–58) 11 vols and index
ASD	*Opera omnia Desiderii Erasmi Roterodami* (Amsterdam 1969–)
Auctarium	*Auctarium selectarum aliquot epistolarum Erasmi Roterodami ad eruditos et horum ad illum* (Basel: Froben August 1518)
Bataillon	Marcel Bataillon *Erasme et l'Espagne* Bibliothèque de l'Ecole des Hautes Etudes Hispaniques, Fasc XXI (Paris 1937)
Benzing	Joseph Benzing *Die Buchdrucker des 16. und 17. Jahrhunderts im deutschen Sprachgebiet* (Wiesbaden 1963)
BHR	*Bibliothèque d'humanisme et renaissance* (Geneva)
Bierlaire	Franz Bierlaire *La familia d'Erasme* (Paris 1968)
BRE	A. Horawitz and K. Hartfelder eds *Briefwechsel des Beatus Rhenanus* (Leipzig 1886; repr 1966)
Copinger	(see Hain)
CSEL	*Corpus scriptorum ecclesiasticorum latinorum* (Vienna/Leipzig 1866–19)
CWE	*The Collected Works of Erasmus* (Toronto 1974–)
E & C	H.C. Porter ed and D.F.S. Thomson trans *Erasmus and Cambridge: The Cambridge Letters of Erasmus* (Toronto 1963)
EHR	*English Historical Review*
Emden BRUC	A.B. Emden *Biographical Register of the University of Cambridge to AD 1500* (Cambridge 1963)
Emden BRUO	A.B. Emden *Biographical Register of the University of Oxford to AD 1500* (Oxford 1957–59) 3 vols; *Biographical Register of the University of Oxford, AD 1501 to 1540* (Oxford 1974)
Epistolae ad diversos	*Epistolae D. Erasmi Roterodami ad diversos et aliquot aliorum ad illum* (Basel: Froben 31 August 1521)
Epistolae ad Erasmum	*Epistolae aliquot illustrium virorum ad Erasmum Roterodamum et huius ad illos* (Louvain: Martens October 1516)
Epistolae elegantes (1517)	*Aliquot epistolae sanequam elegantes Erasmi Roterodami et ad hunc aliorum eruditissimorum hominum* (Louvain: Martens April 1517)

Epistolae elegantes (1518)	*Aliquot epistolae sanequam elegantes Erasmi Roterodami et ad hunc aliorum eruditissimorum hominum* (Basel: Froben January 1518)
Farrago	*Farrago nova epistolarum Des. Erasmi Roterodami ad alios et aliorum ad hunc: admixtis quibusdam quas scripsit etiam adolescens* (Basel: Froben October 1519)
Garanderie	Marie-Madeleine de la Garanderie ed and trans *La Correspondance d'Erasme et de Guillaume Budé* (Paris 1967)
Hain	L.F.T. Hain *Repertorium Bibliographicum ... opera* Ludovici Hain (Stuttgart 1826–38) 2 vols; with Supplement ... in two parts by W.A. Copinger (London 1895–1902) and *Appendices ad Hainii-Coperingi ...* ed Dietericus Reichling (Munich 1905–8)
HE	E. Böcking ed *Epistolae Ulrichi Hutteni* in *Ulrichi Hutteni opera ... omnia* vol 1 (Leipzig 1859; repr 1963)
Jedin	H. Jedin *A History of the Council of Trent* vol 1 tr Dom Ernest Graf (Edinburgh 1957)
Knowles	Dom David Knowles *The Religious Orders in England* III: *The Tudor Age* (Cambridge 1959)
LB	J. Leclerc ed *Desiderii Erasmi Roterodami opera omnia* (Leiden 1703–6) 10 vols
Lupton	J.H. Lupton *A Life of John Colet D.D.* (London 1887)
LP	*Letters and Papers, Foreign and Domestic, of the Reign of Henry VIII* ed J.S. Brewer, J. Gairdner, R.H. Brodie (London 1862–1932) 36 vols
McConica	J.K. McConica *English Humanists and Reformation Politics under Henry VIII and Edward VI* (Oxford 1965)
McNeil	D.O. McNeil *Guillaume Budé and Humanism in the Reign of Francis I* (Geneva 1975)
NK	W. Nijhoff and M.E. Kronenberg eds *Nederlandsche Bibliographie van 1500 tot 1540* (The Hague 1919–)
Opus epistolarum	*Opus epistolarum Des. Erasmi Roterodami per autorem diligenter recognitum et adjectis innumeris novis fere ad trientem auctum* (Basel: Froben, Herwagen, and Episcopius 1529)
Opuscula	W.K. Ferguson ed *Erasmi opuscula: A Supplement to the Opera omnia* (The Hague 1933)
Panzer	G.W. Panzer *Annales Typographici* (Nürnberg 1793–1800; repr 1963–4) 11 vols
Pauly-Wissowa	*Paulys Realencyclopädie der classischen Altertumswissenschaft.* Neue Bearbeitung begonnen von Georg Wissowa (Stuttgart 1894–)
Phillips	M.M. Phillips *The 'Adages' of Erasmus* (Cambridge 1964)
Polain	Louis Polain *Catalogue général des incunables des bibliothèques publiques de France* (Paris 1897–1970) 26 vols

PL	J.P. Migne ed *Patrologiae cursus completus ... series latina* (Paris 1844–1902) 221 vols
Quétif	J. Quétif and J. Echard *Scriptores ordinis fratrum praedicatorum* (Paris 1719–21) 2 vols
RE	L. Geiger ed *Johann Reuchlins Briefwechsel* (Tübingen 1875; repr 1962)
Reedijk	C. Reedijk ed *Poems of Desiderius Erasmus* (Leiden 1956)
Renaudet *Italie*	A. Renaudet *Erasme et l'Italie* (Geneva 1954)
Renaudet *Préréforme*	A. Renaudet *Préréforme et humanisme à Paris pendant les premières guerres d'Italie (1494–1517)* 2nd ed (Paris 1953)
Renouard *Annales*	Antoine A. Renouard *Annales de l'imprimerie des Alde, ou histoire des trois Manuce et de leurs éditions* 3rd ed (Paris 1834 repr 1953)
Renouard *Imprimeurs*	Philippe Renouard *Imprimeurs et libraires parisiens du XVIe siècle: ouvrage publié d'après les manuscrits de Philippe Renouard* Histoire générale de Paris: collection de documents publiée sous les auspices de l'édilité parisienne (Paris 1964–9) 2 vols
Rice	E.F. Rice jr ed *The Prefatory Epistles of Jacques Lefèvre d'Etaples and Related Texts* (New York 1972)
Rogers	E.F. Rogers ed *The Correspondence of Sir Thomas More* (Princeton 1947)
Scarisbrick	J.J. Scarisbrick *Henry VIII* (Berkeley and Los Angeles 1968)
STC	A.W. Pollard and G.R. Redgrave *A Short-Title Catalogue of Books Printed in England, Scotland and Ireland and of English Books Printed Abroad 1475–1640* (London 1926)
SR	*Studies in the Renaissance*
Utopia	The Yale Edition of the Complete Works of St Thomas More vol 4 *Utopia* ed E. Surtz s.j. and J.H. Hexter (New Haven 1965)
de Vocht CTL	H. de Vocht *History of the Foundation and the Rise of the Collegium Trilingue Lovaniense 1517–1550* Humanistica lovaniensia 10–13 (Louvain 1951–5) 4 vols
de Vocht *Literae*	H. de Vocht *Literae virorum eruditorum ad Franciscum Craneveldium 1522–1528* Humanistica lovaniensia 1 (Louvain 1928)
de Vocht MHL	H. de Vocht *Monumenta humanistica lovaniensia* Humanistica lovaniensia 4 (Louvain 1934)
Wegg	J. Wegg *Richard Pace* (London 1932)

Acta contra Lutherum: Acta academiae Lovaniensis contra Lutherum

Adagia: Adagiorum chiliades 1508 (Adagiorum collectanea for the primitive form, when required)

Admonitio adversus mendacium: Admonitio adversus mendacium et obtrectationem

Annotationes de haereticis: Annotationes in leges pontificias et caesareas de haereticis

Annotationes in Novum Testamentum

Antibarbari

Apologia ad Fabrum: Apologia ad Iacobum Fabrum Stapulensem

Apolgia ad Carranza: Apologia ad Sanctium Carranza

Apologia adversus Petrum Sutorem: Apologia adversus debacchationes Petri Sutoris

Apologia adversus monachos: Apologia adversus monachos quosdam hispanos

Apologia adversus rhapsodias Alberti Pii

Apologia contra Latomi dialogum: Apologia contra Iacobi Latomi dialogum de tribus linguis

Apologia contra Stunicam: Apologia contra Lopidem Stunicam

Apologia de 'In principio erat sermo'

Apologia de laude matrimonii: Apologia pro declamatione de laude matrimonii

Apologia de loco 'omnes quidem': Apologia de loco 'Omnes quidem resurgemus'

Apologiae duae

Apologiae omnes

Apologia invectivis Lei: Apologia qua respondet duabus invectivis Eduardi Lei

Apologia monasticae religionis

Apophthegmata

Argumenta: Argumenta in omnes epistolas apostolicas nova

Axiomata pro causa Lutheri: Axiomata pro causa Martini Lutheri

Carmina

Catalogus lucubrationum

Cato

Christiani hominis institutum

Ciceronianus: Dialogus Ciceronianus

Colloquia

Compendium rhetorices

Compendium vitae

Conflictus: Conflictus Thaliae et barbariei

De bello turcico: Consultatio de bello turcico

De civilitate: De civilitate morum puerilium

De conscribendis epistolis

De constructione: De constructione octo partium orationis

De contemptu mundi

De copia: De duplici copia verborum ac rerum

Declamatio de morte

Declamationes
Declamatiuncula
Declamatiunculae
Declarationes ad censuras Lutetiae: Declarationes ad censuras Lutetiae vulgatas
De concordia: De sarcienda ecclesiae concordia
De immensa Dei misericordia: Concio de immensa Dei misericordia
De libero arbitrio: De libero arbitrio diatribe
De praeparatione: De praeparatione ad mortem
De pronuntiatione: De recta latini graecique sermonis pronuntiatione
De pueris instituendis: De pueris statim ac liberaliter instituendis
De puero Iesu: Concio de puero Iesu
De puritate tabernaculi
De ratione studii
Detectio praestigiarum: Detectio praestigiarum cuiusdam libelli germanice scripti
De tedio Iesu: Disputatiuncula de tedio, pavore, tristicia Iesu
Dilutio: Dilutio eorum quae Iodocus Clithoveus scripsit adversus declamationem
    suasoriam matrimonii

Ecclesiastes: Ecclesiastes sive de ratione concionandi
Enarratio in primum psalmum
Enchiridion: Enchiridion militis christiani
Encomium matrimonii
Encomium medicinae: Declamatio in laudem artis medicae
Epigrammata
Epistola ad fratres: Epistola ad fratres Inferioris Germaniae
Epistola consolatoria: Epistola consolatoria in adversis
Epistola contra pseudevangelicos: Epistola contra quosdam qui se falso iactant
    evangelicos
Epistola de apologia Cursii: Epistola de apologia Petri Cursii
Epistola de esu carnium: Epistola apologetica ad Christophorum episcopum
    Basiliensem de interdicto esu carnium
Epistola de modestia: Epistola de modestia profitendi linguas
Exomologesis: Exomologesis sive modus confitendi
Explanatio symboli: Explanatio symboli apostolorum sive catechismus

Formulae: Conficiendarum epistolarum formulae

Gaza: Theodori Gazae grammaticae institutionis libri duo

Hyperaspistes

Institutio christiani matrimonii
Institutio principis christiani

Julius exclusus: Dialogus Julius exclusus e coelis

Liber quo respondet annotationibus Lei: Liber quo respondet annotationibus
    Eduardi Lei

Lingua
Liturgia Virginis Matris: Virginis Matris apud Lauretum cultae liturgia
Lucubrationes
Lucubratiunculae

Methodus
Modus orandi Deum
Moria: Moriae encomium, or Moria

Novum instrumentum
Novum Testamentum

Obsecratio ad Virginem Mariam: Obsecratio sive oratio ad Virginem Mariam in
    rebus adversis
Oratio de pace: Oratio de pace et discordia
Oratio de virtute: Oratio de virtute amplectenda
Oratio funebris: Oratio funebris Berthae de Heyen

Paean Virgini Matri: Paean Virgini Matri dicendus
Panegyricus: Panegyricus ad Philippum Austriae ducem
Parabolae: Parabolae sive similia
Paraclesis
Paraphrasis in Elegantias Vallae: Paraphrasis in Elegantias Laurentii Vallae
Paraphrasis in Novum Testamentum
Paraphrasis in Matthaeum: Paraphrasis in Matthaeum, etc.
Peregrinatio apostolorum: Peregrinatio apostolorum Petri et Pauli
Precatio ad Virginis filium Iesum
Precatio dominica
Precationes
Precatio pro pace ecclesiae: Precatio ad Iesum pro pace ecclesiae
Progymnasmata: Progymnasmata quaedam primae adolescentiae Erasmi
Psalmi: Psalmi (Enarrationes sive commentarii in psalmos)
Purgatio adversus epistolam Lutheri: Purgatio adversus epistolam non sobriam
    Lutheri

Querela pacis

Ratio verae theologiae
Responsio ad annotationes Lei: Responsio ad annotationes Eduardi Lei
Responsio ad annotationem Stunicae: Responsio ad annotationem Iacobi Lopis
    Stunicae
Responsio ad collationes: Responsio ad collationes cuiusdam iuvenis gerontodidas-
    cali
Responsio ad disputationem de diuortio: Responsio ad disputationem cuiusdam
    Phimostomi de diuortio
Responsio ad epistolam apologeticam: Responsio ad fratres Germaniae Inferioris ad
    epistolam apologeticam incerto autore proditam
Responsio ad epistolam Pii: Responsio ad epistolam paraeneticam Alberti Pii

Responsio adversus febricitantis libellum: Responsio adversus febricitantis cuiusdam libellum
Responsio contra Egranum: Responsio apologetica contra Sylvium Egranum

Spongia: Spongia adversus aspergines Hutteni
Supputatio: Supputatio calumniarum Natalis Bedae

Vidua christiana
Virginis et martyris comparatio
Vita Hieronymi: Vita diui Hieronymi Stridonensis

Index

Castille: Prince Charles as king of 95n,
245n

Catharine, mother of Erasmus'
father 403

Catherine of Aragon: Standish and the
divorce 115n

Catherine of Siena, St 16

Catholicon: ungifted theologians resort
to 252

Cato, Marcus Portius 'the censor':
praised by Cicero 136; Octavius
and 381; *see also* Erasmus, translations and editions: Cato

Cato, P. Valerius 388

Catullus 275n

Chalcondyles, Demetrius 81n; taught
Greek to Grocyn 201

Charles of Burgundy, prince (later
Charles v, emperor), archduke of
Austria, duke of Brabant, king of
Aragon and Castile: patron of Erasmus 4, 5n, 35, 56, 83n, 93–4, 100,
108, 124, 128, 175, 177, 212, 240, 291,
333; Erasmus a councillor of 6, 55n,
107, 219, 256, 319, 345, 409; seeks
bishopric for Erasmus 95, 96, 163,
189n; Gomez' poems in praise
of 175; and Treaty of Cambrai 175,
208n, 245, 263; and Erasmus' dispensation 197, 310; Tunstall's mission to 224; Knight's mission
to 250; Erasmus' enemies and 257;
advances learning 263, 269; departure for Spain 271, 294; and imperial
succession 316; council at Ghent
369; Erasmus as 'tutor' of 384;
Egnazio's praise of 384–5

Charles the Rash 245n

Charles VIII, king of France: and Poncher 316; Marzio at court of 348n;
and Lascaris 365

Christ; Jesus Christ: pope as vicar of 5,
29, 30, 310; monks and 9, 16, 18, 20,
28; 'secular' clergy and 24; and secular authority 30, 382; and the
Jews 30; loves freedom 32; rewards
labours 53; philosophy of 69, 182;

acknowledges followers 87; Erasmus' prayer to 133; endured
criticism 158; rebirth in 215; found
in Scriptures, not theology 220, 305;
a peaceful king 246; goal of all
studies 267–8; equality with God
the Father 286–90

Christians: damaged by wars 261

Chrysostom. *See* John Chrysostom, St

Cicero, Marcus Tullius 101; described
by Quintilian 133; praise of
Cato 136; praise of Scaevola 137;
Budé and 151, 239; style of 231, 234,
235; Erasmus compared to 292;
Musurus compared to 338; Paolo
Manuzio's work on 388n

– works: *Ad Herennium* (ascribed
to) 123n; *Brutus* 137n; *De
oratore* 105n, 121, 136n, 137n, 206n;
Epistulae ad Atticum 180n, 393; *Epistulae ad familiares* 320

Cipelli, Giambattista. *See* Egnazio

*Clarorum virorum epistolae ad J.
Reuchlin*: Melanchthon's preface
to 42n

Clava, Antonius (Colve), of Ghent: his
sister's death 211; and Keysere 212;
Gillis' preface to 272n

– letters from 211, 372

– letter to 222

Clement, John: helps Colet with
Greek 80

Cleves 173

Coelius. *See* Ricchieri

Colet, John: and Erasmus 43, 67, 131,
272, 305; admirer of Reuchlin 55n,
56, 85; hesitant about the
Utopia 79n; studies in Greek 80, 87;
copy of Jerome edition 93; and Deloynes 109, 154; studied at
Orléans 154; hesitant about
Reuchlin's Jewish studies 397n, 398

– letter from 398

Colibrantius, Franciscus, secretary of
Antwerp 268n

Colmar: Peter Falck in 37n

Cologne, university: Dominicans